MÜNCHEN auf dem Weg ins 21. Jahrhundert

ISBN 3-932 831-08-X

MÜNCHEN
auf dem Weg ins 21. Jahrhundert

Kunstverlag
Josef Bühn

Copyright
Kunstverlag Josef Bühn
München, 1999

Übersetzungen
Franco Mattoni, München
(italienisch)
Françoise Tardy, München
(französisch)
Inge Wheeler, München
(englisch)

Gestaltung
Wilhelm Zeitlmeir, München

Satz
Hofmann GmbH & Co. KG,
Traunreut

Gesamtherstellung
Lanadruck GmbH, München

Für die Richtigkeit redaktioneller
und bestellter Texte übernimmt
der Verlag keine Haftung.

Alle Rechte der Verbreitung
behält sich der Verlag vor.

München und die Region im Wandel der Zeit
Munich and its Region in the Course of Time
Munich et la région au cours de l'histoire
Monaco e la sua regione nell'evolversi dei tempi

9

Inhalt

Contents

Index

Indice

Kulturstadt München
Munich – a Cultural Centre
Munich – ville culturelle
Monaco – città della cultura

49

Schlösser und Kirchen
Palaces and Churches
Les châteaux et les églises
Castelli e chiese

81

Links und rechts der Isar
Left and Right of the Isar River
Rive gauche et rive droite de l'Isar
A sinistra e a destra dell'Isar

95

Wirtschaftsregion München – Spitzenregion in Europa
The Economic Region of Munich – One of Europe's Top Regions
La région économique de Munich – Une région clé en Europe
Monaco come area economica – di punta nell'economia europea

121

Stadt der Wissenschaft
City of Science
La ville des sciences
La città della scienza

205

Inhalt
Contents
Index
Indice

Unternehmer machen Geschichte
Entrepreneurs Writing History
Les entrepreneurs écrivent l'histoire
Imprenditoriche fanno storia

231

Einkaufen in München
Shopping in Munich
Le shopping à Munich
Fare shopping a Monaco

247

Weltstadt mit „Hub"
Metropolis with Hub
La ville mondiale et sa «plaque-tournante»
Una metropoli e il suo scalo

257

Messeplatz München
Munich – Fair and Exhibition Centre
Munich – Centre de foires et d'expositions
Monaco – Centro fieristico internazionale

263

München – Ziel für die Welt
Munich – International Destination
Munich – une destination pour le monde
Monaco di Baviera – una meta da tutto il mondo

271

Die Münchner Brauereien
Munich's Breweries
Les brasseries munichoises
Le fabbriche di birra di Monaco

295

Zoo der Zukunft: der Münchner Tierpark Hellabrunn
Zoo of the Future: Munich's Tierpark Hellabrunn
Le zoo de l'avenir: le Tierpark Hellabrunn à Munich
Lo zoo del futuro: il Tierpark Hellabrunn di Monaco

305

München – Stadt des Sports
Munich – City of Sports
Munich – ville du sport
Monaco – città dello sport

313

München ist nicht nur München
Munich is not only Munich
Munich n'est pas seulement Munich
Monaco non è solo Monaco

321

Eine Stadt im Aufbruch
A City on the Way to New Horizons
Une ville en plein essor
Una città in atmosfera neopionieristica

331

Autoren und Fotografen
Authors and photographers
Auteurs et photographes
Autori ed fotografi

342

Verzeichnis der PR-Bildbeiträge
Index of PR Photographs
Index des photographies destinées aux relations publiques
Indice delle fotografie PR

343

Nach Grossdingharting & Schäftlarn

*München und die Region
im Wandel der Zeit*

*Munich and its Region
in the Course of Time*

*Munich et la région
au cours de l'histoire*

*Monaco e la sua regione
nell'evolversi dei tempi*

Auf den Anhöhen links und rechts des Flusses hatten sich die Bajuwaren ihre Dörfer gebaut – Föhring wurde 750 erstmals genannt, Moosach 760, Pasing 763, Schwabing und Sendling 782...–, doch von dem Ort, der einmal Mittelpunkt der Region und schließlich des ganzen Landes werden sollte, von München, sprach in den agilolfingischen Zeiten niemand.

Am Ufer der sich in viele Bäche verzweigenden Isar werden zwar ein paar Fischerhütten gestanden haben, etliche Kaufleute dürften hier gelebt haben und sicher auch jene Mönche, denen der Ort später seinen Namen verdankte. Die Spuren dieser Ur-Münchner sind jedoch allesamt verweht.

Im näheren und weiteren Umkreis aber wurden die Archäologen vielfach fündig. Sie buddelten in einer Münchner Kiesgrube Reste eines Ur-Elefanten aus, stießen bei den Osterseen auf Haifischzähne, entdeckten zahlreiche Gräber und Spuren von Siedlungen aus der etwa 3 000 Jahre zurückliegenden Urnenfelderzeit, außerdem Bronzedepots, keltische Viereckschanzen und Bajuwarensiedlungen (unter anderem in Kirchheim und Aschheim). Die Entdeckungen rund um München sind so zahlreich, dass man das Gebiet zu einem „Kernraum Altbaierns" zählt.

In München selbst freilich sind die alten Knochen und Scherben rar – zu oft wurde umgegraben, aufgegraben, zugegraben. Im Alten Hof fand man Mitte der neunziger Jahre unseres Jahrhunderts etliche Keramikreste, die 2500 und 3500 Jahre alt sind. Sie beweisen, dass sich hier, wo später die Wittelsbacher residierten, schon in der Bronze- und Hallstattzeit Menschen aufgehalten haben.

Für die Anfänge dieser Siedlung hat sich lange Zeit niemand sonderlich interessiert. Noch vor 200 Jahren meinte der geschichtssüchtige Professor Westenrieder, dass ihm die ferne Vergangenheit seiner Geburtsstadt „wenig am Herzen liegt".

The Bavarians of old had already built their villages on the hills left and right of the Isar River (Föhring was first mentioned in 750 A. D., Moosach in 760, Pasing in 763, Schwabing and Sendling in 782), but the village that was to become first the centre of the region and later the capital of the entire country – i. e. Munich – was still unknown in the Agilolfingian period.

At that time a few fishermen's cottages had probably been erected on the banks of the Isar, which was divided and subdivided into numerous small brooks; a few merchants might have lived there as well, and certainly monks, who later lent their name to the city. But all traces of these early inhabitants have long since disappeared.

Archaeologists have, however, discovered evidence of this era in Munich's vicinity. In a local gravel pit they dug up the remnants of a primeval elefant; near the Ostersee lakes they hit upon shark teeth; they also found numerous tombs and traces of settlements dating from the urnfield period 3,000 years ago, and they unearthed bronze depots, Celtic entrenchments and Bavarian settlements – for instance in Kirchheim and Aschheim. The finds discovered around Munich are so rich that this area is considered one of Bavaria's major excavation sites.

In the city itself very few ancient bones and shards have been found, since the ground has been dug up, shifted and filled again frequently. In the mid-1990s a few ceramic bits and pieces, estimated to be 2,500 to 3,500 years old, were discovered in the Alte Hof (Old Palace). They go to prove that during the Bronze and Hallstatt Ages people already lived in this part of town where the Wittelsbach Dynasty later built its residential palace.

For a long time nobody was interested in the origins of this settlement. 200 years ago Professor Westenrieder, an expert truly dedicated to historic research, stated that the remote past of his

C'est sur les collines à droite et à gauche du fleuve que les Bajuvares avaient construit leurs villages. Föhring fut mentionnée la première fois en 750, Moosach en 760, Pasing en 763, Schwabing et Sendling en 782... mais de l'endroit qui devait être un jour le cœur de la région et même de l'ensemble du land, à savoir Munich, personne n'en parlait pendant l'époque des Agilolfinger.

Sur les berges de l'Isar se divisant en de nombreux ruisseaux, il y avait certainement quelques cabanes de pêcheurs, de nombreux marchands devaient également y vivre et aussi quelques moines dont la ville hérita plus tard du nom. Les traces de ces premiers Munichois ont toutes été dissipées sans exception.

Mais dans les environs proches et lointains, les archéologues firent de nombreuses découvertes. Dans une gravière munichoise, ils déterrèrent les restes d'un éléphant primitif, trouvèrent dans les lacs d'Ostersee des dents de requins, découvrirent de nombreuses tombes et traces de colonies datant de l'ère des champs d'urnes 3 000 ans auparavant, sans oublier les dépôts de bronze, les fortifications carrées celtes et les colonies des Bajuvares (entre autres à Kirchheim et Aschheim). Les découvertes tout autour de Munich sont si nombreuses que la région compte parmi «les régions clé de l'ancienne Bavière».

A Munich même, les vieux ossements et tessons sont bien entendu rares étant donné que l'on ne compte plus le nombre de fois où la terre a été retournée, fouillée et enterrée. Dans l'Alter Hof, on trouva au milieu des années quatre-vingt-dix de notre siècle de nombreux restes de céramique de 2 500 à 3 500 ans d'âge. Ils prouvent que là où plus tard la famille des Wittelsbach résida, des hommes y habitaient déjà à l'ère de bronze et à l'époque de Hallstatt.

Pendant longtemps, les débuts de cette colonie ne suscitèrent qu'un faible intérêt. Il y a encore 200 ans, le professeur Westen-

I bavari costruirono i loro villaggi sulle colline a destra e a sinistra del fiume – Föhring venne nominato per la prima volta, in un documento, nel 750, Moosach nel 760, Pasing nel 763, Schwabing e Sendling nel 782... - ma del luogo che sarebbe diventato il centro della regione e, infine, dell'intera area geografica, ovvero di Monaco, non parlava nessuno ai tempi di Agilulfo.

Probabilmente, sulle rive del fiume Isar, ramificato in tanti ruscelli, esistevano già un paio di capanne di pescatori, e qui avranno vissuto commercianti e sicuramente anche monaci, ai quali il luogo deve il suo nome ma le cui tracce sono andate completamente perdute.

Gli archeologi, comunque, hanno fatto numerose scoperte nei dintorni vicini e più lontani di Monaco. Scavando in una cava di ghiaia hanno ritrovato i resti di un elefante preistorico; e vicino agli Ostersee dei denti di squalo. Essi, inoltre, hanno scoperto numerose tombe e tracce di insediamenti risalenti ai tempi dei campi delle urne di 3000 anni fa, oltre a magazzini di bronzo, trincee celtiche quadrate ed insediamenti di bavari (anche a Kirchheim e ad Aschheim). I ritrovamenti nei dintorni di Monaco sono talmente numerosi che gli studiosi annoverano questa regione tra i «nuclei dell'antica Baviera».

Nella Monaco stessa, comunque, è molto più raro riuscire a scoprire ossa e frammenti antichi – si è troppo spesso vangato, rivoltato e ricoperto. Intorno alla metà degli anni '90, nel centro storico della città sono stati rinvenuti diversi frammenti di ceramica che risalgono a 2 500 e 3 500 anni fa. Essi dimostrano che questo luogo, che sarebbe diventato più tardi la residenza dei Wittelsbach, era già stato abitato nell'età del bronzo e nell'epoca di Hallstatt.

Per molto tempo nessuno si è interessato più di tanto alle origini di questo insediamento. Ancora 200 anni fa il Professor Westenrieder, un vero patito di storia, affermava che il passato della

Dabei hatte deren Geschichte am 14. Juni 1158, als mit steilen Buchstaben der Name „Munichen" erstmals auf Papier geschrieben wurde, spektakulär begonnen. Kaiser Barbarossa höchstselbst setzte nämlich seinen Namen unter die Urkunde.

Gleichsam als Taufzeugen nahmen an dieser Zeremonie, durch die ein Streit zwischen dem Bischof von Freising und dem Herzog von Bayern geschlichtet wurde, auch noch zwei Erzbischöfe, vier Bischöfe und zwei Markgrafen teil. So wurde der erste Auftritt der Stadt, obwohl es doch nur um eine leidige Steuersache zwischen zwei hohen Herren ging, zu einer veritablen Staatsaktion.

Während die Bauern in den Nachbarorten weiterhin ihre Äcker bestellten und sich die Dörfer kaum ausdehnten, konnte sich das bald schon 17 Hektar große München mit einer ersten und etwa 100 Jahre später – inzwischen erweitert auf 91 Hektar – sogar mit einer zweiten Mauer umgeben. Damit hatte die Stadt

native city "did not excite him very much". Yet Munich's history started in a rather spectacular way when on 14 June 1158 the name "Munichen" was put on paper in tall letters for the first time: it was Emperor Barbarossa in person who put his signature under a document ending the feud between the Bishop of Freising and the Duke of Bavaria. Two archbishops, four bishops and two margraves took part in the ceremony – more or less as "godfathers". Thus the first public appearance of the town turned into a veritable state affair, although one only solved a petty and bothersome tax problem affecting two high dignitaries.

While the peasants living in the neighbouring villages (which hardly increased in size) still tilled their fields, the small town of Munich – soon covering 17 hectares – built its first ring of walls. Only 100 years later, when it already boasted 91 hectares of territory, the town set up a second ring of fortifications which

rieder, pourtant féru d'histoire, avouait que le passé lointain de sa ville natale ne «lui tenait que très peu à cœur». Pourtant son histoire avait commencé de manière spectaculaire le 14 juin 1158 lorsque le nom de «Munichen» fut écrit pour la première fois en lettres raides sur du papier. L'empereur Barberousse en personne apposa son nom au bas du document. En même temps, deux archevêques, quatre évêques et deux margraves avaient participé en tant témoins du baptême à cette cérémonie grâce à laquelle une querelle entre l'évêque de Freising et le duc de Bavière put être réglée. La première entrée en scène de la ville s'avéra une véritable action d'Etat même s'il ne s'agissait que d'une vilaine histoire d'impôt entre deux seigneurs.

Alors que les paysans des villages voisins continuaient de labourer leurs champs et que les villages ne s'agrandissaient guère, Munich, s'étendant entre-temps sur une superficie de 17 hectares,

sua città natale non gli «stava molto a cuore». Eppure, la sua storia aveva avuto un inizio spettacolare quando, il 14 giugno 1158, il nome «Munichen» venne scritto per la prima volta su carta con caratteri diritti. Il documento fu firmato dall'imperatore Barbarossa in persona. Analogamente ai testimoni di un battesimo, parteciparono a questa cerimonia, che compose la controversia tra il vescovo di Freising ed il duca di Baviera, anche due arcivescovi, quattro vescovi e due margravi. Così, la prima «apparizione ufficiale» della città divenne un vero e proprio atto di stato, anche se si trattò soltanto di definire una spiacevole questione di tasse tra due alte personalità del tempo.

Mentre i contadini dei paesini vicini continuavano a coltivare i loro campi ed i loro villaggi si ingrandivano a mala pena, Monaco, che vantava già un'estensione di quasi 17 ettari, si circondava di una prima cinta muraria, alla quale ne seguì una seconda 100 anni più tardi. Nel frattempo, la città si era ampliata fino a raggiungere i 91 ettari di territorio. Questa era destinata a rimanere, per molto tempo, la sua estensione maggiore in quanto le mura non furono soltanto un baluardo, ma costituirono anche una limitazione fino a quando, nel marzo 1791, si diede inizio al cosiddetto «smantellamento».

In quei giorni iniziò una nuova crescita sotto il regno di Carlo Teodoro, e dopo poco più di mezzo secolo l'area della città misurava oltre 1 600 ettari. Que-

Ein Sonntag in der Menterschwaige, 1857

A Sunday at Menterschwaige, 1857

Un dimanche à la Menterschwaige, 1857

Una domenica alla Menterschwaige, 1857

Das Hoftheater - Rückseite - 1827

The Hoftheater - back side - 1827

Le Hoftheater - en arriere - 1827

L'Hoftheater - retro - 1827

für lange Zeit ihre größte Ausdehnung erreicht, denn bis zur so genannten Entfestigung im März 1791 war diese Wallanlage ein Schutz, aber zugleich auch eine Grenze.

Ein neues Wachstum begann in jenen Karl-Theodor-Tagen, und nach wenig mehr als einem halben Jahrhundert umfasste das Stadtgebiet bereits mehr als 1 600 Hektar. Diese Zahl verdoppelte sich an einem einzigen Herbsttag des Jahres 1854, als die Haupt- und Residenzstadt erstmals die Isar übersprang und Nachbargemeinden adoptierte.

Zunächst gaben die Gemeinden Au, Giesing und Haidhausen im (Alten) Rathaus am Marienplatz ihren Schlüssel ab. Zehn Jahre später folgte Ramersdorf, bald danach Sendling, 1890 Neuhausen und das kurz zuvor zur Stadt erhobene Schwabing. Und so ging es weiter, bis zuletzt, 1942, mit Langwied, Aubing und Lochhausen an die 60 einst selbständige Gemarkungen – von A wie Allach bis Z wie Zamdorf – Teile der Stadt waren. Was einst zur Region zählte, wurde eingemeindet, und München war schließlich mit rund 31 000 Hektar die viertgrößte deutsche Stadt.

In 14 Etappen und nach allen Himmelsrichtungen ist der Ausgriff ins Umland erfolgt. Zum Landgericht Dachau hatten Schwabing, Freimann und Sendling gehört, zum Starnberger Landgericht Hadern, Lochham und Puchheim; die Grenze reichte damals bis nahe an Sendling heran. Für Bogenhausen, Denning, Riem und Perlach wiederum war lange das Landgericht Wolfratshausen zuständig gewesen, während Fröttmaning bis ins frühe 19. Jahrhundert dem Landgericht Kranzberg unterstand. Das Bistum Freising aber, ein ausgedehnter Landstreifen entlang der Isar, reichte bis in die Gegend von Bogenhausen.

Diesem Umstand verdankt die Stadt München ihren ersten Auftritt in der Geschichte und ihren frühen Aufstieg: Heinrich der Löwe, eben zum Herzog von Bayern

were to impede Munich's further expansion for a long time to come. For this defense system not only protected Munich from attacks but also served as a rather restrictive borderline until March 1791, when the walls were finally pulled down.

In those days, under the rule of Duke Karl Theodor, a new period of growth started, and about 50 years later the city area already covered 1,600 hectares. This figure was doubled in one single day when in autumn 1854 the capital and residential city of the Wittelsbacher first reached across the Isar and swallowed up several neighbouring communities.

At first the communities of Au, Giesing and Haidhausen turned in their keys at the (old) town hall on Marienplatz. Ten years later Ramersdorf followed suit, shortly afterwards Sendling, and in 1890 Neuhausen and Schwabing which had become a city shortly before. And this incorporation process continued until 1942 when – with the integration of Langwied, Aubing and Lochhausen – almost 60 formerly independent communities (from A like Allach to Z like Zamdorf) had become districts of the city of Munich. What had made up the region until then had been incorporated, so that Munich with 31,000 hectares of city area was Germany's fourth-largest city.

The city's attack on the surrounding country was carried out in 14 sections and in every direction. Schwabing, Freimann and Sendling had belonged to the Landgericht (regional court) of Dachau; Hadern, Lochham and Puchheim to the Landgericht Starnberg, whose limits touched on Sending. The Landgericht Wolfratshausen had for a long time been responsible for Bogenhausen, Denning, Riem and Perlach, while Fröttmaning used to belong to the Landgericht Kranzberg up to the early 19th century. But the Bishopric of Freising – a wide strip of land spreading along the Isar – almost adjoined the Bogenhausen area.

s'entoura d'abord d'une enceinte et 100 ans plus tard avec ses 91 hectares d'une seconde. La ville avait ainsi atteint pour une longue période sa plus grande taille car, jusqu'à la démolition des enceintes en mars 1791, cette fortification représenta non seulement une protection mais encore une frontière.

Une nouvelle croissance commença pendant les journées Karl-Theodor et après à peine plus d'un demi-siècle, la ville englobait déjà plus de 1 600 hectares. Ce chiffre doubla en un seul jour d'automne de l'année 1854 lorsque la ville principale et ville résidentielle sauta pour la première fois l'Isar et adopta des communes voisines.

Ce furent d'abord les communes d'Au, Giesing et Haidhausen qui rendirent leur clé dans (l'ancien) hôtel de ville sur la Marienplatz. Dix ans plus tard, suivit Ramersdorf, puis peu après Sendling, en 1890 Neuhausen et Schwabing élevée peu de temps avant au rang de ville. Et cela continua, jusqu'en 1942 avec Langwied, Aubing et Lochhausen, environ 60 territoires autrefois autonomes, de A comme Allach à Z comme Zamdorf qui étaient des parties de la ville. Ce qui auparavant faisait partie de la région fut incorporée et Munich, avec 31 000 hectares, se rangea finalement au quatrième rang des villes allemandes.

L'avancée dans les régions avoisinantes se fit en 14 étapes et dans toutes les directions. La circonscription du tribunal de Dachau englobait Schwabing, Freimann et Sendling, celle de Starnberg se composait de Hadern, Kochham et Puchheim; la frontière remontait à l'époque jusqu'à proximité de Sendling. La circonscription du tribunal de Wolfratshausen fut longtemps en charge de Bogenhausen, Denning, Riem et Perlach alors que Fröttmaning dépendit jusqu'au début du 19ème siècle de la circonscription du tribunal de Kranzberg. Mais l'évêché de Freising, une longue bande longeant l'Isar,

sto numero fu raddoppiato in un solo giorno d'autunno dell'anno 1854 quando la capitale del regno di Baviera oltrepassò l'Isar ed annesse i comuni vicini.

Inizialmente furono i comuni di Au, Giesing e Haidhausen a deporre le loro chiavi nel (vecchio) municipio sulla Marienplatz. Dieci anni più tardi seguì Ramersdorf, poco dopo Sendling e, nel 1890, Neuhausen e Schwabing, che poco prima era stata elevata al rango di città. Si continuò su questa falsariga finché nel 1942, con l'incorporazione di Langwied, Aubing e Lochhausen, 60 comuni una volta indipendenti – dalla A come Allach alla Z come Zamdorf – erano diventati parte della città. Comuni che in passato facevano parte della regione furono incorporati nella città e Monaco divenne, con i suoi 31 000 ettari, la quarta città della Germania in ordine di grandezza.

La penetrazione nelle aree limitrofe avvenne in 14 tappe e in tutte le direzioni. Schwabing, Freimann e Sendling erano appartenute alla giurisdizione di Dachau, mentre Hadern, Locham e Puchheim erano sotto la giurisdizione di Starnberg; il confine arrivava, all'epoca, fino a Sendling. Per molto tempo la giurisdizione di Wolfsratshausen fu responsabile dei comuni di Bogenhausen, Denning, Riem e Perlach, mentre Fröttmaning rimase sotto la giurisdizione di Kranzberg fino all'inizio del XIX secolo. Per contro, il vescovado di Freising, una lingua di terra estesa lungo l'Isar, arrivava fino al territorio di Bogenhausen.

La città di Monaco deve la sua prima apparizione nella storia e la sua precoce ascesa ad una particolare circostanza: Enrico XII detto il Leone, appena eletto duca di Baviera e Sassonia, guardava con invidia al commercio di sale che avveniva solo a pochi chilometri più a nord del suo regno e che arricchiva il vescovo di Freising al quale veniva pagato il dazio per il passaggio della merce sul ponte di Oberföhring. Un colpo di mano, magari un attentato incendiario contro il ponte, preventivando

berufen, sah mit Neid, wie wenige Kilometer nördlich seines Landes die Salzfuhren an der Oberföhringer Brücke dem Bischof von Freising ihren Zoll entrichteten. Ein Handstreich, vielleicht ein Brandanschlag auf die Brücke, möglicherweise ein paar blessierte bischöfliche Zollwächter – die Brücke war zerstört und eine neue wurde an der Stelle der späteren Ludwigsbrücke geschlagen. Sie führte direkt hinein ins herzogliche, dazumal welfische Land. Das Reichenhaller Salz rollte nun in die bis dahin unbekannte Siedlung München.

Mit den schweren Fuhren kam Geld in die Stadt. Auch wenn davon jeweils ein Drittel als Entschädigung nach Freising geschickt werden musste – München war lange Zeit der mit Abstand größte Steuerzahler im Herzogtum (und auch die höchstbesteuerte Stadt).

Der Brückenschlag brachte den Fürsten Geld, und er machte die Münchner reich. Wer im Rat etwas zu sagen hatte und zum städtischen Patriziat gehörte – Familien wie die Ligsalz, Riedler, Schrenck oder Tulbeck –, verdankte sein Ansehen wie sein Vermögen zumeist Geschäften, die man heute als „Import- und Export-Handel" deklarieren würde. Mit Salz hatte es begonnen, bald schon kam der Wein hinzu (die Weinstraße erinnert daran) und schließlich auch noch das Geschäft mit venezianischen und flandrischen Tuchen.

Herzog Albrecht IV. wusste, was er den Kaufleuten verdankte, und so erlaubte er dem Münchner Kaufmann Heinrich Barth, zwischen Kochel- und Walchensee eine Straße zu bauen. Durch diese steile Kesselbergstraße (auf der noch Goethe nach Italien fuhr) wurde der Weg verkürzt und den häufigen Isarhochwassern ausgewichen. 1492 – dem Jahr, in dem Kolumbus Amerika entdeckte – war die Arbeit abgeschlossen.

Etwa 50 Familien bestimmten im mittelalterlichen München, in einer Stadt von 10 000, 15 000 Einwohnern, die Richtlinien der

To this fact Munich owed its first appearance on the political stage and its early rise to fame: Henry the Lion had barely been made Duke of Bavaria, when he was obliged to watch, enviously, the carts transporting salt paying customs to the Bishop of Freising at the Oberföhring bridge, only a few miles north of his territory. A surprise attack, posssibly a fire laid on the bridge at the cost of the lives of a few customsmen altered the situation: the bishop's bridge was destroyed and another one was built at the location of the later "Ludwigsbrücke". And this bridge led straight into the Ducal, at that time Guelphic territory. Now the salt from Reichenhall was transported into the up to then completely unknown town of Munich.

The heavy salt loads brought money to the town. Although one third had to be paid over to Freising as a compensation, Munich for a long time remained not only the most important taxpayer in the Duchy of Bavaria but also the city subject to highest taxation.

Nevertheless, the new bridge provided the sovereigns of Bavaria with a comfortable income and made the citizens rich. Families like the Ligsalz', Riedlers, Schrencks and Tulbecks, who had a seat in the city council and belonged to the urban patriciate, owed their prestige and wealth mostly to what we would call "import and export trade" today. This business had started with salt; soon the wine trade was added; and finally trade with cloth from Venice and Flanders began to flourish.

Duke Albrecht IV knew quite well how much he owed to the local merchants. He therefore permitted Heinrich Barth, a merchant from Munich, to build a road from Lake Kochelsee to Lake Walchensee. This extremely steep "Kesselberg Road", which Goethe still used when travelling to Italy, was a welcome shortcut and helped to avoid the numerous floods caused by the Isar. The construction of this road was

s'étendait jusqu'aux portes de Bogenhausen.

Cette situation permit à la ville de Munich de faire ses premiers pas dans l'histoire et elle lui doit son essor précoce. Henri Le Lion, nommé duc de Bavière, regardait avec envie à quelques kilomètres seulement au nord de son territoire les transports de sel qui passaient le pont d'Oberföhring et s'acquittaient de leurs droits de douane auprès de l'évêque de Freising. Un coup de main, peut-être l'incendie du pont, éventuellement quelques douaniers épiscopaux blessés – le pont fut détruit et un nouveau fut construit à la place du pont Ludwig d'aujourd'hui. Il conduisait directement dans le territoire ducal en ce temps – là guelfe. Le sel de Reichenhall descendait donc dans la ville de Munich inconnue jusque – là.

Les lourds transports de sel apportèrent de l'argent à la ville. Même si un tiers devait être envoyé en dédommagement à Freising. Munich fut pendant longtemps le plus grand contribuable du duché (et aussi la ville la plus imposée).

La construction du pont apporta de l'argent aux princes et la richesse aux Munichois. Celui qui avait le pouvoir au conseil et appartenait au patriciat municipal – des familles comme les Ligsalz, Riedler, Schreck ou Tulbeck – devait sa réputation et sa richesse le plus souvent à des commerces qu'on appellerait aujourd'hui des magasins d'import-export. Le sel marqua le début des activités, suivit peu après du vin (la route du vin le rappelle) et enfin le commerce des tissus venant de Venise et des Flandres.

Le duc Albrecht IV savait ce qu'il devait aux marchands et il donna l'autorisation au marchand munichois Heinrich Barth de construire une route ente les lacs du Kochelsee et du Walchensee. Cette route montagneuse très raide (que Goethe emprunta pour se rendre en Italie) permit de raccourcir le chemin et d'échapper aux fréquentes inondations de l'Isar. Les travaux furent terminés

anche il ferimento di un paio di doganieri del vescovo ... e il ponte fu distrutto. In compenso ne venne costruito uno nuovo nel punto in cui sarebbe sorta più tardi la famosa Ludwigsbrücke. Il ponte consentiva l'accesso diretto al territorio ducale, allora terra dei franchi salii; e il sale di Reichenhall poté così giungere nell'insediamento di Monaco che era rimasto, fino a quel momento, sconosciuto.

Con i pesanti carri di sale affluì nelle casse della città anche molto denaro, di cui un terzo dovette essere comunque pagato alla città di Freising a titolo di risarcimento – per molto tempo Monaco fu di gran lunga il maggiore contribuente del ducato (ed anche la città maggiormente tassata).

Il duca guadagnò molto denaro dalla costruzione del ponte, facendo ricchi contemporaneamente anche gli abitanti di Monaco stessa. Coloro che avevano voce nel consiglio ed appartenevano al patriziato - famiglie come i Ligsalz, i Riedler, gli Schrenck o i Tulbeck - si guadagnarono la loro reputazione e la loro ricchezza in gran parte conducendo affari che si potrebbe definire oggi con il termine «Import-Export». Tutto ebbe inizio con il sale, cui seguì ben presto il vino (la «Weinstraße» – strada del vino – ne è un ricordo) e, infine, il commercio delle stoffe provenienti da Venezia e dalle Fiandre.

In segno di gratitudine verso i commercianti, il duca Albrecht IV diede il suo benestare ad uno di questi, Heinrich Barth di Monaco, affinché egli potesse costruire una strada tra il lago di Kochel ed il Walchensee. Grazie a questa ripida strada del Kesselberg (sulla quale transitò anche Goethe durante il suo viaggio in Italia), fu possibile abbreviare il tragitto ed aggirare le frequenti piene dell'Isar. I lavori furono ultimati nel 1492, l'anno della scoperta dell'America.

Nella Monaco medievale, una città di 10 000 – 15 000 abitanti, la linea politica fu determinata da circa 50 famiglie che si occupa-

Politik. Sie kümmerten sich ums gemeine wie auch ums eigene Wohl und hatten die Geldtruhen in ihren Häusern allzeit gut gefüllt. Sie hatten aber auch dafür gesorgt, dass sich reichlich Immobiles in Familienbesitz befand – der Griff ins Umland war ein Teil der Geschäfte. Der Augsburger Historiker Pankraz Fried fand heraus, dass im späten 14. Jahrhundert ein Drittel des Grundes im Landgericht Dachau Eigentum von Münchner Bürgern war – eine frühe Art von Eingemeindung also.

Die Patrizier waren reich, und sie schauten sicher herab auf die bäuerlichen Nachbarn in Sendling, Schwabing oder Neuhausen. Diese plagten sich mühsam durchs Leben wie die kleinen Leute überall auf der Welt und waren froh, wenn sie Eier, Schweine oder Fische in die Stadt finished in 1492, the year when Columbus discovered America.

In medieval Munich, when the town already counted 10,000 to 15,000 inhabitants, 50 families were in control of municipal politics. They concentrated on public and private welfare, and made sure that their own money bags were kept full. But they also saw to it that their families acquired plenty of real estate, for the purchasing of land in the city's immediate vicinity was a major part of their business. Pankraz Fried, a historian from Augsburg, found out that in the late 14th century a third of the landed property in the area of the Dachau Regional Court belonged to citizens of Munich – an early version of incorporation.

The patricians were wealthy and certainly looked down on their peasant neighbours in Sendling, Schwabing and Neuhausen. They plodded away laboriously like all the other ordinary people throughout the world and were glad to be able to supply the city with eggs, pigs and fish. It is a fact, however, that the elegantly dressed urbanites of Munich could not match the splendour and business scope of merchant dynasties like the Fugger and en 1492, l'année où Christophe Colomb découvrit l'Amérique.

Au Moyen Age, environ 50 familles définissaient à Munich, une ville de 10 000, 15 000 habitants, les lignes de la politique. Elles s'occupaient du bien-être général et du leur et leurs coffres étaient toujours bien remplis dans leurs maisons. Elles devaient également veiller à ce que les possessions familiales détiennent de nombreux biens immobiliers et acheter des terrains dans les environs faisait partie de leurs activités. L'historien d'Augsbourg, Pankraz Fried découvrit qu'à la fin du 14ème siècle, un tiers des terrains de la circonscription du tribunal de Dachau était aux mains de citoyens munichois – une forme précoce d'incorporation.

Les patriciens étaient riches et regardaient sûrement de haut leurs voisins paysans de Sendling, Schwabing ou Neuhausen. Ceux-ci avançaient difficilement dans la vie comme les petites gens partout dans le monde et étaient contents quand ils pouvaient approvisionner la ville en œufs, cochons ou poissons. Mais les seigneurs munichois bien habillés ne réussirent pas à faire des affaires sensationnelles. Ils ne sou- rono del bene comune così come delle proprie finanze personali, tant'è che i forzieri delle loro case finirono per essere sempre colmi di denaro. Esse si preoccuparono di accrescere anche il loro patrimonio immobiliare – attingere al territorio circostante faceva parte dei loro affari. Lo storico di Augsburg Pankraz Fried scoprì che nel tardo XIV secolo un terzo del territorio che si trovava sotto la giurisdizione di Dachau era di proprietà di cittadini di Monaco – una forma precoce di incorporazione nel comune, dunque.

I patrizi erano ricchi ed ebbero sicuramente poca considerazione per il vicinato contadino di Sendling, Schwabing e Neuhausen. Questi conducevano un'esistenza grama e faticosa come tutta la piccola gente di questo mondo, e si accontentavano di poter vendere i propri prodotti – uova, maiali, pesce – ai mercati della città. Ma nemmeno i signori di Monaco, con le loro ricche vesti, riuscirono alla fine a realizzare degli affari veramente importanti. Infatti, essi non ressero mai il confronto con i Fugger ed i Welser, che fecero affari in tutto il mondo e prestarono denaro persino agli imperatori, né tantomeno con alcuni commercianti di Norinberga.

La ricchezza dei signori della città aveva i suoi limiti, dei quali il re svedese Gustavo Adolfo non doveva essere evidentemente a conoscenza. Infatti, quando fece il suo ingresso nella città la domenica di Pentecoste dell'anno 1632, pretese che i cittadini gli versassero un tributo di 300 000 fiorini quale prezzo da pagare per la salvaguardia della città contro atti incendiari e saccheggiamenti. Ma le casse della città non contenevano nemmeno la metà di tale somma – a dispetto del fatto che la maestà venuta dal profondo nord pensasse che Monaco fosse «una sella d'oro su un vecchio ronzino».

Ma questa frase, se mai fu detta, rispecchiava probabilmente quanto era stato osservato dagli antichi svedesi durante la loro spedizione da Freising a Monaco

Der Schrannenplatz, 1836 – heute Marienplatz

The Schrannenplatz, 1836 – today the Marienplatz

La Schrannenplatz, 1836 – aujourd'hui la Marienplatz

La Schrannenplatz, 1836 – oggi Marienplatz

Das Schwabinger Tor, kurz vor dem 1816/17 erfolgten Abbruch für die Anlage des Odeonsplatzes; rechts die Theatinerkirche

The Schwabinger Tor shortly before it was demolished in 1816/17 to make room for the Odeonsplatz; on the right the Theatiner Church.

Le Schwabinger Tor, peu avant sa destruction en 1816/1817 pour l'aménagement de l'Odeonsplatz; à droite la Theatinerkirche

Lo Schwabinger Tor, poco prima della sua demolizione avvenuta nel 1816/17 per far posto all'Odeonsplatz; a destra, la Theatinerkirche

liefern durften. Zuletzt konnten aber auch die fein gewandeten Münchner Herren die ganz großen Geschäfte nicht machen. Mit den Fuggern und Welsern, die weltweit Handel trieben und auch Kaisern Bares vorstreckten, durften sie sich nicht vergleichen und wahrscheinlich auch nicht mit manchen der Nürnberger Kaufleute.

Der großbürgerliche Wohlstand hatte seine Grenzen, von denen der Schwedenkönig Gustav Adolf offensichtlich nichts wusste. Als er am Pfingstsonntag 1632 in die Stadt einzog, verlangte er nämlich von den Bürgern 300 000 Gulden. Mit diesem Betrag sollte sich die Stadt von Brandschatzung und Plünderung freikaufen. Doch in der Kasse war nicht einmal die Hälfte der Summe – obwohl die Majestät aus dem hohen Norden der Meinung war, München sei „ein goldener Sattel auf einer dürren Mähre".

Doch dieser Satz, wenn er denn so fiel, beschrieb wahrscheinlich nur das, was die alten Schweden auf ihrem Zug von Freising über Ismaning nach München gesehen hatten: dürre Böden mit spärlicher Vegetation. Das Heer ritt nämlich über die Kiese der letzten Eiszeit sowie der Nacheiszeit, auch über die von Ismaning bis Giesing reichende Löss- und Lehmzunge. Am Anfang dieses Marsches aber hatte es jenes Dachauer und Erdinger Moos durchqueren müssen, das München im Norden in weitem Bogen umschließt und früher, wie

Welser, who carried on a worldwide trade and granted loans even to kings and emperors; Munich's patricians were probably unable to compete even with some of the major Nuremberg merchants.

The wealth of Munich's bourgeoisie obviously had its limits – a fact of which Gustav Adolf, the Swedish king who led the Protestant armies during the Thirty Years' War, was not aware. When he entered the city on Whit Sunday 1632, he demanded 300,000 Gulden (gold coins) from the inhabitants as a sort of ransom. By paying this amount they would escape being sacked and having their homes burned to the ground. But the city could not procure even half of this sum, although the Scandinavian invader believed Munich to be "a golden saddle on a scrawny nag". This comparison (if it was really expressed in this way) probably referred to the unattractive country which the old Swedes had crossed on their way from Freising to Ismaning and Munich: dry ground with sparse vegetation. The army had

tenaient pas la comparaison avec les Fugger et les Welser qui commerçaient au niveau mondial et avançaient même de l'argent aux empereurs, et sûrement pas non plus avec certains marchands de Nuremberg.

L'aisance de la grande bourgeoisie avait ses limites qui semblaient apparemment inconnues au roi de Suède Gustav Adolf. Lorsqu'il pénétra dans la ville le dimanche de la Pentecôte 1632, il exigea des bourgeois 300 000 florins. Cette somme devait permettre à la ville d'être à l'abri du rançonnement et des pillages. Mais les coffres ne contenaient même pas la moitié de ce montant, même si sa majesté du Grand Nord était d'avis que Munich «était une selle dorée sur un vieux cheval maigre».

Quand cette phrase fut prononcée, elle ne décrivait sûrement que ce que les vieux Suédois avaient vu en allant de Freising via Ismaning à Munich, à savoir des sols secs et pauvres en végétation. L'armée passa en effet sur les cailloux de la dernière période glaciaire et de la

attraverso Ismaning: terreni aridi con scarsa vegetazione. L'esercito cavalcò infatti sopra la terra ghiaiosa formatasi durante l'ultima era glaciale e post-glaciale, così come sopra la lingua di terra argillosa e di löss che si estendeva da Ismaning a Giesing – una marcia che era iniziata con l'attraversamento delle paludi di Dachau e di Erding che circondavano, con un ampio raggio, la zona a nord di Monaco e che arrivavano allora, così come rivela il nome, fino a Moosach.

Per secoli, queste aree umide funsero da efficace barriera. Qualche decennio dopo il passaggio di Gustavo Adolfo, il pianificatore Johann Joachim Becher sottopose al principe elettore Ferdinando Maria, allora reggente, una proposta per la bonifica della palude di Erding. Egli suggeriva di estrarre la torba del ricco deposito della zona e di trasformare il materiale in olio combustibile. L'idea non venne comunque realizzata, così come non ebbe seguito il piano proposto più tardi di acquisire Manhattan per farne

der Name verrät, bis Moosach reichte.

Jahrhundertelang wirkten diese feuchten Gebiete wie eine Barriere. Dabei hatte der große Pläneschmied Johann Joachim Becher ein paar Jahrzehnte nach Gustav Adolfs Ritt gen München dem regierenden Kurfürsten Ferdinand Maria einen Vorschlag für die gewinnbringende Sanierung des Erdinger Mooses vorgelegt. Die reichen Torflager, meinte er, sollten abgebaut und zu Brennöl verarbeitet werden. Dies wurde allerdings ebenso wenig realisiert wie Bechers später vorgetragener Plan, Manhattan als bayerische Kolonie zu erwerben. Spätere Generationen haben das Terrain nördlich von München auf andere Weise genutzt – sie bauten dort den neuen Münchner Flughafen.

Auf dem näher bei der Stadt gelegenen unfruchtbaren Land, der „dürren Mähre", veranstalteten die bayerischen Herzöge gerne ihre Jagden. Nachdem 1530, beim Besuch Kaiser Karls V., auf der Perlacher Haid 100 Hirsche erlegt worden waren, lobte ein Begleiter der habsburgischen Majestät, dass es in der Umgebung Münchens die schönsten Hirschjagden der Welt gäbe.

Die Reviere rund um die Residenzstadt lohnten auch später noch große Jagdausflüge. So fuhr der Bayernkurfürst Ferdinand Maria 1658 mit Kaiser Leopold I. auf die Garchinger Haid, wo 100 Hirsche aufgetrieben wurden.

Die Zeit der exzessiven Hofjagden ist vorbei, die Hirsche haben sich längst bergwärts zurückgezogen. Und in Garching haben inzwischen Wissenschaftler der Technischen und der Ludwig-Maximilians-Universität, der Europäischen Südsternwarte (ESO) sowie von vier Instituten der Max-Planck-Gesellschaft ihre Forschungsgeräte aufgebaut, um das Größte wie das Kleinste zu jagen. Studiert man hier, knapp außerhalb der nördlichen Stadtgrenze von München, was die Welt im Innersten zusammenhält und die Galaxien auseinandertreibt, will man hinterm südwestlichen Stadtrand, in Martinsried,

ridden along the gravel layer left by the last ice age and postdiluvian age, and further on across the loess and loam tongue spreading from Ismaning to Giesing. The first stage of their progress had led across the "Dachauer and Erdinger Moos", a swampy area which enclosed Munich in the north and which, in former times, reached all the way to Moosach, as the name implies.

For several centuries this wet zone acted as a barrier, even though Johann Joachim Becher, a very ingenious planner, had submitted to Elector Ferdinand Maria a proposal for making the Erdinger Moos more profitable only a few decades after Gustav Adolf's invasion of Munich. What he suggested was exploiting the large peat deposits and to using them for fuel. But neither this idea nor Becher's later suggestion of buying Manhattan and turning it into a Bavarian colony was put into practice. Later generations made use of this area to the north of the city in a different way: they built the new airport there.

The barren land (i.e. Gustav Adolf's "scrawny nag") located close to the city was for centuries the hunting ground of the dukes of Bavaria. When during a visit of Emperor Charles V in 1530 one hundred red deer were bagged on the Perlach Heath, one of the emperor's escorts praised the area as one of the best hunting grounds in the world.

They continued to be rich in game, for in 1658 Elector Ferdinand Maria of Bavaria took Emperor Leopold I to the Garching Heath, where drivers also flushed up 100 stags.

Today the times of the big royal hunts in Munich's region are past, for the red deer withdrew to the mountains a long time ago. And in Garching scientists of the TU (Technical University), Ludwig-Maximilian University, the Europäische Südsternwarte (European Southern Observatory – ESO), and four institutes of the Max-Planck-Gesellschaft have set up their research facilities for "hunting" the tiniest and largest

période post-glaciaire ainsi que sur la langue de lœss et de glaise s'étendant d'Ismaning à Giesing. Au départ de cette marche, elle dut également traverser la zone marécageuse de Dachauer et d'Erdinger Moos qui entoure largement le nord de Munich et s'étendait avant, comme son nom l'indique à Moosach.

Pendant des siècles, ces zones humides fonctionnèrent comme des barrières. Et le grand planificateur Johann Joachim Becher avait, quelques décennies avant la marche de Gustav Adolf sur Munich, soumis une proposition au prince électeur régnant Ferdinand Maria portant sur les bénéfices que présenterait l'assainissement d'Erdinger Moos. D'après lui, les riches tourbières devaient être supprimées et transformées en huile combustible. Cela ne se réalisa pas, pas plus que le plan présenté plus tard par Becher d'acquérir Manhattan comme colonie bavaroise. Les générations ultérieures utilisèrent le terrain au nord de Munich d'une autre manière, à savoir en construisant le nouvel aéroport munichois.

Sur le terrain infertile et proche de la ville, les ducs bavarois organisaient leur chasse. En 1530, lors de la visite de l'empereur Charles V, 100 cerfs furent tués sur la Perlacher Haid, un accompagnateur de sa majesté des Habsbourg loua le fait que les environs de Munich offraient les plus belles chasses au cerf du monde.

Les terrains de chasse autour de la ville résidentielle donnèrent encore plus tard l'occasion à de grandes chasses. Ainsi, le prince électeur de Bavière Ferdinand Maria partit en 1658 avec l'empereur Leopold 1er sur la Garchinger Haid où 100 cerfs avaient été levés.

L'époque des chasses à cour excessives est terminée, les cerfs se sont depuis longtemps repliés dans les montagnes. Et à Garching, les scientifiques de l'université technique et de l'université Ludwig Maximilian, de l'observatoire européen (Europäische

una colonia bavarese. Le generazioni successive hanno poi sfruttato il terreno a nord di Monaco in altro modo, costruendovi il nuovo aeroporto della città.

Sul terreno improduttivo vicino alla città, la cosiddetta «dürre Mähre» («rozza rinsecchita»), i duchi bavaresi si dilettavano ad organizzare le loro battute di caccia. In seguito ad una visita dell'imperatore Carlo V nel 1530, durante la quale furono abbattuti 100 cervi nella riserva di Perlach, un accompagnatore della maestà asburgica elogiò i dintorni di Monaco definendoli le migliori riserve del mondo per la caccia al cervo.

Anche negli anni a seguire, i territori intorno alla residenza ducale furono lo sfondo ideale per grandiose battute di caccia. Nel 1658, durante una di queste battute nella riserva di Garching, alla quale presero parte il principe elettore di Baviera Ferdinando Maria e l'imperatore Leopoldo I, furono abbattuti 100 cervi.

I tempi delle grandiose (ed eccessive) cacce di corte sono ormai passati ed i cervi si sono ritirati, da tempo, verso i monti. Nel frattempo, a Garching gli scienziati del Politecnico e della Ludwig-Maximilians-Universität, dell'Osservatorio Astronomico Europeo «ESO» e di quattro istituti della Max-Planck-Gesellschaft hanno installato i loro strumenti di ricerca per dare la caccia agli elementi più grandi e più piccoli dell'universo. Se qui, appena al di fuori del confine settentrionale della città di Monaco, si studia ciò che tiene insieme la terra a livello infinitamente piccolo e le forze dell'universo che fanno allontanare le galassie, al confine sud-occidentale della città, a Martinsried, due istituti Max Planck dedicano le loro ricerche a decifrare i segreti della vita.

Monaco, metropoli commerciale e, in seguito, anche città d'arte di fama mondiale, è diventata un punto di riferimento di prim'ordine per la ricerca scientifica di rango internazionale grazie anche agli undici istituti della Max-Planck-Gesellschaft, ad

Das Isartor – einziges, weitgehend in seiner Grundform erhaltenes Stadttor Münchens

The Isartor – Munich's only old city gate that has largely preserved its original shape

Isartor – la porte de Munich ayant le mieux conservé sa forme primitive

L'Isartor – l'unica porta della città che ha largamente conservato la sua forma originaria.

in zwei Max-Planck-Instituten die Geheimnisse des Lebens enträtseln.

Die Handels- und später weit gerühmte Kunststadt München ist vor allem auch durch die insgesamt elf Institute der Max-Planck-Gesellschaft sowie durch bedeutende High-Tech-Unternehmen wie Siemens, Dasa, Dornier oder das Deutsche Zentrum für Luft- und Raumfahrt (DLR) in Oberpfaffenhofen zu einem Forschungs-"game": while here, just outside Munich's northern city limits, experts study what holds the interior of our world together and what causes the galaxies to scatter, the scientists working in two Max Planck Institutes in Martinsried (beyond Munich's southwestern limits) try to unravel the mysteries of life.

Munich, first a trade centre and later a widely acclaimed art centre, has by now become a research and science centre of international rank: it boasts not only eleven institutes of the Max-Planck-Gesellschaft, but also important high-tech enterprises such as Siemens, Dasa, Dornier, and the Deutsche Zentrum für Luft- und Raumfahrt (German Center for Air and Space Travel – DLR) in Oberpfaffenhofen.

In about 1830 a city guidebook still stated that "in Munich one finds very few factories and manufacturing companies". It Südsternwarte – ESO) ainsi que des quatre instituts de la société Max Planck déployèrent entretemps leurs instruments de recherche afin de chasser le gigantesque tout comme le minuscule. Ici, on fait des études, juste en dehors des limites nord de la ville de Munich, sur ce qui fait tenir ensemble le cœur du monde et disperse les galaxies alors que derrière la frontière sud-ouest de la ville, à Martinsried, les deux instituts Max Planck élucident les mystères de la vie.

La ville commerciale et plus tard la ville culturelle de Munich jouissant d'une grande réputation devint un site scientifique et de recherche de rang international surtout grâce aux onze instituts de la société Max Planck ainsi qu'aux importantes entreprises de haute technologie comme Siemens, Dasa, Dornier ou au centre allemand pour l'aéronautique et aziende all'avanguardia in campo tecnologico quali la Siemens, la Dasa e la Dornier e, ancora, grazie al Centro Tedesco di Voli Aerospaziali «DLR» di Oberpfaffenhofen.

Nel 1830 si poteva ancora leggere in una guida della città: «A Monaco ci sono poche fabbriche e pochi stabilimenti», e di quel poco si è scritto ancora meno. Ma già a quel tempo, ovvero agli albori dell'industrializzazione, le aziende più importanti avevano stabilito la propria sede in periferia: Joseph Anton von Maffei costruì le sue locomotive a Hirschau a partire dal 1841, la fabbrica di tessuti di Joseph von Utzschneider era situata alle porte della città, la «Königliche Bronce- und Erzgießerei» (Reale Fonderia di Bronzo e Metallo) operava nella Maxvostadt, a Laim si trovavano fabbriche di terraglia, e la manifattura di porcellane

und Wissenschaftsstandort von internationalem Rang geworden.

Um 1830 schrieb ein Stadtführer noch: „Fabriken und Manufakturen zählt München nur wenige", und wenig mehr wurde dann auch darüber berichtet. Aber schon damals, in der Frühzeit der Industrialisierung, waren die größeren Betriebe in Außenbezirken angesiedelt: Joseph Anton von Maffei baute von 1841 an seine Lokomotiven in der Hirschau, Joseph von Utzschneiders Tuchfabrik lag vor dem Einlasstor, die „Königliche Bronce- und Erzgießerei" arbeitete in der Maxvorstadt, Steingutfabriken gab es in Laim, und die um 1750 gegründete Porzellanmanufaktur war von Neudeck nach Nymphenburg gezogen.

20 Jahre später brauchte ein Stadtchronist kaum mehr Zeilen, um alle Fabriken aufzuzählen, „die sich einen Namen gemacht haben". Aber der Autor war zuversichtlich und meinte, München hätte noch immer Platz für zehn, zwölf oder gar noch mehr „großartige Etablissements". Er ahnte nicht, dass diese Zahl sehr bald schon um das Vielfache übertroffen werden würde. Symbole des technischen Aufschwungs waren der Glaspalast und die Große Industrieausstellung 1854.

1275 hatte der Bischof von Freising geschrieben, München sei „ins Unermessliche" gewachsen. Doch mussten von da an noch 300 Jahre vergehen, bis sich die Einwohnerzahl auf 20 000 verdoppelte. Als 1781 dann die erste Volkszählung stattfand, hatte die Stadt 37 840 Einwohner. Nach Überschreiten der 100 000er-Marke aber begann ein Zulauf, der dem Freisinger Bischof selig (seine Nachfolger residieren seit 1821 als Erzbischöfe in München) die Sprache verschlagen hätte: 1862 zählte München 148 000 Einwohner, 1880 bereits 230 000, und 1900 war die halbe Million fast erreicht.

Eine halbe Million in gut 700 Jahren, und diese Zahl verdoppelte sich, obwohl im Zweiten Weltkrieg 30 % der Wohnungen zer-

offered no further information about them. But even at the outset of industrialization several large enterprises had already settled at the periphery: Joseph Anton von Maffei, for instance, built his locomotives in the Hirschau from 1841 on; Joseph von Utzschneider's cloth factory was located in front of the "Einlasstor"; the "Königliche Bronze- und Erzgießerei" (Royal Bronze and Ore Foundry) operated in the Maxvorstadt; in Laim several earthenware factories existed; and the porcelain manufacture founded in 1750 had been moved from Neudeck to Nymphenburg.

20 years later a chronicler would have needed about the same number of pages to list all the factories which had "made a name for themselves" in the meantime. But the author added, optimistically, that Munich still had plenty of room for ten, twelve or even more "large establishments". He had no inkling that these figures would soon be exceeded many times over. The "Glass Palace" and the "Große Industrieausstellung 1854" (a huge industrial exhibition) became symbols of technological progress.

In 1275 the then bishop of Freising had written that "Munich had grown immensely". But it took 300 more years for the population to double in size, i.e. to reach the 20,000 mark. When the first census took place in 1781, the city counted 37,840 inhabitants. After passing the 100,000 mark, the number of inhabitants rose very quickly, a fact that the late Bishop of Freising (his successors have resided as archbishops in Munich since 1821) would hardly have understood: in 1862 the City counted 148,000 people; in 1880 already 230,000, and by the turn of the century nearly half a million.

500,000 new citizens in roughly 700 years was an impressive increase. But even this figure was doubled subsequently in less than sixty years, even though 30 % of the available flats were destroyed in the Second World War.

l'aérospatial (DLR) à Oberpfaffenhofen.

Vers 1830, un guide écrivait encore: «les fabriques et manufactures sont rares à Munich» et le commentaire était encore plus court. Mais à l'époque déjà, aux premiers balbutiements de l'industrialisation, les grands entreprises étaient implantées dans les districts extérieurs: Joseph Anton von Maffei construisit dès 1841 ses locomotives à la Hirschau, la fabrique de tissus de Joseph von Utzschneider se situait à la porte d'entrée, la «fonderie royale de bronze et de minerai» opérait dans la Maxvorstadt, les fabriques de faïence se trouvaient à Laim et la manufacture de porcelaine fondée vers 1750 avait déménagée de Neudeck à Nymphenburg.

20 ans plus tard, un chroniqueur de la ville n'avait guère besoin de plus de place pour énumérer toutes les entreprises «qui s'étaient forgées un nom». Mais l'auteur, plein de confiance, pensait que Munich avait encore de la place pour dix, douze ou même encore plus «d'établissements extraordinaires». Il ne devinait pas que le nombre allait bientôt se multiplier sans fin. Les symboles de l'essor technique furent le palais de verre et la grande exposition industrielle de 1854.

En 1275, l'évêque de Freising écrivait que Munich avait pris des dimensions incroyables. Mais il fallut encore attendre 300 ans pour que le nombre de ses habitants double et passe à 20 000. Lorsqu'en 1781, le premier recensement eut lieu, la ville ne comptait que 37 840 habitants. Le passage de la frontière des 100 000 fut suivi par un afflux qui laissa l'évêque de Freising (ses successeurs résident depuis 1821 comme archevêques à Munich) sans voix. En 1862, Munich comptait 148 000 habitants, en 1880 il y en avait déjà 230 000 et en 1900 le demi million était atteint.

Un demi million en 700 ans et, alors que pendant la Seconde Guerre mondiale 30 % des habita-

fondata nel 1750 venne trasferita da Neudeck a Nymphenburg.

20 anni più tardi, ad un cronista bastarono nuovamente poche righe per elencare tutte le fabbriche «che si erano fatte un nome». Ma l'autore era fiducioso e scrisse che Monaco aveva ancora spazio per 10, 12, e forse ancora più «grandiosi stabilimenti». Non poteva certo sapere che questa cifra sarebbe stata ben presto superata, e di gran lunga. Il Palazzo di Vetro e la Grande Esposizione Industriale del 1854 diventarono i simboli dell'ascesa tecnologica di Monaco.

Nel 1275 il vescovo di Freising aveva scritto che Monaco era cresciuta «a dismisura». Ma dovettero passare ancora 300 anni prima che il numero degli abitanti riuscisse a raddoppiare, arrivando a 20 000 unità. Secondo il primo censimento effettuato nel 1781, la città contava 37 840 abitanti. Dopo aver superato la fatidica soglia dei 100 000 abitanti, verso l'insediamento iniziò un'affluenza che avrebbe ammutolito il vescovo di Freising se fosse stato ancora in vita (gli arcivescovi suoi successori risiedono a Monaco dal 1821): nel 1862 Monaco contava 148 000 abitanti, già nel 1880 arrivava a 230 000 e nel 1900 si raggiunse quasi il mezzo milione di abitanti.

Mezzo milione in 700 anni; e questa cifra era destinata a raddoppiare in soli 60 anni, nonostante la distruzione di circa il 30 % delle abitazioni causate dalla Seconda Guerra Mondiale!

La città, capitale del regno di Baviera, vide l'alba del nuovo secolo con 500 000 abitanti, più o meno la stessa cifra registrata al termine della guerra nel maggio del 1945. Dapprima rientrarono in città i 300 000 cittadini di Monaco che erano stati sfollati o erano fuggiti dai bombardamenti. A questi si aggiunsero i profughi e, dopo la riforma monetaria, quando ebbe inizio il cosiddetto «miracolo economico», si assistette ad un afflusso generalizzato verso Monaco da tutte le regioni della Germania.

stört worden waren, innerhalb von nur sechs Jahrzehnten!

500 000 Einwohner hatte die kgl. bayer. Residenzstadt zu Beginn des Jahrhunderts, und fast genauso viele waren es im Mai 1945, als der Krieg zu Ende ging. Zunächst kehrten wohl die 300 000 Münchner zurück, die evakuiert und vor den Bomben geflohen waren. Dazu kamen Flüchtlinge, und nach der Währungsreform, als das so genannte „Wirtschaftswunder" begann, strömten die Zuzügler aus sämtlichen deutschen Landen herbei.

Und für alle, alte wie neue Einwohner, mussten Wohnungen gebaut werden. 3 000 entstanden 1949, 10 000 kamen 1950 hinzu, nahezu die gleiche Zahl im darauf folgenden Jahr. So ging es weiter, bis im (Olympia-)Jahr 1972 mit 22 000 Wohnungen ein nie wieder erreichter Rekord aufgestellt wurde. Die „heimliche Hauptstadt" stand in der Statistik der neu errichteten Häuser Jahr für Jahr auf dem ersten Platz; sie musste ihn erst für das wiedervereinigte Berlin räumen.

Zunächst wurden vor allem die durch Bomben demolierten Häuser instand gesetzt, doch die Wohnungen reichten nicht aus. München war „boom-town", und so wurde in großem Stil neu geplant. Am eindrucksvollsten wohl am südöstlichen Rand der Stadt, wo die bayerischen Herzöge einst besonders gern gejagt hatten. Der Geograph Philipp Apian wusste vom Wildreichtum in dieser Gegend, denn als er um die Mitte des 16. Jahrhunderts ganz Bayern in 24 Landtafeln erfasste, zeichnete er auf der Perlacher Haid äsende Rehe und springende Hirsche. Das Revier wurde vor mehr als einem halben Jahrhundert eingemeindet und seit 1967 mit rund 16 000 Wohnungen der Trabantenstadt Neuperlach überbaut.

Die erste der insgesamt 17 Großwohnanlagen entstand von 1954 an auf einer Wiese, die zuvor hauptsächlich weidenden Schafen überlassen war. Auf die hier errichtete Parkstadt Bogenhausen folgten: Fürstenried-Ost,

As stated above, the royal residential city and capital of Bavaria had already boasted 500,000 inhabitants at the turn of the century; in May 1945, when the last world war ended, it had only the same number of inhabitants left, for numerous people had been evacuated or had fled to the safer countryside when the bombing started. 300,000 of them returned as soon as the fighting had ceased. They were joined by innumerable displaced persons and refugees and, after the currency reform, when the so-called "Economic Miracle" began, immigrants from all parts of Germany poured into Munich.

Housing had to be provided for all these newcomers. In 1949, 3,000 flats were built, in 1950 10,000 were added, and in the following year 10,000 more. This building boom continued until 1972, when thanks to the Olympic Games a record of 22,000 flats was set, which has not been matched since. Germany's "Secret Capital" took first place in the statistics of newly built housing year after year, until it had to cede this leading position to Berlin, the reunited new German capital.

At first the buildings damaged by bombs were reconstructed, but the housing made available in this way did not suffice. As a "boom-town" Munich started to plan on a bigger scale, particularly at the southeastern fringes of the city where the dukes of Bavaria had liked to hunt. Philipp Apian, a geographer living in the 16th century, knew how rich in game this area was, for when he made 24 plates of Bavaria in the 1550s, he decorated the one showing the Perlach Heath with feeding deer and jumping stags. This hunting preserve was incorporated into the city approximately 50 years ago and from 1967 on has been turned into the satellite city of New Perlach – a housing area containing 16,000 flats.

The first of altogether 17 large housing areas – the park city of Bogenhausen – was built in 1954 on a meadow that had formerly

tions furent détruits, le chiffre doubla en à peine soixante ans!

La ville résidentielle et royale bavaroise comptait 500 000 habitants au début du siècle et en affichait presque autant en mai 1945 lorsque la guerre prit fin. Les 300 000 Munichois évacués et qui avaient fui les bombes revinrent tout d'abord à Munich. Puis les réfugiés arrivèrent et, après la réforme monétaire, lorsque le «miracle économique» se produisit, des gens arrivèrent de tous les coins de l'Allemagne.

Et pour tous, les anciens comme les nouveaux habitants, il fallut construire des appartements. 3 000 virent le jour en 1949, 10 000 vinrent s'ajouter en 1950, et presque le même nombre l'année d'après. Et cela continua jusqu'à ce que l'année des Jeux olympiques, en 1972, vienne battre un record jamais égalé avec 22 000 appartements. «La capitale secrète» caracola pendant des années à la tête des statistiques des maisons neuves, elle laissa sa place à Berlin après la réunification.

Les bâtiments détruits par les bombes furent reconstruits en premier mais la capacité en appartements ne suffisait pas. Munich était en plein boom et la planification se faisait dans le plus grand style. Le côté sud-est de la ville est le plus impressionnant, là où les ducs bavarois aimaient autrefois chasser. Le géographe Philipp Apian connaissait les richesses en gibier de cet endroit car lorsqu'il recensa l'ensemble de la Bavière au milieu du 16ème siècle en 24 tableaux, il dessina sur la Perlacher Haid des chevreuils occupés à brouter et des cerfs en train de courir. Le terrain de chasse fut incorporé il y a plus d'un demi-siècle et, depuis 1967, 16 000 appartements ont été construits dans la ville satellite de Neuperlach.

La première des 17 grandes cités vit le jour en 1954 sur une prairie qui servait avant essentiellement à faire paître les moutons. Après la naissance de la ville-parc de Bogenhausen suivirent Fürstenried-est, Neuaubing-

Per tutti gli abitanti, sia vecchi che nuovi, fu necessario costruire nuove abitazioni. Ne sorsero 3 000 nel 1948, cui se ne aggiunsero altre 10 000 nel 1950 e pressoché lo stesso numero anche nell'anno seguente. La situazione si evolse su questa falsariga fino al 1972 (l'anno dei Giochi Olimpici), quando con la costruzione di 22 000 appartamenti si stabilì un record mai più eguagliato. Anno dopo anno, la «capitale segreta» della Germania rimase al primo posto nella statistica delle città con il maggior numero di nuove costruzioni; un primato che, peraltro, dovette cedere a Berlino solo dopo la riunificazione.

Si iniziò con la ristrutturazione delle case danneggiate dalle bombe, ma le abitazioni non bastavano. Monaco era diventata una «boom town» e quindi si dovette procedere ad una pianificazione in grande stile. Ciò avvenne, in modo impressionante, nella periferia a sud-est della città, zona un tempo prediletta dai duchi bavaresi per la caccia. Il geografo Philipp Apian doveva essere a conoscenza della ricchezza di selvaggina di questa regione quando, intorno alla metà del XVI secolo, disegnò su una delle 24 tavole geografiche interamente dedicate alla Baviera dei daini e dei cervi che brucavano l'erba e saltavano nella zona della riserva di Perlach. Questa riserva è stata incorporata nel comune mezzo secolo fa, e nel 1967 è stata sopraedificata con le oltre 16 000 abitazioni che costituiscono la città satellite di Neuperlach.

Il primo dei 17 grandi centri residenziali, la «città-parco» di Bogenhausen, sorse a partire dal 1954 su un prato che, in precedenza, era stato destinato prevalentemente a pascolo per le pecore. Ad essa seguirono Fürstenried-Est, Neuaubing-Est, Lerchenauer See, Neuabing-Ovest, Cosimapark, Neuforstenried ed infine, a partire dal 1960, il più grande dei centri residenziali, Hasenbergl.

Neuaubing-Ost, Lerchenauer See, Neuaubing-West, Cosimapark, Neuforstenried und schließlich, ab 1960, die größte der Großwohnanlagen, das Hasenbergl.

Die Arbeiten an den 8 600 Wohnungen im Norden Münchens waren noch lange nicht abgeschlossen, als weiter südlich, auf dem Gelände des ehemaligen Flughafens Oberwiesenfeld, die Bauarbeiten für das Olympische Dorf begannen.

Im April 1966 waren die Olympischen Sommerspiele für 1972 nach München vergeben worden. Die Stadt hatte im Laufe der Geschichte mancherlei Titel erhalten. Zuletzt nannte man sie – nachdem im Dezember 1957, also unmittelbar vor Beginn der 700-Jahrfeier, der millionste Einwohner geboren war – das „Millionendorf". Sie ließ sich auch gerne als „Weltstadt mit Herz" feiern und war stolz, als der „Spiegel" sie 1964 „Deutschlands heimliche Metropole" nannte. Und nun also „Olympiastadt".

Der Aufstieg ging im Zeichen der fünf Ringe rasant und auch ein wenig beängstigend weiter. Da die großen freien Flächen auf den 31 000 Münchner Hektaren weitgehend überbaut waren – obwohl man noch Platz für Grünanlagen wie den Ostpark und den Westpark (das ehemalige IGA-Gelände) fand – und die private Motorisierung zugenommen hatte, Straßen ausgebaut und der öffentliche Nahverkehr durch U- und S-Bahnen deutlich verbessert worden waren, gewann das Umland immer mehr an Bedeutung.

In vorolympischen Zeiten hatte man die Region in der Münchner Statistik eingeteilt in „die Stadt" mit einer Million Einwohnern, das daran anschließende „Ergänzungsgebiet" mit den Landkreisen München, Dachau, Fürstenfeldbruck, Starnberg (oder Teilen davon) und schließlich die „verstädterte Zone" sowie die bis in die Landkreise Ebersberg, Erding, Miesbach reichende „Randzone" – insgesamt ein Gebiet mit 1,8 Millionen Einwohnern.

Die Verhältnisse änderten sich, und so wurde München zusammen a sheep pasture. Subsequently, the settlements of Fürstenried-Ost, Neuaubing-Ost, Lerchenauer See, Neuaubing-West, Cosimapark, and Neuforstenried were set up, and finally – from 1960 on – the largest housing area of them all, the "Hasenbergl".

This construction of 8,600 flats in the northern part of Munich was not yet completed, when the city started building the Olympic Village farther south – in the area of the former Oberwiesenfeld Airport.

In April 1966 Munich had been selected as the venue of the Olympic Summer Games of 1972. In the course of its history, many different titles had been bestowed on this city; the last one, used for the first time in 1957, after the millionth inhabitant had been born shortly before Munich's 700th anniversary, was "village with a million inhabitants". But the city also loved being called "metropolis with a heart", and was equally proud when in 1964 the "Der Spiegel" magazine referred to it as "Germany's secret capital". And now it had also become an "Olympic City".

Under the sign of the five (Olympic) rings Munich's rise continued rapidly and even somewhat alarmingly. As most of the large green areas of the 31,000 hectares of city territory had already been built over (even though one had found room for such large parks as the "Ostpark" and "Westpark" (formerly the site of the International Garden Show), and as private motorization had greatly increased, roads been improved, and the public transport system complemented with subways and suburban lines, the outlying districts steadily gained in importance.

In pre-Olympic times statistics had subdivided the Munich region into the "City" with one million inhabitants; the "Ergänzungsgebiet", a supplementary zone comprising the (rural) districts of Dachau, Fürstenfeldbruck and Starnberg, or parts thereof; the est, Lerchenauer See, Neuaubing-ouest, Cosimapark, Neuforstenried et enfin, à partir de 1960, la plus grande des cités: Hasenbergl.

Les travaux des 8 600 appartements au nord de Munich n'étaient pas encore tous terminés quand, plus au sud, sur le terrain de l'ancien aéroport militaire d'Oberwiesenfeld, les travaux de construction du village olympique commencèrent.

En avril 1966, il avait été décidé que les Jeux olympiques d'été de 1972 se tiendraient à Munich. Au cours de son histoire, la ville avait déjà reçu quelques titres. Le dernier lui fut attribué en décembre 1957, juste avant le début de la fête de ses 700 ans, lorsque le millionième habitant vit le jour, «le village d'un million d'âmes». Elle se laissait également appeler volontiers «métropole au grand cœur» et était fière que la revue Spiegel l'ait surnommée en 1964 «la métropole secrète de l'Allemagne». Et voilà qu'elle était maintenant «ville olympique».

A l'instar des cinq anneaux olympiques, son essor fut fulgurant et même un peu inquiétant. Etant donné que les grands terrains libres des 31 000 hectares munichois étaient déjà intensément construits, bien que l'on trouvât encore de la place pour des espaces verts comme le Ostpark et le Westpark (l'ancien terrain de l'IGA), que la motorisation privée avait augmenté, que les routes avaient été agrandies et les transports en commun interurbains nettement améliorés avec le métro et le train interurbain, les environs revêtirent une importance croissante.

Durant la période préolympique, la région avait été rangée dans les statistiques munichois comme «la ville» au million d'habitants et la «zone complémentaire» voisine avec les arrondissements de Munich, Dachau, Fürstenfeldbruck, Starnberg (ou certaines parties), la «zone urbanisée» ainsi que la «zone marginale» allant jusqu'aux arrondissements d'Ebersberg, Erding, Miesbach, I lavori per la realizzazione di 8 600 abitazioni a nord di Monaco erano ancora lontani dall'essere completati quando si diede inizio alla costruzione del villaggio olimpico in una zona più a sud che, qualche decennio prima, era stata occupata dall'aeroporto di Oberwiesenfeld.

Nell'aprile 1966 Monaco si era infatti aggiudicata i Giochi Olimpici Estivi del 1972. In passato, la città aveva ricevuto già parecchi titoli. L'ultimo era stato quello di «paesino da un milione di abitanti», che le era stato conferito dopo la nascita del milionesimo cittadino, un evento che precedette l'inizio dei festeggiamenti per i 700 anni della città. Monaco si faceva anche chiamare «la metropoli con cuore», e fu particolarmente fiera quando, nel 1964, il magazine «Der Spiegel» la definì la «capitale segreta della Germania». A questi appellativi seguiva ora il titolo di «città olimpica».

L'espansione continuò all'insegna dei cinque cerchi: in modo fulmineo ma anche un po' preoccupante. Dato che le grandi aree libere del territorio di 31 000 ettari di Monaco erano in gran parte edificate – pur rimanendo ancora degli spazi verdi come il Parco Est ed il Parco Ovest, ricavato dall'area che aveva ospitato l'Esposizione Internazionale di Giardinaggio «IGA» – e dato che il traffico motorizzato privato era aumentato, la rete stradale era stata ampliata e la rete metropolitana e la ferrovia suburbana veloce avevano migliorato sensibilmente la situazione dei trasporti pubblici su breve distanza, le aree fuori del territorio comunale acquistarono un'importanza sempre maggiore.

Nel periodo pre-olimpico la regione di Monaco era stata ripartita, da un punto di vista statistico, nella «città» con un milione di abitanti, nella limitrofa «area integrativa» comprendente i distretti di Monaco, Dachau, Fürstenfeldbruck, Starnberg (o parti di questo), e, infine, nella «zona urbanizzata» e «zona periferica» che comprendeva persino

men mit 298 umliegenden Gemeinden zur Region 14, in der die Stadt (1996) zwar die Hälfte der Einwohner, 58 % der Arbeitsplätze und sogar 68 % der Beschäftigten, doch nur knapp 6 % der Fläche besaß.

Im Jahre 1784 hatte Lorenz von Westenrieder die Beschreibung einer ungewöhnlichen Exkursion vorgelegt – er erzählte von seiner „fünf mäßige Stunden weiten" Reise an den Starnberger See. Den Münchnern war das Gebiet damals kaum bekannt. Es konnte geschehen, dass der Tourist in der Nähe von Seeshaupt Kinder traf, denen „ganz gewiss nur selten ein Mensch mit unserer Kleidung vor ihre Augen gekommen ist".

München hat inzwischen dreißigmal so viele Einwohner wie in Westenrieders Tagen, und die Kinder von Seeshaupt tragen längst schon dieselbe Kleidung wie die Gleichaltrigen in München und überall in der Welt.

Dr. Hans F. Nöhbauer

"urbanized zone"; and, finally, the "fringe zone" reaching well into the districts of Ebersberg, Erding and Miesbach – altogether an area boasting 1.8 million inhabitants.

But conditions gradually changed, and consequently Munich together with 298 neighbouring communities became "Region 14", in which the city proper (in 1996) claimed half of the entire population, 58 % of the available jobs, and even 68 % of the labour force, but only 6 % of the total city area.

In 1748 Lorenz von Westenrieder had described an unusual excursion, i. e. a journey to Lake Starnberg which took "only five hours". The citizens of Munich knew next to nothing about the lake area. It was also very likely that a tourist straying into Seeshaupt would meet children who "had hardly ever seen someone rigged out in city dwellers' finery".

Today Munich has 30 times the number of inhabitants it had in Westenrieder's time, and the children in Seeshaupt have for a long time worn the same kind of outfits which their contemporaries in Munich and in the rest of the world are wearing.

Dr. Hans F. Nöhbauer

comme formant un ensemble de 1,8 million d'habitants.

Les rapports se modifièrent et, ainsi, Munich avec ses 298 communes voisines devint la région 14 dans laquelle la ville en 1996 comptait certes la moitié des habitants, 58 % des emplois et même 68 % de la population active mais n'occupait que 6 % de la surface.

En 1784, Lorenz von Westenrieder présenta la description d'une excursion extraordinaire. Il raconta son voyage «long de cinq modestes heures» autour du lac de Starnberg. A l'époque, les Munichois connaissait à peine l'endroit. Il pouvait arriver qu'un touriste rencontre des enfants près de Seeshaupt qui «sans aucun doute avaient rarement vu un homme avec nos vêtements».

Maintenant, Munich compte trente fois plus d'habitants qu'aux temps de Westenrieder et les enfants de Seeshaupt portent depuis longtemps les mêmes vêtements que les enfants du même âge à Munich et partout dans le monde.

Dr. Hans F. Nöhbauer

i distretti di Ebersberg, Erding e Miesbach – un territorio con un totale di 1,8 milioni di abitanti.

In seguito, le circostanze cambiarono e Monaco, con i 298 comuni vicini, diventò la regione 14, nella quale la città stessa, pur occupando appena il 6 % dell'area, contava la metà della popolazione (nel 1996), il 58 % dei posti di lavoro e persino il 68 % delle persone occupate.

Nel 1784, Lorenz von Westenrieder aveva presentato il resoconto di un'escursione insolita. Egli raccontò di un gita che lo aveva portato, in cinque ore, fino al Lago di Starnberg. All'epoca questo luogo era sconosciuto alla gran parte degli abitanti di Monaco. Poteva succedere che un turista incontrasse dei bambini nelle vicinanze di Seeshaupt che «sicuramente avevano visto solo raramente persone con un abbigliamento come il nostro».

Nel frattempo, Monaco ha raggiunto un numero di abitanti trenta volte superiore a quello dei tempi di Westenrieder, e i bambini di Seeshaupt indossano già da molto tempo gli stessi abiti dei loro coetanei di Monaco e del resto del mondo.

Dr. Hans F. Nöhbauer

Das Münchner Stadtwappen: 760 Jahre alt wird das Münchner Kindl im Jahr 2000.

Munich's coat of arms: Our "Münchner Kindl" will be 760 years old in the year 2000.

Le blason de la ville de Munich, le Münchner Kindl fêtera ses 760 ans en l'an 2000.

L'emblema di Monaco: nell'anno 2000 il «bambino di Monaco» compie 760 anni.

„Du schöne Münchner Stadt sei tausendmal gegrüßt,
wer einmal g'sehn dich hat dich nimmer mehr vergißt
Immer wieder kommt man gerne hin,
zu dir des Bayernlandes Städtekönigin..."

Ludwig Prell, Isarmärchen

Bavaria mit Ruhmeshalle über der Theresienwiese: Die Ruhmeshalle wurde unter Ludwig I. als Gedenkstätte für „ausgezeichnete Bayern" 1843-53 von Klenze errichtet. Die Enthüllung der Bavaria – von Klenze konzipiert, von Schwanthaler ins Altgermanische abgewandelt, von F. Miller gegossen – erfolgte 1850.

The Bavaria with the pantheon above the Theresienwiese: The pantheon was erected by Klenze 1843-53 under Ludwig I as a memorial for "distinguished Bavarians". The unveiling of the Bavaria – conceived by Klenze, modified by Schwanthaler to Old Germanic style, cast by F. Miller – took place in 1850.

La statue Bavaria avec la Ruhmeshalle surmontant la Theresienwiese : la Ruhmeshalle a été érigée sous Louis 1er par l'architecte von Klenze de 1843 à 1853 comme monument à la mémoire des «noms glorieux de l'histoire bavaroise». Le dévoilement de la Bavaria, conçue par Klenze, modifiée en germanisme ancien par Schwanthaler, fondue par F. Miller, s'est déroulé en 1850.

La statua della Bavaria con la Ruhmeshalle sovrasta la Theresienwiese. La Ruhmeshalle venne costruita da Klenze tra il 1843 e il 1853, su incarico di Ludovico I, come monumento commemorativo dei «bavaresi che si erano distinti». Lo scoprimento della Bavaria – concepita da Klenze, adattata in stile tedesco antico da Schwanthaler e fusa da F. Miller – avvenne nel 1850.

„*Ach, Münchens Skala reicht weiter; wieviel Städte haben so viel Farben auf der Palette, so viel Zwischentöne und Schwingungen.*"

Ernst Penzoldt, Freundschaft mit München

König Ludwig II. von Bayern (1845-86) – Denkmal an der Corneliusbrücke; im Hintergrund die Kirche St. Maximilian

King Louis II of Bavaria (1845-86) - monument at the Cornelius bridge; in the background the St. Maximilian church

Le roi Louis II de Bavière (1845-1886) – monument à sa mémoire sur le pont Cornelius, à l'arrière-plan l'église St. Maximilian

Re Ludovico II di Baviera (1845-86) – monumento sulla Corneliusbrücke; sullo sfondo, la chiesa di St. Maximilian

„Ja, der echte Münchner, das ist ein geradezu hinreißendes menschliches Wunderwerk."

Dieter Hildebrandt, München, Dichter sehen eine Stadt

Die Jakobi-, die Mai- und die Herbstdult am Mariahilfplatz in der Au haben eine lange Tradition und erfreuen sich nicht nur bei den Münchnern alljährlich großer Beliebtheit.

The Dults (Bavarian fairs) on St James' Day, in May and autumn at Mariahilfplatz in the Au district have a long tradition and are not only popular every year with the people in Munich.

Les kermesses Jakobi, de mai et d'automne sur la place Mariahilfplatz dans le district de l'Au reposent sur une longue tradition et font la joie chaque année pas seulement des Munichois.

I mercatini Jakobidult, Maidult e Herbstdult sulla Mariahilfplatz nel quartiere di Au hanno una lunga tradizione e sono molto amati, ogni anno, non solo dai monacensi.

Das Nationaltheater – Bayerische Staatsoper –, der Foyerbau des Neuen Residenztheaters und der Königsbau der Residenz auf dem repräsentativen Max-Joseph-Platz

The Nationaltheater – the Bavarian State Opera –, the foyer of the new Residenztheater and the royal building of the Residenz on the stately Max-Joseph-Platz

Le Nationaltheater – l'opéra bavarvoise – la construction du foyer du nouveau Residenztheater et le bâtiment royal de la résidence sur la place représentative Max-Joseph.

Il Nationaltheater – Opera di Stato Bavarese –, il foyer del Nuovo Teatro della Residenza ed il "Königsbau" della Residenza sull'elegante Max-Joseph-Platz

„Ein bestimmtes Theater für eine bestimmte Stadt bedeutet zum Beispiel für München: Wenn ich nicht Mozart, Strauss und Wagner zu meinen Hausgöttern erkläre, dann bin ich falsch für München..."

August Everding, Die Stadt und ihr Intendant

„In der Traumstadt
ist ein Lächeln steh'n geblieben;
niemand weiß, wem es gehört,
Und ein Polizist hat es
schon dreimal aufgeschrieben,
weil es den Verkehr, dort,
wo es stehngeblieben, stört."

Peter Paul Althaus, In der Traumstadt

Im kleinen Innenhof des alten Singlspieler-
hauses in der Sendlingerstraße steht
man vor einer drei Meter hohen steinernen
Maske an der Wand über einem Brunnen-
becken. Diese Kopie des Gorgonenkopfs
von Didyma wurde von den Bildhauern
Anna und Roman Strobl gestaltet.

On entering the small inner court of the
Singlspielerhaus on Sendlingerstraße
you face a three metre high stone mask
at the wall above the fountain basin. This
copy of a Gorgon head from Didyma
was designed by the sculptors Anna and
Roman Strobl.

Dans la petite cour intérieure de la Singlspielerhaus dans la rue Sendlingerstraße,
on se trouve face à un masque en pierre
de trois mètres de haut placé sur le mur
au-dessus du bassin d'une fontaine. Cette
copie de la tête de Gorgone de Didyme
est l'œuvre de Anna et Roman Strobl.

Nel piccolo cortile interno del vecchio
Singlspielerhaus nella Sendlingerstraße si
può ammirare alla parete, sopra la vasca
di una fontana, una maschera di pietra
alta tre metri. Questa copia della testa
della Gorgone di Didima è stata realizzata
dagli scultori Anna e Roman Strobl.

*Große Fronleichnamsprozession –
seit 1343 – der Dompfarrei in der
Innenstadt*

*The great Corpus Christi procession
which has been performed by the cathedral parish in the city centre since 1343*

*Grande procession de la Fête-Dieu
(depuis 1343) de la paroisse de la
cathédrale au centre ville*

*La grande processione del Corpus Domini
della parrocchia del Duomo nelle vie del
centro, organizzata fin dal 1343*

„*Das will sagen: von einem bestimmten kulturellen Raum geformt: bäuerlich, barock, musikalisch, katholisch, allem Kantisch-Preußischen abgeneigt, allem was Spiel ist zugetan, eigenwillig, immer die Partei des lebendigen Lebens ergreifend.*"

Luise Rinser, München, Dichter sehen eine Stadt

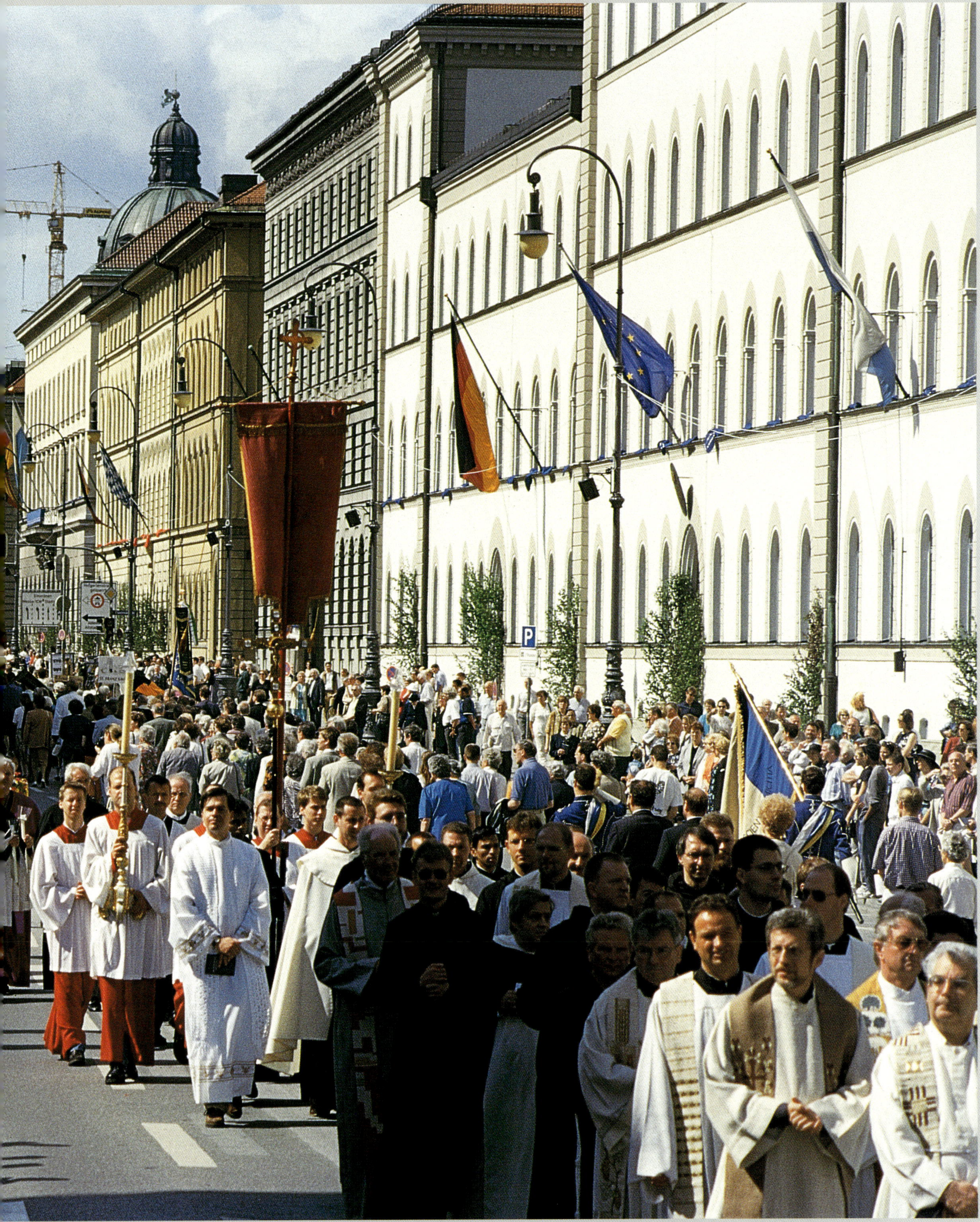

„*Die Kunst blüht, die Kunst ist an der Herrschaft; die Kunst streckt ihr rosenumwundenes Szepter über die Stadt hin und lächelt... München leuchtete.*"

Thomas Mann, Gladius Dei

Münchens beliebteste Graffiti-Meile im Schlachthofviertel für die jung-kreativen Sprayer der Stadt

Munich's most popular graffiti strip in the slaughterhouse quarter for young-creative sprayers of the town

Le lieu préféré de Munich pour les graffiti dans le quartier des abattoirs pour les tagueurs jeunes et créatifs de la ville

La via nei pressi del mattatoio di Monaco preferita dai giovani e creativi autori di graffiti della città

"Stadt der Bergluft und des südlichen Himmels, Pfeiler der Brücke zwischen Deutschland und Italien..."

Ricarda Huch, Unser München

Immer wieder stehen Menschen am Messesee und rätseln, wie die 29 Alpenberge heißen, die in dem 12 m hohen Regal zu sehen sind. Das Objekt „Gran Paradiso" hat der Münchner Künstler Stephan Huber gestaltet.

Frequently people stand by the lake of the exhibition centre and try to think of the names of the 29 alpine peaks which are on display on the 12 metre high shelf. The object "Gran Paradiso" was designed by the Munich artist Stephan Huber.

Des personnes se retrouvent toujours devant le bassin du centre de foire et se demandent comment s'appellent les 29 montagnes bavaroises qui peuvent se voir sur la plaque de 12 mètres de haut. L'œuvre «Gran Paradiso» a été conçue par l'artiste Stephan Huber.

La gente si ritrova sovente attorno al laghetto del Quartiere Fieristico interrogandosi sui nomi delle 29 montagne alpine che si possono amirare nello scaffale alto 12 metri. Questa realizzazione dal titolo «Gran Paradiso» è opera dell'artista monacense Stephan Huber.

39

„Welch ein Genuß, in diesen
prachtvollen Sälen umherzuwandeln...
Gerade die Kunst ist es,
die das Leben erweitert..."

Friedrich Hebbel, Gastfreundliches München

„Der Barberinische Faun", eines der wertvollen Exponate in der Glyptothek am Königsplatz. Die Glyptothek, ein beispielhaftes Werk des Klassizismus für antike und zeitgenössische Plastik

The "Barberinische Faun", one of the most precious exhibits in the Glyptothek at Königsplatz. The Glyptothek is an exemplary classicist building for antique and contemporary sculptures.

«Le Barberinische Faun», une des œuvres les plus précieuses exposées dans la Glyptothek sur la Königsplatz. La Glyptothek, un édifice néoclassique exemplaire pour ses sculptures antiques et contemporaines

«Il Barberinische Faun», uno degli oggetti di maggior valore tra quelli esposti alla Glyptothek sulla Königsplatz. La Glyptothek è un'opera esemplare in stile classico che ospita sculture antiche e contemporanee.

Der Hofgartentempel im herbstlichen Hofgarten, der unter Maximilian I. 1613-17 als italienischer Garten angelegt wurde.

Autumnal hues adorn the gazebo in the Hofgarten which was landscaped under Maximilian I in 1613-17 as an Italian garden.

Le temple du Hofgarten dans le Hofgarten en automne qui fut aménagé sous Maximilian 1er de 1613 à 1617 comme jardin italien.

Il tempietto dell'Hofgarten in autunno. L'Hofgarten venne creato come giardino all'italiana tra il 1613 e il 1617 ai tempi di Maximilian I.

„... *sogar der Novemberwind ist grau angestrichen. Mindestens drei Kilometer lang. Und die Nachmittage sind schläfrig, als hätten sie Veronal genommen...*"

Siegfried Sommer, Großstadt-Impressionen

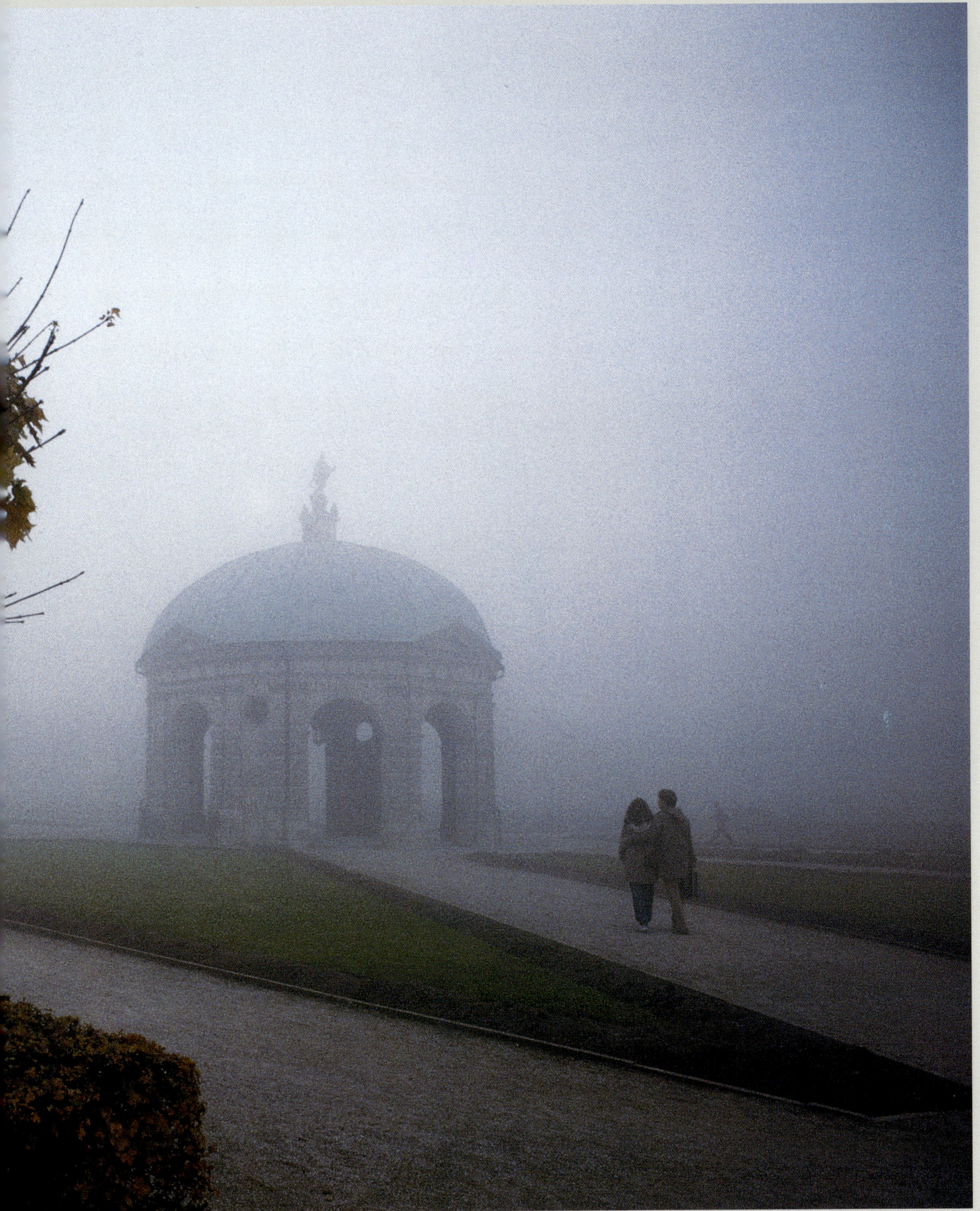

„*Ich habe es stets als eine besondere Gunst meines Geschicks betrachtet, daß mein Leben in jungen Jahren aus dem heimatlichen Berlin nach München verpflanzt wurde.*"

Paul Heyse, Gastfreundliches München

Auch im Winter ein herrlicher Anblick: der Chinesische Turm, 1789/90 als Aussichts- und Musikpagode errichtet, 1944 zerstört, 1951/52 rekonstruiert; inmitten des Englischen Gartens ist er im Sommer ein beliebter Treffpunkt.

A wonderful sight also in winter: the Chinese Tower which was erected in 1789/90 as an observation and music pagoda, destroyed in 1944 and reconstructed in 1951/52; located in the middle of the English Garden it is a popular meeting point in summer.

Un magnifique paysage aussi en hiver: la Tour Chinoise, édifiée en 1789/1790 comme pagode de panorama et de musique, détruite en 1944 et reconstruite en 1951/1952, au centre du Jardin Anglais, c'est un lieu de rencontre apprécié en été.

Una veduta stupenda anche in inverno: la Torre Cinese – realizzata nel 1789/90 come pagoda panoramica e musicale, distrutta nel 1944, ricostruita nel 1951/52 – rappresenta, soprattutto d'estate, un punto d'incontro molto amato nel cuore del Giardino Inglese.

*Ein Engel, der auf den Frieden verweist –
Hoffnung für das 21. Jahrhundert!
Der Friedensengel (eigentlich „Friedensdenkmal") 1899 eingeweiht, ist der optische Abschluss der Prinzregentenstraße zusammen mit der Prinzregententerrasse.*

*An angel referring to peace –
hope for the 21st century!
The Friedensengel, originally called "monument of peace" was inaugurated in 1899; together with the Prinzregententerrasse (patio) it marks the end of Prinzregentenstraße.*

*Un ange qui fait référence à la paix,
espoir pour le 21ème siècle !
Le Friedensengel (en fait le «monument de la paix»), inauguré en 1899, marque la fin optique de la rue Prinzregentenstraße avec la terrasse de la Prinzregenten.*

*Un angelo che evoca la pace –
speranza per il XXI secolo!
Il Friedensengel (la cui definizione ufficiale è «Monumento alla pace»), inaugurato nel 1899, rappresenta, insieme alla Prinzregententerrasse, la conclusione «ottica» della Prinzregentenstraße.*

*„Still, aus den Nebeln blitzt
Glasgrün der Isarfluß
Golden die Schwinge hebt
Stumm jetzt der Engel, schwebt
über der Stadt..."*

Eugen Roth, München im Gedicht

*Kulturstadt
München*

*Munich –
a Cultural Centre*

*Munich –
ville culturelle*

*Monaco –
città della cultura*

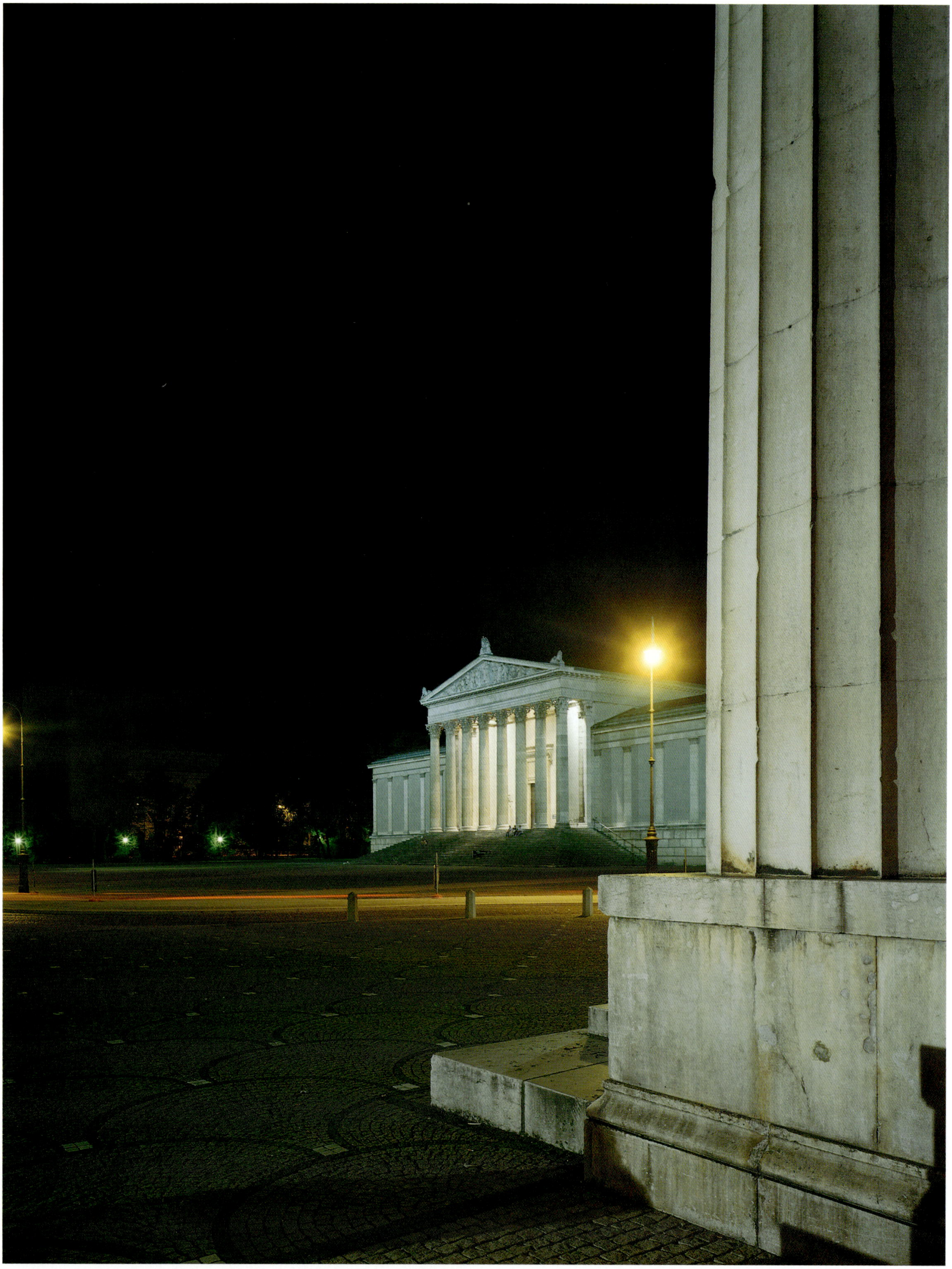

Zeitweise war München „die deutsche Kulturstadt" schlechthin – im vergangenen Jahrhundert beispielsweise, als König Ludwig I. die Baukunst zur Blüte brachte und prächtige Kunstsammlungen präsentierte, aber auch später noch einmal, nach der Jahrhundertwende, als in Münchens Künstlerviertel Schwabing Kunst und Leben eins wurden, als die Künstler-Gruppe „Blauer Reiter" die Moderne einleitete und als in München ein eigenständiger Kunststil entwickelt wurde, der nach der Zeitschrift „Jugend" benannte Jugendstil.

Aber heute? Zehrt die bayerische Landeshauptstadt gegenwärtig nicht ausschließlich oder zumindest weit überwiegend vom Erbe vergangener Zeiten? Haben nicht andere Städte mit aktuelleren Ausstellungen wie der Documenta, mit neueren Museen als den Münchner Pinakotheken, mit aufregenderen Inszenierungen, neuen Kunstformen wie etwa dem Tanztheater, belebteren Jugend-Szenen und einem intellektuell anregenderen, nicht so genusssüchtigen und selbstgenügsamen Klima dem einstigen „Isar-Athen" als Kunststadt längst das Wasser abgegraben?

Diese Zweifel kamen in München jedenfalls auf, als man nach stolzen Zeiten plötzlich der eigenen Defizite gewahr wurde und überdies nach der Wiedervereinigung fürchten musste, dass das so lange geteilte und dadurch gelähmte Berlin jetzt plötzlich nicht nur die größere und politisch wichtigere, sondern auch die gesellschaftlich, kulturell und

Der nach Plänen von Leo von Klenze gestaltete Königsplatz mit der Staatlichen Antikensammlung

The Königsplatz designed by Leo von Klenze with the State Antique Collection

La Königsplatz réalisée selon les plans de Leo von Klenze avec la collection nationale d'antiquités

La Königsplatz, realizzata secondo il progetto di Leo von Klenze, con la Collezione di Stato dell'Antichità Classica

From time to time Munich was the undisputed cultural centre of Germany – in the past century, for instance, when under King Ludwig I architecture flourished and magnificent art collections were amassed; and once more, after the turn of the century, when art and life blended to became a unity in Schwabing, Munich's artists'quarter; at that time the "Blaue Reiter" (Blue Rider) group introduced modern art and Munich created an independent style – the "Jugendstil" (Art Nouveau), called after the "Jugend" magazine.

And what about today? Does the Bavarian capital really live off its heritage from bygone days, exclusively or predominantly? Is it not a fact that other cities have undermined the cultural repute of the former "Isar-Athens" by offering more modern exhibitions such as the "Documenta" and more modern museums than Munich's two Pinakothecas; more exciting productions and new art forms like the dance-theatre; livelier youth scenes and an intellectually more stimulating, less sybaritic and self-sufficient climate?

Doubts like these assailed many local people when after a time of great pride in Munich's successful cultural development they suddenly became aware of the city's deficits and, after reunification, had to fear that the long-divided and therefore paralyzed Berlin would not only be the bigger and politically more important city, but also a socially, culturally and architecturally more significant rival.

These self-doubts afflicted all the people responsible for the cultural climate in Munich during the 1990s. And that was a very good thing. For it would have been fatal in the long run, if pride in our historic heritage had turned Munich's cultural life into a mere administration of valuable objects, and if Munich's title of a cultural centre had thus become a mere catch word for tourism. Thomas Mann already wrote in the 1920s that a cheerful dis-

Munich fut temporairement la «ville culturelle allemande» par excellence. Au siècle dernier par exemple, sous le règne du roi Louis Ier, grand amateur de collections d'objets d'art, qui fit de l'architecture son cheval de bataille. Ou bien encore au début du vingtième siècle, quand Schwabing, le quartier privilégié des artistes, conjuguait art et art de vivre, quand les artistes du mouvement Blauer Reiter (Cavalier bleu) créèrent l'Art moderne, ou bien encore quand Munich devint le berceau du Jugendstil ou Art nouveau, du nom de la revue «Jugend» qui signifie «jeunesse».

Qu'en est-il aujourd'hui? La capitale bavaroise se nourrit-elle exclusivement, ou tout du moins essentiellement, de son héritage historique? L'ancienne «Athènes de l'Isar» n'est-elle pas depuis longtemps menacée par d'autres villes qui se prévalent de foires et salons plus modernes, comme la Documenta, de musées plus récents que les Pinacothèques, de mises en scène plus passionnantes, de formes artistiques innovantes, comme par exemple le Tanztheater, de scènes où la jeunesse est plus présente, plus novatrice ou d'une ambiance intellectuellement plus stimulante, moins épicurienne et moins autosuffisante?

De telles questions se sont imposées lorsque, après avoir connu ses heures de gloire, Munich a soudainement pris conscience de ses propres déficits, lorsque, après la réunification, Berlin, si longtemps divisée et donc paralysée, risquait de devenir subitement non seulement la plus grande ville d'Allemagne, tant sur le plan démographique que politique, mais aussi en termes de société, de culture et surtout d'urbanisme.

Un sujet de réflexion pour tous les responsables de la vie culturelle de Munich dans les années quatre-vingt-dix. Fort heureusement d'ailleurs – en effet, rien n'aurait été plus fatal, à long terme, que de se reposer sur un héritage historique, condamnant ainsi la vie culturelle au statut de

Ci sono stati periodi storici in cui Monaco era «la città tedesca della cultura» per eccellenza – per esempio nel secolo scorso, quando il re Ludovico I portò alla fioritura l'architettura e presentò magnifiche raccolte di opera d'arte. E poi anche più tardi, nuovamente, a cavallo di secolo, quando nel quartiere degli artisti di Schwabing arte e vita divennero tutt'uno, quando le attività del circolo artistico «Il Cavaliere Azzurro» segnarono l'inizio del periodo moderno, e a Monaco si sviluppò uno stile artistico autonomo, il cosiddetto «Jugendstil» (il corrispondente tedesco dell'Art Nouveau) che mutuò il suo nome da quello della rivista «Jugend».

E oggi? Non è vero che il capoluogo della Baviera vive esclusivamente, o almeno quasi in prevalenza, dell'eredità dei tempi passati? Non esistono, forse, altre città con esposizioni più attuali, come la Documenta, con musei più recenti delle pinacoteche monacensi, con allestimenti più avvincenti, con nuove forme artistiche, come il teatro-danza, con scene giovanili più vivaci e con un clima intellettuale più stimolante, non così dedite ai piaceri e poco pretenziose, città che già da molto tempo, ormai, hanno tolto alla città d'arte, all'Atene sull'Isar di un tempo, la sua linfa vitale?

Monaco, in ogni caso, è stata assalita da questi dubbi quando dopo periodi di gloria ci si rendeva conto improvvisamente delle proprie carenze. Inoltre, dopo la riunificazione si è dovuto temere che Berlino, così a lungo divisa e conseguentemente paralizzata, improvvisamente non solo diventasse la città più grande e politicamente più importante, ma anche quella più significativa dal punto di vista sociale, culturale e, sopratutto, architettonico.

Con questi dubbi hanno dovuto fare i conti tutti coloro che, negli anni Novanta, hanno gestito, in veste ufficiale, la vita culturale monacense. E, in fondo, è stato anche giusto così dal momento che, in tempi lunghi, niente sarebbe stato più fatale alla città di un eventuale irrigidimento della vita

51

vor allem städtebaulich bedeutsamere Stadt sein würde.

Solche Selbstzweifel machten allen, die für die Kulturstadt München Verantwortung trugen, in den 90er Jahren durchaus zu schaffen. Das war auch gut so – denn nichts wäre auf Dauer verhängnisvoller, als wenn der Stolz aufs historische Erbe das kulturelle Leben zur bloßen Nachlassverwaltung erstarren lassen würde und der Titel „KulturStadt" langsam zur Floskel der Fremdenverkehrswerbung verkäme. Dass Gemüt und „mir san g'sund" nicht ausreichen, um Münchens Stellung in der Welt vor allem als Kulturstadt zu behaupten, hat Thomas Mann der weiß-blauen Metropole übrigens schon in den 20er Jahren ins Stammbuch geschrieben.

In Wahrheit ist das kulturelle Leben Münchens so vielfältig und unterschiedlich, dass jedes Pauschalurteil verfehlt sein muss. Wer dieser Stadt gerecht werden will, muss schon genau hinsehen und darf weder eitles Selbstlob noch modische Verrisse nach-

position and the local motto "mir san g'sund" (we are well) do not suffice to safeguard internationally the city's status as a cultural centre.

In actual fact, Munich's cultural life is so varied that any generalized statement about it is bound to be wrong. If you want to do justice to the city, you must study it carefully and avoid vain self-praise as well as fashionable criticism – for reality is much more differentiated. An overall view of Munich must, of course, start with the city's cultural heritage, which still strongly influences the town, its appearance and its way of life. Such a description must, however, not be restricted to looking backwards, but has to provide a thorough and up-to-date "panoramic" view.

Let us begin with the historic review: In addition to the historically interesting Antiquarium, the largest profane hall built in the German Renaissance period, the Wittelsbach residence already sheltered three significant temples of high culture: the "Cu-

succession. Le titre de «ville culturelle» serait peu à peu devenu une fleur de rhétorique de la publicité pour touristes. Déjà dans les années 20, Thomas Mann écrivait, dans le livre de la ville, que bonhomie et «mir san g'sund» – une devise bavaroise qui se traduit littéralement par «nous sommes en bonne santé» – ne suffisaient pas pour affirmer la position de Munich dans le monde, et qui plus est, en tant que ville culturelle.

En fait, la vie culturelle de Munich est si diverse et variée que toute généralisation serait déplacée. Quiconque souhaite apprécier cette ville à sa juste valeur se doit d'être particulièrement attentif; il ne doit en aucun cas se complaire dans des compliments présomptueux ou répéter machinalement des critiques à la mode. La réalité est beaucoup plus différenciée. Bien entendu, il faut tout d'abord commencer par étudier l'héritage culturel qui a énormément marqué cette ville, sa physionomie et son art de vivre, aujourd'hui encore

„Rosseführer" von Bleeker, 1930/31, vor der Alten Pinakothek

"Rosseführer" by Bleeker, 1930/31, in front of the Alte Pinakothek

«Rosseführer» de Bleeker, 1930/31, devant l'Alte Pinakothek

«Rosseführer» di Bleeker, 1930/31, davanti alla Vecchia Pinacoteca

Leo von Klenze, kongenialer Baumeister Ludwig I.

Leo von Klenze, ingenious court architect to Ludwig I.

Leo von Klenze, architecte au génie égalant celui de Louis 1er

Leo von Klenze, congeniale architetto di Ludovico I

culturale, provocato dall'orgoglio dell'eredità storica, con conseguente pura amministrazione di tale vita. Il titolo di «città della cultura» avrebbe finito col diventare una frase retorica per pubblicità turistiche. Del resto, il monito che il solo temperamento ed il riaffermare continuamente che «noi siamo sani» non sarebbe stato sufficiente a confermare la

plappern. Die Wirklichkeit ist differenzierter. Und natürlich muss eine Betrachtung mit dem kulturellen Erbe beginnen, das diese Stadt, ihr Stadtbild und ihr Lebensgefühl auch im heutigen Alltag maßgeblich prägt, aber die Betrachtung darf sich nicht auf den Rückblick beschränken, sondern muss einen gründlichen, aktuellen Rundblick versuchen.

Beginnen wir mit dem historischen Rückblick: Schon die Residenz beherbergt neben dem kunstgeschichtlich aufschlussreichen Antiquarium, dem größten Profansaal der deutschen Renaissance, gleich drei bedeutende Tempel der Hochkultur: das Cuvilliéstheater, ein exzellentes Kleinod der Rokoko-Baukunst, das vor einigen Jahren einfühlsam erneuerte Residenztheater und die 1963 nach den ursprünglichen Plänen von Karl von Fischer wieder aufgebaute klassizistische Staatsoper. In der Alten Pinakothek – von Leo von Klenze für den kunstsinnigen König Ludwig I.

villiéstheater", a spledid gem of Rococo architecture; the "Residenztheater", which was restored with subtle intuition a few years ago; and the classicist State Opera, which was reconstructed in 1963 according to the original plans by Karl von Fischer. The "Alte Pinakothek" – designed by Leo von Klenze for art-loving King Ludwig I – shelters numerous works by old masters such as the "Alexanderschlacht" by Altdorfer or Dürer's "Apostles", but also paintings by Leonardo da Vinci, Raphael, Tizian, Tiepolo, Canaletto and – above all – by Dutch and Flemish masters.

By the way, is Munich itself not a work of art comprising all the different art forms? Consider the palaces and gardens, for instance, which were built by the Wittelsbach Electors (primarily by Max Emanuel) in Schleissheim and Nymphenburg; or the neo-classic "Königsplatz", which has – true to style - been recovered with green lawns and now constitutes a magnificent ensemble comprising the "Prophyläen", the "Antikensammlung" (collection of antiques) and the "Glyptothek" (collection of sculptures). During the grand celebration held on Königsplatz for Mikis Theodorakis' 70th birthday my Greek colleague confessed that in all of Athens one could not find a square with a similar Greek atmosphere. Or take Klenze's Ludwigstraße, which Friedrich von Gärtner decorated with the "Feldherrnhalle", "Siegestor" and "Ludwigskirche", and with the State Library and the University constructed in the neo-Romanesque style so typical of Munich. Or look at Maximilianstraße, which architect Friedrich Bürklein planned in the "Maximilianesque" style on order of King Maximilian II, and which finds its crowning end and effect in the "Maximilianeum", set up on the "Isar Height". Or "Prinzregentenstraße", which Prince Regent Luitpold had built in the 1890s; it is Munich's third grand boulevard, lined with such imposing buildings as the National Museum and the "Prinz-

dans la vie de tous les jours. Mais une telle étude ne doit pas se limiter à la rétrospective, un tour d'horizon approfondi sur notre époque contemporaine s'impose également.

Commençons par la rétrospective historique: A elle seule, la Résidence abrite, outre l'Antiquarium, qui vous guide à travers l'histoire de l'art, et la plus grande salle profane de la Renaissance allemande, trois temples de la culture par excellence: le «Cuvilliéstheater», un chef d'œuvre rococo, le «Residenztheater», rénové il y a quelques années avec un savoir-faire empreint de sensibilité, et l'Opéra, un édifice classique, reconstruit en 1963 selon les plans originaux de Karl von Fischer. L'Ancienne Pinacothèque, – conçue par Leo von Klenze pour le roi Louis Ier de Bavière, amoureux des Beaux-Arts – veille sur les plus beaux tableaux des vieux maîtres, tels la Bataille d'Alexandre de Altdorfer ou les Apôtres de Dürer, mais aussi sur les œuvres de Leonard de Vinci, de Raphaël, de Titien, de Tiepolo et de Canaletto et surtout des peintres hollandais et flamands.

Et puis, somme toute: La ville n'est-elle pas elle même une véritable œuvre d'art qui réunit toutes les disciplines? Par exemple dans les châteaux et leurs parcs, édifiés à Schleißheim ou à Nymphenburg par les ducs de la maison Wittelsbach, notamment par Max Emanuel? Ou bien sur la Königsplatz et ses prophylées, de style classique, dont l'aménagement des espaces verts est resté fidèle aux plans originaux, ou bien encore la Collection d'Antiquités et la Glyptothèque? A l'occasion de la somptueuse fête nocturne organisée sur le Königsplatz pour célébrer le 70e anniversaire de Mikis Theodorakis, mon collègue athénien, m'avait avoué que même Athènes ne pouvait s'enorgueuillir d'une telle place ! Ou bien encore la Ludwigstrasse, signée Klenze, et la Feldherrnhalle de Friedrich von Gärtner, le Siegestor (Porte de la Victoire) et la Ludwigskirche, la bibliothèque natio-

posizione vantata da Monaco nel mondo soprattutto come città culturale era stato espresso negli anni Venti, a proposito della metropoli bianco-azzurra, da Thomas Mann.

In verità la vita culturale di Monaco è così multiforme e differente che ogni giudizio globale deve essere sbagliato. Chi vuole render giustizia a questa città deve guardarla più precisamente e non deve ripetere né autoelogi vanesi, né stroncature alla moda. La verità è più differenziata. Naturalmente l'osservazione deve cominciare con l'eredità culturale, che forma questa città, la sua immagine cittadina e la sua gioia di vivere anche al giorno d'oggi in misura rilevante. Ma l'osservazione non si deve limitare ad uno sguardo retrospettivo, ma deve tentare uno sguardo panoramico accurato e attuale.

Cominciamo con la retrospettiva storica: Oltre all'informativo «Antiquarium», concernente la storia dell'arte, alla Sala profana del rinascimento tedesco, la Residenza stessa ospita tre templi significativi dell'alta cultura: il teatro Cuvilliés, un ninnolo eccellente dell'architettura rococò, il Teatro della Residenza, rinnovato con molta sensibilità alcuni anni fa, e l'Opera di Stato, in stile classico, ricostruita nel 1963 secondo i piani originali di Karl von Fischer. Nella Vecchia Pinacoteca – progettata da Leo von Klenze per quel grande conoscitore d'arte che era re Ludovico I – si possono ammirare i dipinti più significativi dei vecchi maestri, la «Battaglia di Alessandro» di Altdorf, per esempio, o «Gli apostoli» di Dürer, ma anche opere di Leonardo da Vinci, Raffaello, Tiziano, Tiepolo e Canaletto nonché di pittori soprattutto olandesi e fiamminghi.

Ma, soprattutto, la città stessa non è, forse, un'opera d'arte completa? Che dire, ad esempio, dei castelli e dei parchi che vennero edificati dai principi elettori dei Wittelsbach, soprattutto da Massimiliano Emanuele, a Schleißheim e a Nymphenburg? O della classica Königsplatz,

53

ALEXANDER M DARIVM VIT: SVPERAT
CA SIS IN ACIE PERSAR: PEDIT C M EQVIT
VERO X M INTERFECTIS. MATRE QVOQVE
CONIVGE LIBERIS DARII REGVM M HAVD
AMPLIVS EQVITIB: FVGA DILAPSI CAPTIS.

entworfen – sind bedeutendste Gemälde alter Meister zu sehen, Altdorfers Alexanderschlacht zum Beispiel oder Dürers Apostel, aber auch Werke Leonardo da Vincis, Raphaels, Tizians, Tiepolos und Canalettos sowie vor allem holländischer und flämischer Maler.

Und überhaupt: Ist nicht die Stadt selbst ein Gesamtkunstwerk? Zum Beispiel in den Schlössern und Anlagen, die von den Wittelsbacher Kurfürsten, vor allem von Max Emanuel, in Schleißheim und Nymphenburg errichtet wurden? Oder auf dem klassizistischen, inzwischen wieder stilgerecht begrünten Königsplatz mit seinen Propyläen, der Antikensammlung und der Glyptothek? Mein Athener Amtskollege hat mir bei dem grandiosen Fest zum 70. Geburtstag von Mikis Theodorakis auf dem nächtlichen Königsplatz gestanden, in ganz Athen gebe es keinen vergleichbar griechischen Platz! Oder in Klenzes Ludwigstraße, die Friedrich von Gärtner mit Feldherrnhalle, Siegestor und Ludwigskirche, mit Staatsbibliothek und Universität im Münchner „Rundbogenstil" bestückte? Oder in der Maximilianstraße, die der Architekt Friedrich Bürklein im Auftrag König Maximilians II. im „maximilianischen Stil" inszenierte – mit dem Maximilianeum auf der Isarhöhe als effektvollem Abschluss? Oder in der Prinzregentenstraße, die Prinzregent Luitpold in den 90er Jahren des letzten Jahrhunderts anlegen ließ als dritte Münchner Prachtallee, an der sowohl das Nationalmuseum als auch das Prinzregententheater,

„Alexanderschlacht"
von Albrecht Altdorfer,
1529 (Alte Pinakothek)

"Alexanderschlacht"
by Albrecht Altdorfer,
1529 (Alte Pinakothek)

«La Bataille d'Alexandre»
par Albrecht Altdorfer, 1529
(Alte Pinakothek)

«La battaglia di Alessandro Magno»
di Albrecht Altdorfer, 1529
(Vecchia Pinacoteca)

regententheater", Germany's most beautiful Art Nouveau theatre. And there are, of course, the numerous churches: the Cathedral in the late-Gothic style, one of Munich's most famous landmarks; the "Theatinerkirche", Munich's first and most beloved Baroque church, initially constructed by Agostino Barelli and completed by Enrico Zuccalli; the Johann-von-Nepomuk Church, erected by the Asam Brothers in Sendlinger Straße, a spacious work of art with a mystic atmosphere and baroque splendour. Finally, we must mention all the palaces of Munich's aristocratic families, the feudal villas of such noble artists as Lenbach and Stuck, and the magnificent patrician buildings dating from the industrial age, which were set up along the Isar River and in the districts enclosing the old city centre.

The "Neue Pinakothek", built by Klenze like the "Alte Pinakothek" and completely destroyed in the Second World War, was reconstructed by architect Alexander von Branca and reopened in 1981. It documents not only the landscape, genre and portrait painting of the 19th century, which still adhered to the older schools (Böcklin, Dillis, Feuerbach, Caspar David Friedrich, Hodler, Kaulbach, Kobell, Leibl, Lenbach and Spitzweg), but also the first awakening of modern art (Bonnard, Cézanne, Degas, Gauguin, Van Gogh, Klimt, Manet and Monet) which reached a spectacular climax in Munich: here Wassily Kandinsky created the first abstract painting in Munich's art quarter of Schwabing, here the artists of the "Blaue Reiter" group (Jawlensky, Kandinsky, Klee, Kubin, Macke, Marc and Gabriele Münter) formed an avant-garde that was faced with widespread hostility. The most important works of the Blaue Reiter Group are exhibited in the "Städtische Galerie im Lenbachhaus", which provides a very attractive background. The same gallery also documents the further development of 20th-century art with

nale et l'université, caractérisée par ses arcades, si typiques à Munich? Ou bien encore la Maximilianstraße, conçue par l'architecte Friedrich Bürklein à la demande du roi Maximilien II dans le style «Maximilien» – qui débouche sur le superbe Maximilianeum, au-dessus de l'Isar? Ou bien encore la Prinzregentenstraße, aménagée dans les années quatre-vingt-dix du siècle dernier, à la demande du prince-régent Leopold, en tant que troisième avenue de Munich, bordée par le Musée national et le Prinzregententheater, le plus beau théâtre de l'Art nouveau en Allemagne? Sans oublier les églises: le dôme du style gothique flamboyant, symbole de la ville, la Theatinerkirche ou l'Eglise des Théatins, première église baroque, si chère aux Munichois, commencée par Agostino Barelli et achevée par Enrico Zuccalli, mais aussi l'Eglise Johann-von-Nepomuk dans la Sendlinger Straße, conçue par les frères Asam, un ouvrage extraordinaire, mystique, un chef d'œuvre de l'exubérance du baroque. Et puis tous les palais érigés par la noblesse, les élégantes villas des grands maîtres Lenbach et Stuck, les magnifiques maisons bourgeoises des années de fondation, construites tout au bord de l'Isar et dans les quartiers autour la vieille ville.

Tout comme l'Ancienne, la Nouvelle Pinacothèque, à l'origine un édifice signé Klenze, entièrement détruite pendant la guerre, documente, dans le nouveau bâtiment postmoderne inauguré en 1981 et conçu par l'architecte Alexander von Branca, non seulement la peinture de paysages, de genre et de portraits du 19ème siècle (Böcklin, Dillis, Feuerbach, Caspar David Friedrich, Hodler, Kaulbach, Kobell, Leibl, Lenbach et Spitzweg), mais aussi la percée de l'art moderne à Munich (Bonnard, Cézanne, Degas, Gauguin, Van Gogh, Klimt, Manet et Monet): ainsi, Wassily Kandinsky créa le premier tableau abstrait de l'histoire de l'art à Schwabing, le quartier des artistes, où se

nel frattempo tornata di nuovo verde secondo il vecchio stile, con i suoi Propilei, la Collezione dell'Antichità Classica e la Gliptoteca? Durante la grandiosa festa per il settantesimo compleanno di Mikis Theodorakis, svoltasi nella notturna Königsplatz, il mio collega ateniese mi ha confessato che in tutta Atene non c'è una piazza analoga in stile greco. O che dire della Ludwigstraße di Klenze, che Friedrich von Gärtner completò con la Sala dei Marescialli («Feldherrnhalle»), la Porta della Vittoria e la Chiesa di Ludovico, con la Biblioteca di Stato e l'università in uno «stile a tutto tondo» tipicamente monacense? O della Maximilianstraße, che l'architetto Friedrich Bürklein realizzò su incarico del re Massimiliano II in «stile massimiliano» – con il Maximilianeum sulla collina sull'Isar per chiudere in bellezza? O della Prinzregentenstraße, che il principe reggente Leopoldo fece costruire negli anni Novanta del secolo scorso come terzo sontuoso viale della città e su cui si affacciano sia il Museo Nazionale, sia il Teatro Prinzregenten, il più bel teatro in stile Art Nouveau della Germania? Per non dimenticare, poi, le chiese: il duomo tardo-gotico come emblema della città, la Chiesa dei Teatini, la prima e la più amata chiesa barocca di Monaco, iniziata da Agostino Barelli e portata a termine da Enrico Zuccalli; o la Chiesa di Johann von Nepomuk dei fratelli Asam, nella Sendlingerstraße, un capolavoro magnifico di grazia mistica in piena magnificenza barocca. E poi tutti i palazzi dell'aristocrazia, le ville graziosamente feudali dei principi-artisti Lenbach e Stuck, le sontuose case borghesi sull'Isar e nei quartieri intorno al centro storico realizzate nel periodo della Rivoluzione industriale.

La Nuova Pinacoteca, originariamente una costruzione dell'architetto Klenze come la Vecchia ma completamente distrutta durante la guerra, documenta, nella sua nuova versione postmoderna dell'architetto Alexander

Deutschlands schönstes Jugendstiltheater liegt? Nicht zu vergessen die Kirchen: der spätgotische Dom als Wahrzeichen der Stadt, die Theatinerkirche als erste und beliebteste Barockkirche Münchens, die Agostino Barelli begann und Enrico Zuccalli vollendete oder die Johann-von-Nepomuk-Kirche der Brüder Asam in der Sendlinger Straße, ein großartiges, mystisch anmutendes Kunstwerk voller Barockpracht. Und dann all die Paläste der Adligen, die feudal anmutenden Villen der Künstlerfürsten Lenbach und Stuck, die prächtigen Bürgerhäuser der Gründerzeit an der Isar und in den Vierteln rund um die Altstadt.

Die Neue Pinakothek, ursprünglich ebenso wie die Alte ein Klenze-Bau, aber im Krieg vollständig zerstört, dokumentiert in ihrem 1981 eröffneten postmodernen Neubau des Architek-

exhibits such as Josef Beuys' installation "Zeige Deine Wunde", works by Andy Warhol, and paintings by the "Junge Wilde" of the 1980s.

As a music centre Munich owes its reputation not only to composers of past centuries like Orlando di Lasso, who in the 16th century was court conductor under Duke Albrecht V and the founder of Munich's history of music, but largely also to the great composers and conductors of the 20th century. This is clearly

„Miracolo" von Marino Marini, 1959/60, vor dem Eingang der Neuen Pinakothek

"Miracolo" by Marino Marini, 1959/60, in front of the entrance of the Neue Pinakothek

«Miracolo» de Marino Marini, 1959/60, devant l'entrée de la Neue Pinakothek

«Miracolo» di Marino Marini, 1959/60, davanti all'entrata della Nuova Pinacoteca

retrouvaient également les artistes avant-gardistes du mouvement «Blauer Reiter» ou Cavalier bleu, victimes des pires critiques (Jawlensky, Kandinsky, Klee, Kubin, Macke, Marc et Gabriele Münter). Les œuvres principales du mouvement du Cavalier bleu sont exposées dans la Galerie municipale du Lenbachhaus, un véritable havre de paix. On peut également y admirer les œuvres d'artistes contemporains, qui témoignent de l'évolution de l'art au 20e siècle, comme par exemple l'installation de Joseph Beuys «Zeige Deine Wunde» («Montre ta blessure») ou des œuvres de Andy Warhol et tableaux des «Jungen Wilden» des années quatre-vingt.

Ville de la musique, Munich ne doit pas seulement sa réputation aux compositeurs des siècles passés, comme par exemple Orlando di Lasso, chef d'orches-

von Branca, non solo la pittura paesaggistica, di genere e ritrattistica che segue le vecchie scuole del XIX secolo (Böcklin, Dillis, Feuerbach, Caspar David Friedrich, Hodler, Kaulbach, Kobell, Leibl, Lenbach e Spitzweg), ma anche l'inizio del periodo moderno (Bonnard, Cézanne, Degas, Gauguin, Van Gogh, Klimt, Manet e Monet), di quello stile moderno che a Monaco raggiunse successi strepitosi. Qui Wassily Kandinsky creò, nel quartiere degli artisti di Schwabing, il primo quadro astratto della storia dell'arte; qui si ritrovarono gli artisti del «Cavaliere Azzurro», in un movimento d'avanguardia all'epoca violentemente combattuto (Jawlensky, Kandinsky, Klee, Kubin, Macke, Marc e Gabriele Münter). I lavori più importanti del Cavaliere Azzurro si possono ammirare nella Galleria Civica della Lenbachhaus, un ambiente

Ludwig Lange: Ideale Ansicht der Akropolis in der Antike, um 1836, Staatliche Graphische Sammlung München

Ludwig Lange: ideal view of the Acropolis in antiquity, painted in about 1836; Staatliche Graphische Sammlung München

Ludwig Lange: Vue magnifique de l'Acropole à Athènes pendant l'Antiquité, vers 1836, Staatliche Graphische Sammlung München

Ludwig Lange: Vista ideale dell'Acropoli di Atene nell'antichità, realizzata attorno al 1836, Staatliche Graphische Sammlung München

Griechenland und Bayern, Athen und München sind in der neueren Geschichte durch eine ganz besondere Beziehung miteinander verbunden: Von 1833 bis 1862 war Prinz Otto aus dem Hause Wittelsbach König von Griechenland. Aus dieser engen Bindung zwischen den beiden Monarchien ergab sich eine vielfältige künstlerische Produktion, deren treibende Kraft König Ludwig I. war. In Zusammenarbeit mit der Nationalpinakothek Athen entstand die Ausstellung „Griechenland und Bayern" im Bayerischen Nationalmuseum in München (28. Oktober 1999 - 30. Januar 2000), die von der **Dresdner Bank** gefördert wird. Gezeigt werden etwa 500 Objekte aus deutschen, griechischen, französischen, englischen und italienischen Sammlungen, darunter jene künstlerischen Hauptwerke, die in dieser Epoche in Athen und München entstanden sind.

In recent history, Greece and Bavaria, Athens and Munich have been linked by very special family ties: Prince Otto of the Wittelsbach Dynasty was King of Greece from 1833 to 1862. This close relation between two kingdoms resulted in a very productive artistic cooperation whose driving force was King Ludwig I of Bavaria. In cooperation with the National Picture Gallery Athens the exhibition "Greece and Bavaria" has been arranged, which has been promoted by the **Dresdner Bank** and will be shown in the National Museum of Bavaria from 28 October 1999 to 30 January 2000. It will display approximately 500 objects from German, Greek, French, English and Italian collections - among them the major works of art which were created in Munich and Athens in that period.

La Grèce et la Bavière, Athènes et Munich sont depuis le siècle dernier liées par un lien très particulier. En effet, de 1833 à 1862, le prince Otto de la famille des Wittelsbach était roi de Grèce. Cette liaison intime entre les deux monarchies entraîna une production artistique variée dont la force motrice était le roi Louis 1er. En collaboration avec la Pinacothèque nationale d'Athènes, l'exposition «la Grèce et la Bavière» vit le jour au Musée national bavarois de Munich (28 octobre 1999 - 30 janvier 2000) et est sponsorisée par la **Dresdner Bank**. Plus de 500 œuvres provenant de collections allemandes, grecques, françaises, anglaises et italiennes sont montrées ici dont des œuvres d'art magistrales ayant été créées à Athènes ou à Munich pendant cette époque.

Nella storia contemporanea, la Grecia e la Baviera, Atene e Monaco vantano dei legami del tutto particolari: dal 1833 al 1862, infatti, il principe Otto del casato dei Wittelsbach fu re della Grecia. Da questo forte trait d'union tra le monarchie dei due Paesi scaturì una produzione artistica molto diversificata, la cui «forza motrice» era rappresentata da re Ludovico I. In collaborazione con la Pinacoteca Nazionale di Atene è nata la mostra «Grecia e Baviera», in programma nel Museo Nazionale Bavarese di Monaco dal 28 ottobre 1999 al 30 gennaio 2000 e patrocinata dalla **Dresdner Bank**. Verranno esposti circa 500 oggetti di collezioni tedesche, greche, francesi, inglesi e italiane, tra cui anche quei capolavori artistici realizzati, nell'epoca sopra menzionata, ad Atene e a Monaco.

ten Alexander von Branca nicht nur die alten Schulen folgende Landschafts-, Genre- und Porträtmalerei des 19. Jahrhunderts (Böcklin, Dillis, Feuerbach, Caspar David Friedrich, Hodler, Kaulbach, Kobell, Leibl, Lenbach und Spitzweg), sondern auch den Aufbruch zur Moderne (Bonnard, Cézanne, Degas, Gauguin, Van Gogh, Klimt, Manet und Monet), zu jener Moderne, die in München epochale Durchbrüche erlebte: Hier schuf Wassily Kandinsky im Künstlerviertel Schwabing das erste abstrakte Gemälde der Kunstgeschichte, hier fanden sich die Künstler des Blauen Reiter zu einer damals heftig angefeindeten Avantgarde zusammen (Jawlensky, Kandinsky, Klee, Kubin, Macke, Marc und Gabriele Münter). Die wichtigsten Werke des Blauen Reiter sind in der Städtischen Galerie im Len-

Staatsgalerie moderner Kunst: „Mädchen unter Bäumen" von August Macke

State Gallery of Modern Art: "Mädchen unter Bäumen" by August Macke

La gallerie de l'Etat de l'art moderne: «Mädchen unter Bäumen» d'August Macke

Galleria di Stato di Arte Moderna: «Mädchen unter Bäumen» di August Macke

shown by the list of honorary citizens in this art sector, comprising such famous names as Richard Strauss, Hans Knappertsbusch, Carl Orff, Werner Egk, and Sergiu Celibidache. In its role as a theatre centre, Munich has frequently acted as a pioneer; this applies not only to important productions in the municipal theatres but also to the extremely varied sector of private theatres, which developed in the 1960s and served as an experimental scene for playwrights like Rainer Werner Fass-

tre à la Cour du duc Albert V au 16e siècle, à l'origine de l'histoire de la musique de Munich, mais aussi essentiellement aux prestigieux compositeurs et chefs d'orchestre du 20ème siècle. Il suffit de jeter un regard sur la liste impressionnante des citoyens d'honneur de Munich dans ce domaine: Richard Strauss, Hans Knappertsbusch, Carl Orff, Werner Egk, Sergiu Celibidache. Fut un temps où Munich faisait même figure de pionnier en matière de théâtre: que ce soit les superbes mises en scène du Schauspielhaus ou les multiples petits théâtres privés créés dans les années soixante et qui étaient le terrain expérimental de Rainer Werner Fassbinder et de Franz Xaver Kroetz par exemple. Munich fut également le berceau du jeune cinéma allemand (Junger Deutsche Film).

espositivo estremamente interessante. Qui viene anche presentato l'ulteriore sviluppo artistico del XX secolo con pezzi d'esposizione considerevoli come, ad esempio, il montaggio «Mostra la tua ferita» di Joseph Beuys oppure opere di Andy Warhol e dipinti dei «giovani selvaggi» degli anni Ottanta.

Monaco deve la sua fama di «città della musica» non solo ai compositori dei secoli passati, come ad esempio Orlando di Lasso, che segnò l'inizio la storia della musica monacense nel XVI secolo come Maestro dell'Orchestra di Corte al servizio del duca Alberto V, ma soprattutto ai grandi compositori e direttori d'orchestra del XX secolo. Ciò viene dimostrato anche solo dalla considerevole lista dei cittadini onorari di Monaco in questo settore: Richard Strauss, Hans Knap-

bachhaus, einem äußerst reizvollen Ambiente, zu sehen. Hier ist auch die weitere Kunstentwicklung des 20. Jahrhunderts mit viel beachteten Exponaten dargestellt, beispielsweise mit der Installation „Zeige Deine Wunde" von Joseph Beuys oder mit Werken von Andy Warhol und Gemälden der Jungen Wilden der 80er Jahre.

Als Musikstadt verdankt München seinen Ruf nicht nur Komponisten vergangener Jahrhunderte wie beispielsweise Orlando di Lasso, der im 16. Jahrhundert als Hofkapellmeister am Hofe Herzog Albrechts V. die Münchner Musikgeschichte begründete, sondern vor allem auch großen Komponisten und Dirigenten des 20. Jahrhunderts. Allein die stattliche Liste der Münchner Ehrenbürger aus diesem Bereich beweist dies: Richard Strauss, Hans

binder, and Franz Xaver Kroetz. The Young German Film also developed in Munich.

The Olympic Games in 1972 helped the already flourishing city to progress even further: at that time Munich became the proud owner of the Olympic Park, boasting the fascinating tent-roof de-

Joseph Beuys und Andy Warhol

Joseph Beuys and Andy Warhol

Joseph Beuys et Andy Warhol

Joseph Beuys ed Andy Warhol

Städtische Galerie im Lenbachhaus

The Städtische Galerie at Lenbachhaus

La Städtische Galerie dans la Lenbachhaus

La Städtische Galerie nella Lenbachhaus

En 1972, les jeux Olympiques ont permis à la ville, déjà en plein essor, de creuser son avantage. A cette époque, Munich fut dotée du Parc Olympique qui doit sa merveilleuse architecture et ses toits en forme de tente à Günter Behnisch et ses associés, mais aussi de la zone piétonne, un

pertsbusch, Carl Orff, Werner Egk, Sergiu Celibidache. Come «città del teatro» Monaco ha svolto, in determinati periodi, addirittura il ruolo di precursore. Ciò vale sia per le grandi rappresentazioni del teatro di prosa dello «Schauspielhaus» che per il panorama teatrale privato straor-

59

Knappertsbusch, Carl Orff, Werner Egk, Sergiu Celibidache. Als Theaterstadt durfte sich München zeitweise sogar als Schrittmacher sehen: Das gilt für große Inszenierungen im Schauspielhaus, aber auch für die ungemein vielfältige Privattheaterszene, die in den 60er Jahren entstand und Experimentierfeld z. B. von Rainer Werner Fassbinder und Franz Xaver Kroetz war. Der Junge Deutsche Film entstand ebenso in München.

Die Olympischen Spiele 1972 brachten die ohnehin florierende Stadt noch einen großen Sprung nach vorn: Damals erhielt München den Olympiapark mit der faszinierenden Zeltdacharchitektur von Günter Behnisch und Partnern, außerdem den vorbildlichen Fußgängerbereich vom Marienplatz bis zum Stachus sowie den damals zukunftsweisenden Münchner Verkehrsverbund mit attraktiven Schnellbahnen. Damals erfand ausgerechnet der Hamburger Spiegel den Ehrentitel „heimliche Hauptstadt".

Der damalige Münchner Hochmut ist inzwischen ebenso passé wie die Depressionen nach der Wiedervereinigung mit der Sorge, die verschlafene Residenzstadt könnte im größer gewordenen Deutschland in eine traurige Randlage geraten, zu einem Provinznest in der Peripherie werden.

Beginnen wir mit der Ausstellungslandschaft: Das städtische Lenbachhaus erhielt mit dem unterirdischen Kunstbau, einem im Zuge des U-Bahnbaus übrig gebliebenen riesigen Hohlraums, eine großartige Erweiterung und Ausstellungsflächen für aktuelle Gegenwartskunst, für Installationen und großformatige Arbeiten. Das „Haus der Kunst", von Hitler für monströse Deutschtümelei missbraucht und hernach nur halbherzig genutzt, wurde in den 90er Jahren von seinem Direktor Christoph Vitali im wahrsten Sinne revitalisiert und ist heute trotz seiner klobigen 20er Jahre-Architektur und seiner NS-Vergangenheit nicht nur Schauplatz großer Retrospektiven, sondern auch Forum der Avantgarde. Und das

signed by Günter Behnisch and his partners; the exemplary pedestrian zone leading from Marienplatz to the Stachus was established; and the future-oriented public transport system of attractive, fast suburban trains

modèle du genre, aménagée entre la Marienplatz et le Stachus et d'un réseau de transport en commun futuriste pour l'époque, avec ses trains interurbains. Munich se vit décerner le titre honorifique de «capitale secrète»,

dinariamente variegato, che è nato negli anni Sessanta e ha rappresentato il campo di sperimentazione, ad esempio, di Rainer Werner Fassbinder e Franz Xaver Kroetz. Anche la giovane cinema-

*Haus der Kunst
in der Prinzregentenstraße*

*The Haus der Kunst
on Prinzregentenstraße*

*La Haus der Kunst
dans la Prinzregentenstraße*

*La Haus der Kunst
nella Prinzregentenstraße*

Wichtigste: Die schon 1906 vom damaligen Oberbürgermeister erhobene Forderung, neben der Alten und der Neuen Pinakothek ein Museum des 20. Jahrhunderts zu errichten, wird jetzt – ein knappes Jahrhundert später – was founded. It was then that the "Spiegel" magazine of Hamburg invented the title of "Heimliche Hauptstadt" (Secret Capital) for Munich.

The vainglory which Munich displayed at that time is just as d'autant plus exceptionnel qu'il fut attribué par le Spiegel de Hambourg.

L'arrogance affichée autrefois par les Munichois fait partie du passé, tout autant que les dépressions déclenchées par la réunification et la crainte de voir la ville assoupie reléguée au second plan dans une Allemagne élargie et devenir un petit village provincial retranché dans ses quartiers.

Commençons tout d'abord par le paysage des expositions: Une énorme cavité, restée inutilisée après la construction du métro, avait permis l'agrandissement du Lenbachhaus, offrant ainsi une surface idéale pour l'exposition des œuvres contemporaines, des installations ou des ouvrages de grand format. La Haus der Kunst ou Maison de l'Art, profanée par Hitler pour ses monstrueuses manifestations nationalistes, fut ensuite utilisée sans grande conviction, avant de retrouver dans les années 1990 un second souffle grâce à Christoph Vitali, son directeur. En dépit de son architecture monumentale des années 20 et de son passé national-socialiste, elle est aujourd'hui, non seulement le théâtre d'importantes rétrospectives, mais aussi le forum de l'avant-garde. Encore mieux: l'Etat libre de Bavière va enfin – un siècle plus tard – concrétiser le souhait de l'ancien maire de Munich, à savoir ériger, aux côtés de l'Ancienne et de la Nouvelle Pinacothèque, un musée du 20ème siècle – selon les plans convaincants du jeune architecte Stephan Braunfels. La Villa Stuck, un ouvrage de l'Art nouveau qui, parallèlement au Lenbachhaus, tografia tedesca ha avuto origine a Monaco.

I Giochi Olimpici del 1972 hanno fatto compiere alla città, di per sé già fiorente, un ulteriore balzo in avanti. All'epoca, a Monaco venne realizzato il Parco Olimpico, con l'affascinante architettura con tetto a tendone dello studio Günter Behnisch e Partner, l'esemplare zona pedonale tra Marienplatz e Stachus nonché la rete monacense di trasporti pubblici integrati, che con i suoi treni suburbani veloci rappresentava già allora una concezione futuribile. All'epoca, addirittura la rivista amburghese «Der Spiegel» inventò per la città il titolo onorario «la capitale segreta della Germania».

L'alterigia di Monaco di allora, comunque, è acqua passata come lo è, ormai, la depressione del dopo-riunificazione, originata dalla preoccupazione che l'addormentata città-residenza potesse venir relegata, in una Germania diventata più grande, in una posizione marginale, che potesse scadere al rango di paesino di provincia della periferia tedesca.

Diamo uno sguardo, ora, alle strutture espositive: La costruzione della metropolitana ha comportato anche un generoso ampliamento della Lenbachhaus civica, con lo sfruttamento di una cavità gigantesca sotterranea realizzata durante i lavori e denominata «Kunstbau» utilizzabile come superficie espositiva per arte contemporanea, per installazioni artistiche e per lavori in grande formato. La «Haus der Kunst» (Casa dell'arte), sfruttata a suo tempo da Hitler per esaltare un «gusto tedesco» dai connotati mostruosi e più tardi utilizzata solo con una certa reticenza, è stata letteralmente rivitalizzata, negli anni Novanta, dal suo direttore Christoph Vitali ed è oggi, nonostante la sua architettura massiccia tipica degli anni Venti ed il suo passato nazista, non solo luogo di svolgimento di grandi retrospettive ma anche foro dei movimenti d'avanguardia. E – cosa forse più importante – la richiesta sollevata nel 1906 dal

vom Freistaat Bayern endlich in die Tat umgesetzt – nach den sehr überzeugenden Plänen des jungen Münchner Architekten Stephan Braunfels. Die Villa Stuck, ein Gesamtkunstwerk des Jugendstils und neben dem Lenbachhaus das zweite große Beispiel für Selbstbewusstsein und Lebensstil der Münchner Malerfürsten, wird derzeit von der Stadt umfassend saniert und erweitert. Auch die „Hypo-Kunsthalle", die von einer bayerischen Bank in der Altstadt gegründet wurde und mit großen Retrospektiven (Braque, Delvaux, Léger, Magritte, Niki de St. Phalle, Tinguély) Publikumserfolge feierte und auch aktueller Kunst Chancen geben wollte, ist zwar vorübergehend dem Umbau des ganzen Häuserblocks zum Opfer gefallen, wird danach aber von den mittlerweile fusionierten bayerischen Großbanken als noch größerer Ausstellungsraum wieder eröffnet. Neben diesen großen Räumen gibt es aber auch ein „dezentrales Museum der Gegenwartskunst", das aus vielen vitalen und durchaus experimentierfreudigen Privatgalerien besteht, nicht nur in der ebenso repräsentativen wie teueren Maximilianstraße, sondern auch in den Stadtteilen Lehel, Maxvorstadt, Schwabing und anderswo.

Die Musikstadt ist keineswegs in der Pflege der Klassiker erstarrt. Für die Münchner Philharmoniker, die unter Sergiu Celibidache zu internationalem Ansehen gekommen sind, konnte mit James Levine wiederum ein weltweit bekannter Dirigent gewonnen werden. Solange Lorin Maazel das Orchester des Bayerischen Rundfunks leitet und Zubin Mehta das Orchester der Staatsoper, hat München ein „musikalisches Dreigestirn", um das es von anderen Musikstädten kräftig beneidet wird. Peter Jonas als Intendant der Staatsoper legt weit mehr Experimentierfreude an den Tag, als manchem Abonnenten recht ist. Auch wenn „musica-viva-Konzerte" keine Publikumsmagnete mehr sind, hat die moderne Musik doch heraus-

much passé as the depressions which afflicted Munich after German reunification; people worried that in a much larger Germany the former residential city might find itself in a desolate fringe position and become a provincial town on the periphery.

Let us continue with the museum and music scene: When the subway was constructed near the Lenbachhaus, this museum was given a huge, left-over cavity to be turned into a subterranean art gallery; it now displays contemporary art in this underground museum, i. e. installations and large-scale works. The "Haus der Kunst", misused by Adolf Hitler for his monstrous Teutomania and afterwards ignored to a large extent, was in the 90s "revitalized" in the true sense of the word by Director Christoph Vitali; in spite of its massive 20th-century architecture and Nazi past it is today not only the scene of large-scale retrospective shows, but also a forum of the avant-garde. The most important piece of news is, however, that the demand made in 1906 by Munich's First Mayor that – in addition to the Old and New Pinakothek – a museum be built to house the art of the 20th-century will now, about one hundred years later, be realized: the Free State of Bavaria has instructed Stephan Braunfels, a young architect from Munich, to make the plans for this new museum. The Villa Stuck, an Art Nouveau masterpiece and, besides the

témoigne du style de vie des peintres munichois, mais aussi de la confiance qu'ils avaient en eux-mêmes, est actuellement restaurée de fond en comble et élargie. La «Hypo-Kunsthalle», fondée dans la vieille ville par une banque bavaroise et dont les importantes rétrospectives (Braque, Delvaux, Léger, Magritte, Niki de St. Phalle, Tinguély), mais aussi les expositions sur l'art contemporain, ont conquis le cœur du grand public, est également provisoirement victime des travaux de rénovation réalisés sur l'ensemble du bâtiment; grâce à la fusion des grandes banques bavaroises, elle rouvrira néanmoins ses portes en offrant au public une salle d'exposition encore plus spacieuse. Outre ces immenses espaces, il existe également un «musée décentralisé de l'art contemporain», composé de nombreuses galeries privées, actives et ouvertes aux nouveautés, implantées non seulement dans la Maximilianstraße, représentative et chère à la fois, mais aussi dans des quartiers, tels Lehel, Maxvorstadt, Schwabing et autres.

Mais la ville de la musique ne s'est pas cantonnée au culte de la musique classique. Pour l'orchestre philharmonique de Munich, qui doit sa renommée internationale au chef d'orchestre Sergiu Celibidache, elle a su gagner les bonnes grâces de James Levine, autre chef d'orchestre mondialement connu. Aussi longtemps que Lorin Maazel dirigera l'orchestre du Bayerischer Rundfunk et Zubin Mehta celui de l'Opéra, Munich pourra s'enorgueillir de ses «trois étoiles musicales», tant convoitées par d'autres villes de musique. Les mises en scène expérimentales encouragées par Peter Jonas, directeur de l'Opéra, ne sont pas toujours du goût des abonnés. Même si les «concerts musica-viva» n'ont plus la même force d'attraction que dans le passé, la musique moderne a encore de beaux jours devant elle: selon le compositeur Werner Henze,

sindaco di allora di realizzare un Museo del XX Secolo vicino alla Vecchia e Nuova Pinacoteca viene finalmente messa in atto ora – appena un secolo più tardi – secondo i progetti molto convincenti del giovane architetto monacense Stephan Braunfels. La Villa Stuck, un capolavoro completo in stile Art Nouveau e secondo grande esempio, oltre alla Lenbachhaus, dell'orgoglio e dello stile di vita dei principi-pittori monacensi, viene attualmente restaurata e completamente ampliata. Anche la «Hypo-Kunsthalle», che era stata costituita nel centro storico da un istituto bancario bavarese e ha registrato considerevoli successi di pubblico con grandi retrospettive (Braque, Delvaux, Léger, Magritte, Niki de St. Phalle, Tinguély) lasciando spazio anche all'arte attuale, è diventata vittima, per un periodo transitorio, di lavori di rifacimento dell'intero caseggiato ma verrà nuovamente riaperta al pubblico, dalle banche bavaresi che nel frattempo si sono fuse, con uno spazio espositivo ancora più grande. Accanto a questi grandi spazi esiste, però, anche un «museo decentrato di arte contemporanea», che consta di numerose gallerie private molto vitali e decisamente orientate verso la sperimentazione, situate non solo sulla rappresentativa ma «costosa» Maximilianstraße ma anche nei quartieri di Lehel, Maxvorstadt, Schwabing e altrove.

La «città della musica» non si è irrigidita nella cura dei classici. Per l'Orchestra Filarmonica di Monaco, che con Sergiu Celibidache ha raggiunto una considerazione internazionale, si è riusciti ad ingaggiare James Levine, anch'egli direttore d'orchestra di fama mondiale. Finché Lorin Maazel dirigerà l'orchestra della Radiotelevisione Bavarese e Zubin Mehta l'orchestra dell'Opera di Stato, Monaco avrà tre «stelle musicali» di prima grandezza da destare invidia ad altre città famose per la loro tradizione musicale. Peter Jonas, direttore dell'Opera di Stato, dimostra di possedere una propensione alla

Die **Münchner Symphoniker** gingen 1990 aus dem 1945 von Kurt Graunke gegründeten Symphonie-Orchester Graunke hervor. Mit ihrem breit gefächerten Programm von Symphoniekonzerten, Opern-, Operetten-, Musical- und Ballettaufführungen, Oratorien und Kirchenmusik sowie zahlreichen Tourneen im In- und Ausland zählen sie heute zu den wichtigsten Kulturträgern ihrer Heimatstadt und des gesamten süddeutschen Raumes.

Die traditionsreichen Spielstätten der Münchner Symphoniker in der bayerischen Landeshauptstadt sind der Herkulessaal, das Prinzregententheater, die Philharmonie am Gasteig und der Brunnenhof der Residenz.

Einen international herausragenden Ruf genießen die Münchner Symphoniker im Bereich der Filmmusik. Eindrucksvoll demonstriert dies der mit 5 Oscars ausgezeichnete Film „Das Schweigen der Lämmer".

Die Zusammenarbeit mit so berühmten Interpreten wie z.B. José Carreras, Placido Domingo, Edita Gruberova und Montserrat Caballé begründen ebenso das hohe Ansehen des Ensembles wie die Nachwuchsförderung junger Solisten und Dirigenten.

Seit 1999 sind die Münchner Symphoniker das Festspiel-Orchester des Chiemgauer Opern-Sommer auf Gut Immling und in Rosenheim.

In 1990 the **Münchner Symphoniker** emerged out of the Symphonic Orchestra Graunke, founded by Kurt Graunke in 1945. With its comprehensive programme of symphonic concerts, opera, operetta, musical and ballet performances, oratorios and church music, and with numerous tours at home and abroad it is today one of Munich's and southern Germany's most significant cultural institutions.

In the Bavarian capital this orchestra performs in such traditional locations as the Herkulessaal, the Prinzregententheater, the Philharmonie am Gasteig, and in the Brunnenhof of the Residential Palace.

The Münchner Symphoniker enjoys an outstanding reputation in the field of film music. This was impressively documented by the movie "The Silence of the Lambs", which received five Oscars.

Not only its cooperation with such famous singers as José Carreras, Placido Domingo, Edita Gruberova and Montserrat Caballé (to mention only a few) has gained the orchestra worldwide fame, but also its promotion of young soloists and conductors.

From 1999 on the Münchner Symphoniker will be the festival orchestra of the Chiemgau Opera Summer Festival, an event taking place at Gut Immling and in Rosenheim.

L'orchestre symphonique de Munich, les **Münchner Symphoniker**, ont été créés en 1990 à partir de l'orchestre symphonique Graunke fondé en 1945 par Kurt Graunke. Avec leur programme varié englobant des concerts symphoniques, opéras, opérettes, comédies musicales et ballets, des oratoires et de la musique sacrée ainsi que de nombreuses tournées en Allemagne et à l'étranger, ils comptent aujourd'hui parmi les plus grands piliers culturels de leur ville et de l'ensemble de l'Allemagne du sud.

Les Münchner Symphoniker se produisent sur des scènes traditionnelles de la capitale bavaroise comme la Herkulessaal, le Prinzregententheater, la Philharmonie am Gasteig et le Brunnenhof de la Résidence.

Les Münchner Symphoniker jouissent d'une excellente réputation internationale dans le domaine de la musique de film. Le film « Le silence des agneaux », récompensé par 5 oscars, en est la preuve éclatante.

La coopération avec des artistes célèbres comme José Carreras, Placido Domingo, Edita Gruberova et Montserrat Caballé témoignent autant de l'immense estime placée dans l'ensemble que la promotion de jeunes solistes et chefs d'orchestre.

Depuis 1999, les Münchner Symphoniker sont l'orchestre du festival d'été de l'opéra en Chiemgau à Gut Immling et à Rosenheim.

I **Münchner Symphoniker** sono scaturiti, nel 1990, dall'Orchestra Sinfonica Graunke fondata da Kurt Graunke nel 1945. Con il loro vasto repertorio di concerti sinfonici, opere, operette, musical e balletto, oratori e musica liturgica nonché con le loro numerose tournee in Germania e all'estero essi vengono annoverati, oggi, tra i principali veicoli culturali della loro città di origine e dell'intera Germania meridionale.

I luoghi ricchi di tradizione in cui i Münchner Symphoniker si esibiscono nel capoluogo bavarese sono la Herkulessaal, il Prinzregententheater, la Philharmonie nel centro culturale del Gasteig ed il Brunnenhof della Residenza.

I Münchner Symphoniker godono di un'eccellente fama a livello internazionale nel settore delle colonne sonore. Lo ha dimostrato, con grande autorevolezza, la pellicola "Il silenzio degli agnelli" vincitrice di 5 premi Oscar.

Il grande prestigio di questo ensemble è motivato sia dalla collaborazione con interpreti della fama di José Carreras, Placido Domingo, Edita Gruberova e Montserrat Caballé sia dalla loro opera di promozione di giovani solisti e direttori d'orchestra.

Dal 1999 i Münchner Symphoniker sono l'orchestra ufficiale dell'Estate Operistica del Chiemgau che si svolge nella tenuta di Immling e a Rosenheim.

Bayerische Staatsoper: Szenen aus „Don Giovanni" (oben) und „L'incoronazione di Poppea" (rechts)

Bavarian State Opera House: Scenes from "Don Giovanni" (above) and "L'incoronatione di Poppea" (right)

L'opéra national de Bavière : scènes tirées de «Don Giovanni» (en haut) et «L'incoronatione di Poppea» (à droite)

Opera di Stato Bavarese: scene tratta dal «Don Giovanni» (in alto) e da «L'incoronazione di Poppea» (a destra)

Bayerische Staatsoper

Bavarian State Opera

L'opéra national de Bavière

Opera di Stato Bavarese

*Das Cuvilliéstheater,
ein Kleinod des Rokoko*

*The Cuvilliéstheater,
a jewel of rococo architecture*

*Le Cuvilliéstheater,
un joyau admirable de l'art rococo*

*Il Cuvilliéstheater,
un gioiello di architettura rococò*

ragende Chancen: „In der ganzen Welt gibt es keine Großstadt, die sich so wie München um die Musik der Zukunft, um den Nachwuchs annimmt", sagte der Komponist Hans-Werner Henze, der im Auftrag der Stadt die Biennale für modernes Musiktheater erfunden und entwickelt hat. Im Alltag freilich hat moderne Musik es schwer – eine Feststellung, die sogar für den inzwischen schon klassischen Jazz gilt. Das Angebot ist großartig, nur die Nachfrage lässt zu wünschen übrig.

Die Theaterszene ist ständigem Wandel unterworfen. Die privaten Theater, die in den 60er Jahren experimentierten und schockierten und dem träge gewordenen Subventionstheater Impulse gaben, sind mittlerweile selbst in die Jahre gekommen. Ihr Problem ist auch, dass die großen Bühnen schnell dazugelernt und viele Talente abgeworben haben

Lenbachhaus, the second imposing example of the self-assurance and luxurious life-style of Munich's feudal painters, is at present being restored and enlarged. But also the "Hypo-Kunsthalle", which was founded by a Bavarian bank in the old city centre and has attracted large crowds by exhibiting works by such retrospective stars as Braque, Delvaux, Léger, Magritte, Niki de St. Phalle and Tinguély, and also wants to make current art popular, has become a victim of the reconstruction of an entire block of buildings. But afterwards it will be reopened in much larger premises by the two main banks of Bavaria, which have fused in the meantime. In addition to these spacious exhibition halls, there is also a "dezentrales Museum der Gegenwartskunst", which comprises numerous active and experiment-oriented private

qui a imaginé et mis au point, à la demande de la ville, la biennale pour les salles de concerts modernes: «Aucune autre ville au monde ne s'occupe, comme Munich, de la musique de l'avenir, de la relève». Bien entendu, la musique moderne a bien du mal à s'imposer au quotidien – ce qui prévaut également pour le jazz, pourtant devenu entre-temps musique «classique». L'offre est exceptionnelle, seule la demande laisse à désirer.

La scène du théâtre est en perpétuelle mutation. Les théâtres privés, qui, dans les années 60, choquaient le public avec leurs mises en scène expérimentales, tout en stimulant un théâtre subventionné plongé dans la torpeur, ont également pris de l'âge. Non seulement les grands théâtres se sont rapidement mis au diapason et ont débauché de nombreux talents, mais le public

sperimentazione superiore alle attese di qualche abbonato. Anche se i concerti della serie «musica viva» hanno perso l'attrattiva un tempo esercitata sul pubblico, la musica moderna continua ad avere eccellenti prospettive. «Non esiste altra grande città al mondo che dedichi tanta attenzione alla musica del futuro, alle nuove leve come fa Monaco», ha detto il compositore Hans-Werner Henze, che su incarico del Comune ha ideato e sviluppato una «Biennale del teatro

65

Prinzregententheater, 1900/01 als Festspielhaus errichtet, 1985-87 vorbildlich restauriert

The Prinzregententheater, a festival opera house built in 1900/01, admirably restored in 1985-87

Le Prinzregententheater, 1900/1901 aménagé comme théâtre et rénové de manière exemplaire de 1985 à 1987

Il Prinzregententheater, edificato nel 1900/01 come teatro per festival e restaurato in maniera esemplare nel 1985/87

Münchner Kammerspiele: Szene aus „Hekabe" von Euripides

The Münchner Kammerspiele: Scene from Euripides' "Hecuba"

Le Münchner Kammerspiele: Scène tirée de «Hécube» de Euripide

I Münchner Kammerspiele: scena di «Ecuba» di Euripide

musicale moderno». Nella quotidianità, tuttavia, la musica moderna ha vita difficile, una constatazione questa che acquista validità addirittura per il jazz ormai diventato classico. L'offerta è consistente, solo la domanda lascia a desiderare.

La scena teatrale sottostà ad un cambiamento continuo. Anche i teatri privati, che negli anni Sessanta sperimentavano e scandalizzavano fornendo nuovi impulsi ai letargici teatri sovvenzionati, risultano, nel frattempo, un po' attempati. Il loro problema di fondo consiste nel fatto che i grandi teatri hanno imparato in fretta ingaggiando numerosi attori di talento; inoltre, il pubblico di Monaco non è eccessivamente entusiasta della sperimentazione a oltranza. Da un lato si desiderano le rappresentazioni teatrali un po' azzardate di registi ed attori famosi – anche perché questa è una prerogativa di una città cul-

und dass Münchens Publikum jedenfalls nicht dauerhaft experimentierfreudig ist: Man möchte schon, dass es gewagte Neuinszenierungen bekannter Regisseure und Schauspieler gibt, weil sich dies für eine Kunststadt gehört, geht aber selber nicht hin, weil man beim Theaterbesuch lieber auf sichere Karten setzt. Aus der Münchner Theaterlandschaft ragen besonders die Münchner Kammerspiele hervor, die mit einem Ensemble voller großer Schauspielerpersönlichkeiten unter der Leitung des Regie führenden Intendanten Dieter Dorn immer wieder den Ehrentitel „bestes deutsches Sprechtheater" einheimsten und zugleich das Kunststück fertigbrachten, eine von wahrer Treue gekennzeichnete Ernsthaftigkeit der künstlerischen Arbeit dem Publikum so nahe zu bringen, dass beinahe jede Vorstellung ausverkauft ist. Das Jugendstil-Schauspielhaus galleries located not only in the representative and much more expensive Maximilianstraße, but also in the city districts of Lehel, Maxvorstadt, Schwabing and in other places.

The Music City has not restricted itself to rigidly cultivating classical composers. The Munich Philharmonic Orchestra, which has gained international renown under Sergiu Celibidache, is now led by James Levine, another conductor acclaimed throughout the world. As long as Lorin Maazel conducts the orchestra of the Bavarian Broadcasting Station and Zubin Mehta the State Opera Orchestra, Munich can call its own a "musical triumvirate" which is the envy of all other leading music centres. Peter Jonas, the present director of the State Opera, enjoys experimenting more than many of the opera subscribers. Even though the "musica viva" concerts no longer attract large crowds, modern music still has oustanding chances in Munich: "Nowhere in the world can you find another big city which promotes the music of the future and the works of young musicians more intensively than Munich", says composer Hans-Werner Henze, who has invented and developed the "Biennale for the Modern Music Theatre" on order of the city. In everyday life, however, modern music has to struggle for survival – a statement which even applies to jazz, which is already regarded as a classic form of music. The offering is fantastic, but demand leaves much to be desired.

The theatre scene is subject to constant change. The private theatres, which experimented and shocked spectators in the 60s and provided new stimuli for the sluggish, subsidized theatres, have become rather "elderly" themselves. They are additionally faced with a number of problems: the large theatres have learned a lot and have recruited many of the new talents, and Munich's audiences are not fond of permanent experimenting; on the one hand they want daring new pro-

est moins friand de pièces expérimentales: chacun s'accorde à reconnaître l'importance de nouvelles mises en scène osées, réalisées par des metteurs en scène et comédiens célèbres, puisque ceci fait partie de l'image d'une ville qui se dit amoureuse de l'art. Il préfère cependant ne pas y aller et miser sur des cartes plus sûres. Les Münchner Kammerspiele, sous la direction du metteur en scène Dieter Dorn, forts d'une troupe qui compte des comédiens hors pair, se distinguent tout particulièrement sur la scène munichoise. Ils se voient régulièrement décerner le titre honorifique du «meilleur théâtre allemand», tout en réussissant à mettre à la portée du public un travail artistique sérieux, basé sur une véritable loyauté, et affichent complet à pratiquement chaque représentation. La salle de théâtre, construite dans le style de l'Art nouveau, a impérativement besoin d'être rénovée; les représentations auront provisoirement lieu dans le nouveau bâtiment de répétition, conçu selon les plans de Gustav Peichl, le célèbre architecte viennois, et achevé en

turale – ma si è poi restii ad assistervi preferendo, invece, andare «sul sicuro». Nel panorama teatrale di Monaco spiccano particolarmente i «Kammerspiele», che con un gruppo di grandi personaggi del mondo del teatro e la regia di Dieter Dorn hanno conseguito, a più riprese, il titolo onorario del migliore teatro tedesco di prosa. Allo stesso tempo, questa struttura ha saputo rendere comprensibile al pubblico una serietà nell'attività professionale connotata da vera fedeltà, con il risultato che quasi ogni rappresentazione registra il «tutto

Das Theater am Gärtnerplatz: Operette, Oper und Musical stehen hier auf dem Programm.

The Theater am Gärtnerplatz, where operetta, opera and musical dominate the scene.

Le Theater am Gärtnerplatz: opérettes, opéras et musicales figurent au programme.

Il Theater am Gärtnerplatz: in cartellone operette, opere e musical

muss dringend saniert werden; vorübergehend wird das Theater auch fürs Publikum im neuen Probengebäude stattfinden, das 1999 nach den Plänen des Wiener Stararchitekten Gustav Peichl fertig gestellt wurde. Insgesamt investierte der Münchner Stadtrat fast 150 Millionen DM in das Schauspielhaus, in Probengebäude und neue Werkstätten: ein deutlicher Beleg für den Rang des Theaters in dieser Stadt. Wie sich das Haus künstlerisch dann weiterentwickelt, hängt stark vom neuen Intendanten Frank Baumbauer ab, der zu den gefragtesten Theaterchefs der Republik zählt und vom neuen Münchner Kulturreferenten Professor Julian Nida-Rümelin trotz hochkarätiger Konkurrenzangebote an die Isar verpflichtet werden konnte. Einer gesicherten Zukunft sieht auch die Schauburg entgegen – Europas wohl bestes Theater für Kinder und Jugendliche und den Dialog der Generationen – mit eigenem Haus (am Schwabinger Elisabethplatz) und eigenem Ensemble. Unklar ist hingegen die Zukunft des Volkstheaters, das nach dem Ausscheiden seiner Prinzipalin Ruth Drexel in schwere Turbulenzen geriet, so dass Ruth Drexel als Retterin in der Not helfen musste und das Heft noch einmal in die Hand nahm. Erste Erfolge mit Franz Xaver Kroetz (diesmal als Regisseur, nicht als Dramatiker) deuten gute Chancen an.

In der Filmstadt München ist man natürlich sehr erschrocken, als die Filmstudios auf dem Bavariagelände infolge der Wiedervereinigung plötzlich Konkurrenz bekamen durch das viel größere Areal in Babelsberg bei Potsdam und als Nordrhein-Westfalen begann, Filmproduktionen noch intensiver zu fördern als der Freistaat Bayern. Trotzdem kann sich München als Filmstadt behaupten, dank einer bedeutenden Geschichte, die mit internationalen Erfolgen wie „Das Boot" oder „Die unendliche Geschichte" oder „Stonk" fortgeschrieben wurde, dank bedeutender Werke der Filmkunst wie etwa der 24-stündi-

ductions by well-known directors and actors, for this is expected of a true "art city"; on the other hand, they do not go to see such performances, for they prefer "a safe bet" for themselves. The "Münchner Kammerspiele" theatre stands out in Munich's theatrescape; with a team of great actors and led by its manager and director Dieter Dorn it has managed to win over and over again the title of "bestes deutsches Sprechtheater" (best German playhouse); and at the same time it has succeeded in communicating its artistic ambitions to the public (by adhering faithfully to its calling) so convincingly that nearly every performance is sold out. This Art Nouveau theatre urgently needs restoration; it will play temporarily in the new rehearsal building, which is just being completed according to the plans of Gustav Peichl, a Viennese star architect. The Munich Municipal Council has invested nearly DM 150 million for the reconstruction of the playhouse, the rehearsal building and new scene shops – a clear proof of the status enjoyed by this theatre. The further artistic development of the Kammerspiele will depend mainly on the new director Frank Baumbauer, one of Germany's most sought after theatre managers. Munich's "Kulturreferent" Prof. Julian Nida-Rümelin was able to entice this expert to Munich, despite the numerous tempting offers made by competitors. The "Schauburg", Europe's assumedly best theatre for children and young people and for the dialogue between different generations which boasts a building (on Schwabing's Elisabethplatz) and a company of its own, also looks forward to a safe future. The future of the "Volkstheater" is, however, rather uncertain; it got into serious trouble after its director, Ruth Drexel, gave up her job. Coming to the rescue, Ruth Drexel took over once more and seems to be rather successful, with Franz Xaver Kroetz assisting her not as a playwright but in his capacity of director.

1999. Le conseil municipal de Munich a, au total, investi près de 150 millions de marks dans la salle de théâtre, le bâtiment de répétition et les nouveaux ateliers: une preuve manifeste de l'importance que la ville de Munich accorde au théâtre. L'évolution artistique de ce théâtre dépend beaucoup de son nouvel intendant, Frank Baumbauer, l'un des directeurs de théâtres les plus convoités de la République et que le professeur Julian Nida-Rümelin, chargé des affaires culturelles, a su convaincre, malgré une concurrence extrêmement compétente. L'avenir de la Schauburg, avec sa propre salle (au cœur de Schwabing sur la Elisabethplatz) et son propre ensemble, sans doute le meilleur théâtre tant pour enfants et adolescents que pour le dialogue entre les générations, est également assuré. En revanche, l'avenir du Volkstheater, qui avait traversé de graves turbulences après le départ de Ruth Drexel, sa directrice, est incertain. Ruth Drexel a donc dû une nouvelle fois intervenir pour le sauver et reprendre les rênes en main. Les premiers succès enregistrés avec Franz Xaver Kroetz (cette fois-ci en tant que metteur en scène et non en tant que dramaturge) sont de bonne augure.

Munich, la ville du septième art, s'est fait une frayeur lorsque les studios de la Bavaria ont dû subitement, après la réunification, défendre leur place, face à la concurrence des studios de Babelsberg près de Potsdam, beaucoup plus spacieux, et lorsque la Rhénanie-du-Nord-Westphalie a commencé à intensifier la promotion des productions cinématographiques beaucoup plus que l'Etat libre de Bavière. Munich peut, malgré tout, s'affirmer en tant que ville privilégiée pour le septième art, grâce à son histoire riche en succès internationaux tels que «Le bateau» ou «Une histoire sans fin» ou «Stonk», grâce à des œuvres remarquables comme la série télévisée - 24 heures de diffusion - «Die zweite Heimat» (La deux-

esaurito». Lo Schauspielhaus in stile Art Nouveau deve venire assolutamente restaurato; per un certo periodo di tempo le rappresentazioni avranno luogo, anche per il pubblico, nel nuovo edificio per le prove che verrà completato nel 1999 su progetto dell'architetto-star viennese Gustav Peichl. Il Comune di Monaco ha investito circa 150 milioni di marchi nello Schauspielhaus, nell'edificio delle prove e nei nuovi laboratori: una prova eloquente del ruolo che il teatro svolge in questa città. L'evoluzione artistica che lo Schauspielhaus conoscerà poi dipenderà, in gran parte, dal nuovo responsabile della struttura Frank Baumbauer, che viene annoverato tra i più ricercati direttori teatrali della Germania e che il nuove assessore alla Cultura di Monaco, il professor Julian Nida-Rümelin, è riuscito a portare nella città sull'Isar nonostante le offerte di grande prestigio avanzate a Baumbauer da città concorrenti. Sembra ormai assicurato anche il futuro della «Schauburg», indubbiamente il migliore teatro in Europa per bambini e giovani e per il dialogo tra le generazioni, con un edificio proprio (sull'Elisabethplatz nel quartiere di Schwabing) e con un proprio ensemble. Tutt'altro che chiaro, invece, è il futuro del «Volkstheater» (Teatro Popolare), che dopo l'uscita di scena della sua direttrice Ruth Drexel è precipitato in gravi turbolenze, al punto da indurre Ruth Drexel ad accorrergli nuovamente in aiuto riassumendo il comando delle operazioni. I primi successi con Franz Xaver Kroetz, stavolta in veste di regista e non di autore drammatico, lasciano intravedere buone prospettive.

Quando, in seguito alla riunificazione, i teatri di posa del Centro della Bavaria si sono improvvisamente trovati ad affrontare la concorrenza delle strutture molto più grandi di Babelsberg vicino Potsdam; e quando il Land del Norreno-Westfalia ha iniziato a promuovere le produzioni cinematografiche più intensamente che il Libero Stato di Baviera,

Krone – der Circus, den die ganze Welt kennt!

„Eure Gunst – unser Streben". Unter diesem Motto begeistert Europas größter Circus seit über 80 Jahren in seinem – nach Plänen des legendären Circuskönigs Karl Krone erbauten – Stammhaus mit 3 000 Sitzplätzen von Dezember bis März sein Publikum mit internationalen Programmen.

Krone – a Circus Known Throughout the World!

"Your Favour – Our Aim". Guided by this motto, Europe's biggest circus has for more than 80 years inspired its spectators with international programmes in its Munich headquarters. This building, constructed after the plans of the legendary "King of the Circus" – Karl Krone – offers 3,000 seats and performances from December to March.

Krone – le cirque connu aux quatre coins du monde!

«Votre plaisir – notre but». Avec ce slogan, le plus grand cirque d'Europe enthousiasme depuis plus de 80 ans son public et lui présente de décembre à mars des programmes internationaux qui se tiennent à son siège de 3 000 places conçu d'après les plans du légendaire roi du cirque, Karl Krone.

Krone – il circo conosciuto in tutto il mondo!

«Il Vostro beneficio è la nostra aspirazione». È con questo motto che da oltre 80 anni il più grande circo d'Europa entusiasma il suo pubblico con i programmi internazionali presentati da dicembre a marzo nella sua sede originaria costruita su progetto del leggendario re del circo Karl Krone e dotata di 3 000 posti a sedere.

◀ *Die schönsten Pferde aus dem weltberühmten Krone-Marstall, präsentiert von Circusdirektorin Christel Sembach-Krone*

The most beautiful horses from the internationally famous Stables Krone-Marstall, presented by Director Christel Sembach-Krone

Les plus beaux chevaux venant de l'écurie mondialement connue Krone-Marstall, présentés par la directrice du cirque, Christel Sembach-Krone

I più bei cavalli della stalla Krone-Marstall, conosciuta in tutto il mondo, vengono presentati dalla direttrice del circo Christel Sembach-Krone.

Installation „in vino vanitas" des Schweizer Künstlers Pavel Schmidt im Palmengarten im Luitpoldblock (September/Oktober 1999)

Installation by the Swiss artist Pavel Schmidt: "in vino vanitas" at the Palmengarten inside the Luitpoldblock (September/October 1999).

Installation de « in vino vanitas » de l'artiste suisse Pavel Schmidt dans le Palmengarten dans le Luitpoldblock (septembre/octobre 1999)

L'installazione «in vino vanitas» dell'artista svizzero Pavel Schmidt nel Palmengarten del Luitpoldblock (settembre/ottobre 1999)

*Rechts/right/à droite/a destra:
Das Literaturhaus am Salvatorplatz*

The Literaturhaus on Salvatorplatz

La Literaturhaus sur la Salvatorplatz

Il Literaturhaus sulla Salvatorplatz

gen Fernsehserie „Die zweite Heimat" von Edgar Reitz, dank international erfolgreicher Akteure wie dem Filmproduzenten Bernd Eichinger (Neue Constantin), der Regisseurin Doris Dörrie (Männer) oder der Schauspielerin Marianne Saegebrecht (Out of

In the Film City of Munich people were shocked when after the reunification the Bavaria film studios were faced with serious competition from the much bigger Babelsberg area near Potsdam, and when North Rhine-Westphalia started to promote

ième patrie) de Edgar Reitz, grâce à des acteurs à renommée internationale, tels le producteur Bernd Eichinger (Neue Constantin), le metteur en scène Doris Dörrie (Männer) ou l'actrice Marianne Saegebrecht (Out of Rosenheim). Le festival du film,

nella Monaco cinematografica lo spavento è stato, naturalmente, grande. Nonostante ciò, Monaco continua ad affermarsi come «città del film», grazie ad un significativo passato che continua con successi internationali come «Das Boot», «La storia infinita» o

70

Rosenheim). Das Filmfest, das alljährlich von Stadt und Staat gemeinsam im Kulturzentrum Gasteig sowie in einigen Programmkinos ausgerichtet wird, konnte sich trotz namhafterer Branchentreffen in Berlin oder Cannes als populäres Publikums-

film production much more generously than the Free State of Bavaria. Thanks to its long tradition Munich was, however, able to hold its own and to continue its long history with successful films like "The Boot", "The Unending Story" or "Stonk". It was

organisé chaque année par la ville et l'Etat dans le centre culturel du Gasteig et quelques salles de cinéma, a pu s'établir durablement et séduire le public et ce, malgré les célèbres festivals de Berlin ou de Cannes; le Filmmuseum, une cinémathèque

«Stonk»; ed anche grazie ad importanti opere di cinema d'essai come, ad esempio, la seria televisiva (della durata di 24 ore) «La seconda patria» di Edgar Reitz; e, ancora, grazie ad esponenti di fama internazionale come il

71

festival dauerhaft etablieren, das städtische Filmmuseum am Jakobsplatz hat internationales Renommee und das von Bernd Eichinger geplante große Multiplex- und Erstaufführungskino wird jetzt zwischen Hauptbahnhof und Stachus auch tatsächlich errichtet, allerdings für andere Betreiber. Eichinger ist gleichwohl unverändert der Shooting-Star der Filmbranche, ging er doch 1999 mit spektakulärem Erfolg an die Börse. Münchens Ruf als Filmstadt lebt aber nicht nur von Kassenerfolgen, zu denen auch noch Sönke Wortmanns „Der bewegte Mann" zu zählen wäre, sondern ebenso von aufsässigen und sperrigen Naturtalenten wie dem mittlerweile 60-jährigen Herbert Achternbusch, der in unzähligen Filmen, aber auch Texten und Bildern seine Hassliebe zur bayerisch-katholischen Heimat bekundet.

Auch wenn das Münchner Publikum, sei es aus katholisch-barocker Tradition oder aus geschmäcklerischer Konsumhaltung heraus, mit Bildern und Szenen mehr anfangen kann als mit Worten und Theorien – schon Thomas Mann klagte, München sei „immer eine Stadt der Maler, nicht der Literatur" gewesen –, ist München doch zur führenden Literaturstadt geworden. Über 14 000 Buchtitel erscheinen hier im Jahr. Doch nicht nur Verlage, auch unzählige Autoren sind hier heimisch geworden. Zu nennen wären neben vielen anderen Carl Amery (Literaturpreisträger 1992), die Schriftstellerin Barbara Bronnen, der eigenbrötlerische Sprachkünstler Uwe Dick, der Dramatiker Tankred Dorst, der immer wieder glänzend analysierende Hans Magnus Enzensberger, die phantasiereiche Barbara König, der satirische Erzähler und Amtsrichter Herbert Rosendorfer, der iranische Exilautor Said, die vom Journalismus kommende Asta Scheib, der Romancier Uwe Timm, der brillante Satiriker Joseph von Westphalen. Viele Autoren bedeuten noch nicht zwangsläufig ein vitales literarisches Leben – doch auch das

also able to survive thanks to important works of film art such as the 24-hour television series "The Second Home" by Edgar Reitz, and thanks to internationally successful players like film producer Bernd Eichinger (Neue Constantin), producer Doris Dörre (Men), or actress Marianne Sägebrecht (Out of Rosenheim). The film festival, which is organized annually by city and state in the Gasteig Culture Centre and in several cinemas, has become well-established in spite of more famous rival events in Berlin or Cannes; the Municipal Film Museum on Jakobsplatz has gained international renown; and the large multiplex and first-performance cinema, initially planned by Bernd Eichinger, is now being set up between the main railway station and the Stachus under different management. Nevertheless, Eichinger is still the shooting star of the film branch, for in 1999 his firm was first quoted at the stock exchange with overwhelming success. But Munich's reputation as a film city does not depend entirely on profitable hits (for instance Sönke Wortmann's film "Der bewegte Mann"), but also on rebellious and difficult natural talents like Herbert Achternbusch (by now 60 years old), who has revealed his love-hate relationship with his Catholic Bavarian homeland in innumerable films, texts and pictures.

Even though the Munich public – maybe because of its Catholic-baroque tradition or a taste-dominated consumer's attitude – prefers pictures and scenes to words and theories (Thomas Mann already complained that Munich "has always been a city of painters and not of literature"), it has become the leading centre of literature. More than 14,000 books are published here every year. But not only publishing firms but also innumerable authors have settled in the city. Besides many others we would like to mention Carl Amery (winner of the Literature Prize of 1992); Barbara Bronnen; Uwe Dick, a

située sur la Jakobsplatz, est connue dans le monde entier et le cinéma multiplex, destiné également aux premières, prévu par Bernd Eichinger, sera effectivement construit entre la gare principale et le Stachus, toutefois pour d'autres exploitants. Eichinger, qui a enregistré en 1999 un succès spectaculaire à la Bourse, reste la «shooting-star» de la branche cinématographique. Mais Munich ne doit pas uniquement sa réputation de ville du septième art aux films qui font recette – citons également «Der bewegte Mann» de Sönke Wortmann – mais aussi à des talents innés, comme Herbert Achternbusch, rebelle et encombrant, entretemps sexagénaire, qui a exprimé dans de nombreux films, mais aussi au travers de ses écrits et images, son amour à double tranchant pour sa patrie, la Bavière catholique.

Même si le public munichois, soit par pure tradition catholique, soit en raison d'un comportement extrêmement exigeant en matière de consommation, est plus sensible aux images et aux scènes qu'aux mots et théories – Thomas Mann se plaignait déjà en affirmant que Munich avait toujours été «une ville des peintres, et non de la littérature» –, Munich est toutefois devenue la première ville des lettres. Plus de 14 000 titres y paraissent chaque année. Les éditeurs, mais aussi les écrivains sont venus s'implanter à Munich. Citons, parmi tant d'autres, Carl Amery (lauréat du prix littéraire en 1992), l'écrivain Barbara Bronnen, l'original Uwe Dick, grand virtuose des mots, le dramaturge Tankred Dorst, le brillant analyste Hans Magnus Enzensberger, Barbara König, débordante de fantaisie, le juge et conteur satirique Herbert Rosendorfer, l'écrivain Said, exilé iranien, Asta Scheib, qui vient du journalisme, le romancier Uwe Timm, le brillant auteur satirique Joseph von Westphalen. Certes, la richesse d'une vie littéraire ne dépend pas obligatoirement du nombre d'auteurs - on la retrouve également chaque jour dans l'une ou l'autre

produttore Bernd Eichinger (della casa «Neue Constantin») o la regista Doris Dörrie («Uomini») o l'attrice Marianne Saegebrecht («Out of Rosenheim»). Il Festival del Cinema, allestito ogni anno dal comune e dallo Stato Bavarese in collaborazione con il centro culturale Gasteig ed alcuni cinema, ha potuto affermarsi durevolmente nonostante l'esistenza, nel settore, di appuntamenti ben più famosi come Berlino o Cannes. Il Museo del Cinema civico nella Jakobsplatz ha fama internazionale, ed il grande cinema multiplex e per prime visioni previsto da Bernd Eichinger verrà ora effettivamente costruito tra la stazione centrale e Stachus, anche se per altri esercenti. Eichinger continua ad essere la shooting-star del cinema, avendo affrontato nel 1999, con un successo spettacolare, anche la quotazione di Borsa della sua società. Ma la fama di Monaco come città del cinema non vive solo di successi di botteghino, tra cui andrebbero ancora annoverati «Der bewegte Mann» di Sönke Wortmann, ma anche di talenti naturali recalcitranti e restii come Herbert Achternbusch (nel frattempo 60enne), che in innumerevoli film nonché testi scritti ed immagini manifesta tutto il suo amore-odio per la sua patria bavarese cattolica. Anche se il pubblico monacense, magari per tradizione cattolico-barocca o per un comportamento di gusto consumistico, ha più dimestichezza con immagini e scene che con parole e teorie – già Thomas Mann lamentava che Monaco fosse sempre stata una città di pittori e non di letteratura – Monaco è diventata un punto di riferimento letterario di prim'ordine: qui vengono pubblicati, ogni anno, 14 mila libri. Qui, tuttavia, non hanno messo le radici solo le case editrici, ma anche innumerevoli autori. Tra gli altri vengono annoverati Carl Amery (vincitore del Premio della Letteratura del 1992), la scrittrice Barbara Bronnen, l'originale artista linguistico Uwe Dick, l'autore drammatico Tankred

Tollwood München

Zweimal im Jahr ist in München „Tollwoodzeit": Ende Juni/Anfang Juli sowie in der Advents- und Weihnachtszeit besuchen hier mehr als 1 Millionen Menschen die unterschiedlichsten Events. Aus einem kleinen Fest, auf dem die Veranstalterin Rita Rottenwallner 1988 Kultur und Ökologie zusammenschweißte, wuchs ein weit über die Grenzen Deutschlands hinaus gerühmtes Kulturfestival, das sich durch seine organisatorische Struktur und sein außergewöhnliches Programmangebot von allen anderen Festivals dieser Art unterscheidet.

Neben hochkarätigen Theater-, Tanz- und Musikveranstaltungen wird im Sommer der Philosophie des Unternehmens entsprechend eine gleich große Zahl an Konzerten und Installationen bei freiem Eintritt geboten.

Im Winter produziert Tollwood ein En-suite-Programm aus Variété und Oper, dessen Höhepunkt die berühmten Weihnachtskonzerte sind.

Neben dem kulturellen Angebot zieht der „Markt der Ideen" mit internationalem Kunsthandwerk und „Weltgastronomie" Hunderttausende – ob Jung oder Alt – in seinen Bann und beweist damit, dass Tollwood inzwischen zu einem Markenzeichen Münchens geworden ist.

Tollwood Munich

Twice a year Munich enjoys "Tollwood Time". In late June and early July, and during the Advent and Christmas season more than 1 million people visit the different events presented to the public under the name of "Tollwood". Originally a small-scale festivity combining culture and ecology, which was first organized by Rita Rottenwallner in 1988, Tollwood has gradually turned into a large festival which is today acclaimed far beyond Germany's limits. It differs from all other festivals of this kind in its organizational structure and its unusual programme.

In summer top-grade theatre, dance and musical performances are offered in accordance with the festival philosophy, in addition to an equal number of concerts and installations – free of charge.

In winter Tollwood produces an ensuite programme of variety shows and operas; its highlights are the famous Christmas concerts.

In addition to the cultural events, the "Market of Ideas" displaying international handicraft and the "Worldwide Gastronomy" event captivate hundreds of thousands of young and old people, proving that Tollwood has become one of Munich's most popular attractions.

Tollwood Munich

Deux fois par an, c'est la période de Tollwood à Munich, d'abord fin juin/début juillet ainsi que pendant la période de l'Avent et de Noël. Plus de 1 million de visiteurs viennent assister aux différents spectacles. La petite fête des débuts, où l'organisatrice Rita Rottenwallner réunissait en 1988 la culture et l'écologie, s'est transformée en un festival culturel dont la réputation a largement dépassé les frontières de l'Allemagne et qui se différencie par l'organisation de sa structure et par son programme étonnant se démarquant de tous les autres festivals de ce genre.

Outre des spectacles de théâtre, danse et musique de grande qualité, un nombre aussi important de concerts et spectacles en plein air répondent en été à la philosophie de l'entreprise.

En hiver, Tollwood produit un programme de variétés et d'opéras dont l'apogée reste les célèbres concerts de Noël.

Outre l'offre culturelle, le «marché des idées» attire des centaines de milliers de jeunes et de moins jeunes avec de l'artisanat international et des spécialités gastronomiques mondiales et prouve ainsi que Tollwood est devenu maintenant une image de marque de Munich.

Tollwood Monaco

Due volte l'anno, a Monaco è «tempo di Tollwood». A fine giugno/inizio luglio nonché nel periodo dell'Avvento e del Natale oltre 1 milioni di visitatori assistono agli eventi più disparati. Da una festa di piccole dimensioni, con la quale l'organizzatrice Rita Rottenwallner voleva fondere nel 1988 i due aspetti «cultura» ed «ecologia», è nato un festival culturale diventato famoso ben oltre i confini tedeschi che, grazie alla sua struttura organizzativa ed al singolare programma proposto, differisce da tutti gli altri festival analoghi.

Oltre a manifestazioni teatrali, di danza e musicali di alto livello, d'estate viene proposta, secondo la filosofia di fondo dell'iniziativa, anche tutta una serie di concerti ed appuntamenti fissi ad ingresso libero.

D'inverno, Tollwood propone un programma «Ensuite» composto da variété ed opera il cui apice è rappresentato dai famosi concerti natalizi.

Oltre all'offerta culturale il «Mercato delle idee» con un artigianato internazionale e la «Gastronomia mondiale» attirano centinaia di migliaia di giovani e vecchi. Cosí Tollwood è diventato un marchio di Monaco.

Blick (oben) und Eingang (rechts) in das Valentin-„Musäum" im Isartor

View of (top) and entrance in (right) the Valentin-"Musäum" in the Isartor

Aperçu (en-haut) et l'entrée (à droite) du Valentin-«Musäum» dans la Isartor

Veduta (in alto) ed entrata (a destra) del Valentin-«Musäum» a Isartor

gibt es: tagtäglich in einer der zahlreichen als Veranstalter aktiven Buchhandlungen, allmonatlich in literarischen Vereinigungen, schließlich bei der Frühjahrsbuchmesse sowie der Bücherschau im Herbst, vor allem aber ganzjährig im Literaturhaus, das die Stadt gemeinsam mit privaten Sponsoren aus Buchhandel und Verlagswesen in der Altstadt am Salvatorplatz errichtet hat. Dieses Haus ist beinahe täglich Ort von Lesungen, Buchpräsentationen und Diskussionen, es bietet Raum für große literarische Ausstellungen sowie Büros für literarische Institutionen. Das Café im Erdgeschoss ist ein beliebter Treffpunkt geworden, aber nur selten mit literarischem Bezug.

Architektonisch leidet München an dem Minderwertigkeitskomplex, nach dem Olympiapark mit der kühnen Zeltdachkonstruk-

cranky language artist; playwright Tankred Dorst; brilliantly analysing Hans Magnus Enzensberger; imaginative Barbara König; Herbert Rosendorfer, a satirical storyteller and judge; exiled Said from Iran; Asta Scheib, who started out as a journalist; romancier Uwe Timm; and the brilliant satirist Joseph von Westphalen. A large number of authors does not automatically guarantee a vital literary life, but Munich can offer that as well: every day in the book shops which also organize literary events; every month in literary societies; at the spring and autumn book fairs; and, above all, throughout the year in the House of Literature which the city has set up at Salvatorplatz in the old city centre – together with private sponsors from the book trade and the publishing sector. In this building readings, book presentations and discussions take place

des nombreuses librairies qui organisent des manifestations littéraires, chaque mois dans des associations littéraires, et enfin à l'occasion du Salon du livre au printemps ou de l'Exposition d'œuvres littéraires en automne, et surtout, tout au long de l'année, dans la Maison de la littérature, créée dans la vieille ville, sur la Salvatorplatz, par la ville et des sponsors privés, venant du commerce du livre ou de l'édition. Cette maison offre pratiquement chaque jour des lectures, présentations de livres et discussions; elle dispose également d'un espace destiné aux grandes expositions littéraires et des bureaux pour des institutions littéraires. Le café au rez-de-chaussée est un point de rencontre privilégié, toutefois rarement en rapport avec la littérature.

En architecture, Munich souffre d'un complexe d'infériorité.

Dorst, Hans Magnus Enzensberger con le sue analisi sempre brillanti, Barbara König con la sua ricchezza di fantasia, l'autore satirico e giudice della Pretura Herbert Rosendorfer, l'autore iraniano in esilio Said, Asta Scheib che proviene dal giornalismo, il romanziere Uwe Timm, il brillante autore satirico Joseph von Westphalen. Certo, la presenza di molti autori non significa automaticamente una vita letteraria vivace – ma c'è anche questa. E si manifesta ogni giorno in una delle innumerevoli librerie che organizzano incontri con gli autori, ogni mese nei circoli letterali, infine nella Fiera del Libro in programma in primavera nonché nella Mostra del Libro in autunno. Ma, soprattutto, è vitale tutto l'anno la «Literaturhaus» (Casa della letteratura), che il Comune ha istituito nel centro storico, nella Salvatorplatz, con l'aiuto di sponsor privati del set-

Bitte nicht Füttern

**99 jährige
in Begleitung
ihrer Eltern
Eintritt frei!**

tion von Professor Günter Behnisch und Partnern sei nichts zukunftsweisendes mehr errichtet worden. Überraschenderweise wird dieses Klagelied besonders oft und laut von Münchner Architekten angestimmt, die sich damit freilich vor allem selber ein Armutszeugnis ausstellen. Ich halte die Kritik für maßlos überzogen und in vielen Fällen für ausgesprochen ungerecht. Dass München kaum mit spektakulärer postmoderner Kulissenschieberei behelligt wurde, halte ich eher für einen Glücksfall – auch wenn die bayerische Landeshauptstadt auf diese Weise längere Zeit auf den Titelseiten der Architekturzeitschriften nicht vertreten war. Dafür zeichnet sich die Stadtplanung ebenso wie der Wohnungsbau durch großes Einfühlungsvermögen in die Wünsche der künftigen Wohnbevölkerung aus: Das ist nicht spektakulär, gewährleistet aber Lebensqualität. Die Wohnanlage „Schwabing am See"

nearly every day; it offers room for large-scale literary exhibitions and for the offices of literary institutions. The café on the ground floor has become a popular meeting place, but only seldom for people connected with literature.

As far as architecture is concerned, Munich has for quite some time been suffering from an inferiority complex, for it is convinced that after the daring Olympic Park tent-roof design by Prof. Günter Behnisch nothing has been constructed which points a way to the future. Surprisingly, Munich's architects have loudly and often joined in this lament, thus revealing their own incapacity. I personally regard this criticism as greatly exaggerated and in many cases unjustified. I consider it a stroke of luck that Munich was hardly affected by the spectacular postmodern scene-shifting, even though the Bavarian capital failed to appear on the title pages of

Aucun autre ouvrage futuriste n'a été construit à Munich après le parc Olympique, avec son toit audacieux en forme de tente, du professeur Günter Behnisch et de ses associés. Le plus surprenant est que ce sont justement les architectes munichois qui se répandent en de telles jérémiades – témoignant ainsi eux-mêmes de leur propre incapacité. Je considère que la critique est exagérée et injuste dans de nombreux cas. A mon avis, Munich peut s'estimer heureuse d'avoir échappé à des coulisses postmodernes spectaculaires – même si la capitale bavaroise était ainsi pendant longtemps absente des couvertures des magazines d'architecture. En revanche, les services compétents en matière d'urbanisme et de construction de logements se distinguent par une grande sensibilité en essayant de répondre aux attentes des futurs habitants: un tel comportement n'a rien de spectaculaire, il garantit toutefois une excellente qualité de vie. La résidence «Schwabing au bord du lac», au nord de l'ancien quartier des artistes, est ainsi devenue l'un des endroits de prédilection; on y trouve, outre les logements du secteur non subventionné, également un pourcentage élevé de logements sociaux. La résidence «Logements intégrés à Gern» du professeur Otto Steidle, qui a pour vocation le regroupement d'individus, tous revenus, milieux et générations confondus, est considérée depuis longtemps comme un exemple du genre. Certains bâtiments industriels et publics témoignent également d'une architecture réussie: la tour BMW, avec ses quatre cylindres, conçue par le professeur Karl Schwanzer, la tour futuriste de la Hypobank, selon les plans de Bea et Walther Betz, achevée en 1981, à Haidhausen, le nouveau bâtiment du Süddeutscher Verlag, qui abrite l'imprimerie, avec ses formes sobres et élégantes, signé par le professeur Peter von Seidlein, le bâtiment administratif de Siemens au sud de Munich, selon les plans de Richard Meier,

tore dell'editoria e del commercio librario. Quasi ogni giorno, questa casa ospita letture, presentazioni di libri e discussioni, offre spazio per grandi mostre letterarie e per uffici di istituzioni dello stesso settore. Il caffè al pianterreno è diventato un apprezzato punto di incontro, anche se raramente l'occasione è di carattere letterario.

Nell'architettura, Monaco soffre un po' di un complesso di inferiorità; infatti, dopo il Parco Olimpico, con l'audace struttura a tendone del suo tetto progettata dallo studio del professore Günter Behnisch e Partner, non è stato più costruito niente di analogamente futuribile. Sorprendentemente, questo lamento viene intonato particolarmente spesso e ad alta voce proprio dagli architetti monacensi, che però, così facendo, finiscono per ridurre i loro meriti. Per quanto mi riguarda considero la critica smisuratamente esagerata e, in molti casi, assolutamente fuori luogo. Anzi, ritengo piuttosto il fatto che Monaco non sia stata interessata da spettacolari cambiamenti di scena un vero colpo di fortuna – sebbene, così facendo, il capoluogo bavarese è stato assente, per lungo tempo dalle copertine delle riviste d'architettura. In compenso, sia le attività urbanistiche che quelle di edilizia abitativa si distinguono per la capacità di immedesimazione nei desideri dei futuri residenti: una politica non certo spettacolare ma orientata a garantire un tenore di vita migliore. La zona residenziale «Schwabing sul lago» a nord del quartiere degli artisti di Schwabing è, ad esempio, una delle zone più ambite; e pensare che oltre all'edilizia liberamente finanziata qui troviamo anche una quota elevata di case popolari. Anche la zona residenziale «Abitare integrato» a Gern, del professore Otto Steidle, che intende amalgamare persone di fasce di reddito, di livello sociale e di generazioni diverse, viene considerata da tempo esemplare. Tra le costruzioni ad uso commerciale e quelle pubbliche esistono esempi molto

im Norden des einstigen Künstlerviertels zählt beispielsweise zu einer der begehrtesten Wohnanlagen; dabei gibt es dort neben dem frei finanzierten Wohnungsbau auch einen hohen Anteil an Sozialwohnungen. Die Wohnanlage „Integriertes Wohnen in Gern" von Professor Otto Steidle, die bewusst Menschen verschiedener Einkommensgruppen, Milieus und Generationen zusammenführen will, gilt ebenso seit längerem als vorbildlich. Und bei den gewerblichen und öffentlichen Bauten gibt es sehr bedeutende Beispiele gelungener Architektur: Wie den BMW-Vierzylinder von Professor Karl Schwanzer, das 1981 fertig gestellte, futuristisch wirkende Hypo-Hochhaus von Bea und Walther Betz, das kühl zweckmäßige und gleichwohl elegante neue Druckereigebäude des Süddeutschen Verlags in Haidhausen von Professor Peter von Seidlein, die Siemens-Verwaltungsgebäude im Münchner Süden von Richard Meier, denen bald am Altstadtring das Siemens-Forum folgen wird, das Terminal 1 des neuen Münchner Flughafens von Professor Busso von Busse, auch wenn dessen filigraner, lichtdurchwirkter „weißer Flughafen im Grünen" zwischenzeitlich durch die großen Gesten des anschließenden „Munich-Airport-Center" von Helmut Jahn etwas bedrängt wird, vor allem aber der Erweiterungsbau der Hypobank, wiederum von Bea und Walther Betz, der meiner Meinung nach in äußerst geglückter Weise an das spektakuläre Hochhaus anschließt, aber eine heute zeitgemäße Architektursprache spricht. Eines ist unleugbar: Die gelungenen Beispiele jüngster Münchner Architektur sind oft schwer zu finden, weil übers ganze Stadtgebiet verstreut. Es gibt halt in München kein brach liegendes Innenstadtareal wie in Berlin nach dem Fall der Mauer. Doch vielleicht ist die weniger spektakuläre Münchner Architektur dafür etwas überzeugender in den Proportionen und in der Rücksichtnahme der Ent-

architectural magazines for a period of some years. As a result, the sector of city planning and housing construction was able to cater with remarkable insight to the wishes of the future population – which is, of course, not spectacular but guarantees quality of life. The housing development "Schwabing am See" in the northern part of this former artists' quarter is, for instance, one of the most popular residential areas, even though it comprises a great amount of publically financed dwellings in addition to the privately financed ones. The settlement "Integriertes Wohnen in Gern", designed by Prof. Otto Steidle, which aims at bringing together people of different income brackets, backgrounds and generations, has also been regarded as an exemplary residential area. Among Munich's industrial and public buildings you also find many examples of outstanding architecture: the "Four-Cylinder" BMW building by Prof. Karl Schwanzer; the futuristic high-rise building of the former Hypobank, which was designed by Bea and Walther Betz and completed in 1981; the functional yet elegant new printing centre of the Süddeutsche publishing firm in Haidhausen, planned by Prof. Peter von Seidlein; the Siemens administration building in the southern part of Munich designed by Richard Meier, which will soon be followed by the "Siemens Forum", to be erected on the Altstadtring; the Terminal 1 of the new Munich Airport by Prof. Busso von Busse, whose transparent "white airport in green surroundings", suffused with light, is unfortunately a bit crowded in by the adjoining, slightly overbearing "Munich Airport Center" designed by Helmut Jahn; and last but not least the Hypobank extension, also planned by Bea and Walther Betz, which in my opinion adjoins in an ideal way the spectacular highrise building, yet shows a very modern architecture. One can, of course, not deny that the most convincing examples of Munich's

„Walking Man" vor der Münchener Rückversicherungs-Gesellschaft an der Leopoldstraße, geschaffen 1995 von dem Amerikaner Jonathan Borofsky

"Walking Man" in front of the Münchener Rückversicherungs-Gesellschaft on Leopoldstraße, by the American artist Jonathan Borofsky, 1995

«Walking Man» devant la Münchener Rückversicherungs-Gesellschaft sur la Leopoldstraße, créé par Jonathan Borofsky en 1995

«Walking Man» davanti all'edificio della Münchener Rückversicherungs-Gesellschaft sulla Leopoldstraße, una creazione dell'americano Jonathan Borofsky del 1995

bientôt le Forum de Siemens sur le périphérique de la vieille ville, le terminal 1 du nouvel aéroport de Munich, conçu par le professeur Busso von Busse, bien que son «aéroport blanc dans la verdure», filigrane et transpercé de lumière, soit entre-temps quelque peu étouffé par les grands «gestes» du «Munich-Airport-Center», tout proche, signé Helmut Jahn, et surtout l'annexe de la Hypobank, toujours de Bea et de Walther Betz, qui, à mon avis, s'aligne admirablement bien sur la tour spectaculaire, tout en

significativi di architettura riuscita: ad esempio, l'«edificio a quattro cilindri» della BMW del professore Carl Schwanzer; il grattacielo di stampo futuristico della Bayerische Hypotheken- und Wechselbank (Hypobank), ultimato nel 1981, opera di Bea e Walther Betz; la nuova tipografia del Süddeutscher Verlag a Haidhausen, opportunamente razionale e allo stesso tempo elegante progettato dal professor Peter von Seidlein; gli edifici amministrativi della Siemens al sud di Monaco di Richard Meier, a cui

werfer auf gewachsene Strukturen.

Zwangsläufig konzentrierte sich dieser Rundblick für die Gäste der Stadt auf das, was Gäste sehen können oder erleben wollen. Die Interessen der Einheimischen kommen dabei zu kurz. Wenn man das kulturelle Leben aus deren Perspektive betrachten würde, träten ganz andere Angebote in den Vordergrund und andere Defizite in Erscheinung: Dann müsste beispielsweise vom vorbildlichen System der städtischen Bibliotheken in sämtlichen

latest architecture are hard to find, because they are scattered all over the city. The fact is that Munich does not have large empty spaces in the city centre at its disposal like Berlin after the fall of the Wall. Munich's architecture might be less spectacular, but it is possibly more convincing in its proportions and in the planners' regard for traditional and naturally-grown structures.

I am well aware that this panoramic view of Munich written for visitors concentrates primarily on what visitors want to see or

représentant néanmoins aujourd'hui une architecture moderne. Une chose est indéniable: difficile de découvrir les derniers exemples réussis de l'architecture munichoise, puisque éparpillés dans toute la ville et ses alentours. Munich ne dispose pas, comme Berlin après la chute du mur, d'un centre-ville «en friche». Toutefois, l'architecture munichoise, moins spectaculaire, est peut-être plus convaincante dans ses proportions et dans le respect des structures existantes par ses concepteurs.

presto seguirà il Siemens-Forum sulla circonvallazione del centro storico; il primo terminale del nuovo aeroporto di Monaco, del professore Busso von Busse, anche se il suo «bianco aeroporto nel verde» con giochi di luce ed effetti in filigrana è stato leggermente scalzato, nel frattempo, dalla viva presenza del «Munich-Airport-Center» di Helmut Jahn. Significativo, tra gli altri, è anche l'ampliamento dell'edificio della Hypobank, anch'esso opera di Bea e Walther Betz, costruito felicemente accanto allo spettaco-

Teilen der Stadt die Rede sein und von der größten Erwachsenenbildungseinrichtung Europas, der Münchner Volkshochschule mit über 6 000 Kursen im Semester. Oder vom Stadtmuseum am Jakobsplatz, das nicht nur Münchner Stadtgeschichte präsentiert, sondern immer wieder in populären Ausstellungen Schwerpunktthemen aufarbeitet. Und es müsste die Rede sein von den kulturellen Aktivitäten in verschiedenen Stadtteilen wie beispielsweise der sehr lebendigen Pasinger Fabrik gleich am S-Bahnhof im Westen der Stadt, von der rührigen Seidl-Villa im Herzen Altschwabings und ähnlichen Orten, die zwar Touristen keine Sensationen bieten können, aber für kulturelle Aktivitäten der jeweiligen Wohnbevölkerung von unschätzbarem Wert sind. Zu den großen und bald schon unverzeihlichen Defiziten gehören meines Erachtens, dass große Neubauviertel wie Neuperlach mit zigtausend Bewohnern immer noch keine eigenen kulturellen Zentren haben, sondern auf das zentrale Angebot der Millionenstadt verwiesen werden. Natürlich ist die Qualität der zentralen Musen-Tempel nicht wiederholbar, aber trotzdem brauchen Viertel, die längst die Einwohnerzahlen mittelgroßer Städte haben, eigene Foren kulturellen Lebens. Hierfür ist noch viel zu tun, ebenso zur Sicherung der Hallenkultur und der Jugendszene, die sich in der Nähe des Ostbahnhofs im mittlerweile international bekannten „Kunstpark Ost" etablieren konnte – mit tausenden von Gästen jeden Abend und internationaler Medienresonanz. Selbstverständlich hat hier nicht jede Aktivität gleich kulturelle Bedeutung, in manchen Hallen findet nur schlichter Diskobetrieb statt. Trotzdem ist das Ensemble von Ateliers und Werkstätten, Tanzschuppen und Nachtlokalen, Konzerten und Performances Ausdruck des Lebensgefühls vor allem der jüngeren Generation und fruchtbarer Humus für viel Kreativität, auch wenn viele sich nur schlicht amüsieren wollen.

experience and thus neglects the interests of the local people. If one regarded Munich's cultural life from their point of view, one would have to focus on other assets and deficits: one would have to mention, for instance, the exemplary public library system in all parts of the city, and the most comprehensive adult education facilities in all of Europe – i. e. the "Münchner Volkshochschule" offering more than 6,000 courses per semester. And one would have to discuss the cultural activities in the different city districts, for example the very lively "Pasinger Fabrik" at the suburban train station in the western part of the city; or the equally creative Seidl-Villa in the heart of Old Schwabing and other similar centres, which do not offer sensational attractions to tourists but are very important to the cultural activities of the people living there. Some of the most acute deficits are, for instance, that huge new housing developments such as "Neuperlach" (with many thousands of inhabitants) still have no cultural centres of their own, but must rely on the events offered by the metropolis of Munich. Of course it is difficult to reach and copy the quality of the city's central temples of the muses, but city districts which have long attained the size and status of medium-sized towns certainly need cultural centres of their own. Much remains to be improved in this sector, and in the fields of safeguarding "hall-culture" and the youth scene as well; the latter has settled near the "Ostbahnhof" (railway station) in the by now internationally known "Kunstpark Ost", which attracts thousands of guests every night and enjoys the acclaim of international media. Not all the centre's activities are of equal cultural significance, for some of the halls serve only as discotheques. Nevertheless, the complex comprising studios, workshops, dance halls and night clubs, and offering concerts and other performances expresses primarily the vital consciousness of the younger generation; and it

Ce tour d'horizon destiné aux visiteurs de la ville se concentre obligatoirement sur ce qu'ils peuvent ou souhaitent voir. A cet effet, les intérêts des Munichois sont quelque peu laissés pour compte. Si les Munichois devaient parler de la vie culturelle de leur ville, le tableau brossé serait sans doute bien différent, tant au niveau des offres que des lacunes. Ils évoqueraient, par exemple, le système exemplaire des bibliothèques municipales dans tous les quartiers de la ville, de l'Institut de formation d'adultes le plus grand d'Europe, l'université populaire de Munich proposant plus de 6 000 cours par semestre. Ou le Stadtmuseum sur la Jakobsplatz, qui présente non seulement l'histoire de la ville de Munich, mais se penche également régulièrement sur certains thèmes essentiels dans le cadre d'expositions très populaires. Ils mentionneraient également les activités culturelles dans certains quartiers, comme par exemple celles de la Pasinger Fabrik, aux nombreuses manifestations, située près de la gare du S-Bahn, à l'ouest de la ville, celles de la Seidl-Villa, aux activités multiples, au cœur du vieux Schwabing et dans d'autres lieux moins touristiques, mais essentielles pour la population concernée. A mon avis, l'une des lacunes les plus flagrantes, et bientôt impardonnable, concerne Neuperlach, un immense quartier composé d'immeubles neufs où vivent des dizaines de milliers d'habitants, toujours sans son propre centre culturel, entièrement dépendant des activités centralisées de la métropole. Bien entendu, il ne sera pas possible de retrouver la qualité des grands musées situés au centre de la ville, toutefois les quartiers, qui correspondent, en nombre d'habitants, à la grandeur de villes moyennes, ont besoin de leurs propres forums culturels. Il reste encore fort à faire, ne serait-ce que pour garantir la culture des «anciennes fabriques» et des scènes «branchées» qui ont pu s'établir à proximité de la Ostbahnhof, dans le «Kunstpark

lare grattacielo ma in grado di parlare, oggi, un linguaggio architettonico al passo coi tempi. Una cosa è innegabile: gli esempi riusciti della giovane architettura monacense sono spesso difficili da trovare, perché sono sparsi in tutta la città. A Monaco non esiste un'area non edificata nel centro della città, come invece a Berlino dopo la caduta del Muro. Ma forse per questo la meno spettacolare architettura di Monaco è più convincente nelle proporzioni e i progettatori hanno tenuto in maggiore considerazione le strutture già esistenti.

Inevitabilmente, questa panoramica effettuata per gli ospiti di Monaco si è concentrata su ciò che essi possono vedere o vogliono sperimentare. In questo modo, però, gli interessi dei monacensi non trovano la giusta considerazione. Se si considerasse la vita culturale dalla loro prospettiva, ben altre offerte acquisirebbero priorità e si manifesterebbero altre carenze. In tal caso, ad esempio, si dovrebbe accennare all'esemplare sistema delle biblioteche comunali distribuite in tutti quartieri della città e della più grande istituzione didattica per adulti in Europa, l'Università Popolare di Monaco che vanta oltre 6 000 corsi ogni semestre. Si dovrebbe considerare, inoltre, lo «Stadtmuseum» nella Jakobsplatz, che oltre a presentare la storia della città tratta anche continuamente, nelle sue divulgative, tutta una serie di argomenti monografici. Si dovrebbe anche parlare delle attività culturali nei diversi quartieri, come la vitalissima «Pasinger Fabrik» nel quartiere omonimo, proprio accanto alla stazione della ferrovia suburbana nell'ovest della città; della vivace Villa-Seidl nel cuore della vecchia Schwabing, e si dovrebbe parlare ancora di posti simili, che non saranno un'attrazione turistica, ma possiedono un valore incalcolabile per le attività culturali della popolazione residente. Delle grandi carenze quasi imperdonabili fa parte, a mio avviso, il fatto che grandi quartieri come quello di Neuperlach di recente

Der Kunstpark Ost ist – wie vorher die Zwischennutzung des alten Flughafens in Riem – leider nur ein Provisorium, die privaten Eigentümer haben andere Pläne. Befriedigende Nachfolgelösungen zu finden, zählt zu den wichtigsten kulturpolitischen Aufgaben in der Stadt. Denn Münchens Kultur lebt in der Tat nicht nur vom großartigen Erbe und dem respektablen Gegenwartsgeschehen, sondern auch von den Entwicklungspotentialen der Jüngeren.

Christian Ude

is a fertile soil for creativity, even though many youngsters only want to have fun. Just like the old airport in Riem, the Kunstpark Ost will unfortunately be used only temporarily, for the owners already have other plans. To find a satisfactory and more permanent solution will be one of the city's most important tasks. For Munich's culture does not subsist exclusively of its grandiose heritage and impressive contemporary achievements, but also of the development potential of its younger citizens.

Christian Ude

Ost», connu entre-temps dans le monde entier, avec chaque soir ses milliers de visiteurs et un impact international dans les médias. Bien entendu, chaque activité ne revêt pas toujours une importance culturelle, certains «hangars» sont tout simplement des discothèques. Et pourtant, l'ensemble des ateliers, des «Tanzschuppen», ces endroits où la jeunesse se rencontre pour danser, et des night-clubs est, notamment pour la plus jeune génération, un terrain propice à la créativité, même si la majeure partie d'entre eux ne viennent que pour s'amuser. Le Kunstpark Ost est malheureusement – comme auparavant l'utilisation temporaire de l'ancien aéroport de Riem – un lieu provisoire, les propriétaires privés ayant d'autres projets. Trouver des solutions de remplacement satisfaisantes fait partie des tâches politico-culturelles majeures de la ville; en effet, la culture munichoise ne se nourrit pas uniquement de son riche héritage et de ses activités actuelles, au demeurant fort respectables, mais aussi du potentiel de créativité des plus jeunes.

Christian Ude

costruzione, con diverse migliaia di abitanti, non dispongono di un centro culturale proprio ma devono sfruttare l'offerta culturale centralizzata della città di Monaco con i suoi milioni di abitanti. Naturalmente, la qualità dei «templi delle Muse» non è ripetibile, ma nonostante ciò i quartieri, che da tempo hanno raggiunto una densità di popolazione di cittadine medio-grandi, necessitano di spazi propri per impiantarvi la loro vita culturale. Al riguardo c'è ancora molto da fare, come pure per la salvaguardia della cultura dei capannoni riadattati a scopi culturali e dell'ambiente giovanile, che si è potuta affermare vicino alla stazione Est, nel «Kunstpark Ost» (Parco Culturale Est) che nel frattempo ha conquistato fama internazionale, ogni sera conta migliaia di ospiti e trova una grande eco dei mass-media. Certo, non ogni attività ha un significato culturale: alcuni capannoni sono solamente adibiti a discoteca. Ciò nonostante, l'insieme di atelier ed officine, di locali da ballo e notturni, di concerti e performance è espressione di gioia di vivere, soprattutto per le giovani generazioni e rappresenta un fertile humus per tanta creatività, anche se molti frequentatori vogliono semplicemente solo divertirsi. Purtroppo, però, il Kunstpark Ost – come era precedentemente avvenuto già con l'utilizzazione del vecchio aeroporto di Riem – rappresenta solo una soluzione provvisoria, i proprietari (privati) hanno altri progetti. La ricerca di soluzioni soddisfacenti per il «dopo» è uno dei compiti politico-culturali più importanti per la città. In verità, infatti, la cultura monacense non vive solo della magnifica eredità e dei rispettabili eventi quotidiani, ma anche del potenziale creativo dei più giovani.

Christian Ude

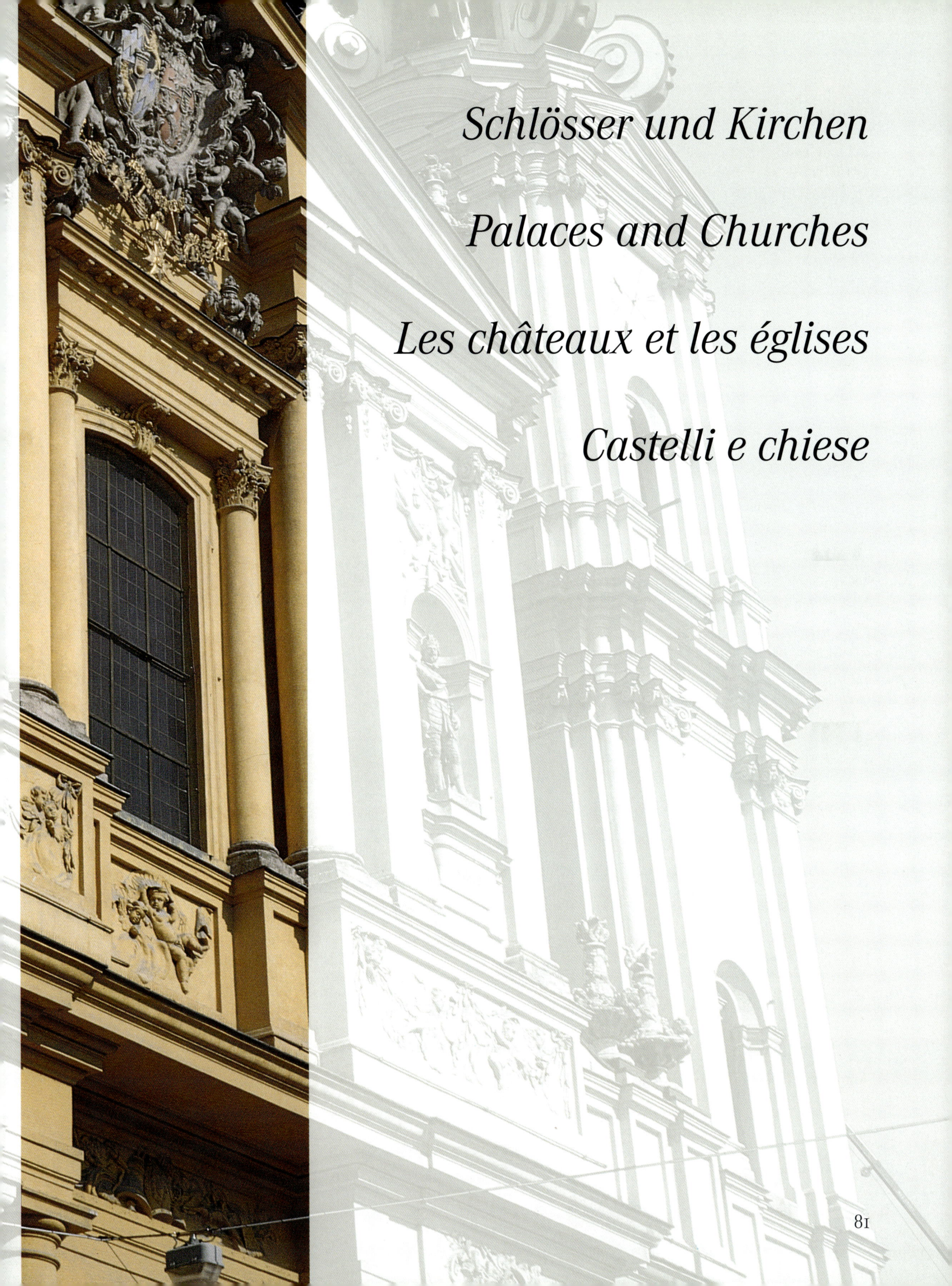

Schlösser und Kirchen

Palaces and Churches

Les châteaux et les églises

Castelli e chiese

Die Geschichte der Schlösser und Kirchen Münchens ist eng an das Haus Wittelsbach gebunden. Seit 1180 waren die Wittelsbacher Herzöge von Bayern, und seit 1255 hatten sie eine ständige Hofhaltung in München. München, wie es sich dem Besucher heute zeigt, ist das München seit der Spätgotik.

Sankt Peter, die älteste Pfarrkirche der Stadt, entstand noch vor der Stadtgründung, wurde im 12. Jahrhundert verändert und im 13. Jahrhundert neu errichtet. Nach dem Stadtbrand von 1327 musste der Chor erneuert werden; die alte Zweiturmfassade wurde durch einen einzigen Turm im Westen ersetzt. 1607 zerstörte ein Blitz Teile der Kirche; sie wurde im Stil des bayerischen Barock wieder aufgebaut und 1646 geweiht. Die Ausstattung des Innenraumes geht vor allem auf das 18. Jahrhundert zurück. Der Hochaltar Gottlieb Nikolaus Stubers reflektiert Berninis Entwürfe der Kathedrale von Sankt Peter in Rom. Die Münchner Peterskirche war ein für das städtische Leben bedeutsamer Ort; die wichtigsten religiösen Bruderschaften hatten hier ihre Altäre und Kapellen; davon zeugt noch heute der Altar für das Maria-Hilf-Bild an der Stirnwand des südlichen Seitenschiffs.

1271 wurde die Frauenkirche zur zweiten Pfarre der Stadt erhoben. In der ersten Hälfte des 13. Jahrhunderts errichtet, galt sie als ein Zeichen für das Selbstbewusstsein der Münchner Bürger; ihre Geschichte ist aber auch eng mit der bayerischen Herzogsfamilie verbunden, die hier ihre Grablege hatte. Am 2. Februar 1468 legten der Bischof von Freising, Johann Tulbeck, und Herzog Sigismund den Grundstein zu einem Neubau. Die Pläne für die dreischiffige Hallenkirche gehen auf Jörg von Halsbach zurück. Von der Ausstattung ist nach der Purifizierung in der Mitte des 19. Jahrhunderts, den Zerstörungen des Zweiten Weltkrieges und den zwei Umgestaltungen nach 1945 kaum mehr etwas erhalten. An der linken Wand hängt heute das

The history of Munich's palaces and churches is closely connected with the Wittelsbach Dynasty. The members of this family were Dukes of Bavaria from 1180 on and set up court in Munich in 1255. The face which Munich shows visitors today has developed since the late-Gothic period.

Sankt Peter – Munich's oldest parish church – was built even before the city was founded; it was altered in the 12th century and rebuilt in the 13th century. After a huge conflagration in 1327 the choir had to be renewed, and the two-spired façade was replaced by a single tower on the western wall. In 1607 lightning struck the church and destroyed a large part of it; it was reconstructed in the Bavarian Baroque style and consecrated in 1646. The decoration of the interior dates back mainly to the 18th century. The high altar created by Gottlieb Nikolaus Stuber reflects Bernini's sketches for the Cathedral of St. Peter's in Rome. Munich's "Peterskirche" played an important part in the town's public life: here the major religious fraternities had their altars and chapels – for instance the altar with the "Maria-Hilf" painting in the southern aisle, which has survived until today.

In 1271 the "Frauenkirche" was elevated to the rank of a second parish church. Erected in the first half of the 13th century, it was regarded as tangible proof of the citizen's self-assurance; but its history is also closely tied to the ducal family of Bavaria, whose members were buried in this church. On 2 February 1468 Bishop Johann Tulbeck of Freising and Duke Sigismund laid the foundation stone for a new building. Jörg von Halsbach made the plans for this three-naved hall-type church. There is hardly anything left of the original interior after the purification measures in the mid-19th century, the destructions during the Second World War, and two alterations after 1945. Today only the former altar painting by Peter Candid still decorates the left wall, and the

L'histoire des châteaux et des églises de Munich est étroitement liée à la dynastie des Wittelsbach. Depuis 1180, les Wittelsbach étaient ducs de Bavière et, depuis 1255, ils résidaient en permanence à Munich. Le Munich familier aux visiteurs d'aujourd'hui se présente ainsi depuis la période du gothique flamboyant.

L'église St Pierre (St. Peterskirche), la plus ancienne église paroissiale de la ville, vit le jour avant la fondation de la ville, fut transformée au 12ème siècle et reconstruite au 13ème siècle. Après l'incendie de la ville en 1327, le chœur dût être rénové; l'ancienne façade à deux tours fut remplacée par une tour unique à l'ouest. En 1607, la foudre détruisit une partie de l'église, elle fut à nouveau reconstruite en style baroque et consacrée en 1646. La décoration de l'intérieur remonte surtout au 18ème siècle. Le maître-autel de Gottlieb Nikolaus Stuber reflète les esquisses de Bernini dans la cathédrale Saint-Pierre à Rome. L'église St Pierre de Munich était un lieu important dans la ville; les communautés religieuses majeures avaient ici leurs autels et chapelles, l'autel de Notre-Dame-de-Bon-Secours sur le mur frontal dans la nef latérale sud en témoigne encore aujourd'hui.

En 1271, l'église Notre-Dame (Frauenkirche) devint la deuxième église paroissiale de la ville. Erigée au cours de la première moitié du 13ème siècle, elle symbolisa l'assurance des citoyens munichois; son histoire est aussi étroitement liée à la famille des ducs de Bavière qui avait ici sa sépulture. Le 2 février 1468, l'évêque de Freising, Johann Tulbeck, et le duc Sigismund posèrent la première pierre de la nouvelle construction. Les plans de l'église à trois nefs furent conçus par Jörg von Halsbach. Mais après la purification au milieu du 19ème siècle, les destructions de la Seconde Guerre mondiale et les deux réaménagements après 1945, il ne reste presque plus rien de la décoration originale. Sur le mur gauche est

La storia dei castelli e delle chiese di Monaco è strettamente legata alla casa dei Wittelsbach. I Wittelsbach furono duchi di Baviera dal 1180, e dal 1255 risiedettero stabilmente nella città. La città, come si presenta oggi al visitatore, è la Monaco del tardo gotico.

San Pietro («St. Peter»), la più antica parrocchiale della città, sorse ancora prima della fondazione della città, venne modificata nel XII secolo e ricostruita nel XIII secolo. Il Coro dovette essere ricostruito in seguito all'incendio che devastò la città nel 1327. L'antica facciata a due torri fu sostituita con un'unica torre posta sul lato occidentale. Nel 1607, un fulmine distrusse parti della chiesa che fu ricostruita in stile barocco bavarese e consacrata nel 1646. Gli allestimenti interni risalgono soprattutto al XVIII secolo. L'altare maggiore di Gottlieb Nikolaus Stuber si rifà agli schizzi del Bernini della Cattedra di San Pietro a Roma. St. Peter era un luogo importante per la vita dei cittadini di Monaco; qui, infatti, le confraternite religiose avevano i loro altari e le loro cappelle. Rimane ancora oggi a testimonianza, sulla parete frontale della navata laterale sud, l'altare per il dipinto di Maria Ausiliatrice.

Nel 1271, la Chiesa di Nostra Signora («Frauenkirche»), dedicata a Nostra Signora, fu elevata al rango di seconda parrocchia della città. Costruita nella prima metà del XIII secolo, divenne il simbolo della città di Monaco. La sua storia è, tuttavia, legata strettamente anche alla famiglia dei duchi di Baviera che trovarono qui sepoltura. Il 2 febbraio 1468 iniziò la ricostruzione ad opera

St. Peter, erste und älteste Pfarrkirche Münchens

St. Peter, Munich's first and oldest parish church

St. Pierre, la première et plus ancienne église paroissiale de Munich

San Pietro la prima e più antica parocchiale de Monaco

83

ehemalige Hochaltarbild Peter Candids. Die Grablege der Wittelsbacher wird durch das Monument Kaiser Ludwigs des Bayern aus dem frühen 17. Jahrhundert bezeichnet.

Von den spätmittelalterlichen herzoglichen Residenzen ist im Stadtzentrum vor allem der Alte Hof zu nennen. Seit 1255 hatten die Wittelsbacher in der Nähe des Marktes einen repräsentativen Sitz; als die Herzöge Christoph und Sigismund hier ihre Wohnung nahmen, wurde er ab 1466 ausgebaut. Der berühmte Wappenerker vor dem Burgstock ist eine Zutat dieser Epoche.

Vor den Toren der alten Stadt, in Obermenzing, liegt das Jagdschloss Blutenburg, das unter Herzog Albrecht III. 1431–1440 entstand. Herzog Sigismund ließ es auf die heutige Größe ausbauen. Mit der ab 1488 errichteten Schlosskapelle hat sich ein kleiner spätgotischer Sakralraum erhalten. Die Altarbilder malte Jan Polack. Der geschlossene Hochaltar zeigt den hl. Bartholomäus, der den knienden Bauherrn seinem Namenspatron, dem hl. Sigismund, empfiehlt.

Der Alte Hof als Regierungssitz der Wittelsbacher wurde von der Neuveste abgelöst, einer zunächst als Fluchtburg errichteten Festung auf dem Gelände des heutigen Apothekenhofes. Seit dem frühen 16. Jahrhundert gewann sie die Bedeutung einer herzoglichen Residenz; noch Herzog Albrecht V. feierte im berühmten Georgssaal die Vermählung seines Sohnes mit Renata von Lothringen; zur selben Zeit jedoch entschloss er sich, in unmittelbarer Nachbarschaft 1568–1571 einen alleinstehenden Sammlungsbau zu errichten. Dieses so genannte Antiquarium enthielt im Erdgeschoss einen großen Festsaal, in dem er antike Skulpturen aus Italien aufstellen ließ; das Obergeschoss beherbergte seine Büchersammlung. Dieser Neubau ist die Keimzelle der Münchner Residenz.

Wittlesbach crypt is dominated by the monument of Emperor Ludwig the Bavarian dating from the early 17th century.

The most impressive of the ducal residences from the late Middle Ages is the "Alte Hof" in the city centre. From 1255 on, the Wittelsbacher owned a very imposing seat near the market. When the dukes Christoph and Sigismund took up residence in this castle, they started improving its appearance (from 1466 on). The famous, coat-of-arms-decorated oriel on the central part of the castle dates from this epoch.

Outside the old city gates, in Obermenzing, Duke Albrecht III from 1431 to 1440 had the Blutenburg hunting lodge built. Duke Sigismund enlarged it to its present size. The palace chapel, whose construction was started in 1488, is a true treasure of late Gothic sacral art. The altar paintings were created by Jan Polack. The closed high altar depicts Saint Bartholomeo recommending the kneeling builder to his patron saint St. Sigismund.

The Alte Hof eventually lost its status as the government seat of the Wittelsbach Dynasty to the "Neuveste" (New Fortress), which had originally been constructed as a refuge on the area of the present-day "Apothekenhof". It became the ducal seat in the early 16th century. Duke Albrecht V celebrated the wedding of his son with Renata of Lorraine in the famous "Georgssaal". But at that time he had already decided to have a large, separate collection building erected in the immediate vicinity. This so-called "Antiquarium" (built between 1568 and 1571) contained a huge banqueting hall on the ground floor, which Albrecht decorated with antique sculptures from Italy; the upper floor sheltered his book collection. This new building was the germ cell of the Munich "Residenz".

Albrecht V's son and successor – Wilhelm V – integrated the

accrochée l'image de l'ancien maître-autel de Peter Candid. La sépulture de la famille des Wittelsbach est appelée le mausolée de l'empereur Louis de Bavière et date du 17ème siècle.

Parmi les résidences ducales de la fin du Moyen Age, il faut

del vescovo di Freising, Johann Tulbeck, e del duca Sigismondo. I progetti per questa chiesa a sala a tre navate erano di Jörg von Halsbach. Degli arredi interni è rimasto ben poco dopo il «ripulisti» avvenuto a metà del XIX secolo, le distruzioni della Se-

*Kapelle St. Sigismund in Schloss Bluten-
burg – ein Kleinod altbayerischer Spätgotik*

*St. Sigismund Chapel in the Blutenburg
Palace – a jewel of Bavarian late Gothic
architecture*

*La chapelle St. Sigismund dans le château
de Blutenburg – un joyau du gothique flamboyant bavarois*

*La cappella St. Sigismund nel castello
di Blutenburg – un gioiello di architettura
bavarese tardo-gotica*

Der Sohn und Nachfolger Albrechts V., Wilhelm V., spannte das Antiquarium zwischen zwei neue Wohntrakte ein, den Grottenhoftrakt und den Schwarzer-Saal-Trakt. Trotz späterer Veränderungen erlebt der Besucher im Grottenhof auch heute noch Antiquarium into two new residential sections, the "Grottenhoftrakt", and the "Schwarzer-Saal-Trakt". Although this complex was altered repeatedly in later days, visitors to the "Grottenhof" can still recognize the spirit of faire une place particulière à l'Alter Hof. Depuis 1255, les Wittelsbach possédaient un château fort représentatif à proximité du marché. Lorsque les ducs Christoph et Sigismund vinrent s'y installer, il fut agrandi à partir de 1466. La célèbre enjolivure sur la conda Guerra Mondiale e i due ammodernamenti seguiti al 1945. Sulla parete sinistra si trova l'antica pala dell'altare maggiore di Peter Candid. All'interno della navata destra si trova il mausoleo dell'imperatore Ludovico IV il Bavaro che risale all'inizio del XVII secolo.

Delle residenze tardo-medievali dei duchi di Baviera è da ricordare soprattutto l'Antica Corte («Alter Hof»), residenza dei Wittelsbach dal 1255, che si trova nel centro storico della città nelle vicinanze del mercato; i lavori di ampliamento iniziarono nel 1466 quando vi si stabilirono i duchi Cristoforo e Sigismondo. La famosa torricella a sporto davanti al «Burgstock» risale a quell'epoca.

Davanti alle porte dell'antica città, ad Obermenzing, sorge il castello di caccia di Blutenburg, costruito tra il 1431 e il 1440 sotto il duca Alberto III ed ampliato dal duca Sigismondo. La cappella, costruita nel 1488, rimane oggi una piccola testimonianza di arte religiosa tardo-gotica. Le pale d'altare sono di Jan Polack. L'altare maggiore, con struttura chiusa, mostra San Bartolomeo che raccomanda il committente, in ginocchio, al suo santo patrono, San Sigismundo.

In seguito, i Wittelsbach lasciarono la residenza dell'Alter Hof per stabilirsi nella Nuova Fortezza («Neuveste»), una costruzione concepita inizialmente come rocca sul terreno dove si trova, oggi, l'Apothekenhof. A partire dal

den Geist einer von Italien beeinflussten Gartenanlage des Manierismus.

Maximilian I., der Sohn Wilhelms V., baute die Anlagen seines Großvaters und Vaters zu einem repräsentativen Fürstensitz aus. Er errichtete die Fassade zur Residenzstraße und mit dem Kaiserhoftrakt einen Gästeflügel, der höchsten Ansprüchen genügte. Zur Ausstattung seiner neuen Residenz gründete er eine eigene Teppichmanufaktur, die nur für seinen Bedarf produzierte und deren großartige Schöpfungen, z. B. die Otto-von-Wittelsbach-Folge, heute in der Residenz zu besichtigen sind. Seine Reliquiensammlung wurde in einem Privatoratorium, der Reichen Kapelle, ausgestellt. Die Ausstattung dieses kleinen Raumes mit bunten Wandfeldern in Scagliolatechnik erinnert an den großen Wert, den Maximilian dieser Sammlung beimaß.

Im Zeitalter der Gegenreformation und der katholischen Reform waren die bayerischen Herzöge mächtige Förderer der katholischen Sache. Albrecht V. hatte in München den Jesuitenorden angesiedelt; Wilhelm V. begann den Bau eines großen Kollegs und einer eigenen Kirche für den Orden. Der Neubau wurde dem

Italy in the mannerist layout of the gardens.

Maximilian I, son of Wilhelm V, enlarged and improved his father's and grandfather's constructions generously, turning them into a magnificent princely residence. He had the façade towards Residenzstraße made and the "Kaiserhoftrakt", a guest wing which lived up to the most exacting wishes and expectations. He set up a rug manufacturing plant of his own which served his own needs exclusively, producing all the rugs for his new residence. The splendid creations of this manufacture – for instance the Otto-von-Wittelsbach series – can be admired in his "Residenz" today. His collection of relics was exhibited in a private oratorium (prayer room), the so-called "Rich Chapel". This room decorated with colourful wall panels in scagliola technique clearly proves how greatly Maximilian cherished his valuable collection.

In the period of the Counter-reformation and the Catholic Reform the Bavarian dukes staunchly supported the Catholic fraction. Albrecht V had already brought the Jesuit Order to Munich. In 1582 Wilhelm V

partie principale du château date de cette époque.

C'est aux portes de la vieille ville, à Obermenzing, que se trouve le château de chasse de Blutenburg qui fut édifié sous le duc Albert III de 1431 à 1440. Le duc Sigismund le fit agrandir à sa dimension actuelle. Avec la chapelle du château érigée dès 1488, un petit joyau sacré du gothique flamboyant a été conservé. Les images de l'autel furent peintes par Jan Polack. Le retable à volets fermés montre le saint Bartholomé qui recommande aux bâtisseurs à genoux son patron, le saint Sigismund.

En tant que siège du gouvernement des Wittelsbach, l'Alter Hof fit place à la Neuveste, une forteresse devant servir à l'origine à se réfugier sur le terrain de l'actuelle Apothenkenhof. Au début du 16ème siècle, elle prit le rang de résidence ducale. Le duc Albert V célébra dans la célèbre salle Georg les noces de son fils avec Renée de Lorraine. A la même époque, il décida cependant, entre 1568 et 1571, de faire construire à proximité immédiate un musée isolé. Cet Antiquarium se composait au rez-de-chaussée d'une grande salle des fêtes dans laquelle il avait fait exposer des sculptures antiques provenant d'Italie, l'étage supérieur

XVI secolo, la Neuveste assurse a residenza ducale e il duca Alberto V vi festeggiò, nella famosa «Georgssaal», il matrimonio del figlio con Renata di Lorena. Nel contempo, egli decise però di costruire nelle immediate vicinanze, tra il 1568 e il 1571, una galleria isolata, il cosiddetto Antiquarium. Questo comprendeva, al piano terra, un grande salone nel quale fece esporre antiche sculture provenienti dall'Italia; il piano superiore ospitava la sua collezione di libri. Questa nuova costruzione rappresentò la prima cellula della Residenza di Monaco.

Il figlio di Alberto V e suo successore, Guglielmo V, aggiunse all'Antiquarium due nuove ale, il Cortile delle Grotte («Grottenhof») e la Sala Nera («Schwarzer Saal»). Nonostante le modifiche apportate successivamente, il visitatore può ancora avvertire, nel cortile del Grottenhof, lo spirito del manierismo italiano.

Massimiliano I, figlio di Guglielmo V, trasformò gli impianti realizzati dal nonno e dal padre in una residenza rappresentativa principesca. Egli fece costruire la facciata che prospetta sulla Residenzstraße e un'ala per gli ospiti, il Kaiserhof, in grado di soddisfare ogni esigenza. Per decorare la sua nuova residenza creò una propria ed esclusiva manifattura di tappeti, le cui splendide creazioni, ad esempio la serie di Otto von Wittelsbach, possono essere oggi ammirate nella Residenza. La sua

Kämpfer der streitbaren Kirche, dem hl. Michael, geweiht. Die Architektur des Baus, der ab 1582 entstand, wurde von Friedrich Sustris entscheidend beeinflusst; sie ist von römischen Eindrücken, vor allem von der Mutterkirche des Jesuitenordens Il Gesù abhängig. Eine große, später nicht ausgeführte Vierungskuppel sollte das Grabmal Wilhelms V. überwölben. Auf der Fassade werden über der kolossalen Statue des heiligen Michael die Ahnen Wilhelms V. gezeigt. So wird die Michaelskirche auch zum genealogischen Monument der bayerischen Herrscher.

1623 gewann Herzog Maximilian für die altbayerische Linie der Wittelsbacher den Titel eines Kurfürsten. Er und seine Nachfolger waren damit berechtigt, den Kaiser des Heiligen Römischen Reiches Deutscher Nation zu wählen. Maximilians Sohn Ferdinand Maria wurde erst geboren, als der Kurfürst schon 63 Jahre alt war. Ferdinand Marias Ehe mit Henriette Adelaide, einer italienischen Prinzessin aus dem Haus Savoyen, blieb zehn Jahre ohne männlichen Erben. 1662 wurde der erste Sohn Max Emanuel geboren. Aus diesem Anlass stiftete Kurfürst Ferdinand Maria am damaligen Stadtrand eine Kirche, die dem Theatinerorden übergeben wurde. Die Kirche variiert den Bautyp der Michaelskirche, wie auch die Mutterkirche des Theatinerordens in Rom, San Andrea della Valle, als eine Weiterentwicklung der römischen Jesuitenkirche Il Gesù gesehen werden muss. Im Inneren dominiert der plastische weiße Stuck. Die Fassade wurde

... im Brunnenhof der Residenz

... in the Brunnenhof of the Residenz

... dans la Brunnenhof de la Résidence

... nella Brunnenhof della Residenza

started to build a huge college and church for them, which was dedicated to the fighter of the militant church, St. Michael. The architecture of this new building was largely determined by Friedrich Sustris; it shows the strong influence of Rome, particularly that of the Jesuit Order's mother church Il Gesù. The large dome, which was planned to rise above the tomb of Wilhelm V at the intersection, was, however, not constructed in the end. The façade shows – above the colossal statue of St. Michael – the ancestors of Duke Wilhelm V. Thus the Church of St. Michael has also become a genealogical monument to the sovereigns of Bavaria.

In 1623 Duke Maximilian won the title of "Elector" for the old-Bavarian Wittelsbach line. He and his successors were thus entitled to elect the emperors of the Holy Roman Empire. Maximilian's son Ferdinand Maria was born when Maximilian was already 63 years old. Ferdinand Maria, who married an Italian princess from the Savoy Dynasty, also had to wait for a male heir for ten years: not until 1662 was his first son – Max Emanuel – born. To celebrate this occasion Elector Ferdinand Maria had a church built at the limits of Munich which was turned over to the Theatine Order. This church is a variation of the Michaelskirche in style, just as the church of San Andrea della Valle, the mother church of the Theatine Order in Rome, was modelled after the Roman Jesuit mother church Il Gesù. Plastic white stucco also dominates the interior of Munich's Theatinerkirche. The façade remained unfinished until Max III Joseph completed it 100 years later.

Ferdinand Maria had a villa built for his Italian wife in the "Hofmark Schwaige", ouside the city gates. The central pavillon of the Palace of Nymphenburg has been altered several times since then, but in the side wings one still finds the original ceiling paintings. Ferdinand Maria's son, Elector Max Emanuel, turned his

était réservé à sa collection de livres. Ce nouvel édifice marqua le point de départ de la résidence (Residenz) de Munich.

Le fils et successeur d'Albert V, Guillaume V, entoura l'Antiquarium de deux nouvelles ailes d'habitation appelées «Grottenhoftrakt» et «Schwarzer-Saal-Trakt». Malgré des transformations ultérieures, le visiteur ressent aujourd'hui encore dans le Grottenhof la conception maniériste des jardins influencée par l'Italie.

Maximilien 1er, le fils de Guillaume V, aménagea les installations de son grand-père et de son père en un siège représentatif des princes électeurs. Il construit la façade sur la rue de la résidence et, le Kaiserhoftrakt, une aile destinée aux invités et satisfaisant les plus grandes exigences. Pour décorer sa nouvelle résidence, il fonda sa propre manufacture de tapisseries qui ne produisait que pour ses besoins et dont les magnifiques créations, p.ex. la série d'Otton von Wittelsbach, peuvent être admirées aujourd'hui dans la résidence. Sa collection de chefs-d'œuvre religieux fut exposée dans une chapelle à part, la Reiche Kapelle. Ce centre spirituel, dont les murs colorés présentent la technique de Scagliola, rappelle l'immense importance que Maximilien accordait à cette collection.

A l'époque de la Contre-Réforme et de la Réforme catholique, les ducs de Bavière étaient les grands partisans de l'église catholique. Albert V avait installé à Munich l'ordre des Jésuites; Guillaume V commença la construction d'un grand collège et d'une église pour cet ordre. Le nouveau bâtiment fut consacré au défenseur de l'Eglise et chef de la milice céleste, le Saint Michel. L'architecture de l'édifice, qui fut érigé dès 1582, fut profondément influencée par Friedrich Sustris, elle rappelle les impressions romaines, en particulier de l'église matrice de l'ordre des Jésuites «Il Gesù». Une grande coupole avec croisée du transept, qui ne fut pas exécutée plus tard, devait

collezione di reliquiari fu esposta in un oratorio privato, la Cappella Ricca («Reiche Kapelle»). L'arredo di questa piccola stanza, che presenta pareti variopinte decorate con la tecnica della scagliola, ricorda il grande valore attribuito da Massimiliano a questa collezione.

Nel periodo della Controriforma e della Riforma cattolica i duchi di Baviera si dimostrarono convinti e potenti promotori della causa cattolica. Alberto V aveva insediato a Monaco l'ordine dei Gesuiti; Guglielmo V iniziò la costruzione di un grande collegio dei Gesuiti e di una chiesa propria dell'ordine. La nuova costruzione fu dedicata al grande combattente della chiesa, San Michele. L'architettura della costruzione, che sorse nel 1582, fu influenzata in modo decisivo da Friedrich Sustris; è di impronta romana, soprattutto sullo stile della Chiesa del Gesù. Una grande cupola sul quadrato, in seguito mai realizzata, avrebbe dovuto coprire a volta la tomba di Guglielmo V. Sulla facciata vengono mostrati gli antenati di Guglielmo V posti sopra la colossale statua di San Michele. Per questo motivo la Michaelskirche può essere anche considerata come monumento genealogico della dinastia dei Wittelsbach.

Nel 1623, il duca Massimiliano ottenne, per la linea alto-bavarese dei Wittelsbach, il titolo di principe elettore. In tal modo, egli ed i suoi successori avevano il diritto di eleggere l'imperatore del Sacro Romano Impero Germanico. Quando nacque il successore di Massimiliano, Ferdinando Maria, il principe elettore aveva già raggiunto l'età di 63 anni. Ferdinando Maria prese in moglie Enrichetta Adelaide, una principessa italiana della casa dei Savoia, ma passarono dieci anni prima della nascita dell'erede maschio, Massimiliano Emanuele, nato nel 1662. Per festeggiare il lieto evento, il principe elettore Ferdinando Maria fece costruire una chiesa alla periferia della città e la donò all'ordine dei Teatini. La chiesa riprende,

erst knapp 100 Jahre später unter Max III. Joseph fertig gestellt.

In der Hofmark Schwaige vor den Toren der Stadt errichtete Ferdinand Maria für seine italienische Gemahlin ein Landhaus. Der Mittelpavillon von Schloss Nymphenburg wurde zwar seitdem mehrmals verändert, in den seitlichen Appartements sind aber immer noch Deckenbilder dieser Erstausstattung zu sehen.

mother's modest villa into a splendid palace, which reflected the impressions he had gained during stays in the Netherlands and in France. In the Nymphenburg Park three small palaces were set up during his reign: the "Badenburg", which shelters a large covered swimming pool; the "Pagodenburg", a Chinese pleasure-house; and the "Magdalenenklause", a fake ruin contain-

recouvrir d'une voûte le tombeau de Guillaume V. Sur la façade, les ancêtres de Guillaume V surplombent la statue de Saint Michel. L'église St Michel devint ainsi un monument généalogique des seigneurs de Bavière.

En 1623, le duc Maximilien reçut le titre de prince électeur de la vieille lignée bavaroise des Wittelsbach. Lui et ses successeurs avaient le droit d'élire l'em-

Barocke Sommerresidenz Schloss Nymphenburg

Nymphenburg Palace, a summer residence in the Baroque style

Une résidence d'été baroque - le château de Nymphenburg

Castello di Nymphenburg, residenza estiva in stile barocco

Der Sohn Ferdinand Marias, Kurfürst Max Emanuel, ließ das Landhaus seiner Mutter in Nymphenburg zu einer repräsentativen Schlossanlage ausbauen; die Erweiterungen spiegeln Eindrücke seiner Aufenthalte in den Niederlanden und in Frankreich wider. Im Park von Schloss Nymphenburg entstanden unter Max Emanuel drei kleine Parkburgen: die Badenburg, die ein großes übering a small chapel which was to express the elector's penitence. Max Emanuel's apartments in the residential palace were later redecorated: the "Reiche Zimmer", planned by Joseph Effner, burned to the ground in the big conflagration of 1729 and were reconstructed by Max Emanuel's son, Karl Albrecht, under the artistic auspices of François Cuvilliés.

pereur du Saint Empire Romain de la nation allemande. Le fils de Maximilien, Ferdinand Maria, venait à peine de naître que le prince électeur était déjà âgé de 63 ans. Le mariage de Ferdinand Maria avec Henriette Adelaide, une princesse italienne de la maison de Savoy, resta dix ans sans héritier mâle. En 1662, le premier fils Max Emanuel naquit. A cette occasion, le prince électeur Ferdinand Maria fit don d'une église érigée aux frontières de l'époque de la ville et qui fut donnée à l'ordre des Théatins. L'église diffère du type de construction de l'église St Michel, tout comme l'église mère de l'ordre des Théatins à Rome, San Andrea della Valle, et doit être considérée comme un prolongement de l'église Jésuite romaine «Il Gesù». A l'intérieur, les sculptures en stuc blanc dominent. La façade ne fut terminée que cent ans plus tard sous Max III Joseph.

Aux portes de la ville, dans la Hofmark Schwaige, Ferdinand Maria fit construire pour son épouse italienne une maison de plaisance. Le pavillon central du château de Nymphenburg fut certes modifié plusieurs fois depuis mais, dans les appartements latéraux, il est encore toujours possible d'admirer les images de plafond de cette décoration d'origine. Le fils de Ferdinand Maria, le prince électeur Max Emanuel, aménagea la maison de campagne de sa mère à Nymphenburg et en fit un château représentatif, les agrandissements reflètent les impressions de ses séjours aux Pays-Bas et en France. Dans le parc du château de Nymphenburg, trois petits châteaux furent érigés sous Max Emanuel: le Badenburg, comprenant une grande piscine couverte, le Pagodenburg, une maison de joie chinoise et le Magdalenenklause, une pseudo-ruine dotée de sa propre chapelle et témoignant de la contrition du prince électeur. Les appartements de Max Emanuel dans la résidence furent modifiés par après; les Reiche Zimmer (chambres riches) dessinées par Josef Effner brûlèrent

seppure con diverse variazioni, il tipo di costruzione della chiesa di San Michele («Michaelskirche») così come la chiesa dell'ordine dei Teatini a Roma dedicata alla Madonna, Sant'Andrea della Valle, deve essere vista come uno sviluppo della chiesa del Gesù dell'ordine dei Gesuiti. All'interno dominano gli stucchi plastici bianchi. La facciata fu completata solo 100 anni dopo sotto Massimiliano III Giuseppe.

Nella pace della campagna davanti alle porte della città, Ferdinando Maria fece costruire, per la moglie italiana, una residenza estiva. Il corpo centrale del castello di Nymphenburg subì da allora molte modifiche, ma negli appartamenti laterali possono essere ancora ammirati i dipinti originali. Il figlio di Ferdinando Maria, il principe elettore Massimiliano Emanuele, ampliò la residenza estiva della madre e la trasformò in un castello di rappresentanza; gli ampliamenti rispecchiano le impressioni che egli doveva aver raccolto durante i suoi soggiorni nei Paesi Bassi e in Francia. Sotto Massimiliano Emanuele sorsero, nel parco del castello di Nymphenburg, tre piccoli padiglioni: la Badenburg, che comprende una grande piscina coperta, la Pagodenburg, un padiglione decorato con cineserie, e la Magdalenenklause, una finta rovina con una cappella privata, espressione della contrizione del principe elettore. Gli appartamenti di Massimiliano Emanuele furono in seguito trasformati; le Camere Ricche («Reiche Zimmer») progettate da Joseph Effner bruciarono completamente durante il grande incendio del 1729 e furono ricostruite dal figlio di Massimiliano Emanuele, Carlo Alberto, sotto la direzione artistica di François Cuvilliés.

La costruzione di chiese in Baviera in stile rococò ebbe due apici assoluti a Monaco. Nel XVIII secolo, Egid Quirin costruì sul suo terreno nella Sendlinger Straße, acquistato negli anni Trenta, una chiesa lunga, a due piani, dedicata a San Giovanni Nepomu-

dachtes Schwimmbecken enthält, die Pagodenburg, ein chinesisches Lusthaus, und die Magdalenenklause, eine Scheinruine mit eigener Kapelle als Ausdruck der Bußfertigkeit des Kurfürsten. Max Emanuels Appartements in der Residenz wurden später umgebaut; die von Joseph Effner geplanten Reichen Zimmer brannten beim großen Residenzfeuer von 1729 aus und wurden von Max Emanuels Sohn Karl Albrecht unter künstlerischer Leitung von François Cuvilliés erneuert.

Der bayerische Kirchenbau des Rokoko brachte in München zwei absolute Höhepunkte hervor. Egid Quirin Asam errichtete auf seinem eigenen in den 1730er Jahren in der Sendlinger Straße erworbenen Grundstück einen länglichen, zweigeschossigen, dem Johann Nepomuk geweihten Kirchenbau. Der Raum wird bestimmt von der böhmischen und römischen Barockarchitektur. Die Wände sind in schwingende, nicht mehr klar zu definierende Flächen aufgelöst, eine warme goldene und rötliche Farbigkeit durchflutet das Innere.

Etwa gleichzeitig mit der Asamkirche entstand St. Michael in Berg am Laim. Auftraggeber war der Bruder des bayerischen Kurfürsten, Clemens August, Kurfürst von Köln. Die Architektur des überkuppelten, aus einem Achteck entwickelten Zentralbaus wurde von Johann Michael Fischer entworfen; die Fresken in der Kuppel schuf Johann Baptist Zimmermann; die Altäre gehen auf Johann Baptist Straub, einen der bedeutendsten Bildhauer der Zeit, zurück.

1743 wurde Kurfürst Karl Albrecht zum Kaiser des Heiligen Römischen Reiches gewählt und in Frankfurt gekrönt. Er musste sein Kaisertum gegen die Ansprüche der späteren Kaiserin Maria Theresia verteidigen. Österreichische Truppen besetzten Bayern; bei seinem Tod 1745 blieben seinem Sohn Max III. Joseph nur Friedensverhandlungen. Der Frieden ist dementsprechend auch das Thema der wichtigsten Baumaßnahme des Kur-

During the Bavarian Rococo period two outstanding churches were created: Egid Quirin Asam, one of Bavaria's most renowned artists, erected on his own ground (purchased in Sendlinger Straße in the 1730s) an oblong, two-storied church, which was dedicated to Johann Nepomuk. In the entire building Bohemian and Roman Baroque architecture dominates. The walls seem to dissolve into oscillating expanses defying definition, and a warm golden and reddish glow suffuses the interior.

At about the same time that the Asamkirche was built, St. Michael in Berg am Laim was erected. It was commissioned by Clemens August, Elector of Cologne, a brother of the Bavarian elector. The architecture of the central building, based on an octagonal outline and topped by a cupola, was designed by Johann Michael Fischer; the dome frescoes were created by Johann Baptist Zimmermann, the altars by Johann Baptist Straub, one of the most famous sculptors of his time.

In 1743 Elector Karl Albrecht was elected Emperor of the Holy Roman Empire and crowned in Frankfurt. But the later Empress Maria Theresia laid claim to the succession, so that Karl Albrecht was forced to defend his empire. As a result, Austrian troops occupied Bavaria. When Karl Albrecht died in 1745 his son Max III Joseph was obliged to start peace negotiations. Thus "Peace" was also the subject of the elector's most important building projects. He had the large hall in the Palace of Nymphenburg redecorated for the third time. François Cuvilliés was responsible for its architecture, and Johann Baptist Zimmermann created the fresco commemorating the "Golden Age".

Max III Joseph was the last member of the old-Bavarian Wittelsbach line. The new sovereigns belonged to the Palatine branch. Max IV Joseph joined the French cause in the Napoleonic Wars and, after the collapse of the Holy

lors de l'incendie qui ravagea la résidence en 1729 et furent rénovées par le fils de Max Emanuel, Karl Albrecht, sous la direction artistique de François Cuvilliés.

La construction bavaroise d'églises de style rococo fut marquée à Munich par deux événements majeurs. Egid Quirin Asam érigea sur son propre terrain, acquis dans les années 1730 dans la rue Sendlinger, une église longue, à deux étages et dédiée au culte de Jean Népomucène. L'édifice est caractérisé par l'architecture baroque tchèque et romaine. Les murs se fondent avec leurs surfaces mal définies, une couleur chaude dorée et rouge traverse l'intérieur.

A Berg am Laim, l'église St Michel (St. Michael) fut construite à peu près à la même époque que l'église Asam, sur l'initiative du frère du prince électeur bavarois Clemens August, prince électeur de Cologne. L'architecture du bâtiment central recouvert d'une coupole et développé à partir d'un octogone est l'œuvre de Johann Michael Fischer, les fresques dans la couple furent créées par Johann Baptist Zimmermann, les autels sont signés Johann Baptist Straub, un des plus grands sculpteurs de l'époque.

En 1743, le prince électeur Karl Albrecht fut élu empereur du Saint Empire romain et couronné à Francfort. Il dut défendre son empire contre les prétentions de la future impératrice Marie Thérèse. Les troupes autrichiennes occupèrent la Bavière; à sa mort en 1745, il ne resta plus à son fils, Max III. Joseph, que de négocier la paix. La paix est également le thème des mesures majeures en matière de construction du prince électeur. Max III Joseph fit, pour la troisième fois, entièrement redécorer la grande salle du château de Nymphenburg. L'architecture est l'œuvre de François Cuvilliés, elle est surmontée par une fresque de Johann Baptist Zimmermann qui évoque la période des temps dorés.

Max III. Joseph marqua la fin de la lignée bavaroise de la dy-

ceno. L'ambiente è caratterizzata dall'architettura barocca boema e romana. Le pareti si perdono in superfici non lineari e un colore caldo, dorato e rosso-bruno inonda l'interno.

Quasi contemporaneamente alla chiesa Asam («Asamkirche») sorse la chiesa di San Michese a Berg am Laim. Il committente fu il fratello del principe elettore di Baviera, Clemente Augusto, principe elettore di Colonia. L'architettura della costruzione centrale su base ottagonale e sormontata da una cupola fu progettata da Johann Michael Fischer; gli affreschi nella cupola portano la firma di Johann Baptist Zimmermann; gli altari sono di Johann Baptist Straub, uno dei maggiori scultori dell'epoca.

Nel 1743, il principe elettore Carlo Alberto fu eletto imperatore del Sacro Romano Impero ed incoronato in Francia. Egli dovette difendere il suo impero dall'imperatrice Maria Teresia che ne rivendicava i diritti. Truppe austriache occuparono la Baviera; alla morte di Carlo Alberto, nel 1745, al figlio Massimiliano III Giuseppe non rimase che concludere le trattative di pace. La pace è conseguentemente anche il tema della sua opera maggiore. Massimiliano III Giuseppe incaricò François Cuvilliés di ricostruire, per la terza volta, il grande salone del castello di Nymphenburg. Questo venne decorato con un affresco di Johann Baptist Zimmermann che riporta indietro la memoria ai tempi d'oro della dinastia dei Wittelsbach.

Con Massimiliano III Giuseppe si estinse la linea alto-bavarese dei Wittelsbach. I nuovi sovrani

Die Asamkirche, eines der großartigsten Kunstwerke der Stadt

The Asamkirche, one of Munich's most impressive works of art

La Asamkirche, un des chefs-d'œuvre les plus imposants de la ville

La Asamkirche, uno delle opere d'arte più imponenti della città

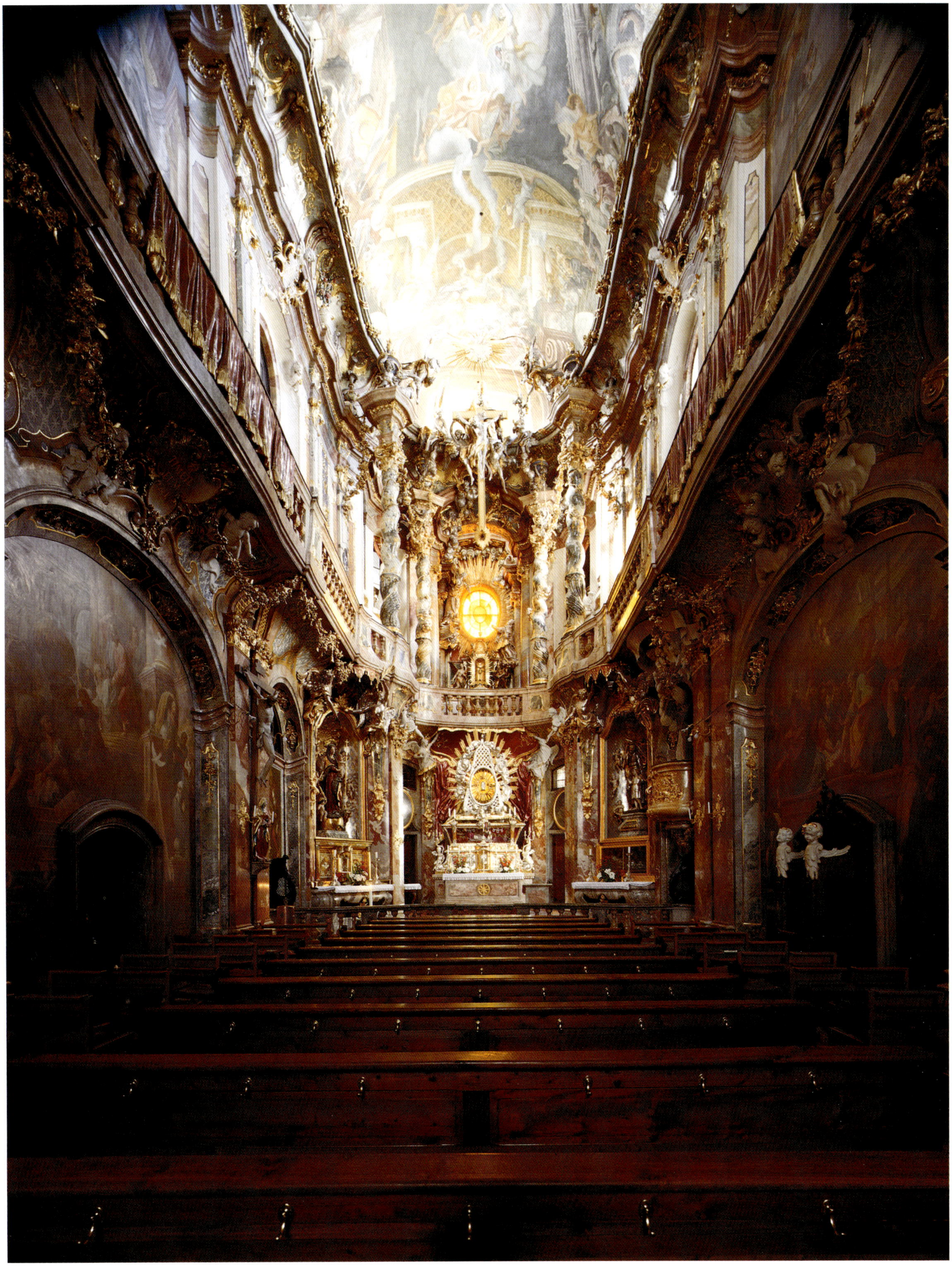

fürsten. Max III. Joseph ließ den großen Saal in Schloss Nymphenburg zum dritten Mal neu ausgestalten. Die Architektur geht auf François Cuvilliés zurück; sie wird von einem Fresko Johann Baptist Zimmermanns überspannt, das die Erinnerung an das Goldene Zeitalter beschwört.

Mit Max III. Joseph starb die altbayerische Linie der Wittelsbacher aus. Die neuen Herrscher kamen aus deren Pfälzer Linien. Max IV. Joseph kämpfte in den Napoleonischen Kriegen auf französischer Seite und machte nach dem Zusammenbruch des Heiligen Römischen Reiches das Herzogtum Bayern zu einem Königreich. Sein Sohn Ludwig I. war der glanzvollste Bauherr im München des 19. Jahrhunderts. Er erweiterte die Residenz und gab ihr zur Stadt hin eine neue, am Palazzo Pitti in Florenz orientierte Fassade. Bau und Innenausstattung gehen auf den Architekten Leo von Klenze zurück. Die Gestaltung der königlichen Wohnung ist beeinflusst von der Antikenmode, wie sie sich seit der Ausgrabung der vom Vesuv verschütteten Stadt Pompeji in Europa verbreitete. Nach Norden schloss Ludwig die Residenz mit dem Festsaalbau, einer Fassade, die Entwürfe des Vicentiner Architekten Andrea Palladio reflektiert.

König Ludwig I. errichtete in München mehrere Kirchen. Die Allerheiligenhofkirche, von der nur mehr die Außenmauern stehen, war die neue Hofkapelle der Residenz und kombiniert Eindrücke aus der Palastkapelle von Palermo mit Motiven aus San Marco in Venedig. Die Ludwigskirche greift Elemente der italienischen Romanik auf; Architekt war Friedrich von Gärtner. Sankt Bonifaz, ein Neubau für den Benediktinerorden, ist eng an der römischen Kirche S. Paolo fuori le Mura orientiert. Die gleichfalls unter Ludwig I. entstandene Maria-Hilf-Kirche in der Au wurde 1831 begonnen; der Architekt Joseph Daniel Ohlmüller gestaltete sie ganz in den Formen der Neugotik.

Roman Empire, turned the Duchy of Bavaria into a kingdom. His son Ludwig I was the most brilliant builder in 19th-century Munich. He enlarged the Residenz and added a new façade – inspired by the Palazzo Pitti in Florenz – to the part facing the city. Leo von Klenze, a renowned architect, was entrusted with the construction and interior decoration. The royal chambers were influenced by antique styles which had become en vogue since the city of Pompeii – buried by the lava streams of Mount Vesuvio in 79 A.D. – had been excavated. The northern part of the palace was finished off with the "Festsaalbau", a banqueting hall whose façade reflects designs by Andrea Palladio, the famous architect from Vicenza in Italy.

King Ludwig I had several churches built in Munich. The "Allerheiligenhofkirche", of which only the outer walls still exist today, became the new court chapel; it combines features of the palace chapel in Palermo with motives from San Marco in Venice. The "Ludwigskirche", based on elements of the Italian Romanesque style, was built by architect Friedrich von Gärtner. "Sankt Bonifaz", a church constructed for the Benedictine Order, was inspired by the church S. Paolo fuori le Mura in Rome. Another project initiated by Ludwig I was the "Maria-Hilf-Kirche" in der Au, whose construction was started in 1831; its architect, Joseph Daniel Ohlmüller designed it in the Neo-Gothic style.

This juxtaposition of different architectural styles in ecclesiastical building was typical of the 19th century. The churches St. Johannes Baptista in Haidhausen and Heilig Kreuz in Giesing were built in the neo-Gothic style; the parish church of St. Anna in the Lehel is a powerful neo-Romanesque building; St. Ursula in Schwabing revives elements of the Italian Renaissance; St. Joseph varies simple Baroque features; and St. Margareth in Sendling

nastie des Wittelsbach. Les nouveaux seigneurs venaient des lignées du Palatinat. Max IV. Joseph lutta pendant les guerres napoléoniennes du côté français et fit, après le déclin du Saint Empire romain, du duché de Bavière un royaume. Son fils, Louis 1er, fut l'architecte le plus pompeux de Munich au 19ème siècle. Il agrandit la résidence et lui donna du côté ville une façade s'orientant sur le Palazzo Pitti de Florence. La construction et la décoration intérieure sont l'œuvre de l'architecte Leo von Klenze. La conception de l'habitat royal est influencée par la mode antique comme elle se répandait en Europe depuis les fouilles de la ville de Pompéi ensevelie par le Vésuve. Au nord, le roi Louis achevait la résidence par la construction de la salle des fêtes, une façade reflétant les esquisses de l'architecte de Vicence Andrea Palladio.

Le roi Louis 1er érigea plusieurs églises à Munich. L'Allerheiligenhofkirche, dont il ne reste plus que les murs extérieurs, était la nouvelle chapelle de la Cour de la résidence et allie les impressions de la chapelle du palais de Palerme avec des motifs de Saint Marc à Venise. L'église Ludwigskirche reprend des éléments de l'art roman italien; l'architecte était Friedrich von Gärtner. L'église Saint Boniface, une nouvelle construction pour l'ordre des Bénédictins, s'oriente étroitement sur l'église romane St Paolo fuori le Mura. La construction de l'église Maria-Hilf dans l'Au, édifiée également sous Louis 1er, débuta en 1831; l'architecte Joseph Daniel Ohlmüller la réalisa entièrement d'après les formes du gothique moderne.

La cohabitation de plusieurs styles différents d'architecture dans la construction des églises est typique du 19ème siècle. Avec St Jean Baptiste à Haidhausen et Heilig Kreuz à Giesing, des églises du gothique moderne virent le jour. L'église paroissiale Ste Anne à Lehel est un édifice imposant de l'art nouveau roman, Ste Ursule à Schwabing reprend des éléments de la re-

provenivano, d'ora in avanti, dalla linea del Palatinato. Massimiliano IV Giuseppe combatté nelle guerre napoleoniche a fianco dei francesi, e in seguito alla caduta del Sacro Romano Impero trasformò il ducato di Baviera in regno. Suo figlio Ludovico I fu il costruttore più brillante nella Monaco del XIX secolo. Egli ampliò la Residenza e le diede una nuova facciata orientata verso la città che ricorda Palazzo Pitti a Firenze. La costruzione e l'allestimento interno sono opera dell'architetto Leo von Klenze. Nell'appartamento reale sono visibili gli influssi della moda per l'antichità che si diffuse in Europa quando fu riportata alla luce la città di Pompei sepolta dalle ceneri del Vesuvio. Sul lato settentrionale, Ludovico chiuse la Residenza con una «Festsaalbau» (un'ala riservata alle feste e alle cerimonie di corte), una facciata che rispecchia gli schizzi dell'architetto vicentino Andrea Palladio.

Il re Ludovico I fece costruire molte chiese a Monaco. La chiesa di Corte di Ognissanti («Allerheiligenhofkirche»), di cui non rimangono oggi che le mura esterne, era la nuova cappella di corte della Residenza e combina motivi della cappella Palatina di Palermo con motivi di San Marco a Venezia. La chiesa di San Ludovico («Ludwigskirche») riprende elementi del romanico italiano; l'architetto fu Friedrich von Gärtner. San Bonifazio («St. Bonifaz»), una nuova costruzione per l'ordine dei Benedettini, si rifà alla chiesa romana di San Paolo fuori le Mura. La costruzione della chiesa di Santa Maria Ausiliatrice («Maria-Hilf-Kirche») nella Au iniziò nel 1831; l'architetto Joseph Daniel Ohlmüller la disegnò completamente con forme del neogotico.

L'accostamento di diversi stili architettonici nella costruzione delle chiese è tipico del XIX secolo. San Giovanni Battista («St. Johannes Baptista») a Haidhausen e la chiesa della Santa Croce («Heilig Kreuz») a Giesing rappresentano esempi di stile

Das Nebeneinander verschiedener Architekturstile im Kirchenbau ist für das 19. Jahrhundert typisch. Mit St. Johannes Baptista in Haidhausen und Heilig Kreuz in Giesing entstehen neugotische Kirchen. Die Pfarrkirche Sankt Anna im Lehel ist ein kraftvoller neuromanischer Bau, St. Ursula in Schwabing greift Elemente der italienischen Renaissance auf, St. Joseph variiert einfache Barockformen, St. Margareth in Sendling wiederholt den Tonnenraum der Michaelskirche.

Zu einem neuen eigenständigen Stil im Kirchenbau kommt es erst nach dem Zweiten Weltkrieg, als in München Zentralbauten entstehen, die weitgehend auf Bauornamentik verzichten. Der asymmetrisch konkav-konvexe Bau der evangelischen Matthäuskirche mit seiner geschwungenen Dachform wurde 1953-1955 nach Plänen von Gustav Gsaenger gebaut. Auch die von Sep Ruf errichtete Kirche Sankt Johann von Capistran reduziert die Bauornamentik. In der 1995 eröffneten griechisch-orthodoxen Allerheiligenkirche an der Ungererstraße wird im Gegensatz zur Reduzierung der fünfziger und sechziger Jahre wiederum auf traditionelle Bauformen zurückgegriffen.

Mit dem Wittelsbacher Palast zog die Neugotik in den Schlossbau ein. König Max II. bewohnte ihn als Kronprinz und nach dessen Abdankung König Ludwig I. Das große, von Ludwig II. im Stil des französischen Barock am Hof Ludwigs XIV. errichtete Appartement in der Residenz wurde im Zweiten Weltkrieg völlig zerstört. Mit dieser Raumfolge ging die Ära der Schlossbauten der Wittelsbacher in München zu Ende. Andere profane Bauaufgaben – Bahnhöfe, Postämter, Bankgebäude – haben den Monumentalbau übernommen. Aus der Masse der Nachkriegsbauten ragt das von Günter Behnisch entworfene Olympiazentrum als Baudenkmal heraus.

Dr. Sabine Glaser

copies the barrel vault shape of the Michaelskirche.

A new and independent style of church architecture was not introduced until after the Second World War, when centralized buildings were set up in Munich which dispensed with ornamental features. The asymmetric concave/convex form of the Protestant "Matthäuskirche" with its curved roof was built between 1953 and 1955 after plans made by Gustav Gsaenger. But also the church "Sankt Johann von Capistran", constructed by Sep Ruf, is characterized by reduced ornamentation. In the Greek Orthodox "Allerheiligenkirche" in Ungererstrasse, on the other hand, which was opened in 1995, one went back to traditional architectural forms.

With the Wittelsbach Palace the neo-Gothic style also conquered the mundane sector of architecture. King Max II lived in it when he was still the crown prince, and after his abdication King Ludwig I took over the building. The large appartment in the "Residenz", which had been established by Ludwig II in the French Baroque style prevailing at the court of Louis XIV, was completely destroyed during the Second World war. This construction concluded the era of palatial architecture of the Wittelsbach. From then on other types of profane edifices such as railway stations, post offices and bank buildings took over the monumental form of construction formerly reserved for churches and palaces. The most impressive post-war building is the Munich Olympic Centre designed by Günter Behnisch, a truly outstanding architectural monument.

Dr. Sabine Glaser

naissance italienne, St Joseph varie des formes baroques simples, Ste Margareth à Sendling reprend la construction voûtée de la Michaelskirche.

Un style nouveau dans la construction des lieux ecclésiastiques ne fait son apparition qu'après la Seconde Guerre mondiale, lorsque des bâtiments centraux voient le jour à Munich renonçant en grande partie aux ornements architecturaux. La construction asymétrique concave et convexe de l'église protestante Matthäus avec son toit de forme élancée fut construite de 1953 à 1955 d'après les plans de Gustav Gsaenger. L'église St Jean de Capistran construite par Sep Ruf limite également les ornements architecturaux. Dans l'église grecque orthodoxe inaugurée en 1995 dans la rue Ungererstraße, il est par contre, à l'inverse des réductions des années cinquante et soixante, à nouveau fait appel aux formes traditionnelles de construction.

Avec le palais des Wittelsbach, le nouveau gothique fit son entrée dans la construction de châteaux. Le roi Max II y habita en tant que prince héritier et, après son abdication, ce fut le tour du roi Louis 1er. Dans la résidence, le grand appartement de Louis II, se présentant dans le style du baroque français à la cour de Louis XIV, fut entièrement détruit pendant la Seconde Guerre mondiale. Avec la réalisation de ces appartements l'ère de la construction des châteaux prit fin. D'autres constructions profanes comme les gares, les bureaux de poste, les banques s'inscrivirent dans la lignée des constructions de monuments. Parmi les édifices construits après la Guerre, le centre olympique, conçu par Günter Behnisch, culmine au niveau des monuments.

Dr. Sabine Glaser

neogotico. La parrocchiale di Sant'Anna a Lehel è una potente esempio di costruzione neoromanica, Sant'Ursula a Schwabing riprende elementi del Rinascimento italiano, San Giuseppe («St. Joseph») varia le semplici forme barocche, Santa Margherita («St. Margareth») a Sendling riprende l'interno a botte della chiesa di San Michele.

Per trovare uno stile completamente nuovo nella costruzione delle chiese bisogna aspettare la fine della Seconda Guerra Mondiale, quando sorsero a Monaco costruzioni centrali che rinunciarono completamente ai fregi architettonici. La struttura concavo-convessa asimmetrica dell'evangelica chiesa di San Matteo («Matthäuskirche») con il suo tetto arcuato fu costruita tra il 1954 e il 1955 sulla base dei progetti di Gustav Gsaenger. Anche la chiesa di San Giovanni di Capistrano («St. Johann von Capistran»), costruita da Sep Ruf, riduce i fregi architettonici. Nella chiesa di Ognissanti («Allerheiligenkirche») greco-ortodossa sulla Ungererstraße, inaugurata nel 1995, vengono riprese le forme tradizionali in contrapposizione alla tendenza alla riduzione formale tipica degli anni Cinquanta e Sessanta.

Il Palazzo dei Wittelsbach è il primo esempio di arte neogotica applicata alla costruzione dei castelli. Vi risedette il re Massimiliano II come principe ereditario e, dopo la sua abdicazione, il re Ludovico I. Il grande appartamento nella Residenza, fatto costruire da Ludovico II nello stile del barocco francese della corte di Luigi XIV, fu distrutto completamente durante la Seconda Guerra Mondiale. Con questi appartamenti terminò l'era delle costruzioni di castelli ed iniziò il periodo di altre costruzioni monumentali, ma profane – stazioni, uffici postali, banche. Dalla massa di costruzioni del dopoguerra si distingue, come monumento architettonico, il Centro Olimpico progettato da Günter Behnisch.

Dr. Sabine Glaser

*Links und rechts
der Isar*

*Left and Right of
the Isar River*

*Rive gauche et rive droite
de l'Isar*

*A sinistra e a destra
dell'Isar*

Wie alle großen deutschen Städte besteht auch München aus vielen ehemaligen Dörfern, heutigen Stadtteilen. Diese haben teilweise noch ein kräftiges Eigenleben.

Die Isar bildet historisch, verkehrsmäßig und psychologisch einen wichtigen Einschnitt in der Stadt. Nur wer ihn mit U- oder S-Bahn unterquert, nimmt ihn nicht wahr. Die Isar war bis zum Beginn ihrer Regulierung um 1800 ein reißender Strom, der ständig sein Bett veränderte. Das Wasser schuf durch seine Eintiefung in die Münchner Schotterebene unsere Landschaft.

Like all the other big German cities Munich consists of numerous former villages which have become city districts by now. Many of them still lead a life of their own.

The Isar River has always made a significant incision in the city area – historically, traffic-wise and psychologically. Only people crossing it by subway or suburban train do not become aware of this fact. Up to its regulation in about 1800 the Isar was a raging torrent which continuously altered its course and created Munich's landscape by deeply burrowing into the city's gravel plain.

Comme toutes les grandes villes allemandes, Munich se compose de plusieurs anciens villages formant aujourd'hui des quartiers. Ils sont quelquefois encore fort animés.

Au niveau de l'histoire, de la circulation et de la psychologie, l'Isar représente une cassure importante dans la ville. Pour ne pas la remarquer, il faut prendre soit le métro soit le train de banlieue. Jusqu'au début de sa régulation vers 1800, l'Isar était un fleuve rapide changeant sans arrêt de lit. En pénétrant dans la surface de pierrailles de Munich, l'eau façonna notre paysage.

Come tutte le grandi città tedesche, anche Monaco è costituita oggi da diversi quartieri che erano, un tempo, dei villaggi autonomi. Parte di questi insediamenti continua a mantenere fino ad oggi una propria forte autonomia.

Sia dal punto di vista storico e psicologico che per quanto riguarda i trasporti, una fenditura importante nella città è formata dal fiume Isar. Solo chi lo attraversa con la metropolitana o con la ferrovia suburbana veloce non se ne accorge. Prima di venir regolato attorno al 1800 l'Isar era un fiume impetuoso che variava continuamente il proprio alveo.

München, erstmals erwähnt 1158, ist einer der jüngsten Orte im ganzen Stadtgebiet. Die meisten ehemaligen Dörfer sind wesentlich älter; so wurden z. B. Aubing, Daglfing, Feldmoching, Giesing, Oberföhring, Pasing, Schwabing, Sendling oder Trudering bereits Anfang des 6. Jahrhunderts gegründet.

Bis 1854 bestand die königliche Landeshaupt- und Residenzstadt München nur aus dem vom Burgfrieden umschlossenen Gebiet von 1600 Hektar, das etwa den heutigen Stadtbezirken 1 (Altstadt-Lehel), 2 (Ludwigsvorstadt-Isarvorstadt) und 3 (Maxvor-

First mentioned in 1158, Munich is one of the "youngest" parts of the city area. Most of the former villages are much older: Aubing, Daglfing, Feldmoching, Giesing, Oberföhring, Pasing, Schwabing, Sendling and Trudering, for instance, were already founded in the early 6th century A.D.

Up to 1854 the royal capital and residential city of Munich comprised an area of only 1,600 hectares protected by the "Burgfrieden", the local jurisdiction. This area corresponded approximately to the city districts 1 (Alt-

Evoquée pour la première fois en 1158, Munich est un des plus jeunes villages de l'ensemble de la ville. La majorité des anciens villages sont nettement plus vieux, ainsi Aubing, Daglfing, Feldmoching, Giesing, Oberföhring, Pasing, Schwabing, Sendling ou Trudering remontent déjà au début du 6ème siècle.

Jusqu'en 1854, Munich, la capitale du land et ville résidentielle royale, se composait uniquement du territoire de 1600 hectares entouré par les remparts de la ville et qui correspond aujourd'hui aux quartiers 1 (Altstadt Lehel), 2 (Ludwigsvorstadt-

Fu proprio l'acqua che, affondando nella pianura ghiaiosa di Monaco, dette forma al paesaggio della nostra città.

Monaco, citata in un documento per la prima volta nel 1158, è uno dei luoghi più recenti di tutto il territorio comunale. La maggior parte degli antichi villaggi risale a molti anni addietro; per citare qualche esempio, Aubing, Daglfing, Feldmoching, Giesing, Oberföhring, Pasing, Schwabing, Sendling e Trudering esistevano già all'inizio del VI secolo d.C.

Fino al 1854 la città di Monaco, residenza eletta dei duchi Wittelsbach ed in seguito

An, in und auf der Isar: verlockende Freizeitangebote - wandern, schwimmen, eine Floßfahrt und vieles mehr

At, in and on the Isar: tempting recreational opportunities - hiking, swimming, gentle river-rafting and many more

Sur les bords, dans et sur l'Isar: un programme de loisirs attrayant - promenade, baignade, ballade en radeau et bien d'autres

Vicino all'Isar, nell'Isar, sull'Isar: allettanti offerte per il tempo libero sotto forma di passeggiate, nuotate, discese in zattera e molto altro ancora

stadt) entspricht. Ursprünglich lagen auf dem restlichen Areal über 29 verschiedene Städte und Gemeinden. Die Eingemeindungen geschahen kontinuierlich seit 1854, als Au, Haidhausen und Giesing zu München geschlagen wurden. Es folgten Ramersdorf (1864), Sendling (1877), Neuhausen und Schwabing (1890), Bogenhausen (1892), Nymphenburg (1899), Laim und Thalkirchen (1900), Forstenried (1912), Milbertshofen, Moosach, Berg am Laim und Oberföhring (1913), Daglfing und Perlach (1930), Freimann (1931), Trudering (1932), Riem (1937), Allach, Feldmoching, Großhadern, Ludwigsfeld, Obermenzing, Pasing, Solln und Untermenzing (1938) sowie schließlich Aubing, Langwied und Lochhausen (1942).

Die Eingemeindungen wurden vollzogen, da die Hauptstadt aufgrund der Industrialisierung Platz brauchte. Anfangs geschah dies mehr oder weniger freiwillig, da die Umlandgemeinden mit ihren Aufgaben, besonders bei Infrastruktureinrichtungen (Schulen, Verkehrsverbindungen, Kanalisation) überfordert waren und durch die Münchner Stadtverwaltung eine Lösung ihrer Probleme erhofften. Erst in der NS-Zeit fanden Zwangseingemeindungen statt (z. B. von Pasing, bis dahin eine der größten Industriestädte Oberbayerns), die lange Zeit nicht von allen Betroffenen akzeptiert wurden.

Seit 1945 gab es – im Gegensatz zu anderen Großstädten – in München keine Eingemeindungen mehr. Politiker und Bürger der Umlandgemeinden wollen nicht zu München gehören, da sie weniger Bürgernähe, Verlust an Identität und eine schlechtere Versorgung befürchten. Den Gemeinden im „Speckgürtel" geht es meist finanziell besser als der Stadt; sie können Lasten auf diese abschieben und deren Vorteile wahrnehmen.

Die Dörfer um München gehörten bis 1802 zu drei verschiedenen Landgerichten (Dachau, Starnberg, Wolfratshausen) im Kurfürstentum Baiern sowie zum stadt-Lehel), 2 (Ludwigsvorstadt-Isarvorstadt) and 3 (Maxvorstadt). Originally, more than 29 different towns and communities covered the rest of the territory; they were gradually integrated into the city after 1854, when Au, Haidhausen and Giesing became parts of Munich. In 1864 Ramersdorf followed; in 1877 Sendling, in 1890 Neuhausen and Schwabing; in 1892 Bogenhausen; in 1899 Nymphenburg; in 1900 Laim and Thalkirchen; in 1912 Forstenried; in 1913 Milbertshofen, Moosach, Berg am Laim and Oberföhring; in 1930 Daglfing and Perlach; in 1931 Freimann; in 1932 Trudering; in 1937 Riem; in 1938 Allach, Feldmoching, Großhadern, Ludwigsfeld, Obermenzing, Pasing, Solln and Untermenzing; and in 1942 Aubing, Langwied and Lochhausen.

These incorporations took place when the capital needed more room to cope with industrialization. At first the communities joined voluntarily, because they were overtaxed by their responsibilities particularly in the sector of infrastructure (i. e. schools, traffic routes and sewerage) and hoped to have their problems solved by the city administration. Coercion was not used until the Nazi era, when Pasing was, for example, incorporated by force, although it had up to then been one of Upper Bavaria's largest industrial towns. Most of these forced integrations were resented by the affected communities and their population for quite some time.

After 1945 no further incorporations took place in the Bavarian capital, contrary to many other big cities. Local politicians and citizens did not relish the thought of becoming a part of Munich, because they feared a loss of identity, an increase of anonymity and a by far worse supply situation. The communities in the so-called "bacon-belt" have always been better off than the city itself, for they are able to unload their burdens on the metropolis while enjoying the city's advantages.

Isarvorstadt) et 3 (Maxvorstadt). A l'origine, plus de 29 villes et communes différentes étaient regroupées sur le reste du territoire. Les incorporations de communes se firent continuellement depuis 1854 lorsque Au, Haidhausen et Giesing furent intégrés à Munich. Suivirent ensuite Ramersdorf (1864), Sendling (1877), Neuhausen et Schwabing (1890), Bogenhausen (1892), Nymphenburg (1899), Laim et Thalkirchen (1900), Forstenried (1912), Milbertshofen, Moosach, Berg am Laim et Oberföhring (1913), Daglfing et Perlach (1930), Freimann (1931), Trudering (1932), Riem (1937), Allach, Feldmoching, Großhadern, Ludwigsfeld, Obermenzing, Pasing, Solln et Untermenzing (1938) ainsi que pour finir Aubing, Langwied et Lochhausen (1942).

Les incorporations continuèrent étant donné que l'industrialisation exigeait beaucoup de place dans la capitale. Au début, cela se fit de manière plus ou moins volontaire. En effet, les communes avoisinantes étaient débordées par leurs tâches, en particulier les questions d'infrastructure (écoles, voies de communication, canalisation) et espéraient que la municipalité munichoise allait apporter une solution à leurs problèmes. Ce n'est que pendant la période nazie que des incorporations forcées eurent lieu (p.ex. celle de Pasing qui était jusque-là une des plus importantes villes industrielles de Haute-Bavière) et les habitants concernés mirent souvent longtemps à les accepter.

Contrairement aux autres grandes villes, aucune incorporation n'eut lieu depuis 1945 à Munich. Les politiciens et les citoyens des communes avoisinantes ne veulent pas appartenir à Munich car ils pensent se sentir moins proches des citoyens, craignent la perte de leur identité et un approvisionnement de moins bonne qualité. Les communes entourant directement Munich se portent généralement financièrement mieux que la ville elle-même, elles peuvent se capitale del regno di Baviera, era costituita solo dal territorio di 1 600 ettari racchiuso all'interno delle mura di fortificazione e che corrisponde, oggi, ai quartieri 1 (Centro storico-Lehel), 2 (Ludwigsvorstadt-Isarvorstadt) e 3 (Maxvorstadt). Originariamente, sull'area restante si trovavano più di 29 diverse città e comuni. Le incorporazioni nel comune di Monaco avvennero gradualmente a partire dal 1854, quando Au, Haidhausen e Giesing furono annesse a Monaco. Seguirono Ramersdorf (1864), Sendling (1877), Neuhausen e Schwabing (1890), Bogenhausen (1892), Nymphenburg (1899), Laim e Thalkirchen (1900), Forstenried (1912), Milbertshofen, Moosach, Berg am Laim e Oberföhring (1913), Daglfing e Perlach (1930), Freimann (1931), Trudering (1932), Riem (1937), Allach, Feldmoching, Großhadern, Ludwigsfeld, Obermenzing, Pasing, Solln e Untermenzing (1938) ed infine Aubing, Langwied e Lochhausen (1942).

La ragione di tutte queste incorporazioni era la necessità della città di acquisire nuovi spazi per lo sviluppo dell'industrializzazione. All'inizio esse avvennero più o meno volontariamente, in quanto ai comuni vicini mancavano la infrastrutture necessarie per rispondere alle esigenze della propria popolazione (scuole, comunicazioni, canalizzazione); pertanto, l'amministrazione comunale di Monaco poteva rappresentare una soluzione ai loro problemi. Solo sotto la dittatura del Nazionalsocialismo furono effettuate delle incorporazioni forzate (ad esempio, nel caso di Pasing, fino all'epoca una delle maggiori città industrializzate dell'Alta Baviera), che per molto tempo non furono accettate da tutti i comuni interessati.

Al contrario di altre metropoli, dal 1945 Monaco non ha più effettuato incorporazioni. Politici e cittadini dei comuni vicini hanno espresso la volontà di non appartenere a Monaco in quanto temono di perdere la propria identità, di ricevere servizi peggiori e, soprattutto, che venga

Im Lehel – Blick von der Steinsdorfstraße mit ihren eleganten Hausfassaden hin zum Turm des Deutschen Museums

In the district Lehel – view from Steinsdorfstraße with its elegant façades towards the tower of the Deutsches Museum

Dans le district de Lehel – vue de la Steinsdorfstraße avec ses élégantes façades jusqu'à la tour du Deutsches Museum

Nel quartiere di Lehel – Veduta della torre del Deutsches Museum dalla Steinsdorfstraße con le eleganti facciate dei suoi edifici

Das Mueller'sche Volksbad, eines der schönsten Jugendstilbäder Deutschlands, in neuem Glanz

The Mueller'sche Volksbad, one of Germany's most beautiful Art Nouveau indoor swimming pools which was refurbished recently

La Mueller'sche Volksbad, la plus belle des piscines en style Art Nouveau après la rénovation

Il Mueller'sche Volksbad, una delle più belle piscine in stile Art Nouveau della Germania, brilla nel suo rinnovato splendore

St. Nikolai am Gasteig, Ursprung 1315, im 16. Jahrhundert Neubau in spätgotischen Formen

St. Nikolai church at the Gasteig has its origins in 1315 and was rebuilt in late Gothic style in the 16th century

L'église St. Nicolai au Gasteig. Son origine remonte à 1315. Le nouveau bâtiment aux formes du gothique tardif date du 16ème siècle.

St. Nikolai al Gasteig, costruita nel 1315 e ristrutturata nel XVI secolo in stile tardogotico

Blick auf die Kirche St. Johann Baptist am Johannisplatz

View of the St. Johann Baptist church at Johannisplatz

Vue sur l'église St. Johann Baptist à la place Johannisplatz

Veduta della chiesa di San Giovanni Battista sulla Johannisplatz

Eines der schmucken Häuser am malerischen Wiener Platz in Haidhausen

One of the charming houses at the picturesque Wiener Platz in the district Haidhausen

Une des plus belles maisons sur la magnifique place Wiener Platz au district de Haidhausen

Una delle graziose case sulla pittoresca Wiener Platz nel quartiere di Haidhausen

Max-II-Denkmal – 1857 dem Bayernkönig Maximilian II. „von seinem getreuen Volke" gestiftet

The Max-II-Denkmal, a monument which was dedicated to the Bavarian king Maximilian II by "his faithful subjects" in 1857

Le Max-II-Denkmal – le monument érigé en 1857 en l'honneur du roi de Bavière Maximilien II. «par son peuple fidèle»

Il monumento di Massimiliano II: venne donato all'omonimo re bavarese, nel 1857, «dal suo fedele popolo»

Das Maximilianeum (Friedrich von Bürklein, 1857-74) – Seit 1949 tagt hier der Bayerische Landtag.

The Maximilianeum (Friedrich von Bürklein, 1857-74), seat of the Bavarian parliament since 1949

Le Maximilianeum (Friedrich von Bürklein, 1857-74) – Le parlement bavarois y siège depuis 1949.

Il Maximilianeum (Friedrich von Bürklein, 1857-74) – Dal 1949 è sede del Parlamento Bavarese.

eigenständigen Territorium des Fürstbistums Freising. Die Orte waren nach Brauchtum, Tracht, Volksmusik und Hausbau unterschiedlich ausgerichtet. Aubing und Feldmoching zählten beispielsweise zum westbaierischen Einflussbereich, während Forstenried und Solln alpenländisch geprägt waren.

Über viele Jahrhunderte war die alte Isarbrücke (die Ludwigsbrücke), über welche die Salzstraße zum Isartor führte, die wichtigste Verbindung der Stadt zu dem Gebiet rechts der Isar. Die Stadtmauer diente dabei nicht nur dem Schutz vor militärischen Angriffen, sondern auch der Abwehr von beruflicher Konkurrenz aus den Vorstädten.

Erst 1854 – vorher hatten die Münchner Eingemeindungsbemühungen aus zum Teil fadenscheinigen Gründen verzögert und verhindert – wurden die Au,

Up to 1802 the villages surrounding Munich belonged to three different regional courts (Dachau, Starnberg and Wolfratshausen) of the Electorate of Bavaria, or to the independent territory of the Prince Bishopric of Freising. All the communitites cultivated customs, costumes, music and house styles of their own. Aubing and Feldmoching, for instance, belonged to the influence sphere of western Bavaria; Forstenried and Solln to the alpine sphere.

For many centuries the old Isar bridge (Ludwigsbrücke), across which the ancient salt road had led to the Isar Gate (Isartor), was Munich's most important connection with the area to the right of the river. The city wall not only protected the town from military attacks, but also kept away commercial competitors from the suburbs.

décharger sur elles de certains problèmes et profiter de certains de ses avantages.

Jusqu'en 1802, les villages autour de Munich appartenaient à trois circonscriptions différentes des tribunaux d'instance (Dachau, Starnberg, Wolfratshausen) dans la principauté du prince électeur de Baiern (Bavière) ainsi qu'au territoire indépendant de la cité épiscopale de Freising. Les villages étaient différemment orientés sur les traditions, les costumes, la musique folklorique et la construction de maisons. Aubing et Feldmoching faisaient par exemple partie du rayon d'action de la Bavière occidentale alors que Forstenried et Solln étaient marqués par la région alpine.

Pendant plusieurs siècles, le vieux pont de l'Isar (le pont Ludwig) sur lequel passait la route du sel en direction de l'Isartor, fut la voie de communication la plus

meno il rapporto di vicinanza tra le autorità comunali e la cittadinanza. Dal punto di vista finanziario, i ricchi comuni della cosiddetta «Cintura di grasso» sono avvantaggiati rispetto alla città; possono scaricare su questa le proprie incombenze ed usufruire dei vantaggi che una grande città può offrire.

Fino al 1802, i villaggi intorno a Monaco appartenevano a tre diverse giurisdizioni (Dachau, Starnberg, Wolfratshausen) del princi-

Giesing mit Harlaching sowie Haidhausen in die Stadt aufgenommen. Grund waren auch ordnungspolitische Überlegungen: Nach der Revolution von 1848, bei der König Ludwig I. durch Tumulte zur Abdankung gezwungen worden war, schien es sicherer, die zum Teil als renitent eingestufte Vorstadtbevölkerung unter die Fuchtel der Münchner Polizei zu bekommen.

Bald entstanden auch auf der anderen Isarseite wichtige Ver-

As the citizens of Munich had foiled former attempts at incorporation with sometimes rather flimsy excuses, the Au, Giesing, Harlaching and Haidhausen were not integrated into the city till 1854. Even then it was mainly political calculation which had led to this measure: after the 1848 revolution, during which King Ludwig I was forced to abdicate owing to public unrest, it was considered safer to get most of the recalcitrant inhabitants of the

importante de la ville avec la rive droite de l'Isar. L'enceinte de la ville ne servait pas seulement à protéger des attaques militaires mais aussi à contrer la concurrence professionnelle venant des banlieues.

Ce n'est qu'en 1854 – les efforts d'incorporations ayant été avant retardés et empêchés pour des raisons quelquefois saugrenues – que Au, Giesing avec Harlaching ainsi que Haidhausen furent intégrés dans la

pato elettore di Baviera e al vescovado sovrano di Freising. Essi erano diversi negli usi e costumi, per quanto riguardava la musica popolare e l'architettura delle proprie case. Aubing e Feldmoching erano, ad esempio, sotto la sfera d'influenza della Baviera occidentale, mentre Forstenried e Solln avevano una chiara impronta alpina.

Per molti secoli il vecchio ponte sull'Isar (oggi Ludwigsbrücke), attraverso il quale la via

sorgungseinrichtungen und Industriebauten. Das „Klinikum rechts der Isar" entwickelte sich aus einem kleinen Bau der Gemeinde Haidhausen, in dem sich vorher das Kaffeehaus einer Witwe befand. Das Maximilianeum, er-

suburbs under the control of the Munich police.

Soon afterwards, important supply facilities and industrial plants were set up on the other side of the river as well. A small building erected by the communi-

ville de Munich. Des réflexions d'ordre politique en furent également la raison. En effet, après la révolution de 1848 – le roi Louis 1er ayant été contraint d'abdiquer en raison des tumultes qu'il avait occasionnés – il paraissait

del sale giungeva all'Isartor (Porta dell'Isar), fu il collegamento più importante della città con il territorio sulla sponda destra del fiume. Le mura cittadine non svolgevano, infatti, solo una funzione protettiva contro eventuali at-

Friedhof bei St. Georg in Bogenhausen: „Da muß man schon „Jemand" g'wesen sein in München, damit man hier seine letzte Ruhe findet."

Cemetery at St. Georg church in the Bogenhausen district: "You had better been an important citizen of Munich to be allowed to rest here."

Le cimetière St. Georg au district Bogenhausen: «Il faut déjà être quelqu'un à Munich pour pouvoir s'y reposer pour l'éternité.»

Cimitero presso San Giorgio nel quartiere di Bogenhausen: «Per trovar qui l'eterno riposo bisogna essere stati qualcuno a Monaco.»

richtet von König Max II. für eine Studienstiftung, dient heute als Sitz des Bayerischen Landtages. Von den in das Steilufer der Isar gebauten Kellern mit den riesigen Bierfabriken der Münchner Brauereien bestehen heute nur noch

ty of Haidhausen, which sheltered a café run by a widow, gradually turned into one of Munich's largest hospitals, the "Klinikum rechts der Isar". The "Maximilianeum", built by King Max II to house a foundation, today serves

possible de mener la population des banlieues, considérée parfois comme récalcitrante, sous la férule de la police munichoise.

De l'autre côté de l'Isar, d'importants centres d'approvisionnement et des industries virent le

tacchi militari, ma anche di difesa contro la concorrenza dei sobborghi vicini.

Solo nel 1854 – dopo che, in precedenza, gli abitanti di Monaco ne avevano ritardato ed impedito gli sforzi di incorporazione per motivi in parte pretestuosi – Au, Giesing, Harlaching e Haidhausen furono inglobate nella città. All'origine dell'iniziativa c'era anche una riflessione di ordine politico: dopo la rivoluzione del 1848, durante la quale il re Luigi I fu costretto dai tumulti ad abdicare, sembrò più sicuro assoggettare la popolazione dei sobborghi, in parte renitente, alla dura disciplina della polizia di Monaco.

Sorsero presto importanti impianti e reti di alimentazione e costruzioni industriali anche sull'altra sponda dell'Isar. Il «Policlinico a destra dell'Isar» si sviluppò da una piccola costruzione del comune di Haidhausen che aveva ospitato, precedentemente, un caffè gestito da una vedova. Il Maximilianeum, costruito dal re Massimiliano II per ospitare una

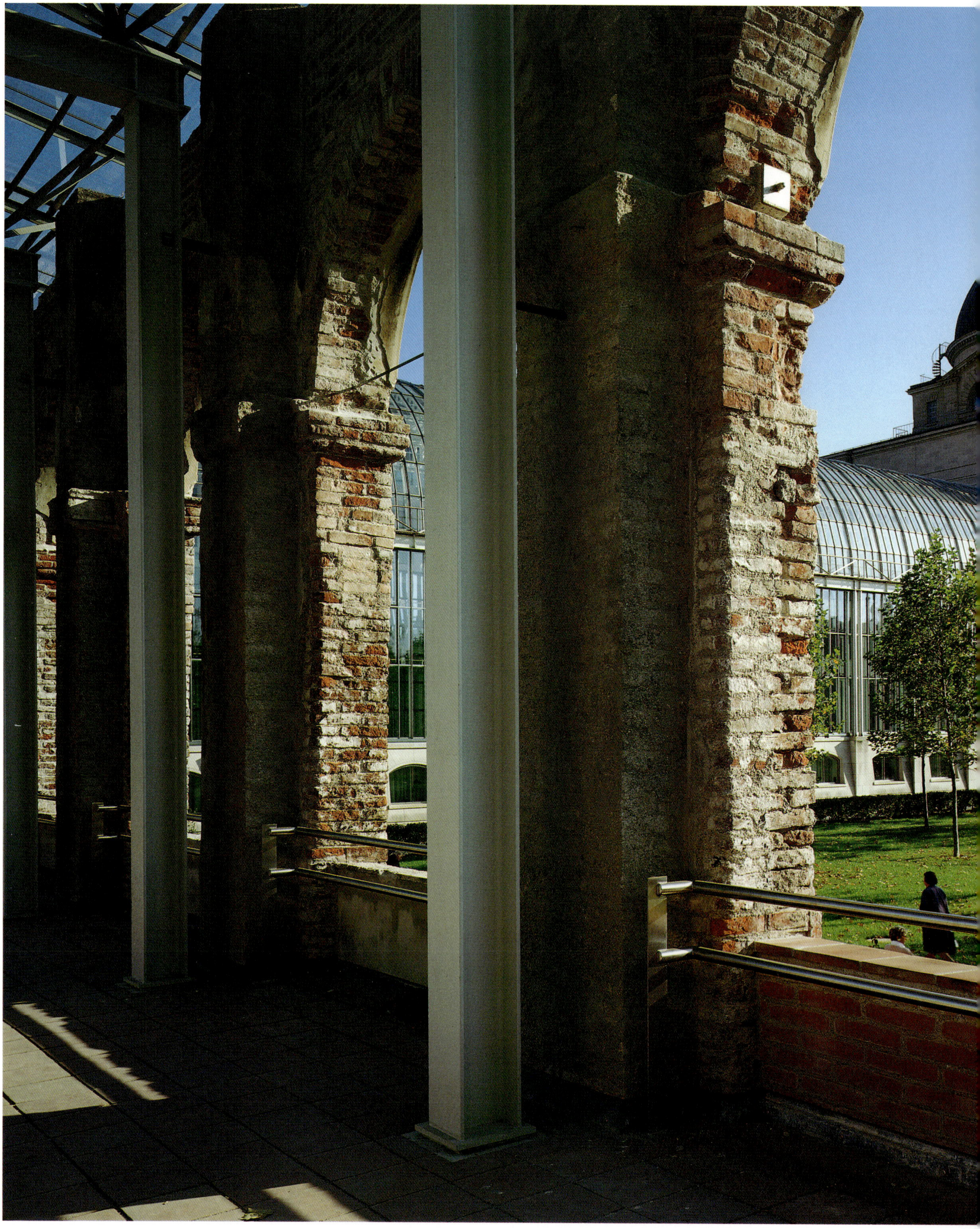

Der 1993 fertiggestellte Neubau der Staatskanzlei am Rande des Hofgartens mit dem integrierten Kuppeltrakt des früheren Armeemuseums

The new Staatskanzlei building, completed in 1993, at the edge of the Hofgarten. Its centerpiece, the cupola, used to house the army museum.

Le nouvel édifice de la chancellerie d'Etat achevé en 1993 en bordure du Hofgarten avec l'aile de l'ancien musée de l'armée portant une coupole

Il nuovo edificio della Cancelleria di Stato, ultimato nel 1993 al confine con il Giardino di Corte, con l'ala con cupola dell'ex-Museo dell'Esercito.

Verweilen vor historischer Kulisse am Odeonsplatz – Hofgartentor und -arkaden

A leisurely break in front of the historical façades at Odeonsplatz – gate at the Hofgarten and arcades

Promenade devant les coulisses historiques de l'Odeonsplatz avec le portique et les arcades du Hofgarten

Sosta davanti allo scenario storico dell' Odeonsplatz – porta e arcate del Giardino di Corte

als Gaststätten der Salvatorkeller in der Au und der Hofbräukeller in Haidhausen. Die Brauereigebäude wurden abgerissen, die Produktion wurde aus der Stadt verlagert.

In den ärmlich-bizarren Herbergsvierteln in Giesing, der Au und Haidhausen entstanden zu-

Rast am Brunnen im Alten Hof

Rest at the fountain in the court of the Alte Hof

Petite pause à la fontaine de l'Alter Hof

Sosta alla fontana nella Vecchia Corte

as the home of the Bavarian "Landtag" (Parliament). Of the former cellars driven into the steep bank of the Isar to shelter the factories of the big Munich breweries only the restaurants "Salvatorkeller" in the Au and the "Hofbräukeller" in Haidhausen have survived till today. The brewery buildings were pulled down and production moved out of the city.

In the shabby but bizarre housing areas of Giesing, the Au and Haidhausen large blocks of flats to let were constructed. After the Franco-Prussian War of 1870/71 the "Franzosenviertel" (French Quarter) at the Ostbahnhof railway station was set up – a huge area of tenement blocks.

But also "Großkopferte" (Bavarian slang for VIPs) built their villas along the bank of the Isar between Harlaching and Bogenhausen. Bankers and businessmen like the Nockhers and

jour. La clinique «Klinikum rechts der Isar» se développa à partir d'un petit bâtiment de la commune de Haidhausen dans lequel se trouvait avant le café d'une veuve. Le Maximilianeum, érigé par Maximilien II pour une fondation d'étudiants, abrite aujourd'hui le siège du parlement bavarois. Des caves construites sur les berges abruptes de l'Isar avec les immenses fabriques de bières des brasseries munichoises, il ne reste aujourd'hui que les restaurants de la Salvatorkeller à Au et la Hofbräukeller à Haidhausen. Les bâtiments des brasseries furent démolis, la production fut délocalisée de la ville.

Dans les quartiers d'hébergement pauvres et bizarres de Giesing, Au et Haidhausen, de plus en plus de maisons de rapport virent le jour. Avec le «quartier français» près de la gare de l'est, on assista, après la guerre de 1870/1871, à la

fondazione scolastica, è oggi la sede della Dieta della Baviera. Delle cantine costruite sull'alta sponda dell'Isar, con le enormi fabbriche di birra di Monaco, rimangono oggi la Salvatorkeller nel quartiere Au e la Hofbräukeller a Haidhausen. Di queste rimangono i locali adibiti alla ristorazione, mentre le fabbriche vere e proprie sono state demolite e gli impianti di produzione trasferiti al di fuori del perimetro della città.

Col passare del tempo, nei quartieri-dormitorio poveri e bizzarri di Giesing, Au e Haidhausen nacquero, in misura sempre maggiore, case d'affitto. Dopo la guerra del 1870/71 venne creata un'enorme area sulla quale furono costruiti i casermoni del «Quartiere Francese» presso la Stazione Est.

Anche i «pezzi grossi» di Monaco hanno costruito le loro ville sulla sponda dell'Isar tra Har-

Ehem. Hauptmünzamt und Münzhof, heute Bayerisches Landesamt für Denkmalpflege

Former mint and mint office, today it is the seat of the Bavarian office for the preservation of monuments

Ancien Office principal des Monnaies et Hôtel des Monnaies, aujourd'hui l'office bavarois de la protection du patrimoine

Ex-Ufficio Centrale della Zecca e cortile dello stesso, oggi Ufficio del Land Baviera per la Tutela delle Belle Arti

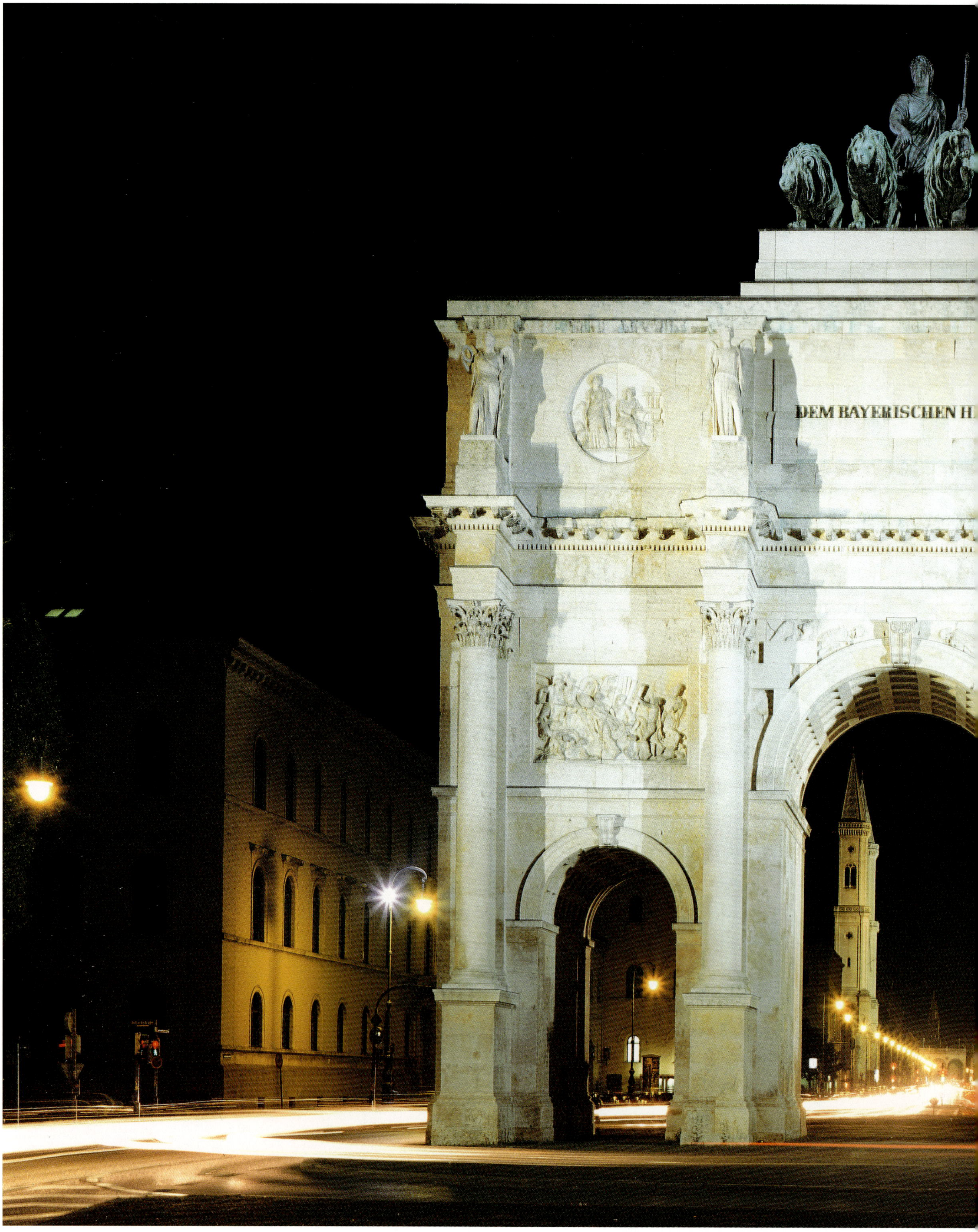
DEM BAYERISCHEN H

Siegestor -
nördlicher Abschluss der Ludwigstraße

The Siegestor -
the northern end of Ludwigstraße

La Siegestor -
la limite nord de la Ludwigstraße

Il Siegestor -
il limite settentrionale della Ludwigstraße

Typische Münchner Jugendstilfassaden ...in der Ainmillerstraße und

Typical Art Nouveau façades in Munich ...on Ainmillerstraße and

Des façades munichoises typiques en Jugendstil ...dans la Ainmillerstraße et

Tipiche facciate monacensi in stile Art Nouveau ...nella Ainmillerstraße e

nehmend Mietshäuser. Mit dem „Franzosenviertel" am Ostbahnhof wurde nach dem Krieg 1870/71 ein riesiges Areal mit „Zins-Schmederers, for instance, thus took up residence in the Au; princely painters such as Eduard von Grützner and Franz von Stuck in Haidhausen; and writer Thomas Mann in Bogenhausen. Here the renowned sculptor Adolf von Hildebrand had his flat and studio in the Hildebrandhaus, which today shelters the Monacensian Library.

In the different districts an individual kind of patriotism either survived or developed. This is particularly noticeable in the towns naissance d'une immense aire avec de «grands immeubles de rapport».

Les riches faisaient bâtir leurs villas également aux bords de l'Isar entre Harlaching et Bogenhausen. Les banquiers et hommes d'affaires comme les Nockher et Schmederer résidaient à Au, les grands peintres comme Eduard von Grützner et Franz von Stuck à Haidhausen et le poète Thomas Mann à Bogenhausen. C'est également ici que vivait et travaillait le célèbre sculpteur laching e Bogenhausen. Banchieri e importanti uomini d'affari, come i Nockher e i Schmederer, hanno risieduto nella Au, grandi pittori come Eduard von Grützner e Franz von Stuck hanno abitato a Haidhausen mentre lo scrittore Thomas Mann risiedeva a Bogenhausen. Qui aveva la sua casa e il suo atelier nella «Hildebrandhaus», che è oggi la sede della Biblioteca Monacensia, anche il famoso scultore Adolf von Hildebrand.

kasernen" aus dem Boden gestampft.

Auch „Großkopferte" errichteten ihre Villen am Isarufer zwischen Harlaching und Bogenhausen. So residierten Bankiers und Geschäftsleute wie die Nockhers und Schmederers in der Au, Malerfürsten wie Eduard von Grützner und Franz von Stuck in Haidhausen oder der Dichter Thomas Mann in Bogenhausen. Hier hatte auch der renommierte Bildhauer Adolf von Hildebrand im „Hildebrandhaus", heute Sitz der Mona-

in der Römerstraße

on Römerstraße

dans la Römerstraße

e nella Römerstraße

that were incorporated at a later date. In old villages like Aubing or Feldmoching even new citizens are much prouder of their home district's history and tradition than the inhabitants of large residential areas such as the Hasen-

Adolf von Hildebrand dans la maison «Hildebrand» où siège aujourd'hui la bibliothèque Monacensia.

Dans les différents quartiers, la notion d'appartenance à un quartier a été conservée ou s'est développée. Cela se ressent fortement dans les quartiers incorporés sur le tard. Dans des vieux villages comme Aubing ou Feldmoching, même les nouveaux habitants sont beaucoup plus fiers de leur histoire et de leur tradition que ceux des grandes agglomérations formées depuis

Nei singoli quartieri della città si è mantenuta o sviluppata una diversa coscienza di appartenenza alle proprie origini. Ciò è sentito, in modo particolare, nei quartieri di più recente incorporazione nel territorio comunale. Nei vecchi villaggi come Aubing o Feldmoching, anche i nuovi cittadini sono più orgogliosi delle proprie origini, della propria storia e delle proprie tradizioni rispetto agli abitanti dei grandi insediamenti sorti a partire dal 1960, come Hasenbergl o Neuperlach.

113

Der Eisbach, Treffpunkt
für unermüdliche Surfer

The Eisbach, meeting place
for energetic surfers

Le Eisbach, le lieu de rencontre
des passionnés de surf

L'Eisbach, punto d'incontro
di instancabili surfisti

Im Englischen Garten – einem der frühesten, größten und bedeutendsten englischen Landschaftsgärten Deutschlands. Blick auf den Monopteros, einem kleinen, offenen Rundtempel von klassischer Schönheit, zu dessen Füßen sich nicht nur Musikanten gerne niederlassen

The English Garden, one of the earliest, biggest and most famous English-style landscaped gardens in Germany. View of the Monopteros, a small, open gazebo of classic beauty, on the steps of which not only musicians like to settle

Dans le Jardin Anglais – un des plus anciens et importants jardins de style anglais d'Allemagne. Vue sur le Monopteros, un petit temple rond ouvert à la beauté classique; où pas seulement que des musiciens viennent s'installer à ses pieds

Impressioni del Giardino Inglese – uno dei primi, più grandi e più importanti parchi del suo genere in Germania. Veduta del Monopteros, un piccolo tempietto circolare di bellezza classica ai cui piedi si ritrovano, spesso e volentieri, musicisti ed altri frequentatori di ogni genere

censia-Bibliothek, Atelier und Wohnung.

In den einzelnen Stadtteilen hat sich ein unterschiedliches Heimatbewusstsein erhalten oder entwickelt. Am deutlichsten wird dies in den spät eingemeindeten Orten. In alten Dörfern wie Aubing oder Feldmoching ist auch bei Neubürgern der Stolz auf Geschichte und Tradition stärker als in den seit 1960 entstandenen Großsiedlungen wie Hasenbergl oder Neuperlach. Noch heute sagen die meisten Pasinger(innen) auf die Frage, wo sie her sind, „aus Pasing", nicht „aus München".

Der bekannteste Stadtteil Münchens ist Schwabing. Das einstige kleine Dorf im Norden der Stadt wurde seit dem Ende des 16. Jahrhunderts Sitz von Schlössern. Anfang des 19. Jahrhunderts begann hier mit der Lokomotivfabrik Maffei im Englischen Garten die Industrialisierung Bayerns. Schwabing wurde die erste Arbeitersiedlung. Durch die Errichtung von Universität und Kunstakademie beim Siegestor kam der Wandel zum Künstlerdorf, das Genies aus aller Welt anzog. Zwischen der Eingemeindung nach München 1890 und dem Ausbruch des Ersten Weltkrieges 1914 erlebte Schwabing einen Bauboom und wurde zum kulturellen Mittelpunkt Deutschlands.

Begehrte Viertel zeigen Wachstumstendenzen. Traditionell glauben so selbst die meisten Bewohner der angrenzenden Maxvorstadt, sie würden in Schwabing leben. Dabei ist diese seit 1808 errichtete, erste planmäßige Vorstadt das eigentliche kulturelle und politische Zentrum Bayerns, denn hier finden sich die meisten Ministerien, Hochschulen, Museen, Bibliotheken und Buchläden.

Milbertshofen bestand bis um 1800 nur aus einem einzigen großen Schwaighof. Erst später entwickelte sich ein Dorf und schließlich eine Industriestadt, die 1913 nach München eingemeindet wurde. Heute ist das Image des Stadtteils besonders

bergl or Neuperlach, both of which developed after 1960. If you ask the people living in Pasing where they come from, most of them will even today answer "from Pasing" and not "from Munich".

Munich's most widely known district is Schwabing. This former small village located to the north of the city boasted numerous small palaces in the late 16th century. When in the early 19th century Bavaria's industrialization started in the English Garden with the construction of the Maffei Locomotive Factory, Schwabing became the first workers' settlement. But when the university and the art academy were established right at the "Siegestor" (a triumphal arch), the district gradually turned into a cultural centre which attracted artists from all parts of the world. In the period between its incorporation into the city in 1890 and the outbreak of the First World War in 1914 Schwabing enjoyed a veritable building boom and became Germany's cultural nucleus.

Munich's most popular districts still show a tendency to grow. Traditionally, most of the inhabitants of the Maxvorstadt (a suburb bordering on Schwabing) also believe that they live in this famous area. Yet the Maxvorstadt, the first officially planned quarter which started to develop in 1808, is the real cultural and political centre of Bavaria, for here one finds most ministries, universities, museums, libraries, and book stores.

Up to about 1800, Milbertshofen consisted of only one large farmstead. Subsequently a village and, finally, an industrial town developed, which was incorporated into Munich in 1913. Today this suburb owes its image largely to BMW and the Olympic site.

The ancient roadside village of Sendling used to be an important central community. Its parish also comprised Schwabing, Neuhausen and Pullach. The village went down into history mainly because of a very tragic event, which is still commemorated by the popu-

1960 comme Hasenbergl ou Neuperlach. Aujourd'hui encore quand on demande à des habitantes et habitants de Pasing d'où ils sont, la plupart répondent «de Pasing» et non «de Munich».

Le quartier le plus connu de Munich est assurément Schwabing. Cet ancien petit village au nord de la ville est devenu, depuis la fin du 16ème siècle, le siège des châteaux. Au début du 19ème siècle, l'industrialisation de la Bavière commença ici avec la fabrique de locomotives Maffei dans le Jardin Anglais. Schwabing fut la première cité ouvrière. Avec la construction de l'université et de l'académie des beaux-arts près du Siegestor (porte de la victoire), Schwabing se métamorphosa en village artistique attirant les génies de toute la planète. Entre son incorporation à Munich en 1890 et le déclenchement de la Première Guerre mondiale en 1914, Schwabing connut un véritable boom de la construction et devint le cœur culturel de l'Allemagne.

Les quartiers convoités présentent des tendances de croissance. Par tradition, la plupart des habitants du quartier voisin de Maxvorstadt croient eux-mêmes qu'ils habitent Schwabing. Mais existant depuis 1808, cette première banlieue planifiée est le véritable centre culturel et politique de la Bavière, car on y trouve la plupart des ministères, universités, musées, bibliothèques et librairies.

Jusqu'en 1800, Milbertshofen se composait uniquement d'une ferme immense. Il devint plus tard d'abord un village puis une ville industrielle intégrée dans Munich en 1913. L'image de ce quartier est aujourd'hui particulièrement marquée par BMW et les installations olympiques.

Le très vieux village-rue de Sendling formait un emplacement central. Sa paroisse englobait également Schwabing, Neuhausen et Pullach. Un événement tragique, très présent aujourd'hui encore dans la mémoire de la population, fit entrer cet endroit dans l'histoire. En 1705, lors de

Ancora oggi, se si chiede loro da dove provengono, la maggior parte degli abitanti di Pasing risponde «da Pasing» e non «da Monaco».

Il quartiere più conosciuto di Monaco è Schwabing. Nell'ex piccolo villaggio a nord della città sono stati costruiti castelli e palazzi fin dalla fine del XVI secolo. Sempre qui è iniziata l'industrializzazione della Baviera all'inizio del XIX secolo, e precisamente con la fabbrica di locomotive Maffei nel Giardino Inglese. Con la costruzione dell'Università e dell'Accademia delle Belle Arti presso la Porta della Vittoria c'è stata una svolta nella storia del villaggio che è divenuto un luogo artistico, meta di geni del settore provenienti da tutto il mondo. Tra l'incorporazione nel comune di Monaco nel 1980 e lo scoppio della Prima Guerra Mondiale nel 1914 Schwabing ha vissuto un vero boom edilizio diventando anche il centro culturale della Germania.

I quartieri più ambiti mostrano una tendenza alla crescita. Tradizionalmente, la maggior parte degli stessi abitanti della vicina Maxvorstadt crede di vivere a Schwabing. Questo primo sobborgo regolare, costruito nel 1808, è il vero e proprio centro politico e culturale della Baviera, in quanto qui si trova la maggior parte dei ministeri, delle università, dei musei, delle biblioteche e delle librerie.

Fino al 1800, Milbertshofen era costituito solo da un'unica grande fattoria. Solo in seguito si è sviluppato un villaggio ed infine una città industriale che è stata incorporata nel comune di Monaco nel 1913. Oggi, l'immagine di questo quartiere è caratterizzata prevalentemente dalla BMW e dagli impianti olimpici.

L'antico villaggio di Sendling era un luogo centrale. La sua parrocchia comprendeva anche Schwabing, Neuhausen e Pullach. Esso è entrato nella storia per un evento tragico ed ancora vivo nella memoria dei suoi abitanti: nel 1705, sotto Natale (ora ricordato come il «Natale insanguinato»),

durch BMW und das Olympiagelände geprägt.

Das uralte Straßendorf Sendling war ein Zentralort. Seine Pfarrei umfasste auch Schwabing, Neuhausen und Pullach. Der Ort ist besonders durch ein tragisches Ereignis – heute noch im Bewusstsein der Bevölkerung lebendig – in die Geschichte eingegangen: Bei der Sendlinger Mordweihnacht im Jahr 1705 wurden mehr als 1000 wehrlose Bauern aus dem Oberland, die ihrem Kurfürsten zur Hilfe eilen wollten, von der damaligen österreichischen Besatzungsarmee niedergemetzelt. Stolz sind die Sendlinger darauf, daß auch die Theresienwiese auf ihrer alten Gemarkung liegt und es eigentlich „Sendlinger Oktoberfest" heißen müsste.

In anderen Stadtteilen kann man sich an bedeutenden Bauten und Anlagen wie dem Schloss Nymphenburg oder der im Kern romanischen Moosacher St. Martinskirche orientieren.

Auch wenn einst eigenständige Gemeinden zu neuen größeren Stadtbezirken vereint wurden, ist damit das Ortsbewusstsein nicht verschwunden. Wehe, man wirft den Obermenzinger Burschenverein mit den Pasingern in einen Topf!

Veränderungen durch Zerstörung im Zweiten Weltkrieg betrafen das Stadtgebiet in unterschiedlichem Maß. Entscheidend geprägt wurden die Stadtteile in den 70er und 80er Jahren. Im Zuge der Aufwertung als „Innenstadtrandgebiet" hat so z.B. Haidhausen sein Gesicht verändert. Aus einem „Kleine-Leute-Viertel" wurde ein „Künstlerviertel" und „Kleines Schwabing" – ein ideales Betätigungsfeld für Immobilienspekulanten. Deshalb engagierten sich zahlreiche Bürger für den Erhalt der gewachsenen Strukturen. Besonders die Planung des gigantischen Kulturzentrums am Gasteig mit Volkshochschule, Stadtbibliothek und Philharmonie erhitzte die Gemüter.

Die meisten Münchner(innen) fühlen sich mit dem Stadtteil, in dem sie leben, gerade in einer lation today: during the "Sendlinger Murder-Christmas" of 1705 more than 1,000 defenseless peasants from the highlands, who wanted to lend assistance to their elector, were slaughtered by the Austrian army occupying the country at that time. The people of Sendling are also proud of the fact that the "Theresienwiese" (the site of the Oktoberfest) is located in their territory, so that the Münchner Oktoberfest should actually be called "Sendlinger Oktoberfest".

In other city districts you can feast your eye on such renowned landmarks as Nymphenburg Palace or the mainly Romanesque church of St. Martin in Moosach.

Even though some formerly independent communities were combined to form new city districts, their inhabitants are still fully aware of their "origin": woe betide you if you cannot tell the difference between the Obermenzing and the Pasing youth clubs.

The destruction occurring in the Second World War affected and altered the city area in different ways and to a different extent. More decisive changes took place in the 1970s and 1980s. Haidhausen's appearance, for instance, was completely altered when the district was "elevated" to the rank of an "Innenstadtgebiet", i. e. when it became part of central Munich's fringe area. This quarter, then housing mostly people of the lower middle class, quickly became an artists' district or "little Schwabing" and, consequently, an ideal playground for real estate speculators. For this reason many citizens started to fight for the preservation of the traditional structures. Particularly the planning of the gigantic cultural centre at the Gasteig – complete with adult education centre, municipal library and a huge concert hall housing the Munich Philharmonic Orchestra – caused a tremendous stir.

Most of the people of Munich feel closely tied to the district in which they live – primarily in our times of uprooting and isolation.

la Sendlinger Mordweihnacht (massacre de la nuit de Noël), plus de 1000 paysans sans défense venant de Haute-Bavière et voulant venir en aide à leur prince électeur furent massacrés par l'occupation autrichienne. Les habitants de Sendling sont fiers que le terrain de la Theresienwiese soit dans leur district et sont d'avis qu'on devrait plutôt parler de « la fête de la Bière de Sendling ».

Dans les autres quartiers, il est possible de s'orienter aux bâtiments ou parcs importants comme le château de Nymphenburg ou, au cœur roman de Moosach, l'église St. Martin.

Même si des communes autrefois indépendantes ont été réunies pour former des quartiers plus importants, la notion d'appartenance à un quartier n'a pas disparu. Pas question de mélanger les associations d'étudiants d'Obermenzing avec celles de Pasing !

Les destructions de la Seconde Guerre mondiale causèrent des dégâts d'ampleur différente dans la ville. Les quartiers furent fortement marqués durant les années 70 et 80. A la suite de sa revalorisation comme « quartier en marge du centre-ville », Haidhausen a par exemple changé de physionomie. Le « quartier des petits gens » est devenu le « quartier des artistes » et le « Petit Schwabing » – un champ d'action idéal pour les promoteurs immobiliers. C'est pourquoi de nombreux citoyens se sont engagés en faveur de la sauvegarde des structures existantes. La planification du gigantesque centre culturel am Gasteig avec l'université populaire, la bibliothèque municipale et la philharmonie fit couler beaucoup d'encre.

La plupart des Munichoises et des Munichois se sentent très proches du quartier dans lesquels ils vivent, justement à une époque de déracinement et d'isolation. Par conséquent, au cours des dernières années, on assista à la naissance d'une multitude d'associations locales s'intéressant au pays et à l'histoire.

più di 1000 contadini inermi, provenienti dall'altopiano e che volevano accorrere in aiuto del loro principe elettore, furono massacrati dall'esercito d'occupazione austriaco. Gli abitanti di Sendling sono orgogliosi del fatto che anche la Theresienwiese rimane all'interno del territorio di Sendling e sostengono che il famoso «Oktoberfest di Monaco» dovrebbe chiamarsi, più propriamente, «Oktoberfest di Sendling».

In altri quartieri della città ci si può orientare con importanti edifici e costruzioni quali il Castello di Nymphenburg o la Chiesa di San Martino, di origine romanica, a Moosach.

Il fatto che comuni un tempo autonomi siano stati uniti a formare nuovi e più ampi quartieri cittadini non ha comportato la perdita della coscienza locale dei loro abitanti. Guai a mettere nello stesso calderone l'associazione studentesca di Obermenzing con quella di Pasing!

Il territorio della città subì modifiche varie e di diversa entità in seguito alle distruzioni causate dalla Seconda Guerra Mondiale. La loro impronta decisiva i quartieri la ricevettero negli anni '70 e '80. Fu il caso di Haidhausen, che ha modificato la propria fisionomia seguendo la tendenza alla rivalutazione delle «aree periferiche del centro». Da «quartiere di piccoli borghesi» esso è diventato un «quartiere di artisti» e una «Piccola Schwabing» – un campo d'azione ideale per gli speculatori immobiliari. È per questo motivo che molti abitanti si sono adoperati attivamente per la salvaguardia delle strutture preesistenti. Soprattutto la progettazione del gigantesco centro culturale del Gasteig, con l'Università Popolare, la Biblioteca Civica e la Filarmonica, ha infervorato gli animi.

Proprio in un periodo di generale sradicamento ed isolamento, la maggior parte degli abitanti di Monaco sente profondamente l'appartenenza al quartiere in cui vive. È per questo motivo che negli ultimi anni sono sorte numerose associazioni di arte e cultura autoctone nonché storiche.

Zeit der Entwurzelung und Vereinsamung, sehr verbunden. Daher entstanden in den letzten Jahren zahlreiche örtliche Heimat- und Geschichtsvereine.

Eine wichtige Rolle für das Stadtteilbewusstsein spielen auch die Bezirksausschüsse. Sie repräsentieren die Bürger und tragen Wünsche aus der Bevölkerung an

Many local history clubs and societies were therefore established in the past few years.

Another important reason for this "local patriotism" are the district committees. They represent the citizens and bring their wishes to the attention of the city administration. When in 1996 the legal status of these "district par-

Les conseils d'arrondissement jouent également un rôle non négligeable au niveau de cette notion d'appartenance à un quartier. Ils représentent les citoyens et transmettent à la municipalité les désirs de la population. La revalorisation légale par référendum, décision du conseil municipal et la première élection

Un ruolo fondamentale per il consolidamento della coscienza di appartenenza al proprio quartiere è svolto anche dai comitati di quartiere. Questi rappresentano i cittadini e fanno loro da tramite con l'amministrazione cittadina. La rivalutazione giuridica ottenuta grazie ai referendum popolari, alle deliberazioni del

„Memoria Historiae",
Stele von Anne und Patrick Poirier
vor dem Stadtarchiv

"Memoria Historiae",
a stele by Anne and Patrick Poirier
in front of the municipal archives

«Memoria Historiae»,
stèle de Anne et Patrick Poirier
devant les archives municipales

«Memoria Historiae»,
stele di Anne e Patrick Poirier
davanti all'Archivio di Stato

die Stadtverwaltung weiter. Die rechtliche Aufwertung durch Volksentscheid, Stadtratsbeschluss und erste Direktwahl der „Stadtteilparlamente" im Jahr 1996 hat die Besinnung auf die Eigenständigkeit gefördert.

**Dr. Reinhard Bauer
Hermann Wilhelm**

liaments" was enhanced through a plebiscite, a city council decree, and a first direct election, the awareness of the districts' independence was also promoted greatly.

**Dr. Reinhard Bauer
Hermann Wilhelm**

directe des «parlements de quartiers» en 1996 encouragea la prise de conscience de l'autonomie.

**Dr. Reinhard Bauer
Hermann Wilhelm**

consiglio comunale e alla prima elezione diretta dei «parlamenti dei quartieri» nel 1996 ha favorito ulteriormente il consolidamento della coscienza della propria autonomia.

**Dr. Reinhard Bauer
Hermann Wilhelm**

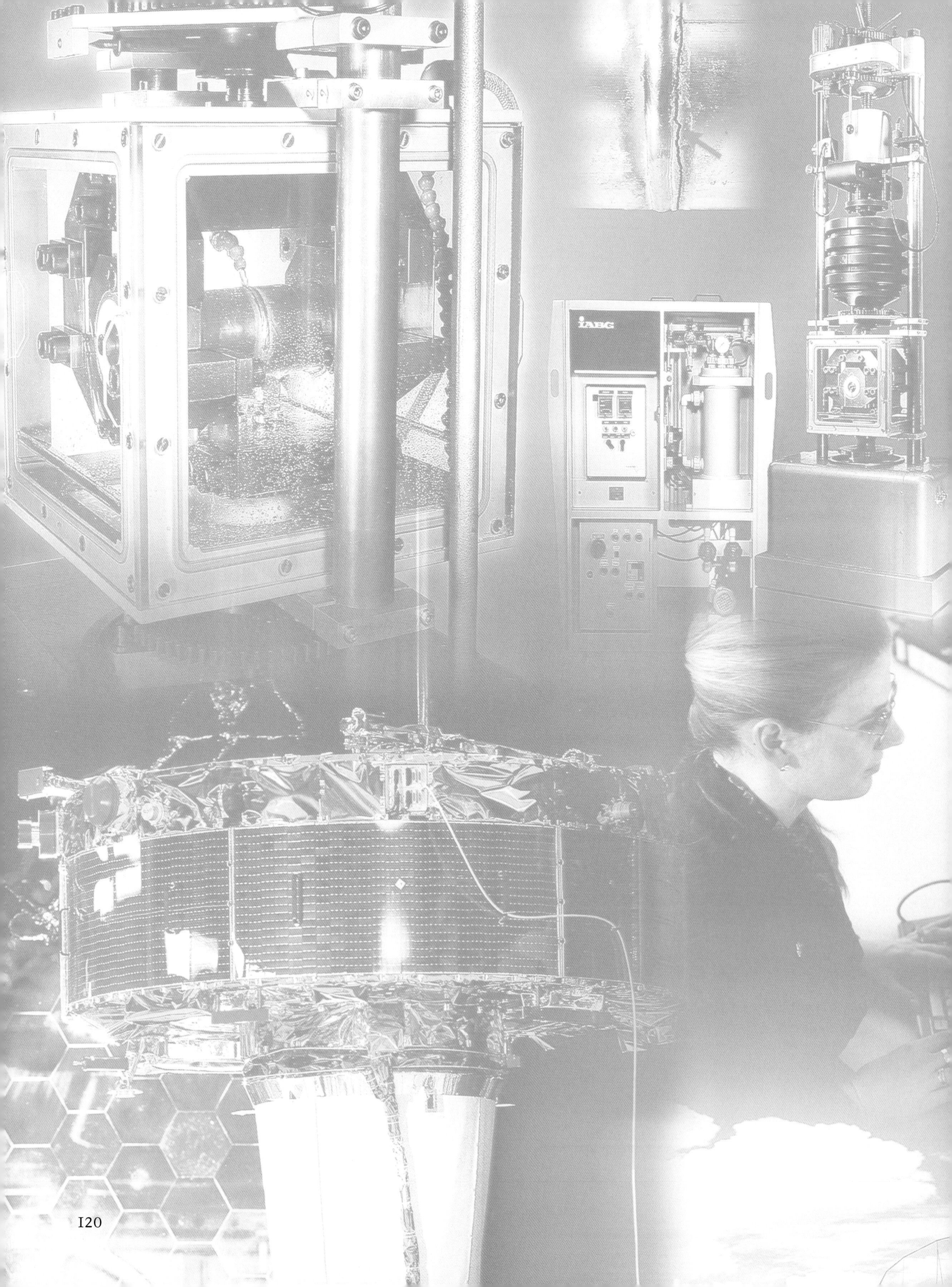
IABG

Wirtschaftsregion München
Spitzenregion in Europa
Vom Salzhandel zum europäischen Hightech-Standort

The Economic Region of Munich
One of Europe's Top Regions
From the Salt Trade to a European Hightech Centre

La région économique de Munich
Une région clé en Europe
Du commerce du sel à un site européen de la haute technologie

Monaco come area economica
di punta nell'economia europea
Dal commercio del sale a capitale europea dell'alta tecnologia

Die gewaltsame Verlagerung des Salzhandelsweges 1158 nach München und die Gründung des Marktes mit Niederlagszwang schufen die Basis der auf dem Salz-, Getreide-, Tuch- und Weinhandel aufbauenden Händler-, Handwerker- und Bürgerstadt. Zudem zog die fürstliche und später kurfürstliche Residenz neben Beamten und Soldaten auch viele Gelehrte und Künstler in die aufstrebende Stadt. Der Fürstenhof wurde somit zur zweiten Säule der wirtschaftlichen Entwicklung Münchens. Mit der Erhebung Bayerns zum Königreich und Münchens zur königlichen Haupt- und Residenzstadt im Jahre 1806 nahm die Konzentration von Politik, Kunst und Kultur, Wissenschaft, Finanzwesen, Wirtschaft und Bevölkerung deutlich zu. Die Abschaffung des Zunftwesens erlaubte neue Arbeitsmethoden und führte zu zahlreichen Firmengründungen. Schwerpunkt der Industrialisierung Münchens war bis in den Anfang des 20. Jahrhunderts hinein die Eisenbahnindustrie. 1837 wurde die Lokomotivenfabrik Maffei, 1852 die Waggonfabrik Rathgeber und 1866 die Lokomotivenfabrik Krauss gegründet. Trotzdem blieb München als Industriestandort im deutschen wie im bayerischen Vergleich (Nürnberg, Augsburg) lange von untergeordneter Bedeutung.

Dieses Manko sollte sich nach dem Zweiten Weltkrieg zusammen mit den durch die deutsche Teilung bedingten Unternehmensverlagerungen als entscheidender Startvorteil in einer sich tertiärisierenden Wirtschaftswelt erweisen. So sorgten die aus Leipzig und Berlin zuziehenden Verlagshäuser gemeinsam mit den heimischen dafür, dass München noch vor New York zur wichtigsten Buchverlagsmetropole der Welt aufstieg – die Basis für den heutigen hochmodernen Medienstandort. Der Umzug von Siemens an die Isar bildete den Nukleus für die Ansiedlung vieler deutscher und internationaler Unternehmen der Elektrotechnik und der Mikroelektronik, die Grundlage jegli-

By shifting the salt route to Munich by force in 1158 and by introducing the market with "Niederlagszwang" (i. e. traders were obliged by law to offer their wares for one day even though they were only travelling through the town) a sound basis was provided for this town of merchants, craftsmen and citizens who relied on the salt, cereal, cloth and wine trade for their livelihood. Additionally, Munich's ducal and later electoral court drew not only officials and soldiers, but also numerous scholars and artists to this quickly developing city. Thus the court became the second pillar of Munich's economic rise. When in 1806 Bavaria became a kingdom and Munich its capital and residential town, the concentration of political power, art, culture, science, banking, and economic influence, as well as the size of the population increased markedly. The abolition of the guild system made new working methods possible and led to the establishment of many new enterprises. One of the focal points of Munich's industrialization was the railway industry, which played a dominating role till the early 20th century. In 1837 the Maffei locomotive factory was founded; in 1852 the Rathgeber railcar factory; and in 1866 the Krauss locomotive factory. Nevertheless, as an industrial location Munich remained insignificant for a long time, compared with other Bavarian cities such as Nuremberg or Augsburg.

After the Second World War this disadvantage – combined with the relocation of numerous enterprises owing to the division of Germany – proved to be an advantage in an economy increasingly dominated by the tertiary sector. The publishing firms moving to Munich from Leipzig and Berlin together with the local ones turned the city into the most significant book printing metropolis on our globe – ranking even before New York; a development that provided the foundation for the present-day ultra-modern media centre. Siemens' move to

En 1158, la délocalisation brutale de la voie du commerce du sel à Munich et la création d'un marché avec obligation d'implantation jetèrent les bases de cette ville de marchands, d'artisans et de bourgeois qui misait sur le commerce du sel, des céréales, des tissus et du vin. Par ailleurs, la résidence d'abord des princes puis ensuite des princes électeurs attira, outre des fonctionnaires et des soldats, également de nombreux intellectuels et artistes dans cette ville en plein essor. La cour des princes devint ainsi le deuxième pilier du développement économique de Munich. En 1806, la Bavière devint un royaume et Munich la capitale et la ville résidentielle. La politique, l'art et la culture, la science, les finances, l'économie et la population connurent alors une forte concentration. La suppression des corporations permit de nouvelles méthodes de travail et entraîna la création de nombreuses entreprises. Jusqu'au début du 20ème siècle, l'industrialisation de Munich se concentra essentiellement sur l'industrie du chemin de fer. En 1837, la fabrique de locomotives Maffei fut fondée, en 1852 ce fut le tour de la fabrique de wagons Rathgeber et en 1866 de la fabrique de locomotives Krauss. Malgré tout, comparée à d'autres sites industriels d'Allemagne ou de Bavière (Nuremberg, Augsbourg), Munich garda longtemps une importance secondaire.

Après la Seconde Guerre mondiale et la délocalisation des entreprises suite à la division de l'Allemagne, ce déficit se révéla un avantage déterminant dans un monde économique en pleine tertiairisation. Ainsi, les maisons d'édition, que ce soit celles nouvellement implantées et venant de Leipzig et Berlin ou les locales, veillèrent à ce que Munich devienne avant New York la capitale mondiale de l'édition du livre – la base du site médiatique ultramoderne d'aujourd'hui. Le déménagement de Siemens aux bords de l'Isar déclencha

Nel 1158, il trasferimento forzato e violento della via del sale su Monaco e la creazione del mercato con l'obbligo di magazzinaggio posero le basi alla creazione di una città di commercianti, artigiani e borghesi che prosperò con il commercio del sale, dei cereali, dei tessuti e del vino. Inoltre, la residenza principesca, che divenne in seguito la residenza del principe elettore, attirò nella città emergente, oltre a funzionari e soldati, anche molti studiosi e artisti. In tal modo la corte principesca divenne il secondo pilastro dello sviluppo economico di Monaco. Con l'elevazione della Baviera a regno e di Monaco a capitale e residenza reale nell'anno 1806, la concentrazione della vita politica, dell'arte e della cultura, della scienza, della finanza e dell'industria, nonché della popolazione aumentò notevolmente. L'abolizione delle corporazioni consentì d'introdurre nuovi metodi di lavoro e portò alla fondazione di numerose aziende. Il fulcro dell'industrializzazione di Monaco fu fino all'inizio del XX secolo l'industria ferroviaria. Nel 1837 venne fondata la fabbrica di locomotive Maffei, nel 1852 la fabbrica di carrozze Rathgeber e nel 1866 la fabbrica di locomotive Krauss. Ciò nonostante, Monaco rimase per molto tempo una città industriale di secondaria importanza in confronto a città concorrenti tedesche e bavaresi (Norimberga, Augusta).

Questa deficienza si sarebbe dimostrata dopo la Seconda Guerra Mondiale, insieme ai trasferimenti delle imprese dovuti alla divisione delle due Germanie, un vantaggio decisivo in un mondo economico sempre più proiettato verso il terziario. Fu così che grazie alle case editrici trasferitesi da Lipsia e da Berlino, e a quelle locali, Monaco assurse al ruolo di maggiore metropoli per l'editoria, più importante persino di New York. Fu questa la base sulla quale si sviluppò l'odierna ultramoderna città dei media. Il trasferimento della Siemens sull'Isar costituì il nucleo per l'insediamento di molte imprese tedesche

KUFNER – Insider der Mode

Das weltweit etablierte Münchner Spezialunternehmen für multifunktionale Bekleidungseinlagestoffe ist auf Gewebe, Gewirke und Vliesstoffe spezialisiert.

23 Tochterfirmen und eigene Büros sowie Repräsentanten in über 70 Ländern sind für die Abnehmer vor Ort einsatzbereit. Aber nicht nur die Ware ist überall verfügbar, sondern auch das Know-how erfahrener Bekleidungstechniker. Kufner-Kunden können sich auf ein weltumspannendes Netz von Lieferlagern und Servicestationen verlassen.

Die Innovationsfreudigkeit des Hauses dokumentieren über 100 weltweit eingetragene Patente. Das Qualitätsmanagement entspricht den Anforderungen ISO 9001.

Kufner ist geblieben, was es im Gründungsjahr 1862 war: ein inhabergeführtes Familienunternehmen mit heute 1 550 Mitarbeitern. Tradition ist bei Kufner die Basis des Fortschritts.

KUFNER – a Fashion Insider

The worldwide established Munich specialist enterprise for multi-purpose interlinings has specialized in woven and nonwoven as well as knitted fabrics.

A total of 23 subsidiaries and company-owned offices as well as representatives in over 70 countries are available to the customers on the spot. But not only the products are readily available, our highly experienced clothing engineers offer their know-how as well. Kufner customers can depend on a global network of warehouses and service offices.

The innovative drive of the company is reflected by more than 100 worldwide registered patents. The quality management meets with the standards of ISO 9001.

Kufner was founded in 1862, and has since then remained a family-run enterprise with 1,550 employees today. Tradition is the foundation for Kufner's success.

KUFNER – le cœur de la mode

Etablie dans le monde entier, l'entreprise munichoise spécialisée dans l'entoilage multifonctionnel pour la confection, est spécialisée dans les entoilages tissés, les entoilages maille et les entoilages non tissés.

23 filiales, des agences et des représentants dans plus de 70 pays sont sur place à la disposition des utilisateurs des produits Kufner. Non seulement les produits sont disponibles partout dans le monde, mais aussi le savoir-faire des techniciens expérimentés de la confection. Les clients de Kufner peuvent compter sur un réseau mondial de dépôts et de cellules.

L'esprit d'innovation de la société est prouvé par plus de 100 brevets déposés. La gestion qualité est conforme à la norme ISO 9001.

Kufner est restée telle qu'elle était en 1862, l'année de sa fondation: une entreprise familiale dirigée par ses propriétaires, avec aujourd'hui 1 550 collaborateurs. Chez Kufner, la tradition est le fondement du progrès.

KUFNER – l'anima della moda

L'azienda specializzata Kufner di Monaco di Baviera, ormai impostasi in tutto il mondo, produce tessuti multifunzionali di rinforzo per l'abbigliamento ed è specializzata nella produzione di stoffe, tessuti di maglia e veli.

23 società affiliate, uffici propri e rappresentanti in oltre 70 paesi sono a disposizione dei clienti locali. Non solo la merce è disponibile in tutto il mondo, ma anche il know-how di tecnici esperti nel settore dell'abbigliamento. I clienti della Kufner possono contare su una rete internazionale di magazzini di fornitura e di stazioni per il servizio di assistenza.

Lo spirito innovativo della casa è documentato dagli oltre 100 brevetti depositati in tutto il mondo. Il Servizio Qualità e Sicurezza è conforme alle norme ISO 9001.

Dal 1862, anno della sua fondazione, la Kufner è sempre rimasta un'impresa a conduzione familiare che conta oggi ben 1 550 dipendenti. Per la Kufner, la base del progresso è rappresentata dalla tradizione.

IMAGE

cher Hochtechnologie. Auch eine hervorragende wissenschaftliche Infrastruktur mit zahlreichen Forschungsinstituten und einer guten technischen Ausbildung durch die Münchner Universitäten war idealer Nährboden für diese Entwicklung, die schließlich zum größten deutschen Industriestandort führte.

Für das richtige Image sorgten die Olympischen Sommerspiele 1972, ein städtebaulicher wie wirtschaftlicher Glücksfall. Sie verbreiteten weltweit das Bild einer heiteren, weltoffenen Stadt mit hohem Freizeitwert, die bis heute Touristen und zuzugswillige hochqualifizierte Arbeitskräfte aus aller Welt anzieht. Der wirtschaftliche und kulturelle Reichtum, die großen Investitionen in die ökonomische und wissenschaftliche Infrastruktur, die Förderung der Wachstumsbranchen Neue Medien und Biotechnologie werden helfen, die Position Münchens als europäische Spitzenregion zu festigen und auszubauen.

Stadt und Region

In einer sich globalisierenden Welt verlieren Verwaltungsgrenzen zunehmend an Bedeutung. Aus wirtschaftlicher Sicht konkurrieren heute nicht mehr einzelne Städte, sondern ökonomisch homogene Großräume miteinander, deren Grenzen fließend sind und sich den jeweiligen Entwicklungen anpassen. Zudem wächst in der Regel mit der räumlichen Distanz des Betrachters der Umgriff einer Region. Während ein Unternehmer aus Rosenheim unter der Wirtschaftsregion München allenfalls den Bereich des S-Bahn-Netzes begreift, versteht eine amerikanische oder japanische Firma darunter gesamt Ober- oder gar Südbayern also einschließlich unseres Rosenheimer Unternehmers, der sich

the city on the Isar induced many German and international enterprises of the electrical engineering and microelectronic sectors (which are preconditions for any hightech development) to settle in Munich as well. The city's excellent scientific infrastructure boasting numerous research institutes and universities providing good technological training was an ideal breeding ground for this development, which eventually led to Munich's becoming the biggest industrial centre of Germany.

The Olympic Summer Games of 1972 – which constituted an architectural and economic boom – gave Munich a very fitting image: The city was presented to the world as a cheerful and open-minded town of great recreational value. It still attracts tourists and people from all parts of the world who are willing to settle and work here. Munich's economic and cultural wealth, generous investments in the local economic and scientific infrastructure, and the promotion of growth sectors like the new media and biotechnology will probably contribute their share to securing and improving Munich's status as a leading European region.

City and Region

Administrative centres continue to lose in significance in our globally-oriented world. Economically, it is no longer cities which compete with one another but homogeneous areas with flexible borders which are able to adapt to current developments. Furthermore, the farther one gets away from a region the more the concept of its size grows. An entrepreneur from Rosenheim will probably define the limits of Munich's short-distance railway network as the periphery of the Munich region, while an American or Japanese businessman is bound to include Upper Bavaria or even southern Bavaria – including our Rosenheim entrepreneur who is convinced that he lives outside this "inner circle".

l'implantation de nombreuses sociétés allemandes et internationales de l'électronique et de la microélectronique, la base de toute haute technologie. L'excellente infrastructure scientifique dotée d'une multitude d'instituts de recherche et d'une bonne formation technique donnée par les universités munichoises fut la base idéale à ce développement qui en fit le plus important site industriel d'Allemagne.

Les Jeux olympiques d'été de 1972 vinrent peaufiner son image, un coup de chance aussi bien pour l'urbanisme que pour l'économie. Ils diffusèrent à travers le monde l'image d'une ville gaie et ouverte accordant une place conséquente aux loisirs et qui attire aujourd'hui encore des touristes et une main-d'œuvre hautement qualifiée venant des quatre coins du monde. La richesse économique et culturelle, les grands investissements dans l'infrastructure économique et scientifique, la promotion des secteurs de croissance comme les nouveaux médias et la biotechnologie permettront d'étayer et de développer la position de Munich comme une région clé européenne.

La ville et la région

Dans un monde en pleine mondialisation, les frontières administratives perdent de plus en plus de leur importance. D'un point de vue économique, ce ne sont plus quelques villes mais des agglomérations économiques homogènes qui se font concurrence et leurs frontières s'adaptent aux différents développements. En règle générale, plus un observateur est éloigné et plus la notion de région est vaste. Alors que pour un entrepreneur de Rosenheim, la région économique de Munich englobe au maximum le réseau interurbain, il s'agit pour une société américaine ou japonaise de toute la Haute-Bavière ou même du sud de la Bavière, donc y compris

ed internazionali specializzate nel campo dell'elettrotecnica e della microelettronica e il fondamento per ogni sviluppo futuro dell'alta tecnologia. Questo fu favorito inoltre da un'eccellente infrastruttura economica forte della presenza di numerosi istituti di ricerca e di tecnici altamente preparati dalle università di Monaco. Fu così che Monaco divenne il maggiore centro industriale della Germania.

Un bel tocco all'immagine della città fu dato dai Giochi Olimpici Estivi del 1972, un vero e proprio colpo di fortuna, sia per l'urbanistica che per l'economia. Diffusero nel mondo l'immagine di una città allegra, aperta, che attribuisce un alto valore al tempo libero: un'immagine che attira ancora oggi turisti e lavoratori altamente qualificati di tutto il mondo. La ricchezza economica e culturale, i grandi investimenti nelle infrastrutture economiche e scientifiche, la promozione di settori in espansione quali i nuovi mezzi di comunicazione e la biotecnologia, tutto questo contribuirà a consolidare ed ampliare ulteriormente la posizione di Monaco come regione di primaria importanza.

Città e regione

In un mondo che si sta sempre più globalizzando, i confini amministrativi perdono sempre più importanza. Dal punto di vista economico, attualmente la concorrenza non si svolge più tra singole città, ma tra vaste aree omogenee con confini fluttuanti che si adeguano di volta in volta agli sviluppi del momento. Inoltre, l'estensione di una regione cresce di norma in rapporto alla distanza esistente tra essa e il suo osservatore. Mentre un imprenditore di Rosenheim ritiene che la regione economica di Monaco corrisponde tutt'al più alla zona della rete della ferrovia urbana, per una ditta americana o giapponese essa corrisponderebbe all'intera Alta e Bassa Baviera, compreso quindi il nostro imprenditore di Rosenheim che si

Europa- und Deutschlandzentrale in Holzkirchen bei München

Corporate and German headquarters located in Holzkirchen close to Munich

Siège social pour l'Europe et l'Allemagne à Holzkirchen près de Munich

La sede centrale per l'Europa e la Germania a Holzkirchen presso Monaco

NAiS *Bildverarbeitungssysteme*

NAiS *Machine Vision Systems*

Systèmes de vision **NAiS**

Sistemi di elaborazione immagine **NAiS**

Die **Matsushita Electric Works (Europe) AG** ist ein bayerisches Unternehmen mit neun Tochterfirmen und zwei Produktionsstätten in Europa unter dem Dach des japanischen Großkonzerns Matsushita Electric Works, Ltd.

Sie entwickelt, fertigt und vertreibt elektromechanische und elektronische Bauteile, Komponenten und Systeme für die Automatisierungs- und Messtechnik sowie die zugehörige Software. Ihre Kunden und Partner sind vorwiegend im Hightech-Bereich tätig. Mit Universitäten und Forschungsinstituten wird ein enger Erfahrungsaustausch gepflegt.

Das Firmenlogo **NAiS** tragen mittlerweile auch Produkte für den Endverbraucher auf den Gebieten Medizin und Hygiene.

Mit ihren Produkten leistet die Matsushita Electric Works (Europe) AG einen Beitrag zu mehr Sicherheit, erhöhter Lebensqualität und wachsendem Umweltschutz für die Zukunft unserer Gesellschaft.

Matsushita Electric Works (Europe) AG is a Bavarian enterprise with nine sales and marketing subsidiaries and two manufacturing plants in Europe under the umbrella of the global Japanese group Matsushita Electric Works, Ltd.

The company develops, manufactures and distributes electro-mechanical and electronic parts, components and systems for automation and measuring techniques as well as the necessary software. The company, whose customers are primarily in high technology industries, also maintains close collaborative relationships with universities and research institutions.

The company's logo **NAiS** will gradually also be used on medical, hygiene and consumer type products.

As a supplier of environmentally considerate products Matsushita Electric Works (Europe) AG helps contribute to improvements in living standards and safety.

Matsushita Electric Works (Europe) AG est une entreprise bavaroise regroupant neuf filiales et deux unités de production en Europe et fait partie du groupe japonais Matsushita Electric Works, Ltd.

Elle conçoit, fabrique et commercialise des composants électromécaniques et électroniques, des systèmes d'automatisme et de mesure ainsi que les logiciels associés.

Ses clients et partenaires travaillent, pour la plupart, dans le secteur des technologies de pointe. Elle entretient, en outre, des contacts étroits avec les Universités et les Instituts de Recherche.

Le logo de la société, **NAiS**, est porté maintenant également par des produits paramédicaux destinés au grand public.

Par ses produits, la société Matsushita Electric Works (Europe) AG contribue à davantage de sécurité, une amélioration de la qualité de vie et une protection accrue de l'environnement.

Matsushita Electric Works (Europe) AG è un'azienda bavarese con nove affiliate e due siti produttivi in Europa appartenente al grande gruppo giapponese Matsushita Electric Works, Ltd.

Essa sviluppa, produce e distribuisce componenti elettromeccanici ed elettronici, componenti e sistemi per l'industria dell'automazione e di misura, nonché il relativo software.

I suoi clienti e partner operano principalmente nel settore high tech. Il gruppo intrattiene una stretta collaborazione con atenei ed istituti di ricerca.

I prodotti vengono distribuiti in Europa con il marchio **NAiS**, sia quelli industriali che quelli destinati al mercato di consumo.

La Matsushita Electric Works (Europe) AG presta la massima attenzione al miglioramento della qualità della vita e alla tutela ambientale.

Deutsche Fertigung und europäisches Zentrallager in Pfaffenhofen/Ilm

German production and central warehouse facility in Pfaffenhofen/Ilm

Usine allemande et stock central européen à Pfaffenhoffen/Ilm

Il settore produzione per la Germania ed il magazzino centrale per l'Europa a Pfaffenhofen/Ilm

Der Geschäftsbereich Halbleiter der **Motorola GmbH** hat seinen Sitz seit Ende 1987 in München-Moosfeld. In dem dreistöckigen Gebäude befinden sich auf insgesamt 16 000 m² neben den administrativen Abteilungen die europäischen Design- und Entwicklungszentren für Automobilelektronik und die Computergroup.

Schwerpunkt der Entwicklungsaktivitäten ist der Entwurf von Mikroprozessoren und dazugehöriger Peripheriebausteine, die in Kraftfahrzeugen Einsatz finden. Mit dieser Investition in Halbleiteranwendungen wurde der ständig steigenden Bedeutung der Automobilindustrie Rechnung getragen.

The semiconductor sector of **Motorola GmbH** has been based in Munich-Moosfeld since late 1987. The three-storied building boasting a floor space of 16,000 square metres shelters – in addition to the administrative departments – the European design and development centres for car electronics and the computer group.

Development focuses on designing microprocessors and the appropriate peripheral modules used in motor vehicles. With this investment in semiconductor application the firm has taken into account the steadily increasing significance of the automotive industry.

Le secteur des semiconducteurs de la société **Motorola GmbH** siège depuis la fin de l'année 1987 à Munich-Moosfeld. Outre les services administratifs, les 16 000 m² du bâtiment à trois étages abritent les centres de design et de développement pour l'électronique automobile ainsi que le groupe informatique.

Les activités de développement se concentrent particulièrement sur la mise au point de microprocesseurs ainsi que les éléments périphériques inhérents trouvant leur utilisation dans l'automobile. Cet investissement dans les applications des semiconducteurs est à mettre au compte de l'importance croissante de l'industrie automobile.

«Advanced Interconnection Systems Laboratory» (AISL) de Motorola a construit à Munich un centre européen pour la technique avancée de construction et de raccordement des semiconducteurs. La mission de ce laboratoire est d'aider les clients lors du développement d'applications futures de systèmes en mettant au point et en intégrant de nouveaux concepts de boîtiers pour les composants microélectroniques. C'est pourquoi, dans le «packaging lab» AISL-Europe, toutes les conditions ont été réunies au cours de l'année 1997 pour développer de nouvelles technologies de boîtiers. Les installations permettent

La divisione operativa «Semiconduttori» della **Motorola GmbH** ha la propria sede, fin dalla fine del 1987, a Monaco di Baviera-Moosfeld. Oltre agli uffici amministrativi, l'edificio di tre piani ospita, su una superficie totale di 16 000 mq, anche i centri europei di progettazione e sviluppo di componentistica elettronica per il settore automobilistico ed il gruppo informatico.

Il baricentro delle attività di sviluppo è rappresentato dalla progettazione di microprocessori e relativi componenti periferici impiegati negli autoveicoli. Con questo investimento nelle applicazioni dei semiconduttori si è voluto tener conto del crescente significato che questo settore ha per l'industria automobilistica.

L'«Advanced Interconnection Systems Laboratory» (AISL) della Motorola ha realizzato, a Monaco, un centro europeo di tecnica avanzata di installazione e collegamento dei microprocessori. Il compito di questo laboratorio consiste nel fornire un supporto ai clienti nello sviluppo di applicazioni future di sistema attraverso l'elaborazione e l'integrazione di nuove concezioni di alloggiamenti per componentistica microelettronica. Per questo motivo, nel «Packaging Lab» di AISL- Europa sono state create, nel corso del 1997, tutte le premesse per lo sviluppo di nuove tecnologie di alloggiamento. Gli impianti installati

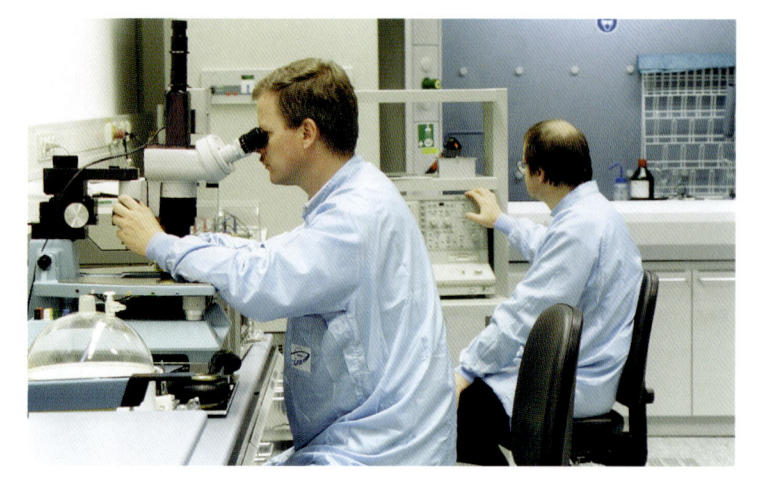

Motorolas „Advanced Interconnection Systems Laboratory" (AISL) hat in München ein europäisches Zentrum für die fortschrittliche Aufbau- und Verbindungstechnik von Halbleitern errichtet. Die Aufgabe dieses Labors besteht darin, Kunden bei der Entwicklung künftiger Systemanwendungen durch die Erarbeitung und Integration neuer Gehäusekonzepte für mikroelektronische Bauelemente zu unterstützen. Im „Packaging Lab" von AISL-Europa wurden deshalb im Laufe des Jahres 1997 alle Voraussetzungen für die Entwicklung neuer Gehäusetechnologien geschaffen. Die installierten Anlagen ermöglichen es, den gesamten Entwicklungszyklus neuer Gehäusekonzepte in München durchzuführen und den Kunden fortschrittliche Gehäuseplattformen zu liefern, die - zusammen mit den hervorragenden Halbleiterprodukten von Motorola - wesentliche Systemvorteile bieten.

Der Bereich „Transportation" umfasst ein breites Spektrum an Produkten und Lösungen für Kfz-Antriebssysteme, intelligente Verkehrssysteme, Sicherheits- und Fahrwerksysteme sowie Komfortelektronik und Sensortechnologien. In manchen Automobilen realisiert Motorola über 80 % der embedded Elektroniklösungen. Dies erfolgt in enger Zusammenarbeit mit Kfz-Herstellern zunächst für Fahrzeuge der Luxusklasse, die sich durch überragende Eigenschaften hinsichtlich Sicherheit, Komfort und Bordinformationssysteme auszeichnen und wird später auch auf andere Fahrzeuge übertragen.

Motorola's "Advanced Interconnection Systems Laboratory" (AISL) has set up in Munich a European centre for the progressive construction and linkage technology of semiconductors. This laboratory is responsible for aiding customers in the development of future system applications by designing and integrating new cases for microelectronic units. In 1997 AISL - Europe's "packaging lab" - provided the preconditions for developing new case technologies. The installed plants make it possible to carry out the entire development cycle of new case concepts in Munich and to supply customers with progressive case platforms which offer - together with Motorola's excellent semiconductor products - considerable system advantages.

The transportation sector comprises a wide range of products and solutions for motor car driving units; intelligent traffic systems; safety and moving gear systems; comfort electronics, and sensor technology. For some cars Motorola provides 80 % of the embedded electronic solutions - in close cooperation with car manufacturers of, primarily, luxury standard vehicles which boast exceptional safety and bord information systems as well as outstanding comfort. These innovations are later transferred to other makes and models as well.

d'exécuter à Munich tout le cycle de développement des nouveaux concepts de boîtiers et de fournir aux clients des plates-formes avancées de boîtiers offrant, avec les excellents produits de semiconducteurs de Motorola, de sérieux avantages au niveau des systèmes.

Le secteur «transportation» comprend la large gamme de produits et solutions pour les systèmes d'entraînement dans l'automobile, des systèmes de circulation intelligents, des systèmes de sécurité et de roulement ainsi qu'une électronique de confort et des technologies de senseurs. Dans certaines voitures, Motorola réalise plus de 80 % des solutions électroniques embarquées. Cela se fait en collaboration étroite avec les fabricants automobiles d'abord pour les véhicules de la classe de luxe qui se caractérisent par des qualités exceptionnelles de sécurité, confort et systèmes d'information de la planche de bord; le transfert aux autres véhicules se fera plus tard.

permettono di effettuare, a Monaco, l'intero ciclo di sviluppo delle nuove concezioni degli alloggiamenti e fornire ai clienti piattaforme di alloggiamenti avanzati che, unitamente agli eccellenti semiconduttori Motorola, offrono considerevoli vantaggi di sistema.

La divisione «Trasporti» comprende un ampio ventaglio di prodotti e soluzioni per sistemi di propulsori automobilistici, sistemi di traffico intelligenti, sistemi di sicurezza ed assetto nonché dispositivi elettronici confort e le tecniche dei sensori. In alcune automobili vengono realizzate da Motorola attraverso l'80 % delle soluzioni elettroniche embedded. Ciò avviene in stretta collaborazione con le case automobilistiche, inizialmente per vetture della fascia di lusso, che si distinguono per le eccellenti proprietà dei dispositivi di sicurezza, del confort e dei sistemi di informazione di bordo, e in un secondo tempo anche per veicoli di altre fasce.

selbst außerhalb dieses Raumes sieht.

Auch wenn mit der Region 14 ein gemeinsames Planungsinstrument existiert, hinken Politik und Verwaltung aufgrund der vorhandenen Rechtslage hinter dieser Entwicklung her. Dementsprechend schwierig ist es, für alle Bereiche homogene Daten zu erhalten, weil diese nicht nach den Wirtschaftsräumen, sondern nach den Verwaltungsgrenzen erhoben werden.

Das städtische Wirtschafts- und Tourismusmarketing berücksichtigt diese globalisierende Sichtweise seit vielen Jahren und präsentiert die Leistungen der gesamten Region. Denn auch wenn der Landeshauptstadt das eigene (finanzielle) Hemd am nächsten ist, weiß auch sie den Vorteil zu schätzen, wenn sich ein US-Unternehmen in einer Umlandgemeinde Münchens ansiedelt, statt irgendwo anders in Deutschland oder Europa. Die Wirtschaftsregion München konkurriert heute mit aufstrebenden Großräumen wie Mailand, Lyon oder Barcelona um einen absoluten Spitzenplatz in Europa. Lediglich der Status von Metropolen wie London oder Paris ist wegen der dort vorhandenen Konzentration von Bevölkerung, wirtschaftlicher und politischer Macht außer Reichweite.

Although Munich shares a joint planning instrument with Region 14 (comprising the central part of Upper Bavaria), the current legal situation is responsible for the fact that politics and administration lagg far behind in this development. Thus it is very difficult to obtain homogeneous data about the various sectors: They are not collected according to economic areas but according to administrative limits.

The city's economic and touristic marketing has paid consideration to this global view for many years and has always referred to the performances of the entire region. Even though the Bavarian capital, too, thinks that "charity begins at home", it also appreciates the advantages for the city whenever an American enterprise settles in the vicinity of Munich instead of in another part of Germany or Europe. Today the economic region of Munich competes with such up-and-coming large areas as Milano, Lyon or Barcelona for attaining and holding an absolutely leading position in Europe. To vie for the status held by metropolises like London or Paris is, of course, not realistic, because of their enormous population and their tremendous economic and political power.

Highlights of the Munich Economic Region

Attributes like "European high-tech metropolis", "media capital", "all-finance centre number 1", "biotechnology centre", "important fair and exhibition site", "Germany's city of craftsmen", "German research centre", or "European mecca of venture capital" clearly indicate that today Munich is not only an internationally acclaimed stronghold of culture and leisure-time activities but also Germany's most important economic region.

According to the conclusions of renowned economic institutes such as "empirica", "Prognos" and "ifo", Bavaria with its capital of Munich has for years retained

notre entrepreneur de Rosenheim qui se voyait lui-même en-dehors de cet espace.

Même s'il existe pour la région 14 un instrument commun de planification, la politique et l'administration traînent derrière ce développement, en raison de la législation existante. Il est par conséquent difficile d'obtenir des données homogènes pour tous les secteurs étant donné qu'elles ne sont pas saisies en fonction des espaces économiques mais d'après les frontières administratives.

Le marketing municipal économique et touristique prend depuis plusieurs années en considération le thème de la mondialisation et présente les performances de l'ensemble de la région. Car même si la capitale du land regarde en premier ses intérêts (financiers), elle apprécie également quand une entreprise américaine s'installe dans une commune voisine de Munich et non pas ailleurs en Allemagne ou en Europe. La région économique de Munich est aujourd'hui en concurrence avec de grandes agglomérations montantes comme Milan, Lyon ou Barcelone pour être une place absolument clé en Europe. Le statut de capitales comme Londres ou Paris, connaissant une concentration de la population et une puissance économique et politique, est inaccessible.

Les atouts de la région économique de Munich

Métropole européenne de la haute technologie, capitale médiatique, place N° 1 de la bancassurance, centre de la biotechnologie, place de foires et de commerce importante, ville allemande de l'artisanat, centre de recherche allemand, Mecque européenne du capital à risque, tels sont les attributs illustrant le fait que Munich n'est pas seulement aujourd'hui un fief de la culture et des loisirs mais la ré-

ritiene al di fuori di quest'area.

Anche se con la Regione 14 esiste un comune strumento di pianificazione, la politica e l'amministrazione zoppicano dietro a questo sviluppo a causa della situazione giuridica esistente. Risulta quindi difficile ottenere dati omogenei per tutti i settori in quanto questi non vengono stabiliti sulla base delle aree economiche, bensì sulla base dei confini amministrativi.

Dal punto di vista economico e turistico, Monaco tiene conto da molti anni di questa tendenza alla globalizzazione e si presenta per questo motivo all'interno di una regione unitaria. In quanto, anche se la capitale bavarese privilegia i propri interessi (finanziari), sa comunque apprezzare il vantaggio derivante dal fatto che un'impresa statunitense scelga un comune periferico di Monaco ove stabilire la propria sede, piuttosto che un altro luogo della Germania o dell'Europa. Monaco, come regione economica, concorre oggi con grandi ed importanti aree quali Milano, Lione o Barcellona per il primo posto in assoluto in Europa. Solo lo status di metropoli come Londra o Parigi è fuori portata a causa dell'eccezionale concentrazione in queste città di popolazione e del potere economico e politico.

Neles Automation in Oberhaching ist die deutsche Tochtergesellschaft der finnischen Neles Automation Inc. und Mitglied der durch Fusion per 1. Juli 1999 entstandenen Metso Gruppe.

Neles Automation gehört weltweit zu den führenden Anbietern von Prozessleitsystemen, Informationssystemen, Qualitätsleitsystemen und Applikationen für die Papier- und Zellstoffindustrie. Ebenso werden hochwertige Mess-, Regel- und Analysengeräte sowie Automatik- und Regelventile für den Weltmarkt gefertigt.

Die deutsche Vertretung ist zuständig für die Marktsegmente Deutschland, Schweiz und Niederlande und beschäftigt an vier Vertriebs- und Servicezentren 75 Mitarbeiter. Für 1998 wies Neles Automation einen konsolidierten Nettoumsatz von über 595 Millionen EUR aus.

Neles Automation located in Oberhaching is the German subsidiary of the Finnish Neles Automation Inc. and member of the Metso Group which was established through a merger as of 1 July 1999.

Neles Automation is one of the leading suppliers in the world for process control systems and applications for the paper and pulp industry. In addition Neles Automation supplies a global market with high quality instruments for measuring, controlling and analysing as well as automatic and control valves.

The German subsidiary services the market segments Germany, Switzerland und the Netherlands and employs 75 persons in four distribution and service centres. A consolidated net turnover of more than 595 million EUR was produced in 1998.

A Oberhaching, **Neles Automation** est la filiale allemande de la société finnoise Neles Automation Inc. et est membre du groupe Metso né par fusion le 1er juillet 1999.

Neles Automation fait partie, à l'échelle mondiale, des prestataires majeurs de systèmes de contrôle du processus, de systèmes d'information, de systèmes de contrôle de la qualité et d'applications pour l'industrie du papier et de la cellulose. De même, des appareils de mesure, de réglage et d'analyse tout comme des soupapes automatiques et de régulation sont fabriqués pour le marché mondial.

La représentation allemande est en charge du marché allemand, suisse et néerlandais et emploie sur ses quatre centres de distribution et de service 75 collaborateurs. Pour 1998, Neles Automation a réalisé un chiffre d'affaires net consolidé dépassant 595 millions d'euros.

La **Neles Automation** di Oberhaching è l'affiliata tedesca dell'azienda finlandese Neles Automation Inc. e fa parte del Gruppo Metso formatosi il 1º luglio 1999 in seguito ad una fusione.

La Neles Automation è una delle principali aziende su scala mondiale nel settore dei sistemi di gestione di processo, sistemi informatici, sistemi di gestione della qualità ed applicazioni per l'industria della carta e della cellulosa. Inoltre, vengono anche fabbricati per il mercato internazionale pregevoli apparecchi di misurazione, regolazione ed analisi nonché valvole automatiche e di regolazione.

Alla rappresentanza tedesca, che conta quattro centri di vendita ed assistenza clienti e 75 dipendenti, competono i segmenti di mercato Germania, Svizzera e Paesi Bassi. Nell'esercizio 1998 la Neles Automation ha registrato un fatturato netto consolidato di oltre 595 milioni di Euro.

◀ *Dreharbeiten in der Sierra Nevada. Teammitglieder (u.a.) von links: Walter H. Spohn, Regisseur/Rolf Homann, Geschäftsführer und Produktionsleiter/Günter Euringer, Chefkameramann/Stefan Baur, Kameraassistent (1.unit)/Charly Namendorf, Kameraassistent (2. unit)*

Shooting in the Sierra Nevada. The crew members include (l. to r.) Walter H. Spohn, director; Rolf Homann, company CEO and production manager; Günter Euringer, director of photography; Stefan Baur, assistant cameraman (1st unit); Charly Namendorf, assistant cameraman (2nd unit).

Am 15. Dezember 1982 tauchte die cine motion GmbH in der Münchner Filmszene auf. Mit dem Film „Königsschlösser Ludwig II" gelang gleich ein Senkrechtstart.

Neben der Produktion von Fernsehfilmen und TV-Dokumentationen entwickelte die cine motion sehr bald einige Spezialitäten – Filme für Industrieanwendungen, für Firmenpräsentationen, Marketing und Werbung.

Heute produziert die cine motion GmbH sowohl am Standort München als auch weltweit im Verbund mit internationalen renommierten Partnern.

On December 15, 1982, cine motion appeared on Munich's film scene, taking off like a skyrocket with the motion picture "Ludwig II's Royal Castles".

In addition to television feature and documentary production, cine motion soon developed a couple of specialties – industrials, films for corporate presentations, marketing and advertising.

Today cine motion produces both at its Munich base as well as worldwide in cooperation with internationally renowned partner companies.

**cine motion
Film- und Fernsehproduktion GmbH**
Haar bei München

Glanzlichter der Wirtschaftsregion München

Europäische Hightech-Metropole, Medienhauptstadt, Allfinanzplatz Nr. 1, das Biotechnologiezentrum, wichtiger Messe- und Handelsplatz, die deutsche Handwerksstadt, deutsches Forschungszentrum, europäisches Mekka des Wagniskapitals – Attribute, die illustrieren, dass München heute nicht nur eine weltbekannte Kultur- und Freizeithochburg ist, sondern auch die bedeutendste deutsche Wirtschaftsregion.

Nach allen Aussagen renommierter Wirtschaftsinstitute wie empirica, Prognos und ifo behauptet sich Oberbayern mit seiner Landeshauptstadt München seit Jahren als Topstandort unter 267 europäischen Regionen. Verglichen werden dabei Kriterien wie Wachstumsdynamik, Qualifikationsniveau der Arbeitskräfte, Verkehrsanbindung, Lohnniveau und Lebensqualität. Kennzeichen einer „Eurometropole" ist auch its status as a top location among 267 European regions. In their studies they compared criteria like growth dynamics, the qualification level of working people, traffic and transport connections, the wage level, and the quality of life. One of the characteristics of an "Eurometropolis" is also its significance as an "entrepreneurial centre". Eight of the 125 biggest European groups have their headquarters in Munich. This fact puts Munich in fourth place on the list of leading European cities.

The following comparative values are to illustrate Munich's national top ranking: From 1993 to 1997 the number of industrial enterprises increased from 78,500 to just over 98,000 – a positive balance of 20,000 firms. Every year more than 10,000 new enterprises are being founded. The achieved nominal per capita gross domestic product reaches approximately 200 % and the purchasing power 132 % of the German average.

gion économique majeure de l'Allemagne.

Selon tous les résultats des instituts économiques renommés comme empirica, Prognos et ifo, la Haute-Bavière ainsi que sa capitale du land Munich font depuis des années partie du peloton de tête des 267 régions européennes. Pour cela, des critères comme le dynamisme de croissance, le niveau de qualification du personnel, les liaisons de communication, le niveau des revenus et la qualité de la vie sont comparés. Une métropole européenne se caractérise également par la concentration de ses entreprises. Parmi les 125 groupes européens majeurs, huit ont leur siège principal dans la capitale bavaroise. Avec ce chiffre, Munich se range à la quatrième place des villes européennes.

Quelques valeurs comparatives doivent souligner l'excellente position nationale de Munich. Le nombre des entreprises industrielles est passé de 1993 à 1997

I fasti della regione economica di Monaco

Metropoli europea dell'alta tecnologia, capitale dell'informazione, piazza finanziaria n° 1, centro della biotecnologia, primaria piazza fieristica e commerciale, città tedesca per eccellenza dell'artigianato, centro tedesco per la ricerca, mecca europea del capitale di rischio – sono tutti attributi che illustrano come la Monaco di oggi sia non solo una roccaforte della cultura e del tempo libero conosciuta in tutto il mondo, ma anche la più importante regione economica della Germania.

Secondo tutte le dichiarazioni di rinomati istituti di ricerca economica quali empirica, Prognos e ifo, l'Alta Baviera, con la sua capitale, si afferma da anni quale sede privilegiata tra 267 regioni europee. Come termine di paragone si considerano criteri quali la dinamica della crescita, il livello di qualifica della manodopera, i

ihre Bedeutung als Unternehmenszentrale. Von den 125 größten europäischen Konzernen haben acht in der bayerischen Landeshauptstadt ihren Hauptsitz. München liegt mit dieser Zahl unter den europäischen Städten an vierter Stelle.

Einige Vergleichswerte sollen Münchens nationale Spitzenstellung verdeutlichen: Die Zahl der Gewerbebetriebe stieg von 1993 bis 1997 von 78 500 auf knapp 98 000, ein positiver Saldo von beinahe 20 000 Firmen. Jahr für Jahr werden mehr als 10 000 neue Unternehmen gegründet. Das hier erzielte nominale Pro-Kopf-Bruttoinlandsprodukt erreicht ca. 200 %, und die Kaufkraft liegt bei 132 % des deutschen Durchschnittswertes.

Auch in puncto Beschäftigungsniveau und -entwicklung ist München führend. Es hat die niedrigste Arbeitslosenquote aller deutschen Großstädte. 1998 lag sie im Jahresdurchschnitt bei 5,8 % nach EU-Standard, ziemlich genau der Hälfte des deutschen Mittelwertes. Mit insgesamt fast 900 000 Beschäftigten wird München nach absoluten Zahlen nur von der dreimal so großen Hauptstadt Berlin und nach relativen Zahlen (Verhältnis Beschäftigte/ Einwohner) nur von Frankfurt übertroffen. An das Qualifikationsniveau, das mehr als doppelt so hoch ist wie der Bundesdurchschnitt, reicht keine andere Stadt heran. Eine FOCUS-Studie kommt zu dem Schluss, dass München-Land und München-Stadt die Standorte Nr. 1 und 2 für neue Arbeitsplätze in Deutschland sind.

Zu dieser positiven Entwicklung und dem heutigen Status als deutscher Wirtschaftsstandort Nr. 1 haben auch die städtischen Weichenstellungen entscheidend beigetragen. So sind die kommunalen Investitionen pro Einwohner fast doppelt so hoch wie im Durchschnitt aller deutschen Großstädte. Das garantiert, dass Münchens Infrastruktur für die Zukunft gerüstet ist, die Wirtschaft ein beispiellos großes kommunales Auftragsvolumen erhält und vor Ort so viele Ar-

But also as far as the employment level and development are concerned Munich takes the lead. It boasts the lowest unemployment rate of all major German cities: in 1998 its yearly average amounted to 5,8 % EU-standard – almost to the point one half of the German average. With altogether nearly 900,000 employees, Munich is surpassed – according to absolute figures – only by Berlin, the German capital, which is three times the size of Munich; and according to relative figures (relation of employees to inhabitants) only by Frankfurt. No other city can match Munich as far as the level of employee qualification is concerned, for this is twice as high as the German average. A "Focus" study concludes that Munich-country and Munich-city rank first and second throughout Germany in the sector of new working places.

Municipal initiative has also contributed greatly to this positive development and to Munich's becoming Germany's leading economic location. For communal investments per inhabitant are nearly twice as high in Munich than in any other German city. This means that Munich's infrastructure will be able to meet any future challenge, that the local economy will receive a so far unmatched communal order volume, and that as many working places as possible will be safeguarded. This very generous investment rate was achieved at the expense of Munich's former status as the German city with the lowest per capita debts, but it still is better placed than the average city.

GROWTH BRANCHES AS A MOTOR OF DEVELOPMENT

The Hightech Region of Munich

The modern global economy is gradually turning into a service, information and know-how economy. Advanced knowledge and

HAUTE TECHNOLOGIE

de 78 500 à 98 000, donc une augmentation de près de 20 000 sociétés. Chaque année, plus de 10 000 nouvelles sociétés sont créées. Le produit national brut nominal par habitant atteint environ 200 % et le pouvoir d'achat dépasse de près de 132 % la moyenne allemande.

En ce qui concerne le niveau et le développement de l'emploi, Munich arrive aussi en tête. Elle affiche le taux de chômage le plus bas de toutes les grandes villes allemandes. En 1998, son taux annuel moyen s'élevait à 5,8 % (standard UE) soit donc presque la moitié de la moyenne nationale. Avec une population active de 900 000 personnes, Munich n'est dépassée en chiffres absolus que par la capitale Berlin, trois fois plus importante, et en chiffres relatifs (rapport population active/habitants) que par Francfort. Aucune autre ville n'atteint le degré de qualification, qui est plus de deux fois supérieur à la moyenne allemande. Une étude de FOCUS démontre que la ville et la campagne de Munich sont les sites N° 1 et 2 pour les nouveaux emplois en Allemagne.

Ce développement positif et le statut actuel comme premier site économique allemand sont également à mettre au compte de la municipalité. Ainsi, les investissements communaux par habitant sont deux fois supérieurs à la moyenne de toutes les

collegamenti tramite i servizi di trasporto, il livello delle retribuzioni e la qualità della vita. Segno distintivo di un'«eurometropoli» è anche il suo significato come sede centrale per le imprese. Dei 125 maggiori gruppi europei, ben otto hanno la loro sede principale nella capitale bavarese, un numero che la colloca al quarto posto tra le città europee.

Alcuni valori comparativi per illustrare la posizione di primo piano che Monaco detiene sulla scena nazionale: Il numero di aziende è salito dal 1993 al 1997 da 78 500 a quasi 98 000, un saldo positivo di quasi 20 000 ditte. Di anno in anno sono state fondate più di 10 000 nuove aziende. Il prodotto interno lordo nominale pro capite ha raggiunto ca. il 200 % e la forza d'acquisto corrisponde al 132 % della media nazionale.

Monaco è leader anche per quanto riguarda il livello e lo sviluppo dell'occupazione. Presenta infatti il tasso di disoccupazione più basso rispetto a tutte le grandi città tedesche. Nel 1998 si trovava con un valore medio annuale pari al 5,8 % (lo stanard della UE), esattamente al centro della media nazionale. Con un totale di quasi 900 000 lavoratori, Monaco viene battuta in assoluto solo dalla capitale Berlino, che vanta una grandezza di tre volte maggiore, e in cifre relative (rapporto lavoratori/abitanti) solo da Francoforte. Ma il livello di qualifica, doppio rispetto alla media federale, non è raggiunto da nessun'altra città. Uno studio di FOCUS ha stabilito che la zona e la città di Monaco sono le località n° 1 e 2 in ordine di importanza per quanto riguarda la creazione di nuovi posti di lavoro in Germania.

A questo sviluppo positivo e al primato economico di cui sopra hanno contribuito in modo determinante anche le agevolazioni concesse dall'amministrazione cittadina. Ad esempio, gli investimenti comunali pro abitante sono il doppio rispetto alla media di tutte le grandi città tedesche. Ciò garantisce che l'infrastruttura di Monaco sia pronta per affrontare

beitsplätze wie möglich gesichert werden. Der Preis dieser hohen Investitionstätigkeit ist, dass München seine einstige positive Spitzenstellung als die deutsche Großstadt mit der geringsten Pro-Kopf-Verschuldung eingebüßt hat, aber noch deutlich besser als der Durchschnitt liegt.

WACHSTUMSBRANCHEN ALS MOTOR DER ENTWICKLUNG

Hightech-Region München

Die moderne Weltwirtschaft wandelt sich immer mehr zu einer Dienstleistungs-, Informations- und Wissensökonomie. Im internationalen Wettbewerb werden Wissen(svorsprung) sowie eine daraus resultierende schnelle Umsetzung in vermarktbare Produkte und Dienstleistungen zunehmend eine größere Rolle spielen. Die Informations- und Kommunikationstechnologie nimmt dabei die Schlüsselrolle ein. Der Großraum München besitzt all jene erfolgsentscheidenden Faktoren, die globale Hightech-Regionen kennzeichnen: eine international anerkannte Forschungslandschaft, die Vernetzung der Wissenschaft mit Industrie und Dienstleistern, optimale Finanzierungsmodalitäten und eine überlegene Infrastruktur.

Technologieunternehmen in München

1998 waren im Raum München über 4 000 Unternehmen im Bereich Neue Technologien tätig. Allein 2 500 Firmen arbeiten hier in den Schlüsseltechnologien Mikroelektronik, Software und Hardware. Jeder zehnte Beschäftigte der deutschen EDV- und Elektro-

the resulting quick translation into marketable products and services will play an increasingly significant part in international competition. Here information and communication technologies will take the lead. Greater Munich boasts all the factors promising success which are typical of a global hightech region: an internationally acclaimed researchscape; a science sector closely linked with industry and service enterprises; optimum financing methods; and a superior infrastructure.

Technological Enterprises in Munich

In 1998 more than 4,000 enterprises of the sector "new technologies" were located in Munich. No less than 2,500 of them work in such key technologies as microelectronics, software and hardware. Every tenth person employed in the German data-processing and electronics industries earns his keep in Munich. Thanks to its leading position in these important sectors in Europe, Munich is known, worldwide, as the "Isar Valley". Every year relocating firms and company foundings account for a growth rate of roughly 8 %.

Not only the headquarters of such huge groups as Siemens, Siemens Nixdorf, DaimlerChrysler Aerospace and Rohde & Schwarz can be found in Munich. Numerous other global players – for example, Apple, Compaq-DEC, Intel, Microsoft, Oracle, Silicon Graphics, Sun Microsystems and Texas Instruments also have their main offices in Munich. No enterprise operating on an international basis can afford not to have an address in the Bavarian capital. But in addition to sheltering these large groups Munich houses primarily innovative small and medium-sized companies.

Further technological branches which are strongly represented in Munich are space engineering; medical engineering; energy technology; information and commu-

grandes villes allemandes. Cela garantit que l'infrastructure munichoise soit équipée pour l'avenir, que l'économie reçoive une quantité extrêmement conséquente d'ordres communaux et que, sur place, le maximum d'emplois soit assuré. Cette forte activité d'investissement se solde pour Munich par la perte de son ancienne position de grande ville allemande avec l'endettement le plus faible par habitant mais elle reste toujours nettement mieux placée que la moyenne.

LES SECTEURS DE CROISSANCE COMME MOTEURS DU DEVELOPPEMENT

Munich, la région de la haute technologie

L'économie mondiale moderne se transforme de plus en plus en une économie de prestations, d'informations et de connaissances. Au niveau de la concurrence internationale, les connaissances (inédites) ainsi que leur transformation rapide en produits et services commerciaux s'avèrent prépondérantes. La technologie de l'information et de la communication joue ici un rôle clé. La grande agglomération de Munich détient tous ces facteurs de réussite qui caractérisent les régions globales de haute technologie, à savoir une recherche reconnue au niveau international, la liaison de la science avec l'industrie et les prestataires de services, des modalités de financements optimales et une infrastructure de premier choix.

Les entreprises technologiques à Munich

En 1998, Munich et sa région comptaient plus de 4 000 entreprises opérant dans le secteur des nouvelles technologies. 2 500 sociétés travaillent ici dans les technologies clé comme la microélectronique, le logiciel et

il futuro, grazie anche ad una politica economica comunale che conferisce un volume di ordini senza precedenti alle industrie della città e assicura il maggior numero possibile di posti di lavoro sul posto. Il prezzo da pagare per questa intensa attività di investimenti è l'aver perso il primato positivo di grande città tedesca con il minore debito pro capite, pur rimanendo decisamente al di sotto della media nazionale.

I SETTORI DI CRESCITA COME MOTORE DELLO SVILUPPO

Monaco – regione dell'alta tecnologia

L'economia mondiale moderna si sta trasformando sempre più in un'economia dei servizi, dell'informazione e della conoscenza. Quest'ultima (e i vantaggi che ne derivano) e la sua rapida conversione in prodotti e servizi commercializzabili avranno un ruolo sempre più importante nel panorama della concorrenza internazionale. La tecnologia dell'informazione e della comunicazione assumono in questo un ruolo chiave. La grande area di Monaco possiede tutti quei fattori determinanti per il successo e che contraddistinguono le regioni ad alta tecnologia: un terreno di ricerca riconosciuto a livello internazionale, l'intreccio della scienza con l'industria e i servizi, ottime modalità di finanziamento e un'infrastruttura superiore.

Le imprese tecnologiche di Monaco

Nel 1998 più di 4 000 aziende erano attive nella zona di Monaco nel settore delle Nuove Tecnologie. Di queste solo 2 500 ditte lavorano nei settori chiave della microelettronica, del software e dell'hardware. Una persona su 10 impiegate nell'industria dell'elaborazione dati e dell'elettronica in Germania lavora nell'area economica di Monaco. Grazie alla

Mitten in München liegt einer der schönsten klassizistischen Saalplätze, der Wittelsbacherplatz. An seiner Nordseite befindet sich der Firmensitz von **Siemens**, *einem der größten Unternehmen der Welt für Elektronik und Elektrotechnik – und in München mit rund 37 000 Mitarbeitern der größte private Arbeitgeber.*

Wittelsbacherplatz, one of Munich's most beautiful neo-classical squares, is located in the heart of the city. The building flanking Wittelsbacherplatz in the north, houses the headquarters of **Siemens**, *one of the world's biggest enterprises in the field of electronics and electrical engineering. With about 37,000 employees Siemens is the most important private employer in Munich.*

Une très belle place en style classique au cœur de Munich: la Wittelsbacherplatz. La firme **Siemens** *- l'une des plus grandes entreprises d'électronique et d'électrotechnique et l'un des plus importants fournisseurs d'emplois de Munich (37 000 employés) a établi son siège principal sur le côté nord de la Wittelsbacherplatz.*

Nel cuore di Monaco di Baviera si trova una delle più belle piazze-salotto in stile classico, la Wittelsbacherplatz. Sul lato nord di questa piazza si trova la sede della **Siemens**, *una delle maggiori aziende mondiali di elettronica ed elettrotecnica – che a Monaco, con circa 37.000 dipendenti, costituisce il maggiore datore di lavoro privato.*

Zu einem Streifzug durch die Welt der Elektrotechnik und Elektronik wird ein Besuch im SiemensForum am Oskar-von-Miller-Ring 20.

The "SiemensForum" located Oskar-von-Miller-Ring 20 gives visitors the opportunity to explore the world of electronics and electrical engineering.

Une visite du «SiemensForum» installé Oskar-von-Miller-Ring 20 représente une incursion dans le monde de l'électronique et de l'électrotechnique.

Una visita al «SiemensForum», Oskar-von-Miller-Ring 20, diventa un'escursione nel mondo dell'elettronica e dell'elettrotecnica.

Compaq – vom PC-Verkäufer zum Technologieführer und strategischen Unternehmenspartner

Die Compaq Computer Corporation wurde 1982 gegründet. Mit der Übernahme von Digital im Juni 1998 avancierte das Fortune-100-Unternehmen zum zweitgrößten Computerunternehmen der Welt und Marktführer. Aus dem ehemaligen PC-Verkäufer ist ein Technologieführer und strategischer Unternehmenspartner geworden.

Compaq arbeitet mit einem Netzwerk von weltweit 100 000 Vermarktungspartnern zusammen und verfügt mit 29 000 eigenen IT-Experten sowie 60 000 Service-Mitarbeitern bei seinen Partnern über eine der größten Service- und Support-Organisationen der Welt.

Während der Hauptsitz in Houston, Texas, liegt, befindet sich die Zentrale diesseits des Atlantiks in Dornach bei München. Zirka 800 Mitarbeiter aus fast 30 Nationen steuern von hier aus sämtliche Aktivitäten von *Compaq Europa, Nahost und Afrika (EMEA);* das ist ein Gebiet, das sich von Finnland bis Südafrika und von Irland bis Russland erstreckt. Mehr als 22 000 Menschen erwirtschaften hier 40 % des gesamten Unternehmensumsatzes.

Neben kommerziellen Desktops, tragbaren Rechnern und PCs für den privaten Anwender bietet Compaq heute vor allem fehlertolerante, geschäftskritische Lösungen und Dienstleistungen im Bereich Informationstechnologie für Unternehmen jeder Größe an.

Compaqs Zielsetzungen sind, global der beste Computerpartner zu sein und bis zum Jahr 2000 weltweit die Nummer 1 im boomenden Internet-Geschäft zu werden.

Compaq – from PC dealer to leading technological enterprise and strategic business partner

In 1995, Compaq Computer Corporation became the largest manufacturer of Personal Computers in the world. A year later, the Company announced its intention to become one of the top three computer companies in the world by the turn of the century. Eighteen months ahead of that goal, following the acquisitions of Tandem and Digital Equipment Corporation, Compaq became the second largest computer company, while maintaining its position as the largest global supplier of personal computers.

These days, Compaq is far more than just a manufacturer of PCs. Compaq now develops and markets hardware, software, solutions, and services, including industry-leading enterprise computing solutions, fault-tolerant business-critical solutions, enterprise and network storage solutions, commercial desktop and portable products and consumer PCs. Compaq enables everyone from individual consumers to the largest corporations to experience the Internet, communicate and operate globally and take advantage of the latest in computing technology by being "open for business" 24 hours a day, seven days a week, 365 days a year.

The integration of the customer service organizations of Compaq, Tandem and Digital offered the unique combination of Compaq's high volume channel service approach, Tandem's mission-critical experience and Digital's multivendor and enterprise background.

The combined strengths, plus the capabilities and reach of Compaq's 25,000 reseller and service partners, have established the company as a powerful IT service provider. Compaq's service offerings now contribute 22 percent of overall EMEA business and are growing fast. The corporation's worldwide services mission is to become a $15 billion per year business by the year 2002 and number one or number two in the focused services segments of Network and Systems Integration Services (NSIS), Operations Management Services (OMS), and Customer Services.

Compaq Computer EMEA BV, headquartered in Munich, is responsible for all of the Company's operations across Europe, Middle East and Africa and accounted for more than $14 billion revenue in 1998. Compaq EMEA employs more than 21,000 people across the 360 locations in 95 countries.

Compaq – du vendeur de PC au chef de file en technologie et au partenaire stratégique d'entreprises

En 1995, Compaq devenait le plus grand constructeur d'ordinateurs à usage personnel. Un an plus tard, la société annonçait son intention de faire partie des 3 plus grands constructeurs d'ordinateurs d'ici l'an 2000. 18 mois avant l'échéance de cette date, après les acquisitions successives de Tandem et Digital, Compaq devenait No 2 dans ce domaine, et maintenait sa position de plus grand fournisseur d'ordinateurs destinés à usage personnel.

Désormais, Compaq est bien plus qu'un simple constructeur de PC's. Compaq maintenant développe et commercialise aussi du matériel informatique, des logiciels, toute une gamme de produits et services destinés au secteur de l'informatique. Compaq permet à chacun, consommateur individuel ou grande société, de se servir d'Internet, opère de façon globale, utilise les dernières technologies dans ce secteur en étant «ouvert pour le business» 24 heures sur 24, 7 jours sur 7, et 365 jours par an.

L'intégration des services à la clientèle de Compaq, Tandem et de Digital a permis de combiner de manière unique l'expertise de chacun: Compaq a apporté son savoir-faire dans les services à vastes réseaux de distribution, Tandem son expérience dans les applications critiques, et Digital son héritage auprès des vendeurs multiples.

Les forces combinées des 3 entreprises, ajoutées aux différentes capacités de chacune et à la performance de Compaq envers ses revendeurs et partenaires dans les services, ont permis à la société de devenir un puissant fournisseur de services en informatique. Ce que Compaq offre comme services contribue à 22 % du commerce total en Europe et ce chiffre augmente rapidement. La mission de la société est de devenir un «business» de $ 15 millards par an d'ici l'an 2002, et numéro un ou numéro deux dans les segments suivants: NSIS, OMS et Service Client.

Compaq Computer EMEA BV, dont le siège social est à Munich, est responsable des opérations de la société en Europe, au Moyen-Orient et en Afrique et représente plus de $ 14 millards de revenus en 1998. Compaq EMEA emploie plus de 21 000 personnes réparties dans 360 sites différents dans 95 pays.

Compaq – da venditore di PC a leader tecnologico e partner aziendale strategico

La Compaq Computer Corporation è stata fondata nel 1982. Con l'acquisizione della Digital Equipment Corporation nel giugno 1998 la Compaq, all'epoca una delle prime100 aziende nella classifica stilata della rivista «Fortune», è diventata la seconda maggiore impresa di computer del mondo e leader del mercato. Quella che un tempo era una semplice azienda venditrice di PC è diventata, così, un leader tecnologico ed un partner aziendale strategico.

La Compaq collabora con una rete di 100 000 partner di vendita sparsi in tutto il mondo e dispone, con i suoi 29 000 esperti di informatica ed i 60 000 dipendenti del servizio assistenza distribuiti presso i suoi partner commerciali, di una delle maggiori organizzazioni del mondo per quanto attiene i servizi di assistenza e di supporto tecnico.

Mentre la sede principale dell'azienda si trova a Houston, nel Texas, la centrale europea è situata a Dornach, nelle vicinanze di Monaco. Da qui circa 800 dipendenti provenienti da quasi 30 nazioni del mondo gestiscono tutte le attività di *Compaq Europa, Vicino Oriente e Africa (EMEA);* si tratta di un'area che si estende dalla Finlandia al Sudafrica e dall'Irlanda alla Russia. Più di 22 000 persone realizzano qui il 40 % dell'intero fatturato dell'azienda.

Oltre a desktop commerciali, calcolatori portatili e PC per l'utente privato, la Compaq offre oggi soprattutto soluzioni ad hoc e servizi nel settore dell'informatica applicata ad aziende di tutte le dimensioni.

L'obiettivo della Compaq è quello di essere il migliore partner informatico a livello globale e di diventare entro il 2000 il Numero 1 al mondo nella fornitura dei servizi Internet attualmente in forte espansione.

135

nikindustrie hat im Wirtschaftsraum München sein Auskommen. Wegen seiner in Europa führenden Stellung in diesen wichtigen Geschäftsfeldern ist München weltweit als „Isar Valley" bekannt. Dabei werden Jahr für Jahr Wachstumsraten von jeweils rund 8 % durch Zuzüge und Existenzgründungen erreicht.

In München stehen nicht nur die Konzernzentralen von Siemens, Siemens Nixdorf, Daimler-Chrysler Aerospace, Rohde & Schwarz. Viele weitere Global Players haben hier ihren europäischen oder deutschen Hauptsitz wie Apple, Compaq-DEC, Intel, Microsoft, Oracle, Silicon Graphics, Sun Microsystems und Texas Instruments. Kein weltweit agierendes Unternehmen dieser Branche kann es sich leisten, auf eine Münchner Adresse zu verzichten. Neben diesen Großunternehmen ist München aber insbesondere Zentrum für innovative Klein- und mittelständische Unternehmen.

Weitere stark vertretene Technologiefelder sind Luft- und Raumfahrttechnik, Medizintechnik, Energietechnik, Nachrichten- und Kommunikationstechnik, Mess-, Prüf-, Steuerungs- und Regelungstechnik, Umwelttechnik, Neue Werkstoffe sowie technologierelevante und wissensintensive Dienstleistungen.

Boombranche der Zukunft

Der Wirtschaftsstandort München ist auch führend in der Biotechnologie. Dies bestätigt der erste Platz im Wettbewerb „BioRegio" des Bundesforschungsministeriums (BMBF). Auf den Wurzeln der langjährigen Forschung ist der Raum München mit seinen zahlreichen Großunternehmen sowie der enormen Kapazität an Forschungsvolumen der größte Biotechnologiestandort Deutschlands und nach dem Großraum London die Nr. 2 in Europa. Zu den klangvollen Namen im Biotechnologiesektor zählen unter anderen Boehringer Mannheim, Bayer Diagnostics, Amgen, Bax-

BIOTECHNICAL CENTRE

nication engineering; mensuration, testing and control technology; environmental engineering; new materials; and technology-relevant, knowledge-intensive services.

A Booming Branch of the Future

The economic centre of Munich also leads in biotechnology, a fact which has been emphasized by Munich winning first place in the "Bio-Regio Competition" organized by the Federal Research Ministry (BMBF). Relying on a foundation of comprehensive research, Munich with its numerous large enterprises and its enormous research volume is at present Germany's biggest biotechnical centre, ranking second (after Greater London) in Europe. This sector comprises such renowned firms as Boehringer Mannheim; Bayer Diagnostics; Amgen; Baxter; Biomer; Bristol-Myers Squibb; Biogen; and Hoechst Marion Roussel. These enterprises and several other international firms based in Munich with its German headquarters employed more than 2,500 persons in this region in 1998. Since the introduction in 1996 of the "Bio^M AG" – an initiative for founding new companies which is promoted by the city – the number of biotechnical enterprises has doubled in the Munich area.

le matériel. En Allemagne, un employé sur dix dans le secteur de l'informatique et de l'électronique perçoit ses revenus de l'espace économique de Munich. Par sa position de leader en Europe dans ces domaines importants, Munich est connue mondialement comme la «Isar Valley». Chaque année, des taux de croissance de 8 % sont obtenus par des délocalisations et des créations d'entreprises.

A Munich, il n'y a pas seulement les sièges des groupes Siemens, Siemens Nixdorf, DaimlerChrysler Aerospace, Rhode & Schwarz. Beaucoup d'autres global players ont ici leur siège européen ou allemand comme Apple, Compaq-DEC, Intel, Microsoft, Oracle, Silicon Graphics, Sun Microsystems et Texas Instruments. Aucune entreprise de rang international et active dans ce secteur peut se permettre de ne pas être présente à Munich. Outre ces grandes entreprises, Munich est surtout le centre des petites et moyennes entreprises novatrices.

Les autres secteurs technologiques fortement représentés sont la technique aéronautique et aérospatiale, la technique médicale, la technique énergétique, la technique de l'information et de la communication, la métrologie, la technique d'essai, de commande et de réglage, la technique écologique, les nouvelles matières ainsi que les prestations inhérentes à la technologie et demandant des connaissances intenses.

Le secteur en plein boom de l'avenir

Le site économique de Munich arrive également en tête en biotechnologie. Cela est confirmé par la première place obtenue au concours «BioRegio» du ministère fédéral de la recherche. Basé sur une recherche existant depuis de nombreuses années, l'espace de Munich avec ses nombreuses grandes entreprises ainsi que son énorme capacité de volume de recherche est le site biotechno-

sua posizione di leader in Europa in questi importanti settori economici, Monaco è conosciuta in tutto il mondo con il nome di «Isar Valley», raggiungendo ogni anno tassi di incremento di circa l'8 % grazie a trasferimenti e costituzioni di nuove imprese.

A Monaco non si trovano solo le sedi centrali dei gruppi Siemens, Siemens Nixdorf, Daimler-Chrysler Aerospace e Rohde & Schwarz. Anche molti altri «global player», quali Apple, Compaq-DEC, Intel, Microsoft, Oracle, Silicon Graphics, Sun Microsystems e Texas Instruments hanno la loro sede principale tedesca in questa regione. Nessuna azienda operante in questo settore a livello mondiale può permettersi di rinunciare ad avere una propria sede a Monaco. Ma oltre a questi grandi gruppi, Monaco è un centro importante soprattutto per piccole e medie imprese innovative.

Altri settori tecnologici presenti qui in forma massiccia sono quelli delle tecniche applicate all'aeronautica e all'astronautica, alla medicina e all'energia, delle tecniche dell'informazione e delle comunicazioni in generale, di quelle impiegate negli strumenti di misurazione, controllo, comando e regolazione, infine i settori delle tecniche applicate alla protezione dell'ambiente, dei Nuovi Materiali e dei servizi in ambito tecnologico e scientifico.

Il settore del «boom» del futuro

Monaco è anche leader nel campo della biotecnologia. Ciò è confermato dal primo posto ottenuto al concorso «BioRegio» organizzato dal Ministero Federale per la Ricerca (BMBF). Grazie ai lunghi anni dedicati in passato alla ricerca, la regione di Monaco, con le numerose grandi aziende ivi presenti e l'enorme potenzialità di ricerca di cui dispone al momento, è la sede maggiore per la biotecnologia in Germania e la seconda in Europa dopo Londra. Alcuni dei grandi nomi nel settore della biotecnologia sono Boehrin-

Blick in eine Montagestation

View of a mounting station

Vue dans une station de montage

Una stazione di montaggio

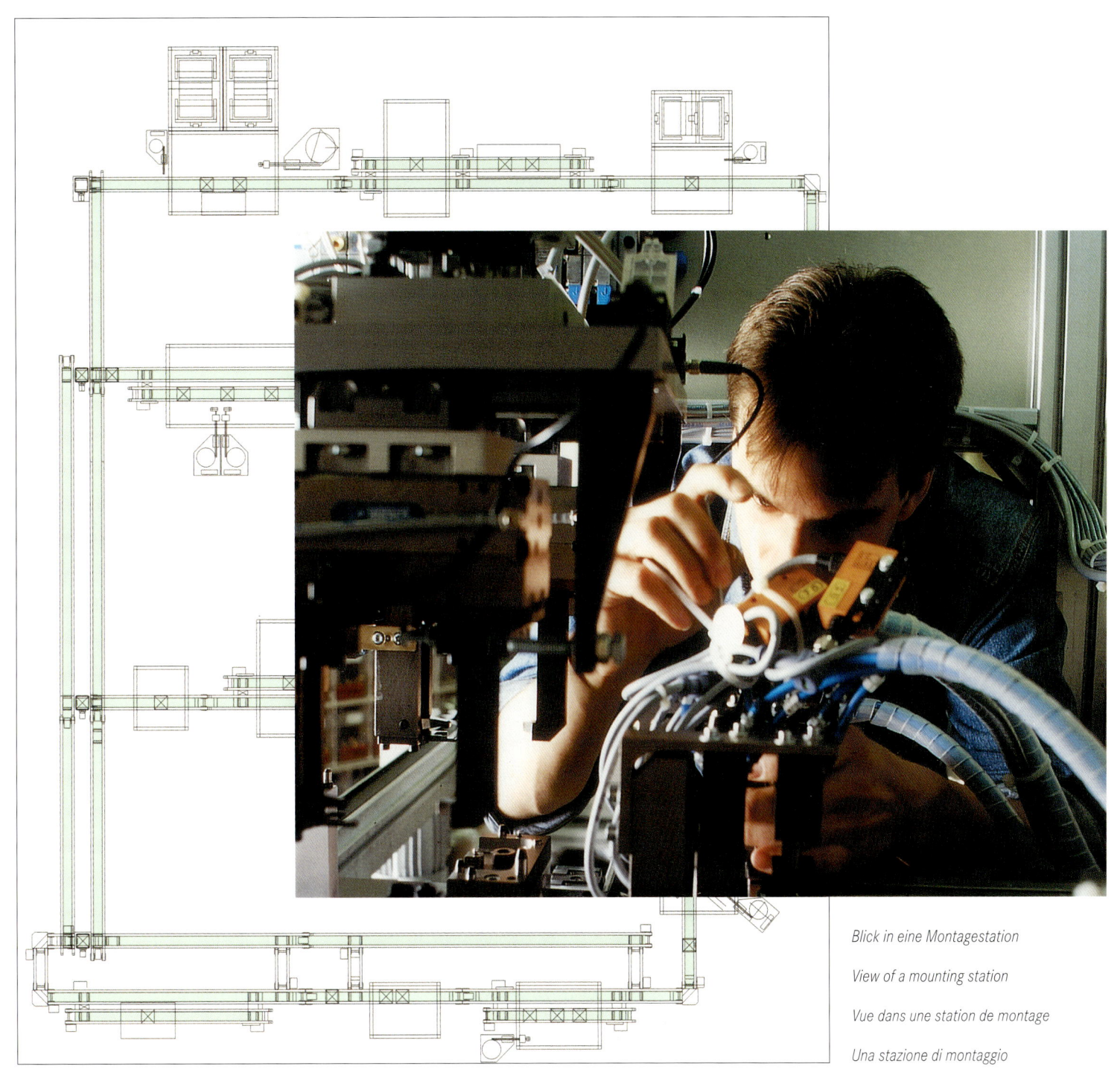

Rettinger Präzisions-Anlagenbau-München
Automatisierung nach Ihren Wünschen

Innovative technische Lösungen sind die Stärke des Unternehmens, das Spezialmaschinen für die Fertigungsautomatisierung, die Handhabungs-, Montage- und Messtechnik sowie Werksplanung anbietet. Nach Jahren kontinuierlichen Wachstums und umsichtiger Konsolidierung konnte sich die Johann Rettinger GmbH, wie sie seit 1985 firmiert, einen erheblichen Marktanteil in Deutschland sichern. Hauptkunden sind die Automobilzuliefer- und Elektroindustrie.

Rettinger Präzisions-Anlagenbau-München
Automation meeting your personal requirements

Innovative technical solutions are the strong point of this enterprise which offers special machines for production automation, for handling, mounting and measurement techniques, and plant layout. After years of continuous growth and careful consolidation, Johann Rettinger GmbH (as it has been called since 1985) was able to win a considerable share of the German market. Its main customers are suppliers of the automotive industry and the electrical industry.

Rettinger Präzisions-Anlagenbau-München
L'automatisation selon vos désirs

Des solutions techniques novatrices sont les atouts de cette entreprise qui propose des machines spéciales pour l'automatisation de la production, la technique de maniement, de montage et de mesure ainsi que la planification des ateliers. Après des années de croissance continue et de consolidation prudente, Johann Rettinger GmbH, le nom de la société depuis 1985, a pu s'assurer une part de marché considérable en Allemagne. Ses clients principaux sont les sous-traitants automobiles et l'industrie électrique.

Rettinger Präzisions-Anlagenbau-München
Automazione secondo i vostri desideri

Le soluzioni tecniche innovative costituiscono il punto di forza di questa azienda che propone macchinari speciali per l'automazione dei processi di produzione, per la tecnica della manipolazione, di montaggio e di misura, oltre alla progettazione completa di stabilimenti. Dopo anni di crescita continua e di avveduto consolidamento, la Johann Rettinger GmbH – questa la denominazione sociale dell'azienda dal 1985 – si è potuta assicurare una quota notevole del mercato tedesco. I suoi maggiori clienti sono l'indotto automobilistico e l'industria elettrotecnica.

ter, Biomer, Bristol-Myers Squibb, Biogen, Hoechst Marion Roussel. Diese und weitere internationale Unternehmen, die hier mit ihrem deutschen Hauptsitz vertreten sind, beschäftigten 1998 über 2 500 Arbeitnehmer in der Region. Seit dem Start der von der Stadt unterstützten Existenzgründungsinitiative Bio^M AG 1996 hat sich die Zahl der Biotechnologieunternehmen im Münchner Raum verdoppelt.

Gebündelte Offensiven für das dritte Jahrtausend

Die Bio^M AG ist bei weitem nicht die einzige Initiative, an der die Stadt beteiligt ist, um den Wirtschaftsstandort für die Herausforderungen des dritten Jahrtausends fit zu machen. Mit der *Software Offensive Bayern* will die Bayerische Staatsregierung in enger Zusammenarbeit mit Wirtschaft, Wissenschaft und Politik die Position Bayerns als führenden europäischen Standort für Entwicklung, Beratung und Vertrieb von Software durch die Schaffung eines sogenannten Software-Campus im Umfeld der Technischen Universität München weiter ausbauen. Ziel der *GründerRegio M* ist es, eine nachhaltige Gründerkultur an den Münchner Hochschulen und Forschungseinrichtungen durch die Integration von Coaching-, Qualifizierungs- und Beratungsangeboten für technologieorientierte Existenzgründungen zu etablieren. Der von der Unternehmensberatung

Combined Efforts and Strategies for the Third Millennium

Bio^M AG is certainly not the only initiative supported by the city which is to prepare Munich for the challenges of the third millennium. With the help of *"Software Offensive Bayern"* and in close cooperation with industry, science and politics the Bavarian state plans to secure and further improve Bavaria's position as a leading European location for the development, consulting and sale of software; for this purpose it will set up a so-called "software campus" in the vicinity of the Munich Polytechnic. The *"GründerRegio M"* aims at establishing an effective company-founding programme at Munich's universities and research facilities by integrating coaching, qualifying and advisory courses for technology-oriented entrepreneurs into their curriculum. The *"Münchner Businessplan-Wettbewerb" (Business Plan Competition),* first introduced in 1996/97 by the McKinsey & Company Inc. consulting firm as a joint project of Munich's universities and several other institutions, represents another important step taken in the same direction. Here one should emphasize the concept of a competition-immanent networking set up by experienced coaches, entrepreneurs and investors. This initiative concentrates on quickly growing enterprises of the hightech sector. Bavaria is investing DM three billion in the project *"Offensive Zukunft Bayern" (Future of Bavaria Offensive),* whose goal it is to secure the country's future as a hightech location. A package of concerted measures is to promote future-oriented further development in the scientific-technological sphere. Most of these projects will be carried out in Munich.

Incubators for Hightech Enterprises

The quantity and quality of innovative company foundings are

logique majeur d'Allemagne et, après la grande agglomération de Londres, le N° 2 européen. Parmi les noms célèbres du secteur de biotechnologie citons entre autres Boehringer Mannheim, Bayer Diagnostics, Amgen, Baxter, Biomer, Bristol-Myers Squibb, Biogen, Hoechst Marion Roussel. Ceux-ci tout comme d'autres entreprises internationales possédant ici leur siège allemand employaient en 1998 plus de 2 500 personnes dans la région. Depuis le commencement en 1996 de l'initiative Bio^M AG soutenue par la ville et portant sur les créations d'entreprises, le nombre des entreprises de biotechnologie a doublé dans l'espace munichois.

Des offensives communes pour le troisième millénaire

La Bio^M AG n'est absolument pas la seule initiative à laquelle participe la ville afin que le site économique soit prêt à affronter les défis du troisième millénaire. Avec la *Software Offensive Bayern*, le gouvernement bavarois, en coopération étroite avec l'économie, la science et la politique, veut affirmer la position de la Bavière comme site européen leader pour le développement, le conseil et la distribution de logiciel en créant un campus de logiciel dans le voisinage de l'Université Technique de Munich. L'objectif de la *GründerRegio M* est d'établir une culture permanente de créations d'entreprise dans les universités et les centres de recherche de Munich en intégrant des propositions de coaching, de qualification et de conseil pour les créateurs d'entreprise à caractère technologique. Le projet *Münchner Businessplan-Wettbewerb*, une initiative commune de la société conseil McKinsey & Company, Inc. comme projet commun des universités de Munich ainsi que de nombreuses autres institutions est un important pas dans cette direction. Il faut ici particulièrement souligner l'idée de l'augmentation de la compétitivité en

ger Mannheim, Bayer Diagnostics, Amgen, Baxter, Biomer, Bristol-Myers Squibb, Biogen e Hoechst Marion Roussel. In queste ed altre aziende internazionali, che hanno qui la loro sede principale tedesca, erano occupate nel 1998 oltre 2 500 abitanti della regione. Da quando ha preso avvio nel 1996 l'iniziativa per la creazione di nuove imprese in questo settore, chiamata Bio^M AG e che può contare sul supporto della città, il numero delle aziende operanti nel settore della biotecnologia nell'area di Monaco è raddoppiato.

Offensive coordinate per il terzo millennio

La Bio^M AG non è certo l'unica iniziativa alla quale la città partecipa per prepararsi ad affrontare le sfide del terzo millennio. Con la *«Software Offensive Bayern»*, il governo della Baviera intende ampliare ulteriormente la posizione della Baviera come sede europea per lo sviluppo, la consulenza e la commercializzazione di software operando in stretta collaborazione con economia, scienza e politica, e attraverso la creazione di un cosiddetto «Software-Campus» collegato al Politecnico di Monaco. L'obiettivo della *GründerRegio M* è di creare una forte cultura imprenditoriale nelle università e negli istituti di ricerca di Monaco attraverso l'integrazione di offerte di addestramento, qualificazione e consulenza per la costituzione di nuove imprese orientate verso il settore tecnologico. Il concorso *«Businessplan»* di Monaco, promosso per la prima volta nel 1996/97 dalla società di consulenza per imprese McKinsey & Company Inc. come progetto comune tra le università di Monaco e di molte altre istituzioni, può essere considerato come un passo importante in questa direzione. Deve essere messa qui in risalto soprattutto l'idea di creare una sinergia di istruttori, imprenditori e finanziatori, esperti ciascuno nel proprio campo. L'iniziativa punta sulle imprese in rapida espansione nel

BUSINESS SERVICES

◀ Ein Teil des Produktportfolios
Part of the product portfolio

Die **Firma Omega SEE Software Vertriebs GmbH** hat sich seit 1986 auf die Lokalisierung und Vermarktung ausgewählter Software und intelligenter PC-Lösungen in Zentraleuropa fokussiert.

Für die optimale Kundenbetreuung und bestmögliche technische Unterstützung bietet Omega SEE GmbH heute dem Markt folgende Produkte:

PowerQuest: DriveImage (professionelles Festplatten-Imaging und Duplizieren), Partition Magic (Festplattenpartitionen erstellen, verschieben, verändern), Lost & Found (Wiederherstellen verlorener Daten), Data Keeper (permanentes und automatisches Backup Ihrer Daten), Server Magic (Partitionierung von Novell-Server), Second Chance (Systemwiederherstellung per Mausklick)

Panda Antivirus Deutschland: Panda Platinum (umfassender Virenschutz für 24 h an 365 Tagen) insbesondere für Netzwerke und Internetanbindungen

Correx 2000: Jahr-2000-Prüfung und Problembehebung für das BIOS

Cybersitter: Organisation und Reporting der Arbeit im Internet.

Omega See GmbH ist ein dynamischer Unternehmensverbund mit den Abteilungen Vertrieb, Marketing und Support. Mit immer neuen innovativen Produkten bietet Omega SEE GmbH dem Markt ein umfassendes Angebot an Software sowie beste technische Unterstützung für Installation, Pflege und Weiterentwicklung der firmeninternen PC Landschaft. Die Kunden der Omega SEE GmbH in der Abteilung Direktvertrieb sind Firmen wie Adam Opel AG, Siemens Nixdorf Retail & Banking Systems GmbH, GRZ Nord, DeTeCSM GmbH u.v.a. In der Abteilung Fachhandelsbetreuung arbeitet Omega SEE GmbH mit dem Großhandel sowie Systemhäusern und technisch orientierten Kaufhausgruppen.

Gemeinsam mit den Partnern bietet Omega SEE GmbH ein durchdachtes Konzept im Bereich der PC Software sowie der Großrechneranbindung mit den Produkten von PowerQuest, Panda und Correx 2000.

Since 1986 the **Omega SEE Software Vertriebs GmbH** has specialized on the localization and sale of selected softwares and intelligent solutions for PCs in central Europe.

For optimal customer care and best technical support possible the Omega SEE GmbH offers the following products:

PowerQuest: DriveImage (professional hard disk imaging and duplicating), Partition Magic (creating, shifting and changing of hard disk partitions), Lost & Found (Retrieval of lost data), Data Keeper (constant and automatic backup of your data), Server Magic (partitioning of Novell Servers), Second Chance (restores the system with a mouse-click)

Panda Antivirus Deutschland: Panda Platinum (comprehensive virus protection around the clock every single day of the year) especially for networks and Internet hook-ups

Correx 2000: Year 2K check and problem solving for BIOS

Cybersitter: Organization and reporting of Internet work.

The Omega See GmbH is a dynamic association of businesses comprising the departments sales, marketing and support. Omega SEE GmbH constantly supplies the market with a comprehensive offer of new and innovative softwares as well as excellent technical support for installation, maintenance and development of the individual company's computer environment. Customers of Omega SEE GmbH's direct sales department include companies such as the Adam Opel AG, Siemens Nixdorf Retail & Banking Systems GmbH, GRZ Nord, DeTeCSM GmbH and many more. The department for the specialized trade services wholesalers as well as system stores and technology-minded department stores.

Together with its partners the Omega SEE GmbH offers smart concepts for PC softwares and with the products from PowerQuest, Panda and Correx 2000, hook-up to large-scale computers.

◀ Das Team in der Freizeit
The team off duty

Ende der sechziger Jahre gründeten die beiden renommierten Elektrokonzerne Robert Bosch in Stuttgart und Siemens AG in Berlin und München als Joint Venture die damalige Bosch-Siemens Hausgeräte GmbH. Das seit 1998 in **BSH Bosch und Siemens Hausgeräte GmbH** umfirmierte Unternehmen ist heute marktführend in Deutschland und Europa. Die Expansionsstrategie der BSH beinhaltet die Vision, im Konzert der Global Player das wettbewerbsstärkste und damit erfolgreichste Unternehmen der Weißen Ware-Branche zu werden. Neugründungen und Akquisitionen auf der ganzen Welt sind Beweis für den Erfolg dieses grenzüberschreitenden Handelns. Insgesamt erwirtschafteten in 1998 34 000 Mitarbeiter in 37 Werken 10,3 Milliarden Mark. Darüber hinaus garantiert ein dichtes Kundendienstnetz rund um den Globus schnelle und kompetente Hilfe, wo immer sie benötigt wird.

In the late 1960s the two renowned electrical groups Robert Bosch in Stuttgart and Siemens AG in Berlin and Munich founded the then Bosch-Siemens Hausgeräte AG as a joint venture. Today the enterprise – since 1998 renamed **BSH Bosch und Siemens Hausgeräte GmbH** – is a market leader in Germany and Europe. The firm's expansion strategy focuses on the BHS' becoming the most competitive and therefore most successful enterprise for electrical equipment in the "concert of global players". Newly founded companies and acquisitions throughout the world are evidence of the success of the firm's cross-border activities. In 1998 34,000 employees working in 37 plants achieved a turnover amounting to approximately DM 10.3 billion. Additionally, a dense network of customer services spanning the globe guarantees quick and efficient assistance wherever it is needed.

A la fin des années 60, les deux groupes d'électroménager renommés Robert Bosch à Stuttgart et Siemens AG à Berlin et Munich créèrent une joint venture qui s'appelait à l'époque la Bosch-Siemens Hausgeräte GmbH. Portant depuis 1998 le nom de **BSH Bosch und Siemens Hausgeräte GmbH**, l'entreprise est aujourd'hui leader en Allemagne et en Europe. La stratégie d'expansion de la BSH englobe la vision d'être dans le groupe des global players la société la plus concurrentielle et connaissant la plus grande réussite dans le secteur de l'électroménager. A l'échelon mondial, les nouvelles créations et les reprises d'entreprises prouvent le succès transfrontalier de cette société. En 1998, 34 000 collaborateurs travaillant dans les 37 usines réalisèrent un chiffre d'affaires de 10,3 milliards de DM. De plus, la densité du réseau de service après-vente à travers le monde garantit, chaque fois que le besoin s'en fait sentir, une aide rapide et compétente.

Era la fine degli anni Sessanta quando due rinomate aziende elettriche, la Robert Bosch di Stoccarda e la Siemens AG a Berlino e Monaco, decidevano di dare vita a una joint venture che avrebbe preso il nome di Bosch-Siemens Hausgeräte GmbH. La società, che nel 1998 ha cambiato la ragione sociale in **BSH Bosch und Siemens Hausgeräte GmbH**, é oggi leader sul mercato tedesco e più in generale su quello europeo. La strategia di espansione adottata dalla BSH si basa essenzialmente sulla visione di diventare l'azienda più forte e di successo a livello mondiale nel settore degli elettrodomestici. La costituzione di nuove società e la campagna di acquisizioni portata avanti a livello globale sono indice del successo di questa attività internazionale. Complessivamente, nel 1998, con una forza lavoro di 34 000 dipendenti distribuiti in 37 stabilimenti, l'azienda ha conseguito un utile di circa 10,3 miliardi di marchi. Oltre a ciò, la fitta rete di centri di assistenza tecnica ben distribuiti in tutto il mondo garantisce un servizio rapido e competente per rispondere a tutte le esigenze dei clienti.

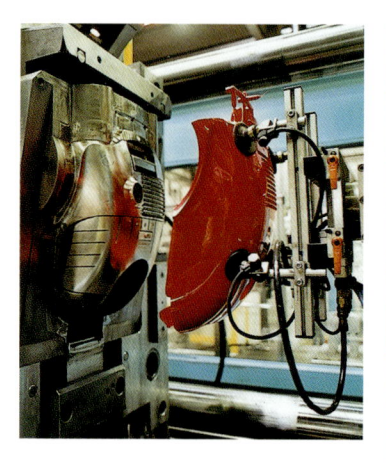

Modernste Produktionstechnik für Staubsauger in Bad Neustadt

Up-to-date: Hoover production in Bad Neustadt

La technique la plus moderne de production pour les aspirateurs à Bad Neustadt

La più moderna tecnica di produzione degli aspirapolveri a Bad Neustadt

Unsere Trocknerfabrik in Nauen gewährt Einblick in die moderne Technik eines Trockners.

Our factory in Nauen gives a view insight the modern technology of a dryer.

L'usine à Nauen donne un aperçu de la technique moderne d'un sèche-linge.

Nella fabbrica di lavatrici a Nauen si ha una visione della tecnica moderna di una lava-asciuga.

Eleganz und Funktionalität:
Das „Vario-Programm" von Gaggenau

Mit den Hauptmarken BOSCH und SIEMENS, den Spezialmarken CONSTRUCTA, GAGGENAU, NEFF und UFESA sowie 11 weiteren regionalen Marken verbinden unzählige Verbraucher hohe Qualität und Funktionalität sowie die Erfüllung ihrer Wünsche nach einem angenehmeren Leben.

Besonderes Engagement übernimmt die BSH GmbH im Rahmen ihres konzernweiten Umweltmanagements für ein umweltbewusstes und Ressourcen schonendes Wirtschaften.

Um das Ziel „best in class" zu erreichen, sollen die Mitarbeiter in einer veränderten Unternehmensstruktur der Eigenverantwortung und Innovationsfreude im Rahmen der so genannten top-Bewegung aktiv den Arbeitsprozess mitgestalten.

Elegance and functionality:
The "Vario-programme" of Gaggenau

For a great number of consumers the main brand names BOSCH and SIEMENS, the special trademarks of CONSTRUCTA, GAGGENAU, NEFF, and UFESA, and 11 further regional trademarks stand not only for top-quality and functionality, but also for the fulfillment of their longing for a more pleasant and comfortable life.

BSH GmbH concentrates particularly on environment-friendly and resource-friendly operation within the sphere of its group-wide management.

To reach the company's goal of becoming "the best in class" the employees are encouraged to contribute actively to the working process in a changed company structure relying on individual responsibility and an innovative attitude – within the scope of so-called "top-movement".

Elégance et fonctionnalité:
Le «programme Vario» de Gaggenau

Les marques principales BOSCH et SIEMENS, les marques spécialisées CONSTRUCTA, GAGGENAU, NEFF et UFESA ainsi que 11 marques supplémentaires régionales proposent à de nombreux clients une qualité et une fonctionnalité élevées et répondent à leur désir d'une vie plus agréable.

Dans le cadre du management écologique au sein du groupe, la BSH GmbH s'engage tout particulièrement pour une économie écologique et protégeant les ressources.

Afin d'atteindre l'objectif de «best in class», les collaborateurs doivent activement participer, dans le cadre du mouvement «top», à la conception des procédés de travail dans une structure d'entreprise changée au niveau de l'auto-responsabilité et du plaisir d'innovation.

Eleganza e funzionalità:
Il «Programma Vario» di Gaggenau

Grazie all'unione tra i marchi principali BOSCH e SIEMENS e i marchi speciali CONSTRUCTA, GAGGENAU, NEFF e UFESA, ai quali vanno ad aggiungersi altri 11 marchi regionali, un numero elevatissimo di consumatori può sempre contare su prodotti di alta qualità e perfetta funzionalità che offrono la comodità tanto desiderata.

La BSH GmbH è inoltre impegnata nell'ambito della tutela ambientale che viene attesa come impegno di tutta l'azienda, per favorire un'economia più rispettosa dell'ambiente e delle risorse naturali.

Al fine di raggiungere l'obiettivo «best in class», ai collaboratori é chiesto di partecipare in modo attivo alla configurazione del processo di lavoro, operando all'interno di una struttura aziendale nuova che si basa sulla responsabilità individuale e sull'innovazione nell'ambito del cosiddetto «top-movement».

McKinsey & Company, Inc. als Gemeinschaftsprojekt der Münchner Hochschulen sowie vieler weiterer Institutionen 1996/97 erstmalig initiierte *Münchener Businessplan-Wettbewerb* gilt als wichtiger Schritt in diese Richtung. Hervorzuheben ist hierbei vor allem der Gedanke der wettbewerbsimanenten Vernetzung durch erfahrene Coaches, Unternehmer und Kapitalgeber. Die Initiative zielt auf schnell wachsende Unternehmen im Hightech-Bereich ab. Rund drei Milliarden Mark investiert das Land im Rahmen seines Konzeptes *Offensive Zukunft Bayern* in die Zukunft Bayerns als Hightech-Standort. Ein Bündel gezielter Maßnahmen soll die zukunftsorientierte Weiterentwicklung im wissenschaftlich-technologischen Bereich fördern. Der größte Teil dieser Projekte wird im Wirtschaftsraum München realisiert.

Brutkästen für Hightech-Unternehmen

Voraussetzung für den langfristigen Erfolg eines Wirtschaftsstandortes sind Quantität und Qualität innovativer Unternehmensgründungen. Die Aussage, die Erfolgsstory von Apple wäre in Deutschland wegen restriktiver Bau- und Gewerbeordnungen nicht möglich gewesen, trifft zumindest auf München nicht zu. Denn Landeshauptstadt und Freistaat bieten mit ihren Gründerzentren den optimalen Nährboden. Das MTZ-Münchner Technologiezentrum mit seinem Full-Service erweist sich seit Jahren als idealer „Durchlauferhitzer" für Existenzgründer und Forschergruppen, insbesondere der Informations- und Kommunikationstechnologie. Aus allen Nähten platzt auch das IZB-Innovations- und Gründerzentrum Biotechnologie in Martinsried, so dass es laufend erweitert werden muss. Mit zielgenauer Infrastruktur für junge innovative Unternehmen der Biotechnologie ausgestattet, liegt es

RESEARCH CENTRE

preconditions for an economic centre's lasting success. The statement that the Apple success story could not have taken place in Germany owing to restrictive building and business regulations does not apply to Munich. For the Bavarian capital and the Free State of Bavaria provide an excellent breeding ground in their founding centres. The Munich Technology Center (MTZ) with its full service programme has for years proved to be a perfect "flow heater" for company founders and research groups – particularly for the branches of information and communication technology. But also the "IZB" (Innovation and Founding Centre Biotechnology) in Martinsried is expanding so rapidly that it must be enlarged continuously. Furnished with an infrastructure exactly suited to young innovative entrepreneurs in the field of biotechnology, this centre is located in the immediate vicinity of the biomedical campus.

Science and research

The status of the hightech region of Munich is based on an exceptional infrastructure. The first asset to be mentioned is the university and research landscape which is unique in all of Germany. Thus Munich is regarded as Germany's science capital.

More than 100,000 students are registered in Munich's ten universities and "Fachhochschu-

faisant jouer ensemble coaches, entreprises et investisseurs expérimentés. L'initiative vise des entreprises à croissance rapide actives dans le domaine de la haute technologie. Dans le cadre de son concept *Offensive Zukunft Bayern*, le land investit environ trois milliards dans l'avenir de la Bavière comme site de la haute technologie. Un paquet de mesures doit promouvoir le développement futur dans le secteur scientifique et technologique. La majeure partie de ces projets est réalisée dans l'espace économique de Munich.

Des incubateurs pour les entreprises de haute technologie

La durée du succès d'un site économique est conditionnée par la quantité et la qualité des créations d'entreprises novatrices. Les propos selon lesquels l'histoire du succès de Apple n'aurait pas été possible en Allemagne en raison d'une réglementation restrictive sur la construction et le code de législation industriel, ne concernent tout au moins pas Munich. Car la capitale de Bavière et l'Etat libre de Bavière offrent, grâce à leurs centres de créations d'entreprise, un terrain optimal. Avec sa palette complète de services, le centre de technologie de Munich, MTZ-Münchner Technologiezentrum s'avère depuis des années la première étape idéale pour les créateurs d'entreprise et les groupes de recherche, en particulier dans la technologie d'information et de communication. A Martinsried, le centre d'innovation et de création d'entreprise de biotechnologie, IZB, est plein à craquer et doit être constamment agrandi. Doté d'une infrastructure optimale pour de jeunes entreprises novatrices de la biotechnologie, il est situé à proximité immédiate du campus de biomédecine.

settore dell'alta tecnologia. La Baviera ha investito circa tre miliardi di marchi nel progetto *«Offensive Zukunft Bayern»* (Offensiva per il futuro della Baviera) che si pone come obiettivo l'affermazione del Land bavarese come sede dell'industria high-tech. Sarà inoltre messa in atto una serie di misure mirate per promuovere lo sviluppo futuro nel settore tecnologico-scientifico. La maggior parte di questi progetti sarà realizzata nell'area economica di Monaco.

Incubatrici per aziende high-tech

Le premesse per un successo a lungo termine di un'area industriale sono la quantità e la qualità delle imprese innovative presenti sul territorio. Quanto si racconta della storia del successo della Apple, ovvero del fatto che non sarebbe stato possibile in Germania a causa della legislazione troppo restrittiva in materia di edilizia e impresa, non trova riscontro almeno per quanto riguarda Monaco. In quanto la capitale bavarese e il Land stesso offrono il terreno ottimale per la fondazione di nuove imprese grazie alla possibilità di rivolgersi a dei centri per l'avviamento di nuove imprese. Il Centro per le Tecnologie di Monaco (MTZ) si dimostra da anni, grazie al suo servizio di assistenza completa, come il partner ideale per nuovi soggetti imprenditoriali e gruppi di ricerca, soprattutto nel settore delle tecnologie dell'informatica e delle telecomunicazioni. Sta letteralmente scoppiando anche il Centro per l'Avviamento e l'Innovazione nel settore della Biotecnologia (IZB) a Martinsried, tanto che deve essere continuamente ampliato. Quest'ultimo è dotato di un'infrastruttura mirata per giovani imprese innovative del settore della biotecnologia e si trova nelle immediate vicinanze del campus per la biomedicina.

Die EMPRISE Consulting München GmbH

Die EMPRISE Consulting München GmbH gehört zur EMPRISE Unternehmensgruppe. Ihr Erfolg beruht auf einem ganzheitlichen Beratungsansatz, der zu optimalen Lösungen führt:

- Internet Geschäftsprozessoptimierung (IGPO) - die effiziente Gestaltung und optimale Abstimmung von Geschäftsprozessen

- Veränderungsmanagement zur frühzeitigen Berücksichtigung der Wirkung innovativen Lösungsdesigns auf Anwender und Kunden

- Überzeugende und bessere Lösungen durch systematische Zusammenführung von Datenverarbeitung und Kommunikation

Ihr Nutzen - Solutions for tomorrow

Der Kunde steht im Mittelpunkt unseres Handelns. Seine Zufriedenheit und die Steigerung seines Unternehmenserfolges ist unsere Zielsetzung. Um unserem Anspruch, „soviel Individualität wie nötig, soviel Standard wie möglich", gerecht zu werden, kooperieren wir mit ausgewählten Technologielieferanten.

Unsere Ziele erreichen wir durch:

- Innovation und Qualität auf höchstem Niveau
- Erhebliche Reduzierung der Prozessdurchlaufzeiten und -kosten
- Lösungsdesign mit hoher Akzeptanz
- Erhöhten Nutzen durch die Zusammenführung von Sprache und Daten

Die EMPRISE Unternehmensgruppe

Ein signifikantes Merkmal des IT-Marktes ist sein rasanter Wandel. Doch weitaus rascher verändert sich die EMPRISE Unternehmensgruppe. Weil wir eingefahrene Wege verlassen, innovative Lösungen konsequent umsetzen und Trends in der Internet-Technologie forcieren. Jahr für Jahr erzielen wir ein Wachstum, das deutlich über der Entwicklung des Marktes liegt. Heute sind wir mit über 300 Mitarbeitern an 7 Standorten in Deutschland, der Schweiz und England vertreten. Und wir wachsen mit innovativen Geschäftsideen weiter:

Internet-Systemintegration, Hochgeschwindigkeits-Funktechnik sowie die Entwicklung innovativer Software und e-Commerce-Lösungen sind Bestandteil unseres Portfolios.

EMPRISE Consulting München GmbH

EMPRISE Consulting München GmbH is part of the EMPRISE GROUP AG. The holistic consulting services approach is part of its success. Excellent solutions are generated by:

- Internet Business Process Reengineering (IBPR) - the efficient design and fine-tuning of business processes

- Change Management to ensure early participation of customers as well as end users. Change Management also generates higher acceptance of innovative application design.

- Convincing integration of Information and Communication Technology improves application efficiency and usability

Your Advantage - Solutions for tomorrow

Emprise Consulting München GmbH is customer driven. Our goal is customer satisfaction. Our pride is excellence in improving our customers performance.

We cooperate with leading technology suppliers to meet our aspiration "as much individuality as neccessary, as much open standards as possible".

We achieve our objectives

- with innovation und excellent quality
- by significantly reducing process time and cost
- with highly accepted design and solutions
- by combining voice and data in a single application

The EMPRISE Group

One of the significant characteristics of the IT market is its rapid change. However faster is the change of the EMPRISE Group. We do not follow trotten paths but create consistently innovative solutions and actively shape the Internet technology market. Our annual results grow steadily, always outperforming the market. Today we employ more than 300 people in seven locations in Germany, Switzerland and United Kingdom and we continue to grow. You can expect innovative solutions in the following areas:

Internet-System-Integration, High speed wirelss technology, Client/Server Software, eCommerce Solutions

MAN Nutzfahrzeuge,
mit Wasserstoff sauber in die Zukunft. „Wasserstoffbusse" am Flughafen München fahren nahezu schadstofffrei.

MAN Nutzfahrzeuge,
a clean-burning fuel for the buses of tomorrow. Shown is a hydrogen-powered bus in operation at Munich Airport. The bus emits virtually no pollutants.

MAN Nutzfahrzeuge,
des véhicules utilitaires, fonctionnant à l'hydrogène et assurant un avenir propre. Des «bus à l'hydrogène» à l'aéroport de Munich roulent sans presque émettre de polluants.

MAN Nutzfahrzeuge,
veicoli industriali ad idrogeno, il motore del futuro. Gli «autobus ad idrogeno» dell' aeroporto di Monaco di Baviera funzionano senza quasi emettere gas nocivi.

Zwei von vier Schiffsgetrieben in Leichtbauweise für eine schnelle Katamaran-Fähre in Australien, Gesamtleistung 28 320 kW. **RENK** bietet Antriebstechnik für höchste Leistungen. Zum Beispiel ist das Unternehmen Weltmarktführer bei automatischen Kettenfahrzeuggetrieben und Gleitlagern.

Two of four marine gear units of leightweight design for a fast catamaran ferry in Australia, total power 28,320 kW. **RENK** offers propulsion technology for maximum performances. The enterprise is for example leader on the world market for automatic tracked vehicle transmissions and slide bearings.

Deux de quatre réducteurs marins de construction légère pour un catamaran ferryboat rapide en Australie, puissance totale 28 320 kW. **RENK** offre de la technologie de propulsion pour des rendements maximaux. L'entreprise est par exemple leader sur le marché mondial pour des transmissions automatiques de véhicules chenillées et paliers lisses.

Due di quattro riduttori navali di costruzione leggera per un catamarano traghetto veloce in Australia, potenza totale 28 320 kW. **RENK** offre una tecnologia di propulsione per rendimenti massimi. L'impresa è per esempio leader sul mercato mondiale per trasmissioni automatiche di veicoli a catena e cuscinetti di scivolamento.

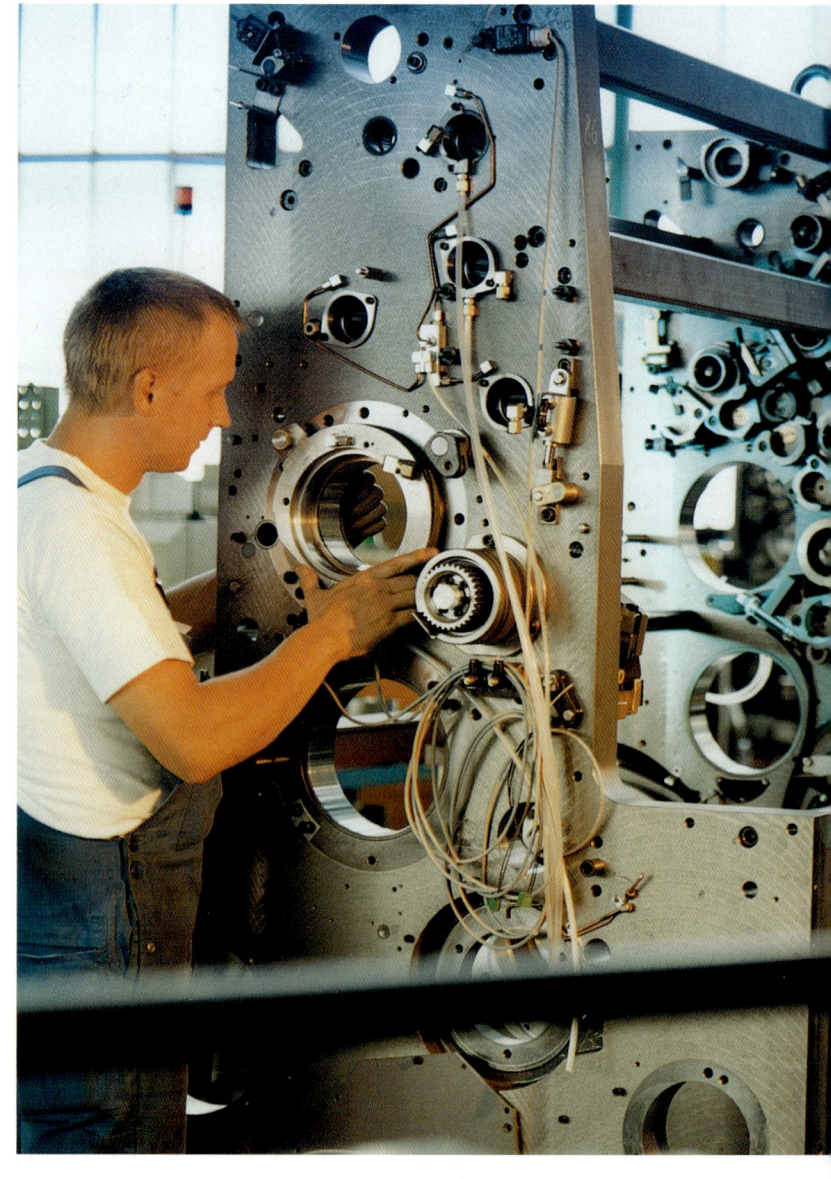

Motor 6L50MC aus Frederikshavn. Über 80 Millionen PS aus 5 250 Motoren sind die beeindruckende Verkaufsbilanz der MC-Baureihe der **MAN B&W Diesel**.

This 6L50MC engine was produced at our facilities in Frederikshavn. The **MAN B&W Diesel** *MC line of engines has put together some very impressive figures. 5,250 engines have been sold. Their collective output: more than 80 million HP.*

Le moteur 6L50MC de Frederikshavn. Plus de 80 millions de CH de 5 250 moteurs sont les chiffres de vente impressionnants de la série MC de **MAN B&W Diesel**.

Motore 6L50MC prodotto a Frederikshavn. Più di 80 milioni di CV prodotti da 5 250 motori sono il bilancio impressionante delle vendite della Serie MC della **MAN B&W Diesel**.

Montage der „Roland 700" in Offenbach. „Jeder kann jedem in die Karten sehen" – Motto und Ergebnis einer tiefgreifenden Veränderung der Arbeitsorganisation bei **MAN Roland Druckmaschinen**. *Die Transparenz von Abteilungs- und Prozessverantwortung mittels Vernetzung ist Ziel des Projekts „Vom Zulieferer zum Systempartner".*

The "Roland 700" model printing press is assembled at our facility in Offenbach. "Everyone knows – and can see – what everybody else is doing." And that's thanks to the changes made in how **MAN Roland Druckmaschinen** *operates, changes which have networked every department and every area of responsibility into a unified entity. Objective of these changes: the transforming of MAN Roland from a supplier into a partner providing entire systems.*

Montage du «Roland 700» à Offenbach. Ici, on joue cartes sur table – le slogan et le résultat d'une mutation profonde de l'organisation du travail chez **MAN Roland Druckmaschinen**. *La transparence de la responsabilité des départements et des processus au moyen d'une mise en réseau est le but du projet «Du sous-traitant au partenaire système».*

Montaggio della «Roland 700» ad Offenbach. «Ognuno può vedere le carte dell'altro» – questo lo slogan ed il risultato di un profondo cambiamento nell'organizzazione del lavoro alla **MAN Roland Druckmaschinen**. *La trasparenza nella ripartizione delle responsabilità di reparto e di produzione mediante collegamenti in rete è l'obiettivo del progetto «Da fornitore a partner di sistema».*

Produktionsanteil 14 %. **MAN Technologie** *ist heute der größte deutsche und außerhalb Frankreichs der bedeutendste Zulieferer für das ARIANE-5-Programm. Für den Bau des Raumfahrtbahnhofs ELA 3 in Kourou/Französisch-Guyana war MAN Technologie als Generalunternehmer verantwortlich. MAN-Fahrzeuge transportieren die Raketen zum Startplatz.*

14 % of all products supplied to the ARIANE 5 program stem from **MAN Technologie**, *making the company the largest supplier in Germany and the most important one outside of France. MAN Technologie was the general contractor handling the construction of the ELA 3 space station, located in Kourou, French Guyana. MAN-made vehicles transport the rockets to their launching pad.*

Pourcentage à la production: 14 %. **MAN Technologie** *est aujourd'hui le sous-traitant allemand majeur et, en dehors de la France, le plus important du programme ARIANE 5. Pour la construction de la gare aérospatiale ELA 3 à Kourou/Guyane française, MAN Technologie était responsable en tant qu'entreprise générale. Les véhicules MAN transportent les fusées jusqu'au point de lancement.*

Una quota di produzione del 14 %. **MAN Technologie** *è oggi il maggiore fornitore tedesco del programma ARIANE 5 e il più importante al di fuori della Francia. La MAN Technologie è stata capocommessa nell'esecuzione dei lavori di costruzione del centro spaziale ELA 3 di Kourou nella Guiana francese. I veicoli MAN effettuano il trasporto dei razzi alla piattaforma di lancio.*

in unmittelbarer Nachbarschaft des biomedizinischen Campus'.

Wissenschaft und Forschung

Basis der Hightech-Region München ist eine hervorragende Infrastruktur. An erster Stelle sei hier die in Deutschland einzigartige Hochschul- und Forschungslandschaft genannt. So gilt München als Wissenschaftshauptstadt Deutschlands.

In den zehn Münchner Universitäten und (Fach-)Hochschulen sind über 100 000 Studenten eingeschrieben, davon rund 20 % in naturwissenschaftlich-technischen Studiengängen. Der Freistaat Bayern baut die deutsche Spitzenposition Münchens mit hohen Investitionen aus, um sie trotz des immer härter werdenden internationalen Wettbewerbs zu sichern. Auf dem naturwissenschaftlich-technischen Campus in Garching verfügt die Technische Universität München über die modernste Maschinenbaufakultät Europas. Die dort in Bau befindliche politisch umstrittene Neutronenquelle wird der Grundlagenforschung insbesondere bei der Entwicklung neuer Materialien zusätzliche Impulse verleihen. In Großhadern-Martinsried wächst zügig das neue biomedizinische Zentrum der Ludwig-Maximilians-Universität, welches das Life-Sciences-Zentrum Freising-Weihenstephan hervorragend ergänzt.

Neben der Generalverwaltung der Max-Planck-Gesellschaft sowie fünf ihrer naturwissenschaftlichen Institute und der Zentralverwaltung der Fraunhofer-Gesellschaft, len" (institutes of higher learning), about 20% of them being enrolled in courses of natural science and technology. The Free State of Bavaria has persistently supported Munich's leading position in Germany by means of generous funding in order to secure this significant rank in spite of increasing international competition. With the scientific-technical campus in Garching the Munich Polytechnic owns Europe's most modern faculty for machine construction. The neutron source, which is still under construction there and has caused considerable political controversies, will provide additional stimuli – particularly in the development of new materials. In Großhadern-Martinsried the new biomedical centre of the Ludwig-Maximilians-Universität is taking shape, which will be an ideal complement to the Centre of Life Sciences in Freising-Weihenstephan.

Not only the main administration of the Max-Planck-Gesellschaft with five of its naturalscience institutes and the central administration of the Fraunhofer-Gesellschaft and two of its institutes of natural Science as well as the Fraunhofer Management Gesellschaft are based in the region of Munich, but also the GSF-Forschungszentrum Umwelt und Gesundheit GmbH (Research Centre for Environment and Health) and the DLR Deutsches Zentrum für Luft- und Raumfahrt e.V. (German Centre for Aviation and Space Travel), employing approximately 6,000 persons.

Additionally, Munich is a leading centre for research and development of private business. In addition to Siemens and BMW, where more than 20,000 people conduct research and development, we should also mention DaimlerChrysler Aerospace (DASA), IBM, Krauss-Maffei, MAN-Technology, Rohde & Schwarz, and Kraft-Jakobs-Suchard.

In addition to other institutions, 15 technology transfer points at the universities, the Fachhochschule and the Cham-

La science et la recherche

La région de la haute technologie de Munich se base sur son excellente infrastructure. Citons ici en premier l'extraordinaire constellation d'universités et de recherche. Ainsi, Munich est la capitale scientifique de l'Allemagne.

Les dix universités et écoles supérieures (de technologie) de Munich comptent plus de 100 000 étudiants dont 20 % dans des filières Sciences naturelles et Technique. L'Etat libre de Bavière étaye l'excellente position de Munich en Allemagne avec de forts investissements pour la prémunir contre la concurrence internationale de plus en plus aiguë. A Garching, sur le campus scientifique et technique, l'université technique de Munich dispose de la faculté de construction mécanique la plus moderne d'Europe. La source de neutrons en cours de construction et donnant lieu à de nombreuses polémiques apportera de nouvelles impulsions à la recherche fondamentale surtout au niveau du développement de nouvelles matières. A Großhadern-Martinsried, le nouveau centre biomédical de l'université Ludwig Maximilian grandit rapidement et s'avère un complément idéal au centre Life-Sciences de Freising-Weihenstephan.

Outre l'administration centrale de la société Max Planck et cinq de ses instituts de sciences naturelles, l'administration centrale de la société Fraunhofer et deux de ses instituts de sciences naturelles ainsi que la société Fraunhofer Management, la région de Munich abrite également le centre de recherche sur l'environnement et la santé GSF-Forschungszentrum Umwelt und Gesundheit GmbH et le DLR Deutsches Zentrum für Luft- und Raumfahrt e.V. (centre allemand de l'aéronautique et l'aérospatial) qui emploie 6 000 personnes.

Munich est en plus un centre leader pour la recherche et le développement de l'économie privée. Outre Siemens et BMW où plus de 20 000 collaborateurs se

Scienza e ricerca

Il fondamento su cui si basa la regione di Monaco come area specializzata nell'alta tecnologia è un'infrastruttura eccellente. È opportuno ricordare in primo luogo la presenza di università ed istituti di ricerca unica nel suo genere in Germania e che fa di Monaco la capitale tedesca delle scienze.

Nelle dieci università di Monaco (compresi gli Istituti Tecnici e il Politecnico) sono iscritti più di 100 000 studenti, di cui circa il 20 % ha scelto un indirizzo tecnico-naturalistico (tecnica applicata alle scienze naturali). La Baviera sta rafforzando con notevoli investimenti la posizione di punta che Monaco ha saputo conquistarsi a livello nazionale, in modo tale da salvaguardare il suo primato economico nonostante il fatto che la concorrenza internazionale si stia facendo sempre più agguerrita. L'Università tecnica di Monaco dispone della facoltà di Ingegneria Meccanica più moderna d'Europa, e che si trova fisicamente nel campus per le scienze tecnico-naturalistiche di Garching. Il reattore che si trova oggi in fase di costruzione presso questo campus, nonostante il progetto sia stato contestato politicamente, darà nuovi impulsi alla ricerca basilare, soprattutto per quanto riguarda lo sviluppo di nuovi materiali. A Großhadern-Martinsried si lavora rapidamente alla realizzazione del Centro per la Biomedicina dell'Università Ludwig Maximilian che andrà a completare in modo perfetto il Centro di Scienze Naturali di Freising-Weihenstephan.

Oltre all'amministrazione generale della Max-Planck Gesellschaft, inclusi cinque dei suoi istituti per le scienze naturali, e all'amministrazione centrale della Fraunhofer Gesellschaft, inclusi due dei suoi istituti per le scienze naturali e la Fraunhofer Management Gesellschaft, hanno la loro sede nella regione di Monaco anche il GSF-Forschungszentrum Umwelt und Gesundheit GmbH (Centro di Ricerche GSF per

ENTWICKLUNG

Die **IABG Industrieanlagen-Betriebsgesellschaft mbH** in Ottobrunn ist ein führendes technisches Dienstleistungsunternehmen in Europa. Auf der Grundlage jahrzehntelanger Erfahrung und unter dem Einsatz moderner Werkzeuge analysieren und lösen wir technische, wirtschaftliche und planerische Aufgabenstellungen. Unsere Kunden aus Wirtschaft und Behörden schätzen uns als unabhängigen Partner für innovative systemtechnische Dienstleistungen mit hoher Qualität. Dabei reicht unser Angebotsspektrum von Beratung, Forschung und Analysen über Simulation und Test bis zur Systemintegration. Das Ergebnis unserer Arbeit sind ganzheitliche Lösungen in den zukunftsorientierten Bereichen Information und Kommunikation, Luft- und Raumfahrt, Verteidigung, Umwelt- und Managementsysteme, Verkehr sowie Fertigung und Logistik.

IABG Industrieanlagen-Betriebsgesellschaft mbH in Ottobrunn is one of Europe's leading technological service enterprises. Backed by several decades of experience and by ultra-modern facilities, we analyse and solve technical, economic and planning problems. Our customers from industry and the public sector appreciate us as inpartial partners for top-grade innovative systems engineering services. Our programme comprises everything from consulting, research and analyses to simulation, tests and system integration. The results of our efforts are complete solutions in such future-oriented fields as information technology and communications, aerospace, defence, environment and management systems, transportation, manufacturing and logistics.

La société **IABG Industrieanlagen-Betriebsgesellschaft mbH** sise à Ottobrunn est une des sociétés leader en services techniques en Europe. Sur la base d'une expérience gagnée pendant des dizaines d'années et l'utilisation d'outils modernes, nous analysons des problèmes dans le domaine de la technique, de l'économie et de la conception et en apportons des solutions. Nos clients du secteur économique ou administratif, nous apprécient en tant que partenaire indépendant en ce qui concerne les services innovatifs d'une grande qualité relatifs à l'ingénierie de systèmes. La gamme des services que nous vous proposons ne comprend pas seulement la consultation, la recherche et les analyses mais aussi les simulations, les essais et l'intégration de systèmes. Par notre travail, nous vous proposons des solutions globales dans les domaines d'avenir comme l'information et la communication, l'aéronautique et l'astronautique, la défense, les systèmes de l'environnement et les systèmes de gestion, les transports, la fabrication et la logistique.

La **IABG Industrieanlagen-Betriebsgesellschaft mbH** è un'azienda di servizi leader in Europa per il campo tecnico. Sulla base della nostra esperienza decennale e grazie all'impiego di attrezzature estremamente moderne, analizziamo e risolviamo problemi tecnici, economici e di programmazione. I nostri clienti provengono dal mondo dell'economia e delle istituzioni e ci stimano quali partner indipendenti in grado di offrire servizi integrati innovativi e di alta qualità. Il raggio della nostra offerta comprende servizi di consulenza, ricerca e analisi mediante simulazione e test fino ad arrivare ad una completa integrazione di sistema. Il risultato del nostro lavoro è rappresentato da soluzioni complessive nei settori di maggiore possibilità di sviluppo quali quello dell'informazione e della comunicazione, dell'aeronautica e delle imprese spaziali, della difesa, dei sistemi ambientali e di gestione, del traffico, della produzione e della logistica.

zwei ihrer naturwissenschaftlichen Institute sowie der Fraunhofer Management Gesellschaft sind in der Region München auch das GSF-Forschungszentrum Umwelt und Gesundheit GmbH und die DLR Deutsches Zentrum für Luft- und Raumfahrt e. V. mit rund 6 000 Beschäftigten ansässig.

Zudem ist München ein führendes Zentrum für Forschung und Entwicklung der Privatwirtschaft. Hervorzuheben sind außer Siemens und BMW, bei denen über 20 000 Mitarbeiter in München forschen und entwickeln, auch DaimlerChrysler Aerospace (DASA), IBM, Krauss-Maffei, MAN-Technologie, Rohde & Schwarz sowie Kraft-Jakobs-Suchard.

Für eine intensive Kooperation zwischen Forschung und Wirtschaft sorgen neben anderen Institutionen allein 15 Technologietransferstellen bei den Universitäten, der Fachhochschule und den Wirtschaftskammern, die im Technologie-Transfer-Verbund Oberbayern zusammenarbeiten.

Technologiemessen München

Einen weiteren Kristallisationspunkt der Hightech-Branchen bildet die Münchner Messe. Mit den Veranstaltungen SYSTEMS, SEMICON, Produktronica, electronica, LASER, Analytica, Ceramitec, IFAT und Drinktec/Interbrau, die das Ziel von über einer halben Million Fachbesuchern und mehr als 11 000 Ausstellern aus über 100 Staaten sind, zählt sie zu den führenden Standorten internationaler Technologiemessen. Von dem Zusammenspiel zwischen der Neuen Messe in Riem und dem Internationalen Congresszentrum München (ICM) einerseits sowie den Hightech-Unternehmen der Wirtschaftsregion München andererseits werden kräftige Impulse erwartet.

München das europäische Patentzentrum

Mit dem Europäischen Patentamt, dem Deutschen Patentamt, dem

FAIRS

bers of Commerce – all of which cooperate in the "Technologie-Transfer-Verbund Oberbayern" – make sure that research and industry keep in constant touch with each other.

Technology Fairs in Munich

The Munich Fair is another focal meeting place of the hightech branches. Thanks to events like SYSTEMS, SEMICON, Produktronica, electronica, LASER, Analytica, Ceramitec, IFAT and Drinktec/Interbrau, which attract more than half a million professional visitors and more than 11,000 exhibitors from more than 100 nations, it is one of the leading locations of international technology fairs. Further strong incentives are expected to be provided by the cooperation of the "Neue Messe" in Riem and the "Internationales Congresszentrum München" (ICM) on the one hand, and Munich's hightech enterprises on the other.

Munich – European Patent Centre

With the European Patent Office, the German Patent Office, the German Patent Court, the "Patentstelle für die Deutsche Forschung der Fraunhofer-Gesellschaft" and the "Max-Planck-Institut für internationales und ausländisches Patent- Urheber- und Wettbewerbsrecht" – all of which are based in Munich – the city offers innovation-oriented enterprises another important locational advantage which is unique in Europe.

MUNICH – MEDIA REGION

The media industry is one of the economic branches which enjoys an impressive boom worldwide and – in view of increasing leisure-time – promises rising growth

concentrent sur la recherche et le développement à Munich, citons aussi DaimlerChrysler Aerospace (DASA), IBM, Krauss-Maffei, MAN-Technologie, Rhode & Schwarz ainsi que Kraft-Jakobs-Suchard.

Pour une coopération intensive entre la recherche et l'économie, citons parmi les autres institutions rien que 15 centres de transfert de technologie dans les universités, l'école supérieure de technologie et les chambres économiques qui coopèrent dans l'association du transfert de technologie en Haute-Bavière.

Les salons de technologie à Munich

Un autre point de cristallisation des secteurs de la haute technologie est le centre de foires et expositions de Munich. Avec les foires SYSTEMS, SEMICON, Produktronica, electronica, LASER, Analytica, Ceramitec, IFAT et Drinktec/Interbrau qui accueillent plus d'un demi million de visiteurs et plus de 11 000 exposants venant de plus de 100 pays, Munich fait partie des sites leaders au niveau des foires et expositions technologiques internationales. La combinaison d'une part de la Neue Messe à Riem et du Centre International des congrès (ICM) et d'autre part des entreprises de haute technologie de la région économique de Munich laisse espérer de fortes impulsions.

Munich – centre européen des brevets

Avec l'Office européen des brevets, l'Office allemand des brevets, le tribunal allemand des brevets, l'Office des brevets pour la recherche allemande de la Fraunhofer-Gesellschaft et l'Institut Max Planck pour les législations internationales et étrangères en matière de brevets, de concurrence commerciale et de droits d'auteurs, Munich jouit d'un atout supplémentaire pour les entreprises aimant l'innova-

l'Ambiente e la Salute) e il DLR Deutsches Zentrum für Luft- und Raumfahrt e. V. (Centro Tedesco per l'Aeronautica e l'Astronautica) per un totale di circa 6 000 persone impiegate.

Inoltre, Monaco è un centro di primaria importanza per la ricerca e lo sviluppo dell'economia privata. Oltre alla Siemens e alla BMW, presso cui lavorano oltre 20 000 ricercatori e sviluppatori, spiccano anche DaimlerChrysler Aerospace (DASA), IBM, Krauss-Maffei, MAN-Technologie, Rohde & Schwarz e Kraft-Jakobs-Suchard.

La cooperazione intensiva tra i settori della ricerca e dell'economia è resa possibile, oltre che da altre istituzioni, attraverso 15 punti di trasferimento di tecnologie situati presso le università, il Politecnico e le Camere di Commercio che collaborano nell'Unione dell'Alta Baviera per il Trasferimento delle Tecnologie.

Le fiere tecnologiche di Monaco

Un ulteriore punto di cristallizzazione dei settori high-tech è costituito dalla Fiera di Monaco. Con le diverse fiere e manifestazioni SYSTEMS, SEMICON, Produktronica, electronica, LASER, Analytica, Ceramitec, IFAT e Drinktec/Interbrau, che sono la meta di più di mezzo milione di visitatori selezionati e di oltre 11 000 espositori provenienti da più di 100 stati, la Fiera di Monaco può essere considerata come uno dei maggiori centri fieristici internazionali per il settore tecnologico. Tutti si aspettano forti impulsi dalla cooperazione tra la Nuova Fiera di Riem e il Centro Congressi Internazionale di Monaco (ICM) da un lato e le aziende dell'area economica di Monaco specializzare nell'alta tecnologia dall'altro.

Monaco – centro europeo dei brevetti

Un altro motivo per cui Monaco può essere preferita a qualsiasi altra città europea come sede per

Verleger Dr. Hubert Burda

Publisher Dr. Hubert Burda

L'éditeur Dr. Hubert Burda

L'editore Dr. Hubert Burda

Seit 1983 sitzt die strategische Konzernführung von Hubert Burda Media in der Münchner Arabellastraße.

Since 1983 the strategic management of Hubert Burda Media has been based at Arabellastraße in Munich.

Depuis 1983, la direction stratégique du Hubert Burda Media siège à Munich, dans la Arabellastraße.

Dal 1983 la direzione strategica del Hubert Burda Media ha la sua sede a Monaco, nella Arabellastraße.

An der Schwelle zu einer Gesellschaft des Wissens wächst der Bedarf an Information. Kommunikation wird schneller, individueller. Die Medien selbst werden dabei zu Motoren des ökonomischen Umbruchs. **Hubert Burda Media** hat diese Entwicklung erkannt und expandiert in vielen Teilen der Welt in neue Märkte. Ihre unternehmerischen Schwerpunkte sind das Verlagsgeschäft, das Druckgeschäft und die Neuen Medien. Weltweit gibt der Konzern heute mehr als 100 Zeitschriften heraus, davon 55 in eigener redaktioneller Verantwortung. Neben dem Printbereich zählt Hubert Burda Media als Anbieter von Onlinediensten zu den größten Content Providern unter den deutschen Verlagen. Mit seinem gesamten Engagement im Bereich der Kommunikation und Information erreichte das Unternehmen 1998 einen konsolidierten Konzernumsatz von über zwei Milliarden Mark.

Standing on the threshold of a new knowledgeable society, we need more and more information. Communication is becoming more rapid and more individualized. The media themselves are turning into motors of economic change. **Hubert Burda Media** has quickly recognized this trend and is therefore trying to conquer new markets in many parts of the world. The group's key sectors are the publishing business, printing, and the new media. Today the group publishes worldwide more than 100 magazines and is responsible for the editorial work in 55 of them. In addition to its printing sector, Hubert Burda Media offers online services and is thus one of the most significant content providers of the German publishing sector. In 1998 the activities in the fields of communication and information led to a consolidated turnover of more than DM two billion.

En passant à une société se distinguant par la connaissance, le besoin en information augmente. La communication se fait plus rapide et individuelle. Les médias se transforment en moteurs de la mutation économique. **Hubert Burda Media** a compris ce développement et se lance dans de nouveaux marchés presque aux quatre coins de la terre. Ses points forts se concentrent sur l'édition, l'imprimerie et les nouveaux médias. Au niveau mondial, le groupe publie aujourd'hui plus de 100 revues et est responsable pour 55 d'entre elles de la partie rédactionnelle. Outre l'imprimerie, Hubert Burda Media, propose des services en ligne et fait partie, parmi les éditeurs allemands, des plus grands fournisseurs d'informations. Grâce à son engagement dans la communication et l'information, la société a réalisé en 1998 un chiffre d'affaires consolidé dépassant deux milliards de DM.

Sulla soglia della società del sapere il fabbisogno di informazione cresce continuamente. La comunicazione diventa sempre più rapida e personalizzata. In questo contesto, sono i media stessi a farsi motore della svolta economica. **Hubert Burda Media** ha individuato questo sviluppo e si espande in molte parti del mondo aprendo nuovi mercati. I punti focali della sua attività imprenditoriale sono l'editoria, la stampa ed i nuovi media. Oggi, il gruppo pubblica oltre 100 riviste, 55 delle quali sotto la propria responsabilità redazionale. Oltre al settore «print» Hubert Burda Media fa parte, come fornitore di servizi online, dei maggiori content provider tra le case editrici tedesche. Con il suo impegno globale nel settore della comunicazione e dell'informazione l'azienda ha ottenuto, nel 1998, un fatturato consolidato superiore ai due miliardi di marchi.

Das redaktionelle Herz der **Süddeutschen Zeitung** schlägt seit der ersten Ausgabe am 6. Oktober 1945 im Zentrum Münchens, in der Sendlinger Straße. Dort beginnt die Redaktionskonferenz täglich um halb elf mit der Kritik am vorliegenden Blatt. Danach besprechen Ressortleiter und Redakteure die Konzeption der nächsten Ausgabe.

Seit 1988 wird die „Süddeutsche" im hauseigenen Druckzentrum in München-Steinhausen gedruckt. Mittlerweile hat sie eine verkaufte Auflage von 430 040 (Montag bis Samstag, IVW II/99).

Since the first edition of the **Süddeutsche Zeitung** appeared on 6 October 1945 the "editorial heart" of this newspaper has been beating in Sendlinger Straße, in Munich's city centre. Every day at 10.30 a.m. the editors meet there to criticise the latest edition. Afterwards the department heads and editors discuss the concept of the next edition.

Since 1988 the "Süddeutsche" has been printed in the company's own printing centre in München-Steinhausen. At present it sells 430,040 copies daily (Monday to Saturday, IVW II/99).

Le cœur de la rédaction du quotidien **Süddeutsche Zeitung** bat depuis le premier jour, le 6 octobre 1945, au centre de Munich, dans la rue Sendlinger Straße. C'est là que se tient tous les jours à 10 heures et demie la conférence rédactionnelle avec la critique de la dernière édition. Les chefs de départements et les rédacteurs discutent ensuite la conception de la prochaine édition.

Depuis 1988, le «Süddeutsche» est imprimé dans sa propre imprimerie à München-Steinhausen. Il se vend maintenant à 430 040 exemplaires (du lundi au samedi, IVW II/99).

Fin dalla prima edizione, il 6 ottobre 1945, il cuore della redazione della **Süddeutsche Zeitung** batte nel centro di Monaco, nella Sendlinger Straße. Qui, tutte le mattine, alle dieci e mezzo, ha inizio la riunione di redazione con i commenti sul giornale uscito qualche ora prima e la discussione tra i direttori di sezione e i redattori sulla bozza per l'edizione successiva.

Dal 1988 la «Süddeutsche» viene pubblicata nel centro di stampa proprio del giornale a München-Steinhausen. Attualmente il quotidiano vanta una tiratura di 430 040 copie vendute (da lunedí a sabato, IVW II/99).

Deutschen Patentgericht, der Patentstelle für die Deutsche Forschung der Fraunhofer-Gesellschaft und dem Max-Planck-Institut für internationales und ausländisches Patent-, Urheber- und Wettbewerbsrecht verfügt München über einen weiteren Standortvorteil für innovationsfreudige Unternehmen, der in Europa seinesgleichen sucht.

MEDIENREGION MÜNCHEN

Die Medienwirtschaft gehört zu den weltweit boomenden Branchen und verspricht angesichts steigender Freizeit hohe Wachstumsraten für die Zukunft. Da es sich zudem um eine saubere „Industrie" handelt, sind Medienunternehmen überall hochwillkommen. Entsprechend hart ist der Wettbewerb unter den Medienstandorten Hamburg, Köln, Berlin und München, der von einigen Bundesländern mit hohen Subventionen forciert wird.

Medienhauptstadt Deutschlands

Die Medienwirtschaft am Standort München ist auf Wachstum programmiert. Von 1988 bis 1995 stiegen die Zahl der Medienunternehmen in Stadt und Landkreis um 60 %, der Umsatz um 47 %. Mittlerweile befindet sich jeder zehnte Arbeitsplatz im Raum München in der Medienbranche.

Stark im Print

Mit mehr als 13 500 Neuerscheinungen im Jahr ist die Landeshauptstadt die führende Buchverlagsstadt der Welt, in der eine international renommierte Literaturszene zu Hause ist. Als neues Highlight wurde 1997 das Münchner Literatur- und Medienhaus eröffnet, ein Partnerschaftsprojekt von Stadt und Medienwirtschaft. Mit fünf Tageszeitungen – darunter die Süddeutsche Zeitung als auflagenstärkste deutsche meinungsbildende Tageszeitung – ist die bayerische Metropole auch

rates in future too. Since they are regarded as "clean", media enterprises are welcome everywhere. Consequently, competition is very tough between the German media centres of Hamburg, Cologne, Berlin and Munich, particularly as it is aggravated by means of high investments by several German states.

Germany's Media Capital

In Munich the media industry is growth-oriented. From 1988 to 1995 the number of media enterprises in urban and rural Munich increased by 60 %, and their turnover by 47 %. Today every tenth job in the Munich area is offered by the media sector.

Strong in Printing

With more than 13,500 new publications per year the Bavarian capital is the world's leading publishing city, which shelters an internationally renowned literary scene. Its newest highlight is the "Münchner Literatur- und Medienhaus", a project which was initiated jointly by the city and the media industry and opened in 1997. With five daily papers – among them the "Süddeutsche Zeitung" as the daily with the highest circulation in Germany – Munich is also one of the leading newspaper centres. According to the number of editors, publishers and publications, Munich also takes the lead in Germany's magazine market – together with Hamburg.

A City of Films, Television and Music

Products from Munich are used

FILM AND TV

MEDIATIQUE

tion qui s'avère absolument unique en Europe.

MUNICH – REGION MEDIATIQUE

L'économie médiatique fait partie des secteurs connaissant un boom à l'échelle mondiale et escompte, en raison de l'augmentation des loisirs, une hausse des taux de croissance pour l'avenir. Comme il s'agit en plus d'une «industrie» propre, les entreprises médiatiques sont les bienvenues partout. La concurrence que se livrent les sites médiatiques de Hambourg, Cologne, Berlin et Munich est particulièrement dure et est fortement subventionnée par certains länder.

Capitale médiatique d'Allemagne

Sur le site de Munich, l'économie médiatique est programmée sur la croissance. De 1988 à 1995, le nombre des entreprises médiatiques a augmenté dans la ville et le land de 60 % et le chiffre d'affaires de 47 %. Actuellement, un emploi sur dix dans l'espace de Munich se trouve dans le secteur médiatique.

Une position forte dans l'imprimerie

Avec plus de 13 500 nouvelles parutions par an, la capitale du land est leader mondial pour les maisons d'édition de livres et jouit d'un cercle littéraire de renom international. Un nouvel atout est venu s'ajouter en 1997, à savoir le centre de littérature et des médias de Munich, un projet de partenariat de la ville et du monde médiatique. Avec cinq quotidiens, dont le Süd-

la costituzione di un'azienda innovativa è rappresentato dalla presenza dell'Ufficio Europeo dei Brevetti, dell'Ufficio Tedesco Brevetti, del Tribunale Tedesco per i Brevetti, del Reparto Brevetti per la Ricerca Tedesca della società Fraunhofer e dall'Istituto Max Planck per la salvaguardia dei diritti d'autore così come del diritto dei brevetti e della concorrenza, sia a livello internazionale che estero.

MONACO – LA REGION DEI MEDIA

L'industria dei media appartiene ai settori di maggiore espansione a livello mondiale e si può prevedere per il futuro un ulteriore crescita di rilevanti proporzioni grazie alla possibilità di poter disporre di periodi sempre maggiori di tempo libero. Inoltre, dato che si tratta di una «industria» pulita, la costituzione di nuove imprese di questo tipo è particolarmente benvenuta. Ne consegue che vi è una forte concorrenza tra le città che si contendono il titolo di capitale dei media, tra cui Amburgo, Colonia, Berlino e Monaco, dove tale concorrenza viene forzata in alcuni Länder con cospicue sovvenzioni statali.

Capitale tedesca dei media

L'industria dei media a Monaco è in forte crescita. Dal 1988 al 1995, il numero delle aziende operanti in questo settore con sede a Monaco o all'interno del suo distretto regionale è aumentato del 60 % e il fatturato del 47 %. Nel frattempo, nell'area di Monaco un lavoratore su dieci è impiegato in questo settore.

Un punto di forza – l'editoria

Con più di 13 500 novità editoriali all'anno, la capitale bavarese è leader nel mondo per quanto riguarda il settore dell'editoria e presenta uno scenario letterario conosciuto e apprezzato a livello internazionale. L'evento principale del 1997 è stato l'apertura

*Ein Wahrzeichen Münchens – das Hochhaus des **Bayerischen Rundfunks**, gleich neben dem Münchner Hauptbahnhof*

*One of Munich's landmarks – the high-rise building of the **Bayerische Rundfunk**, the Bavarian Radio Station next to the Munich Main Railway Station*

*Un symbole de Munich – la tour du **Bayerischer Rundfunk**, l'établissement bavarois de radiodiffusion, domine dans le voisinage immédiat de la gare principale de Munich.*

*Un simbolo di Monaco – il grattacielo della **Bayerischer Rundfunk**, nelle immediate vicinanze della stazione centrale della città*

Der Intendant des Bayerischen Rundfunks, Professor Albert Scharf, verteilt während der Medientage München Autogramme an seine jüngsten Fans.

The manager of the Bavarian Radio Station, Professor Albert Scharf, signs autographs for his youngest fans during the Munich Media Days.

Le professeur Albert Scharf, directeur du Bayerischer Rundfunk, distribue pendant les journées médiatiques de Munich des autogrammes à ses jeunes fans.

Il direttore della Radiotelevisione Bavarese, Professor Albert Scharf, mentre distribuisce autografi ad alcuni giovani appassionati durante le Giornate dei Media di Monaco di Baviera.

Der „Tatort" aus München mit den drei Kommissaren Udo Wachtveitl, Miro Nemec und Michael Fitz - eines der erfolgreichsten Produkte des Bayerischen Rundfunks

The "Tatort" series from Munich, starring the three police superintendents Udo Wachtveitl, Miro Nemec, and Michael Fitz, is one of the station's most successful products.

La série policière «Tatort» de Munich avec les trois commissaires Udo Wachtveitl, Miro Nemec et Michael Fitz - un des produits les plus réussis du Bayerischer Rundfunk

La serie «Tatort», prodotta a Monaco, ed i suoi i tre commissari Udo Wachtveitl, Miro Nemec e Michael Fitz - uno dei prodotti di maggiore successo della Bayerischer Rundfunk

Modernste Fernsehtechnik beim Bayerischen Rundfunk. Deutschlands erstes voll digitales Fernsehstudio (Bildregie) in München-Unterföhring

The latest television technology at Bayerischer Rundfunk. Germany's first all-digital television studio (image control) in München-Unterföhring

La technologie la plus moderne de télévision au Bayerischer Rundfunk. Le premier studio purement digital en Allemagne (contrôle des images) à München-Unterföhring

Tecnica televisiva d'avanguardia presso la Bayerischer Rundfunk: il primo studio televisivo completamente digitale (regia d'immagini) a München-Unterföhring

153

ProSieben Media AG, Unterföhring

Galileo, das Wissensmagazin, mit Aiman Abdallah

Galileo, the information programme with Aiman Abdallah

Galileo, le magazine de l'information avec Aiman Abdallah

Galileo, il magazine dell'informazione condotto da Aiman Abdallah

ProSieben – mit Bildern bewegen

Die ProSieben Media AG gilt als eines der innovativsten und erfolgreichsten Medienunternehmen Europas.

1989 ging ProSieben auf Sendung und ist heute Deutschlands Spielfilmsender Nummer eins. Journalistische Magazine und Talkshows ergänzen sein unverwechselbares Profil. 1992 folgte Kabel 1, der inzwischen erfolgreichste Sender der zweiten Generation.

Neben dem Fernsehen hat sich ProSieben Media AG mit den Geschäftsfeldern Multimedia und Merchandising klar positioniert und verfügt damit über erhebliche Wachstumsreserven in den Zukunftsmärkten der audiovisuellen Kommunikation.

Mit einem Umsatz von fast 2 Milliarden DM in 1998 ist das Unternehmen eines der ertragsstärksten Medienhäuser Europas.

ProSieben – Moving with Pictures

ProSieben Media AG is regarded as one of Europe's most innovative and successful media enterprises.

ProSieben started operating in 1989 and is Germany's leading feature film broadcaster today. Journalistic reports and talkshows complement the station's unmistakable profile. In 1992 the Kabel 1 channel was set up, which at present is the most successful one of the second generation.

In addition to television, ProSieben Media AG has become firmly established in the sectors of multimedia and merchandising, and can thus depend on considerable growth reserves in the future markets of audiovisual communication.

With a turnover of nearly DM 2 billion in 1998 ProSieben Media AG is one of Europe's most profitable media enterprises.

ProSieben – émouvoir avec les images

La société ProSieben Media AG est une des entreprises médiatiques les plus novatrices et connaissant la plus grande réussite en Europe.

En 1989, ProSieben fut lancée et occupe aujourd'hui la première place en Allemagne comme chaîne montrant des longs métrages. Les magazines journalistiques et les talkshows viennent compléter son profil unique en son genre. En 1992, suivit Kabel 1, devenu entre-temps la chaîne de télévision de la deuxième génération et remportant le plus grand succès.

Outre la télévision, ProSieben Media AG s'est nettement positionnée dans le secteur du multimédia et du merchandising et dispose ainsi d'énormes réserves de croissance dans les marchés de l'avenir de la communication audiovisuelle.

Avec un chiffre d'affaires frôlant les 2 milliards de DM en 1998, la société est une des entreprises médiatiques les plus performantes d'Europe.

ProSieben – commuovere con le immagini

La ProSieben Media AG è considerata una delle aziende più innovative e di maggior successo nel panorama europeo dei mass media.

ProSieben mandò in onda le prime trasmissioni nel 1989 ed è oggi, in Germania, l'emittente numero uno per la programmazione di film a lungo metraggio. La sua inconfondibile fisionomia viene completata da magazine di alto livello giornalistico e talkshow. Nel 1992 è seguita, poi, Kabel 1, ormai diventata l'emittente di maggior successo tra quelle della seconda generazione.

Oltre all'attività televisiva, la ProSieben Media AG ha raggiunto un chiaro posizionamento di mercato anche nei settori multimedia e merchandising disponendo, in tal modo, di notevoli riserve di crescita nei mercati del futuro della comunicazione audiovisiva.

Con un fatturato di quasi 2 miliardi di marchi conseguito nel 1998 l'azienda è una delle case europee che consegue il maggior utile nel settore dei media.

eine führende Zeitungsstadt. Auf dem Zeitschriftenmarkt steht München gemessen an der Zahl der Redaktionen, Titel und Verlage zusammen mit Hamburg an der Spitze in Deutschland.

Film-, Fernseh- und Musikstadt

Wenn große Filme gedreht werden, dann ist fast immer ein Münchner Produkt dabei. Filmtechnik – Kamera, Licht und Kamerasupport – aus München nimmt eine internationale Spitzenstellung ein. So genießt die Technik von ARRI weltweit Renommee.

Auch in der deutschen Film- und Fernsehproduktion dominiert München. 34 % des deutschen Branchenumsatzes werden in Bayern erwirtschaftet, der größte Teil davon in der Landeshauptstadt. Das Gelände der Bavaria Film GmbH gehört zu den führenden Produktionsstätten in Deutschland. In der Postproduktion sowie im Filmlizenzhandel – die Kirch-Gruppe unterhält eines der weltweit größten Lager für sendefertiges Filmmaterial – zählt München zu den europäischen Top-Adressen.

Musik zu verlegen, zu produzieren, zu verwerten und zu vertreiben ist in München ein Geschäftszweig mit Gewicht. Tonträgerbetriebe, Musikverlage, Künstler-, Musik- sowie Konzertagenturen machen die Stadt zu einem führenden Zentrum der Musikwirtschaft. Größtes Unternehmen ist die BMG Ariola Musik GmbH mit Sitz in München, ebenso wie eine der größten deut-

in nearly every big film made. Cinematics – cameras, lights and camera supports – from Munich rank at the top internationally. ARRI technology, for instance, is renowned throughout the world.

But Munich also dominates in German film and TV production. 34% of this branch's turnover in Germany is earned in Bavaria, the lion's share being clained by the state capital. The studio lot of the Bavaria Film GmbH is one of Germany's leading production centres. In post products and in the license trade (the Kirch group maintains one of the world's largest stocks of pre-recorded film material) Munich is also one of Europe's top addresses.

The business of publishing, producing, commercializing and selling music carries much weight in Munich. Thanks to numerous sound engineering enterprises, music publishers, artists, music and concert agencies the city is also a leading centre of the music industry. Not only is the largest enterprise in this branch – BMG Ariola Musik GmbH – based in Munich, but also one of the largest German concert agencies – MAMA Concerts & Rau GmbH.

Radio and New Media are Tops in Munich

A further innovation was born in Munich: the first German television station – the Munich-based ProSieben Media AG, quoted at the stock exchange. It is Munich's biggest private station but not the only one: Kabel 1, RTL 2, TM 3, and DSF are further national transmitters. These are complemented by international programmes such as Eurosport, MTV Europe, and TV 5, which also have their main offices in Munich. "TV München" and "M1 – Fernsehen für München" concentrate on local events. Additionally, there are the "Bayerische Rundfunk" and the ZDF Landesstudio – TV stations under public law.

At present Munich's inhabitants can receive the private local radio programme on five frequen-

deutsche Zeitung qui est le quotidien allemand au plus fort tirage, la métropole bavaroise occupe ici aussi une position de leader. Sur le marché des revues, Munich arrive en Allemagne en tête avec Hambourg si l'on compare le nombre des rédactions, titres et maisons d'édition.

Ville du film, de la télévision et de la musique

Quand de grands films sont tournés, on peut être sûr qu'il s'agit d'un produit munichois. La technique cinématographique venant de Munich, qu'il s'agisse de la caméra, de l'éclairage ou du support de caméra, prend une position internationale clé. Ainsi, la technique de la société ARRI jouit d'une renommée mondiale.

Au niveau de la production cinématographique ou télévisée, Munich domine également. 34 % du chiffre d'affaires allemand sont réalisés en Bavière, la majeure partie d'ailleurs dans la capitale du land. La Bavaria Film GmbH fait partie des studios de production les plus importants d'Allemagne. Dans la postproduction ainsi que dans le commerce des licences de films – le groupe Kirch possède un des plus grands entrepôts mondiaux de films prêts à envoyer – Munich compte parmi les meilleures adresses européennes.

Editer de la musique, la produire, l'exploiter et la distribuer est un secteur de poids à Munich. Les sociétés d'enregistrement, les maisons d'édition musicales, les agences d'artistes, de musique et de concerts font de la ville un centre leader de l'économie de la musique. L'entreprise principale est la BMG Ariola Musik GmbH qui siège à Munich, tout comme une des plus grandes agences de concerts allemandes, la MAMA Concerts & Rau GmbH.

Top niveau à Munich – radio et nouveaux médias

Encore une fois, une nouveauté part de Munich. La société

della Casa della Letteratura e dei Media, un progetto realizzato dall'amministrazione cittadina insieme alle aziende del settore. Con ben cinque quotidiani – tra i quali la Süddeutsche Zeitung come giornale di opinione con maggiore tiratura in Germania – la metropoli bavarese è anche una città leader nel settore dell'informazione su carta. Insieme ad Amburgo, Monaco è al primo posto nel mercato dei periodici in Germania per numero di redazioni, titoli e case editrici.

Città del cinema, della televisione e della musica

Quando vengono girati dei film importanti, si tratta quasi sempre di un prodotto di Monaco. La tecnica cinematografica di Monaco – cinepresa, luci e macchinari di supporto – occupa una posizione di rilievo a livello internazionale. Un esempio è la tecnica di ARRI, conosciuta ed apprezzata in tutto il mondo.

Monaco domina anche nel settore della produzione cinematografica e televisiva. Il 34 % del fatturato tedesco in questo settore proviene dalla Baviera, e la maggior parte di questo viene prodotto a Monaco. Uno dei maggiori studi di produzione in Germania è quello della Bavaria Film GmbH. Monaco è inoltre uno degli indirizzi europei principali per quanto riguarda la postproduzione e la vendita dei diritti sui film – il gruppo Kirch possiede uno dei più grandi magazzini in tutto il mondo per materiale cinematografico pronto per la proiezione.

L'edizione, la produzione, la valorizzazione e la commercializzazione della musica è uno dei settori commerciali più importanti a Monaco. Imprese di portanti audio, case editrici musicali, agenzie artistiche, musicali e concertistiche fanno della città uno dei maggiori centri dell'industria musicale. Hanno infatti la propria sede a Monaco la BMG Ariola Musik GmbH, una delle aziende maggiori nel settore musicale, e la MAMA Concerts & Rau GmbH,

**KirchMedia –
ein Unternehmensporträt**

KirchMedia baut auf über 40 Jahre Erfahrung, Know-how und Wachstum der Kirch-Gruppe im Film- und Fernsehgeschäft. Die wichtigsten Betätigungsfelder auf einen Blick:

Rechtehandel
Fußballweltmeisterschaften und Erfolgsserien, Hollywood-Blockbuster und Dokumentationen – mit mehr als 85 000 Stunden Programm verfügt die KirchMedia über eine der größten Film- und Fernsehbibliotheken der Welt und ist Marktführer im Rechteverkauf in Deutschland. Alle wichtigen Fernsehsender gehören zu ihren Kunden.

Free-TV
KirchMedia ist an Fernsehveranstaltern in Deutschland, Spanien und Italien beteiligt. Dazu gehören der zweitstärkste deutsche Privatsender SAT.1 und das SportFernsehen DSF, Spaniens Telecinco-Gruppe und die italienische Mediaset.

Produktion
Das Unternehmen engagiert sich seit den achtziger Jahren erfolgreich in der Produktion von Kinofilmen, TV-Movies und Fernsehserien sowie der Entwicklung neuer Sendeformate und ist einer der großen internationalen Koproduzenten von Film- und Fernsehunterhaltung. Ein Schwerpunkt der Expansion liegt auf der Spielfilmproduktion.

Filmtechnologie
Die KirchMedia betreibt das modernste filmtechnische Dienstleistungszentrum Europas und unterhält eines der weltweit größten Lagersysteme für Filme. Der Service reicht von der Restauration und Farbkorrektur bis hin zu Internetdesign und der Entwicklung neuer Technologien.

**KirchMedia –
A Company Profile**

KirchMedia counts on more than 40 years of experience, know-how and growth of the KirchGruppe in film and TV business. An overview of the most important segments:

Rights Trade
Soccer World Cup and successful series, Hollywood blockbusters and documentaries – with more than 85,000 program hours, KirchMedia has one of the largest film and TV libraries in the world at its disposal. It numbers all major TV stations among its customers.

Free-TV
KirchMedia has interests in television operators in Germany, Spain and Italy. They include Germany's SAT.1, the German sports television channel DSF, Spain's Telecinco Group and Italy's Mediaset.

Production
Since the Eighties, the company has been successfully involved in the production of feature films, made-for-TV-movies and television series as well as in the development of new formats. It is one of the leading international co-producers of movie and television entertainment. In expanding its operations, it attaches particular emphasis to strengthening the feature film production.

Film Technology
KirchMedia operates a state-of-the-art film technology service center, the most advanced of its type in Europe, and maintains one of the largest film-storage systems in the world. Its services extend from film restoration and color correction to Internet design work and the development of new technologies.

oben/top/en-haut/in alto:
Kommissar Rex
Gedeon Burkhard, Schäferhund Rex

rechts/right/à droite/a destra:
Der Graf von Monte Christo
Gérard Depardieu, Ornella Muti

KirchMedia – portrait d'entreprise

KirchMedia s'appuie sur plus de 40 ans d'expérience, de savoir-faire et de croissance du KirchGruppe dans les secteurs du film et de la télévision. Aperçu des champs principaux d'activité:

Commercialisation des droits
Championnats du monde de football et séries à succès, les Blockbuster d'Hollywood et les documentaires, avec un programme de plus de 85 000 heures, la KirchMedia dispose d'une des plus grandes bibliothèques mondiales du cinéma et de la télévision et arrive en tête sur le marché de la vente des droits en Allemagne. Toutes les grandes chaînes de télévision font partie de sa clientèle.

Free-TV
KirchMedia détient des participations dans les chaînes télévisées en Allemagne, Espagne et Italie. La deuxième chaîne privée allemande SAT.1 et la chaîne de sports DSF, le groupe espagnol Telecinco et la société italienne Mediaset en font partie.

Production
Depuis les années quatre-vingt, l'entreprise s'engage avec succès dans la production de films cinématographiques, de films et de séries pour la télévision ainsi que dans le développement de nouveaux concepts d'émissions. Elle est également un des plus grands coproducteurs internationaux de films cinématographiques et télévisés. Un des points forts de l'expansion réside dans la production de films.

Technologie du film
KirchMedia opère dans le centre tertiaire le plus moderne d'Europe au niveau de la technique cinématographique et télévisée et gère un des plus grands systèmes mondiaux de stockage de films. Le service s'étend de la restauration et de la correction des couleurs au design Internet et au développement de nouvelles technologies.

KirchMedia – il ritratto di un'azienda

La KirchMedia può fare affidamento su 40 anni di esperienza, di know-how e di crescita del KirchGruppe nel settore cine-televisivo. I principali campi di attività dell'azienda, sono riportati, a colpo d'occhio, qui di seguito:

Commercio di diritti cine-televisivi
I campionati del mondo di calcio e le serie televisive più gettonate, i successi di cassetta di Hollywood ed i grandi documentari: con oltre 85 000 ore di programmi la KirchMedia dispone di una delle più grandi biblioteche cine-televisive del mondo ed è leader di mercato in Germania nella vendita di diritti. Della sua clientela fanno parte tutte le principali emittenti televisive.

Free-TV
La KirchMedia vanta partecipazioni in aziende televisive in Germania, Spagna e Italia. Tra esse figurano la seconda maggiore emittente privata tedesca SAT.1 ed il canale sportivo DSF, il Gruppo spagnolo Telecinco e l'italiana Mediaset.

Produzioni
Fin dagli anni Ottanta l'azienda è impegnata con successo nella produzione di pellicole cinematografiche, televisive e serial nonché nello sviluppo di trasmissioni di nuove concezione ed è uno dei maggiori coproduttori internazionali di intrattenimento cine-televisivo. Uno dei settori più rilevanti nella strategia di espansione è rappresentato dalla produzione di lungometraggi.

Servizi tecnici cinematografici
La KirchMedia gestisce il più moderno centro di servizi tecnici cinematografici in Europa e dispone di uno dei maggiori depositi di film del mondo. Il ventaglio dei servizi spazia dal restauro e correzione cromatica fino all'Internet design e allo sviluppo di nuove tecnologie.

oben/top/en-haut/in alto:
Balzac – Leidenschaften eines Lebenskünstlers
Gérard Depardieu, Katja Riemann

links/left/à gauche/a sinistra:
Verlockende Falle (Entrapment)
Catherine Zeta-Jones, Sean Connery

DSF – Wir sind der Sport!

Seit 1993 bereichert DSF mit dem größten Sport-TV-Angebot die deutsche Medienlandschaft und hat sich seither vom Newcomer zu einem der profilstärksten Sender Deutschlands entwickelt. Mit hochwertigen Sportrechten, journalistisch fundierter Berichterstattung und unverwechselbaren Eigenformaten liefert DSF anerkannte Qualität im TV-Sport.

Mit der Fokussierung auf Männer, mit langfristigen Investitionen oder dem technisch einzigartigen Produktionsniveau – realisiert durch die 100 %ige DSF-Tochter PLAZAMEDIA – hat DSF in vielerei Hinsicht Maßstäbe gesetzt.

Doch DSF hat sich nicht nur als TV-Sportmedium etabliert, sondern steht heute für ein prosperierendes Unternehmen, das auf unterschiedlichen Geschäftsfeldern wie Internet überaus erfolgreich agiert.

DSF – Sports Are Us!

With the greatest offer of sports events on TV DSF has been a valuable asset to the German media since 1993, and has turned from newcomer to one of today's high-profile TV-stations. It is widely recognized as a high quality sports channel because it holds excellent licenses to cover sports events, presents high quality journalism and has characteristic formats that are unmistakably DSF.

Thanks to its focus on the male audience, long-term investments or because of its state-of-the-art product level-made possible with the wholly-owned subsidiary PLAZAMEDIA, DSF has been able to set a level of excellence in many ways.

But DSF is not only a sports channel on TV, it is a booming enterprise in various areas such as the Internet.

DSF – Nous sommes le sport!

Avec son offre unique de programmes télévisés sportifs, DSF enrichit depuis 1993 le paysage médiatique allemand et le nouveau venu compte maintenant parmi les chaînes les plus rentables d'Allemagne. Avec ses retransmissions de grands événements sportifs, ses reportages montrant un journalisme fondé ainsi que ses propres tournages bien reconnaissables, DSF apporte une qualité reconnue à l'actualité télévisée sportive.

En se concentrant sur les hommes, avec des investissements à long terme et un niveau technique de production unique en son genre – réalisé par la filiale à 100 % de DSF, la PLAZAMEDIA – DSF a posé de nouveaux jalons.

Mais DSF ne s'est pas uniquement établie comme média sportif, elle symbolise aujourd'hui une entreprise prospère agissant avec succès sur des champs d'action différents comme Internet.

DSF – Lo sport siamo noi!

Dal 1993 DSF arricchisce il panorama tedesco dei media con la più grande offerta televisiva di sport, e da allora si è trasformata da matricola ad emittente dal profilo più marcato in Germania. Con diritti sportivi di grande pregio, un giornalismo di profondo valore e trasmissioni dal formato inconfondibile, DSF propone sport in TV di riconosciuta qualità.

Focalizzandosi sugli uomini, con investimenti a lungo termine o con un livello di produzione unico nel suo genere da un punto di vista tecnico – realizzato attraverso la società controllata PLAZAMEDIA – DSF ha definito, sotto molti aspetti, veri e propri standard.

Ma DSF non si è imposta solo come emittente televisiva sportiva ma è diventata anche sinonimo di prospera azienda che agisce con grande successo nei differenti campi di attività tra cui figura anche Internet.

Mittendrin statt nur dabei – Faszination Sport in DSF

Right in the middle, not just from the outside – the fascination of sports on DSF

Plus que participer, être en plein milieu – la fascination du sport sur DSF

Eventi vissuti dal di dentro, anziché da spettatore – il fascino dello sport su DSF

Produktion auf höchstem Niveau: die mehrfeedige Übertragung der Formel 1 durch PLAZAMEDIA

State-of-the-art production: Formula 1 multi-camera transmission by PLAZAMEDIA

Production à un excellent niveau: exploitation numérique des images de la Formule 1 par PLAZAMEDIA

Produzioni ai massimi livelli: la telecronaca delle gare di Formula Uno effettuata da PLAZAMEDIA con più inquadrature contemporanee sullo schermo

PLAZAMEDIA –
Wir produzieren gute Ideen

Die PLAZAMEDIA GmbH Film- und TV-Produktion in Ismaning bei München hat sich in kürzester Zeit von einer reinen Produktionsgesellschaft zu einem Full-Service-Anbieter im TV-Bereich entwickelt. Das komplett digitale Sendezentrum zählt zu den modernsten Europas und garantiert TV-Produktionen auf höchstem technischen Niveau. Seit 1998 bietet das Unternehmen auch sämtliche Dienstleistungen im Bereich der Außenproduktionen an. Abgerundet wird das Leistungsspektrum durch die Bereiche Spotproduktion, Postproduktion und Programmabwicklung.

PLAZAMEDIA bietet maßgeschneiderte Dienstleistungen aus einer Hand und ist insbesondere für komplexe Aufgaben der ideale Partner in einer digitalen TV-Zukunft.

PLAZAMEDIA –
We Produce Good Ideas

The PLAZAMEDIA GmbH Film- und TV-Produktion in Ismaning on the outskirts of Munich has turned in the shortest possible time from a company limited to production to a full-service provider in the TV segment. The fully digital broadcasting facilities belong to the most modern in Europe and guarantee state-of-the-art productions. Since 1998 the company has also offered comprehensive services for extern productions. To complete the range of services PLAZAMEDIA also offers the production of commercials and image clips.

PLAZAMEDIA offers customized comprehensive services and is the ideal partner for the digital TV future particularly for complex projects.

PLAZAMEDIA –
Nous produisons de bonnes idées

Située à Ismaning, la société de production cinématographique et télévisée, PLAZAMEDIA GmbH Film- und TV-Produktion, est passée en peu de temps d'une société de production à part entière à un prestataire complet de services dans le secteur télévisé. L'émetteur entièrement numérique compte parmi les plus modernes d'Europe et garantit des productions télévisées d'un excellent niveau technique. Depuis 1998, la société propose tout un éventail de services dans le secteur de la production extérieure. La gamme de ses activités est complétée par le domaine de la production de sports qui fabrique des spots publicitaires et des films d'image.

PLAZAMEDIA propose des services taillés sur mesure et s'avère, en particulier pour des missions complexes, le partenaire idéal pour l'avenir de la télévision numérique.

PLAZAMEDIA –
Produciamo delle buone idee

La PLAZAMEDIA GmbH Film- und TV-Produktion di Ismaning presso Monaco si è trasformata, in brevissimo tempo, da pura società di produzione ad operatore full service in campo televisivo. Il suo centro trasmissioni completamente digitale viene annoverato tra i più moderni d'Europa e garantisce produzioni televisive ai massimi livelli tecnici. Dal 1998 esso offre anche tutti i servizi di ripresa esterna. Il ventaglio di prestazioni viene completato dalla divisione «Produzione spot», che realizza spot pubblicitari e filmati istituzionali.

PLAZAMEDIA offre servizi «su misura» di prima mano e rappresenta, soprattutto per l'espletamento di mansioni complesse, il partner ideale del futuro televisivo digitale.

schen Konzertagenturen, die MAMA Concerts & Rau GmbH.

Rundfunk und Neue Medien – in München top

Wieder nimmt ein Novum von München seinen Ausgang: Mit der ProSieben Media AG hat der erste an der Börse notierte deutsche Fernsehsender seinen Sitz an der Isar. Er ist der größte private Fernsehsender in München, aber nicht der einzige: Kabel 1, RTL 2, TM 3 und DSF sind die weiteren nationalen Anbieter. Dazu kommen noch internationale Sender wie Eurosport, MTV Europe und TV 5, die ihren deutschen Hauptsitz in München haben. Das lokale Geschehen ist Thema der Sender „tv München" und „M1 – Fernsehen für München". Hinzu kommen der Bayerische Rundfunk sowie das Landesstudio des ZDF als öffentlich-rechtliche Fernsehanstalten.

Privaten lokalen Hörfunk können die Münchner derzeit auf fünf Frequenzen empfangen. Sehr erfolgreich agiert insbesondere Antenne Bayern, der bundesweit größte private Hörfunksender. Der Bayerische Rundfunk hat als erster deutscher Sender einen Nachrichtenkanal – B5 aktuell – eingerichtet.

Neue Inhalte bietet auch H.O.T., der Fernsehsender, der das Teleshopping in Deutschland publik machen will. Der Vorreiter für die technisch neuen Möglichkeiten des digitalen Fernsehens hat ebenfalls in München seinen Sitz. DF1 ist mit seinem Angebot von Spartenkanälen und aktuellen Spielfilmen seit 1996 am Markt. Der Bayerische Rundfunk startete im Januar 1998 den Bildungskanal BR-alpha, ein Spartenfernsehprogramm mit bildungsspezifischen Inhalten und multimedialer Verknüpfung.

Die Entwicklung des Wachstumsmarktes Neue Medien unterstützt auch die öffentliche Hand mit dem Programm „Bayern Online". 100 Millionen DM stellt der Freistaat zur Förderung von Zukunftsprojekten, z. B. für die cies. One of the most successful stations is "Antenne Bayern", the largest private sound broadcasting station in the Federal Republic of Germany. The "Bayerische Rundfunk" was the first German radio station to set up a special news channel – "B5 aktuell".

H.O.T., a TV station which intends to introduce teleshopping in Germany, also offers new ideas. The pioneer of the new technical opportunities offered by digital television is also based in Munich. Since 1996 DF1 has been in the market with its programme of special channels and current feature films. In January 1998 the Bavarian Broadcasting Station started the educational BR-alpha channel, a special TV programme offering education-specific themes and multi-media connections.

The authorities also support the development of the new media market with the "Bayern Online" programme. The Free State of Bavaria has made available DM 100 million for the promotion of future projects such as the setting up of a high-speed data network.

Advertising Centre of the Future

Although Munich with billings amounting to DM 2.1 billion at present takes only fourth place after Frankfurt, Düsseldorf and Hamburg, the growth potential of the advertising agencies located in the Bavarian metropolis lies far above the German average.

Central Location for Media Training

Munich is a leading education centre for Germany's media industry. Noted further education institutes like the "Institut für Kommunikationswissenschaften", "Hochschule für Fernsehen und Film", "Bayerische Akademie der Werbung", "Deutsche Journalistenschule", "Akademie der Bayerischen Presse", "Akademie des Deutschen Buchhandels", ProSieben Media AG, la première chaîne de télévision allemande cotée en bourse, siège aux bords de l'Isar. C'est la plus grande chaîne privée de Munich mais pas la seule: Kabel 1, RTL 2, TM 3 et DSF sont les autres chaînes nationales. Viennent ensuite s'ajouter les chaînes internationales comme Eurosport, MTV Europe et TV 5 qui ont leur siège allemand à Munich. Les chaînes «tv München» et «M1 – Fernsehen für München» sont régionales. Citons également les chaînes publiques: la Bayerischer Rundfunk ainsi que le studio bavarois de la ZDF.

Actuellement, les Munichois peuvent écouter les radios privées locales sur cinq fréquences. Antenne Bayern, la plus grande radio privée allemande, connaît un grand succès. La Bayerischer Rundfunk a été la première radio allemande à installer un canal d'informations, B5 aktuell.

La chaîne télévisée H.O.T. propose un nouveau programme et veut rendre populaire le téléachat en Allemagne. Le précurseur des nouvelles possibilités techniques offertes par la télévision numérique siège également à Munich. Avec son programme de canaux à thèmes et de films actuels, DF1 est depuis 1996 sur le marché. En janvier 1998, la Bayerischer Rundfunk a commencé un programme de formation BR-alpha, un programme télévisé de thèmes avec des sujets inhérents à la formation et une liaison multimédiale.

L'opinion publique soutient également le développement du marché de croissance Nouveaux Médias avec le programme «Bayern Online». L'Etat libre met à la disposition 100 millions de DM pour la promotion de projets d'avenir, par exemple le développement d'un réseau grande vitesse de données.

Site publicitaire de demain

Avec des opérations de l'ordre de 2,1 milliards de DM, Munich occupe actuellement certes la una delle maggiori agenzie di concerti della Germania.

Radiodiffusione e nuovi mezzi di comunicazione – il top dei top a Monaco

Ancora una volta una novità parte da Monaco: ProSieben Media AG, con sede sull'Isar, è la prima emittente televisiva tedesca quotata in borsa e la maggiore emittente televisiva privata a Monaco, ma non l'unica: seguono infatti, sempre a carattere nazionale, Kabel 1, RTL 2, TM 3 e DSF. A queste vanno aggiunte altre emittenti internazionali che hanno la loro sede principale tedesca a Monaco, ovvero Eurosport, MTV Europe e TV 5. Le notizie locali vengono trasmesse da «tv München» e «M1 – Fernsehen für München». Infine, vanno ricordati gli enti televisivi pubblici, ovvero la Radiotelevisione bavarese e la sede regionale della ZDF.

Le emittenti radiofoniche private locali utilizzano cinque frequenze. Quella che riscuote maggiore successo è Antenne Bayern, la maggiore emittente radiofonica privata della Germania. La Radio bavarese è stata la prima emittente tedesca ad istituire un canale di giornale radio: B5 aktuell.

Nuovi contenuti sono offerti anche da H.O.T., l'emittente televisiva che vuole rendere pubbliche le televendite in Germania. Anche il precursore delle nuove possibilità tecniche della televisione digitale, la DF1, ha la propria sede a Monaco. DF1 è presente sul mercato dal 1996 con la sua offerta di canali specializzati e di film attuali. La Radio bavarese ha inaugurato nel Gennaio 1998 il canale di cultura BR-alpha, un programma televisivo multimediale che tratta argomenti di carattere educativo e culturale.

La crescita del mercato dei nuovi mezzi di comunicazione viene finanziata anche pubblicamente attraverso il programma «Bayern Online». La Baviera mette infatti a disposizione 100 milioni di marchi per la promozione di progetti futuri e, ad es., per lo svi-

*Im Bankenzentrum am Promenadeplatz steht das um die Jahrhundertwende errichtete Gebäude der **Dresdner Bank AG** in München.*

*Constructed at the turn of the century, the building of the **Dresdner Bank AG** in Munich stands on the Promenadeplatz in the banking district.*

*Construit au début du siècle, le bâtiment de la **Dresdner Bank AG** à Munich borde la Promenadeplatz, le quartier de la finance.*

*Nel centro bancario sulla Promenadeplatz si trova l'edificio della **Dresdner Bank AG** a Monaco, costruito al principio del secolo.*

Entwicklung eines Datenhochgeschwindigkeitsnetzes, zur Verfügung.

Werbestandort der Zukunft

Zwar liegt München mit 2,1 Milliarden DM Billings derzeit hinter Frankfurt, Düsseldorf und Hamburg nur auf Platz vier, aber die Werbeagenturen in der bayerischen Metropole wachsen seit Jahren deutlich über dem bundesdeutschen Durchschnitt.

Standort für Medienausbildung

München ist ein führendes Ausbildungszentrum für die Medienwirtschaft in Deutschland. Ansässig sind namhafte Fortbildungsstätten wie das Institut für Kommunikationswissenschaften, die Hochschule für Fernsehen und Film, die Bayerische Akademie für Fernsehen, die Bayerische Akademie der Werbung, die Deutsche Journalistenschule, die Akademie der Bayerischen Presse, die Akademie des Deutschen Buchhandels, das Berufsbildungszentrum für Druck, Grafik und Fotografie, die Fachakademie für Fotodesign und das Medienforum München für interdisziplinäre Medienprojekte.

Die 1998 gegründete „virtuelle" Münchner Multimedia-Akademie (MMA) koordiniert die vorhandenen Kapazitäten im Bereich Multimedia-Aus- und Weiterbildung. Im ebenfalls neuen Medienzentrum „Media Works Munich (MWM)" finden Institutionen der Medienwirtschaft, überwiegend aus dem Bereich der Aus- und Fortbildung, auch räumlich zusammen und profitieren von den dort entstehenden Synergien.

Plattform für Medien-Events

München ist mit einer Vielzahl von Veranstaltungen Treffpunkt der nationalen wie internationalen Medienbranche. Neben dem Münchner Filmfest sind vor allem die Medientage München – der "Berufsbildungszentrum für Druck, Grafik und Fotografie", "Fachakademie für Fotodesign", and the "Medienforum München für interdisziplinäre Medienprojekte" are all based in Munich.

The virtual "Münchner Multimedia-Akademie" (MMA), founded in 1998, coordinates the existing capacities in the field of multimedia training and further education. In the newly established "Media Works Munich" (MWM) institutions of the media sector mainly concentrating on education and further eduction enjoy close contact and profit from the resulting synergies.

A Platform for Media Events

Thanks to a great number of events, Munich is a favourite meeting place of the national and international media industries. In addition to the "Münchner Filmfest" it is primarily the "Medientage München" (Germany's most important media-political congress), the "Werbegipfel München" (Advertising Summit) and the "Internationale Fachmesse für Filmtechnik" (CINEC) which must be mentioned in this connection. With the "DigiGlobe", Deutsche Telekom and the FOCUS magazine in 1998 awarded prizes for outstanding multimedia developments for the first time. "Corporate New Media", one of the most renowned media competitions, moved to the Bavarian capital in 1998 as well.

EUROPEAN FINANCE CENTRE

A Branch Undergoing Radical Changes

Globally, there is no business sector in this late 20th century which is undergoing more radical structural changes than the financial sector. Nearly every week one hears of new dramatic fusions. Most of these mergers take place within a special field in which a bank or finance company was poorly represented so far and quatrième place, loin derrière Francfort, Düsseldorf et Hambourg mais les agences publicitaires de la métropole bavaroise enregistrent depuis des années une croissance nettement supérieure à la moyenne fédérale.

Site pour la formation médiatique

Munich est un centre de formation principal pour l'économie médiatique en Allemagne. Des centres renommés de formation siègent ici comme l'institut pour les sciences de la communication, l'école supérieure de la télévision et du cinéma, l'académie bavaroise de la télévision, l'académie bavaroise de la publicité, l'école allemande de journalisme, l'académie de la presse bavaroise, l'académie de la librairie allemande, le centre de formation professionnelle pour l'impression, le graphisme et la photographie, l'académie technique du design photographique et le forum médiatique de Munich pour les projets interdisciplinaires médiatiques.

Fondée en 1998, l'académie virtuelle de Munich sur les multimédias (MMA) coordonne les capacités présentes dans le domaine de la formation et du perfectionnement professionnel multimédial. Le nouveau centre médiatique «Media Works Munich (MWM)» rassemble des institutions du monde médiatique principalement actives dans le secteur de la formation et du perfectionnement professionnel. Elles profitent ainsi des synergies.

Plate-forme des événements médiatiques

Avec son programme intense, Munich est le point de rencontre du secteur médiatique national et international. Outre le festival du cinéma, citons surtout les journées médiatiques de Munich, le plus important congrès allemand sur les médias, le sommet publicitaire de Munich et CINEC, le salon spécialisé international sur la technique de film. Pour la luppo di un network ad alta velocità di trasmissione.

Piazza pubblicitaria del futuro

Al momento Monaco è solo al quarto posto dietro a Francoforte, Düsseldorf e Amburgo, con un budget amministrato di 2,1 miliardi di marchi, ma le agenzie pubblicitarie nella metropoli bavarese stanno crescendo da anni decisamente oltre la media nazionale.

Sede per la formazione nel settore dei mezzi dicomunicazione

Monaco è un centro di primaria importanza in Germania per la formazione nel settore dei mezzi di comunicazione. È sede di rinomate scuole di perfezionamento quali l'Istituto per le Scienze della Comunicazione, l'Istituto Superiore per la Televisione e la Cinematografia, l'Accademia Bavarese per la Televisione, l'Accademia Bavarese della Pubblicità, la Scuola Tedesca per Giornalisti, l'Accademia Bavarese della Stampa, l'Accademia Tedesca per l'Editoria, il Centro di Formazione Professionale per Stampa, Grafica e Fotografia, l'Accademia per Design Fotografico e il Forum di Monaco dei Mezzi di Comunicazione per progetti interdisciplinari.

L'Accademia «virtuale» di Monaco per il Multimediale (MMA), fondata nel 1998, coordina la formazione e il perfezionamento nel settore dei mezzi di comunicazione multimediali. Nel nuovo centro per il multimediale «Media Works Munich (MWM)» lavorano a stretto contatto varie istituzioni operanti nel settore dell'industria multimediale, soprattutto nell'ambito della formazione e della specializzazione, in modo tale da poter approfittare delle sinergie che nascono inevitabilmente da tale vicinanza.

*Seit ihrer Gründung im Jahr 1951 verfolgt die **LfA Förderbank Bayern** (Bayerische Landesanstalt für Aufbaufinanzierung) das Ziel, die Leistungs- und Wettbewerbsfähigkeit der bayerischen Wirtschaft zu steigern und damit zur Schaffung und Sicherung von Arbeitsplätzen beizutragen. Dafür stehen ihr Förderinstrumente in Form von Darlehen, Bürgschaften und Beteiligungskapital zur Verfügung. In Zusammenarbeit mit den Hausbanken verhilft die LfA gewerblichen Unternehmen bei Gründungs-, Wachstums-, Innovations-, Konsolidierungs- und Umweltschutzvorhaben zu einer optimalen Finanzierung. Rund 300 hochqualifizierte Mitarbeiter setzen sich für das Erreichen des Unternehmenszieles ein.*

*Since its founding in 1951 **LfA Förderbank Bayern** (Bayerische Landesanstalt für Aufbaufinanzierung) has concentrated on increasing the efficiency and competitive strength of Bavaria's economy and on contributing its share to creating and securing jobs in this way. For this purpose it employs promotional tools like loans, guarantees and participation capital. In cooperation with the local banks the LfA procures optimum financing conditions for industrial enterprises intending to enlarge, modernize, consolidate or improve the environment-friendliness of their firms. Approximately 300 highly qualified employees make every effort to realize the company's aims.*

*Depuis sa création en 1951, la **LfA Förderbank Bayern** (Bayerische Landesanstalt für Aufbaufinanzierung) vise à augmenter la performance et la compétitivité de l'économie bavaroise et contribue ainsi à la création et au maintien d'emplois. Pour y arriver, elle met à disposition ses instruments de promotion, à savoir des prêts, des cautions et du capital placé en participations. En coopération avec les banques des entreprises, la LfA soutient les entreprises industrielles dans tous leurs projets de création, de croissance, d'innovation, de consolidation et de protection de l'environnement en leur proposant un financement optimal. Environ 300 collaborateurs qualifiés se mobilisent pour réaliser l'objectif de l'entreprise.*

*Fin dalla sua costituzione avvenuta nel 1951, la **LfA Förderbank Bayern** (Bayerische Landesanstalt für Aufbaufinanzierung) persegue l'obiettivo di incrementare l'efficienza e la competitività dell'economia bavarese e, dunque, di contribuire a creare ed assicurare numerosi posti di lavoro. Per ottenere ciò essa ha a disposizione strumenti di promozione sotto forma di mutui, fideiussioni e capitale di partecipazione. In collaborazione con le banche delle aziende commerciali interessate la LfA coadiuva queste ultime nella predisposizione di finanziamenti mirati alla costituzione di società, all'attuazione di progetti di crescita, di innovazione, di consolidamento e di tutela dell'ambiente. Circa 300 dipendenti sono costantemente impegnati nel raggiungimento di questo obiettivo.*

Im Süden Münchens, im Zentrum Neuperlachs, befindet sich die Hauptverwaltung der Versicherungs- und Finanzdienstleistungsgruppe **Bayerische Beamten Versicherungen (BBV)**. Die Palette dieser in der Bundesrepublik und in Südeuropa tätigen Gruppe umfasst neben Lebens-, Kranken- und Sachversicherungen auch geschlossene Immobilien- und Mobilienleasingfonds sowie Renten- und Aktienfonds. Das Angebot auf dem Finanzdienstleistungssektor wird abgerundet durch die Beteiligung an einer namhaften Bank.

The headquarters of the **Bayerische Beamten Versicherungen (BBV)**, an insurance and financial services group, is located in the centre of Neuperlach in the southern part of Munich. The programme of this group operating in the Federal Republic of Germany and in southern Europe comprises - in addition to life, health and property insurance - locked real estate and mobile leasing funds, as well as bond and share funds. These activities in the sector of financial services are rounded off by a participation in a renowned bank.

C'est au sud de Munich, au cœur de Neuperlach que se trouve le centre administratif du groupe d'assurances et de prestations financières **Bayerische Beamten Versicherungen (BBV)**. Opérant en Allemagne et dans le sud de l'Europe, ce groupe propose outre les assurances vie, maladie et de dommages aux biens également des fonds de leasing sur l'immobilier et les valeurs mobilières ainsi que des fonds de pensions et d'actions. Dans le secteur des prestations financières, l'offre est complétée par une participation dans une banque de renom.

A sud di Monaco, al centro del quartiere di Neuperlach, si trova la sede centrale del gruppo assicurativo e di servizi finanziari **Bayerische Beamten Versicherungen (BBV)**. La gamma di prodotti offerta da questo gruppo, che opera nella Repubblica Federale Tedesca e nel sud dell'Europa, comprende, oltre ai rami assicurativi vita, malattie e danni, anche fondi immobiliari chiusi e fondi di leasing mobiliare nonché fondi obbligazionari ed azionari. L'offerta nel settore dei servizi finanziari viene completata dalla partecipazione in un noto istituto bancario.

Rund 600 Mitarbeiter sind in der BBV-Hauptverwaltung an modernen, freundlichen, funktionell gestalteten Arbeitsplätzen tätig.

Approximately 600 persons work at modern, pleasant and functional working places in the BBV headquarters.

Environ 600 personnes occupent, dans le centre administratif de la BBV, des postes modernes, agréables et conçus de manière fonctionnelle.

Nella sede centrale BBV operano, in postazioni di lavoro moderne, gradevoli e funzionali, circa 600 dipendenti.

„Kunst in Neuperlach" heißt eine seit mehr als zehn Jahren praktizierte kulturelle Aktivität der BBV: die inzwischen in der Münchner Kunstszene etablierte „Galerie im BBV-Haus".

"Art in Neuperlach" is the term used for a cultural BBV programme which was introduced ten years ago: here the Gallery in the BBV House, an art gallery which has by now become an integral part of Munich's art scene.

«L'art à Neuperlach», tel est le nom d'une activité culturelle pratiquée depuis plus de dix ans par la BBV : la «Galerie dans la maison de la BBV» est maintenant bien établie dans le milieu artistique munichois.

«Arte a Neuperlach», questo il motto con cui da oltre dieci anni la BBV organizza tutta una serie di attività culturali: la «Galleria nella casa della BBV», diventata ormai un punto di riferimento fisso nella scena artistica monacense.

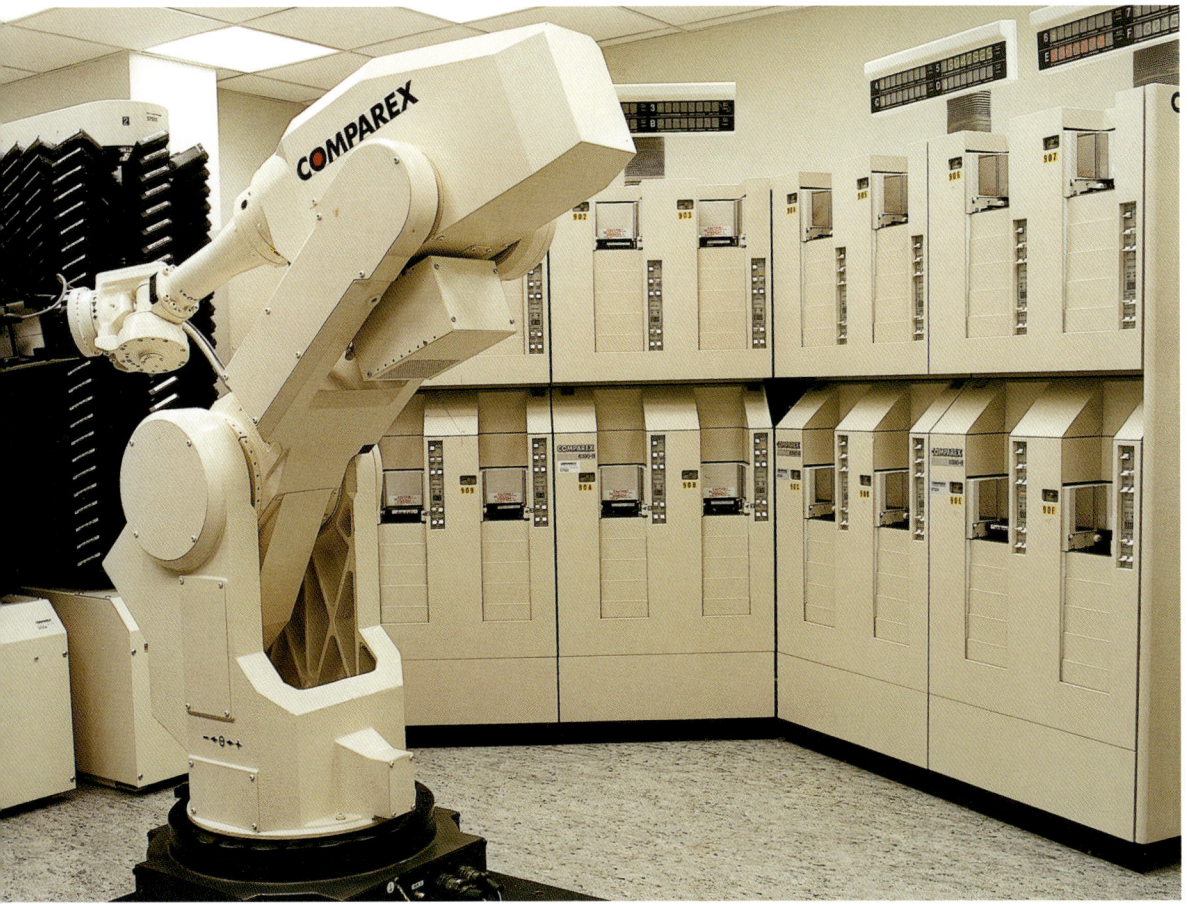

Technische Schaltzentrale ist das Rechenzentrum. Es sorgt mit modernster Technik für schnelle, sichere, fehlerfreie Abläufe.

The computing centre is the technical control station. With ultra-modern equipment it guarantees quick, safe and error-free processes.

Le centre informatique est la centrale technique opérant l'ensemble des calculs. Grâce à sa technique moderne, il permet des transactions rapides, sûres et sans erreur.

La «stanza dei bottoni», a livello tecnico, è rappresentata dal centro meccanografico. Grazie all'impiego delle tecniche più moderne esso assicura procedure rapide, sicure ed esatte.

wichtigste medienpolitische Kongress Deutschlands –, der Werbegipfel München und die internationale Fachmesse für Filmtechnik CINEC zu nennen. Deutsche Telekom und FOCUS verliehen 1998 mit dem „DigiGlobe" erstmals Preise für herausragende Multimedia-Entwicklungen. „Corporate New Media", einer der renommiertesten Wettbewerbe der Medienbranche, zog im selben Jahr in die bayerische Landeshauptstadt um.

EUROPÄISCHES FINANZZENTRUM

Eine Branche im Umbruch

Weltweit gesehen gibt es gegen Ende des 20. Jahrhunderts keine Branche, die einen tiefgreifenderen Strukturwandel durchläuft als der Finanzsektor. Beinahe wöchentlich werden neue schlagzeilenträchtige Fusionen gemeldet. Meist sind Zusammenschlüsse innerhalb eines Bereiches zu beobachten, um die jeweilige Position auf Märkten zu verstärken, auf denen man bislang schwach vertreten war. Andererseits gibt es eine Tendenz zur Bildung von Allfinanzkonzernen, die alle Bereiche des Finanzsektors abdecken. In Europa muss man diesen Konzentrationsprozess vor dem am 1.1.1999 eingeläuteten Euro-Zeitalter sehen. Dabei darf man neben den sich für München ergebenden Chancen die Risiken – insbesondere für den Arbeitsmarkt – nicht außer Acht lassen. Schließlich now wants to improve its market position. On the other hand, there is a trend towards setting up "all-finance groups" which cover all fields of the financial sector. In Europe one must consider this concentration process in connection with the new "Euro Age", which was rung in on 1 January 1999. But one should not let the hoped-for chances blind one for the risks which may affect Munich – particularly for the labour market. For more than 60,000 persons are employed by banks and insurance companies in the city on the Isar River.

Munich – the Number 1 All-Finance Centre

In this battle for a new position Munich holds an excellent starting position. In view of the ample variety (as far as quality and quantity is concerned), which the city offers in the sector of banks, insurance companies, leasing and venture capital firms, it shares the rank of Germany's leading finance centre with Frankfurt.

Munich – An Insurance Centre

Munich is also Germany's first-ranking insurance centre, as far as the number of enterprises, employees and insurance contributions are concerned. Evaluated according to premium income, Munich holds first place worldwide, surpassing even New York and London. In addition to numerous other companies, Munich shelters the "Münchner Rück", the largest reinsurer worldwide; "Allianz", the biggest internationally operating insurance company of our globe and one of the largest direct-writers worldwide; and the Ergo Group, the second-largest insurance company Germany's. The decision of the Italian Generali Group in future to handle all their German transactions from their Munich branch, has greatly reinforced the city's special status.

The dominance in quality of the insurance centre can only be première fois en 1998, Deutsche Telekom et FOCUS ont récompensé avec le «DigiGlobe» des développements multimédiaux extraordinaires. «Corporate New Media», un des concurrents les plus renommés du monde médiatique, a déménagé pour s'installer la même année dans la capitale du land de Bavière.

CENTRE FINANCIER EUROPEEN

Un secteur en mutation

Au niveau mondial, il n'existe à la fin du 20ème siècle aucun secteur connaissant une si profonde mutation structurelle que le secteur des finances. Il ne se passe pas une semaine sans qu'il ne soit question de fusions faisant la une des journaux. Il faut la plupart du temps observer les fusions au sein d'un secteur afin de confirmer sa position sur les marchés sur lesquels on était faiblement représenté jusqu'à présent. Il existe aussi une tendance à former des groupes de bancassurance couvrant tous les domaines du secteur financier. En Europe, ce processus de concentration doit être considéré avant le glas de l'ère de l'euro (1er janvier 1999). Outre les opportunités qui s'offrent à Munich, il ne faut pas perdre de vue les risques en résultant, en particulier pour le marché de l'emploi. En effet, plus de 60 000 personnes travaillent dans la ville aux bords de l'Isar dans des banques et assurances.

Munich – place N° 1 de la bancassurance

Dans cette lutte pour se forger une nouvelle position, Munich part d'une base excellente. Etant donné le grand éventail qu'offre la capitale du land au niveau de la quantité et de la qualité dans les secteurs des banques, assurances, leasing, fonds et capital de risque, elle prévaut avec Francfort comme place financière allemande.

Piattaforma per eventi nel settore delle comunicazioni

Monaco ospita numerosi eventi e manifestazioni e può essere considerata per questo il punto d'incontro del settore delle comunicazioni, sia a livello nazionale che internazionale. Oltre al Festival del Cinema di Monaco, sono da ricordare soprattutto le Giornate per la Comunicazione di Monaco – il congresso più importante della Germania a livello di politica e comunicazione –, il «summit» della Pubblicità di Monaco e la Fiera internazionale per la Tecnica Cinematografica (CINEC). La Deutsche Telekom e FOCUS hanno conferito per la prima volta nel 1998 un premio – il «DigiGlobe» – al migliore prodotto multimediale dell'anno. Nello stesso anno «Corporate New Media», uno dei concorsi più rinomati del settore delle comunicazioni, è stato trasferito nella capitale bavarese.

CENTRO FINANZIARIO DI LEVATURA EUROPEA

Un settore in trasformazione

Dal punto di vista globale, alla fine del XX secolo non esiste un settore che stia attraversando una svolta strutturale più radicale di quello finanziario. Quasi ogni settimana vengono annunciate nuove fusioni clamorose. Per la maggior parte si tratta di unioni all'interno di uno stesso settore allo scopo di rafforzare la propria posizione su mercati in cui si era fino a quel momento scarsamente rappresentati. Dall'altra parte, c'è una tendenza a creare gruppi finanziari che coprano tutti i campi del settore finanziario. In Europa questo processo di concentrazione deve essere visto prima dell'era dell'Euro inaugurata l'1.1.1999. Ma, oltre alle possibilità che si sono aperte per Monaco, non si può non prendere in considerazione i rischi che ne derivano, soprattutto per il mercato del lavoro. In fin conti, solo nelle banche e presso gli istituti di assicurazione della

Die **Bayerische Landesbank** - eine der bedeutendsten deutschen Universalbanken - hat ihren Hauptsitz in München. Sie ist Hausbank des Freistaates Bayern und Zentralbank der bayerischen Sparkassen. Ihr Kapital wird von beiden zu gleichen Teilen gehalten.

Als nationale und internationale Geschäftsbank ist die Bayerische Landesbank an allen wichtigen Finanzplätzen der Welt vertreten. Sie ist das zweitgrößte Emissionshaus Deutschlands und bietet sowohl Großunternehmen als auch privaten und institutionellen Anlegern sämtliche Finanzdienstleistungen.

Erstklassige Bonität, außergewöhnliche Plazierungs- und Innovationskraft sowie weltweite Verbindungen sichern den Kunden internationalen Erfolg.

Neben Bankgeschäften übernimmt die Bayerische Landesbank mit großem Engagement soziale Verantwortung. So unterstützt sie mit viel Einsatz die Benefizaktion „Sternstunden - Wir helfen Kindern".

Eine hauseigene Kunstgalerie ist außerdem fester Bestandteil ihrer kulturellen Verpflichtung.

The **Bayerische Landesbank** - one of Germany's most important universal banks - has its headquarters in Munich. It is the official bank of the Free State of Bavaria and the central bank of the Bavarian savings banks. Its capital is held in equal shares by both.

As a nationally and internationally operating commercial bank, the Bayerische Landesbank is represented in all important finance centres throughout the world. Additionally, it is Germany's second-largest issuing house and offers all kinds of financial services to large-scale enterprises as well as to private and institutional investors.

Excellent reliability, outstanding innovative and placement strength and worldwide relations safeguard our clients' international success.

In addition to its banking business the Bayerische Landesbank also concentrates intensively on its social obligations. It supports, for instance, very generously the programme "Sternstunden - Wir helfen Kindern", a benefit drive for children in need.

Furthermore, the bank maintains an art gallery of its own as a major contribution to the local cultural scene.

La **Bayerische Landesbank**, une des banques universelles allemandes les plus importantes, siège à Munich. Elle est la banque de l'Etat libre de Bavière et l'institut de crédit des caisses d'épargne bavaroises qui détiennent d'ailleurs chacun la moitié de son capital.

En tant que banque commerciale nationale et internationale, la Bayerische Landesbank est représentée sur toutes les places financières importantes du monde. De plus, elle est la deuxième banque d'émission d'Allemagne et offre aussi bien aux grandes entreprises qu'aux particuliers et aux institutions la gamme complète des prestations financières.

Une solvabilité de premier ordre, un potentiel de placement et d'innovation extraordinaire ainsi que des relations internationales garantissent à ses clients un succès international.

Outre les affaires bancaires, la Bayerische Landesbank prend son rôle social très au sérieux. Elle encourage avec beaucoup d'engagement l'action d'aide à l'enfance «Sternstunden - Wir helfen Kindern».

Par ailleurs, sa galerie d'art fait partie intégrante de ses obligations culturelles.

La **Bayerische Landesbank** - una delle più importanti banche universali della Germania - ha la sua sede centrale a Monaco di Baviera. È la banca ufficiale del Land Baviera e banca centrale delle casse di risparmio bavaresi. Entrambe le entità detengono una quota identica del capitale della banca.

Come banca commerciale nazionale ed internazionale, la Bayerische Landesbank è rappresentata su tutte le piazze finanziarie del mondo. Essa è, inoltre, la seconda banca emittente tedesca in ordine di importanza ed offre un'assistenza finanziaria completa sia alle grandi imprese che agli investitori privati ed istituzionali.

Solidità, servizi di prima qualità, potenzialità di collocamento titoli e di innovazione fuori dell'ordinario garantiscono ai clienti un successo internazionale.

Accanto alle attività bancarie, la Bayerische Landesbank è fortemente impegnata nel sociale: essa appoggia e sostiene, infatti, la campagna di beneficenza per bambini «Sternstunden - Wir helfen Kindern».

La Bayerische Landesbank avverte, inoltre, una forte responsabilità nella salvaguardia del patrimonio culturale e possiede, a tal fine, una propria galleria d'arte.

Verwaltungsgebäude der DEMOS in München

Headquarters of DEMOS in Munich

Siège de la Société DEMOS à Munich

Sede amministrativa DEMOS a Monaco

DEMOS heißt auf griechisch „das Volk" und steht für unserenUnternehmenszweck, nämlich Wohneigentum preiswert für möglichst viele Menschen zu schaffen und dafür zugleich das Bestmögliche an Qualität zu bieten. Dieses ehrgeizige Ziel verfolgt DEMOS nun seit mehr als 30 Jahren. Bis zum heutigen Tag wurden ca. 8 000 Häuser und Wohnungen in und um München errichtet.

Bundesweit zeigen sogar mehr als 10 000 gebaute Wohnungen, Reihenhäuser und Gewerbeeinheiten den Erfolg unserer Idee und das Vertrauen unserer Kunden. DEMOS-Wohnanlagen findet man in ausgewählten, werthaltigen Lagen in beinahe allen Münchner Stadtvierteln und im Einzugsbereich der Stadt München. Seit 1993 sind wir mit unseren Firmen DEMOS Spreegrund und DEMOS Sachsengrund auch in den Großräumen Berlin und Leipzig tätig.

Zur Philosophie des Hauses DEMOS gehört eine hervorragende Leistung – zufriedene Kunden und Geschäftspartner sind das Ergebnis. Gesellschaftlichen Veränderungen begegnen wir mit neuen Konzepten wie dem Betreuten Wohnen, das der wachsenden Anzahl von Senioren, die selbstständig und unabhängig leben wollen, Rechnung trägt, oder Reihenhäusern, die jungen Familien ein ihrem Geldbeutel entsprechendes Eigenheim ermöglichen.

Doch der Service bleibt auch zukünftig das Herz unseres Geschäfts. Deshalb verlangen wir von jedem einzelnen Mitarbeiter umfassende Servicebereitschaft und unternehmerisches Denken. Dafür setzen wir auf eine moderne Unternehmensorganisation mit flachen Hierarchien und Strukturen, bei der die Verantwortungsbereit-

DEMOS means "the people" in Greek; but it also stands for our enterprise's aim to provide reasonably priced housing for as many people as possible, and to offer at the same time the best quality possible. DEMOS has pursued this goal for more than 30 years. Up to now approximately 8,000 houses and flats have been constructed in and around Munich.

Nationwide, more than 10,000 newly built flats, detached houses and industrial units prove the success of our idea and the trust our customers put in us. You find DEMOS housing estates in selected locations (which retain their value) in nearly all districts of Munich and throughout the city's region. Since 1993 we have also been represented in the areas of Berlin and Leipzig by our companies DEMOS Spreegrund and DEMOS Sachsengrund.

The DEMOS philosophy centers on extraordinary efficiency and performance standards which, in turn, lead to satisfied customers and business partners. We meet

DEMOS signifie en grec «le peuple» et symbolise le but de notre société, à savoir créer des logements bon marché pour un plus grand nombre de personnes et proposer en même temps une bonne qualité. DEMOS poursuit depuis plus de 30 ans cet objectif ambitieux, en effet jusqu'à aujourd'hui, plus de 8 000 maisons et appartements ont été construits à Munich et aux environs.

En Allemagne, la construction de plus de 10 000 appartements, maisons individuelles et unités commerciales prouvent l'aboutissement de ce but, et la confiance apportée par notre clientèle. Les emplacements de nos habitations ont été préalablement choisis, de valeur confirmée dans les quartiers munichois et les environs. Depuis 1993, grâce à nos sociétés DEMOS Sachsengrund et DEMOS Spreegrund nous sommes actifs dans de grandes agglomérations comme Berlin et Leipzig.

La philosophie de notre société est d'être performant et de satisfaire nos clients ainsi

DEMOS, in greco, significa «popolo» ed è anche il nome della nostra azienda, in quanto il nostro scopo è quello di creare case accessibili al maggior numero di persone, offrendo loro contemporaneamente la migliore qualità possibile. Ormai la DEMOS persegue questo ambizioso obiettivo da oltre 30 anni. Fino ad oggi a Monaco di Baviera e dintorni sono state costruite circa 8 000 case e appartamenti.

Più di 10 000 appartamenti, villini monofamiliari e fabbricati commerciali sparsi su tutto il territorio tedesco testimoniano del successo della nostra idea e della fiducia dei nostri clienti. È possibile trovare fabbricati residenziali DEMOS in quasi tutti i quartieri di Monaco e nella periferia della città, sempre in zone estremamente selezionate il cui valore è destinato a durare nel tempo. Dal 1993 siamo presenti anche nel comprensorio di Berlino e di Lipsia con le nostre filiali DEMOS Spreegrund e DEMOS Sachsengrund.

1 Perlach „Blumenhof", Gustav Heinemann-Ring

2 Holzkirchen, Josef-Kammerloher-Straße

3 Perlach „Am kleinen See", Gustav Heinemann-Ring

schaft jedes Einzelnen zählt. Da vornehmlich die Lage einer Immobilie deren Wert bestimmt, wählen wir die Standorte für unsere Projekte mit großer Sorgfalt aus und achten beispielsweise auf gute Anbindung an öffentliche Verkehrsmittel, auf schnelle und leichte Erreichbarkeit von Erholungsflächen, Geschäften, Schulen und Kindergärten. Deshalb wohnen Menschen gerne in unseren Häusern und Wohnungen, und auch Investoren können sicher sein, dass sich ihre DEMOS-Objekte bestens vermieten lassen und zu einer rentablen Kapitalanlage werden.

social changes with new concepts such as "Betreutes Wohnen" (Housing cum Care) which pays consideration to the growing number of elderly people who prefer to live independently; or with detached houses which enable young families to acquire homes suited to their incomes.

But good service will remain the core of our business. We therefore expect every one of our employees to display service-orientation and an enterprising spirit. We therefore rely on a modern company organization with simple hierarchies and structures which encourages and relies on individual responsibility and commitment. As it is the location which, as a rule, determines the value of real estate, we choose our project sites very carefully and pay particular attention to the availability of public transport and to the proximity of recreational areas, shops, schools and kindergartens. For that reason most people like to live in our houses and flats. Investors can count on letting their DEMOS objects easily, so that they become a profitable capital investment.

que nos partenaires. Nous faisons face aux mutations sociales en mettant au point de nouveaux concepts tels que l'habitat assisté, qui permet aux personnes agées de vivre de manière indépendante, et aux familles de s'offrir une maison correspondant à leurs moyens.

Cependant, le service reste pour l'avenir la priorité essentielle. C'est pourquoi nous demandons à nos collaborateurs de respecter cette valeur et de faire preuve d'ésprit d'initiative. Pour cela nous avons misé sur une organisation d'entreprise moderne présentant des hièrarchies et des structures planes qui mettent en avant la responsabilité de chacun. Nous prenons grand soin au choix de nos emplacements, car nous pensons que c'est ce qui en fait sa valeur, comme par exemple la proximité des transports en commun, les accès aux espaces de loisirs, les commerces, les écoles et les jardins d'enfants.Ce qui explique pourquoi les gens se sentent bien dans nos habitations, c'est ce qu'ont compris les investisseurs, en effet DEMOS s'avère un investissement rentable.

Della filosofia DEMOS fa parte il concetto del massimo rendimento – la soddisfazione dei nostri clienti e dei nostri partner d'affari ne è il risultato. Affrontiamo le trasformazioni sociali creando nuovi concetti quali l'abitazione con assistenza a domicilio, che tiene conto del numero crescente di anziani che desiderano continuare a condurre una vita autonoma ed indipendente, o le villette singole che consentono alle giovani coppie di possedere una proprietà adeguata alle loro possibilità finanziarie.

Il cuore della nostra attività sarà rappresentato, anche in futuro, dall'assistenza professionale. È per questo motivo che richiediamo a tutti i nostri collaboratori una disponibilità completa all'assistenza ed uno spirito imprenditoriale. La nostra azienda fa leva su una struttura organizzativa moderna, priva di gerarchie e sovrastrutture, nella quale conta la disponibilità del singolo ad assumersi le proprie responsabilità. Poiché il valore di un immobile è dato prevalentemente dalla sua posizione, l'ubicazione dei nostri progetti viene scelta con grande cura tenendo conto, ad esempio, della presenza di buoni collegamenti con i mezzi pubblici e della possibilità di raggiungere velocemente e facilmente spazi ricreativi, negozi, scuole, ed asili. È per tutti questi motivi che i nostri clienti sono soddisfatti di vivere nei nostri appartamenti e case. Anche gli acquirenti-investitori possono essere certi che il loro immobile DEMOS può venir ottimamente affittato e costituisce, in ogni caso, un ottimo investimento.

sind an der Isar allein bei Banken und Versicherungen über 60 000 Arbeitnehmer beschäftigt.

München – der Allfinanzplatz Nr. 1

München hat bei diesem Kampf um eine Neupositionierung eine hervorragende Ausgangsbasis. Angesichts der großen Bandbreite, die die Landeshauptstadt hinsichtlich Quantität und Qualität in den Bereichen Banken, Versicherungen, Leasing, Fonds und Wagniskapital zu bieten hat, gilt sie zusammen mit Frankfurt als der deutsche Finanzplatz.

München – die Versicherungsstadt

München ist sowohl nach Anzahl der Unternehmen und Beschäftigten als auch hinsichtlich der Beitragseinnahmen Versicherungsstandort Nummer eins in Deutschland. Gemessen an den Prämieneinnahmen hat München weltweit die Spitzenstellung inne – noch vor New York und London. So haben neben vielen anderen die Münchner Rück, der größte Rückversicherer der Welt, die Allianz, der größte international tätige Versicherer der Welt und einer der weltweit größten Erstversicherer, sowie die Ergo-Gruppe, der zweitgrößte deutsche Versicherungskonzern, ihren Hauptsitz an der Isar. Die Entscheidung der italienischen Generali-Gruppe, ihre gesamten Deutschlandaktivitäten künftig von ihrer Münchner Dependance aus zu steuern, stärkt zudem die Ausnahmestellung.

Die qualitative Dominanz des Versicherungsstandortes München wird erst dann voll ersichtlich, wenn man bedenkt, dass zumindest die Grundzüge der Kapitalanlage- und Beteiligungsstrategie ebenso in den Konzernzentralen vorgegeben werden wie die generellen Annahmerichtlinien im eigentlichen Versicherungsgeschäft. Wo immer auf der Welt und in welcher Form diese gewaltigen Kapitalien – allein der Allianz-Konzern verwaltet 382 Mil-

INSURANCE CENTRE

appreciated fully, if one takes into consideration that not only the basic features of the capital investment and participation strategies are determined in the group headquarters, but also the conditions of acceptance in the insurance business proper. Where and in which manner these enormous amounts of money are to be invested – the Allianz Group alone administers DM 382 billion – is lastly decided in the Bavarian capital. But from the viewpoint of national economics it is even more momentous that Munich decides what is nationally and internationally insurable or not.

Second-important Banking Centre of Germany

Although the Munich banks achieve only half of the balance sheet total of the Frankfurt banks, they boast twice the amount of Düsseldorf, which ranks next in size. In the mortgage sector, however, Munich holds the top position: The institutes located in Munich issue the largest number of mortgage bonds and have bigger holdings of mortgages than the Frankfurt banks.

Two of Germany's six largest banks operating on a supraregional and international basis – the HypoVereinsbank and the Bayerische Landesbank – control their business from their Munich headquarters. 1998 after the fusion of the former Bayerische Vereinsbank and the Bayerische Hypotheken-und Wechselbank to form

Munich – la ville des assurances

Aussi bien au niveau du nombre des compagnies et des employés qu'au niveau du montant des primes encaissées, Munich est le site N°1 de l'assurance en Allemagne. Comparée au niveau de l'encaissement des primes, Munich prend la première place mondiale, avant New York et Londres. A côté de beaucoup d'autres, la Münchner Rück, la plus grande compagnie de réassurance du monde, l'Allianz, le plus grand assureur international du monde et un des plus grands assureurs directs du monde, ainsi que le groupe Ergo, le deuxième groupe d'assurances allemand, ont leur siège ici. La décision du groupe italien Generali de coordonner l'ensemble de ses activités allemandes à partir de son bureau de Munich vient encore renforcer cette position.

La domination qualitative de Munich, en tant que site du monde de l'assurance devient particulièrement sensible si l'on réfléchit que les caractères fondamentaux d'une stratégie d'investissements de capitaux et de participation sont définis dans les centrales des groupes tout comme les lignes générales des opérations d'assurance. Où que se fassent les investissements et quelle que soit leur forme – le groupe Allianz gère 382 milliards de DM – la décision est prise aux bords de l'Isar. Du point de vue de l'économie nationale, il est encore plus important que Munich décide de ce qui sera assuré ou pas au niveau national et mondial.

La deuxième place bancaire

Certes, le total du bilan des banques munichoises représente juste la moitié des établissements financiers de Francfort, mais c'est quand même le double de Düsseldorf, le grand site voisin. Une excellente position que Munich maintient avec des opérations bancaires hypothécaires. Les instituts établis ici émettent

città sull'Isar sono impiegati oltre 60 000 lavoratori.

Monaco – la piazza finanziaria globale n° 1

Monaco dispone di un eccezionale punto di partenza in questa lotta per il riordinamento delle posizioni. In considerazione della sua ampia offerta, sia per quanto riguarda quantità che qualità, nei settori bancario, assicurativo, del leasing, dei fondi e del capitale di rischio, la capitale bavarese è considerata insieme a Francoforte come la piazza finanziaria della Germania.

Monaco – città delle assicurazioni

Sia per il numero delle aziende e delle persone ivi impiegate che per gli introiti complessivi del settore assicurativo, Monaco può essere considerata la sede n° 1 in Germania per quanto riguarda le assicurazioni. Se si considerano i premi incassati, Monaco mantiene la prima posizione a livello mondiale, anche davanti a New York e a Londra. Ecco perché, oltre a tante altre, hanno qui la loro sede principale la Münchner Rück, la maggiore compagnia riassicurativa del mondo, la Allianz, la più grande compagnia assicurativa del mondo operante a livello internazionale e una delle maggiori compagnie assicurative dirette del mondo, e il Gruppo Ergo, il secondo gruppo assicurativo tedesco. La decisione del gruppo italiano Generali, di dirigere in futuro tutte le sue attività relative all'ambito tedesco dalla filiale di Monaco rafforza ulteriormente la posizione di eccezionale importanza della città.

Il dominio qualitativo della piazza assicurativa di Monaco viene evidenziato pienamente soltanto se si considera che almeno le linee fondamentali delle strategie riguardanti gli investimenti di capitale e le compartecipazioni vengono indicate nelle sedi centrali dei gruppi così come le direttive generali di accettazione sono

Die **INVESTA UNTERNEHMENSGRUPPE** ist seit 1972 Partner für private Bauherren, für Industrie und Handel, kommunale Körperschaften sowie für institutionelle Anleger, wenn es um die Entwicklung, Planung, Finanzierung und Errichtung schlüsselfertiger Gewerbe-, Industrie- und Wohnbauprojekte geht.

In der bankenunabhängigen Gruppe werden die Unternehmen einzelverantwortlich, unter erfolgsorientierten und sozialen Vorgaben geführt, was die Voraussetzung und Gewähr für einen gleichmäßig hohen Leistungsstandard bietet.

Since 1972 the **INVESTA UNTERNEHMENSGRUPPE** has been a partner of private home builders, industry and trade, communal corporations and institutional investors wherever the development, financing and construction of turnkey projects for industry and the housing sector are required.

In this group – independent of banks – the individual enterprises are managed on the basis of individual responsibility, success-orientation and social commitment, principles which are at the same time preconditions and the guarantee of a high standard of performance.

▲
In Münchens absoluter Bestlage befindet sich das Büro- und Geschäftshaus Maximilianstraße 35, das von der INVESTA UNTERNEHMENSGRUPPE initiiert wurde. Der Kopfbau, im Stil Friedrich Bürkleins neu errichtet, ist Teil des schönsten und besterhaltenen neugotischen Ensembles aus der Mitte des 19. Jahrhunderts – der Maximilianstraße. Der anschließende Hauptbau greift den Rhythmus der alten Fassade auf und fügt sich mit seiner unverwechselbaren Komposition ästhetisch in das Stadtbild ein. Der Bau wurde 1997 fertiggestellt und ist an mehrere namhafte Unternehmen vermietet.

The office and business centre of the INVESTA UNTERNEHMENSGRUPPE is located in 35 Maximilianstraße, one of Munich's best addresses. The head building, newly constructed in the style of Friedrich Bürklein, forms a part of the most beautiful and best preserved neo-Gothic ensemble dating from the mid-19th century – i.e. of Maximilianstraße. The adjoining main building takes up the rhythm of the old façade and with its unmistakable composition blends aesthetically with the overall cityscape. The edifice was finished in 1997 and has been let to several noted enterprises since then.

◄ Im Herzen der Landeshauptstadt München liegt das ehemalige Telegrafenamt, das von der INVESTA UNTERNEHMENSGRUPPE 1997 erworben und in aufwendiger Arbeit innen und außen sorgfältig saniert und renoviert wurde. Die neue Konzeption des Gebäudes bietet sowohl Büronutzern als auch Einzelhändlern die Möglichkeit, sich in nostalgischem Ambiente repräsentativ darzustellen.

In the centre of the state capital of Munich the former Telegraph Office is located which was purchased by the INVESTA UNTERNEHMENSGRUPPE in 1997; it was restored and reconstructed inside and outside with the utmost care. The newly refurbished building offers firms and retailers the possibility to present themselves impressively in a nostalgic ambiance.

liarden DM – investiert werden, entscheidet sich letztendlich an der Isar. Unter volkswirtschaftlichen Gesichtspunkten ist jedoch noch gewichtiger, dass von München aus bestimmt wird, was national und international versicherbar ist und was nicht.

Zweitwichtigster Bankenplatz

Zwar erreicht die Bilanzsumme der Münchner Banken gerade einmal die Hälfte der Frankfurter Geldhäuser, aber immerhin das Doppelte des nächst größten Standorts Düsseldorf. Eine Spitzenposition hält München im Hypothekenbankgeschäft. Die hier ansässigen Institute emittieren die meisten Hypothekenpfandbriefe und haben einen größeren Hypothekenbestand als die Frankfurter Institute.

Zwei der sechs größten, überregional und international tätigen Banken Deutschlands lenken ihre Geschäfte aus einer Münchner Zentrale; dies sind die HypoVereinsbank und die Bayerische Landesbank. Nach der 1998 durchgeführten Fusion zwischen der Bayerischen Hypotheken- und Wechselbank und der Bayerischen Vereinsbank ist die neue HypoVereinsbank die zweitgrößte Universalbank in Deutschland, der größte Immobilienfinanzierer in Europa und gehört nach der Bilanzsumme zu den Top Ten der Welt.

Zentrum des (Immobilien-) Leasings

Auch im Immobilienleasing dominiert die bayerische Landeshauptstadt. Mit der KGAL GmbH & Co, der Hannover HL Leasing GmbH & Co KG, der LHI Leasing für Handel und Industrie GmbH sowie der BMW Leasing GmbH haben vier der zehn größten deutschen Leasingfirmen ihren Sitz im Münchner Raum.

CONSULTING

the HypoVereinsbank, this new institute is the second-largest universal bank in Germany, the biggest institute financing real estate in Europe, and it ranks – according to its balance sheet total – among the top ten banks of our globe.

Leasing Centre

The Bavarian capital also dominates in real estate leasing. Four of Germanies ten most eminent leasing firms are based in the Munich area: KGAL GmbH & Co, Hannover HL Leasing GmbH & Co KG, LHI Leasing für Handel und Industrie GmbH, and BMW Leasing GmbH.

Mecca of Venture Capital

As a finance centre with Munich as its hub Bavaria takes the lead in the allocation of public promotion funds and private venture capital. Three of Germany's top ten companies working in this field (which are also called risk, venture or chance capital companies) are based in Munich. Here venture capital is so abundant that investors are by now looking for new marketable hightech ideas instead of vice versa. Munich thus offers young entrepreneurs veritable dream conditions.

AN ATTRACTIVE NEIGHBOURHOOD FOR CONSULTANTS

For quite some time the service sector has been the driving force in providing additional employment, as it accounts for about 75% of the working population. Particularly company-related services, the so-called business services, have increased above average. Chartered accountants, lawyers, engineering offices, management consultants, software enterprises, schools, advertising agencies, market research institutes, real estate services and other freelancers find a very fertile soil in

la plupart des obligations foncières et leur portefeuille hypothécaire est plus important que celui des instituts francfortois.

Pour deux des six grandes banques supra-régionales et opérant sur la scène internationale, leurs affaires partent directement de leur centrale munichoise, il s'agit de la Hypo-Vereinsbank et de la Bayerische Landesbank. Depuis la fusion en 1998 de la Bayerische Hypotheken- und Wechselbank et de la Bayerische Vereinsbank, la nouvelle HypoVereinsbank est la deuxième banque universelle d'Allemagne, le plus grand financier immobilier d'Europe et fait partie avec son total de bilan des 10 premières banques mondiales.

Le centre du leasing (immobilier)

La capitale du land bavarois domine également dans le leasing immobilier. Avec la KGAL GmbH & Co, la HL Leasing GmbH & Co KG de Hanovre, la LHI Leasing für Handel und Industrie GmbH et la BMW Leasing GmbH, quatre des dix plus grands du secteur du leasing en Allemagne ont leur siège dans l'espace économique de Munich.

La Mecque du capital à risque

Avec sa centrale à Munich, la place financière de Bavière arrive en tête en Allemagne pour l'attribution de moyens publics comme le venture capital privé. Trois des dix premières sociétés allemandes, appelées également sociétés de capitaux à risque, siègent ici. Il y existe tellement de capital-risque que les investisseurs sont à la recherche de nouvelles idées de haute technologie et non pas l'inverse – des conditions idéales pour des créateurs d'entreprise novateurs.

indicate nell'operazione d'assicurazione vera e propria. In quale parte del mondo e in quale forma debbano essere investiti questi ingenti capitali – soltanto il Gruppo Allianz amministra 382 miliardi di marchi – viene deciso in ultima istanza proprio qui, sulle sponde dell'Isar. Tuttavia, dal punto di vista politico-economico è ancora più importante che partendo da Monaco si decida quanto possa o non possa essere assicurato a livello nazionale ed internazionale.

Al secondo posto come piazza bancaria

È vero che il totale del bilancio delle banche di Monaco raggiunge soltanto la metà di quello delle banche di Francoforte, ma rimane comunque il doppio della piazza bancaria successiva, ovvero di Düsseldorf. Monaco detiene il primato per quanto riguarda il settore delle banche di credito ipotecario. Gli istituti bancari con sede a Monaco emettono la maggior parte dei titoli ipotecari ed hanno un portafoglio ipotecario più grande rispetto agli istituti di Francoforte.

Due delle sei maggiori banche tedesche operanti a livello sovraregionale ed internazionale dirigono i loro affari dalla sede centrale di Monaco; si tratta della HypoVereinsbank e della Bayerische Landesbank. In seguito alla fusione tra la Banca di Credito Ipotecario e di Sconto Bavarese (Bayerische Hypotheken- und Wechselbank) e la Banca Cooperativa Bavarese (Bayerische Vereinsbank) avvenuta nel 1998, la nuova HypoVereinsbank è la seconda banca universale della Germania, il più grande finanziere dell'Europa e appartiene ai «top ten» del mondo per quanto riguarda il totale del bilancio.

Centro del leasing (immobiliare)

La capitale bavarese domina anche nel settore del leasing immobiliare. La KGAL GmbH & Co, la HL Leasing GmbH & Co KG

Die neueste Kirby-Generation: der Gsix. Offizielle Markteinführung in Deutschland und Österreich im August 1999

The latest Kirby generation: the Gsix. Officially it will be launched on the German and Austrian market in August 1999.

La dernière génération Kirby: le Gsix. Lancement officiel sur les marchés allemands et autrichiens en août 1999

La nuova generazione Kirby è rappresentata dal Gsix. Commercializzazione ufficiale in Germania e Austria: agosto 1999

Kirby – der Fast-Alleskönner aus Ohio

Inspiriert von den erfolglosen Bemühungen seiner Mutter, das Haus staubfrei zu halten, erfand Jim Kirby in den dreißiger Jahren das revolutionäre Reinigungssystem Kirby. Das Gerät erfüllt bis zu 80 Funktionen und erfreut sich seit mehr als 15 Jahren auch in Deutschland großer Beliebtheit. Von Oberhaching bei München, dem deutschen Firmensitz, aus betreut Supervisor Wolfgang Mahling ca. 1 000 Mitarbeiter.

Der außerordentliche Erfolg von Kirby beruht auf der Tatsache, dass das Produkt seit Anbeginn an seinem Einsatzort – zu Hause – verkauft wird. Heute verfügt das zur Firmengruppe Scott Fetzer gehörende Unternehmen gleichen Namens über ein weltweit verzweigtes Netz von Vertragshändlern und Systemberatern, die das Allround-Talent dem Kunden in seinen eigenen vier Wänden präsentieren und weltweit einen Jahresumsatz von einer Milliarde USD erwirtschaften.

Kirby – the Allround-Genius Made in Ohio

Inspired by his mother's futile attempts to keep the house dust-free Jim Kirby invented the revolutionary cleaning system Kirby in the 1930s. The multi-purpose appliance has up to 80 applications and has been well accepted on the German market for more than 15 years. The seat of the German headquarters is in Oberhaching not far from Munich where Wolfgang Mahling supervises approximately 1,000 employees.

The reason for Kirby's extraordinary success is the fact that the product has been sold right from the beginning where it would eventually be used: at home. Today the company, also called Kirby, belongs to the Scott Fetzer group and has a global net of authorized dealers and system consultants that demonstrate the allround-genius to customers in their own place producing an annual turnover of 1 billion US dollars.

Kirby – le multi-talent de l'Ohio

Inspiré par les vains efforts de sa mère à épousseter dans la maison, Jim Kirby créa durant les années trente le système Kirby, offrant un nettoyage révolutionnaire. L'appareil remplit jusqu'à 80 fonctions et est, depuis plus de 15 ans, très apprécié également en Allemagne. C'est à Oberhaching près de Munich que le directeur Wolfgang Mahling gère les quelques 1 000 employés.

L'immense succès de Kirby s'explique par le fait que le produit est vendu, depuis ses débuts, là où il est employé, à savoir à la maison. L'entreprise, appartenant au groupe d'entreprises Scott Fetzer et portant le même nom, dispose aujourd'hui d'un réseau mondial et diversifié de concessionnaires et de conseillers en systèmes qui présentent au client le multi-talent dans ses quatre murs et réalisent un chiffre d'affaires annuel d'un milliard de dollars.

Kirby – il quasi tuttofare dell'Ohio

Traendo ispirazione dai vani sforzi della madre di tenere lontana la polvere dalla casa, Jim Kirby inventò, negli anni Trenta, il rivoluzionario sistema di pulizia Kirby. L'apparecchio svolge fino a 80 funzioni e viene molto apprezzato, da oltre 15 anni, anche in Germania. Da Oberhaching presso Monaco, dove è situata la sede dell'azienda, il supervisore Wolfgang Mahling si prende cura di circa 1 000 dipendenti.

Lo straordinario successo di Kirby è riconducibile al fatto che il prodotto viene venduto, fin dall'inizio, nel luogo in cui viene poi utilizzato: a casa. Oggi l'azienda, che reca lo stesso nome e fa capo al Gruppo Scott Fetzer, dispone di una rete ramificata in tutto il mondo di rivenditori autorizzati e consulenti di sistema, che presentano questo multitalento al cliente nelle sue quattro mura domestiche e conseguono ogni anno, in tutto il mondo, un fatturato di un miliardo di dollari.

Die Bertelsmann Buch AG in München: Kreativität und Vielfalt aus dem größten Buchhaus der Welt

Mitgliedsstarke Buch- und Musikclubs, erfolgreiche Verlage und dynamische Direktvertriebe in über 25 Ländern machen die Bertelsmann Buch AG zum größten Buchunternehmen weltweit. Die Zahl der Mitarbeiter lag im Geschäftsjahr 1997/98 bei 18 400; der Umsatz von 7,3 Milliarden DM wurde zu je einem Drittel im deutschen Sprachraum, im übrigen Europa und in Nordamerika erzielt. Auch auf den Zukunftsmärkten in Asien und Lateinamerika wächst das Engagement der Clubs und Verlage kontinuierlich.

Weltweit bieten die Buch- und Musikclubs 25 Millionen Mitgliedern preisgünstige, exklusive Programme und einen umfangreichen Service.

Die publizistische Unabhängigkeit und die Autonomie der Verleger im Hause Bertelsmann ermöglichen es, literarische Vielfalt und künstlerische Qualität miteinander zu verbinden. Zahlreiche preisgekrönte Autoren, darunter eine Vielzahl von Literaturnobelpreisträger (z.B. Toni Morrison und Gabriel García Marquez), belegen eindrucksvoll das Renommee der Verlage.

Bertelsmann Buch AG in Munich: creativity and variety from the world's largest book centre

Book and music clubs with numerous members, successful publishing firms, and dynamic direct sales companies in more than 25 countries make Bertelsmann Buch AG the largest book enterprise worldwide. In the business year of 1997/98 it employed 18,400 persons. One third of its turnover amounting to DM 7.3 billion was earned in Germany, one third in the rest of Europe, and one third in North America. In the future markets of Asia and South America the activities of clubs and publishing firms are also increasing steadily.

Worldwide, the book and music clubs offer 25 million members low-priced and exclusive programmes, as well as comprehensive service.

The publishers' independent and autonomous status in the Bertelsmann enterprise makes it possible to combine literary variety and artistic quality. Numerous authors who have received awards and eight winners of the Nobel Prize of Literature (Toni Morrison and Gabriel García Marquez, for instance) underline in an impressive way the renown of the Bertelsmann publishing firms.

La Bertelsmann Buch AG à Munich: créativité et variété de la plus grande maison de livres du monde

Des clubs de livres et de musique comptant un grand nombre d'adhérents, des maisons d'édition à succès et des voies directes de distribution dynamiques dans plus de 25 pays font de la Bertelsmann Buch AG la plus grande société de livres du monde. Au cours de l'exercice 1997/98, la société comptait 18 400 collaborateurs, le chiffre d'affaires de 7,3 milliards de DM a été réalisé à part égale dans les pays germanophones, dans le reste de l'Europe et en Amérique du Nord. Dans les marchés d'avenir, en Asie et en Amérique Latine, l'engagement des clubs et des maisons d'édition croît de manière continue.

A l'échelle internationale, les clubs de livres et de musique offrent à leurs 25 millions de membres des programmes avantageux, exclusifs et un vaste service.

L'indépendance des publications et l'autonomie des éditeurs au sein de la maison Bertelsmann permettent d'associer la variété littéraire à la qualité artistique. De nombreux auteurs récompensés par des prix, dont huit prix Nobel de littérature (p.ex. Toni Morrison et Gabriel García Marquez), témoignent avec force de la renommée des maisons d'édition.

La Bertelsmann Buch AG di Monaco: la più grande casa libraria del mondo propone creatività e molteplicità

Numerosi club del libro e musicali con un gran numero di iscritti, case editrici di successo e dinamiche organizzazioni di vendita diretta in oltre 25 Paesi fanno della Bertelsmann Buch AG la maggiore azienda libraria del mondo. Nell'esercizio 1997/98 il numero dei dipendenti era di 18 400 unità; il fatturato è stato conseguito per un terzo nell'area di lingua tedesca, per un terzo nel resto d'Europa e per un terzo nel Nordamerica. Anche nei mercati del futuro dell'Asia e America Latina l'impegno dei club e delle case editrici cresce costantemente.

In tutto il mondo, i club del libro e quelli musicali propongono a 25 milioni di iscritti programmi economici ed esclusivi oltre ad un servizio assistenza molto vasto.

L'indipendenza in campo pubblicistico e l'autonomia degli editori all'interno della casa Bertelsmann permettono la simbiosi tra la molteplicità letteraria e la qualità artistica. Tutta una serie di autori di prestigio, tra cui anche otto Premi Nobel (ad esempio, Toni Morrison e Gabriel García Marquez) provano l'alta considerazione goduta dalle case editrici del Gruppo.

und Industrie GmbH und der BMW Leasing GmbH haben vier der zehn bedeutendsten Leasing-Anbieter Deutschlands ihren Sitz im Wirtschaftsraum München.

Mekka des Wagniskapitals

Der Finanzplatz Bayern mit seiner Zentrale München ist in der Bundesrepublik führend in der Vergabe öffentlicher Fördermittel wie privatem Venture Capital. Drei der „Top-Ten"-Gesellschaften in Deutschland, die auch Risiko-, Wagnis- oder Chancen-Kapitalgesellschaften genannt werden, sitzen hier. An der Isar steht so viel Risikokapital zur Verfügung, dass mittlerweile die Anleger nach neuen vermarktbaren High-Tech-Ideen fahnden und nicht umgekehrt – paradiesische Verhältnisse für innovative Existenzgründer.

ATTRAKTIVES UMFELD FÜR BERATER

Der Motor des Beschäftigungswachstums in München liegt seit längerem im Dienstleistungsbereich, dem inzwischen ca. 75% der Arbeitnehmer zuzurechnen sind. Insbesondere die unternehmensbezogenen Dienstleistungen – sogenannte Business Services – haben überdurchschnittlich zugenommen. Wirtschaftsprüfer, Rechtsanwälte, Ingenieurbüros, Unternehmensberater, Softwarehäuser, Bildungsinstitute, Werbeagenturen, Marktforschungsinstitute, Immobiliendienste und die anderen Freien Berufe finden hier den richtigen Nährboden: zahlreiche Unternehmen der Informations- und Kommunikationstechnologie, Biotechnologie und Multimedia. Da diese Firmen schneller wachsen als der Durchschnitt haben sie auch einen erhöhten Beratungsbedarf. Zum anderen sind Business Services auf hochqualifizierte und kreative Mitarbeiter angewiesen. Und diese sind in München und für München leichter zu gewinnen als in allen anderen Munich's numerous enterprises working in the sectors of information, communications, biotechnology and the media. As these firms grow more rapidly than most other enterprises, they require more comprehensive consulting. On the other hand, business services are dependent on highly qualified and creative personnel, which can be found in and for Munich much easier than in all other German cities and for other locations.

By employing external consultants and experts more frequently, the local enterprises boost their efficiency and effectiveness. The resulting gain in competitiveness and performance in turn generates growth and creates additional demand for advisory services. It is therefore not surprising that since 1980 business services have increased unproportionally (as regards turnover and number of employees) in relation to the overall private service sector. Munich benefits greatly from this development: Since consultants rely primarily on common synergies, rapid communication and availability, they prefer to settle in the city.

CHANCES OFFERED BY TOURISM

The decline of pure sightseeing and recreational tourism, which has become noticeable in the past few years, is accompanied by a pronounced trend towards more mobility and a thirst for more adventure and new experiences: People are getting more interested in shopping, musicals, event tourism, fun and sports. According to the forecasts of the World Travel & Tourism Council and the World Tourism Organization, tourism in the coming years will become the number one growth

UN ENVIRONNEMENT ATTRAYANT POUR LES CONSEILLERS

Le moteur de la croissance de l'emploi à Munich se trouve depuis longtemps dans le secteur tertiaire qui emploie maintenant 75% de la population active. Les services orientés vers les entreprises, que l'on appelle également business services, ont enregistré une croissance au-dessus de la moyenne. Les commissaires aux comptes, avocats, bureaux d'ingénieurs, conseillers d'entreprises, sociétés de logiciel, instituts de formation, agences publicitaires, instituts d'études de marché, promoteurs immobiliers et autres professions libérales trouvent ici un terrain idéal, à savoir une multitude d'entreprises de la technologie de l'information et de la communication, de la biotechnologie et du multimédia. Comme ces entreprises croissent plus rapidement que la moyenne, elles ont un énorme besoin en conseil. De plus, les business services dépendent de collaborateurs hautement qualifiés et créatifs. Il est plus facile de les trouver à Munich ou de les faire venir ici que dans les autres villes allemandes.

L'intervention renforcée de conseillers et d'experts externes auprès des entreprises entraîne une augmentation de l'efficacité et de l'efficience. En augmentant ainsi leur degré de compétitivité et de performance, les entreprises assurent la croissance et, par conséquent, une demande supplémentaire de prestations de conseil. Il n'est donc pas étonnant que, depuis 1980, les services proches des entreprises aient connu, au niveau du chiffre d'affaires et du nombre des employés, une augmentation disproportionnée par rapport à l'ensemble des prestations privées et économiques. Cette évolution est exemplaire pour Munich. Comme les conseillers sont absolument dépendants de synergies communes, de communication rapide et d'une di Hannover, la LHI Leasing für Handel und Industrie GmbH e la BMW Leasing GmbH, quattro delle maggiori compagnie di leasing della Germania, hanno la propria sede nell'area economica di Monaco.

Mecca del capitale di rischio

La piazza finanziaria bavarese con sede centrale a Monaco è al primo posto in Germania sia per quanto riguarda l'assegnazione di finanziamenti pubblici che per quanto riguarda il capitale di rischio privato. Tre delle maggiori compagnie tedesche, chiamate anche società di capitale di rischio o di venture capital, hanno qui la loro sede. Sull'Isar c'è a disposizione così tanto capitale di rischio che sono gli investitori che vanno alla caccia di nuove idee sull'alta tecnologia da poter finanziare e non vice versa – una situazione a dir poco paradisiaca per imprenditori innovativi e con spirito di iniziativa.

Un ambiente attraente per le attività di consulenza

Il motore della crescita dell'occupazione a Monaco è da molto tempo il settore dei servizi nel quale è impiegato circa il 75% dei lavoratori. In modo particolare, la crescita dei servizi relativi alle imprese – i cosiddetti business services – è stata superiore alla media. Revisori contabili, avvocati, ingegneri, consulenti aziendali, case di software, istituti di formazione, agenzie pubblicitarie, istituti di ricerca di mercato, servizi immobiliari e tutte le altre categorie di liberi professionisti trovano qui un terreno fertile: ovvero numerose aziende nei settori delle tecnologie informatiche, della comunicazione, della biotecnologia e dei multimedia. Dato che queste ditte crescono più velocemente rispetto alla media, sentono anche maggiormente l'esigenza di rivolgersi a servizi di consulenza. Dall'altra parte trovano degli interlocutori altamente

In München und in über 170 Städten weltweit:	In Munich and in more than 170 cities worldwide:	A Munich et dans plus de 170 villes du monde:	A Monaco ed in più di 170 città del mondo:
Brems- und Sicherheitssysteme für Metros, Stadtbahnen, Schnellbahnen und Nutzfahrzeuge vom führenden Hersteller mit dem Hauptsitz in München	**Brake and safety systems for metros, suburban railways, high-speed railways, and utility vehicles by the leading manufacturer with headquarters in Munich**	**Des systèmes de freins et de sécurité pour métros, trains interurbains, trains de banlieue et véhicules utilitaires produits par le leader avec siège central à Munich**	**Sistemi frenanti e di sicurezza per la metropolitana, la ferrovia suburbana veloce et per veicoli industriali dal produttore leader con sede centrale a Monaco**

Seit über 50 Jahren hat die **KNORR-BREMSE AG**, 1905 von Georg Knorr in Berlin gegründet, ihren Stammsitz in München.

Die Schwerpunkte des Unternehmens, das mit 40 Gesellschaften auf allen Kontinenten vertreten ist, liegen in Entwicklung, Produktion und Vertrieb modernster Brems- und Sicherheitssysteme für Schienen- und Nutzfahrzeuge. Mit einem hohen Anteil an Forschung und Entwicklung sichert sich die Firmengruppe ihren technologischen Führungsanspruch.

Knorr-Brems- und Fahrdynamikregelungen werden zusammen mit den weltweit bedeutendsten Nutzfahrzeugherstellern entwickelt.

Knorr-Bremssysteme für Schienenfahrzeuge finden sich in allen Hochgeschwindigkeitszügen der Welt, in den längsten und schwersten Kohle- und Erzzügen sowie in den Metros und Stadtschnellbahnen von über 170 Großstädten. Allein in München verlassen sich täglich 1,8 Millionen Fahrgäste in S-Bahn, U-Bahn, Straßenbahn und Stadtbussen auf Knorr-Brems- und Sicherheitssysteme.

Die KNORR-BREMSE AG beschäftigt heute weltweit über 7 300 Mitarbeiter, davon über 2 400 in Deutschland, und erzielte 1998 mehr als zwei Milliarden DM Umsatz.

Over 50 years **KNORR-BREMSE AG** which was founded in 1905 by Georg Knorr in Berlin has had its headquarters in Munich.

The enterprise which is represented with 40 companies on all continents specializes in research and development, manufacture and distribution of state-of-the-art brake and safety systems for rail cars and utility vehicles. With particular emphasis on R&D the group successfully secures its leading role for state-of-the-art technology.

Together with world-leading manufacturers of utility vehicles Knorr develops brake dynamic controls and controls for the dynamics of vehicle movement.

All high-speed trains throughout the world, the longest and heaviest coal and ore carrying trains as well as metros and city railways in more than 170 big cities are equipped with Knorr brake systems. In Munich alone 1.8 million people riding the S-Bahn and U-Bahn trains, the street cars and busses every day rely on brake and safety systems made by Knorr.

The KNORR-BREMSE AG employs more than 7,300 persons worldwide, of which 2,400 jobs are in Germany, and produced a turnover in 1998 exceeding 2 billion DM.

Fondée à Berlin en 1905 par Georg Knorr, la société **KNORR-BREMSE AG** possède depuis plus de 50 ans son siège à Munich.

Les atouts de l'entreprise, représentée à travers le monde par 40 sociétés, se trouvent dans le développement, la production et la distribution de systèmes de freins et de sécurité ultramodernes pour les véhicules ferroviaires et utilitaires. Avec son fort pourcentage de recherche et de développement, le groupe d'entreprises s'assure une place de leader technologique.

Les réglages Knorr des freins et de la dynamique de conduite sont développés en commun avec les plus grands fabricants mondiaux de véhicules utilitaires.

Les systèmes de freins Knorr pour les véhicules ferroviaires se trouvent dans tous les trains à grande vitesse du monde, dans les plus longs et les plus lourds trains de transport de charbon et de minerai ainsi que dans les métros et trains interurbains de plus de 170 villes. Rien qu'à Munich, 1,8 million de voyageurs dans les trains interurbains, le métro, les tram et les bus font tous les jours confiance aux systèmes de freins et de sécurité Knorr.

La KNORR-BREMSE AG emploie aujourd'hui plus de 7 300 collaborateurs à l'échelle mondiale, dont 2 400 en Allemagne et a réalisé en 1998 un chiffre d'affaires dépassant deux milliards de DM.

Da oltre 50 anni la **KNORR-BREMSE AG**, fondata nel 1905 da Georg Knorr a Berlino, ha la sua sede centrale a Monaco.

Il «baricentro» dell'attività dell'azienda, che con 40 società è presente in tutti i continenti, è rappresentato dallo sviluppo, dalla produzione e vendita di modernissimi sistemi frenanti e di sicurezza per veicoli industriali e su rotaia. Il gruppo si assicura la sua leadership tecnologica con un'elevata quota di ricerca e sviluppo.

I sistemi Knorr di regolazione dei freni e della dinamica di guida vengono sviluppati in collaborazione con i più importanti produttori di veicoli industriali su scala mondiale.

I sistemi frenanti Knorr per i veicoli su rotaia vengono impiegati in tutti i treni ad alta velocità del mondo, nei convogli più lunghi e pesanti per il trasporto di carbone e ferro nonché nelle metropolitane sotterranee e in quelle di superficie di oltre 170 grandi città. Nella sola Monaco sono 1,8 i passeggeri che giornalmente fanno affidamento sui sistemi frenanti e di sicurezza Knorr nei convogli della ferrovia suburbana veloce, della metropolitana, nei tram e negli autobus cittadini.

La KNORR-BREMSE AG dà lavoro oggi, in tutto il mondo, a 7 300 dipendenti, di cui oltre 2 400 in Germania, e ha ottenuto, nel 1998, un fatturato superiore ai due miliardi.

ren deutschen Städten oder für andere Standorte.

Die verstärkte Einschaltung externer Berater und Experten bei den Unternehmen führt zu einer Steigerung von Effektivität und Effizienz. Die dadurch erhöhte Wettbewerbs- und Leistungsfähigkeit der Firmen sorgt für Wachstum und somit für zusätzliche Nachfrage nach Beratungsleistungen. Es verwundert daher nicht, dass die unternehmensnahen Dienstleistungen hinsichtlich Umsatz und Anzahl der Beschäftigten im Verhältnis zum gesamten privatwirtschaftlichen Dienstleistungsbereich seit 1980 überproportional wachsen. Diese Entwicklung ist für München sehr vorteilhaft. Da die Berater in besonderem Maße auf gemeinsame Synergien, schnelle Kommunikation und gute Erreichbarkeit angewiesen sind, siedeln sie sich bevorzugt in der Stadt an.

CHANCEN IM TOURISMUS

Die in den letzten Jahren abnehmende Bedeutung des reinen Besichtigungs- und Erholungstourismus geht einher mit einem Trend zu mehr Mobilität und Erlebnishunger (Shopping, Musical, Event-Tourismus, Fun und Sport). Nach Schätzungen des World Travel & Tourism Council und der World Tourism Organization wird sich der Tourismus in den nächsten Jahren weltweit zur Wachstumsbranche Nummer 1 entwickeln und zu einer der wichtigsten Schlüsselbranchen der Zukunft werden.

Schon heute weist München mit fast 6,5 Millionen Übernachtungen in gewerblichen Betrieben unter allen deutschen Städten die höchste Fremdenverkehrsintensität (Übernachtungen pro 100 Einwohner) auf und liegt damit im Spitzenfeld der europäischen Metropolen. Beinahe 60 Millionen Besucher pro Jahr sorgen für einen touristischen Umsatz von über sechs Milliarden Mark und sichern 68 000 Arbeitsplätze, insbesondere im Hotel- und Gaststättengewerbe sowie im Handel.

branch worldwide and will eventually turn into one of the key industries of the future.

Today Munich with about 6.5 million overnight stays in hotels and boarding houses already boasts the highest rate of touristic intensity (i. e. overnight stays per 100 inhabitants) of all German cities and ranks among the top group of European metropolises. Nearly 60 million visitors per year generate a touristic turnover of more than DM six billion; they safeguard 68,000 jobs mainly in the hotel sector and in trade.

The Munich Airport is turning into a European air turnstile, and the Neue Messe with the ultra-modern Congress Centre will promote further growth just as effectively as international top events like the European Light Athletics Championships in 2002 and the Federal Garden Show in 2005. The Municipal Tourist Office is responsible for some of the most important touristic functions: It not only organizes top attractions like the October Festival, the Christmas Market, and various "Dulten" (village fairs), which together attract about 8.8 million visitors, but also 3,500 other events. New programmes like the internet with 600 pages and more than six million contacts per year; innovations like the "Key to Munich"; "Hits for Kids"; and the "Welcome Card" appeal to new target groups and thus promote a stable and varied touristic structure.

INFRASTRUCTURE

The quality of the local infrastructure is a decisive factor in the international competition among industrial locations. The most important components are accessibility and supply. In addition to its interior mobility and smoothly flowing economic traf-

accessibilité facile, ils s'installent de préférence en ville.

OPPORTUNITES DU TOURISME

Au cours des dernières années, la baisse de l'importance du tourisme s'intéressant uniquement aux visites ou aux loisirs va de pair avec la tendance vers une plus grande mobilité et un désir d'aventure (shopping, comédie musicale, tourisme dans le cadre d'une manifestation, fun et sport). D'après les estimations du World Travel & Tourism Council et de la World Tourism Organisation, le tourisme deviendra au cours des prochaines années le secteur de croissance N° 1 et sera un des secteurs clé de l'avenir.

Aujourd'hui déjà, Munich, avec près de 6,5 millions de nuitées en hôtels ou pensions, présente la plus forte intensité touristique (nuitées par 100 habitants) des villes allemandes et arrive dans le peloton de tête des métropoles européennes. Environ 60 millions de visiteurs par an permettent de réaliser un chiffre d'affaires touristique dépassant six milliards de mark et assurent 68 000 emplois, en particulier dans l'hôtellerie et la gastronomie ainsi que dans le commerce.

Le développement de l'aéroport de Munich en une plate-forme aérienne européenne et la Neue Messe avec son centre des congrès moderne assureront cette croissance tout comme les grandes manifestations internationales, à savoir les championnats du monde d'athlétisme en 2002 et l'exposition d'horticulture en 2005. Une fonction principale du tourisme à Munich est à la charge de l'office municipal du tourisme qui n'organise pas seulement la fête de la Bière, le marché de Noël et les kermesses attirant plus de 8,8 millions de visiteurs mais s'occupe chaque année de plus de 3 500 manifestations. De nouvelles offres comme Internet avec 600 pages et enregistrant plus de six millions d'accès par an, la Mün-

qualificati e creativi in grado di offrire un servizio ottimo e più facilmente accessibile a Monaco e per Monaco rispetto ad ogni altra città tedesca.

Il sempre maggiore intervento di consulenti ed esperti esterni nelle attività delle aziende porta ad un aumento dell'effettività e dell'efficienza. L'accresciuta concorrenzialità ed efficienza delle ditte produce a sua volta uno sviluppo e quindi una richiesta maggiore di servizi di consulenza. Non meraviglia quindi che i servizi connessi alle aziende siano cresciuti in modo sproporzionato dal 1980 ad oggi per quanto riguarda fatturato e numero di addetti in rapporto all'intero settore dei servizi economico-privati. Questo sviluppo è molto vantaggioso per Monaco. Infatti, dato che questo tipo di lavoro si basa in modo particolare su sinergie comuni, su una comunicazione veloce ed una buona raggiungibilità, i consulenti preferiscono stabilirsi direttamente in città.

Le prospettive nel turismo

Il puro turismo ricreativo e le classiche visite turistiche stanno perdendo importanza negli ultimi anni e questa tendenza va di pari passo con una maggiore mobilità e con il desiderio di fare nuove esperienze (shopping, eventi musicali, manifestazioni, divertimento e sport). Secondo quanto stabilito dal World Travel & Tourism Council e la World Tourism Organization, il turismo si svilupperà nei prossimi anni fino a diventare il settore di maggiore espansione a livello mondiale ed uno dei più importanti settori chiave del futuro.

Già oggi Monaco presenta con i suoi quasi 6,5 milioni di pernottamenti la maggiore intensità di afflusso turistico (n° di pernottamenti per 100 abitanti) tra tutte le città tedesche, inserendosi al primo posto delle metropoli europee. Quasi 60 milioni di visitatori all'anno contribuiscono a produrre un fatturato di oltre sei

Die Entwicklung des Flughafens München zu einem europäischen Luftdrehkreuz und die Neue Messe mit dem modernen Kongresszentrum werden dieses Wachstum genauso fördern wie die internationalen Großveranstaltungen Leichtathletik-Europameisterschaften 2002 und Bundesgartenschau 2005. Eine wichtige Funktion im Tourismus Münchens obliegt dem städtischen Fremdenverkehrsamt, das nicht nur die Magneten Oktoberfest, Christkindlmarkt und Dulten mit insgesamt rund 8,8 Millionen Besuchern organisiert, sondern Jahr für Jahr etwa 3 500 Veranstaltungen betreut. Neue Angebote wie das Internet mit 600 Seiten und über sechs Millionen Zugriffen pro Jahr, der München-Schlüssel, Hits for Kids und Welcome Card gewinnen neue Zielgruppen und fördern so eine stabile, vielfältige Besucherstruktur.

INFRASTRUKTUR

Die Qualität der Infrastruktur ist mit entscheidend im internationalen Standortwettbewerb. Bedeutsam sind hier vor allem die Komponenten Erreichbarkeit und Versorgung. Abgesehen von der inneren Mobilität und einem flüssigen Wirtschaftsverkehr wird die Erreichbarkeit Münchens nach internationalen Kriterien insbesondere durch die Qualität des Flughafens, der Hochgeschwindigkeitszüge, der Autobahnverbindungen sowie nicht zuletzt der Telekommunikationsnetze bestimmt.

München beflügelt

Am 17. Mai 1992 wurde der neue Münchner Flughafen in Betrieb genommen, der sich seitdem als zweites nationales Gateway im deutschen Luftverkehrssystem etabliert hat. Überproportionales Wachstum mit zweistelligen Zuwachsraten brachte München 1997 mit 17,9 Millionen Fluggästen erstmals in den Kreis der zehn größten europäischen Flughäfen. Jede Million Passagiere fic, Munich is easily accessible according to international criteria, thanks to the quality of its airport, its high-speed trains, its excellent autobahn connections, and – last but not least – to its telecommunication network.

Munich Takes to the Air

On 17 May 1992 the new Munich Airport was put into service and has turned into a second national gateway of the German air traffic system. In 1997 its above-average growth (based on two-digit growth rates) and 17.9 million passengers elevated Munich to the level of Europe's largest airports for the first time. Every million passengers secures approximately 1,000 working places at the airport itself and a further 1,000 jobs in the airport vicinity. In 1999 the construction of a second terminal was started.

Munich already holds the position of an important railway junction in the heart of Europe. An ICE line leading to Nuremberg via Ingolstadt is under construction; a high-speed line connecting Paris and Budapest via Munich – the "Magistrale" – is still in the planning stage; further projects which are to increase the attractiveness and efficiency of the railway junction of Munich are the "Brennerbasistunnel" (which will provide a faster connection to Italy) and the "Bahn-21-Konzept", which envisages putting the Munich Main Railway Station underground for transit traffic.

Thanks to seven autobahns, five of which are already connected by an "autobahn ring", road access to Munich and from the city to other German and foreign destinati- chener-Schlüssel, Hits for Kids et la Welcome Card attirent de nouveaux groupes cibles et encouragent ainsi une structure stable et variée des touristes.

L'INFRASTRUCTURE

La qualité de l'infrastructure est décisive pour la compétitivité internationale d'un site. Les composants comme l'accessibilité et l'approvisionnement sont capitaux. Outre la mobilité interne et une circulation économique rapide, l'accès à Munich est déterminé entre autres par des critères internationaux comme la qualité de l'aéroport, les trains à grande vitesse, les accès autoroutiers ainsi que les réseaux de télécommunication.

Munich anime

Le 17 mai 1992 marqua l'entrée en fonction du nouvel aéroport de Munich qui s'est depuis établi au deuxième rang des aéroports nationaux. Un essor extraordinaire avec des taux de croissance à deux chiffres porta Munich en 1997 avec 17,9 millions de passagers pour la première fois parmi le cercle des dix plus grand aéroports européens. Chaque million de passagers assure environ 1 000 emplois dans l'aéroport ainsi que 1 000 autres dans ses environs. Les travaux du deuxième terminal ont déjà commencé en 1999.

Aujourd'hui déjà, Munich est un axe ferroviaire important au cœur de l'Europe. La ligne ICE en cours de construction et reliant Nuremberg via Ingolstadt, les projets «Magistrale für Europa», une ligne ferroviaire à grande vitesse entre Paris et Budapest via Munich, le tunnel du Brenner ainsi que le concept Bahn 21, qui mettrait sous terre la gare principale et en ferait une gare de passage, continuent d'augmenter l'attractivité et l'efficience de Munich comme axe ferroviaire.

Grâce à sept autoroutes dont maintenant cinq d'entre elles sont reliées par un anneau autoroutier, aller à Munich et en partir milioni di marchi, garantendo 68 000 posti di lavoro, soprattutto nell'industria alberghiera e nel commercio.

Lo sviluppo dell'aeroporto di Monaco in uno snodo europeo per il traffico aereo e la Nuova Fiera con il moderno Centro Congressi favoriranno questa crescita così come le grandi manifestazioni internazionali previste per i primi anni del duemila, ovvero i Campionati Europei di Atletica Leggera del 2002 e la Mostra Nazionale dei Giardini del 2005. Un'importante funzione nel turismo di Monaco è svolta dall'Ente del Turismo della città che non organizza solo i famosi Oktoberfest, Christkindlmarkt (Mercatino di Natale) e i balli per un totale di circa 8,8 milioni di visitatori, ma si occupa di organizzare anche di anno in anno circa 3 500 manifestazioni ed eventi. Nuove offerte quali Internet con 600 pagine e oltre sei milioni di accessi all'anno, la Chiave di Monaco, gli «Hits for Kids» e la Welcome Card hanno raggiunto e continuano a raggiungere nuovi target turistici contribuendo a promuovere un turismo variegato e quindi più stabile.

L'INFRASTRUTTURA

La qualità dell'infrastruttura è di importanza fondamentale nella concorrenza tra Monaco e le sue antagoniste internazionali. I componenti più rilevanti sono l'accessibilità e la distribuzione. A parte la mobilità interna ed un traffico commerciale scorrevole, l'accessibilità di Monaco viene determinata secondo criteri internazionali tenendo conto soprattutto della qualità dell'aeroporto, dei treni ad alta velocità, dei collegamenti autostradali e, non da ultimo, delle reti di telecomunicazione.

Monaco mette le ali

Il nuovo aeroporto di Monaco è stato inaugurato il 17 Maggio 1992 ed è diventato da allora il secondo gateway nazionale nel sistema tedesco dei trasporti aerei. La crescita sproporzionata

Das multifunktionale Arabellahaus im gleichnamigen Stadtteilpark

The multi-functional Arabellahaus in Arabella Park

La Arabellahaus, un bâtiment multifonctionnel situé dans le parc du même nom

Arabellahaus, l'edificio multifunzionale che sorge nel parco del quartiere omonimo

Das denkmalgeschützte Stachus-Rondell am Karlsplatz

The Stachus-Rondell on Karlsplatz - a protected monument

Classée monument historique, la place en demi-cercle du Stachus sur la Karlsplatz

L'emiciclo dello Stachus sulla Karlsplatz, posto sotto la tutela delle opere d'arte

Die Geschichte einer Stadt ist immer auch die Geschichte ihrer Gebäude, Plätze und Menschen. Mit ihrem Bauträger- und Immobilienengagement leistet die **Schörghuber Unternehmensgruppe** seit Jahrzehnten einen wichtigen Beitrag für ein attraktives Stadtbild und eine lebenswerte Stadtkultur in München.

The history of a city is at the same time the history of its buildings, squares and people. The **Schörghuber Corporate Group** - concentrating on construction and real estate - has for several decades contributed a significant share to creating an attractive cityscape and a valuable city culture in Munich.

L'histoire d'une ville est toujours étroitement liée à l'histoire de ses bâtiments, places et de ses habitants. Avec son engagement en tant qu'entreprise de construction et agent immobilier, le **Groupe d'entreprises Schörghuber** contribue depuis des décennies à rendre attrayant l'image de la ville et apporte une culture citadine vitale à Munich.

La storia di una città è sempre anche la storia dei suoi edifici, degli angoli caratteristici e delle persone. Con la sua gestione di progetti edili ed immobiliare il **Gruppo Schörghuber** presta da decenni un importante contributo alla realizzazione, a Monaco di Baviera, di una fisionomia urbanistica accattivante e di una cultura urbana degna di essere vissuta.

Das Einkaufs- und Freizeitzentrum Elisenhof gleich gegenüber dem Hauptbahnhof

The Elisenhof shopping and recreation centre opposite the main railway station

Le centre commercial et de loisirs Elisenhof en face de la gare principale

Il centro commerciale e per il tempo libero Elisenhof di fronte alla stazione centrale

MESSEPLATZ

sichert etwa 1 000 Arbeitsplätze am Flughafen sowie weitere 1 000 in dessen Umfeld. 1999 wurde mit dem Bau eines zweiten Terminals begonnen.

Bereits heute ist München ein wichtiger Schienenknotenpunkt im Herzen Europas. Die im Bau befindliche ICE-Strecke über Ingolstadt nach Nürnberg, die geplanten Projekte Magistrale für Europa – eine Hochgeschwindigkeitsbahnlinie zwischen Paris und Budapest über München – und der Brennerbasistunnel sowie das Bahn-21-Konzept, wonach der Hauptbahnhof als Durchgangsbahnhof unter die Oberfläche verlegt werden soll, werden die Attraktivität und Effizienz des Bahnknotenpunktes München weiter steigern.

Dank sieben Autobahnen, von denen mittlerweile fünf durch einen Autobahnring miteinander verbunden sind, ist auch auf der Straße der Weg nach München und von der Stadt hinaus in das In- und Ausland kürzer geworden.

Neue Messe München – ein „flagship project"

Strategische Entwicklungsprojekte können der Wirtschaft eines Raumes neue Impulse geben. So hat die Verlagerung des Flughafens unter anderem auch der Zukunftsinvestition in das im Februar 1998 eröffnete Internationale Messe- und Kongresszentrum in der neuen Messestadt Riem sowie dem stadtpolitisch bedeutsamen Nachfolgeprojekt auf der Theresienhöhe den Weg bereitet. Aufgrund der starken Nachfrage musste bereits ein Dreivierteljahr nach der Eröffnung des Messe- und Kongresszent-

ons has also become less time-consuming.

Neue Messe München – a Flagship Project

Strategic development projects can provide new stimuli for the economy of a region. Thus shifting the airport from Riem to Erding has paved the way for the International Fair and Congress Centre (an investment for the future), opened in February 1998 in Riem, and for the successor project on "Theresienhöhe", which is of particular importance to the city. Because of heavy demand it was necessary – only nine months after the inauguration of the Fair and Congress Centre – to start building two more exhibition halls. From autumn 2000 on the Munich fair site will boast a hall capacity of 165,000 square metres. These so-called flagship projects normally increase confidence in a certain location and, consequently, in the region's entrepreneurial investments.

A Shopping Centre with Italian Flair

Nowhere in Germany do people spend as much money per square metre of retail floor space as in the city centre of Munich. For that reason turnover and employee figures remained relatively stable in this Bavarian metropolis with Italian flair even during years when in other German cities pronounced drops in turnover were observed. Munich also seems to be well prepared for future developments: It plans to further liberalize business hours; and it relies on increasing electronic on-line trade by means of the internet, and on event centres which combine shopping, gastronomy and entertainment in covered malls. On Willy-Brandt-Platz in the new fair-city of Riem such an urban entertainment centre will be set up at the beginning of the new millennium.

pour aller vers le reste de l'Allemagne et l'étranger prend moins de temps.

Neue Messe München – un projet clé

Les projets stratégiques de développement peuvent donner de nouvelles impulsions à l'économie d'un espace. Ainsi, le déménagement de l'aéroport, sans oublier l'investissement du futur dans le centre international de congrès et de foires ouvert en février 1998 dans la nouvelle ville de foires et expositions de Riem ainsi que l'important projet sur la Theresienhöhe ont préparé le terrain. Neuf mois seulement après l'ouverture du centre de congrès et de foires, il a fallu commencer la construction de nouveaux halls en raison de l'ampleur de la demande. A partir de l'automne 2000, la place de foires de Munich affichera une capacité de halls de 165 000 m². Ces projets clé encouragent la confiance placée dans le site et aussi les investissements des entreprises dans la région.

Ville du shopping au flair italien

Nulle part ailleurs en Allemagne, le chiffre d'affaires par mètre carré de surface commerciale n'est aussi important que dans le centre ville de Munich. Ainsi, dans la métropole de l'Isar au flair presque italien, les chiffres d'affaires et les nombres des employés sont restés relativement stables même les années où ailleurs de nets reculs ont été observés. Munich semble aussi équipée pour les développements futurs, qu'il s'agisse de la libéralisation des heures d'ouverture des magasins, de la croissance du commerce en ligne via Internet ainsi que des centres commerciaux regroupant shopping, gastronomie et programme d'animation dans des galeries couvertes. Sur la place Willy Brandt dans la nouvelle ville de foire de Riem, un tel centre Urban Entertainment

dei traffici aerei, con tassi di incremento a due cifre, ha portato Monaco a raggiungere nel 1997 i 17,9 milioni di passeggeri e ad entrare per la prima volta nel circuito dei dieci maggiori aeroporti europei. Ogni milione di passeggeri garantisce circa 1 000 posti di lavoro nell'aeroporto ed altrettanti 1 000 nel suo indotto. Nel 1999 è stata iniziata la costruzione di un secondo terminale.

Già oggi Monaco è un importante snodo ferroviario nel cuore dell'Europa. Il tratto dell'ICE al momento in costruzione che attraverserà Ingolstadt fino a raggiungere Nürnberg, i progetti per la linea ferroviaria principale per l'Europa – una linea ferroviaria ad alta velocità che collegherà Parigi e Budapest attraverso Monaco –, il tunnel del Brennero e il progetto Bahn-21, in cui si prevede di spostare la stazione principale sotto la superficie, incrementeranno ulteriormente l'attrattiva e l'efficienza dello snodo ferroviario di Monaco.

Grazie a sette autostrade, di cui nel frattempo cinque sono state collegate mediante un anello autostradale, sono stati raccorciati anche i collegamenti via strada ed autostrada per e da Monaco verso le altre città tedesche e verso i Paesi esteri.

La Nuova Fiera di Monaco – un «flagship project»

Progetti strategici di sviluppo possono dare nuovi impulsi all'economia di una determinata area. Ad esempio, il trasferimento dell'aeroporto ha aperto la strada anche all'investimento successivo del Centro Congressi e Fiere inaugurato nel Febbraio 1998 nella nuova città fieristica di Riem e al progetto futuro sulla Theresienhöhe, importante dal punto di vista politico della città. In seguito a forti richieste, già dopo nove mesi dall'inaugurazione del Centro Congressi e Fiere è stato necessario iniziare con la costruzione di due ulteriori capannoni. A partire dall'autunno del 2000, il Centro Fiere di Monaco avrà

Hochleistungs-Schmierstoffe von Optimol

Optimol wurde 1920 als eigenständiges deutsches Unternehmen in München gegründet und ist seit 1990 eine Tochter der weltweit tätigen Burmah Castrol Gruppe.

Von Anfang an setzte man bei Optimol auf technische Innovationen im Bereich der Tribologie. Das Unternehmen entwickelte sich schnell zum Spezialisten für Hochleistungs-Schmierstoffe. Zahlreiche Patente belegen den Anspruch, den Optimol in der eigenen Forschung und Entwicklung an sich stellt. Heute präsentiert sich der Schmierstoff-Spezialist als ein international aktives Unternehmen mit rund 80 Mitarbeitern vor Ort und über 50 Ländervertretungen weltweit.

Optimol bietet seinen Kunden nicht nur Hochleistungs-Schmierstoffe in Form von Ölen, Fetten und Pasten, sondern auch eine fachkundige Beratung, die einen effizienten und umweltgerechten Einsatz von Schmierstoffen sicherstellt. Optimol Produkte werden in vielen Industriebereichen wie z.B. Lebensmittel, Getränke, Automobil, Kunststoff, Textil, Druck, Papier, Glas und Chemie eingesetzt.

High Performance Lubricants from Optimol

In 1920 Optimol was founded as an independent German enterprise in Munich. Since 1990 it has been a subsidiary of the worldwide operating Burmah Castrol Group.

Optimol relied from its beginnings on technological innovations in the field of tribology. The enterprise quickly turned into a specialist for high performance lubricants. Numerous patents are evidence of the high standard which Optimol sets in its own research and development. Today this lubricant expert presents itself as an internationally operating company with, locally, about 80 employees and more than 50 agencies worldwide.

Optimol offers its customers not only high performance lubricants in the form of oils, greases and pastes, but also expert advice in how to employ them in an efficient and environmentally friendly way. Optimol products are used in many industrial branches, for instance in the food, beverage, automotive, plastics, textile, printing, paper, glass and chemical industries.

Les lubrifiants hautement performants d'Optimol

Optimol fut créé à Munich en 1920 comme entreprise allemande autonome et est depuis 1990 une filiale du groupe Burmah Castrol opérant au niveau mondial.

Dès le début, Optimol s'est concentré sur les innovations techniques dans le secteur de la tribologie. L'entreprise se transforma rapidement en un spécialiste de lubrifiants de hautes performances. Les nombreux brevets obtenus témoignent combien Optimol est exigeant au niveau de la recherche et du développement. Le spécialiste des lubrifiants se présente aujourd'hui comme une entreprise active à l'échelle internationale, comptant 80 collaborateurs sur place et plus de 50 représentations à l'étranger.

Optimol propose à ses clients des lubrifiants de hautes performances sous forme d'huiles, de graisses et de pâtes et elle offre en plus du conseil technique assurant une utilisation efficace et écologique des lubrifiants. Les produits Optimol sont utilisés dans de nombreux secteurs industriels, qu'il s'agisse de la production de produits alimentaires, de boissons, de l'automobile, des plastiques, du textile, de l'imprimerie, du papier, du verre et de la chimie.

Lubrificanti ad elevate prestazioni Optimol

Optimol è stata fondata a Monaco di Baviera, come azienda autonoma tedesca, nel 1920 e dal 1990 è una società affiliata della Burmah Castrol, gruppo operante sul mercato a livello mondiale.

Fin dall'inizio, Optimol ha concentrato i suoi sforzi nello sviluppo di innovazioni tecniche nel settore della tribologia e si è sviluppata velocemente come azienda specializzata in lubrificanti ad elevate prestazioni. Numerosi brevetti testimoniano dell'ambizione dell'azienda nel campo della ricerca e sviluppo. Optimol si presenta oggi come un'azienda specializzata operante a livello internazionale, con 80 dipendenti in sede ed oltre 50 rappresentanze in tutto il mondo.

Optimol offre ai propri clienti non solo lubrificanti ad elevate prestazioni sotto forma di oli, grassi e paste, bensì anche un servizio di consulenza competente al fine di garantire un impiego efficiente ed ecologico dei lubrificanti. I prodotti Optimol vengono impiegati in diversi settori industriali quali, ad esempio, quello delle bevande, delle materie plastiche, della stampa, della carta, del vetro, oltre all'industria alimentare, tessile, automobilistica e chimica.

Firmensitz der Optimol in München

The Optimol Headquarters in Munich

Le siège social d'Optimol à Munich

La sede della Optimol a Monaco di Baviera

Produktion von Hochleistungs-Schmierstoffen nach QS 9000

Production of high performance lubricants in accordance with QS 9000

La production de lubrifiants de hautes performances conformément à QS 9000

Produzione di lubrificanti ad elevate prestazioni secondo la norma QS 9000

rums mit dem Bau von zwei weiteren Hallen begonnen werden. Ab Herbst des Jahres 2000 wird der Messeplatz München eine Hallenkapazität von 165 000 m² besitzen. Diese sogenannten „flagship projects" fördern das Vertrauen in den Standort und schließlich die unternehmerischen Investitionen in der Region.

Einkaufsstadt mit italienischem Flair

Nirgendwo in Deutschland wird mehr Geld pro Quadratmeter Einzelhandelsfläche umgesetzt als in der Münchner Innenstadt. So blieben in der Isarmetropole mit fast italienischem Flair Umsätze und Beschäftigtenzahlen auch in den Jahren relativ stabil, in denen anderenorts deutliche Rückgänge zu beobachten waren. München scheint auch für künftige Entwicklungen gerüstet zu sein: weitere Liberalisierung der Ladenöffnungszeiten, zunehmender elektronischer Online-Handel über das Internet sowie Erlebniszentren, die Einkaufen, Gastronomie und Unterhaltungsangebote in überdachten Malls vereinen. Am Willy-Brandt-Platz in der neuen Messestadt Riem wird Anfang des neuen Jahrtausends ein solches Urban Entertainment Center entstehen.

Münchner Meisterstück

Eine der Säulen der Münchner Wirtschaftsstruktur stellen die kleinen und mittelständischen Betriebe (KMU) vor allem des Handwerks dar. Nicht zuletzt wegen der mit über 15 000 Firmen mit rund 130 000 Beschäftigten größten

Munich's Masterpiece

One of the pillars of Munich's economic structure are the so-called "KMU" – small and medium-sized enterprises, primarily of the trades and crafts. Because of the extreme density of these enterprises in the Bavarian capital (more than 15,000 firms employing 130,000 persons), this economic structure is called the "Munich Mix". Small and medium-sized companies are not only far less prone to cyclical fluctuations than large-scale enterprises, but they also safeguard the supply of the local population with products and services; besides, they train by far more apprentices than their number of employees would warrant.

It is therefore one of the essential aims of Munich's economic policy to promote the growth potential of the KMUs. Not only customer-oriented and – above all – service-oriented enterprise-consulting is to help achieve this goal; but also the safeguarding and expanding of traditional sites, and the full exploitation of existing and the development of new industrial areas. The municipal offering includes not only newly opened up and well-alloted plots (for instance in the industrial zones of the fair and exhibition town of Riem), but also rental space in the so-called "Gewerbehöfe" (industrial parks).

For many firms with location problems these industrial parks offer the only means to find suitable and affordable plots near their original location in order to safeguard the long-term existence of their businesses. By employing an extremely dense

Center verra le jour au début du prochain millénaire.

Chef d'œuvre munichois

Les petites et moyennes entreprises (PME) constituent un des piliers de la structure économique munichoise, en particulier pour l'artisanat. Les quelques 15 000 entreprises comptant 130 000 employés forment la plus grande densité d'entreprises artisanales d'Allemagne et on parle de la «mixité munichoise» particulière de l'économie. Les petites et moyennes entreprises sont plus résistantes à la conjoncture que les grandes entreprises. Elles approvisionnent localement la population en produits et services et, par rapport au nombre de leurs employés, leur contribution à la formation est énorme.

Un objectif essentiel de la politique économique de Munich est d'ailleurs d'encourager les potentiels de croissance des PME. Cela englobe, outre un conseil des entreprises orienté sur la clientèle et le service, tout particulièrement le maintien et l'agrandissement des sites artisanaux existant depuis longtemps ainsi que la médiation d'espaces commerciaux existants et le développement de nouveaux. «L'offre municipale» comprend ici aussi bien les espaces commerciaux accordés récemment et exactement morcelés, p.ex. dans les zones industrielles de la ville de foires de Riem que les surfaces louées dans les centres artisanaux.

Pour de nombreuses entreprises connaissant des problèmes avec leur site, les centres artisanaux représentent l'unique possibilité pour obtenir des surfaces appropriées à un prix abordable, à proximité de leur ancien site et pour assurer ainsi l'existence à long terme de l'entreprise. Avec leur construction dense, les centres artisanaux ont une utilisation optimale des petites surfaces de terrain et réduisent ainsi les coûts ce qui permet de conserver la mixité habitat et travail. Par les

una capacità espositiva di ben 165 000 mq. Questi cosiddetto «flagship projects» alimentano la fiducia nella città e, di conseguenza, aumentano gli investimenti imprenditoriali nella regione.

Città dello shopping con «flair» italiano

In nessun'altra parte della Germania si realizzano così tanti guadagni per metro quadrato di superficie commerciale (negozi di vendita al dettaglio) come nel centro di Monaco. È così che nella metropoli sull'Isar dal «flair» italiano i fatturati e il numero di persone occupate nel settore sono rimasti relativamente stabili anche in quegli anni in cui si osservavano chiari segni di recesso nelle altre città. Monaco sembra inoltre preparata per affrontare anche gli sviluppi del futuro: l'ulteriore liberalizzazione degli orari di apertura dei negozi, l'aumento delle vendite in linea attraverso Internet e i centri commerciali o «isole pedonali al coperto« che riuniscono shopping, gastronomia e divertimento. Anche sulla Piazza Willy Brandt nella nuova città fieristica di Riem sorgerà all'inizio del nuovo millennio un «Urban Entertainment Center« dello stesso tipo.

Il capolavoro di Monaco

Uno dei pilastri della struttura economica di Monaco è rappresentato dalle piccole e medie aziende – identificate in tedesco dalla sigla KMU –, soprattutto nel settore dell'artigianato. Non da ultimo per il fatto che la densità di imprese artigianali è la maggiore in Germania con oltre 15 000 ditte e circa 130 000 persone impiegate, si parla di una particolare «formula Monaco» dell'economia. Piccole e medie imprese sono fondamentalmente più resistenti alle congiunture rispetto alle grandi imprese, garantiscono alla popolazione una fornitura di prodotti e servizi locali e offrono in proporzione migliori possibilità di formazione ad un numero mag-

Der Firmensitz des Weltunternehmens in München. **OSRAM** *ist einer der drei international führenden Lampenhersteller mit rund 30 000 Mitarbeitern und einem Weltumsatz von über 7 Milliarden DM. OSRAM beliefert Kunden in über 140 Ländern und produziert in 52 Fertigungsstätten in 18 Ländern.*

The Munich headquarters of a global company. **OSRAM** *is one of the three leading lamp manufacturers in the world with a turnover of more than 7 billion, employing about 30,000 people. OSRAM supplies customers in more than 140 countries and has 52 production facilities in 18 countries.*

Le siège munichois d'une société internationale. Avec un chiffre d'affaires de plus de 7 milliards de DM. **OSRAM** *est l'un des trois principaux fabricants de lampes de la planète et emploie 30 000 personnes. La société compte ses clients dans plus de 140 pays et dispose dans le monde entier de 52 usines situées dans 18 pays différents.*

La sede dell'azienda, che opera su scala mondiale a Monaco. **OSRAM** *è una delle tre aziende leader a livello internazionale nella produzione di lampade con un turnover di oltre 7 miliardi di marchi, e conta circa 30 000 dipendenti. La OSRAM rifornice clienti in oltre 140 Paesi e produce in 52 stabilimenti distribuiti in 18 Paesi.*

Innovative Mini-Leuchtstofflampen haben einen Durchmesser von nur noch 7 mm. Die OSRAM-Forscher haben das Ziel, Lichtquellen zu entwickeln, die immer kleiner, energiesparender, umweltfreundlicher und langlebiger sind.

Innovative miniature fluorescent lamps have a tube diameter of only 7 mm. OSRAM experts try to develop light sources which constantly become smaller in size, save more energy, are environment-friendly and have a longer life span.

Les tubes fluorescents miniaturisés affichent un diamètre de 7 mm seulement. Le but des chercheurs de chez OSRAM est de mettre au point des sources lumineuses toujours plus petites, écologiques, de plus longue durée et consommant encore moins d'énergie.

Le innovative minilampade fluorescenti hanno ormai un diametro di 7 mm. I ricercatori OSRAM perseguono l'obiettivo di sviluppare fonti di luce con consumi di energia sempre più ridotti, più ecologiche e longeve.

183

Dichte an Handwerksbetrieben in Deutschland spricht man von einer besonderen „Münchner Mischung" der Wirtschaft. Kleine und mittelständische Betriebe sind wesentlich konjunkturresistenter als Großunternehmen, sie gewährleisten eine wohnortnahe Versorgung der Bevölkerung mit Produkten und Dienstleistungen und bilden im Verhältnis zur Anzahl der Beschäftigten überproportional aus.

Daher ist es ein wesentliches Ziel der Münchner Wirtschaftspolitik, die Wachstumspotentiale bei den KMUs zu fördern. Dazu gehören neben einer kunden- und serviceorientierten Beratung der Unternehmen vor allem die Sicherung und Erweiterung angestammter Betriebsstandorte sowie die Vermittlung bestehender und die Entwicklung neuer Gewerbeflächen. Das „städtische Angebot" umfasst hier sowohl Gewerbeflächen, die neu ausgewiesen und maßgerecht parzelliert werden, z. B. in den Gewerbegebieten der Messestadt Riem, als auch Mietflächen in den Gewerbehöfen.

Für viele Firmen mit Standortproblemen sind Gewerbehöfe die einzige Möglichkeit, passende und bezahlbare Flächen in der Nähe des bisherigen Standortes zu erhalten und damit die langfristige Existenz des Betriebes zu sichern. Gewerbehöfe nutzen durch verdichtete Bauweise die knappen Grundstücksflächen besser aus und reduzieren so die Kosten, wodurch es möglich wird, die Mischung von Wohnen und Arbeiten zu erhalten. Durch Agglomerationsvorteile und Synergieeffekte verbessern sie die Entwicklungschancen der untergebrachten Betriebe. Das städtische Gewerbehofnetz umfasst mittlerweile fünf Gewerbehöfe, in denen 180 Betriebe mit über 1 500 Beschäftigten eine neue Heimat gefunden haben.

style of construction, these industrial parks make the best possible use of small plots and thus reduce costs; this enables them to preserve a mixture of living and working space. Agglomeration advantages and synergy effects improve the chances for developing the resident firms. The municipal network of industrial parks at present comprises five such facilities, where 180 businesses employing 1,500 persons have found a new home so far.

An Old and New Company for Munich

To be able to compete with private suppliers should the price of electricity continue to decline in future, too, the "old" Stadtwerke München (an owner-operator) was turned 1998 into the "new" Stadtwerke München GmbH (SWM GmbH) – one of Munich's largest enterprises boasting a balance sheet total of DM seven billion. But SWM GmbH will also be able to profit from the concentration process accompanying liberalization if it offers its customers better products and more reasonable prices than its competitors.

"SOFT" LOCATION FACTORS – MUNICH SHINES

The so-called "soft" location factors – i.e. art and culture, leisure-time and sports, scenic beauty and climate – play an increasingly important part in the global competition of the individual regions to attract enterprises of the hightech sector. Here a very simple rule applies: The more attractive the soft factors are, the easier it is to draw highly-qualified and thus highly-paid personnel to a certain location. The reconstructed "Schrannenhalle" on Viktualienmarkt; the revitalisation of the "Alte Hof"; the promotion

avantages de l'agglomération et les effets de synergie, ils améliorent les possibilités de développement des entreprises installées. Le réseau municipal des espaces commerciaux englobe maintenant cinq centres artisanaux dans lesquels 180 sociétés avec plus de 1 500 employés ont trouvé un nouvel emplacement.

Une ancienne et nouvelle société pour Munich

Pour pouvoir, malgré la chute des prix de l'électricité, continuer d'être compétitif face aux prestataires privés, «l'ancienne» société Stadtwerke München a fait place en 1998 à la «nouvelle» Stadtwerke München GmbH, une des entreprises majeures de Munich avec un total de bilan dépassant sept milliards de mark. La SWM GmbH peut également profiter du processus de concentration engendré par la libéralisation du marché de l'énergie pour proposer à ses clients de meilleurs produits à des prix plus intéressants que la concurrence.

FACTEURS OBJECTIFS DU SITE – MUNICH BRILLE

Les facteurs objectifs du site comme l'art et la culture, les loisirs et le sport, le charme du paysage et le climat, jouent un rôle de plus en plus important dans la bataille globale que se livrent les régions pour attirer des entreprises du secteur de haute technologie. La règle suivante est à respecter: plus les facteurs objectifs du site sont attrayants et plus il est facile pour un site d'attirer une main-d'œuvre hautement qualifiée et par conséquent très bien payée. La reconstruction de la Schrannenhalle au Viktualienmarkt ou la revitalisation de l'Alter Hof, la promotion d'installations culturelles comme les musées, théâtres et salles de

giore di lavoratori rispetto alle grandi aziende.

Questo è il motivo per cui un obiettivo essenziale della politica economica di Monaco è favorire la crescita delle piccole e medie imprese, offrendo loro un servizio di consulenza attraverso il quale possono essere informate sulle effettive esigenze dei clienti e, soprattutto, salvaguardando ed ampliando le loro sedi tradizionali, mettendo a loro disposizione superfici industriali già esistenti o creando nuove aree commerciali. L'«offerta cittadina» comprende sia nuove aree industriali adeguatamente lottizzate, come è stato fatto ad es. per i terreni adibiti ad uso commerciale nella città fieristica di Riem, che aree disponibili per la locazione nei centri commerciali.

Per molte aziende con problemi logistici, i centri commerciali rappresentano l'unica possibilità di trovare spazi adeguati ad un costo equo nelle vicinanze della sede originaria, in modo tale da garantire la continuità dell'azienda. I centri commerciali sfruttano al meglio gli spazi ridotti riducendo in tal modo le spese e consentendo di mantenere la combinazione di edificio adibito ad abitazione e posto di lavoro. Inoltre le possibilità di sviluppo delle aziende migliorano grazie ai vantaggi offerti dall'agglomerazione e dalla sinergia dei diversi settori artigianali. La rete cittadina di centri commerciali comprende nel frattempo cinque centri che ospitano 180 aziende in cui lavorano oltre 1 500 persone.

Una vecchia nuova azienda per Monaco

Per poter concorrere anche in futuro con le aziende private in una situazione di netto ribasso dei prezzi dell'energia elettrica, la «vecchia» azienda autonoma municipalizzata «Stadtwerke München» è stata trasformata nel 1998 nella nuova «Stadtwerke München GmbH», una delle maggiore aziende di Monaco con un

1946 von Dr.-Ing. Georg Spinner gegründet, ist die **Spinner GmbH** heute weltweit als Spezialist im Bereich der Hochfrequenztechnik bekannt. Telekommunikation und Rundfunk, optische Übertragungssysteme und Bauelemente für die physikalische Grundlagenforschung werden mit modernster Technik entwickelt und gefertigt. Mit Werken in Westerham/Bayern und Lauenstein/Sachsen ist das Unternehmen heute in der Lage, schnell und innovativ alle Kundenwünsche zu erfüllen. Bekannt für überdurchschnittliche Qualität, ist Spinner seit 1994 nach ISO 9001 zertifiziert.

Today **Spinner GmbH**, founded by Dr.-Ing. Georg Spinner in 1946, is a specialist in high-frequency engineering. It develops and manufactures telecommunication and radio systems, optical transmission systems and elements for physical fundamental research with state-of-the-art technology. The enterprise with operating plants in Westerham/Bavaria and Lauenstein/Saxony is today able to meet all customer demands quickly and innovatively. Well-known for its above-average quality, Spinner has been certified in accordance with ISO 9001 since 1994.

Fondée en 1946 par l'ingénieur Dr. Georg Spinner, la société **Spinner GmbH** est connue aujourd'hui au niveau international comme spécialiste dans la technique des hautes fréquences. La télécommunication et la radio, les sytèmes optiques de transmission et les éléments de construction servant à la recherche de base en physique sont développés et fabriqués à l'aide de la technique la plus sophistiquée. Possédant des usines à Westerham/Bavière et Lauenstein/Saxe, l'entreprise est aujourd'hui à même de répondre à tous les désirs de sa clientèle de manière innovative et rapide. Réputée pour son excellente qualité, Spinner est certifiée depuis 1994 conformément à l'ISO 9001.

Fondata nel 1946 dall'Ing. Georg Spinner, la **Spinner GmbH** è oggi nota in tutto il mondo come azienda specializzata nel settore della tecnica ad alta frequenza. Telecomunicazioni e radiotelevisione, sistemi ottici di trasmissione ed elementi per la ricerca di base nel campo della fisica vengono sviluppati e fabbricati con le tecniche più moderne. Con stabilimenti a Westerham, in Baviera, e Lauenstein, in Sassonia, l'azienda è oggi in grado di soddisfare tutti i desideri dei clienti in maniera rapida ed innovativa. Nota per la sua qualità superiore alla media, la Spinner è certificata, fin dal 1994, secondo la norma ISO 9001.

Die unter Denkmalschutz stehende Villa „Belle Maison" – 1907/08 von dem Architekten Gustav von Cube für den Schriftsteller Carl Sternheim erbaut – ist seit 1995 der Firmensitz der Schoeller-Gruppe.

The mansion "Belle Maison" is a protected historical site which was built by the architect Gustav von Cube for the writer Carl Sternheim in 1907/08. It has been the seat of the Schoeller group since 1995.

Schoeller Packaging Systems GmbH in Pullach zählt zu den Pionieren innovativer Transport- und Lagerverpackungen. Unter dem Motto „Mehrweg statt Einweg" arbeitet das Unternehmen seit Jahrzehnten erfolgreich an zukunftsweisenden Lösungen, die längst ihren Siegeszug rund um die Welt angetreten haben.

Seit Ende des 18. Jahrhunderts war die aus Düren stammende Schoeller-Familie führend am Aufbau der Papier-, Zucker- und Textilindustrie in Deutschland beteiligt. Zunächst in Schlesien und nach dem Zweiten Weltkrieg ab 1948 in Göttingen nahm Alexander Schoeller aus der fünften Generation die Produktion von Getränkeverpackungen auf. Während die ersten Flaschenkästen noch aus Holz waren, gelang dem Gründer des heutigen Unternehmens 1958 mit der Entwicklung des Kunststoff-Flaschenkastens der Durchbruch. Von Deutschland ausgehend wurden von 1961 bis heute mehr als eine Milliarde Schoeller-Flaschenkästen weltweit in Eigenproduktion und über ein breites Lizenznehmernetz produziert und an Kunden wie Coca-Cola, Pepsi-Cola, Heineken, Beck's und South African Breweries ausgeliefert.

Von diesem Erfolg ausgehend, entwickelte sich Schoeller bis heute zum führenden Anbieter von Gesamtlösungen für die Technik der Warenströme. Vom Behälter bis zu der entsprechenden Logistikplanung und Dienstleistung ermöglicht das Unternehmen den modernen und umweltschonenden Warenstrom. Durch Joint Ventures, z. B. mit der amerikanischen Firma General Electric und der japanischen Mitsubishi-Gruppe, treten diese Konzepte ihren Weg um die Welt an.

Schoeller Packaging Systems GmbH in Pullach is one of the pioneers of innovative transport and store-room packagings. With the motto "returnable instead of disposable" the enterprise has found trend-setting solutions for decades which have been highly successful around the world.

Since the end of the 18th century the Schoeller family from Düren participated actively in the development of Germany's paper, sugar and textile industry. At first in Silesia and after World War II as of 1948 in Göttingen Alexander Schoeller, a member of the fifth generation, started the production of beverage packagings. While the first bottle crates were still made of wood, the founder of today's enterprise reached a break-through with the development of plastic crates in 1958. Since 1961 until today more than a billion Schoeller crates have been manufactured in domestic production in Germany as well as through license holders worldwide and delivered to customers such as Coca-Cola, Pepsi-Cola, Heineken, Beck's and South African breweries.

With this success as the cornerstone Schoeller has become the current leading supplier of comprehensive technological solutions to control the movement of goods. From the containers to the individually required logistic planning as well as services the company enables a state-of-the-art and environmentally sensible flow of goods. Through joint ventures with ie the American company General Electric or the Japanese Mitsubishi group these solutions are applied globally.

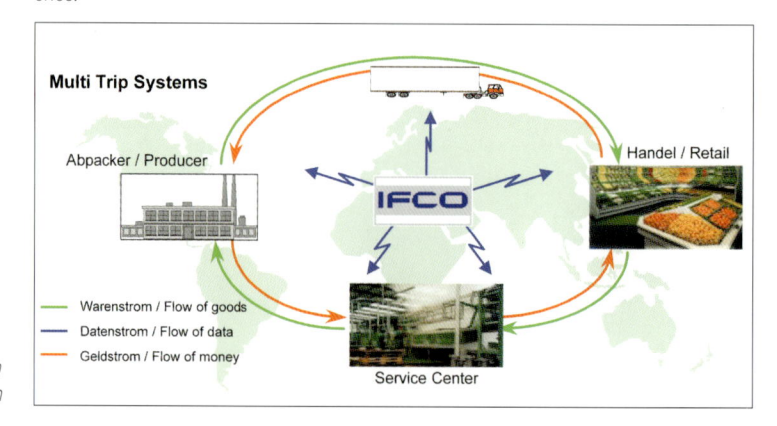

Eine alte neue Gesellschaft für München

Um bei fallenden Strompreisen auch künftig mit privaten Anbietern konkurrieren zu können, wurde 1998 aus dem „alten" Eigenbetrieb Stadtwerke München die „neue" Stadtwerke München GmbH, eines der größten Münchner Unternehmen mit einer Bilanzsumme von über sieben Milliarden Mark. Von dem mit der Liberalisierung einhergehenden Konzentrationsprozess auf dem Energiemarkt kann die SWM GmbH aber auch profitieren, wenn sie den Kunden bessere Produkte und günstigere Preise bietet als die Konkurrenz.

WEICHE STANDORT FAKTOREN – MÜNCHEN LEUCHTET

Die sogenannten weichen Standortfaktoren - Kunst und Kultur, Freizeit und Sport, landschaftlicher Reiz und Klima - spielen im globalen Wettkampf der Regionen um Unternehmen aus dem Hochtechnologiesektor eine immer größere Rolle. Dabei gilt folgende Faustregel: Je attraktiver die weichen Standortfaktoren sind, desto leichter lassen sich hochqualifizierte und somit auch hochbezahlte Arbeitskräfte für einen Standort gewinnen. Die Wiedererrichtung der Schrannenhalle am Viktualienmarkt oder die Revitalisierung des Alten Hofs, die Förderung kultureller Einrichtungen wie Museen, Theater und Musikhallen und nicht zuletzt eine moderne, zukunftweisende Architektur sollen die Attraktivität der Stadt noch steigern. Dass sich Verbesserungen und neue Attraktionen in diesen Bereichen auch auf den Tourismus positiv auswirken, ist ein angenehmer Nebeneffekt.

Die drei Dirigenten

James Levine, Lorin Maazel, Zubin Mehta - ein musikalisches Triumvirat, das seinesgleichen sucht. Keine Stadt der Welt wartet mit of cultural institutions such as museums, theatres and music halls; and last but not least a modern future-oriented architecture are to enhance Munich's flair even more. The fact that improvements and new attractions in this field will also have a beneficial influence on tourism will be a pleasant side-effect.

The Three Conductors

James Levine, Lorin Maazel, and Zubin Mehta form a musical triumvirate which has no equal anywhere. No other city can offer such a concentration of prominent musicians - a fact that is certainly not due to a lucky coincidence or to delusions of grandeur on the part of Munich. For orchestra leaders of international renown are only attracted by equally acclaimed orchestras - like the Münchner Philharmoniker, the Symphonieorchester des Bayerischen Rundfunks, and the orchestra of the Bavarian State Opera. With the "Musikhochschule München" and the "Richard-Strauss-Konservatorium" (well-known music schools) the state capital owns two globally acclaimed training centres which attract numerous foreign students, especially from East Asia and from Central and Eastern Europe.

Art Buildings and Building Art

While in other cities theatres and museums have to be closed because of a lack of funds, our "Isar-Athens" sets up one highlight after the other – from the "Kunstbau am Lenbachhaus", the "Hypo-Kunsthalle" and the reopening of the reconstructed Prinzregententheater to the completely renewed "Alte concert sans oublier une architecture moderne et futuriste doivent encore rendre la ville plus attrayante. Le fait que des améliorations et de nouvelles attractions dans ces secteurs aient un impact positif sur le tourisme est un effet secondaire fort appréciable.

Les trois chefs d'orchestre

James Levine, Lorin Maazel, Zubin Mehta, un triumvirat musical absolument unique. Aucune ville au monde peut se targuer de chefs d'orchestre aussi prestigieux. Il n'est pas question ici de hasard ou de folie des grandeurs. Des chefs d'orchestres de réputation mondiale sont attirés par des orchestres renommés à l'échelle internationale comme l'orchestre philharmonique de Munich, l'orchestre symphonique de la Bayerischer Rundfunk et l'orchestre de l'opéra national bavarois. Avec l'école supérieure de musique de Munich et le conservatoire Richard Strauss, la capitale du land possède deux piliers de réputation mondiale attirant une foule d'étudiants étrangers en particulier d'Asie de l'est ainsi que d'Europe centrale et de l'est.

Bâtiments artistiques et architecture

Alors que dans d'autres villes, les théâtres et musées ferment en raison de la précarité de leur budget, l'Athènes de l'Isar offre un événement après l'autre, à commencer par le bâtiment am Lenbachhaus, la galerie de l'Hypo-Kunsthalle et la réouverture du théâtre entièrement reconstruit du Prinzregent, en passant par l'assainissement général de l'Alte Pinakothek jusqu'à la nouvelle construction de la Pinatkothek des Modernes. Avec près de 22 000 m², la construction du musée devant abriter l'art moderne de la Staatsgalerie, l'art appliqué de la Neue Sammlung, le musée de l'architecture et la Graphische Sammlung sera le plus grand du 20ème siècle en Allemagne. Le musée de la fan- totale di fatturato pari ad oltre sette miliardi di marchi. Ma la nuova SWM GmbH può anche approfittare della liberalizzazione e del contemporaneo processo di concentrazione che si sta verificando nel mercato dell'energia elettrica offrendo ai clienti prodotti migliori e a prezzi più vantaggiosi.

FATTORI «MORBIDI» – MONACO RISPLENDE

I cosiddetti fattori «morbidi» - arte e cultura, tempo libero e sport, bellezza paesaggistica e clima - hanno un ruolo sempre maggiore nella corsa globale tra le regioni per accaparrarsi le aziende del settore dell'alta tecnologia. La regola di base è questa: quanto maggiore è l'attrattiva dei fattori «morbidi», tanto più facilmente i lavoratori più qualificati e quindi più pagati si lasceranno convincere a trasferirsi in tale sede. Il compito di aumentare ulteriormente l'attrattività della città è affidato alla ricostruzione del mercato coperto del «Viktualienmarkt» o alla revitalizzazione della Vecchia Corte (Alter Hof), alla promozione di istituzioni culturali quali musei, teatri e sale da concerto e, non da ultimo, ad un'architettura moderna e futuristica. Il fatto che questi interventi di miglioramento e le nuove attrazioni nei settori summenzionati abbiano un influsso positivo anche sul turismo è un effetto secondario di cui non ci si può che rallegrare.

I tre direttori d'orchestra

James Levine, Lorin Maazel, Zubin Mehta: un triumvirato musicale unico al mondo. Nessuna città del mondo può vantarsi di avere una simile concentrazione di eminenti direttori d'orchestra. E non si tratta qui di puro caso o addirittura di manie di grandezza. Infatti, i direttori di orchestra di fama mondiale vengono attratti solo da orchestre rinomate a livello internazionale, proprio come i filarmonici di Monaco, l'orchestra sinfonica della Radio

einer solch geballten Dirigentenprominenz auf. Von Zufall oder gar Größenwahn kann hier keine Rede sein. Denn Orchesterchefs von Weltruf werden nur von international renommierten Orchestern angezogen wie den Münchner Philharmonikern, dem Symphonieorchester des Bayerischen Rundfunks und dem Orchester der Bayerischen Staatsoper. Mit der Musikhochschule München und dem Richard-Strauss-Konservatorium besitzt die Landeshauptstadt zwei Kaderschmieden von Weltruf, die zahlreiche ausländische Studenten vor allem aus Ostasien sowie aus Mittel- und Osteuropa an die Isar ziehen.

Kunstbauten und Baukunst

Während in manch anderen Städten aufgrund prekärer finanzieller Haushaltslagen Theater und Museen geschlossen werden, bietet das Isar-Athen ein neues Highlight nach dem anderen, angefangen vom Kunstbau am Lenbachhaus, der Hypo-Kunsthalle und der Neueröffnung des wiederhergestellten Prinzregententheaters über die Generalsanierung der Alten Pinakothek bis zum Neubau der Pinakothek der Moderne. Mit seinen nahezu 22 000 m² wird der für die Staatsgalerie moderner Kunst, die Neue Sammlung angewandter Kunst, das Architekturmuseum und die Graphische Sammlung gedachte Museumsbau der größte des 20. Jahrhunderts in Deutschland sein. Mit Lothar Buchheims Museum der Phantasie in Bernried im Münchner Süden entsteht eine Heimstatt für eine der weltweit bedeutendsten Sammlungen expressionistischer Kunst. Nächstes – aber bestimmt nicht letztes – Prunkstück wird die bis 2001 geplante Realisierung des Museums der Mobilität, eine Dependance des Deutschen Museums, in drei denkmalgeschützten Messehallen auf der Theresienhöhe werden. Keinesfalls vergessen darf man hier die Muffathalle, einen der wohl attraktivsten Veranstal-

Pinakothek" and the newly constructed "Pinakothek der Moderne". Covering nearly 22,000 square metres, this new museum containing the State Gallery of Modern Art, the New Collection of
Commercial Art, the Museum for Architecture and the Graphic Collection will be the biggest 20th-century-museum in Germany. Lothar Buchheim's "Museum of Phantasie" in Bernried (in the southern part of Munich), which is still under construction, will shelter one of the world's most significant collections of expressionist art. The next but certainly not last showpiece of this scene will be the " Museum of Mobility" which is to be finished in 2001; it will be an annex of the "Deutsche Museum", located at "Theresienhöhe" in three exhibiton halls protected as monuments. We must, of course, also mention the "Muffathalle", one of Munich's most attractive locations for great events.

Hall Culture and Culture-Halls

The metropolis on the Isar offers outstanding attractions to the younger generations of inhabitants as well. After finding an abode in former military barracks and in the premises of the old airport in Riem, Munich's hall-culture has now settled in the "Pfanni" area, the site of a former producer of potato dumplings. In the "Kunstpark Ost" – Germany's most popular and best-known recreational area covering 80,000 square metres – young people find a unique assortment of attractions: They can amuse themselves in concert halls, music clubs, discotheques, bars and cinemas; additionally they can enjoy the "Kunstpark Ost 2000 – Millennium Lightyears", a light-architectural artistic concept; Munich's largest flea, art and antiques market; a skating hall; Bavaria's largest indoor beach-volley-ball facility; and Europe's highest indoor climbing wall.

taisie de Lothar Buchheim à Bernried au sud de Munich accueille une des plus impressionnantes collections mondiales d'art expressionniste. Le prochain chef-d'œuvre, qui ne sera certainement pas le dernier, est la réalisation du musée de la mobilité prévue pour 2001, une dépendance du Musée allemand, qui se composera de trois halls de foire classés monuments historiques sur la Theresienhöhe. La salle Muffathalle mérite d'être signalée ici, une des salles de concerts les plus attrayantes de Munich.

La culture des halls et les halls culturels

La métropole de l'Isar ne propose au public jeune et créatif que des superlatifs. Après l'utilisation prolongée des terrains de casernes et de l'ancien aéroport de Munich, la culture des halls de Munich s'est maintenant installée sur le terrain de l'ancien producteur alimentaire Pfanni. Les 80 000m² du Kunstpark Ost, le parc de loisirs le plus connu d'Allemagne, offrent un spectre unique d'animations. Les visiteurs peuvent en effet se rendre dans plusieurs salles de concerts, discothèques, clubs de musique bars et cinémas. «Kunstpark Ost 2000 Millenium Lightyears», un concept global d'architectures lumineuses, le plus grand marché aux puces, marché d'œuvres d'art et d'antiquités de Munich, une salle de roller, le plus grand centre couvert de beachvolleyball ainsi que le plus haut mur d'escalade en salle viennent compléter l'offre.

bavarese e l'orchestra dell'Opera di Stato bavarese. La capitale bavarese ha due centri di formazione musicale di fama mondiale, il Conservatorio di Monaco e il Conservatorio Richard Strauss, che attirano qui numerosi studenti stranieri soprattutto dall'Asia orientale e dai paesi dell'Europa centrale ed orientale.

Opere d'arte e architettura

Mentre in altre città vengono chiusi teatri e musei a causa di situazioni finanziarie precarie, l'«Atene sull'Isar» offre un nuovo evento straordinario dopo l'altro, a partire dal «Kunstbau» della Galleria Lenbach, dalla Galleria d'Arte Hypo e dall'inaugurazione del restaurato Prinzregententheater (Teatro del principe reggente) al risanamento generale della Vecchia Pinacoteca fino alla costruzione della Nuova Pinacoteca. Con i suoi circa 22 000 mq, il complesso museale che ospiterà la Galleria Nazionale di Arte Moderna, la Nuova Collezione per l'Arte applicata, il Museo di Architettura e la Collezione nazionale di Arte grafica sarà il più grande della Germania del Secolo XX. Il Museo della Fantasia di Lothar Buchheim, che sorgerà a Bernried a sud di Monaco, ospiterà una delle maggiori collezioni d'arte espressionista del mondo. Il pezzo forte successivo – ma certamente non l'ultimo – sarà la realizzazione nel 2001 del Museo della Mobilità, che farà parte del «Deutsches Museum» e sarà allestito in tre padiglioni sulla Theresienhöhe che si trovano sotto la tutela delle Belle Arti. Ma non deve essere assolutamente dimenticata la Muffathalle, uno degli spazi espositivi più affascinanti che Monaco può offrire.

La cultura da capannone e i capannoni della cultura

La metropoli sull'Isar ha offerte superlative anche per il pubblico più giovane e creativo. Dopo le caserme militari fuori uso e il vecchio aeroporto di Riem, la cultura da capannone di Monaco

COMMERCE

Die Bauunternehmung Mühlbauer Baugruppe ist seit über 70 Jahren in München zu Hause und arbeitet mit Niederlassungen im gesamten Bundesgebiet sowie in Österreich.

Die umfangreiche Baupalette umfasst die Bereiche: Kabelbau, Kanalbau, Straßen- und Pflasterbau, Gleisbau, Spritzbeton, Tunnel- und Stollenbau und Horizontalbohrungen.

Die Mühlbauer Baugruppe bietet dem anspruchsvollen Kunden schnell und zuverlässig maßgeschneiderte Lösungen „aus einer Hand". Oberstes Ziel ist die Kundenzufriedenheit. Sie wird erreicht durch den Einsatz hoch qualifizierter Projektleiter und motivierter Mitarbeiter. Produktqualität ist selbstverständlich.

Mühlbauer Baugruppe – denn Sympathie schlägt Konditionen!

The Mühlbauer Baugruppe is a firm of builders and contractors that has had its seat in Munich for over 70 years and has offices throughout Germany as well as Austria.

The exhaustive range of services includes the following areas: cable, sewer and road construction and paving, track construction, air-placed concrete, tunnelling as well as horizontal drilling.

The Mühlbauer Baugruppe offers its discerning customers all-encompassing, quick, custom-made and reliable service. Customer satisfaction is our greatest priority. It is achieved through highly qualified project managers and motivated employees. The high quality of our products is a matter of course.

Mühlbauer Baugruppe – because sympathy beats terms and conditions!

L'entreprise du bâtiment Mühlbauer Baugruppe siège à Munich depuis plus de 70 ans et opère avec ses filiales dans l'ensemble de la République fédérale d'Allemagne et en Autriche.

La vaste palette de construction englobe les domaines: construction de câbles, d'égouts, de rues et de pavés, de voies ferrées, de béton armé, de tunnels et de galeries ainsi que les forages horizontaux.

Le groupe Mühlbauer Baugruppe offre à ses clients exigeants des solutions rapides et taillées sur mesure qu'il exécute d'un bout à l'autre. L'objectif prioritaire est d'avoir des clients entièrement satisfaits. Il est réalisé grâce à l'engagement de chefs de projets hautement qualifiés et de collaborateurs motivés. La qualité des produits va de soi.

Mühlbauer Baugruppe – car la sympathie dépasse les conditions!

L'impresa edile Mühlbauer Baugruppe ha la propria sede a Monaco da oltre 70 anni ed opera con delle filiali nell'intero territorio tedesco nonché in Austria.

L'ampia gamma di prestazioni comprende i seguenti settori: costruzione di cavi, di canali, costruzioni di strade e strutture viarie in catrame, costruzione di rotaie, calcestruzzo a proiezione, costruzione di tunnel e gallerie di miniera nonché perforazioni direzionali orizzontali.

La Mühlbauer Baugruppe propone, con rapidità ed affidabilità, soluzioni su misura «di prima mano» ad una clientela altamente esigente. Obiettivo prioritario rimane la soddisfazione del cliente. Essa viene conseguita grazie alla disponibilità di responsabili di progetto altamente qualificati e di dipendenti motivati. Con tali presupposti, la qualità del prodotto diventa una conseguenza logica.

Mühlbauer Baugruppe – quando la simpatia prevale sulle condizioni generali!

tungsräume, den München zu bieten hat.

Hallenkultur und Kulturhallen

Auch dem jüngeren, kreativen Publikum bietet die Isarmetropole nur Superlative. Nach ausgedienten Kasernengeländen und dem alten Flughafen Riem hat die Münchner Hallenkultur nun auf dem Areal des ehemaligen Kartoffelknödelproduzenten Pfanni eine neue Heimstatt gefunden. Auf mehr als 80 000 m² gibt es im Kunstpark Ost, dem deutschlandweit wohl bekanntesten Freizeitgelände, ein einzigartiges Unterhaltungsspektrum: Die Besucher können sich in mehreren Konzerthallen, Diskotheken, Musikklubs, Bars und Kinos vergnügen. „Kunstpark Ost 2000 – Millennium Lightyears", ein lichtarchitektonisches Gesamtkonzept, der größte Floh-, Kunst- und Antiquitätenmarkt Münchens, eine Skaterhalle, Bayerns größte Indoor-Beachvolleyball-Anlage sowie Europas höchste Indoor-Kletterwand runden das Angebot ab.

Olympia hautnah

Sowohl die aktiven als auch die passiven Sportangebote kennen in und um München herum keine Grenzen. Die Palette des Kunstparks Ost und der FC Bayern München, einer der bekanntesten Sportvereine der Welt, seien hier stellvertretend genannt. Seit diesem Jahr ist München um eine weltweit bislang einzigartige Attraktion reicher: Es schließt sich der Kreis von den Olympischen Sommerspielen des Jahres 1972 zu Olympic Spirits, einem audiovisuellen olympischen Erlebnis-Center mit interaktivem virtuellem Angebot. In der ehemaligen olympischen Radsportarena lassen Simulatoren die Besucher einen den Eiskanal von Nagano hinunterrasenden Bob oder ein Tennismatch gegen einen Weltklassespieler erleben.

Olympia – Proximate

There is no limit to active and passive sports offered in and around Munich. Let me mention only two examples – the attractions of the Kunstpark Ost and the FC Bayern München – one of the world's most renowned sports clubs. Since 1999 Munich has boasted one more highlight which is unique throughout the world and connects with the Olympic Summer Games of 1972: the "Olympic Spirits" audiovisuel event centre offering an interactive virtual programme. In the former Olympic cycling arena simulators allow visitors to experience the race of a bobsled, chasing down the ice channel in Nagana at breakneck speed, or a tennis match against one of the world's top champions.

CHALLENGES OF THE FUTURE

Labour Market

In international competition the rank and future chances of an economic region are also evaluated according to its educational and qualification offers. Because of its importance to economic growth and social peace, employment promotion is an integral part of municipal economic policy. In view of the still extremely high unemployment rate, limited municipal funds, and the fact that nation-wide skeleton conditions

Près de l'Olympie

Les possibilités de sport actif ou passif ne connaissent à Munich et dans les environs aucune limite. L'offre du Kunstpark Ost et du FC Bayern München, un des clubs sportifs les plus connus au monde, ne sont ici cités qu'à titre d'exemples. Depuis cette année, Munich dispose d'une attraction absolument unique au monde: elle se range dans la ligne des Jeux olympiques de 1972 et s'appelle Olympic Spirits, un centre d'aventures audiovisuel et olympique avec une offre virtuelle interactive. Dans l'ancien vélodrome olympique, les simulateurs permettent aux visiteurs de vivre un bob dévalant la piste glacée de Nagano ou un match de tennis contre un joueur de classe mondiale.

LES DEFIS DE L'AVENIR

Le marché de l'emploi

La valeur et les chances d'avenir d'une région économique au sein de la concurrence internationale se mesurent aussi à ses offres en matière de formation et de qualification. En raison de son importance pour la croissance et la paix sociale, la promotion de l'emploi fait partie intégrante de la politique économique municipale. Vu le taux toujours trop élevé de chômage, les moyens financiers municipaux limités et les conditions-cadre de la politique de l'emploi fixées à l'échelle fédérale, la politique de l'emploi et de qualification ne peut commencer qu'à titre d'exemple. Vaste et différencié, le «programme de Munich sur l'emploi et la qualification» améliore les perspectives individuelles des employés et des chômeurs sur le marché du travail. Il doit mettre fin aux «carrières négatives», comme être tributaire depuis des années de l'aide sociale, la dépréciation des connaissances, la maladie et la pauvreté. Parallèlement ces projets touchent aussi de nouveaux segments de marché et développent de nou-

ha trovato ora una nuova sede nell'area dell'ex produttore di gnocchi di patata Pfanni. Il Kunstpark Ost, il parco divertimenti più conosciuto in tutta la Germania che si estende su più di 80 000 mq, offre una gamma di divertimenti unica nel suo genere: i visitatori possono divertirsi in diverse sale da concerto, discoteche, club musicali, bar e cinema. Il «Kunstpark Ost 2000 – Millennium Lightyears» – un progetto di illuminazione architettonica che si estende su tutto il parco –, il più grande mercato delle pulci, dell'antiquariato e di oggetti d'arte di Monaco, un padiglione per gli amanti dei pattini, il più grande impianto di beach volley indoor e la più alta parete da scalata al coperto dell'Europa completano l'offerta.

A stretto contatto con le Olimpiadi

Sia le offerte attive che passive nel campo dello sport non conoscono limiti a Monaco e nei dintorni. Ricordiamo qui, a titolo di esempio, il Kunstpark Ost e la squadra del FC Bayern di Monaco, uno dei sodalizi sportivi più conosciuti del mondo. Da quest'anno Monaco può vantare un'attrazione finora unica al mondo: si chiude il cerchio dei Giochi Olimpiaci Estivi del 1972 con Olympic Spirits, un centro divertimenti audiovisivo tutto improntato alle olimpiadi e con una ricca offerta interattiva e virtuale. Nell'arena ciclistica che fu usata per le gare di ciclismo è possibile rivivere grazie a dei simulatori l'emozione di scendere giù in picchiata con il bob attraverso il canale di ghiaccio di Nagano o di giocare un match a tennis contro un giocatore di classe internazionale.

LE SFIDE DEL FUTURO

Il mercato del lavoro

Il valore di una regione economica e le sue possibilità per il futuro all'interno della concorrenza internazionale si misurano

MULTI–MEDIA CENTRE

HERAUSFORDERUNG DER ZUKUNFT

Arbeitsmarkt

Stellenwert und Zukunftschancen einer Wirtschaftsregion im internationalen Wettbewerb bemessen sich auch nach den vorhandenen Bildungs- und Qualifizierungsangeboten. Wegen der Bedeutung für Wachstum und sozialen Frieden ist Beschäftigungsförderung ein integraler Bestandteil der städtischen Wirtschaftspolitik. Angesichts der nach wie vor zu hohen Arbeitslosigkeit, der begrenzten städtischen Finanzmittel wie auch der auf Bundesebene gesetzten beschäftigungspolitischen Rahmenbedingungen kann die kommunale Beschäftigungs- und Qualifizierungspolitik nur exemplarisch ansetzen. So verbessert das umfangreiche und differenzierte „Münchner Beschäftigungs- und Qualifizierungsprogramm" (MBQ) die individuellen Perspektiven von Arbeitnehmern und Arbeitslosen auf dem Arbeitsmarkt. Dadurch werden sogenannte „negative Karrieren", d.h. ein Abstieg in jahrelangen Sozialhilfebezug, Entwertung von Kenntnissen, auch Krankheit und Armut, durchbrochen. Und ganz nebenbei erschließen diese Projekte auch neue Marktsegmente und entwickeln neue Berufsfelder; Beispiele hierfür sind Kfz-Recycling und Elektronikschrottverwertung.

Gefördert werden Pilotprojekte, die den Strukturwandel unterstützen. So hilft die Stadt Erwerbstätigen und Unternehmen, sich auf Veränderungen des Arbeitsmarktes und deren Auswirkungen vorausschauend einzustellen. Es werden nicht nur die negativen sozialen Folgen beim Verlust veralteter Arbeitsplätze abgefedert, sondern auch zukunftsorientierte Bereiche wie die Medienbranche forciert. Weitere beschäftigungspolitische Ansätze beziehen sich auf die berufliche Gleichstellung von Frauen auf dem Arbeitsmarkt und die Verbesserung der beruflichen Chancen von Jugendlichen, auf Möglichkeiten zur Arbeit jen-

must be observed, the communal labour and qualification policy can be applied only in an exemplary manner. Thus the "Münchner Beschäftigungs- und Qualifizierungsprogramm" (MBQ) tries to improve the individual perspectives of employees and unemployed people in the labour market. It helps to prevent, completely or partly, so-called "negative careers" – i.e. the drop to long-term dependence on public assistance, devaluation of knowledge, or even illness and poverty. Additionally, these projects open up new market segments and develop new professional fields; two examples are the recycling of motor cars and electronic waste.

Pilot projects which support structural change are generously promoted. The city assists, for instance, working people and enterprises to adjust to imminent changes in the labour market and their aftereffects. One does not only try to cushion off the negative consequences of losing an outdated job, but also pushes future-oriented branches like the media sector. Further labour-political efforts aim at the professional emancipation of women; at improving the professional chances of young people; at finding possibilities for employment beyond traditional job profiles; and at defining the city's part in the promotion of the communication between the labour-political players.

The virtual "Münchner Multimedia-Akademie" (MMA), which since 1998 has coordinated, optimized qualitatively, and expanded according to demand the existing capacities in the field of multi-media education and further education, will serve as an internationally outstanding education and further education centre for the multi-media sector. MMA is ideally complemented by the "Media Works Munich" (MWM) centre, where primarily education and further education institutions of the media industry use synergies that arise out of close contact, joint infrastructural facilities, the positive effects achieved by a

L'AVENIR

veaux champs professionnels, par exemple le recyclage en mécanique automobile et la valorisation des déchets électroniques.

Un soutien est apporté aux projets pilotes étayant la mutation structurelle. Ainsi, la ville aide la population active et les entreprises à s'adapter à l'avance aux changements du marché du travail et à ses conséquences. Il s'agit non seulement de réduire les conséquences sociales négatives lors de la perte d'emplois tombés en désuétude mais encore d'approfondir les secteurs prometteurs comme le secteur médiatique. D'autres points de la politique de l'emploi se concentrent sur l'égalité des droits de la femme sur le marché du travail, sur l'amélioration des chances professionnelles des jeunes, sur les possibilités de travail autres que professionnelles et sur le rôle de la ville lors de la promotion de la communication entre les différents acteurs du marché de l'emploi.

Avec la Münchner Multimedia-Akademie (MMA) coordonnant depuis 1998 les capacités présentes dans le secteur du multimédia pour la formation et le perfectionnement professionnel, les optimisant qualitativement et les orientant en fonction de la demande, un excellent centre de formation (inter)national de formation et le perfectionnement professionnel est en train de voir le jour. La MMA est complétée par le centre médiatique «Media Works Munich (MWM)» où les institutions de formation et de perfectionnement professionnel du monde médiatique utilisent les synergies résultant de la réunion spatiale et des infrastructures communes, de l'effet positif produit par l'image et la qualité de l'adresse ainsi que de coopérations éventuelles.

anche sulla base delle offerte di formazione e di qualificazione che questa può presentare. Per l'importanza che ha per lo sviluppo e la tranquillità sociale, il sostegno all'occupazione è una parte integrante della politica economica della città. In considerazione del livello di disoccupazione ancora troppo elevato, dei mezzi finanziari limitati della città e delle condizioni di base politico-occupazionali poste su base nazionale, la politica comunale dell'occupazione e della qualificazione può intervenire solo in alcuni casi. Ad esempio, l'ampio e differenziato «Programma di Monaco per l'occupazione e la qualificazione» (MBQ) migliora le prospettive individuali relative al mondo del lavoro di lavoratori e disoccupati. In questo modo si cerca di stroncare le cosiddette «carriere negative», ovvero il declino nell'assistenza sociale, con la svalorizzazione delle conoscenze e anche malattia e povertà. Parallelamente, questi progetti aprono anche nuovi segmenti di mercato e sviluppano nuove categorie professionali. Ne sono un esempio il riciclaggio delle autovetture e la riutilizzazione di rottami elettronici.

La città promuove soprattutto quei progetti pilota che mirano ad assistere lavoratori e aziende ad affrontare la trasformazione strutturale, ovvero a prevenire i cambiamenti del mercato del lavoro e a prepararsi ad affrontare i suoi effetti. Non solo vengono ammortizzate le conseguenze negative derivanti dalla perdita di posti di lavoro obsoleti, ma ci si preoccupa anche di forzare i settori più orientati al futuro come quello dei mezzi di comunicazione. Altre formule politico-occupazionali si riferiscono all'equiparazione professionale tra uomini e donne e al miglioramento delle possibilità professionali per i giovani, alle possibilità del lavoro non-profit e al ruolo della città come promotrice della comunicazione tra i diversi attori del mondo politico e del mercato del lavoro.

L'Accademia «virtuale» di Monaco per il Multimediale (MMA)

SANKYO PHARMA GmbH mit Sitz in München ist die europäische Marketing- und Vertriebszentrale von Sankyo Co., Ltd. Tokio.

Sankyo Tokio – 1899 gegründet – ist heute das zweitgrößte pharmazeutische Unternehmen in Japan.

Sankyo Pharma München erschließt und bearbeitet die pharmazeutischen Märkte in Europa für die vorhandenen und noch folgenden Sankyo Arzneimittel. Die Sankyo Pharma GmbH beschäftigt mehr als 1100 Mitarbeiter einschließlich der Zentrale in München, der zehn europäischen Tochtergesellschaften und der Produktionsbetriebe in Deutschland und Frankreich.

The **SANKYO PHARMA GmbH** with its seat in Munich is the European administrative centre for marketing and distribution of the Sankyo Co., Ltd. Tokyo.

Today Sankyo Tokyo – founded in 1899 – is the second biggest pharmaceutical enterprise in Japan.

Sankyo Pharma Munich services the pharmaceutical markets in Europe and opens up new ones with its existing and future Sankyo pharmaceuticals. The Sankyo Pharma GmbH employs more than 1,100 persons, who work at the headquarters in Munich, the ten European subsidiaries and the production plants in Germany and France.

SANKYO PHARMA GmbH siège à Munich et est la centrale européenne de marketing et de distribution de Sankyo Co., Ltd. Tokyo.

Fondée en 1899, Sankyo Tokyo est aujourd'hui le deuxième plus grand groupe pharmaceutique du Japon.

Sankyo Pharma München prospecte et travaille les marchés pharmaceutiques européens pour les médicaments Sankyo existants et à venir. La Sankyo Pharma GmbH emploie plus de 1100 collaborateurs y compris la centrale de Munich, les dix filiales européennes et les usines de production en Allemagne et en France.

La **SANKYO PHARMA GmbH** con sede a Monaco è la sede centrale per l'Europa delle attività di marketing e di vendita della Sankyo Co., Ltd. di Tokio.

La Sankyo Tokio – fondata nel 1899 – è, oggi, la seconda maggiore azienda farmaceutica del Giappone.

La Sankyo Pharma di Monaco apre e cura i mercati farmaceutici in Europa per i farmaci Sankyo già disponibili e per quelli futuri. Compresa la sede centrale di Monaco, le dieci affiliate europee e le unità produttive in Germania e Francia, la Sankyo Pharma GmbH conta oltre 1100 addetti.

60 Kilometer nördlich von München, in der Kleinstadt Pfaffenhofen/Ilm – inzwischen auch ein bekannter Industriestandort – befinden sich die Produktionsstätten der SANKYO PHARMA GmbH München. Diese sind mit modernster Technologie ausgestattet und produzieren mit über 230 Mitarbeiterinnen und Mitarbeitern unter strenger Beachtung der GMP-Vorschriften (Good Manufacturing Practice) Arzneimittel. Mehr als 22 Millionen Packungen – Tabletten, Dragees, Salben, Gele, Lösungen – werden dort jährlich produziert und in über 60 Länder versandt.

The production plants of the SANKYO PHARMA GmbH Munich are 60 km north of Munich, in the small town of Pfaffenhofen/Ilm – which over time has become a popular location for industries. They feature state-of-the-art technology and a staff of 230 plus produces pharmaceuticals in compliance with the strict GMP-regulations (Good Manufacturing Practice). Every year over 22 million packets – pills, tablets, salves, gels, solutions – are produced and distributed to more than 60 countries.

C'est à 60 kilomètres au nord de Munich, dans la petite ville de Pfaffenhofen/Ilm devenue maintenant un site industriel connu, que se trouvent les usines de production de la SANKYO PHARMA GmbH Munich. Equipées d'une technologie ultramoderne, elles produisent avec 230 collaboratrices et collaborateurs des médicaments en respectant scrupuleusement la réglementation GMP (Good Manufacturing Practice). Plus de 22 millions d'emballages, qu'il s'agisse de tablettes, dragées, pommades, gels ou de solutions, sont produits chaque année et exportés dans plus de 60 pays.

60 chilometri a nord di Monaco, nella cittadina di Pfaffenhofen/Ilm – che nel frattempo è diventata anche un conosciuto sito industriale – si trovano i siti produttivi della SANKYO PHARMA GmbH Monaco. Essi sono attrezzati con tecnologie modernissime e producono farmaci avvalendosi di oltre 230 dipendenti e in stretta osservanza delle norme GMP (Good Manufacturing Practice). Qui vengono prodotti ogni anno e spediti in oltre 60 Paesi più di 22 milioni di confezioni: pastiglie, confetti, pomate, gel medicali e soluzioni.

seits der Erwerbsarbeit und auf die Rolle der Stadt bei der Förderung der Kommunikation zwischen den arbeitsmarktpolitischen Akteuren.

Mit der virtuellen Münchner Multimedia-Akademie (MMA), die seit 1998 die vorhandenen Kapazitäten im Bereich Multimedia Aus- und Weiterbildung koordiniert, qualitativ optimiert und nachfrageorientiert ausbaut, entsteht ein (inter)national herausragendes Weiter- und Ausbildungszentrum für Multimedia. Eine reale Ergänzung findet die MMA in dem Medienzentrum „Media Works Munich (MWM)", wo vor allem Aus- und Fortbildungsinstitutionen der Medienwirtschaft Synergien nutzen, die sich aus dem räumlichen Zusammenschluss und den gemeinsamen Infrastruktureinrichtungen, dem positiven Effekt der Image- und Adressbildung sowie möglichen Kooperationen ergeben.

Rund 500 Schulen, von der Grundschule bis zur Europäischen Schule, sind die Bildungsbasis Münchens. Stadt und Freistaat leisten viel, um die im Bundesvergleich überdurchschnittliche Qualifikation zu halten und auszubauen. Letztes Beispiel hierfür ist das 1998 eingeweihte Berufsbildungszentrum an der Bergsonstraße für Elektroinstallationstechnik und -mechanik, Solartechnik, Industrie- sowie Kommunikationselektronik – eine 109-Millionen-Mark-Investition der Landeshauptstadt. Mit der Münchner Volkshochschule (MVHS) ist zudem das größte und vielfältigste kommunale Weiterbildungszentrum Europas mit jährlich über 400 000 Teilnehmern in der Landeshauptstadt beheimatet.

Gründeroffensive

Im internationalen Vergleich hinkt die Bundesrepublik bei Existenzgründungen hinterher. Im Gegensatz zu den USA gibt es hierzulande keine Selbstständigen- und Gründerkultur, die fest in Wirtschaft und Gesellschaft verwurzelt ist. Gründerinitiativen wie der Münchener Businessplan-

common image and address, and possible cooperations.

About 500 schools – from elementary to European level – constitute Munich's educational foundation. The city and the Free State of Bavaria make every effort to maintain and improve Munich's above-average level of educational qualifications (compared with the rest of Germany). The most recent example of this endeavour is the Vocal Education Centre at Bergsonstraße, which was inaugurated in 1998; this institute, in which the Bavarian capital invested DM 109 million, concentrates on special training in the sectors of electrical installation technology and mechanics; solar technology; industrial and communications electronics. The "Münchner Volkshochschule" (MVHS) is Europe's biggest and most variable communal adult education centre, instructing more than 400,000 students every year.

Company-founding Campaign

In the sector of founding new enterprises the Federal Republic of Germany is lagging behind international competition. Unlike the United States, Germany has no enterprise-founding "culture" which is firmly rooted in the local economy and society. Initiatives like the "Munich Business Plan Competition", "the Bio^M AG" and the "GründerRegio M" try to bring about a change of attitude at universities and

COMPANY-FOUNDING

A Munich, environ 500 écoles, de l'école primaire à l'école européenne servent de base à la formation. La ville et l'Etat Libre font de gros efforts afin de maintenir et de confirmer le niveau de qualification nettement au-dessus de la moyenne fédérale. Le dernier exemple ici est le centre de formation inauguré en 1998 dans la Bergsonstraße pour la technique et la mécanique des installations électriques, la technique solaire, l'électronique industrielle et de communication – un investissement de 109 millions de mark de la capitale du land. Avec l'université populaire de Munich, la capitale du land détient le plus grand et le plus varié des centres communaux de perfectionnement professionnel d'Europe enregistrant chaque année 400 000 participants.

L'offensive des créateurs d'entreprise

En comparant à l'échelon international, la République fédérale est à la traîne au niveau des créateurs d'entreprise. Contrairement aux USA, il n'existe pas ici une culture des professions libérales et des créateurs d'entreprise fortement ancrée dans l'économie et la société. Les initiatives de créations d'entreprise comme la Münchener Businessplan-Wettbewerb, la Bio^M AG et la GründerRegio M veillent à un changement des mentalités dans les universités et les centres de recherche mais visent exclusivement le secteur de la haute technologie.

Un boom continu des créations d'entreprise ne peut cependant être atteint que par une multitude de petites et moyennes entreprises nouvelles – venant principalement du secteur tertiaire. C'est pourquoi, la ville de Munich a mis au point avec d'autres partenaires un vaste éventail d'offres en capital, terrains et savoir-faire pour les jeunes entrepreneurs.

Avec la Stadtsparkasse, elle a donné naissance à un programme de crédit offrant sans bureaucratie aux créateurs d'entreprises,

coordina dal 1998 la formazione e il perfezionamento nel settore dei mezzi di comunicazione multimediali, ottimizzando qualitativamente le capacità esistenti sulla base dell'orientamento delle richieste. Con questa si sta formando un centro eccezionale della formazione multimediale (inter)nazionale. La MMA trova il suo completamento reale nel centro mediale «Media Works Munich (MWM)», in cui le istituzioni di formazione e di perfezionamento dell'economia mediale utilizzano soprattutto le sinergie derivanti dalla vicinanza e dall'uso di infrastrutture comuni, dall'effetto positivo della creazione di un'immagine e di un nome così come dalle possibili cooperazioni.

Circa 500 scuole, dalla scuola elementare alla Scuola Europea, costituiscono la base dell'istruzione di Monaco. Città e Land fanno molto per mantenere e perfezionare le qualifiche che risultano al momento superiori alla media nazionale. L'ultimo esempio è il Cento di formazione professionale nella Bergsonstraße, inaugurato nel 1998 e nel quale si studiano la tecnica e la meccanica delle installazioni elettriche, la tecnica solare, l'elettronica industriale e applicata ai sistemi di comunicazione – un investimento di 109 milioni di marchi della capitale bavarese. A Monaco si trova inoltre il centro di perfezionamento comunale più grande e differenziato d'Europa – l'Università popolare di Monaco (MVHS) – che vanta un'affluenza annuale di oltre 400 000 studenti.

L'offensiva dei nuovi imprenditori

Rispetto al panorama internazionale, la Repubblica Federale Tedesca è in netto ritardo per quanto riguarda la creazione di nuove imprese. Al contrario di quanto accade negli Usa, qui da noi la cultura imprenditoriale e del lavoro in proprio non è radicata saldamente nell'economia e nel tessuto sociale. Iniziative quali il concorso «Businessplan» di

Wettbewerb, die Bio^M AG und GründerRegio M sorgen für einen Bewusstseinswandel an Universitäten und Forschungseinrichtungen, zielen aber nur auf den Hochtechnologiesektor.

Doch ein nachhaltiger Existenzgründungsboom ist nur durch viele neue kleine und mittlere Unternehmen – vor allem aus dem Dienstleistungsbereich – zu erzielen. Die Stadt München hat deshalb in Kooperation mit anderen Partnern ein breites Spektrum an Kapital-, Flächen- und Know-how-Angeboten für Jungunternehmer entwickelt.

Zusammen mit der Stadtsparkasse hat sie ein Kreditprogramm ins Leben gerufen, das auf unbürokratischem Wege Existenzgründern – insbesondere aus der Dienstleistungsbranche – ein Startdarlehen von bis zu 50 000 DM offeriert. Bei der Entscheidung der Kreditvergabe steht die Persönlichkeit und Geschäftsidee des Gründers im Vordergrund und nicht die sonst übliche Frage nach Sicherheiten.

Bezahlbare und klein parzellierte Mietflächen für Jungunternehmer bietet die Münchner Gewerbehof- und Technologiezentrumsgesellschaft mbH, eine Beteiligungsgesellschaft der Landeshauptstadt. In fünf Gewerbehöfen und dem Münchner Technologiezentrum erwartet die Mieter neben einer maßgeschneiderten Gebäudeinfrastruktur auch ein Full-Service. Es ist geplant, diese Infrastruktur weiter auszubauen, z. B. durch ein Dienstleistungs- und Existenzgründerhaus, das sich in hohem Maße an Frauen richten wird.

Im MEB-Münchner Existenzgründungsbüro hat die Stadt gemeinsam mit der Industrie- und Handelskammer für München und Oberbayern eine zentrale Anlaufstelle für alle geschaffen, die den Schritt in die berufliche Selbstständigkeit wagen. Dort erhalten Existenzgründerinnen und -gründer kostenlose Beratung und Informationen zu allen Fragen der Unternehmensgründung. Außerdem vermittelt das Beraterteam auch Seminare und Veranstaltun-

research institutes, but focus only on the hightech sector.

A lasting boom in company-founding can, however, be brought about only if numerous small and medium-sized firms are newly established, primarily in the service sector. Therefore the city of Munich has developed – together with other partners – a comprehensive offering of capital, plots and know-how for young entrepreneurs.

Together with the "Stadtsparkasse" it has set up a credit programme which provides – in a very unbureaucratic way – starting loans of up to DM 50,000 for entrepreneurs concentrating particularly on the service sector. Here it is the personality and the business acumen of the founder that decide who receives a loan, and not the usual demand for securities.

Reasonably-priced and small rental space for young entrepreneurs can be found at the "Münchner Gewerbehof- und Technologiezentrumsgesellschaft mbH", a holding company of the Bavarian state capital. In five industrial parks and the Munich Technology Center tenants find not only a "custom-made" building infrastructure but also a full service offer. The management plans to improve the infrastructure even further by adding a service and entrepreneurial building which will mainly cater to women.

With the "MEB" (Münchner Existenzgründungsbüro) the city – in cooperation with the Chamber of Commerce and Industry for Munich and Upper Bavaria – has set up a central contact point for all persons who are prepared to take the risk of setting up a business of their own. In this office male and female company-founders are given advice and information, free of charge, in all questions concerning the setting up of a firm. Additionally, the team of advisors arranges seminars and courses for company-founders and more specific consulting.

Furthermore, "Verbund Strukturwandel GmbH" (also a munici-

ENTREPRISE

en particulier dans le secteur tertiaire, une aide de départ allant jusqu'à 50 000 DM. Le crédit est accordé en fonction de la personnalité et de l'idée commerciale du créateur et non, comme d'habitude, d'après les garanties fournies.

Des petites surfaces à louer à un prix raisonnable pour de jeunes entrepreneurs sont proposées par la société munichoise Münchner Gewerbehof- und Technologiezentrumsgesellschaft mbH, une société à participation de la ville de Munich. Dans cinq espaces artisanaux et dans le centre de technologie de Munich, les locataires disposent, outre d'un bâtiment à l'infrastructure taillée sur mesure, d'une gamme complète de services. Il est prévue d'agrandir encore cette infrastructure, par exemple avec un centre de prestations de service et de créations d'entreprise destiné en premier lieu aux femmes.

Dans le MEB-Münchner Existenzgründungsbüro, la ville en coopération avec la chambre de commerce et d'industrie de Munich et de Haute-Bavière ont créé un centre pour tous ceux qui osent se lancer dans une profession libérale. Les créatrices et les créateurs d'entreprise y reçoivent un conseil gratuit, des informations sur toutes les questions inhérentes à la création d'entreprise. Par ailleurs, l'équipe de conseillers propose également des séminaires et des conférences pour les créateurs d'entreprise ainsi que des offres de conseil plus spécialisés.

En outre le Verbund Strukturwandel GmbH, une société communale également à participation, propose, en coopération avec le bureau BfE pour les créations

Monaco, la Bio^M AG e la GründerRegio M mirano a far nascere un nuovo spirito imprenditoriale a livello universitario e di istituti di ricerca, ma si rivolgono solo al settore dell'alta tecnologia.

Il boom tanto auspicato della creazione di nuove imprese potrà avvenire solo attraverso le piccole e medie imprese – soprattutto nel settore dei servizi. È per questo motivo che la città di Monaco ha sviluppato insieme ad altri partner un ampio spettro di offerte per giovani imprenditori relative alla possibilità di finanziamenti, di reperimento di aree industriali e commerciali e di acquisizione del know-how.

Con la collaborazione della cassa di risparmio municipale, è stato portato in vita un programma di finanziamento che non segue le solite vie burocratiche ed offre ai nuovi imprenditori – soprattutto del ramo dei servizi – un credito standard fino ad un massimo di 50 000 DM. Questo viene concesso non più sulla base delle garanzie prodotte al momento della richiesta, bensì sulla base della personalità dell'imprenditore e del suo progetto commerciale.

Inoltre, la Gewerbehof- und Technologiezentrumsgesellschaft mbH di Monaco, una società finanziaria della capitale bavarese, offre la possibilità ai giovani imprenditori di affittare ad un prezzo equo un'area commerciale suddivisa in piccoli lotti. I locatari troveranno nei cinque centri commerciali e nel Centro Tecnologico di Monaco un'infrastruttura pensata su misura per loro ed un'offerta completa di servizi. In futuro si progetta di ampliare ulteriormente questa infrastruttura, che comprenderà una sezione rivolta soprattutto alle giovani imprenditrici.

Nell'ufficio di avviamento per nuove imprese MEB di Monaco, la città ha creato insieme alla Camera dell'Industria e del Commercio di Monaco e dell'Alta Baviera un punto di partenza centrale per tutti coloro che intendono fare il primo passo come imprenditori autonomi. I nuovi

INNOVATION

gen für Existenzgründer sowie weiterführende fachspezifische Beratungsangebote.

Daneben bietet die Verbund Strukturwandel GmbH, ebenfalls eine städtische Beteiligungsgesellschaft, in Kooperation mit dem BfE-Büro für Existenzgründungen des Arbeitsamtes München eine Existenzsicherungsberatung an, die Jungunternehmern in den ersten schwierigen Jahren nach der Gründung mit Rat und Tat zur Seite steht.

In keiner anderen deutschen Stadt haben Existenzgründer so gute Startbedingungen wie an der Isar. Fast 20 000 neue Gewerbebetriebe in den Jahren 1993 bis 1997 sprechen eine eindeutige Sprache.

Europäische Städtepolitik

Angesichts der wachsenden internationalen Konkurrenz muss sich die Stadt klar darüber sein, welche Rolle sie in der europäischen Städtehierarchie weiter spielen will: Absicherung der Position als „Euro-Metropole"? Ausbau ihrer globalen Qualitäten zugunsten einer Stärkung der Position in der Städtehierarchie?

Da internationale Investitionen verstärkt zu internationalen Städten tendieren, scheint es sinnvoll und notwendig, dass die Stadt ihre globalen Qualitäten ausbaut. Dazu gehören insbesondere Erreichbarkeit, Telekommunikation, Internationalisierung der Wissenschafts-, der politischen und administrativen Beziehungen. Erforderlich sind zudem ein verstärktes internationales Marketing, vor allem auch in den neuen Ostmärkten, in den asiatischen und südamerikanischen Wachstumsmärkten, sowie eine Stär-

pal holding company) offers – in cooperation with the BfE-Bureau for Company-Founding of the Munich Labour Exchange – consulting in safeguarding the existence of young company founders, and it assists them during the first difficult years after the founding.

Young entrepreneurs find similarly promising starting conditions in no other German city. The fact that nearly 20,000 new businesses were set up in Munich between 1993 and 1997 speaks for itself.

European City Policy

In view of increasing international competition Munich must make up its mind which role it wants to play in the hierarchy of European cities: Does it want to safeguard its position as a "Eurometropolis"? Or does it plan to increase its global qualities for consolidating its position in the hierarchy of cities?

As international investments tend to concentrate on international cities it seems more logical for Munich to improve its global qualities. This will include improving its accessibility and telecommunications, and the internationalization of its scientific, political and administrative relations. Additionally, it will be necessary to increase international marketing – primarily in the east-European markets and in the Asian and South-American growth markets – and to intensify cooperation with European cities ranking in the same league and boasting a high innovative potential such as Amsterdam/Rotterdam, Barcelona, Milano, Manchester, Lyon and Vienna.

To attain an international position, it will be necessary for Munich to present itself as a global economic centre; to introduce international marketing at fairs and other events; and to take over the function of a "doorhandle" for the local enterprises on international markets. To be able to assess its own competitive position in relation to rival

d'entreprise de l'agence nationale pour l'emploi, un conseil devant aider les jeunes entrepreneurs à surmonter les difficultés des premières années de démarrage.

Aucune autre ville allemande n'offre d'aussi bonnes conditions de départ aux créateurs d'entreprise que la ville aux bords de l'Isar. Près de 20 000 nouvelles entreprises industrielles entre 1993 et 1997; un chiffre qui en dit long.

La politique municipale européenne

Face à la concurrence internationale croissante, la ville doit bien clarifier le rôle qu'elle veut jouer dans la hiérarchie des villes européennes: maintenir la position de «capitale européenne»? Développement de ses qualités globales en faveur d'une affirmation de sa position dans la hiérarchie des villes?

Comme les investissements internationaux tendent de plus en plus vers des villes internationales, il semble nécessaire que la ville développe ses qualités globales. Il s'agit en particulier de son accessibilité, de sa télécommunication, de l'internationalisation de ses relations scientifiques, politiques et administratives. De plus, une focalisation doit s'opérer sur un marketing international plus poussé, en particulier dans les marchés de l'est, dans les marchés de croissance d'Asie et d'Amérique du Sud ainsi que sur le renforcement de la coopération avec les villes européennes de même «statut» et dotées d'un énorme potentiel novateur comme Amsterdam/Rotterdam, Barcelone, Milan, Manchester, Lyon et Vienne.

Les mesures pour le positionnement international de Munich concernent la présentation en tant que site économique global, un marketing international sur les foires et manifestations ainsi que le rôle «d'ouvreur» pour les entreprises régionales sur les marchés internationaux. Pour juger sa compétitivité par rapport

imprenditori e le nuove imprenditrici possono ricevere qui un servizio di consulenza gratuito e informazioni su ogni tipo di problematica relativa alla costituzione di un'impresa. Inoltre, il team di consulenti organizza per loro anche seminari e manifestazioni ed offre anche in seguito servizi di consulenza specialistici.

Un altro aiuto è offerto dalla Verbund Strukturwandel GmbH. Si tratta anche in questo caso di una società finanziaria cittadina che offre in cooperazione con l'ufficio dell'Ente federale per gli aiuti di sviluppo (BfE) dell'Ufficio del Lavoro di Monaco un servizio di consulenza che assisterà i giovani imprenditori con le parole e coi fatti durante i primi anni difficili di attività.

Nessun'altra città tedesca offre delle condizioni così buone per l'avviamento. Lo confermano le quasi 20 000 nuove aziende fondate tra il 1993 e il 1997.

La politica europea della città

In considerazione della crescente concorrenza internazionale, la città deve aver ben chiaro quale ruolo intende continuare ad avere nella gerarchia europea delle città, ovvero se intende assicurare la propria posizione come «metropoli europea» o potenziare le sue qualità globali a favore di un rafforzamento della propria posizione nella gerarchia delle città.

Dato che gli investimenti internazionali tendono fortemente a concentrarsi su città internazionali, sembra sensato e necessario che la città potenzi le sue qualità globali. Queste comprendono soprattutto la facilità di accesso, le telecomunicazioni e l'internazionalizzazione delle relazioni scientifiche, politiche e amministrative. Si richiede inoltre un marketing forte a livello internazionale, anche e soprattutto nei nuovi mercati dell'Est e nei mercati di sviluppo asiatici e sudamericani, oltre ad un rafforzamento della cooperazione con le altre città europee della stessa statura e con alto poten-

kung der Kooperation mit europäischen Städten der gleichen „Liga" mit hohem Innovationspotential wie Amsterdam/Rotterdam, Barcelona, Mailand, Manchester, Lyon und Wien.

Maßnahmen zur internationalen Positionierung Münchens sind die Präsentation als globaler Wirtschaftsstandort, ein internationales Marketing auf Messen und Veranstaltungen sowie die Rolle einer Türöffnerfunktion für die heimischen Unternehmen auf internationalen Märkten. Zur Einschätzung der eigenen Wettbewerbsposition im Verhältnis zu konkurrierenden Städten und Regionen – Stichwort Benchmarking – muss München die internationale erfolgreiche Politik aber auch Fehlschläge von Stadtregionen aufmerksam verfolgen, um daraus zu lernen (Förderung von „best-practice") und die Mitarbeit in internationalen Kooperationen sowie Städtenetzwerken ausbauen. Ein Katalysator hierfür ist die konsequente Nutzung von EU-Projekten.

Regionale Zusammenarbeit

Nicht zuletzt gehören dazu verstärkte Anstrengungen, um mit der Region zu einer abgestimmten wirtschaftlichen Strategie und Präsentation nach außen zu gelangen. Stadt und Umland sind inzwischen zu einem funktionalen Wirtschaftsraum vernetzt, wobei das relative wirtschaftliche Gewicht des Umlands zunimmt. In Zukunft werden nationale Grenzen in einem vereinten Europa an Bedeutung verlieren, die Regionen sind die wichtigen Akteure. Zentren von Metropolregionen sind Global oder Metropolitan Cities. Sie müssen eingebettet sein in den großen räumlichen Zusammenhang des regionalen Umfelds.

Der Wettbewerb der Regionen, der zusehends den Wettbewerb zwischen Städten überlagert, erfordert eine bessere Koordination der Infrastrukturpolitik, der strategischen Entwicklungsziele und der entsprechenden Maßnahmen bis hin zum regionalen Marketing.

cities and regions (called benchmarking in professional lingo) Munich must carefully watch successful international policies as well as eventual failures to gain experience (i.e. promotion of best practice), and it must intensify its work in international cooperations and city networks. Taking part consistently in EU projects will be an excellent catalyst in this field.

Regional Cooperation

This includes increased efforts to develop – together with the region – a well-coordinated economic strategy and image. The city and its environs have by now turned into a closely interwoven, functional economic unit in which the relative economic importance of the region is increasing. In the united Europe of the future national borders will lose their significance and regions will become the true players. Global or metropolitan cities will then become the centres of such "metropolregions", and will have to be safely embedded in their larger environment.

The competition between regions, which increasingly overshadows competition between cities, requires a better coordination of infrastructural policies, of strategic development aims, and of corresponding measures – right up to regional marketing. Increased regional cooperation is also compulsory with regard to the future "Europe of regions" – particularly in view of the further development of the regional infrastructure, of a regional area management, of regional marketing and tourism, and

aux villes et régions concurrentes (benchmarking), Munich doit suivre avec attention la politique internationale, les succès comme les échecs des régions urbaines afin d'en tirer des leçons (promotion de «best practice») et renforcer la collaboration dans des coopérations internationales et des réseaux urbains. L'utilisation conséquente des projets de l'UE peut servir de catalyseur.

Coopération régionale

Il va également falloir renouveler ses efforts pour arriver à définir avec la région une stratégie et une présentation vers l'extérieur. La ville et ses environs forment maintenant un espace économique fonctionnel et le poids économique des environs s'accentue.

A l'avenir, les frontières nationales perdront de leur importance dans une Europe unifiée, les régions deviendront les acteurs principaux. Les centres des régions sont des «global ou metropolitan cities». Elles doivent être bien placées dans le vaste environnement régional.

La concurrence entre les régions remplaçant de plus en plus la concurrence entre les villes exige une meilleure coordination de la politique d'infrastructure, des objectifs stratégiques de développement et des mesures inhérentes jusqu'à la mise en place d'un marketing régional. Une coopération régionale renforcée

ziale innovativo, ovvero Amsterdam/Rotterdam, Barcellona, Milano, Manchester, Lione e Vienna.

I provvedimenti adottati per posizionare Monaco ad un livello internazionale sono la sua presentazione come sede di un'economia globale, operazioni di marketing internazionale condotte attraverso numerose fiere e manifestazioni, infine il ruolo svolto dalla città nell'apertura dei mercati internazionali a favore delle aziende locali. Per valutare la propria posizione in rapporto alle altre città e regioni concorrenti – parola d'ordine: «bench marking» – è però opportuno che Monaco segua con attenzione non solo i successi ma anche gli insuccessi della politica internazionale, per imparare dagli errori (politica della «best practice») e potenziare la collaborazione con cooperazioni internazionali e reti cittadine. Un catalizzatore per tutte queste iniziative possono essere i progetti finanziati dall'Unione Europea.

Collaborazione regionale

Non da ultimo sono da ricordare gli sforzi sempre maggiori per presentarsi sulla scena internazionale insieme alla propria regione e con una strategia economica comune. Nel frattempo, la città e le zone circostanti hanno sviluppato una fitta rete di collegamenti divenendo un'area economica funzionale e comportando un aumento del peso economico relativo della regione. In futuro i confini nazionali perderanno importanza all'interno di un'Europa unita, e il ruolo di attore principale passerà alle regioni. I centri delle regioni metropolitane saranno le «global» o «metropolitan cities», che dovranno essere inserite nel contesto più ampio della regione.

La concorrenza tra le regioni, che si sovrappone e supera decisamente quella tra le città, richiede un coordinamento migliore della politica infrastrutturale, degli obiettivi strategici di sviluppo e dei relativi provve-

Zwingend ist eine verstärkte regionale Kooperation auch mit Blick auf das „Europa der Regionen", vor allem hinsichtlich der Weiterentwicklung der regionalen Infrastruktur, eines regionalen Flächenmanagements, des Regionalmarketings und Tourismus sowie der Abstimmung der Entwicklungsvorstellungen und Perspektiven bzw. Strategien für die Gesamtregion.

Eine intensivere Zusammenarbeit, insbesondere im Regionalmarketing, sowie eine Stärkung der Wettbewerbsfähigkeit der Region auf internationaler Ebene verfolgt auch der 1995 gegründete Verein „Wirtschaftsraum Südbayern. München. Augsburg. Ingolstadt. (MAI) e.V." mit dem Ziel, die wirtschaftliche Entwicklung in Südbayern und die Bekanntheit des Raumes zum Nutzen aller Beteiligten zu fördern. Nur durch konsequente Lobbyarbeit sowie Bündeln der vielfältigen Energien und Synergieeffekte öffentlicher und privater Akteure kann sich die Wirtschaftsregion weiterentwickeln und konkurrenzfähig bleiben. Eine Region, die sich gegenseitig stärkt, wird eine Zukunftsregion in Europa sein.

Verwaltungsreform

Im Zuge der Globalisierung muss auch Münchens Stadtverwaltung den Konkurrenzkampf nicht nur gegen andere Kommunen, sondern auch gegen private Mitbewerber aufnehmen. Das heißt, die städtischen Dienstleistungen müssen für Bürger und Unternehmen sowohl im internationalen Vergleich mit anderen Städten als auch vor Ort gegenüber privaten Angeboten wettbewerbsfähig werden. Dies gilt z. B. für das Baureferat, für die Rechtsabteilungen, für das Amt für Abfallwirtschaft. Aber auch für die Lokalbaukommission,

of coordinating the conceptions of development, and the perspectives and strategies for the entire region.

The society "Wirtschaftsraum Südbayern. München. Augsburg. Ingolstadt. (MAI) e.V.", founded in 1995, also promotes more intensive cooperation (particularly in regional marketing) and the region's competitive edge on an international level. It aims at promoting the economic development and popularity of southern Bavaria in the interest of all participants. Only consistant lobby work and the combining of energy and synergy effects contributed by public and private agents will enable the region to develop further and remain competitive. Only a region whose parts support and strengthen one another will become a future "region of Europe".

Administrative Reform

In the course of globalization Munich's city administration will also have to take up a competitive battle not only against other communities but also against private rivals. This means that municipal services must become acceptable to citizens and enterprises – not only in international comparison with other cities but also in comparison with private local offerers. This applies, for instance, to the construction department, to the legal department, and to the office for waste disposal. But it also refers to the local building commission, whose services and ploddy procedures (building permits) will in future

s'avère indispensable encore plus si l'on considère «l'Europe des régions», en particulier le développement de l'infrastructure régionale, d'un management régional, d'un marketing régional et du tourisme ainsi que la concertation des idées de développement et des perspectives ou stratégies pour l'ensemble de la région.

Une coopération plus intense, en particulier au niveau du marketing régional, ainsi que le renforcement de la compétitivité de la région à l'échelon international sont également la mission de l'association fondée en 1995 «Wirtschaftsraum Südbayern. München. Augsburg. Ingolstadt. (MAI) e.V.» (espace économique de la Bavière du sud. Munich. Augsbourg. Ingolstadt) qui vise la promotion du développement économique du sud de la Bavière et la notoriété de l'espace ce dont profitent tous les participants. Ce n'est qu'avec un travail de lobby conséquent ainsi que la réunion d'énergies et d'effet synergiques divers des acteurs publics et privés que la région économique pourra poursuivre son développement et rester concurrentielle. Une région qui s'épaule mutuellement est une région d'avenir en Europe.

Réforme administrative

Suite à la mondialisation, la gestion municipale de Munich doit affronter la concurrence non seulement des autres communes mais aussi des concurrents privés. En d'autres termes, les services municipaux doivent être concurrentiels pour les citoyens et les entreprises aussi bien à l'échelle internationale en comparant avec d'autres villes qu'à l'échelle locale par rapport aux prestataires privés. Cela prévaut p.ex. pour le service de l'urbanisme, les services juridiques, le service du traitement des déchets. Mais également pour la commission locale de construction dont le service et la durée de procédure pour l'octroi des permis de construire devra

dimenti fino ad arrivare al marketing regionale. Ciò che risulta assolutamente necessario è rafforzare la cooperazione regionale anche in vista dell'«Europa delle regioni», ma soprattutto per quanto riguarda lo sviluppo dell'infrastruttura regionale, di una gestione regionale delle aree, del marketing regionale e del turismo, concordando le idee, le prospettive di sviluppo e le strategie per l'intera regione.

Una collaborazione più intensiva, soprattutto nel marketing regionale, e il rafforzamento della concorrenzialità della regione a livello internazionale sono anche l'obiettivo dell'associazione «Wirtschaftsraum Südbayern. München. Augsburg. Ingolstadt. (MAI) e.V.» fondata nel 1995 al fine di promuovere lo sviluppo economico dell'Alta Baviera e di accrescere la notorietà della regione a vantaggio di tutti i membri dell'associazione. La regione economica potrà continuare a svilupparsi e a rimanere concorrenziale solo unendo le forze, le energie e gli effetti di sinergia delle diverse parti in causa, pubbliche e private. Solo una regione in cui le diverse parti si rafforzano reciprocamente potrà essere una regione del futuro in Europa.

La riforma dell'amministrazione

Nell'ambito della globalizzazione, anche l'amministrazione cittadina di Monaco deve mettersi in concorrenza non solo contro altri comuni, ma anche contro concorrenti privati. Ovvero, i servizi cittadini devono diventare competitivi per cittadini ed imprese sia in confronto con le altre città internazionali che in rapporto alle offerte private locali. Quanto sopra vale, ad es. per l'Ufficio tecnico, gli uffici legali e per l'ufficio per lo smaltimento dei rifiuti. Ma anche per la commissione edilizia locale, i cui servizi saranno confrontati in futuro con quelli degli altri comuni europei, così come la durata dei procedimenti per le concessioni edilizie.

deren Service und Verfahrensdauer bei Baugenehmigungen sich künftig mit anderen europäischen Kommunen messen lassen muss.

Um das zu erreichen, brauchen wir eine grundlegende Reform der Verwaltung mit dem Ziel, wirtschaftlicher zu werden, die Serviceleistungen zu verbessern sowie den Bedürfnissen der Münchner stärker Rechnung zu tragen. Alle städtischen Mitarbeiter und Münchner Bürger sind aufgerufen, sich aktiv an diesem Umsetzungsprozess zu beteiligen, in dem es keine Tabus geben darf und der vom Mut zu Veränderung getragen sein muss. Um unsere Arbeit künftig bürgerfreundlicher, wirtschaftlicher und mitarbeiterorientierter leisten zu können, übernimmt die Verwaltung erprobte Steuerungsmechanismen der Wirtschaft: Abbau hierarchischer Strukturen, kooperativer Führungsstil, Produktentwicklung, Kosten- und Leistungsrechnung, Controlling, Berichtswesen und Outputbudgetierung.

**Dr. Reinhard Wieczorek
Jürgen Kuhr**

be compared with those of other European communities.

To reach this aim we need a thorough reform of our administration; it must become more economical, must improve its services and must pay more attention to the needs and requirements of the local population. All public servants and citizens are called upon to actively take part in this restructuring process, which must not be handicapped by taboos and should accept changes courageously. To be able to carry out our tasks in a more citizen-friendly, economical and colleague-oriented manner, the administration must rely on proven control mechanisms employed by the economy: on discarding hierarchic structures, on a cooperative type of management, on product development, on cost and performance accounting, on controlling, on reporting and on output budgeting.

**Dr. Reinhard Wieczorek
Jürgen Kuhr**

se mesurer à l'avenir aux autres communes européennes.

Pour y arriver, nous avons besoin d'une réforme fondamentale de l'administration afin de devenir plus économiques, d'améliorer les prestations de service et afin de répondre encore mieux aux besoins des Munichois. Le personnel de la ville et les citoyens munichois sont appelés à participer activement à ce processus de transformation qui ne devra connaître aucun tabou et devra être porté par une volonté de changement. Afin que son travail devienne à l'avenir encore plus agréable pour le citoyen, plus efficace, et plus orienté sur ses collaborateurs, l'administration reprend des mécanismes ayant fait leur preuve dans l'économie, à savoir suppression des structures hiérarchiques, encadrement coopératif, développement de produit, calcul des coûts et résultats, controlling, rapport et budgétisation.

**Dr. Reinhard Wieczorek
Jürgen Kuhr**

Per raggiungere tutto ciò è necessaria una riforma radicale dell'amministrazione al fine di renderla più snella ed economica, di migliorarne i servizi e di venire incontro in modo più incisivo alle esigenze dei cittadini. Tutti i collaboratori e gli abitanti della città sono chiamati a partecipare in modo attivo a questo processo di trasformazione, nel quale non dovrà esserci alcun tabù e che dovrà essere affrontato con coraggio e senza timore dei cambiamenti. Per poter fare il nostro lavoro in futuro con maggiore soddisfazione di cittadini e collaboratori e in modo più economico, l'amministrazione adotta i meccanismi di gestione collaudati dell'economia: smantellamento delle strutture gerarchiche, stile di comando cooperativo, sviluppo del prodotto, calcolo dei costi e dei rendimenti, controlling, bilancio e pianificazione della produzione.

**Dr. Reinhard Wieczorek
Jürgen Kuhr**

DAS HANDWERK – MÜNCHENS VIELSEITIGSTER WIRTSCHAFTSBEREICH

Jeden Tag um 11, 12 und 17 Uhr, wenn sich Touristen aus aller Welt auf dem Münchner Marienplatz am Glockenspiel des Neuen Rathauses erfreuen, wird mit dem Schäfflertanz an den ältesten Handwerkerbrauch der Isarmetropole erinnert. Er geht zurück auf das Pestjahr 1517, als sich die Münchner Fassmacher nach einer verheerenden Epidemie als erste wieder auf die Straßen trauten und durch ihren Tanz und Gesang Frohsinn in die Gemäuer der Stadt zurückbrachten. Auch heute noch dokumentiert der Schäfflertanz – täglich auf dem Rathausturm und alle sieben Jahre live zu bewundern – die Lebendigkeit des Handwerks, dieses vielseitigsten Wirtschaftsbereiches in München.

Das Handwerk hat über Jahrhunderte den Charakter und das Erscheinungsbild der Stadt geprägt. Münchens Baudenkmäler sind ebenso wie die weltweit bekannten Schmankerl des Nahrungsmittelhandwerks wie die Münchner Weißwurst Zeugen altbewährter Handwerkskunst. Heute präsentiert sich das Handwerk der Landeshauptstadt wie sie selbst, sowohl traditionsbewusst als auch dynamisch und modern. Das Handwerk bedient sich modernster sowie traditioneller Techniken gleichermaßen selbstverständlich. Dabei ist das Wesen handwerklicher Produktion trotz des rasanten Wandels im wirtschaftlichen Umfeld gerade in München im Kern erhalten geblieben: Qualitätsbewusstsein und individuelle Fertigung von dauerhaften Produkten haben sich als unverzichtbar und zeitlos erwiesen. Diese Stärken basieren im wesentlichen auf der hohen Qualifikation der Mitarbeiter, allen voran der Handwerksmeister.

Mehr denn je bildet der Wirtschaftszweig Handwerk das leistungsstarke Herzstück der Münchner Wirtschaft und Gesell-

THE CRAFTS – MUNICH'S MOST VARIABLE ECONOMIC SECTOR

Every day at eleven, twelve and 17 hours – when tourists from all parts of the world look forward to watching the carillon in the New Town Hall on Marienplatz – the "Schäfflertanz" (Dance of the Coopers) commemorates Munich's oldest craftsmen's custom. It dates back to 1517, the year when after a horrible epidemic of the plague Munich's coopers were the first to venture out into the streets; dancing and singing, they tried to bring a bit of cheerfulness back into the city. Even today the "Schäfflertanz" – which can be watched daily on the tower of the town hall and every seven years live on Marienplatz – emphasizes the fact that the crafts are still very much alive and Munich's most variable economic sector.

For centuries the trades and crafts have shaped the character and appearance of the city. Munich's architectural monuments are as much evidence of long-established craftsmen's skill as the internationally known and appreciated delicacies of the food trade – such as the "Weißwurst". Today the crafts present themselves just like the city shows itself – proud of its tradition but also dynamic and modern. They employ traditional and ultra-modern techniques with the same expertise. Nevertheless the gist of craft production has remained unaltered, in spite of the rapid changes taking place all around it: top quality and the individual making of durable products have proved to be indispensible and timeless assets. They rely primarily on the excellent qualifications of the craftsmen, particularly on those of the masters of the crafts.

Now more than ever the crafts are the efficient heart piece of Munich's economy and society. More than 15,000 businesses employing far more than 110,000

L'ARTISANAT – LE SECTEUR ECONOMIQUE LE PLUS DIVERSIFIE DE MUNICH

Chaque jour à onze heures, midi et 17 heures lorsque le carillon du nouvel hôtel de ville sur la Marienplatz de Munich est admiré par les touristes du monde entier, il rappel avec la Schäfflertanz (danse des tonneliers), la plus vieille tradition artisanale de la métropole aux bords de l'Isar. Elle remonte à l'année de la peste en 1517 lorsque les tonneliers osèrent s'aventurer en premier dans les rues après une épidémie ravageuse et ramenèrent par leur danse et leur chant la gaieté dans les murs de la ville. Aujourd'hui encore, la Schäfflertanz que l'on peut apprécier tous les jours sur la tour de la mairie et tous les sept ans en direct, prouve la vie de l'artisanat, le secteur économique le plus diversifié de Munich.

Pendant des siècles, l'artisanat a marqué le caractère et l'image de la ville. Les édifices munichois tout comme les spécialités culinaires mondialement connues de la gastronomie artisanale, comme les saucisses blanches munichoises, démontrent un talent artisanal ayant fait ses preuves. Aujourd'hui, l'artisanat de la capitale du land se présente tel qu'il est, attaché aux traditions mais aussi dynamique et moderne. L'artisanat se sert pareillement des techniques modernes et traditionnelles. Malgré la mutation rapide marquant le monde économique, la production artisanale est restée ancrée dans sa tradition: le sens de la qualité et une fabrication individuelle de produits durables se sont avérés indispensables et intemporels. Ces atouts se basent principalement sur le haut degré de qualification des collaborateurs, et tout spécialement des maîtres artisans.

Plus que jamais, le secteur économique de l'artisanat s'avère le cœur puissant de l'économie et de la société munichoises. Plus de 15 000 exploitations comptant plus de 110 000 employés réali-

L'ARTIGIANATO – IL SETTORE ECONOMICO MONACENSE PIU VARIEGATO

Ogni giorno, quando alle ore undici, dodici e alle cinque del pomeriggio in punto i turisti di tutto il mondo si godono, sulla Marienplatz monacense, lo spettacolo del carillon del Municipio Nuovo, si ricorda il «Ballo dei bottai», la più antica tradizione artigianale della metropoli sull'Isar. Tale tradizione risale al 1517, anno in cui a Monaco infuriava la peste. Dopo che questa tremenda epidemia aveva mietuto un gran numero di vittime, i bottai furono i primi a ripresentarsi nelle strade; e con il loro ballo e canto essi riportarono un po' di buonumore nelle mura della città. Ancora oggi, il ballo dei bottai, che può venir ammirato giornalmente sulla torre del Municipio e ogni sette anni in una rievocazione dal vivo, documenta la vitalità dell'artigianato, di questo settore economico considerato il più variegato di Monaco.

L'artigianato ha lasciato, per secoli, un'impronta tangibile sul carattere e sull'immagine della città. Una testimonianza di questa arte artigiana ormai consolidata viene fornita dai monumenti architettonici monacensi nonché dalle delicatezze alimentari conosciute in tutto il mondo come il salsicciotto bianco. Oggi, l'artigianato del capoluogo bavarese si presenta con connotati analoghi a quelli della città: con la consapevolezza della tradizione, ma anche con dinamismo e modernità. L'artigianato si serve, con grande naturalezza, sia delle tecniche più moderne che di quelle tradizionali. Tuttavia, nonostante i rapidi cambiamenti che interessano il panorama economico in cui questo settore opera, l'essenza della produzione artigianale è rimasta, proprio a Monaco, inalterata. La consapevolezza della qualità e la fabbricazione personalizzata di prodotti duraturi si sono dimostrati elementi irrinunciabili e senza tempo. Questi pun-

schaft. In über 15 000 Betrieben mit weit über 110 000 Beschäftigten werden rund 13,5 Milliarden DM (6,9 Mrd. Euro) Umsatz jährlich erwirtschaftet und knapp 7 000 Lehrlinge ausgebildet.

Sieben Tage im Jahr, wenn die Internationale Handwerksmesse (I.H.M.) ihre Pforten öffnet, ist die bayerische Landeshauptstadt Schaufenster für das Handwerk in aller Welt. Die I.H.M. ist übrigens die älteste und größte alljährlich stattfindende Messeveranstaltung in München.

Das Sprachrohr des Handwerks gegenüber der Münchner Politik und Öffentlichkeit ist die Handwerkskammer für München und Oberbayern, die im Jahre 2000 ihr 100-jähriges Jubiläum feiert. Gerade kleine und mittlere Betriebe sind auf eine starke Organisation angewiesen, um ihre Interessen durchzusetzen. Die Handwerkskammer ist vor allem auch kompetenter Dienstleister für ihre Mitgliedsbetriebe. Sie berät diese kostenlos in allen für die Betriebsführung relevanten Fragen. Zudem bietet sie Handwerkern, Lehrlingen, Gesellen und Meistern in eigenen Berufsbildungs- und Technologiezentren und drei Akademien des Handwerks qualifizierte Weiterbildung.

Heinrich Traublinger

persons achieve a turnover amounting to approximately DM 13.5 billion (6.9 billion Euro) and train just about 7,000 apprentices.

On seven days of the year, when the International Trade Fair (I.H.M.) opens its gates, the Bavarian capital becomes an international "shop window", where the crafts display their products from all parts of the world. The I.H.M. is, in fact, Munich's oldest and biggest annual fair event.

The "Handwerkskammer für München and Oberbayern" (Chamber of Crafts for Munich and Upper Bavaria), which will celebrate its centenary in the year 2000, is the official mouthpiece of the crafts in their dealings with the political sector and the public. Particularly small and medium-sized businesses are dependent on a strong organization to protect their interests. But the chamber of crafts also provides services very efficiently for its members: it advises them free of charge in all questions concerning management; and offers craftsmen, apprentices, journeymen and masters qualified further education in vocational training and technology centres of its own and in three craft academies.

Heinrich Traublinger

sent chaque année 13,5 milliards de mark (6,9 milliards d'euro) de chiffre d'affaires et forment 7 000 apprentis.

Sept jours par an, quand la foire internationale de l'artisanat (Internationale Handwerksmesse, I.H.M.) ouvre ses portes, la capitale de la Bavière est la vitrine de l'artisanat du monde entier. Par ailleurs, l'I.H.M. est le plus ancien et le plus grand salon ayant lieu chaque année à Munich.

La chambre des métiers de Munich et de Haute-Bavière sert de porte-parole à l'artisanat auprès de la politique et du public munichois. En l'an 2000, elle fêtera ses 100 ans. Les petites et moyennes entreprises ont besoin d'une organisation puissante pour faire valoir leurs intérêts. La chambre des métiers est avant tout un prestataire de service compétent pour les entreprises membres. Elle les conseille gratuitement dans toutes les questions touchant la gestion d'entreprise. De plus, elle propose aux artisans, apprentis, compagnons et maîtres un perfectionnement professionnel qualifié dans ses propres centres de formation professionnelle et de technologie et dans les trois académies de l'artisanat.

Heinrich Traublinger

ti di forza sono essenzialmente il risultato dell'elevata preparazione dei dipendenti, primo fra tutti del mastro artigiano.

Il ramo economico dell'artigianato rappresenta, oggi più che mai, il cuore efficiente dell'economia e della società monacensi. Le oltre 15 000 aziende con più di 110 000 dipendenti raggiungono complessivamente un fatturato annuo di circa 13,5 miliardi di marchi (6,9 miliardi di Euro) ed offrono una possibilità di imparare il mestiere a poco meno di 7 000 apprendisti.

Sette giorni all'anno, durante la Fiera Internazionale dell'Artigianato (I.H.M.), il capoluogo bavarese diventa la vetrina dell'artigianato di tutto il mondo. Per inciso, l'I.H.M. è la manifestazione fieristica più antica e più grande tra tutte le rassegne in programma annualmente a Monaco.

Il «megafono» dell'artigianato nei confronti del mondo politico e dell'opinione pubblica di Monaco è la Camera dell'Artigianato di Monaco e dell'Alta Baviera, che nell'anno 2000 festeggia il suo centenario di fondazione. Per poter imporre i propri interessi, proprio le aziende piccole e medie necessitano di una forte organizzazione. La Camera dell'Artigianato opera con competenza, per le aziende ad essa iscritte, soprattutto nel settore dei servizi. Il sodalizio camerale presta opera di consulenza gratuita in tutte le questioni rilevanti della gestione aziendale. Inoltre, in centri di istruzione professionale e tecnologici da essa gestiti ed in tre accademie la Camera offre ad artigiani, apprendisti, artigiani diplomati e maestri corsi qualificati di aggiornamento professionale.

Heinrich Traublinger

Die **Handwerkskammer für München und Oberbayern** ist kompetenter Partner für Handwerksbetriebe und berät kostenlos in allen Fragen, die sich im Betrieb ergeben.

Beratungsleistungen der Handwerkskammer:
Betriebswirtschaftliche Beratung
Betriebsbörse
Technische Betriebsberatung
Technologie-Transfer-Beratung
EDV-Beratung
Umweltschutzberatung
Rechtsberatung
Arbeits- und Sozialrechtsberatung
Ausbildungsberatung
Weiterbildungsberatung
Formgebungs- und Denkmalpflegeberatung

The **Chamber of Crafts for Munich and Upper Bavaria** is an effcient partner of craftsmen's enterprises and offers advice free of charge in all managerial questions.

Consulting services offered by the Chamber:
Business administration consulting
Business exchange
Technical business consulting
Technology transfer consulting
EDP consulting
Environmental protection consulting
Legal consulting
Labour law and social law consulting
Educational guidance
Further education guidance
Style and monument protection consulting

La **chambre des métiers de Munich et de Haute-Bavière** est un partenaire compétent pour les entreprises artisanales et elle les conseille gratuitement pour toutes les questions inhérentes à l'entreprise.

Les activités conseil de la chambre des métiers :
Conseil en matière de gestion d'entreprise
Bourse aux entreprises
Conseil technique
Conseil en matière de transfert de technologie
Conseil en informatique
Conseil sur la protection de l'environnement
Conseil juridique
Conseil en droit du travail et social
Conseil de formation
Conseil de perfectionnement professionnel
Conseil en matière de conception et de sauvegarde du patrimoine

La **Camera dell'Artigianato di Monaco e dell'Alta Baviera** è un partner competente delle aziende artigianali ed offre una consulenza gratuita per tutte le questioni riguardanti il funzionamento dell'azienda.

Queste le consulenze offerte dalla Camera dell'Artigianato:
Consulenza di economia aziendale
Borsino delle aziende
Consulenza nella gestione tecnica
Consulenza sul trasferimento tecnologico
Consulenza EDP
Consulenza di tutela ambientale
Consulenza legale
Consulenza di diritto del lavoro e diritto sociale
Consulenza di aggiornamento professionale
Consulenza nella modellatura e nella tutela dei monumenti

Die Handwerkskammer für München und Oberbayern ist das Sprachrohr des Handwerks gegenüber Politik und Öffentlichkeit.

Zum Durchsetzen ihrer Interessen sind gerade kleine und mittlere Betriebe auf eine starke Organisation angewiesen. Die Handwerkskammer für München und Oberbayern vertritt die Interessen objektiv und sachgerecht.

Die Handwerkskammer vertritt als Selbstverwaltungseinrichtung die Interessen des Handwerks in allen politischen Fragen, berät in allen Fragen, die von einem Handwerksbetrieb gelöst werden müssen.

Die Beratung der Kammer-Mitglieder wird dabei großgeschrieben. Zudem bietet die Kammer Kurse der Aus-, Fort- und Weiterbildung an. Denn: Nur qualifizierte Handwerker können sich der Konkurrenz gelassen stellen.

The Chamber of Crafts for Munich and Upper Bavaria represents the crafts in their dealings with politics and the public.

Particularly small and medium-sized businesses are dependent on a strong organization to protect their interests. The chamber represents these interest objectively and adequately.

As an autonomous institution, the chamber of crafts safeguards the interests of the crafts in all political issues, and offers advice and help in solving any problems craftsman's enterprises are confronted with.

Counselling chamber members has priority. Additionally, the chamber offers training, further education and adult education courses. For it is only qualified craftsmen who can meet competition serenely.

Die Handwerkskammer fördert die berufliche Aus-, Fort- und Weiterbildung.

Die Wettbewerbssituation verlangt vom Handwerker lebenslanges Lernen. Die Handwerkskammer bietet jedem Handwerker deshalb eine Fülle von Weiterbildungsmöglichkeiten an, denn Wissen wird für Handwerker zum entscheidenden Wettbewerbsfaktor:

Die Handwerkskammer unterhält
7 Berufsbildungs- und Technologiezentren
9 Meisterschulen
3 Akademien des Handwerks.

The Chamber of Crafts promotes professional training, further education and adult education.

The rules of competition force craftsmen to keep learning throughout their lives. Thus the chamber offers every craftsman numerous opportunities for further education and training. A high degree of qualification enables craftsmen to be competitive.

The Chamber of Crafts operates
7 Professional training and technology centres
9 Master schools
3 Academies of the crafts.

La chambre des métiers de Munich et Haute-Bavière est le porte-parole de l'artisanat auprès de la politique et de l'opinion publique.

Pour faire valoir leurs intérêts, les petites et moyennes entreprises ont besoin d'une organisation puissante. La chambre des métiers de Munich et de Haute-Bavière représente les intérêts de manière objective et adéquate.

En tant qu'institution d'autogestion, la chambre des métiers représente les intérêts de l'artisanat pour toutes les questions politiques, elle le conseille sur toutes les questions auxquelles doit répondre une entreprise artisanale.

Le conseil des membres de la chambre arrive en tout premier plan. De plus, la chambre propose des cours de formation professionnelle, de formation continue et de perfectionnement professionnel. Car seuls des artisans qualifiés peuvent affronter tranquillement la concurrence.

La Camera dell'Artigianato di Monaco e dell'Alta Baviera rappresenta il «megafono» del settore nei confronti del mondo politico e dell'opinione pubblica.

Per imporre i propri interessi, proprio le aziende piccole e medie necessitano di una forte organizzazione. La Camera dell'Artigianato di Monaco e dell'Alta Baviera tutela gli interessi in maniera obiettiva e consona alle esigenze degli iscritti.

Istituzione autogestita, la Camera dell'Artigianato tutela gli interessi dell'artigianato in tutte le questioni di carattere politico ed offre la sua consulenza in tutte le questioni che devono venir risolte da un'azienda artigianale.

In questo contesto, la consulenza degli iscritti al sodalizio camerale assume una valenza di prim'ordine. Inoltre, la Camera offre corsi di formazione ed aggiornamento professionale. Infatti, solo artigiani qualificati possono affrontare la concorrenza senza eccessivi patemi.

La chambre des métiers encourage la formation professionnelle, la formation continue et le perfectionnement professionnel.

En raison de la concurrence, l'artisan doit apprendre toute sa vie. C'est pourquoi, la chambre des métiers propose à chaque artisan une foule de possibilités de perfectionnement professionnel car le savoir pour un artisan est un atout décisif au niveau de la concurrence :

La chambre des métiers subventionne
7 centres de formation professionnelle et de technologie
9 écoles de maîtres
3 académies de l'artisanat.

La Camera dell'Artigianato promuove la formazione e l'aggiornamento professionale.

La situazione concorrenziale esige dall'artigiano un apprendimento vita natural durante. La Camera dell'Artigianato offre pertanto a ciascun artigiano tutta una serie di possibilità di aggiornamento professionale; infatti, il disporre di un vasto bagaglio di conoscenze diventa, per gli artigiani, un fattore concorrenziale di importanza decisiva.

La Camera dell'Artigianato gestisce le seguenti strutture:
7 Centri di istruzione professionale e tecnologici
9 Scuole tecniche professionali
3 Accademie dell'artigianato.

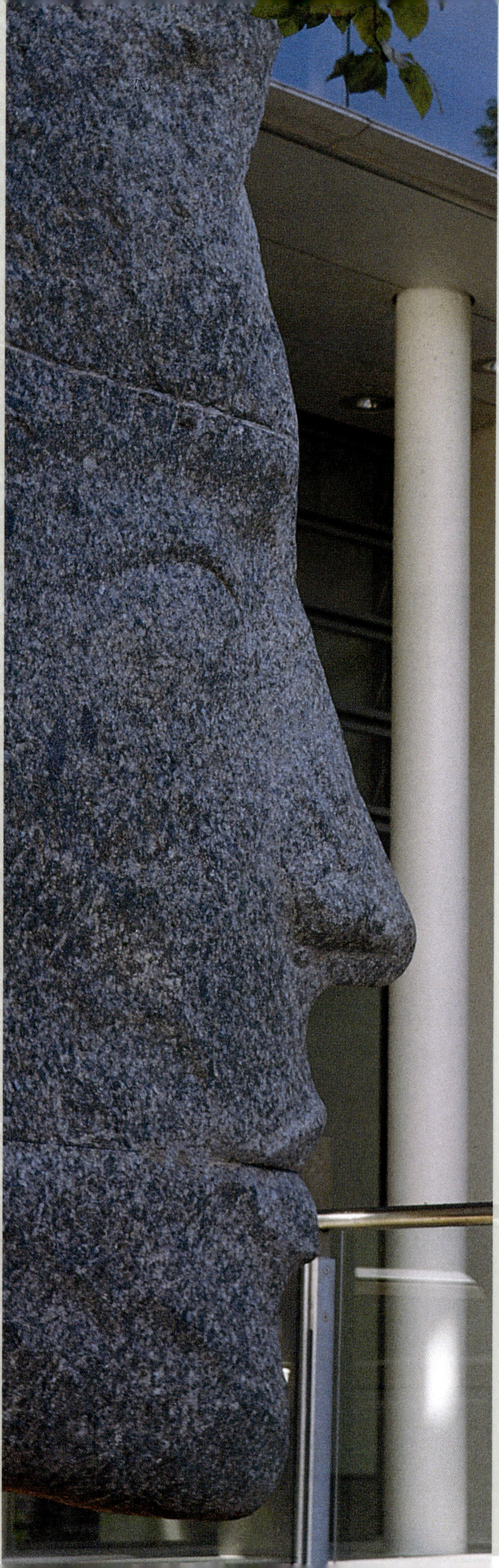

Stadt der Wissenschaft

City of Science

La ville des sciences

La città della scienza

Wissenschaft begegnet einem in München auf Schritt und Tritt. Am besten bedient man sich der U-Bahn und nimmt sich Zeit, an den verschiedenen Haltepunkten auszusteigen. Beginnen wir an der Station „Universität" – sie hält, was sie verspricht. Nach welcher Seite man auch immer aussteigt, man betritt an der Oberfläche ein Gebäude der Ludwig-Maximilians-Universität. Der Geschwister-Scholl-Platz, den sie umrahmen, erinnert an Sophie und Hans Scholl, die Gründer der Gruppe „Weiße Rose", die 1943 hier zum Widerstand gegen die Nazionalsozialisten aufriefen.

Über das Alter der LMU lässt sich streiten. Rechnet man es von 1472 an, dem Jahr ihrer Gründung in Ingolstadt durch Herzog Ludwig den Reichen, so gehört sie zweifellos zu den ältesten Universitäten im deutschen Sprachraum. Da sie aber erst 1826 nach München verlegt wurde, mutet dies ein wenig als Koketterie an, war sie doch lange die größte Universität Deutschlands und kann in der Liste ihrer Professoren mit Namen aufwarten, die ihresgleichen suchen: Max von Pettenkofer, Justus von Liebig, Conrad Wilhelm Röntgen, Adolf von Baeyer, Richard Willstätter, Feodor Lynen oder Adolf Butenandt sowie die Physiker Arnold Sommerfeld, Heinz Maier-Leibnitz, Rudolf Mössbauer oder der Biologe Karl von Frisch (der mit den Bienen!). Die Institute der LMU sind über die ganze Stadt verteilt.

Verzichtet man auf die U-Bahn und läuft vom Hauptgebäude der LMU auf der Ludwigstraße in Richtung Feldherrnhalle, so kommt man zunächst an der Bayerischen Staatsbibliothek vorbei. Sie wurde 1558 von dem Wittelsbacher Herzog Albrecht V. gegründet und birgt eine der weltweit bedeutendsten Handschriftensammlungen. Ein wenig weiter, am Odeonsplatz, steht die Generalverwaltung der Max-Planck-Gesellschaft zur Förderung der Wissenschaften, eine der großen Forschungsförderorganisationen unseres Landes.

In Munich you come across science wherever you go. The easiest way to discover the individual points of interest is to take the subway and the time to get out at the appropriate stations. Let us start with the "University" stop. No matter at which side of the street you come to the surface, you will find yourself in one of the buildings of the Ludwig-Maximilians-Universität (LMU). Its different faculties circle "Geschwister-Scholl-Platz", a large square commemorating Sophie and Hans Scholl who founded the "White Rose Group" in the university as an instrument to fight the National Socialists.

The true age of the LMU has always been a moot point: If you take 1472 – the year when the university was established by Duke Ludwig the Rich in Ingolstadt – as its founding year it is certainly one of the oldest universities of the German-speaking part of Europe. But since it was not moved to Munich till 1826 this seems to be somewhat unprincipled, for the LMU was for a long time Germany's largest university, and its list of professors contains many prominent names: Max von Pettenkofer, for instance, Justus von Liebig, Conrad Wilhelm Röntgen, Adolf von Baeyer, Richard Willstätter, Feodor Lynen, Adolf Butenandt, the physicists Arnold Sommerfeld, Heinz Maier-Leibnitz, and Rudolf Mössbauer, or biologist Karl von Frisch (the one with the bees!). The different LMU institutes are spread throughout the city.

If you ignore the subway and walk from the LMU main building along Ludwigstraße towards Feldherrnhalle, you first pass the Bavarian State Library. It was founded in 1558 by Duke Albrecht V of Wittelsbach and shelters one of the world's most valuable collections of manuscripts. A little further on you find the general administration of the "Max-Planck-Gesellschaft zur Förderung der Wissenschaft", one of Germany's largest organizations for promoting the sciences.

La science nous accompagne partout à Munich. Le mieux est de prendre le métro et d'avoir le temps de descendre à différentes stations. Commençons à la station «Universität». Elle tient ses promesses. Quelque soit la sortie que l'on prenne, on voit en sortant un bâtiment de l'université Ludwig Maximilian. La place Geschwister Scholl-Platz qui se trouve au centre rappelle Sophie et Hans Scholl, les fondateurs du groupe «Weiße Rose», qui en 1943 appela à résister contre les nationaux socialistes.

L'âge de l'université nourrit des discussions. Si l'on part de 1472, l'année de sa création à Ingolstadt par le duc Louis le Riche, elle fait sans aucun doute partie des plus anciennes universités allemandes. Mais, comme elle n'a été transférée à Munich qu'en 1826, il semble s'agir d'un pur effet de coquetterie. Quoi qu'il en soit, elle a été pendant longtemps la plus grande université d'Allemagne et peut se targuer que sa liste des professeurs contienne des noms illustres comme Max von Pettenkofer, Justus von Liebig, Conrad Wilhelm Röntgen, Adolf von Baeyer, Richard Willstätter, Feodor Lynen ou Adolf Butenandt ainsi que les physiciens Arnold Sommerfeld, Heinz Maier-Leibnitz, Rudolf Mössbauer ou le biologiste Karl von Frisch (le passionné des abeilles!). Les instituts de la LMU sont répartis dans toute la ville.

Si l'on ne prend pas le métro, on part du bâtiment principal de la LMU sur la Ludwigstraße en direction de la Feldherrnhalle, on passe d'abord devant la Bayerische Staatsbibliothek (Bibliothèque nationale bavaroise). Fondée en 1558 par le duc Albrecht V de la famille des Wittelsbach, elle abrite une des plus importantes collections mondiales de manuscrits. Un peu plus loin, à l'Odeonsplatz, se trouve l'administration générale de la société Max-Planck-Gesellschaft pour la promotion des sciences, une des organisations majeures du pays pour la promotion de la recherche.

A Monaco la scienza la si incontra a ogni piè sospinto. È sufficiente anche solo prendere la metropolitana e scendere alle diverse stazioni. Cominciamo con la stazione «Università»: questa mantiene ciò che il suo nome promette. Infatti, sia che si scenda da un lato della fermata che dall'altro, si accede ad uno degli edifici della Ludwig-Maximilians-Universität (LMU). Essi circondano la Geschwister-Scholl-Platz, una piazza dedicata a Sophie e Hans Scholl, i fondatori del gruppo della «Rosa bianca» che nel 1943 esortarono, proprio qui, la popolazione ad opporsi al regime nazista.

La questione concernente l'età della LMU è dibattuta. Se la si calcola a partire dal 1472, l'anno della sua fondazione ad Ingolstadt ad opera del duca Ludovico il Ricco, la LMU appartiene senza dubbio alle più antiche università dei Paesi di lingua tedesca. Tuttavia, visto che essa fu trasferita a Monaco solo nel 1826, fregiarsi di tale titolo può sembrare una civetteria. Per molto tempo, comunque, la LMU è stata la più grande università della Germania ed annovera nella lista dei suoi professori personalità di tutto rispetto quali: Max von Pettenkofer, Justus von Liebig, Conrad Wilhelm Röntgen, Adolf von Baeyer, Richard Willstätter, Feodor Lynen e Adolf Butenandt, così come i fisici Arnold Sommerfeld, Heinz Maier-Leibnitz, Rudolf Mössbauer e il biologo Karl von Frisch (divenuto famoso per le sue ricerche sulle api!). Gli istituti della LMU sono sparsi in tutta la città.

Rinunciando a risalire sulla metropolitana, ci si lascia alle spalle l'edificio principale della LMU percorrendo la Ludwigstraße in direzione della «Loggia dei Marescialli» (Feldherrnhalle). Il primo edificio che si incontra è la Biblioteca di Stato Bavarese (Bayerische Staatsbibliothek). Istituita nel 1558 dal duca Alberto V del casato dei Wittelsbach essa conserva una delle più importanti raccolte di manoscritti del mondo. Un po' più avanti, sulla

Zwei Schalenbrunnen vor der Universität; 1840-44 nach einem Entwurf von Friedrich von Gärtner errichtet

Two basin fountains in front of the university; erected in 1840-44 after a model by Friedrich von Gärtner

Les deux fontaines devant l'université ; construites de 1840 à 1844 d'après une esquisse de Friedrich von Gärtner

Due fontane a guscio davanti all'Università, realizzate tra il 1840 ed il 1844 su progetto di Friedrich von Gärtner

Auf dem Weg entlang des Hofgartens passieren wir die Bayerische Akademie der Wissenschaften. Ihre Statuten gehen auf das Jahr 1759 zurück, als diese Landesakademie von Kurfürst Maximilian III. Joseph gegründet wurde. In der Akademie war und ist alles vertreten, was in der deutschen Wissenschaft Rang und Namen hatte und noch hat.

Geht man vom Odeonsplatz in die Briennerstraße hinein, so befindet sich rechts der Wittelsbacherplatz mit dem rosa Gebäude der Siemens AG. Dieses Weltunternehmen darf hier nicht fehlen, steht doch sein Name auch für ein Zentrum der Industriefor-

Walking along the "Hofgarten", we pass the Bavarian Academy of Science, whose statutes date back to 1759, when this institution was founded by Elector Maximilian III Joseph. In this academy everyone is represented who has ever enjoyed high rank or an illustrious name in German science.

If you turn from Odeonsplatz into Briennerstraße, you find at your right the "Wittelsbacherplatz", a large square dominated by the pink building of the Siemens AG. This internationally operating enterprise must certainly be mentioned here, for it lends its name to a centre of

Bayerische Staatsbibliothek an der Ludwigstraße

The Bavarian State Library on Ludwigstraße

La bibliothèque nationale bavaroise sur la Ludwigstraße

La Biblioteca di Stato Bavarese nella Ludwigstraße

En longeant le Hofgarten, nous passons devant la Bayerische Akademie der Wissenschaften (académie bavaroise des sciences). Ses statuts remontent à l'an 1759, lorsque l'académie du land fut fondée par le prince électeur Maximilian III Joseph. L'académie

Odeonsplatz, si trova la rappresentanza generale della Max-Planck-Gesellschaft, una delle maggiori organizzazioni per la promozione della ricerca scientifica in Germania.

Lungo la strada che costeggia il «Giardino di Corte» (Hofgarten) si passa davanti all'Accademia Bavarese delle Scienze (Bayerische Akademie der Wissenschaften). I suoi statuti risalgono al 1759, l'anno in cui essa fu istituita dal principe elettore Massimiliano III Giuseppe. Nell'accademia erano e sono tuttora rappresentate le maggiori scoperte scientifiche della Germania.

Foto: Springorum

Fraunhofer Management GmbH – Partner für Technologie- und Innovationsmanagement

Die Fraunhofer Management GmbH (FhM), München, ist eine rechtlich selbstständige Tochterfirma der Fraunhofer-Gesellschaft zur Förderung der angewandten Forschung e.V. und der Roland Berger & Partner GmbH. Sie berät Ministerien, öffentliche Einrichtungen, Forschungsinstitute, Technologiezentren sowie Unternehmen, die im Bereich Forschung und Entwicklung tätig sind oder für die Technologietransfer von entscheidender Bedeutung ist.

Neben der wirtschaftlichen und technologischen Beratung bietet FhM auch die Realisierung ihrer Empfehlungen an. Der modulare Aufbau des Dienstleistungsspektrums ermöglicht sowohl die Übernahme von kurzfristigen Aufträgen als auch die Lösung mehrjähriger komplexer Aufgaben.

Das international erfahrene Team arbeitet interdisziplinär. Funktionsübergreifende Problemlösungen werden zielorientiert erarbeitet und gemeinsam mit dem Kunden umgesetzt.

Die Dienstleistungen der Fraunhofer Management GmbH umfassen:

- Beratung in allen betriebswirtschaftlichen und technologischen Fragen
- Technologiepolitische Analysen
- Machbarkeitsstudien
- Projekt- und Standortentwicklung
- Konzeption, Realisation und Management von Technologieeinrichtungen
- Projektträgerschaften, Projektmanagement
- Umstrukturierungen, Turnaround-Management
- Finanzierungskonzepte, Beratung von Banken und Beteiligungsgesellschaften
- Bauprojekte im Technologiebereich
- Evaluierung von FuE-Einrichtungen oder Programmen
- Trainingsprogramme, Fachveranstaltungen und Messebegleitung
- Internationale Projekte

Fraunhofer Management GmbH – Partner for Technology and Innovation Management

The Fraunhofer Management GmbH (FhM) in Munich is a legally independent subsidiary of the Fraunhofer society for the promotion of applied research and development (Fraunhofer-Gesellschaft zur Förderung der angewandten Forschung e.V.) and Roland Berger & Partner GmbH. Counsel is offered to ministries, public institutions, research institutes, technology centres as well as enterprises with activities in the field of research and development or decisive interest in technology transfer.

In addition to economic and technological counsel FhM also helps to put into practice the recommendations offered. The modular structure of the services allows the performance of orders made on short notice as well as the solution of complex tasks which might take several years.

The internationally experienced team works on an interdisciplinary basis. Problem solutions requiring the expertise of several disciplines evolve from focus teams and are implemented together with the customer.

The services offered by the Fraunhofer Management GmbH comprise:

- Counsel concerning all business-related and technological issues
- Technological-political analyses
- Feasibility studies
- Project and location development
- Conception, realization and management of technological institutions
- Implementation and management of projects
- Restructuring, turnaround-management
- Financing models, technology consulting of banks and finance companies
- Building projects in the field of technology
- Evaluation of R&D-institutes or programmes
- Training programmes, special events, trade fair accompaniment
- International projects

Hauptsitz des Europäischen Patentamtes in München

European Patent Office, Munich Headquarters

Siège de l'Office européen des brevets à Munich

Fotos: Gregor Feindt, Ottobrunn

Das **Europäische Patentamt (EPA)** ist eine zwischenstaatliche Organisation. Es wurde auf der Grundlage des am 5. Oktober 1973 in München unterzeichneten und am 7. Oktober 1977 in Kraft getretenen Europäischen Patentübereinkommens errichtet. Neben dem Sitz in München unterhält das Amt Dienststellen in Den Haag, Berlin und Wien.

Das EPA ist das Ergebnis einer modellhaften Zusammenarbeit zwischen den Staaten Europas auf dem Gebiet des gewerblichen Rechtsschutzes. Der Europäischen Patentorganisation (EPO), deren Exekutivorgan das EPA ist, gehören zur Zeit 19 Staaten an, nämlich alle Mitgliedstaaten der EU sowie Liechtenstein, die Schweiz, das Fürstentum Monaco und Zypern. Darüber hinaus kann die Schutzwirkung europäischer Patentanmeldungen und Patente auch auf eine Reihe mittel- und osteuropäischer Staaten erstreckt werden.

Aufgabe des EPA ist die Erteilung europäischer Patente nach einem einheitlichen und zentralisierten Verfahren. Dabei genügt es, eine Patentanmeldung in einer der drei Amtssprachen, Deutsch, Englisch und Französisch, einzureichen, um Patentschutz in allen Mitgliedstaaten der Organi-

The **European Patent Office (EPO)** is an international patent-granting authority established under the European Patent Convention (EPC), which was signed in Munich on 5 October 1973 and came into force on 7 October 1977. The EPO has its headquarters in Munich, a branch in The Hague, and sub-offices in Berlin and Vienna.

The EPO was established as a result of exemplary co-operation between the states of Europe in the industrial property field. The European Patent Organisation, for which the European Patent Office acts as executive arm, currently has 19 member states: all the EU countries plus Cyprus, Liechtenstein, Monaco and Switzerland. The protection conferred by European patent applications and patents can also be extended to a number of central and eastern European states.

The EPO grants European patents under a unitary and centralised procedure. By filing a single patent application in any of the three official languages – English, French or German – an applicant can obtain patent protection in all EPO member and extension states. In 1998, the EPO received 113, 400 applications.

L'**Office européen des brevets (OEB)** est une administration internationale, créée sur la base de la Convention sur le brevet européen, signée le 5 octobre 1973 à Munich et entrée en vigueur le 7 octobre 1977. L'Office a son siège à Munich, un département à la Haye ainsi qu'une agence à Berlin et à Vienne.

La création de l'OEB est le fruit d'une coopération exemplaire entre les Etats européens dans le domaine de la protection de la propriété industrielle. L'Organisation européenne des brevets, dont l'OEB est l'organe exécutif, compte actuellement 19 Etats membres, à savoir tous les Etats membres de l'UE ainsi que le Liechtenstein, la Principauté de Monaco, la Suisse et Chypre. En outre, il est également possible d'étendre la protection conférée par les demandes et les brevets européens à plusieurs Etats d'Europe centrale et orientale.

L'OEB a pour mission de délivrer des brevets européens selon une procédure uniforme et centralisée. Pour obtenir une protection par brevet dans tous les Etats membres de l'Organisation européenne des brevets, il suffit de déposer une demande dans l'une des trois langues officielles de l'Office, à savoir l'allemand,

sation zu erlangen. 1998 nahm das EPA rund 113 400 Anmeldungen entgegen.

Als Gegenleistung für das ausschließliche Nutzungsrecht an seiner Erfindung legt der Anmelder sein technisches Wissen offen. Deshalb gehören Patentanmeldungen stets zu den aktuellsten Dokumenten über technische Innovationen. Vor dem Hintergrund des intensiven Wettbewerbs um Schlüsseltechnologien gewinnt die Informationsfunktion von Patenten immer stärker an Bedeutung. Über die CD-ROM-Serie ESPACE®, die INPADOC-Datenbanken und den Internet-Dienst esp@cenet® erschließt das EPA in enger Zusammenarbeit mit den nationalen Patentämtern das in Patenten enthaltene technische Wissen für die Benutzer. Mit mehr als 30 Millionen Dokumenten, die in allen Amtssprachen der EPO-Staaten abgefragt werden können, ist esp@cenet® der weltweit umfangreichste kostenlose Patentinformationsdienst im Internet. Weiterführende Informationen über Patente vermitteln die 120 Patentinformationszentren (PATLIB-Zentren) der Mitgliedstaaten, deren Angebot speziell auf die Bedürfnisse der Erfinder, der kleineren Betriebe und der mittelständischen Industrie, der Forschungszentren und der Universitäten ausgerichtet ist.

Das Europäische Patentübereinkommen ist mit dem Vertrag über die internationale Zusammenarbeit auf dem Gebiet des Patentwesens (PCT) verknüpft, der in über 120 Ländern ein vereinfachtes Anmeldeverfahren bietet. Europäische Patente können auch auf nach dem PCT eingereichte internationale Anmeldungen erteilt werden.

In return for the right to control the use of his invention, the applicant is required to disclose his idea to the public. As a result, patent applications contain some of the most up-to-date information on technical innovations. Against a backdrop of intense competition for key technologies, the information aspect of patents is becoming increasingly important. With its ESPACE® CD-ROM series, INPADOC databases and esp@cenet® Internet services, the EPO makes the technical knowledge in patents available to the public in close co-operation with national patent offices. esp@cenet® – the world's biggest free patent information service on the Internet – contains over 30 million documents which can be accessed in any official language of the EPO member states. Further information on patents is provided by 120 PATLIB patent information centres throughout the member states, offering services catering specially to the needs of inventors, small and medium-sized firms, research centres and universities.

The EPC is linked to the Patent Co-operation Treaty (PCT), which offers a unitary, simplified filing procedure in more than 120 countries. European patents may be granted in respect of international applications filed under the PCT.

l'anglais et le français. En 1998, environ 113 400 demandes de brevet ont été déposées auprès de l'OEB.

En contrepartie du droit d'exploitation exclusif de son invention, le demandeur en divulgue le contenu. Les demandes de brevet représentent donc les documents les plus actuels sur les innovations techniques. Les technologies de pointe donnant lieu à une vive concurrence, la fonction informative des brevets revêt une importance sans cesse grandissante. Grâce à la série de CD-ROM ESPACE®, aux bases de données INPADOC et au service Internet esp@cenet®, l'OEB, opérant en étroite collaboration avec les offices nationaux, permet aux utilisateurs d'accéder aux connaissances techniques contenues dans les brevets. Avec plus de 30 millions de documents pouvant être consultés dans les langues officielles de tous les Etats membres de l'Organisation européenne des brevets, esp@cenet® est le service gratuit d'informations brevets sur Internet le plus complet dans le monde. Des informations plus détaillées sur les brevets peuvent être obtenues auprès des 120 centres d'information brevets (centres PATLIB) implantés dans les Etats membres, et dont les produits sont spécialement axés sur les besoins des inventeurs, des PME/PMI, des centres de recherche et des universités.

La Convention sur le brevet européen est liée au Traité de coopération en matière de brevets (PCT), qui offre dans plus de 120 pays une procédure de dépôt uniforme et simplifiée. Des brevets européens peuvent également être délivrés sur la base de ces demandes internationales.

PschorrHöfe mit einem Kunstwerk von Hannsjörg Voth: „Zwischen Sonnentor und Mondplatz" - Europäisches Patentamt, München

European Patent Office Munich-Pschorr-Höfe building with Hannsjörg Voth's work of art: "Between Sun Gate and Moon Court"

Office européen des brevets, Munich-PschorrHöfe: œuvre d'art de Hannsjörg Voth: «Entre la Porte du Soleil et la Place de la Lune»

Foto: Thomas Luettge, Wolfratshausen

Technische Universität München (TU)

Munich's technical university (TU)

L'université technique de Munich (TU)

Politecnico di Monaco (TU)

schung, das in der Welt seinesgleichen sucht.

Linker Hand über den Platz der Opfer des Nationalsozialismus kommen wir zum Maximiliansplatz mit den Denkmälern zweier Münchner Fürsten der Wissenschaft: Max von Pettenkofer und Justus von Liebig. Sie sitzen sich gegenüber, getrennt lediglich durch die Max-Joseph-Straße. Max von Pettenkofers Forschungen zur Hygiene haben entscheidend zur Ausrottung der Cholera und anderer Infektionskrankheiten beigetragen. Liebig wurde vor allem durch seine Arbeiten zur Mineraldüngung bekannt. Mit seinen Untersuchungen zu den Spurenelementen stellte er die Welternährung auf eine neue Grundlage und schuf die Voraussetzungen für die heutige Bevölkerungsentwicklung. Viele später berufene Chemiker waren nicht weniger bedeutend, darunter die Nobelpreisträger Adolf von Baeyer, Richard Willstätter sowie Heinrich von Wieland.

Der Franzose Clémenceau soll einmal geäußert haben, die Deutschen liebten das Leben weniger als den Tod. Um das zu widerlegen, soll unser Weg nun von den Denkmälern weg und am Karolinenplatz vorbei zur Technischen Universität führen. Sie lebt im besten Sinne des Wortes. Den Namen trägt sie allerdings erst seit 1970. Ihre Gründung im Jahre

industrial research which is unrivalled throughout the world.

Continuing on the left side of the street, we cross the square dedicated to the victims of National Socialism and reach Maximiliansplatz; here we find the monuments of two princes of science – Max von Pettenkofer and Justus von Liebig. They face each other across Max-Joseph-Straße. Max von Pettenkofer's research of hygienic conditions have greatly contributed to eliminating cholera and other contagious diseases. Liebig became famous primarily

a accueilli et accueille toujours tous les grands noms allemands de la science.

En partant de l'Odeonsplatz en direction de la rue Brienner Straße, on trouve à droite de la place Wittelsbacherplatz, le bâtiment rose de la Siemens AG. Cette société mondiale ne doit pas manquer ici, son nom symbolisant un centre de recherche industrielle unique au monde.

Sur la gauche, juste après la place Opfer des Nationalsozialismus, nous arrivons à la Maximiliansplatz avec les deux monu-

Entrando dalla Odeonsplatz nella Briennerstraße si incontra, sulla destra, la Wittelsbacherplatz con l'edificio rosa della Siemens AG. Questa azienda di fama mondiale, qui, non poteva davvero mancare, visto che il suo nome è diventato un punto di riferimento imprescindibile per la ricerca scientifica che non ha uguali al mondo.

Continuando a sinistra si attraversa la Piazza delle Vittime del Nazionalsocialismo (Platz der Opfer des Nationalsozialismus) per giungere alla Maximiliansplatz

1868 durch König Ludwig II. fällt in eine Zeit der ersten Blüte der technischen Chemie und Ingenieurwissenschaft. Die TU ist kleiner als die LMU, aber wie diese mit ihren Einrichtungen über die ganze Stadt verteilt. Wir werden ihr vor allem an der Endstation der U 6 in Garching wieder begegnen. Ihre Arme reichen bis Freising, wo sich die „grünen" Fakultäten (Landwirtschaft, Gartenbau, Brauwesen, Lebensmitteltechnologie und Milchwirtschaft) befinden.

for discovering mineral fertilizers. By analyzing micronutrients he based international nutrition on a new foundation and provided the preconditions for today's population development. Many of the later chemical scientists were equally important – among them the Nobel Prize winners Adolf von Baeyer, Richard Willstätter and Heinrich von Wieland.

It was Clémenceau, a French politician, who is supposed to have said that the Germans love life less than death. To contradict

ments en l'honneur des princes munichois de la science, à savoir Max von Pettenkofer et Justus von Liebig. Ils sont assis face à face, simplement séparés par la rue Max-Joseph. Les recherches de Max von Pettenkofer sur l'hygiène ont largement contribué à la disparition du choléra et d'autres maladies infectieuses. Liebig fut surtout célèbre pour ses travaux sur les engrais minéraux. Avec ses recherches sur les éléments de la chaîne, il jeta une nouvelle base à l'alimentation mondiale et créa les conditions pour le développement démographique actuel. De nombreux chimistes nommés plus tard professeurs sont tout aussi importants, parmi eux citons les prix Nobel Adolf von Baeyer, Richard Willstätter ainsi que Heinrich von Wieland.

Il paraît que le Français Clémenceau a dit une fois que les Allemands préféraient plus la mort à la vie. Pour prouver le contraire, notre chemin doit quitter ces deux mémoriaux, longer la place Karolinenplatz et mener à l'Université Technique (TU). Elle vit dans le meilleur sens de ce terme. Elle ne porte cependant ce nom que depuis 1970. Sa création en 1868 par le roi Louis II tombe à une époque du premier apogée de la chimie technique et des sciences de l'ingénieur. La TU est plus petite que la LMU mais à son instar, ses bâtiments sont dispersés à travers la ville. Nous la retrouverons surtout au terminal de la ligne U6 à Garching. Ses bras vont jusqu'à Freising où se trouvent les facultés «vertes» (agriculture, paysagerie, technique de la brasserie, technologie alimentaire et technologie laitière).

Retournons à la ligne U6 et partons en direction d'une des deux stations terminales. Commençons par Großhadern, où le regard se porte sur l'immense bâtiment de la clinique universitaire. Il abrite une des meilleures cliniques universitaires du monde. Et parmi tous les superlatifs, les cliniques de transplantation ainsi

con i suoi monumenti dedicati ai due «principi» della scienza di Monaco di Baviera: Max von Pettenkofer e Justus von Liebig. Siedono l'uno di fronte all'altro, separati solo dalla Max-Joseph-Straße. Le ricerche di Max von Pettenkofer sull'igiene hanno contribuito, in modo determinante, ad estirpare il colera ed altre malattie infettive. Liebig è conosciuto soprattutto per i suoi lavori sulla concimazione minerale. Con le sue ricerche sugli oligoelementi egli ha posto le nuove basi per l'alimentazione mondiale e ha creato i presupposti dell'attuale sviluppo demografico. A Pettenkofer e a Liebig sono seguiti molti altri chimici di importanza non minore, tra i quali i Premi Nobel Adolf von Baeyer, Richard Willstätter e Heinrich von Wieland.

Il francese Clémenceau sembra che una volta abbia detto che i tedeschi amano la vita meno della morte. Per confutare questa tesi lasciamo questi monumenti alle nostre spalle e, passando davanti alla Karolinenplatz, arriviamo al Politecnico (Technische Universität, TU). Questa istituzione è «viva» nel vero senso della parola. Il nome attuale, tuttavia, le è stato attribuito solo nel 1970. La sua istituzione nel 1868 ad opera del re Ludwig II risale al primo periodo di maggiore splendore della chimica tecnica e dell'ingegneria. La TU è più piccola della LMU, ma come questa ha i propri istituti dislocati su tutto il territorio della città. La reincontreremo soprattutto al capolinea della metropolitana U6 a Garching. Le diramazioni della TU arrivano fino a Freising, dove si trovano le facoltà «verdi» (Agraria, Orticoltura, Industria della Birra, Tecnologia Alimentare e Industria Casearia).

Ritorniamo alla U6 e dirigiamoci verso uno dei capolinea. Iniziamo con Grosshadern. Lo sguardo cade sull'immenso edificio che ospita alcune delle migliori cliniche universitarie del mondo. Tra le molte strutture di assoluta eccellenza figurano le cliniche per i trapianti ed il «Cen-

Kehren wir nun zurück zur U 6 und fahren zu einer der beiden Endstationen. Beginnen wir mit Großhadern, wo der Blick auf das riesige Gebäude des Universitätsklinikums fällt. Es beherbergt eine

Der 1999 bezogene Neubau der Max-Planck-Gesellschaft am Marstallplatz

The new building on Marstallplatz to which the Max Planck Society moved in 1999

Le nouveau bâtiment servant depuis 1999 de la société Max Planck sur la Marstallplatz

Il nuovo edificio della società Max Planck sulla Marstallplatz preso in consegna nel 1999

this statement, we shall now leave this monument and pass Karolinenplatz on our way to the Technical University (TU). It "flourishes" in the best sense of the word, although it was not granted the rank of a university until 1970. Its founding in 1868 by King Ludwig II coincided with the first golden age of technical chemistry and engineering. The TU is smaller than the LMU, but its institutes are also distributed throughout the city. We will meet it once more when we reach the terminal of the U 6 subway line in Garching. The arms of the TU stretch all the way to Freising,

que le centre Carreras pour les leucémies, tirant son nom du célèbre ténor, soigné ici avec succès sont spectaculaires.

Une petite marche à pied nous amène aux instituts de la société Max Planck pour la biochimie et la psychiatrie. En 1998, l'institut de biochimie fêta ses 25 ans d'existence. C'est là que furent réalisés les célèbres travaux sur la photosynthèse qui furent récompensés en 1988 par le prix Nobel de médecine et de physiologie décerné à Robert Huber, Johann Deisenhofer et Hartmut Michel.

tro Carreras» per le terapie leucemiche, divenuto famoso per aver curato con successo il noto tenore omonimo.

A poca distanza si trovano gli istituti della Max-Planck-Gesellschaft per la Biochimica e la Psichiatria. Il primo ha festeggiato, nel 1998, il suo 25° anniversario. Qui sono stati effettuati i famosi lavori sulla fotosintesi che sono stati premiati, nel 1988, con il Premio Nobel per la Medicina e la Fisiologia conferito a Robert Huber, Johann Deisenhofer e Hartmut Michel.

„Es gibt unzählige Möglichkeiten, Liebe zu zeigen. Ein neues Medikament ist eine davon."

Eine neue pharmazeutische Gruppe
sanofi~synthelabo
Das Wichtigste ist die Gesundheit

„Jeden Tag forschen unsere 5000 Wissenschaftler in den wichtigen Gebieten der Medizin: Herz- und Gefäßerkrankungen, Neurologische Störungen, Krebs und andere Erkrankungen der Inneren Medizin. Denn für uns bedeutet eine weltweit führende Rolle im Gesundheitswesen auch, in der Forschung neue Wege zu finden."

Im Mai 1999 ist durch die Fusion von Sanofi und Synthelabo ein neues pharmazeutisches Unternehmen von weltweiter Bedeutung entstanden: **Sanofi-Synthelabo**.

In Frankreich ist Sanofi-Synthelabo das zweitgrößte Pharmaunternehmen, in Europa rangiert die neue Gruppe auf Rang sechs, und in Deutschland zählt das Unternehmen zu den zehn größten Arzneimittelherstellern.

Die deutsche Tochtergesellschaft Sanofi-Synthelabo GmbH verlegt Anfang des Jahres 2000 ihren Firmensitz nach Berlin. Mit über 1 000 Mitarbeitern und einem Umsatzvolumen von knapp einer Milliarde DM wird dort die Ausgangsbasis für ein weiteres Wachstum geschaffen.

Sanofi-Synthelabo verfügt über ein breites Produktportfolio von verschreibungs- und apothekenpflichtigen Präparaten, das größtenteils aus der eigenen Forschung stammt und sich auf vier therapeutische Gebiete konzentriert:
Herz-Kreislauf/Thrombose
Zentrales Nervensystem
Onkologie
Innere Medizin

Sanofi-Synthelabo stellt für Patienten und Ärzte Medikamente zur Verfügung, die wirklich helfen, die Lebensqualität zu verbessern, denn...

„Das Wichtigste ist die Gesundheit"

When in May 1999 Sanofi and Synthelabo merged, a new world class pharmaceutical group was established – **Sanofi-Synthelabo**.

Sanofi-Synthelabo is the second-largest pharmaceutical company in France; in Europe 6th and in Germany Sanofi-Synthelabo is one of the ten biggest producers of medicaments.

In the year 2000 the German subsidiary Sanofi-Synthelabo GmbH will move its headquarters from Munich to Berlin. With more than 1,000 employees and sales of approximately DM one billion the firm will lay the foundation for further growth in the new German capital.

Sanofi-Synthelabo boasts a wide range of prescription medicines sold in pharmacies; most of them have been developed in the enterprise's own research department and are mainly used in four therapeutical fields:
cardiovascular/thrombosis
central nervous system
oncology
internal medicine

Sanofi-Synthelabo mission is to provide innovative medicines for patients and physicians which really help to improve the quality of life,

"Because health matters"

En mai 1999, la fusion de Sanofi et Synthelabo donna le jour à un noveau groupe pharmaceutique de taille mondiale : **Sanofi-Synthelabo**.

En France, Sanofi-Synthelabo est la deuxième entreprise pharmaceutique, en Europe le groupe occupe la sixième place et, en Allemagne, il compte parmi les dix plus grands sociétés pharmaceutiques.

La filiale allemande Sanofi-Synthelabo GmbH transférera a son siège à Berlin au début de l'an 2000. Comptant plus de 1 000 collaborateurs et réalisant un chiffre d'affaires de près d'un milliard de DM, elle forgera, à partir de Berlin, la base à une croissance supplémentaire.

Sanofi-Synthelabo dispose d'une vaste gamme de medicaments éthiques qui sort en majorité de sa propre recherche et se concentre sur quatre domaines thérapeutiques :
cardiovasculaire/thrombose
le système nerveux central
l'oncologie
la médecine interne

Sanofi-Synthelabo met à la disposition des patients et des médecins des médicaments qui aident vraiment à améliorer la qualité de vie, parce-que ...

«L'essentiel c'est la santé»

Nel maggio 1999 è nata, in seguito ad una fusione tra la Sanofi e la Synthelabo, una nuova azienda farmaceutica di levatura mondiale: la **Sanofi-Synthelabo**.

In Francia, Sanofi-Synthelabo è la seconda maggiore azienda farmaceutica, mentre in Europa il nuovo Gruppo occupa il sesto posto e in Germania è tra le dieci maggiori case produttrici.

All'inizio dell'anno 2000 la filiale tedesca Sanofi-Synthelabo GmbH trasferirà la propria sede a Berlino. Qui, con oltre 1 000 dipendenti ed un fatturato di quasi inferiore al miliardo di marchi si creeranno le basi per l'ulteriore crescita di questa realtà imprenditoriale.

Sanofi-Synthelabo dispone di un vasto portafoglio di prodotti che annovera preparati venduti solo dietro presentazione di ricetta medica o in farmacia; essi, in massima parte, sono il risultato della propria attività di ricerca e sono imperniati su quattro settori terapeutici:
cardio-vasculare/trombosi
sistema nervoso centrale
oncologia
medicina interna

La Sanofi-Synthelabo mette a disposizione di pazienti e medici farmaci che aiutano veramente a migliorare la qualità della vita. Infatti...

«La salute è la cosa più importante»

der weltweit besten Universitätskliniken. Spektakulär unter den vielen Superlativen sind die Transplantationskliniken sowie das Carreras-Zentrum für Blutkrebserkrankungen, benannt nach dem berühmten Tenor, der hier erfolgreich behandelt wurde.

Einen kurzen Fußmarsch entfernt findet man die Institute der Max-Planck-Gesellschaft für Biochemie und für Psychiatrie. 1998 feierte das Institut für Biochemie sein 25-jähriges Jubiläum. Hier entstanden die bekannten Arbeiten zur Photosynthese, die 1988

Blütenpracht im Botanischen Garten

A festival of blossoms at the botanical gardens

Splendeur florale dans le jardin botanique

Magnificenza floreale nel Giardino Botanico

where the "green" faculties – i. e. agriculture, horticulture, brewing, food technology and dairy farming – are located.

Let us now return to the U6 line and go to one of its two terminals. We start with Großhadern, where the huge building of the "Universitätsklinikum" catches the eye immediately you leave the subway station. It houses one of the globe's best university hospitals. The many outstanding clinics comprise the spectacular transplantation ward and the "Carreras Center" for blood cancer, called after the famous tenor who was treated there successfully.

After a short walk we reach the institutes of the Max-Planck-Gesellschaft for Biochemistry and Psychiatry. In 1998 the Institute for Biochemistry celebrated its 25th anniversary. Here such famous work as the research on

Pendant de nombreuses années, la clinique de Großhadern et les instituts Max Planck furent isolés aux limites de la ville de Munich jusqu'à ce que le gouvernement bavarois décide en 1989 d'installer ici les instituts de sciences naturelles de la LMU. Le centre génétique de Munich fut le premier à être inauguré en 1994. Il est issu d'un centre de recherche sur la technique génétique financé par l'Etat. Puis suivirent les facultés de chimie et de pharmacie. En gagnant le concours BioRegio en 1995, un autre centre pour les sociétés de biotechnologie vint s'ajouter. Par manque de place, beaucoup de ces sociétés sont depuis installées dans le quartier voisin de Martinsried.

Comme un reflet de miroir, près de l'autre station terminale de la ligne U6, se trouve Garching

Per molti anni le cliniche di Grosshadern e gli Istituti Max Planck sono rimasti isolati al confine del territorio comunale di Monaco, fino a quando, nel 1989, il governo bavarese ha deciso di costruire qui gli Istituti delle Scienze Naturali della LMU. Per primo è stato inaugurato, nel 1994, il Centro di Genetica di Monaco di Baviera, scaturito da un centro di ricerche per l'ingegneria genetica finanziato dalla Repubblica Federale Tedesca. Ad esso sono seguite le facoltà di Chimica e di Farmacia. Con la vittoria del Concorso di Biologia tra le Regioni nel 1995 si è aggiunto, poi, anche un centro per nuove aziende del settore biotecnologico. Molte di queste, nel frattempo, hanno dovuto trasferirsi nella vicina Martinsried per mancanza di spazio.

Nourypharma
Partner der Gynäkologie

Die Firma Nourypharma in Oberschleißheim bei München ist eine Tochter des AKZO-Nobel-Konzerns. Sie zählt im Bereich der Frauenheilkunde zu den führenden Firmen in der Bundesrepublik Deutschland. Mit Nourypharma verbindet man anerkannte Produkte für die unterschiedlichsten gynäkologischen Therapiebereiche.

Anlass für die Gründung der Nourypharma am 8. Mai 1968 war die Einführung eines völlig neuartigen Kontrazeptivums, das im Stammhaus der Nourypharma in Oss/Niederlande entwickelt worden war. Heute kommen die fast 30 verschiedenen Arzneimittel sowohl aus eigener Forschung als auch von Lizenzgebern aus Italien, der Schweiz und Japan. Das Sortiment beinhaltet orale Kontrazeptiva, Intrauterinpessare, Produkte der Hormonersatztherapie, Anti-infektiva, Klinikpräparate zur Geburtsvorbereitung, Onkologika sowie Diagnostika.

Der Erfolg der Nourypharma basiert zum einen auf innovativen Präparaten, zum anderen auf der wissenschaftlichen Information und Beratung der Ärzte, aber auch Patientinnen. Die Frauenärzte der medizinischen Abteilung stehen rund um die Uhr für telefonische Anfragen zur Verfügung. Nachwuchswissenschaftler zu unterstützen sowie nationale und internationale wissenschaftliche Arbeitskreise zu gynäkologischen Inhalten auszurichten, sieht die Firma ebenfalls als eine ihrer wesentlichen Aufgaben an.

Nourypharma
Partner for Gynaecology

The Nourypharma company in Oberschleißheim near Munich is a subsidiary of the AKZO-Nobel Group. It is one of the leading firms in Germany in the sector of gynaecology. The name Nourypharma stands for acclaimed products used in various fields of gynaecological therapy.

Nourypharma was founded on 8th May 1968, after the introduction of an innovative contraceptive which had been developed in Nourypharma's parent company in Oss/Netherlands. Today the company's nearly 30 different medicaments are provided by its own research department or by licencers from Italy, Switzerland and Japan. The product range comprises oral contraceptives, intra-uterine pessaries, products used in hormone replacement therapy, anti-infectives, prenatal clinical medicaments as well as oncological drugs and diagnostics.

Nourypharma's success is based on innovative preparations on the one hand, and on providing scientific information and consultation services to physicians and patients on the other. The gynaecologists in the medical department are ready to answer questions concerning gynaecology on the telephone round the clock. The company also considers it a major responsibility to support young scientists and to organize national and international scientific study groups addressing gynaecological affairs.

Nourypharma
Partenaire de la gynécologie

Implantée à Oberschleißheim près de Munich, la société Nourypharma est une filiale du groupe AKZO-Nobel. Elle compte parmi les sociétés leaders en République fédérale d'Allemagne dans le domaine de la gynécologie. Nourypharma symbolise des produits reconnus destinés à des secteurs de thérapie gynécologiques les plus divers.

C'est l'élaboration, au siège social de Nourypharma à Oss/Pays-Bas, d'un contraceptif tout à fait nouveau qui entraîna la création de Nourypharma le 8 mai 1968. Les 30 médicaments différents sortent aujourd'hui soit des propres laboratoires de recherche soit des laboratoires agréés implantés en Italie, Suisse et au Japon. La gamme comprend des contraceptifs oraux, des stérilets intra-utérins, des produits de l'hormonothérapie de substitution, des anti-infectieux, des préparations cliniques pour la préparation à l'accouchement, des produits oncologiques ainsi que des produits à visée diagnostique.

Le succès de Nourypharma se base, d'une part, sur des préparations novatrices et, d'autre part, sur l'information scientifique et le conseil des médecins mais aussi des patientes. Les gynécologues du département médical sont à votre service 24 heures sur 24 au téléphone pour répondre à vos questions. Aider les futurs scientifiques et organiser des groupes de travail scientifiques à l'échelle nationale et internationale sur des thèmes touchant la gynécologie constituent pour la société une de ses tâches essentielles.

Nourypharma
Partner della ginecologia

La Nourypharma di Oberschleißheim presso Monaco di Baviera è una società affiliata del Gruppo AKZO-Nobel ed è una delle aziende leader in Germania nel settore della ginecologia. Al marchio Nourypharma sono collegati prodotti largamente apprezzati ed impiegati in diversi settori della terapia ginecologica.

La Nourypharma è stata fondata l'8 maggio 1968 in occasione della commercializzazione di un contraccettivo del tutto innovativo sviluppato presso la casa madre con sede ad Oss, nei Paesi Bassi. Attualmente, i quasi 30 medicinali diversi, prodotti con il marchio Nourypharma, provengono sia dai laboratori di ricerca Nourypharma che da titolari di licenze italiani, svizzeri e giapponesi. L'assortimento comprende contraccettivi orali, pessari intrauterini, prodotti per la terapia ormonale sostitutiva, farmaci contro le infezioni, medicinali clinici di preparazione al parto, oncologici e diagnostici.

Il successo della Nourypharma si basa, da un lato, sui suoi preparati innovativi, dall'altro sull'informazione e sulla consulenza scientifica per i medici, ma anche per i pazienti. I ginecologi del reparto di medicina sono a disposizione telefonica degli interessati 24 ore su 24. L'azienda ritiene, inoltre, che uno dei suoi maggiori compiti consista nella formazione di nuove leve della scienza e nell'organizzazione di gruppi di ricerca scientifica finalizzata al settore della ginecologia sia a livello nazionale che internazionale.

**Das Deutsche Museum –
Technik hautnah erleben**

Wie vielleicht kein anderes naturwissenschaftlich-technisches Museum dieser Welt spiegelt das Deutsche Museum den technischen Fortschritt und die technisch-naturwissenschaftlichen Errungenschaften dieses Jahrhunderts, aber auch den damit verbundenen gesellschaftlichen Wandel wider. Es ist das erste naturwissenschaftliche Museum der Welt mit dem größten Bestand an wertvollen technischen und naturwissenschaftlichen Originalexponaten. Mit rund 50 000 m² Ausstellungsfläche ist es nicht nur eines der größten Museen der Welt, es ist auch eines der erfolgreichsten: Jährlich besuchen ca. 1,3 Millionen Menschen aus aller Welt das Deutsche Museum und sind fasziniert und begeistert. Gerade angesichts der immer schneller voranschreitenden Entwicklungen in Technik und Wissenschaft ist das, was die englisch sprechende Welt public understanding of science nennt, dringend notwendig. Erst ein Grundverständnis von Wissenschaft und Technik ermöglicht eine Orientierung in einer komplexen Welt. Seit fast 100 Jahren ist es der Anspruch des Deutschen Museums, Wissenschaftlichkeit mit Anschaulichkeit zu verbinden und Grundwissen über naturwissenschaftlich-technische Zusammenhänge spannend und populär zu vermitteln.

**The Deutsches Museum –
Hands-On Technology Experience**

Perhaps like no other science and technology museum in the world the Deutsches Museum reflects not only the technical progress and the technical-scientific achievements of this century, but also the changes they have brought about in society. It is the first scientific museum in the world with the greatest display of rare original exhibits pertaining to the natural sciences and the industry. With an exhibition space of approximately 50,000 square metres it is not only one of the biggest museums worldwide but, also one of the most successful: every year ca. 1.3 million people from around the globe come to visit the Deutsches Museum and are fascinated and thrilled by it. Especially in the face of the constant flow of new technical and scientific developments a public understanding of science is of paramount importance. Only if the basics of the natural sciences and technology are understood it is possible to find a way through our complex world. For almost 100 years the Deutsches Museum has endeavoured to make the sciences a hands-on experience and to communicate fundamental knowledge about scientific and technical contexts in an exciting and popular way.

*Blick in die Schifffahrt –
Fischewer „Maria", 1880*

*View of the ships and boats department –
Fischewer "Maria", 1880*

*La navigation maritime –
Fischewer «Maria», 1880*

*Un'occhiata al mondo della navigazione –
Fischewer «Maria», 1880*

Le Deutsches Museum –
Une technique à la portée de tous

Comme aucun autre musée technique et scientifique du monde, le Deutsches Museum reflète non seulement les progrès techniques et les succès scientifiques de ce siècle, mais aussi les transformations qu'ils ont engendrées par cette évolution dans notre société. Il s'agit là du plus grand musée scientifique du monde avec le plus grand nombre d'objets techniques et scientifiques originaux exposés. Avec une superficie de près de 50 000 m², il n'est pas seulement le plus grand musée du monde, mais il figure également parmi les musées qui connaissent le plus grand succès. En effet, près de 1,3 million de visiteurs enthousiastes et fascinés viennent du monde entier visiter le Deutsches Museum. Face aux évolutions toujours plus rapides enregistrées dans le monde technique et scientifique, ce que les anglophones appellent public understanding of science nous apparaît absolument nécessaire. Seule une bonne connaissance de base des sciences et des techniques permet une orientation optimale dans un monde de plus en plus complexe. Depuis plus d'un siècle, le Deutsches Museum s'attache à démocratiser les sciences et à en propager les connaissances fondamentales et leurs interactions d'une façon attrayante et populaire.

Il Deutsches Museum –
La tecnica da toccare con mano

Non esiste, forse, altro museo tecnico-scientifico al mondo in grado di rispecchiare il progresso tecnico e le conquiste tecnico-scientifiche di questo secolo e, conseguentemente, i cambiamenti sociali occorsi come il Deutsches Museum. È il primo museo scientifico a livello internazionale e vanta il più grande assortimento di pregevoli oggetti originali esposti provenienti dal settore della tecnica e della scienza. Con la sua superficie di 50 mila metri quadrati esso non è solo uno dei più grandi musei del mondo ma anche uno di quelli di maggior successo. Ogni anno circa 1,3 milioni di persone di ogni parte del globo visitano il Deutsches Museum, restandone entusiaste e affascinate. Proprio in considerazione degli sviluppi sempre più rapidi che si registrano nel mondo della tecnica e della scienza è assolutamente necessario promuovere ciò che il mondo di lingua inglese definisce il public understanding of science. Infatti, solo una comprensione basilare di queste due branche permette di orientarsi in un mondo che si fa sempre più complesso. Da circa cento anni il Deutsches Museum aspira a creare un trait d'union tra la scienza e la sua rappresentazione visiva fornendo, in una maniera avvincente e contemporaneamente divulgativa, una conoscenza basilare sui nessi scientifici e tecnici.

Das Deutsche Museum auf der Isarinsel

The Deutsches Museum on the island in the Isar river

Le Deutsches Museum sur une île de l'Isar

Il Deutsches Museum sull'Isola dell'Isar

Das Zweigmuseum mit der historischen Flugwerft von 1912 auf dem ältesten erhaltenen Flugplatz Deutschlands ergänzt die Luft- und Raumfahrtausstellung des Deutschen Museums.

The subsidiary museum with the historical aviation department dating from 1912 on the oldest still existing airfield in Germany completes the space and aviation department of the Deutsches Museum.

Le musée annexe avec ses ateliers de construction aéronautique historiques de 1912, implantés sur le plus ancien aérodrome d'Allemagne viennent compléter judicieusement l'exposition aéronautique et spatiale du Deutsches Museum.

La sezione distaccata del museo, con lo storico cantiere aeronautico del 1912 nel più antico campo d'aviazione conservato in Germania, integra la mostra sul settore aerospaziale del Deutsches Museum.

Das Genzentrum der Ludwig-Maximilians-Universität kurz nach seiner Einweihung im Juni 1994

The centre for bioengineering run by the Ludwig Maximilian university shortly after its inauguration in June 1994

Le centre génétique de l'université Ludwig Maximilian peu après son inauguration en juin 1994

Il centro di ricerche genetiche dell'Università Ludwig Maximilian poco dopo la sua inaugurazione nel giugno 1994

mit der Verleihung des Nobelpreises für Medizin und Physiologie an Robert Huber, Johann Deisenhofer und Hartmut Michel ausgezeichnet wurden.

photosynthesis was carried out, which in 1988 was honoured with the Nobel Prize for Medicine and Physiology, awarded to Robert Huber, Johann Deisenhofer and Hartmut Michel.

avec différents instituts de la TU de Munich ainsi que la société Max Planck. Impossible de rater l'œuf atomique, visible déjà de l'autoroute Nuremberg-Munich. Le centre construit autour du ré-

In posizione diametralmente opposta, vicino all'altro capolinea della U6, si trova la cittadina di Garching con diversi istituti della TU di Monaco e della Max-Planck-Gesellschaft. Sorge qui l'immenso

Fermenteraum des Genzentrums in Großhadern/Martinsried

Fermentation room at the centre for bio-engineering in Großhadern/Martinsried

Pièce de fermentation du centre génétique à Großhadern/Martinsried

La sala dei fermentatori del centro di ricerche genetiche di Großhadern/Martinsried

Lange Jahre hindurch waren das Klinikum Großhadern und die Max-Planck-Institute an der Stadtgrenze Münchens isoliert, bis die Bayerische Staatsregierung 1989 entschied, hier die

For many years the Klinikum Großhadern and the Max-Planck-Institutes were located in splendid isolation at the city limits, until in 1989 the Bavarian State Government decided to establish

acteur de recherche (Forschungsreaktor München; FRM) fut dirigé les dix premières années par le Prof. Dr. Heinz Maier-Leibnitz. Il en fit un nec plus ultra de la physique. Comptant parmi l'élite

centro di ricerche nucleari conosciuto con il nome di «uovo atomico», dalla forma caratteristica di uno degli edifici visibile già dall'autostrada Norinberga-Mo-

naturwissenschaftlichen Institute der LMU zu errichten. Als Erstes wurde 1994 das Genzentrum München eingeweiht, hervorgegangen aus einem vom Bund finanzierten Forschungszentrum für Gentechnik. Es folgten die Fakultäten für Chemie und Pharmazie. Mit dem Gewinn des Bio-Regio-Wettbewerbs im Jahre 1995 kam noch ein Gründerzentrum für Biotech-Firmen hinzu. Viele dieser Unternehmen sind inzwischen aus Platzmangel in das nahe gelegene Martinsried ausgewichen.

Spiegelbildlich gewissermaßen, nahe der anderen Endstation der U 6, findet sich der Standort Garching mit verschiedenen Instituten der TU München und der Max-Planck-Gesellschaft. Unübersehbar ist hier schon von der Autobahn Nürnberg-München aus das so genannte Atomei. Das um den Forschungsreaktor München (FRM) herum gebaute Zentrum wurde in den ersten zehn Jahren von Prof. Dr. Heinz Maier-Leibnitz geleitet. Er machte es zu einer physikalischen Kaderschmiede ersten Ranges. Von den Besten ihres Faches, die hier forschten und forschen, seien beispielhaft die Nobelpreisträger Rudolf Mössbauer und Clifford G. Shull genannt. Inzwischen kommt das Atomei in die Jahre und soll nun durch eine neue, wesentlich intensivere Neutronenquelle ersetzt werden, den FRM II. Sie wird nicht nur der Grundlagenforschung im Bereich Neuer Materialien dienen, sondern vor allem auch bei den Biowissenschaften eingesetzt werden.

Vor lauter Neutronenforschung gehen in Garching die anderen Bereiche ein wenig unter: die neue Fakultät für Maschinenwesen der TU, die Fakultät für Chemie der TU und die diversen Max-Planck-Institute, darunter eins für Quantenoptik und eins für Plasmaphysik, die alle Weltrang genießen.

Das abnehmende Interesse an den Naturwissenschaften zeigt sich im allgemeinen an den rückläufigen Studentenzahlen. Nicht so in München, wo die erwähnten

the natural science institutes of the Ludwig-Maximilians-Universität in the vicinity. First the Gene Centre Munich was inaugurated, which had developed out of a research centre for gene technology financed by the Federation. The faculties of chemistry and pharmacy followed shortly after. By winning the Bio-Regio-Competition in 1995, Munich also received a centre for new biotechnical firms; but due to lack of space, many of these enterprises have relocated to nearby Martinsried.

More or less mirror-reverted, several institutes of the TU and the Max-Planck-Gesellschaft are situated near the other U 6 subway terminal in Garching. If you follow the Nuremberg-Munich autobahn, the so-called "Atomei" (Atomic Egg) rises right in front. The centre built around Munich's research reactor (FRM) was run by Prof. Dr. Heinz Maier-Leibnitz in the first ten years. He turned it into a top-grade physical training facility. Let me mention just two of the experts who have conducted research in this centre, i. e. the Nobel Prize winner Rudolf Mössbauer and Clifford G. Shull. By now the Atomic Egg has aged considerably and is to be replaced by a new, much more intensive neutron source – the FMR II. It will not only be used for fundamental research in the field of new materials, but also in the bio-sciences.

With emphasis being put on neutron research, Garching's other fields are less conspicuous: the TU's new faculty for engineering and for chemistry, for instance, as well as several Max-Planck-Institutes (including the centre for quantum optics and one for plasma physics), all of which enjoy international renown.

The steadily decreasing interest in the natural sciences documented by declining student figures in other universities is not noticeable in Munich: Here these faculties are extremely popular, particularly with foreign students.

Can one find "science for the masses" in Munich? Of course.

de leur spécialisation, ils ont fait et font ici des recherches, citons par exemple les prix Nobel Rudolf Mössbauer et Clifford G. Shull. Depuis, l'œuf atomique, prenant quelques «rides», doit être remplacé par une nouvelle source de neutrons nettement plus intense, le FRM II. Il servira non seulement à la recherche de base dans le secteur des Nouvelles Matières mais sera surtout utilisé dans les sciences biologiques.

L'importance de la recherche sur les neutrons fait légèrement de l'ombre aux autres secteurs: la nouvelle faculté de mécanique de la TU, la faculté de chimie de la TU et les divers instituts Max Planck, dont un spécialisé dans l'optique quantique et un dans la physique plasmique, qui jouissent tous d'une réputation internationale.

Le manque croissant d'intérêt pour les sciences naturelles se voit en général dans le nombre d'étudiants en baisse. Ce n'est pas le cas à Munich où les instituts mentionnés sont très prisés en particulier par l'étranger.

Peut-on également palper la science à Munich? Mais bien sûr! Nous vous donnons ici quatre bonnes adresses: le Musée allemand de la technique situé sur l'île Museumsinsel est connu de tous mais tout le monde ne connaît pas sa dépendance sur la Oberwiesenfeld où l'on peut visiter des avions fascinants. Le Jardin Botanique de la LMU avec ses buissons de rhododendrons fleurissant au printemps vaut bien une visite. Et, à proximité, le Musée Homme et Nature dans le château de Nymphenburg avec ses intéressantes expositions sur l'écologie et la technique génétique.

Munich brille. C'est ce qu'a dit une fois Thomas Mann, sans penser spécialement à la science. Mais elle l'aurait mérité. Tout n'a pas pu être cité ici, par exemple les instituts de la Fraunhofer-Gesellschaft, Graf Rumford à qui nous devons le Jardin Anglais, le grand Romano Guardini dont les cours sur la morale et l'éthique à la LMU étaient un impératif, les

naco. Nei primi dieci anni di attività questa struttura, costruita intorno al reattore di ricerche di Monaco (FRM), è stata diretta dal professor Dr. Heinz Maier-Leibnitz che ne ha fatto un centro di formazione di assoluta eccellenza per studiosi di fisica. Tra i migliori di questo campo, che hanno condotto e conducono tuttora importanti ricerche, ricordiamo, ad esempio, i Premi Nobel Rudolf Mössbauer e Clifford G. Shull. Nel frattempo l'«uovo atomico» comincia ad invecchiare e dovrà essere sostituito da un nuovo reattore molto più potente, l'FRM II. Quest'ultimo non servirà solo alla ricerca basilare nel settore dei Nuovi Materiali, ma troverà impiego soprattutto nel campo delle scienze biologiche.

Rispetto alla grande attività di ricerca in campo nucleare gli altri settori presenti a Garching sono in leggero declino: le nuove facoltà di Meccanica e di Chimica della TU e i diversi istituti Max Planck, tra i quali ne figura uno dedicato all'ottica quantistica ed uno per la fisica del plasma, che godono tutti di fama internazionale.

Il calo di interesse nei confronti delle scienze naturali si manifesta fondamentalmente nella diminuzione delle iscrizioni. Ciò non vale, tuttavia, per le strutture di Monaco, dove gli istituti sopra menzionati registrano una grande affluenza di studenti provenienti anche e soprattutto dall'estero.

Esistono anche istituzioni a Monaco dove è possibile «toccare la scienza con mano»? Certamente! Eccovi quattro suggerimenti, alcuni peraltro già noti a molti. Ad esempio, il Museo Tedesco della Scienza e della Tecnica (Deutsches Museum) sull'Isola del Museo, che tutti conoscono. Un po' sconosciuta, invece, è la sua dépendance sull'Oberwiesenfeld dove è possibile ammirare aerei affascinanti. Vale anche la pena di visitare il Giardino Botanico (Botanischer Garten) della LMU, con i suoi cespugli di rododendri che fioriscono in primavera. E da qui non si è lontani dal Museo Uomo e Natura (Museum Mensch

Institute großen Zulauf haben, auch und gerade aus dem Ausland.

Gibt es in München auch die Wissenschaft zum Anfassen? Selbstverständlich! Hier vier Geheimtips, die allerdings so geheim nicht sind: Das Deutsche Museum auf der Museumsinsel kennt jeder; aber nicht jeder kennt seine Dependance auf dem Oberwiesenfeld, wo man faszinierende Flugzeuge besichtigen kann. Auch der Botanische Garten der LMU mit seinen im Frühjahr blühenden Rhododendronbüschen ist einen Besuch wert. Und damit ist es nun nicht mehr weit zum Museum Mensch und Natur im Nymphenburger Schloss mit seinen interessanten Ausstellungen zu Themen der Ökologie und Gentechnik.

München leuchtet. So hat es Thomas Mann einmal ausgedrückt, ohne im Speziellen an die Wissenschaft zu denken. Sie hätte es aber verdient. Vieles konnte hier aus Platzmangel nicht erwähnt werden: so etwa die Institute der Fraunhofer-Gesellschaft, Graf Rumford, dem wir den Englischen Garten verdanken, der große Romano Guardini, dessen Vorlesungen zu Moral und Ethik an der LMU ein Muss waren, die Biochemiker Buchner und Bücher, von denen leider nur Buchner für die Entdeckung der zellfreien alkoholischen Gärung den Nobelpreis für Medizin erhielt, oder schließlich Alois Alzheimer, der große Psychiater, dessen Bruder übrigens die Münchener Rückversicherung gründete. Ebenso Abt Odilo von St. Bonifaz an der Karlstraße. Er sprach einmal auf einer Zeremonie zur Verleihung des Bayerischen Verdienstordens über den „Bayerischen Himmel". Vielleicht liegt hier der Ursprung dessen, was die immer währende Blüte der Wissenschaft in München ausmacht.

Prof. Ernst-Ludwig Winnacker

Let me give you a few personal tips which are actually nothing special: everybody knows the German Museum on Museum Island in the Isar, but few people are familiar with its annex in Oberwiesenfeld, where you can admire fascinating airplanes. The Botanical Garden run by the university is well worth a visit, particularly in spring when the rhododendrons are in bloom. And from this garden it is only a few steps to the "Museum Mensch und Natur" (Man and Nature) in the Palace of Nymphenburg, which offers very interesting exhibitions about ecology and gene technology.

"Munich shines" is one of the most famous quotations by Thomas Mann, who loved Munich but probably did not refer to its science sector with this statement. This sector would, however, have earned this praise. Unfortunately lack of space does not allow me to mention many other important and deserving facts: the institutes of the Fraunhofer-Gesellschaft, for instance; Count Rumford to whom we owe the English Garden; the great Romano Guardini whose lectures on morals and ethics were a must for every student at the LMU; Buchner and Bücher, two biochemists who discovered the cellfree alcoholic fermentation, but for which only Buchner received the Nobel Prize of Medicine; and, finally, Alois Alzheimer, a famous psychiatrist, whose brother founded the "Münchner Rückversicherung" insurance company. But we must also mention Abbot Odilo of St. Bonifaz in Karlstraße. At a ceremony during which the "Bayerische Verdienstorden", a Bavarian order of merit, was awarded, he spoke of the "Bavarian Heaven". Maybe this is the source of the everlasting flourishing of science in Munich.

Prof. Ernst-Ludwig Winnacker

biochimistes Buchner et Bücher dont malheureusement seul Buchner reçut le prix Nobel de médecine pour sa découverte sur la fermentation alcoolique sans cellule, ou alors Alois Alzheimer, le grand psychiatre dont le frère fonda d'ailleurs la société de réassurance Münchener Rückversicherung. De même pour le père Odilo von St. Bonifaz dans la rue Karlstraße. Il a tenu, lors d'une cérémonie de remise de l'ordre du mérite bavarois, un discours sur le «Ciel Bavarois». Voilà peut-être les origines de l'ère constamment glorieuse de la science à Munich.

Prof. Ernst-Ludwig Winnacker

Minerva, römische Göttin der Wissenschaft, von Fernando de la Jara vor dem Eingang der Max-Planck-Gesellschaft am Marstallplatz

Minerva, Roman goddess of the arts, by Fernando de la Jara, at the entrance of the Max Planck Society at Marstallplatz

Minerva, déesse romaine de la science, œuvre de Fernando de la Jara devant l'entrée de la société Max Planck sur la Marstallplatz

Minerva, dea romana della scienza, nella realizzazione di Fernando de la Jara davanti all'ingresso della società Max Planck sulla Marstallplatz

und Natur) nel castello di Nymphenburg, con le sue mostre interessanti su temi relativi all'ecologia e all'ingegneria genetica.

Monaco risplende. Così la descrisse una volta Thomas Mann, senza peraltro riferirsi in modo particolare alle attività scientifiche della città. Anche se essa lo avrebbe meritato. Per mancanza di spazio abbiamo dovuto sorvolare su tutta una serie di altri aspetti e personaggi non meno interessanti: ad esempio sugli Istituti della Fraunhofer-Gesellschaft, su Graf Rumford, al quale dobbiamo il Giardino Inglese, sul grande Romano Guardini, le cui lezioni sulla morale e l'etica alla LMU erano un «must», sui biochimici Buchner e Bücher, dei quali purtroppo solo Buchner ricevette il Premio Nobel per la Medicina per aver scoperto che si può ottenere un estratto esente da cellule viventi ma ugualmente capace di provocare la fermentazione alcolica; o, infine, su Alois Alzheimer, il grande psichiatra, il cui fratello ha fondato tra l'altro la compagnia di riassicurazione «Münchener Rückversicherung». Non va dimenticato nemmeno l'abate Odilo della chiesa di San Bonifacio sulla Karlstrasse. Questi, in occasione di una cerimonia per il conferimento dell'Ordine al merito della Baviera, ha parlato del «cielo bavarese». Ed è forse da ricercarsi proprio qui l'origine di quella continuità di splendore che caratterizza le scienze di Monaco.

Prof. Ernst-Ludwig Winnacker

München – ein Zentrum der Luft- und Raumfahrtindustrie

Der Traum vom Fliegen hat die Menschen zu allen Zeiten und allerorten fasziniert. Als Zeitgenossen Otto Lilienthals entwarfen auch Münchner Pioniere – etwa Gustav Koch und Alois Wolfmüller – unermüdlich neue Flugmaschinen, um sich wie ein Vogel in die Lüfte erheben zu können. Bayerische Könige und Regenten förderten die Luftfahrt von Anfang an. So entstand Bayerns erster Flugplatz in Puchheim 1909 als „Akademie für Luftfahrt", 1912 wurde die erste Fliegerkompanie der bayerischen Armee gegründet.

Gleich zu Beginn des Wiederaufbaus der deutschen Luft- und Raumfahrtindustrie gelang es der Bayerischen Staatsregierung, den Luftfahrtpionier Ludwig Bölkow nach München zu holen. In Ottobrunn wurde der Grundstein für den Technologiekonzern Messerschmitt-Bölkow-Blohm (MBB) gelegt. Heute ist dort der Sitz der DaimlerChrysler Aerospace AG (Dasa). Zudem entstand vor den Toren der Stadt in Oberpfaffenhofen eine Niederlassung von Dornier und ein Zentrum der Deutschen Forschungsanstalt für Luft- und Raumfahrt.

Munich – a Centre of Aerospace Industry

The dream of flight has fascinated people at all times and in all places. Contemporaries of Otto Lilienthal such as the Munich pioneers Gustav Koch and Alois Wolfmüller, who were untiring inventors of new flying machines, had one desire: to take to the skies like a bird. And Bavaria's kings and regents promoted aviation from its very beginnings. As early as 1909, for example, Bavaria's first aerodrome was established in Puchheim under the name of "Academy of Aviation", and 1912 saw the foundation of the first flying corps of the Bavarian Army.

At the beginning of the reconstruction period after the Second World War the Bavarian State Government succeeded in attracting Ludwig Bölkow, an aeronautics pioneer, to Munich. The foundation was then laid for the Messerschmitt-Bölkow-Blohm (MBB) high-tech group at Ottobrunn, which is now the registered office of DaimlerChrysler Aerospace AG (Dasa). In addition, a facility of Dornier was set up at Oberpfaffenhofen on the outskirts of the city, along with a branch of the German Aerospace Center.

Munich – un centre de l'industrie aéronautique et l'aérospatiale

Depuis toujours, voler fait rêver et fascine les hommes de toutes origines. Contemporains d'Otto Lilienthal, des pionniers munichois comme Gustav Koch et Alois Wolfmüller ne ménagèrent pas leurs efforts pour construire des appareils devant leur permettre de s'élever dans les airs comme un oiseau. Dès le début, l'aviation reçut le soutien des rois et des dirigeants bavarois. Le premier aérodrome de Bavière fut construit à Puchheim en 1909 sous le nom d'«académie de l'aviation», et c'est en 1912 que naquit la première compagnie d'aviation de l'armée bavaroise.

Dès le début de la reconstruction de l'industrie aérospatiale allemande, le gouvernement bavarois réussit à faire venir à Munich le pionnier de l'aviation Ludwig Bölkow. C'est à Ottobrunn que furent posés les premiers jalons du groupe de technologie Messerschmitt-Bölkow-Blohm (MBB). C'est aujourd'hui le siège de DaimlerChrysler Aerospace AG (Dasa). De plus, une filiale de Dornier et un centre de recherche allemand des techniques aérospatiales virent le jour aux portes de la ville à Oberpfaffenhofen.

Munich – un centro de la industria aeronáutica y espacial

Desde siempre, los hombres han estado fascinados por el sueño de poder volar. Los contemporáneos de Otto Lilienthal, los pioneros Gustav Koch y Alois Wolfmüller de Munich, también dedicaron todos sus esfuerzos a desarrollar nuevas máquinas aéreas para poder elevarse por los aires como aves voladoras. Los reyes y regentes bávaros fomentaron la aeronáutica desde sus comienzos. Así, en 1909 se inauguró el primer aeropuerto bávaro en Puchheim, bajo el nombre de «Academia de Aviación», y en 1912 se fundó la primera compañía de aviadores del ejército bávaro.

Desde los inicios de la reconstrucción de la industria aeronáutica y espacial alemana, el gobierno bávaro incitó al pionero de la aviación Ludwig Bölkow a trasladarse a Munich. En Ottobrunn se fundó el consorcio tecnológico Messerschmitt-Bölkow-Blohm (MBB). Actualmente es la sede de la DaimlerChrysler Aerospace AG (Dasa). Además, a las puertas de la ciudad, en Oberpfaffenhofen, se creó una sucursal de Dornier y un centro del Instituto Alemán de Investigación Aeronáutica y Espacial.

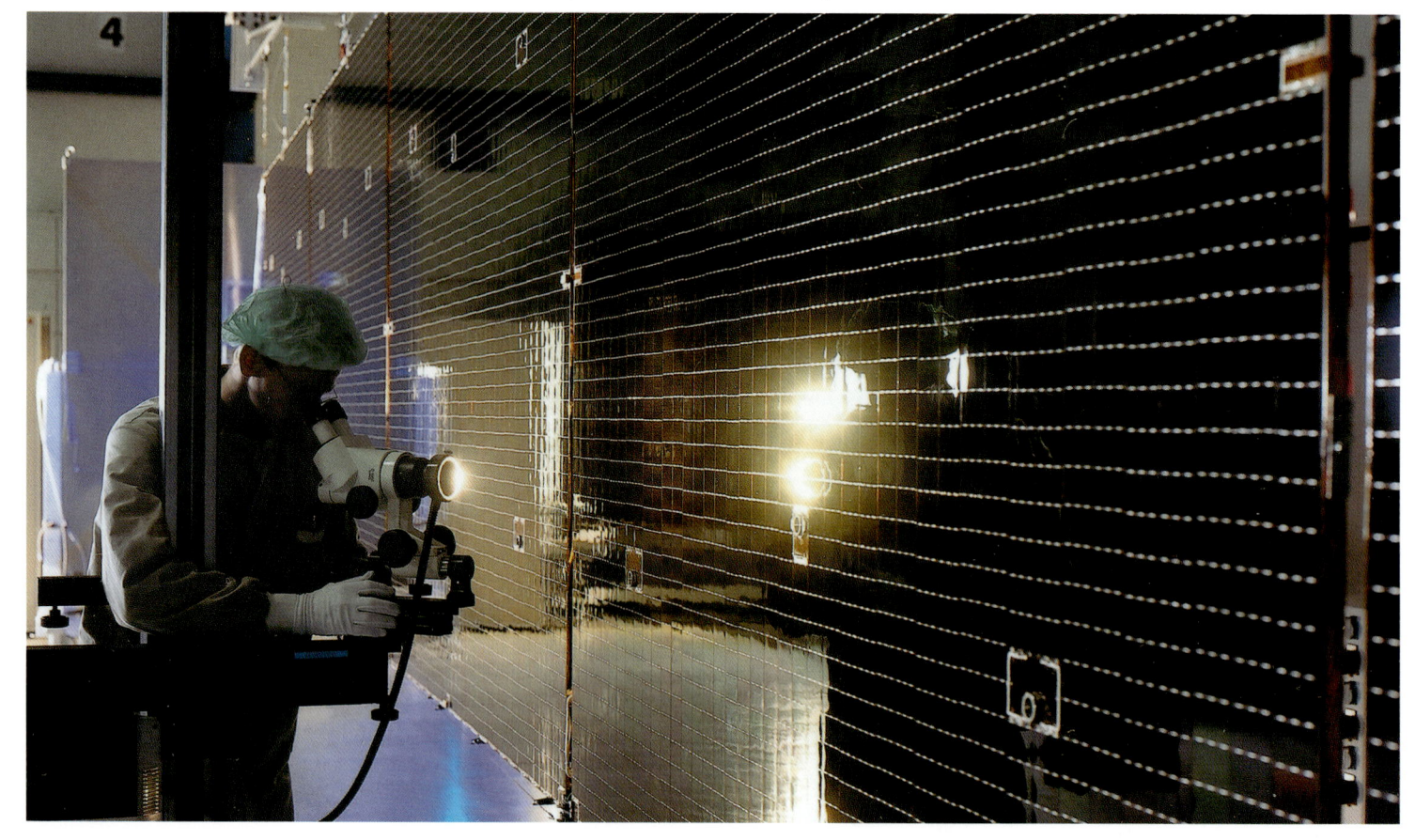

Prüfung eines Solarpanels für die Globalstar-Satellitenflotte: Im Ottobrunner Fertigungszentrum der zur DaimlerChrysler Aerospace gehörenden Dornier Satellitensysteme GmbH werden Solarzellen für die verschiedensten Satellitentypen entwickelt und gebaut.

Checking a solar panel for the Globalstar satellite fleet: solar cells for various types of satellites are developed and constructed at the Ottobrunn production center of Dornier Satellitensysteme GmbH, a subsidiary of DaimlerChrysler Aerospace.

Contrôle d'un panneau solaire pour la flotte de satellites Globalstar. Dans ce centre de fabrication d'Ottobrunn de la société Dornier Satellitensysteme GmbH appartenant à DaimlerChrysler Aerospace, des cellules solaires sont mises au point et fabriquées pour les types de satellite les plus divers.

Control de un panel solar para la flota de satélites Globalstar: en el centro de producción de Ottobrunn de la empresa Dornier Satellitensysteme GmbH, que pertenece a DaimlerChrysler, se desarrollan y fabrican células solares para los más diversos tipos de satélites.

Ein „bestseller" aus Donauwörth: Die bayerische Polizei besitzt neun moderne Leichthubschrauber vom Typ EC 135, die vom deutsch-französischen Unternehmen Eurocopter gebaut werden.

A bestseller from Donauwörth: the Bavarian police own nine modern light-duty helicopters of the type EC 135; they are built by the Franco-German joint venture Eurocopter.

Un «bestseller» de Donauwörth: la police bavaroise possède neuf hélicoptères légers modernes de type EC 135 construits par l'entreprise franco-allemande Eurocopter.

Un «bestseller» de Donauwörth son los nueve helicópteros modernos y ligeros modelo EC 135 de la policía bávara, fabricados por la empresa franco-alemana Eurocopter.

Die Luft- und Raumfahrtindustrie nimmt eine technologische Schlüsselrolle ein und hat damit entscheidenden Einfluss auf die wirtschaftliche Zukunft der hochindustrialisierten Länder. Da sie über Spitzentechnologien wie Mikroelektronik, Materialtechnik, Mikrosystemtechnik, Sensorik, Informationsverarbeitung und das zugehörige Know-how in der Fertigung und Integration verfügt, ist sie Impulsgeber für den technologischen Fortschritt in vielen anderen Bereichen.

Seit ihrer Gründung 1989 bündelt die DaimlerChrysler Aerospace die Luftfahrt-, Raumfahrt- und Verteidigungsaktivitäten der Traditionsunternehmen Dornier, Messerschmitt-Bölkow-Blohm (MBB), MTU Motoren- und Turbinen-Union und Telefunken Systemtechnik (TST).

Die DaimlerChrysler Aerospace zählt weltweit zu den innovativsten und leistungsfähigsten Unternehmen der Luft- und Raumfahrtindustrie. Als einziges europäisches Unternehmen bietet die Dasa ein Produktspektrum vom Flugzeugtriebwerk bis zur Raumstation an. In allen Geschäftsbereichen kann die DaimlerChrysler Aerospace auf eine technologische Erfahrungsspanne bis zu den Anfängen der Luft- und

The aerospace industry holds a key position in technology and decisively influences the economic future of highly-industrialized countries. As it can draw upon a wealth of state-of-the-art technologies such as microelectronics, material technology, microsystems technology, sensor systems, information processing and the associated know-how in production and integration, it also provides an impulse for technological progress in many other fields.

Since its foundation in 1989, under its roof Dasa has concentrated the aeronautical, space and defense activities of the traditional enterprises Dornier, Messerschmitt-Bölkow-Blohm (MBB), MTU Motoren- und Turbinen-Union, and Telefunken Systemtechnik (TST).

DaimlerChrysler Aerospace is one of the most innovative and efficient enterprises in the aerospace sector worldwide. Dasa is the only European company to offer the whole range of products from aircraft engines to space platforms. In all sectors of its business the company can look back on a wealth of experience – reaching back to the origins of aviation and space technology in Europe. It employs approximately 47,000 persons in 27 locations throughout

L'industrie aérospatiale occupe un rôle clé au niveau technologique. Elle exerce ainsi une influence déterminante sur l'avenir économique des pays fortement industrialisés. Disposant des technologies de pointe comme la microélectronique, la technique des matériaux, la technique des systèmes hyperminiaturisés et des capteurs, le traitement des données et le savoir-faire inhérent à la fabrication et l'intégration, elle donne des impulsions au progrès technologique dans de nombreux autres secteurs.

Depuis sa création en 1989, la société DaimlerChrysler Aerospace fédère les activités aérospatiales et de défense des entreprises de longue tradition Dornier, Messerschmitt-Bölkow-Blohm (MBB), MTU Motoren- und Turbinen-Union ainsi que Telefunken Systemtechnik (TST).

A l'échelle mondiale, la société DaimlerChrysler Aerospace compte parmi les entreprises les plus novatrices et performantes de l'industrie aérospatiale. La Dasa est la seule entreprise européenne à offrir une gamme de produits allant des moteurs d'avion à la station spatiale. Dans tous les secteurs d'activité, la sté. DaimlerChrysler Aerospace s'appuie sur une expérience en technologie remontant au tout début de

La industria aeronáutica y espacial desempeña un papel clave en la tecnología; así tiene también una influencia fundamental en el futuro económico de los países altamente industrializados. Al disponer de tecnologías claves como la microelectrónica, la técnica de materiales, la técnica de microsistemas, el análisis sensórico, el procesamiento de la información, así como del correspondiente know-how en la fabricación y la integración, se convierte en el impulsor del desarrollo tecnológico de muchos otros sectores.

Desde su fundación en 1989, la empresa DaimlerChrysler Aerospace agrupa las actividades aeronáuticas, espaciales y de defensa de empresas de gran tradición como Dornier, Messerschmitt-Bölkow-Blohm (MBB), MTU Motoren-und-Turbinen-Union y Telefunken Systemtechnik (TST).

La DaimlerChrysler Aerospace se encuentra entre las empresas más innovadoras y productivas de la industria aeronáutica y espacial del mundo. La Dasa es la única empresa europea que ofrece una gama de productos que se extiende desde el motor para aviones hasta un módulo espacial. En todas las áreas de operacione, la DaimlerChrysler Aerospace puede ofrece

Raumfahrt in Europa zurückblicken. Das Unternehmen beschäftigt rund 47 000 Mitarbeiter an 27 Standorten in ganz Deutschland sowie in Marktgesellschaften und Büros im Ausland.

Die Dasa ist der deutsche Partner der europäischen Erfolgsprogramme Airbus (37,9 %), Eurofighter (30 %) und Ariane (10,4 %) und ist am deutsch-französischen Hubschrauberunternehmen Eurocopter mit 40 % beteiligt. Im Oktober 1999 haben die Dasa und die französische Aerospatiale Matra ihre Fusion angekündigt. Der European Aeronautic, Defense and Space Company (EADS) will auch die spanische CASA beitreten.

Dr. Manfred Bischoff

Germany and in operational units and offices abroad.

Dasa is the German partner of the successfull European programmes Airbus (37.9 %), Eurofighter (30 %), and Ariane (10.4 %), and it also holds a 40 % share of the Franco-German helicopter joint venture Eurocopter. In October 1999, Dasa and the French group Aerospatiale Matra have announced their merger. CASA of Spain also intends to become a member ot the European Aeronautic, Defense and Space Company (EADS).

Dr. Manfred Bischoff

Beim Eurofighter-Triebwerk EJ200 – hier in der Endmontagelinie der MTU in Karlsfeld – ist das Münchner Unternehmen deutscher Systemführer.

MTU in Munich is the German systems' leader for the Eurofighter engine EJ200 – shown here on the MTU final assembly line in Karlsfeld.

Le propulseur EJ200 de l'Eurofighter – ici la fin du montage en ligne de la MTU à Karlsfeld – la société munichoise est le leader allemand des systèmes.

La empresa de Munich es el líder alemán de sistemas en la constucción del motor EJ200 – en el foto se ve en la línea de montaje final de la MTU en Karlsfeld.

Die sieben Prototypen umfassende Eurofighter-Erprobungsflotte in den vier Partnerländern Deutschland, Großbritannien, Italien und Spanien hat mittlerweile mehr als 1 000 Testflüge absolviert. Der Jungfernflug des ersten Prototyps startete vom Erprobungszentrum der DaimlerChrysler Aerospace in Manching bei Ingolstadt aus.

The Eurofighter test fleet in the four partner countries Germany, Great Britain, Italy and Spain, which comprises seven prototypes, has already carried out more than 1000 test flights. The maiden flight of the first prototype was started from the test centre of DaimlerChrysler Aerospace in Manching near Ingolstadt.

La flotte d'essai d'Eurofighter composée de sept prototypes dans les quatre pays partenaires, à savoir l'Allemagne, la Grande-Bretagne, l'Italie et l'Espagne, a réalisé jusqu'à maintenant plus de 1 000 vols d'essai. Le premier vol du premier prototype a eu lieu au centre d'essai de DaimlerChrysler Aerospace à Manching près d'Ingolstadt

Los siete prototipos que forman la flota experimental Eurofighter en los cuatro países socios, Alemania, Gran Bretaña, Italia y España, en la actualidad han realizado más de 1 000 vuelos de prueba. El primer vuelo del prototipo se realizó desde el centro de pruebas de DaimlerChrysler Aerospace en Manching, cerca de Ingolstadt.

l'histoire de l'aéronautique et astronautique en Europe. L'entreprise emploie environ 47 000 personnes sur 27 sites répartis dans toute l'Allemagne ainsi que dans des sociétés et des bureaux à l'étranger.

La Dasa est le partenaire allemand des programmes européens ayant enregistré un grand succès comme Airbus (37,9 %), Eurofighter (30 %) et Ariane (10,4 %) et elle détient 40 % de l'entreprise franco-allemande de construction d'hélicoptères Eurocopter. Au mois d'octobre 1999, le groupe allemand Dasa et Aerospatiale Matra ont annoncé leur fusion. La société espagnole CASA envisage également de rejoindre la société European Aeronautic, Defense and Space Company (EADS).

Dr. Manfred Bischoff

una gran experiencia que tiene sus orígenes en los comienzos de la navegación aérea y espacial en Europa. La empresa cuenta con cerca de 47 000 empleados en 27 delegaciones en toda Alemania, así como con sociedades comerciales y oficinas en el extranjero.

La Dasa es el socio alemán en programas europeos de gran éxito como el Airbus (37,9%), el Eurofighter (30%) y el Ariane (10,4%) y participa con un 40% en el proyecto franco-alemán de helicópteros Eurocopter. Dasa y la empresa francesa Aerospatiale Matra han anunciado su fusión en octubre de 1999. También la sociedad española CASA desea incorporarse a la European Aeronautic, Defense and Space Company (EADS).

Dr. Manfred Bischoff

Das Rumpfheck, das größte zusammenhängende Bauteil der Airbus-Flugzeuge, wird komplett bei der DaimlerChrysler Aerospace Airbus in Hamburg montiert und mit allen flugwichtigen Systemen versehen. Die Dasa-Werke in Augsburg und Donauwörth liefern wesentliche Komponenten für die erfolgreiche Airbus-Familie.

The rear fuselage, the largest single assembly of the Airbus aircraft, is completely integrated and equipped with all the important flight systems at DaimlerChrysler Aerospace Airbus in Hamburg. The Dasa plants in Augsburg and Donauwörth supply essential components for the successful Airbus family.

Le fuselage, tronçon d'un seul tenant de la plus grande taille des avions Airbus, est entièrement monté par DaimlerChrysler Aerospace Airbus à Hambourg et est doté de tous les systèmes de vol importants. Les usines Dasa à Augsbourg et Donauwörth fournissent les composants essentiels au succès de la famille Airbus.

El cono de cola es el elemento conjunto más grande de los aviones Airbus y se fabrica completamente en la DaimlerChrysler Aerospace Airbus en Hamburgo, donde también se realiza el montaje de todos los sistemas de navegación importantes. Las fábricas de Dasa en Augsburgo y Donauwörth suministran los componentes esenciales para la exitosa familia Airbus.

Die Oberstufe EPS der europäischen Trägerrakete Ariane 5 wird in Bremen integriert. Der Geschäftsbereich Raumfahrt Infrastruktur ist verantwortlich für die Entwicklung und Produktion der Ariane 5 Oberstufe EPS. Die Brennkammer des Vulcain-Triebwerks der Zentralstufe und das Aestus-Triebwerk der Oberstufe der Ariane 5 wurden bei der Dasa in Ottobrunn entwickelt und werden hier produziert.

Integration of the EPS upper-stage of the European Ariane 5 launcher is carried out at Bremen. The Space Infrastructure business unit is responsible for the development and production of the Ariane 5 upper-stage EPS. The combustion chamber for the Vulcain engine of the central stage and the Aestus engine of the upper stage of Ariane 5 were both developed by Dasa in Ottobrunn and are still being produced there.

L'étage supérieur EPS du lanceur européen Ariane 5 est intégré à Brême. Le secteur d'activité „infrastructure aérospatiale" est en charge du développement et de la production de l'étage supérieur EPS d'Ariane 5. C'est ici à Ottobrunn que la Dasa développe et produit la chambre de combustion du propulseur Vulcain de l'étage central et le propulseur Aestus de l'étage supérieur d'Ariane.

La etapa superior EPS del cohete portador europeo Ariane 5 se integra en Bremen. El sector Infraestructura Espacial es responsable del desarrollo y de la producción de la etapa superior EPS del Ariane 5. La cámara de combustión del motor Vulcain de la etapa central y el motor Aestus de la etapa superior del Ariane 5 se desarrollaron y se producen en la Dasa en Ottobrunn.

Hauptsitz der MTU ist München; hier das Verwaltungsgebäude an der Dachauer Straße 665

MTU's headquarters are located in Munich: the above photograph shows the administration building at 665 Dachauer Straße.

Le siège social de MTU est à Munich (ci-dessus les bâtiments administratifs, Dachauer Straße 665)

Il quartier generale MTU è a Monaco; qui vediamo gli uffici amministrativi siti in Dachauer Straße 665

MTU München
Deutschlands führender Triebwerkhersteller

Die MTU München befasst sich mit der Entwicklung, Fertigung, Vermarktung und Betreuung von Triebwerken für zivile und militärische Anwendungen. Zusammen mit ihren Tochtergesellschaften beschäftigt sie rund 6 700 Mitarbeiter.

Für die nächsten Jahre hat sich die MTU das Ziel gesetzt, in allen Tätigkeitsfeldern zu wachsen. Sie wird ihre Ressourcen auf die Kernkompetenzen konzentrieren und dabei den Globalisierungsprozess vorantreiben. Im Vordergrund steht die Errichtung von Fertigungs- und Wartungs-Joint-Ventures mit Schwerpunkten in Asien und Nordamerika.

Gleichzeitig wird sich die MTU auch künftig im Verbund mit Partnern an Triebwerken aller Schub- und Leistungsklassen beteiligen. Das Gesamt-Know-how im zivilen und militärischen Triebwerkbau wird weiterhin bei ihr liegen.

Der Instandhaltung ziviler Triebwerke misst das Unternehmen besondere Bedeutung bei, da hier in Zukunft hohe Wachstumsraten zu erwarten sind. Die MTU hat sich

MTU München
Germany's Leading Aero Engine Manufacturer

Together with its subsidiary companies, MTU München has a workforce of some 6,700 and engages in the design, development, production, sales and support of aero engines for commercial and military applications.

MTU's objective for the next few years is to grow in all fields of activity. To achieve this target, it will be focusing its resources on its core competencies and will continue to establish a presence around the world, by setting up production and maintenance joint ventures primarily in Asia and in North America.

At the same time, MTU, in collaboration with partners, will take stakes in emerging aircraft propulsion systems in all power and thrust classes and will maintain its overall propulsion system expertise, both in the field of commercial and military engines

MTU concentrates its efforts on the repair and overhaul (R&O) of commercial aircraft engines, a field of activity that holds promise of particularly high growth rates. MTU is

MTU München
le plus important constructeur allemand de moteurs aéronautiques

Les secteurs d'activité de MTU München sont les études, le développement, la fabrication et l'entretien de moteurs aéronautiques pour applications civiles et militaires. Son effectif toutes filiales comprises est d'environ 6 700 personnes.

Pour les années à venir, MTU s'est fixé l'objectif d'une croissance soutenue dans tous ses secteurs d'activité. La société concentrera ses ressources sur ses compétences clés tout en mettant l'accent sur le processus de mondialisation. Dans ce contexte la priorité est accordée à la mise en place de joint ventures axées sur la fabrication et la maintenance avec une concentration sur l'Asie et l'Amérique du Nord.

Par ailleurs, MTU participera avec ses partenaires à la réalisation de moteurs de toutes les catégories de poussée et de puissance soulignant ainsi sa compétence globale dans le domaine des moteurs d'aviation civiles et militaires.

La société attache une importance particulière à l'entretien des moteurs civils,

MTU München
Il produttore di propulsori leader in Germania

MTU München è attiva nella progettazione, produzione, commercializzazione e assistenza di propulsori per applicazioni civili e militari. Con le sue società affiliate, occupa circa 6 700 dipendenti.

Per i prossimi anni, MTU si è posta l'obiettivo di espandersi in tutti i settori d'attività. Concentrerà, infatti, le proprie risorse sulle competenze chiave, accelerando il processo di globalizzazione. La priorità sarà l'istituzione di joint venture per la produzione e la manutenzione, principalmente in Asia e in Nord America.

Nel contempo, MTU istituirà in futuro delle partnership per realizzare propulsori di ogni classe di spinta e di potenza. MTU continuerà comunque a detenere il know-how complessivo per la produzione di propulsori per applicazioni civili e industriali.

L'azienda attribuisce particolare importanza alla manutenzione dei propulsori per usi civili, dato che in futuro in questo comparto si prevedono elevati tassi di crescita. MTU si è quindi posta l'obiettivo di raddoppiare nei prossimi quattro anni il fatturato

deshalb vorgenommen, in den nächsten vier Jahren den Umsatz dieses Bereiches zu verdoppeln und das weltweit führende unabhängige Unternehmen in der Wartung und Betreuung ziviler Triebwerke zu werden. Zusätzliche Leistungen und neue Wartungsprogramme sowie die Präsenz der MTU „vor Ort" beim Kunden sind wesentliche Ziele.

Die zivile Instandhaltung der MTU teilen sich derzeit drei Tochtergesellschaften: Die MTU Maintenance Hannover, eine 100 %ige Tochtergesellschaft der MTU München (ca. 900 Mitarbeiter), ist mit der Betreuung, Wartung und Reparatur ziviler Großtriebwerke befasst. Die MTU Maintenance Berlin-Brandenburg, ebenfalls eine 100 %ige Tochter der MTU München (rund 300 Mitarbeiter), betreut, wartet und repariert Luftfahrtantriebe im unteren Leistungsbereich sowie Industriegasturbinen. Hinzugekommen ist die MTU Maintenance Canada in Vancouver, British Columbia (ca. 250 Mitarbeiter), die ebenfalls zivile Triebwerke des mittleren und oberen Schubbereichs betreut.

accordingly aiming to double its sales in this field within the next four years and to become the world's leading independent commercial engine R&O provider. To achieve this goal, the company intends to expand its service offerings, to add new programs to its maintenance portfolio and to establish an MTU presence right at the customer's doorstep.

MTU's commercial aircraft engine maintenance is spread over three subsidiary companies at present: MTU Maintenance Hannover, a wholly-owned subsidiary of MTU München with an approximate workforce of 900 engages in the support, maintenance and repair of commercial large-scale engines. MTU Maintenance Berlin Brandenburg, another wholly-owned MTU München subsidiary, has an approximate workforce of 300 and engages in the support, maintenance and repair of aircraft propulsion units in the lower thrust/power categories as well as industrial gas turbines. The newly formed MTU Maintenance Canada in Vancouver, British Columbia, with a workforce of some 250 is likewise engaged in the repair and overhaul of medium-scale and large-scale engines.

Hochqualifizierte Fachleute – wie beispielsweise in der Endmontage – sind im Triebwerkbau unerlässlich.

A highly qualified workforce is essential in aero engine construction, e.g. in the final assembly area.

Des spécialistes compétents: un facteur indispensable dans la construction de moteurs aéronautiques – ici, par exemple le montage final

Nella produzione dei propulsori, per esempio nell'assemblaggio finale, sono indispensabili tecnici altamente qualificati.

Die MTU kann an ihren Standorten auch auf Prüfstände für zivile Triebwerke zurückgreifen. Hier eine solche Einrichtung bei der MTU Maintenance Canada in Vancouver.

Test facilities for commercial engines are available at all MTU locations. The photograph shows an engine undergoing testing at MTU Maintenance Canada in Vancouver.

Sur ses différents sites, MTU dispose de bancs d'essais pour moteurs civils. Voici l'un de ces équipements chez MTU Maintenance Canada à Vancouver

Nei propri stabilimenti, MTU può disporre anche di banchi di prova per propulsori per usi civili. Qui vediamo le apparecchiature utilizzate a Vancouver da MTU Maintenance Canada.

secteur où sont attendus des taux de croissance considérables. Elle envisage de doubler son chiffre d'affaires dans ce secteur dans les quatre années à venir pour devenir la plus importante entreprise indépendante au monde dans la maintenance de moteurs civils. Des services supplémentaires et de nouveaux programmes d'entretien ainsi que la présence de MTU sur place auprès du client sont autant d'objectifs essentiels.

A l'heure actuelle, trois filiales se partagent les activités de maintenance de MTU: MTU Maintenance Hannover, filiale à 100 % de MTU München (effectif environ 900 personnes) assure l'entretien, la maintenance et la réparation des gros réacteurs d'avions civils. MTU Maintenance Berlin-Brandenburg, elle aussi filiale à 100 % de MTU München (effectif environ 300 personnes) entretient et répare les moteurs aéronautiques de puissance inférieure ainsi que les turbines à gaz industrielles. S'y ajoute désormais MTU Maintenance Canada à Vancouver, Colombie britannique (environ 250 personnes) chargée de la maintenance de moteurs civils des catégories de poussée moyennes et supérieures.

di questo comparto, e di diventare l'azienda indipendente leader mondiale nella manutenzione e nell'assistenza dei propulsori per usi civili. Gli obiettivi principali saranno nuovi servizi e nuovi programmi di manutenzione, cosí come la presenza di MTU «sul posto», ossia direttamente presso la clientela.

Al momento, il comparto della manutenzione dei propulsori per usi civili è ripartito fra tre società affiliate. MTU Maintenance Hannover, società partecipata al 100 % di MTU München (ca. 900 dipendenti), è attiva nell'assistenza, nella manutenzione e nella riparazione dei grandi propulsori per usi civili. MTU Maintenance Berlin-Brandenburg, anch'essa società partecipata al 100 % di MTU München (circa 300 dipendenti) è attiva nell'assistenza, nella manutenzione e nella riparazione di propulsori per l'industria aeronautica con classe di potenza inferiore e di turbine a gas per usi industriali. MTU Maintenance Canada di Vancouver, nel British Columbia (ca. 250 dipendenti), infine, è attiva nell'assistenza di propulsori per usi civili con classe di spinta media e superiore.

*Unternehmer
machen Geschichte*

*Entrepreneurs
Writing History*

*Les entrepreneurs
écrivent l'histoire*

*Imprenditori
che fanno storia*

Wer München besucht, kann sie schnell kennenlernen, die bedeutenden Unternehmer dieser Stadt: Maffeistraße, Rodenstockplatz, Kustermannpark, Freystraße, Carl-von-Linde-Straße, Messerschmittstraße. Die Liste ließe sich beliebig fortsetzen – die Namen sind jedem geläufig, aber sie verraten nicht immer, welche Persönlichkeiten und unternehmerischen Leistungen sich dahinter verbergen. Dabei sind diese umso bemerkenswerter, bedenkt man, dass die meisten Gründungen bis weit in das 19. Jahrhundert zurückreichen – also in eine Zeit, in der die Bedingungen hierfür in München nicht gerade ideal waren. Die Stadt bot keine schiffbaren Wasserstraßen und lag fernab wichtiger Rohstoff- und Energiequellen. Als Unternehmer entschied man sich in Süddeutschland eher für die Konkurrenzstädte Augsburg oder Nürnberg, in denen das Bankwesen besser etabliert war. Auch von staatlicher Seite wurde der Strukturwandel der heutigen Metropole wenig gefördert. König Ludwig I. sträubte sich lange gegen die Ansiedlung von Industrien, da ihm die Lebensumstände des sich herausbildenden Industrieproletariats zutiefst zuwider waren. All diese Umstände konnten jedoch echte Unternehmerpersönlichkeiten nicht davon abhalten, sich München als Gründungsstandort auszusuchen.

1838 gründete Joseph Anton von Maffei „auf der grünen Wiese" in der Hirschau ein Eisenwerk. Drei Jahre später stellte er die erste bayerische Lokomotive, den „Münchner", vor. 1847 baute er sein erstes Dampfschiff, dem später ganze Flotten für den Starnberger- und den Ammersee folgten. Den internationalen Durchbruch schaffte Maffei mit der Lok „Bavaria", mit der er einen von der k.u.k. Österreichischen Staatsbahn ausgeschriebenen Wettbewerb gewann. Keine drei Jahrzehnte nach der Gründung beschäftigte das Unternehmen fast 800 Arbeiter. Bis dahin waren über 500 Lokomotiven, mehr als 100 stationäre

If you visit Munich you will quickly get to know the city's most renowned entrepreneurs, for numerous streets have been named after them: Maffeistraße, for instance, Rodenstockplatz, Kustermannpark, Freystraße, Carl-von-Linde-Straße, or Messerschmittstraße. One could easily continue this list. You may know the names but not what kind of personality or accomplishments they stand for. And considering that most of the enterprises were founded in the 19th century, these achievements appear even more stunning. At that time the city offered no navigable waterways and was far removed from important sources of raw material and energy. Entrepreneurs from southern Germany normally preferred the rivalling cities of Augsburg and Nuremberg as a location for settlement, where banking had already been established earlier. Even the government did very little to promote structural changes in Munich. King Ludwig I resisted the settling of industries for a long time, as he abhorred the life style of the quickly developing industrial proletariat. But all these impediments did not prevent true entrepreneurs from establishing their enterprises in Munich.

In 1838 Joseph Anton von Maffei founded an iron works "in green surroundings" in the Hirschau. Three years later he presented the first Bavarian locomotive, the so-called "Münchner". In 1847 he built his first steamship which was subsequently followed by a whole fleet of steamers connecting the towns and villages on Lake Starnberg and Lake Ammersee. Maffei gained international renown with the steam engine "Bavaria" which won a public competition held by the k.u.k. Österreichische Staatsbahnen (Austrian Railways). Less than 30 years later the enterprise was employing nearly 800 workers. By that time more than 500 locomotives, more than 100 stationary steam engines and several steamship engines had left the Maffei factory.

En visitant Munich, il est facile de faire connaissance avec les entrepreneurs importants de cette ville: Maffeistraße, Rodenstockplatz, Kustermannpark, Freystraße, Carl-von-Linde-Straße, Messerschmittstraße. La liste est encore longue, des noms connus de tous mais qui ne dévoilent pas toujours les personnalités et les prestations audacieuses des entreprises cachées derrière. Et pourtant elles sont d'autant plus remarquables si l'on réfléchit que la création de la plupart de ces entreprises remonte au 19ème siècle, donc à une époque où les conditions n'étaient pas absolument idéales à Munich. La ville n'offrait en effet aucune voie fluviale navigable et était éloignée des sources importantes de matières premières et d'énergie. En tant qu'entrepreneur, on choisissait en Allemagne du sud plus volontiers les villes concurrentes, à savoir Augsbourg ou Nuremberg dans lesquelles le secteur bancaire était mieux affirmé. Au niveau étatique, la mutation structurelle de la métropole actuelle ne reçut guère d'encouragements. Le roi Louis 1er s'opposa longtemps à l'implantation d'industries étant donné que les conditions de vie du prolétariat industriel qui en résultaient lui répugnaient énormément. Toutes ces circonstances ne firent cependant pas reculer les vraies personnalités d'entrepreneurs à venir s'implanter à Munich.

En 1838, Joseph Anton von Maffei créa une aciérie dans la Hirschau qui se situait encore à la périphérie. Trois ans plus tard, il présentait la première locomotive bavaroise, la «Munichoise». En 1847, il construit son premier bateau à vapeur, puis s'ensuivirent des flottes entières pour les lacs de Starnberg et de Ammersee. Maffei réussit à percer au niveau international avec la locomotive «Bavaria» grâce à laquelle il gagna un concours organisé par les chemins de fer autrichiens, la k.u.k. Österreichische Staatsbahn. A peine trois décennies

Chi visita Monaco impara ben presto a conoscere i grandi imprenditori della città: Maffeistraße, Rodenstockplatz, Kustermannpark, Freystraße, Carl-von-Linde-Straße, Messerschmittstraße. E la lista potrebbe continuare a piacimento. Tutti conoscono i nomi, ma pochi ricordano le personalità e le imprese che si nascondono dietro di essi. Eppure queste risultano ancora più sorprendenti se si considera che la maggior parte delle aziende furono fondate già nel XIX secolo, vale a dire in un periodo in cui, a Monaco, le condizioni generali per l'attività imprenditoriale non erano proprio ideali. La città non disponeva di corsi d'acqua navigabili ed era lontana da importanti giacimenti di materie prime e fonti di energia. Per impiantare un'attività l'imprenditore della Germania meridionale preferiva orientarsi verso le città rivali Augusta o Norimberga, che disponevano anche di un sistema bancario più sviluppato. Anche il governo fece poco per favorire i cambiamenti strutturali nell'odierna metropoli. Il re Ludovico I si oppose a lungo all'insediamento delle industrie in quanto aveva una vera e propria repulsione verso il nascente proletariato industriale. Tuttavia, queste circostanze non poterono impedire che grandi personalità imprenditoriali scegliessero proprio Monaco come sede delle loro imprese.

Nel 1838, su un prato verde nella Hirschau, Josef Anton von Maffei fondò una ferriera. Tre anni più tardi presentò la prima locomotiva bavarese, la «Münchner». Nel 1847 costruì la sua prima nave a vapore, alla quale seguirono più tardi delle intere flotte destinate alla navigazione sui laghi di Starnberg e Ammer. Maffei raggiunse il successo internazionale con la costruzione della locomotiva «Bavaria» con la quale vinse un concorso bandito dalle Ferrovie di Stato Austroungariche. Dopo nemmeno tre decenni dalla sua fondazione, l'impresa di Maffei occupava quasi 800 operai ed aveva prodotto più di 500 locomotive, oltre

Das heutige Böhmler Einrichtungshaus in München, Tal 11

The present-day Böhmler Einrichtungshaus in 11 Tal, Munich

Empfangshalle der Firma J.G. Böhmler vor der Zerstörung im Zweiten Weltkrieg

Entrance hall of the J.G. Böhmler enterprise before its destruction in the Second World War

Die hohe Kultur des Wohnens
Porträt eines traditionsreichen Familienunternehmens

Die Firma Böhmler wurde 1875 in München gegründet. Trotz der ruinösen Folgen beider Weltkriege hat sie sich zu einem der größten deutschen Spezialunternehmen auf dem Gebiet des Einrichtens, des Innenausbaus und der Fußbodentechnik entwickelt. Der Name Böhmler steht weit über die Landesgrenzen hinaus für Leistung und Qualität. Der Aufstieg des Hauses und seine internationale Marktgeltung beruhen letztlich auf der kompromisslosen Befolgung der gleichen Geschäftsgrundsätze, die den Begriff „Made in Germany" begründet haben:

„Unablässiges Streben nach Leistung mit dem Ziel, dem Menschen bestmöglich zu dienen, weil sich nur auf diese Weise das Vertrauen des Marktes gewinnen und ein dauerhafter Geschäftserfolg erzielen lässt."

Dieser Maxime des Firmengründers Georg Böhmler, dessen kaufmännischer Weitblick vom damaligen Prinzregenten durch Ernennung zum Königlich Bayerischen Hoflieferanten gewürdigt wurde, fühlt sich das Triumvirat seiner Urenkel Georg, Stephan und Thomas Böhmler, in deren Händen heute die Geschäftsleitung liegt, uneingeschränkt verpflichtet.

Beredter Ausdruck dafür war die Entscheidung, die angestammte Fachgeschäftstradition trotz des sich nach Kriegsende stürmisch entwickelnden Massenkonsums konsequent fortzusetzen und damit der Qualität auf allen Gebieten den Vorrang einzuräumen. Das beginnt beim Warenangebot und dessen geschmacklicher Ausrichtung und reicht bis zu den Dienstleistungen.

Ein Team von Innenarchitekten und Einrichtungsberatern begleitet Sie von der Planung über die Realisation bis zur Einweihung Ihrer neuen Einrichtung!

Unsere großen Fachabteilungen:
Möbel - Küchen - Teppiche - Bodenbeläge - Gardinen - Tapeten - Glas und Porzellan - Meisterschreinerei sowie alle dazugehörigen Dienstleistungen.

Cultivating the Art of Home Decor
Portrait of a Family Enterprise with a Long Tradition

The Böhmler enterprise was founded in Munich in 1875. Despite the devastating consequences of two world wars it has turned into one of Germany's largest firms specializing in furnishings, interior decoration and floor technology. The name of Böhmler is a synonym of efficiency and quality far beyond the state limits. The firm's rise and international repute are largely based on its consistent adherence to the business principles which created the concept of "Made in Germany":

"To strive persistently for achievement, with the purpose of serving people in the best manner possible, for this is the only way to gain confidence and lasting success in business."

This maxim of the firm's founder, Georg Böhmler, whose commercial farsight was honoured by the Prince Regent who bestowed the title of a "Royal Bavarian Court Purveyor" on him, is still the guiding principle of the founder's three greatgrandsons – Georg, Stephan, and Thomas Böhmler – who are responsible for the management today.

Their attitude was clearly demonstrated when after the Second World War they decided – in spite of a rapidly developing trend for mass consumption – to continue with the original business tradition: to give priority to quality in all sectors, starting with the product offering and its style and ending with services.

A team of interior decorators and furnishing experts assists customers from planning and realizing their projects to the final presentation of the new decor.

Our store comprises the following branches:
furniture - kitchens - rugs - floor coverings - curtains - wallpaper - glassware and china - carpenter's shop and the appropriate services.

BMW Group, München
Das im Volksmund „Vierzylinder" genannte BMW Haus ist die Zentrale des weltweit agierenden BMW Konzerns. Es wurde 1972 nach Plänen des Architekten Karl Schwanzer gleichzeitig mit den olympischen Anlagen in unmittelbarer Nachbarschaft erbaut.

BMW Group, Munich
The BMW Building – called the "Four-Cylinder" in the vernacular – is the headquarters of the worldwide operating BMW Group. It was constructed in 1972 according to plans made by architect Karl Schwanzer, at the same time as the Olympic facilities were built in its immediate vicinity.

BMW Group, Munich
Le «Quatre Cylindres», le nom que les Munichois ont donné au bâtiment BMW, abrite le siège du groupe BMW opérant à l'échelle mondiale. Il fut construit en 1972 d'après les plans de l'architecte Karl Schwanzer en même temps que le parc olympique dans son voisinage immédiat.

BMW Group, Monaco
L'edificio BMW, comunemente chiamato il «quattro cilindri», è la sede centrale cui fanno capo le filiali sparse in tutto il mondo del Gruppo BMW. Fu costruita nel 1972 su progetto dell'architetto Karl Schwanzer in concomitanza con la costruzione degli impianti olimpici e nelle vicinanze degli stessi.

◀ Das Ende der achtziger Jahre fertiggestellte BMW-Forschungs- und Ingenieurzentrum (FIZ) ist die modernste Einrichtung ihrer Art. Rund 6 000 hochqualifizierte Fachleute sind hier für den gesamten Entwicklungsprozess der Automobile und Motorräder des BMW Konzerns verantwortlich.

The BMW Research and Engineering Centre (FIZ), completed in the late 1980s, is the most modern facility of its kind. Here approximately 6,000 highly qualified experts are responsible for developing BMW automobiles and motorcycles.

Achevé à la fin des années quatre-vingt, le centre de formation et d'ingénierie (FIZ), est l'espace le plus moderne en son genre. Plus de 6 000 experts hautement qualifiés sont responsables ici de l'ensemble du processus de développement des automobiles et des motos du groupe BMW.

Il Centro di Ricerca e di Ingegneria della BMW (FIZ), costruito alla fine degli anni '80, è il più moderno nel suo genere. Vi lavorano circa 6 000 tecnici e specialisti altamente qualificati e responsabili dell'intero processo di sviluppo delle automobili e delle motociclette del Gruppo BMW.

Das Unternehmen BMW wurde im Jahre 1916 im Münchner Norden gegründet. Hier befindet sich auch heute noch das BMW-Stammwerk, in dem die Fahrzeuge der 3er Reihe und Motoren gebaut werden. Mit über 25 000 Mitarbeitern, davon allein 12 000 im Werk, ist BMW einer der größten Arbeitgeber in München.

The BMW enterprise was founded in the northern part of Munich in 1916. Today this area is still the home of the parent plant, where vehicles of the 3-series and engines are constructed. Employing more than 25,000 persons – 12,000 of them in the plant – BMW is one of Munich's biggest employers.

L'entreprise BMW a été fondée en 1916 au nord de Munich. C'est également là que se situe aujourd'hui encore l'usine principale de BMW qui fabrique les automobiles de la série 3 et les moteurs. Comptant plus de 25 000 collaborateurs, dont 12 000 en usine, BMW est un des employeurs majeurs de Munich. ▶

L'azienda BMW è stata fondata nel 1916 nella parte settentrionale di Monaco. Qui si trova ancora oggi il primo stabilimento nel quale vengono fabbricati i veicoli della 3™ serie e i motori. Con i suoi 25 000 dipendenti, di cui solo 12 000 impiegati nello stabilimento, la BMW è una delle maggiori aziende di Monaco.

◀ Das BMW-Museum, direkt neben dem Verwaltungshochhaus gelegen, gehört zu den meistbesuchten Museen in München. Es zeigt die Faszination der Marke BMW, die Meilensteine der Unternehmensgeschichte und gibt darüber hinaus Auskunft über Themen, die heute und in der Zukunft entscheidende Bedeutung für den Fahrzeugbau und den Straßenverkehr haben.

The BMW Museum, adjoining the high-rise building housing the administration, is one of Munich's most frequented museums. It shows the fascination of the BMW models, the milestones of the enterprise's history, and provides information about subjects which still have – and will have in future too – a decisive influence on car manufacture and road traffic.

Le musée BMW, situé directement à côté de la tour administrative, fait partie des musées les plus fréquentés de Munich. Il montre la fascination exercée par la marque BMW, les étapes de l'histoire de l'entreprise et donne, en outre, des informations sur des thèmes s'avérant aujourd'hui et demain d'une importance déterminante pour la construction de véhicules et la circulation routière.

Il Museo della BMW, situato direttamente vicino al grattacielo in cui si trovano gli uffici amministrativi, è uno dei musei più visitati di Monaco. Esso mostra le pietre miliari della storia di questa azienda e il fascino che ha da sempre esercitato il marchio BMW. Inoltre mette a disposizione informazioni su temi di grande importanza riguardanti la costruzione degli autoveicoli ed il traffico stradale.

Dampfmaschinen und etliche Maschinen für Dampfboote durch das Werkstor der Maffei'schen Fabrik gegangen.

Da ließ die Konkurrenz nicht auf sich warten. Am Thalkirchner Bahnhof entstand 1866 die Lokomotivenfabrik Krauss & Comp. Zusammen mit der Eisenbahnwaggonfabrik Rathgeber bildete sich so ein erster Schwerpunkt in der damaligen regionalen Wirtschaftsstruktur heraus: die Maschinen- und Eisenindustrie.

Mit dem Ausbau der Eisenbahn wurde München allmählich zu einem wichtigen Knotenpunkt.

Its success called the rivals on to the scene. At the Thalkirchen railway station the locomotive factory Krauss & Comp. was set up in 1866. Together with the "Eisenbahnwaggonfabrik Rathgeber" (a plant making railway carriages) they formed the first nucleus of the regional industrial structure of those days: the machine and iron industry.

With the growing railway network Munich eventually became an important traffic junction. Additionally, the liquidity of the local economy improved considerably after King Ludwig I had

après sa création, l'entreprise comptait presque 800 employés. Entre-temps, plus de 500 locomotives, plus de 100 machines à vapeur stationnaires et de nombreuses machines pour les bateaux à vapeur passèrent par les ateliers de l'usine Maffei.

En 1866, la concurrence ne se fit pas attendre. C'est à la Thalkirchner Bahnhof (gare de Thalkirchen) que fut créée l'usine à locomotives Krauss & Comp. Avec l'usine de wagons de chemin de fer Rathgeber, un premier pilier important se cristallisa dans la structure économique autrefois

100 macchine a vapore fisse e tutta una serie di motori per vaporetti.

La concorrenza, però, non si fece attendere a lungo. Nel 1866, ad esempio, presso la stazione ferroviaria di Thalkirchen venne fondata la fabbrica di locomotive Krauss & Comp. Insieme alla fabbrica per vagoni ferroviari Rathgeber si creò, così, una prima concentrazione industriale nella struttura economica dell'epoca: l'industria meccanica e siderurgica.

Con il potenziamento delle ferrovie Monaco divenne gradual-

Züge verbinden München mit ganz Europa.

Trains connect Munich with destinations throughout Europe.

Les trains relient Munich avec toute l'Europe.

I treni collegano Monaco a tutta l'Europa.

Zudem verbesserte sich die Liquidität der Wirtschaft, nachdem König Ludwig I. 1835 die Bayerische Hypotheken- und Wechselbank gegründet hatte. Sie gewann große Macht durch das Recht zur Notenausgabe und war ein wichtiges Instrument der königlichen Wirtschaftspolitik.

Die Textilindustrie war – bis auf ein paar unbedeutende Baumwollspinnereien – praktisch noch nicht entwickelt. In dieser Branche hatte Johann Georg Frey mit seinem Unternehmen großen Erfolg. Im Alter von 21 Jahren erwarb er 1842 die Weberei-founded the "Bayerische Hypotheken-und Wechselbank" in 1835. This bank gained greatly in significance when it was granted the right to issue bank notes and thus became an important tool of the royal economic policy.

Except for a few insignificant cotton mills practically no textile industry existed in Munich. In this branch Johann Georg Frey became extremely successful with his enterprise. At 21 he bought the "Gerechtsame" weaving mill in 1842 and at first produced simple woolen materials with only ten looms. One year later he was régionale, à savoir l'industrie mécanique et du rail.

Avec la construction des chemins de fer, Munich devint peu à peu un point d'intersection important. De plus, la trésorerie de l'économie s'améliora après la création par Louis 1er de la Bayerische Hypotheken- und Wechselbank en 1835. Elle était dotée d'un énorme pouvoir en recevant le droit d'émettre des billets et était un instrument majeur de la politique économique royale.

A l'exception de quelques filatures de coton d'importance négligeable, l'industrie textile n'était pratiquement pas encore développée. Dans ce secteur, Johann Georg Frey remporta un énorme succès avec son entreprise. A l'age de 21 ans, il se porta acquéreur en 1842 de l'atelier de tissage «Gerechtsame» et produisit d'abord avec dix métiers à tisser de simples tissus. Un an plus tard, il reçut le droit de tisser le lin et construisit alors une grande usine. En 1845, il employait déjà 100 tisseurs manuels, en 1847 il reçut à l'exposition universelle de Paris le premier prix avec son tissu Loden. Sa création en 1878 du premier tissu Loden imperméable fut révolutionnaire. Loden-Frey est le plus vieux fabricant allemand de Loden et possède de nombreux centres de production en Allemagne et à l'étranger.

mente un importante nodo ferroviario. Inoltre, l'economia trasse vantaggio dalla fondazione della Bayerische Hypotheken- und Wechselbank (Banca di credito ipotecario e di sconto) voluta dal re Ludovico I nel 1835. La banca divenne molto potente avendo ottenuto l'autorizzazione all'emissione delle banconote e diventando, ben presto, uno strumento importante della politica economica regia.

Fatta eccezione per qualche insignificante cotonificio, l'industria tessile non era ancora sviluppata. In questo settore ebbe grande successo l'impresa di Johann Georg Frey. Nel 1842, all'età di 21 anni, egli acquistò la fabbrica di tessuti «Gerechtsame» ed iniziò a fabbricare semplici stoffe di lana con soli dieci telai. L'anno seguente ottenne la licenza di fabbricazione di tessuti di lino e costruì una grande fabbrica che già nel 1845 occupava 100 tessitori a mano. Nel 1847, in occasione dell'Esposizione Mondiale di Parigi gli venne consegnato il primo premio per il suo tessuto loden. L'invenzione, avvenuta nel 1878, del primo loden impermeabile si rivelò rivoluzionaria. Loden-Frey è il più antico fabbricante tedesco di loden, che viene prodotto oggi in numerosi stabilimenti sia in Germania che all'estero. Il suo punto vendita monacense si trova, ancora oggi, nella Maffeistraße.

Robert Friedrich Metzeler, un imprenditore coraggioso, creò un settore completamente nuovo per l'epoca in cui visse. Egli iniziò la sua attività nel 1863 con il commercio di vari articoli di gomma. Sempre in cerca di nuove idee, volle entrare di persona nel campo della produzione. Dopo varie traversie con l'amministrazione comunale poté finalmente realizzare il suo progetto e fondò così, nel 1871, la prima fabbrica di caucciù di Monaco. Il suo fu davvero un lavoro pionieristico in quanto riuscì a sviluppare delle tecniche produttive sensazionali. Inventò, ad esempio, un metodo per gommare a più strati i tessuti di lino e di cotone. Riuscì, in tal

Betty Bauch (Gründerin) mit Sohn Magnus und Schwiegertochter Parwathi

Betty Bauch (foundress) with her son Magnus and daughter-in-law Parwathi

Betty Bauch (fondatrice) avec son fils Magnus et sa belle-fille Parwathi

Betty Bauch (fondatrice) con il figlio Magnus e la nuora Parwathi

Belegschaft vor dem Firmensitz in der Thalkirchner Straße in München

The staff in front of the Bauch headquarters in Thalkirchner Straße, Munich

Le personnel devant le siège de la société dans la Thalkirchner Straße à Munich

Dipendenti davanti alla sede dell'azienda nella Thalkirchner Straße di Monaco

Großmetzgerei Magnus Bauch

Am 1. Oktober 1953 gründeten Betty und Magnus Bauch ihre Metzgerei in München. Aus dem kleinen Familienbetrieb entwickelte sich innerhalb von 30 Jahren ein Unternehmen mit 74 Mitarbeitern, davon 14 Meister. Auf modernsten Produktionsanlagen werden täglich 15 Tonnen Wurst allererster Qualität für höchste Ansprüche erzeugt. Bei der Herstellung der weit über 100 Wurstsorten hat Frische absolute Priorität.

Heute wird der Betrieb von Magnus Bauch jun. und dessen Ehefrau Parwathi geleitet. Gründerin Betty Bauch ist nach wie vor aktiv im Unternehmen tätig.

Die Großmetzgerei in der Thalkirchner Straße 63 ist inzwischen weit über die Grenzen der Stadt hinaus bekannt. Spezialität des Hauses und Flaggschiff der bayerischen Wurstproduktion ist die Weißwurst, die traditionsgemäß – auch samstags frisch hergestellt wird.

Der Kundenkreis erstreckt sich vom Privatkunden über den Einzelhandel bis hin zur Gastronomie und Hotellerie. Seit Jahrzehnten ist Magnus Bauch einer der Hauptlieferanten des Münchner Oktoberfests, worauf das Unternehmen besonders stolz ist.

Seit 1995 betreiben Magnus und Parwathi Bauch außerdem ein 5-Sternehotel auf Bali, das dank gewissenhafter Führung und eines hohen Qualitätsstandards ausgesprochen erfolgreich ist.

Butcher Store Magnus Bauch

On 1 October 1953 Betty and Magnus Bauch opened a butcher shop in Munich. Within 30 years this small family enterprise turned into a large firm employing 74 persons, 14 of them master craftsmen. Every day modern plants produce 15 tonnes of top-grade sausage which meets the most exacting demands. Freshness has priority in the production of more than 100 types of sausage.

Today the enterprise is managed by Magnus Bauch jun. and his wife Parwathi. Betty Bauch, one of the founders, is still working actively in the firm.

This large-scale butcher store located in 63 Thalkirchner Straße has become well-known far beyond the city limits. The firm's specialty and "flagship" of Bavarian sausage production is the "Weißwurst", which is traditionally made fresh on Saturdays too.

Bauch's clientele comprises private customers, retail stores, restaurants and hotels. Magnus Bauch has been one of the major suppliers of the "Oktoberfest" for several decades, a fact of which the enterprise is particularly proud.

Since 1995 Magnus and Parwathi Bauch have also operated a five-star hotel on the island of Bali, which is extremely successful thanks to an efficient management and a high standard of quality.

La boucherie Magnus Bauch

Le 1er octobre 1953, Betty et Magnus Bauch fondèrent leur boucherie à Munich. En une trentaine d'années, la petite entreprise familiale se transforma en une entreprise comptant 74 collaborateurs, dont 14 maîtres-charcutiers. Des installations ultramodernes de production permettent de fabriquer chaque jour 15 tonnes de charcuterie de toute première qualité satisfaisant les plus hautes exigences. Pour la production de la centaine de sortes de charcuterie, la fraîcheur est une priorité absolue.

Aujourd'hui, la société est dirigée par Magnus Bauch fils et sa femme Parwathi. La fondatrice, Betty Bauch, continue de travailler dans l'entreprise.

La réputation de la boucherie, située dans la Thalkirchner Straße 63, a entre-temps largement dépassé les frontières de la ville. La spécialité de la maison et l'élément fondamental de la production de saucisses bavaroises est la saucisse blanche, qui, conformément à la tradition, est également fabriquée le samedi.

La clientèle comprend la clientèle privée, le commerce de détail, sans oublier la gastronomie et l'hôtellerie. Depuis des décennies, Magnus Bauch est un des principaux fournisseurs de la Fête de la Bière de Munich et la société en est particulièrement fière.

En outre, Magnus et Parwathi Bauch dirigent à Bali depuis 1995 un hôtel cinq étoiles qui, grâce à une gestion soignée et un standard de qualité élevé, connaît un grand succès.

Macelleria Magnus Bauch

Betty e Magnus Bauch hanno fondato la loro macelleria a Monaco il 1 Ottobre 1953. Dalla piccola azienda a conduzione familiare si è sviluppata, nel giro di 30 anni, un'impresa che conta 74 dipendenti, di cui 14 mastri macellai. Mediante l'impiego di impianti produttivi all'avanguardia vengono prodotte, ogni giorno, 15 tonnellate di salumi della migliore qualità per soddisfare le richieste dei clienti più esigenti. Nella produzione degli oltre 100 tipi di salumi, la freschezza ha la priorità assoluta.

Oggi l'azienda è diretta da Magnus Bauch junior e da sua moglie Parwathi. La fondatrice Betty Bauch continua a collaborare attivamente alla conduzione dell'azienda.

Nel frattempo, la macelleria nella Thalkirchner Straße 63 si è fatta conoscere oltre i confini della città. La specialità della casa e portabandiera della produzione bavarese di salumi è la salsiccia bianca che viene prodotta secondo i metodi tradizionali ed è in vendita, fresca, anche di sabato.

La cerchia clientelare va dal cliente privato, al quale l'azienda si rivolge attraverso il commercio al dettaglio, alle gastronomie e agli alberghi. Da decenni la Magnus Bauch è la fornitrice principale per l'Oktoberfest di Monaco, cosa di cui va particolarmente fiera.

Inoltre, dal 1995 Magnus e Parwathi Bauch gestiscono un albergo a 5 stelle a Bali che riscuote grande successo grazie ad una amministrazione attenta e scrupolosa e ad un alto standard di qualità.

▲ Weit über die Grenzen Bayerns berühmt: Das Flaggschiff der Bauch'schen Wurstproduktion – die Weißwurst

Famous far beyond Bavaria's limits: the flagship of Bavarian sausage production – the "Weißwurst"

Célèbre bien au-delà des frontières bavaroises: l'élément fondamental de la production de saucisse de la maison Bauch: la saucisse blanche.

Conosciuta oltre i confini bavaresi: il portabandiera della produzione di salumi della Baviera – la salsiccia bianca

◀ Ein Teil des Großverkaufes – im Hintergrund ein Bild des Gründers, Magnus Bauch

Part of the whole-sale sales office – with a portrait of the founder, Magnus Bauch, in the background

Une partie de la vente en gros – à l'arrière-plan un portrait du fondateur, Magnus Bauch

Una parte della vendita all'ingrosso – sullo sfondo un quadro del fondatore, Magnus Bauch

„Gerechtsame" und fertigte zunächst mit zehn Webstühlen einfache Wollstoffe. Ein Jahr später erhielt er das Leineweberrecht und errichtete daraufhin eine große Fabrikanlage. 1845 beschäftigte er bereits 100 Handweber, 1847 gewann er bei der Pariser Weltausstellung den ersten Preis mit seinem Lodenstoff. Revolutionär war seine Entwicklung des ersten wasserdichten Lodenstoffes 1878. Loden-Frey ist der älteste deutsche Lodenhersteller und betreibt zahlreiche Produktionsstätten im In- und Ausland. Sein Münchner Verkaufshaus befindet sich bis heute in der Maffeistraße.

Eine damals völlig neue Branche begründete der wagemutige Unternehmer Robert Friedrich Metzeler. Er startete 1863 mit dem Handel von Gummiwaren aller Art. Ständig auf der Suche nach neuen Ideen, wollte er jedoch selbst in die Produktion einsteigen. Nach einigem Hin und Her mit der Stadtverwaltung konnte er sein Vorhaben realisieren und gründete 1871 Münchens erste Kautschukfabrik. Er leistete wahrlich Pionierarbeit, und es gelang ihm, einige Aufsehen erregende technische Verfahren zu entwickeln. So fand er eine Methode, Gewebe aus Leinen oder Baumwolle vielschichtig zu gummieren. Die bis dato nie erreichte Dichte des Gewebes war wiederum Voraussetzung für die Konstruktion von Ballons und Luftschiffen größerer Reichweite. Auch entwickelte und produzierte er einen „Fliegerstoff", mit dem Tragflächen und Rümpfe der damaligen Flugapparate überzogen wurden. Schließlich durfte er den Titel „Königlich Bayerischer Hoffabrikant für Gummi- und Guttaperchawaren" tragen.

Die fortschreitende Industrialisierung, infrastrukturelle Verbesserungen, die Ausweitung des Bankensystems und nicht zuletzt die seit 1886 gewährte Gewerbefreiheit brachten der wirtschaftlichen Entwicklung neue Impulse. Die so genannte Gründerzeit brach an. München war auf dem besten Weg, eine überregional granted the right to weave linen and, subsequently, had a large factory built. In 1845 he already employed 100 hand weavers, and in 1847 his Loden material was awarded the first prize at the World Fair in Paris. In 1878 he developed the first waterproof Loden - a revolutionary feat. Thus "Loden-Frey" is Germany's oldest Loden producer, which operates numerous manufacturing plants at home and abroad. But its parent store is still located in Maffeistraße.

A very daring entrepreneur, Robert Friedrich Metzeler, founded an entirely new industrial branch. In 1863 he started trading with rubber articles of all kinds. Constantly on the lookout for new ideas, he was determined to start manufacturing by himself. After some disputes with the city administration he was able to put into practice his ambitious plans: In 1871 he founded Munich's first caoutchouc factory. A true pioneer, he developed some sensational technical processes. He discovered, for example, a method of rubberizing linen and cotton fabrics. The up to then unmatched density of the material made it possible to construct balloons and airships with a bigger flying range. Metzeler also developed and produced a special airplane material with which the wings and fuselage of the first flying apparatuses were covered. He was eventually granted the title of a "Königlich Bayerischer Hoffabrikant für Gummi- und Guttaperchawaren" - Royal Bavarian Court Manufacturer for Rubber and Gutta-Percha Products.

Progressing industrialization, infrastructural improvements, the expansion of banking and - last but not least - freedom of trade (which was granted in 1886) greatly stimulated economic development. The industrial "golden age" - i. e. the so-called "Gründerzeit" - began. Munich was on its way to becoming a metropolis of supraregional significance. By the turn of the century a great number of mostly A Munich, sa boutique se situe aujourd'hui encore dans la Maiffeistraße.

L'entrepreneur Robert Friedrich Metzeler s'engagea courageusement dans un secteur absolument nouveau à l'époque. En 1863, il commença le commerce d'articles en caoutchouc de tout genre. Cherchant constamment de nouvelles idées, il voulut cependant se lancer dans la production. Après quelques négociations avec la municipalité, il put réaliser son projet et fonda en 1871 la première industrie de caoutchouc de Munich. En faisant vraiment un travail de pionnier, il arriva à mettre au point quelques procédés techniques remarquables. Il trouva ainsi une méthode pour engommer sur plusieurs couches des tissus en lin ou coton. L'épaisseur jusque là tout à fait inédite du tissu était la condition sine qua non pour la construction de ballons et d'aéronefs de grande ampleur. De même, il mit au point et produisit une «matière pour voler» qui servit à recouvrir les surfaces et les ailes des avions d'autrefois. Il put également porter le titre de «fabricant de la cour royale de Bavière d'articles en caoutchouc et gutta-percha».

Les progrès de l'industrialisation, l'amélioration des infrastructures, l'élargissement du système bancaire et enfin le libre exercice d'une profession commerciale, industrielle ou artisanale instaurée depuis 1886 donnèrent de nouvelles impulsions au développement économique. L'ère de la création d'entreprises commença. Munich était en train de devenir une capitale suprarégionale représentative. Jusqu'au début du siècle, des entreprises importantes, la plupart de taille moyenne, venant de secteurs les plus divers s'étaient installées.

C'est pendant cette période que l'inventeur génial, ingénieur et entrepreneur sur le tard, Carl von Linde, opéra. Il inventa en 1875, la machine à glace à l'ammoniac et fonda en 1879 sa société «Gesellschaft für Lindes Eismachinen AG». En 1895, il modo, a produrre tessuti con uno spessore mai raggiunto prima, e ciò rappresentò, a sua volta, la premessa per la progettazione di palloni aerostatici e dirigibili di portata maggiore. Metzeler, inoltre, inventò e produsse la cosiddetta «stoffa per aerei» con la quale venivano rivestite le superfici alari e le fusoliere dei velivoli del tempo. Infine gli venne conferito il titolo di «Fabbricante della Corte reale di Baviera per articoli di gomma e guttaperca».

Il progresso dell'industrializzazione, il miglioramento delle infrastrutture, l'evoluzione del sistema bancario e, non da ultima, la liberalizzazione delle attività commerciali concessa nel 1886 portarono nuovi impulsi allo sviluppo economico. Iniziò, così, la cosiddetta «seconda industrializzazione tedesca». Monaco era sulla buona strada per diventare una metropoli di importanza sovraregionale. A cavallo dei due secoli qui si erano già insediate diverse importanti imprese industriali dei settori più vari e, per lo più, di medie dimensioni.

In questo periodo operò anche un inventore geniale: l'ingegnere e futuro imprenditore Carl von Linde. Nel 1875 egli inventò la gelatiera ad ammoniaca e nel 1879 fondò la «Gesellschaft für Lindes Eismaschinen AG» (Società per Gelatiere Linde S.p.A.). Nel 1895 e nel 1902 mise a punto due procedimenti per la fabbricazione rispettivamente di aria liquida e di ossigeno liquido, e l'anno seguente costruì il primo apparecchio per la fabbricazione di azoto puro. Queste invenzioni non furono solo rivoluzionarie ma ebbero un impatto anche su altri settori. Ad esempio, ebbe inizio la produzione della birra su scala industriale che comportò una ristrutturazione delle fabbriche di birra e la nascita della grande industria birraria. La nuova tecnica di refrigerazione, insieme ad un migliorato sistema dei trasporti, aprì la strada verso nuovi mercati di sbocco, addirittura oltreoceano. Nel 1893 Georg Pschorr fu il primo proprietario di una fabbrica di birra a fare

wichtige Metropole zu werden. Bis zur Jahrhundertwende hatten sich bedeutende, überwiegend mittelständische Industriebetriebe der unterschiedlichsten Branchen angesiedelt.

In dieser Zeit wirkte der geniale Erfinder, Ingenieur und spätere Unternehmer Carl von Linde. Er erfand 1875 die Ammoniak-Eismaschine und gründete 1879 seine „Gesellschaft für Lindes Eismaschinen AG". 1895 erfand er ein Verfahren zur Herstellung von flüssiger Luft, 1902 von flüssigem Sauerstoff, ein Jahr später konstruierte er den ersten Apparat zur Herstellung reinen Stickstoffs. Nicht allein, dass seine Entwicklungen revolutionär waren, sie hatten auch Auswirkungen auf andere Bereiche. Die Industrialisierung der Biererzeugung und damit eine Umstrukturierung des Brauereigewerbes kam ins Rollen, die heutigen Großbrauereien entstanden. Die neue Kühltechnik in Verbindung mit besseren Transportmöglichkeiten eröffnete weitere Absatzmärkte – sogar bis nach Übersee. Als erster Brauereibesitzer ließ Georg Pschorr 1893 auf Dampfschiffen Kühlräume für den Nordamerikaverkehr einrichten, die den Bierexport auch im Sommer ermöglichten.

Der zunehmende technische Fortschritt führte Anfang des 20. Jahrhunderts zu neuen Schwerpunkten in der optischen, feinmechanischen und elektrotechnischen Industrie, im Fahrzeug- und Flugzeugbau.

In der optisch-feinmechanischen Industrie entstanden mehrere Unternehmen, die auf den Erkenntnissen der berühmten Institute von Fraunhofer und Reichenbach aufbauen konnten. Für diese auf der Verbindung wissenschaftlicher Forschung und handwerklicher Kunstfertigkeit basierende Industrie war der Standort München bestens gerüstet. Bereits um 1900 war die Stadt führend in der Herstellung von astronomischen und geodätischen Instrumenten, Fotoobjektiven und Fernrohren. Auf den engagierten Unternehmer Joseph Rodenstock übte München daher

medium-sized companies of all industrial branches had settled in the city.

In this period Carl von Linde – an ingenious inventor, engineer and, later, entrepreneur – played an important part in the city. In 1875 he invented the ammonia-based ice machine and in 1879 founded his "Gesellschaft für Lindes Eismaschinen AG". In 1895 he developed a process for producing liquid air, in 1902 a process for producing liquid oxygen, and one year later he constructed the first apparatus for producing pure nitrogen. Not only were his inventions revolutionary, they also had their impact on other fields: They brought about the industrialization of beer production and, consequently, the restructuring of the entire brewing sector, a change that led to the development of our present-day large-scale breweries. The new cooling techniques together with improved means of transport opened up new sales markets – even beyond the oceans. Georg Pschorr was the first brewer who in 1893 had refrigeration rooms installed in the steamships travelling to North America; thus it became possible to export beer in summer too.

Technological progress led to remarkable upswings in the sectors of optics, fine-mechanics, electrical engineering, and vehicle and airplane construction in the early 20th century.

In the optical industry and in precision mechanics several firms were established which relied on the findings of the famous Fraunhofer and Reichenbach institutes. The industry based on this combination of scientific research and commercial art was well-placed in Munich. As early as 1900 the city held a leading position in the manufacture of astronomical and geodetic instruments, camera lenses and telescopes. For this reason Munich was particularly attractive to the dedicated entrepreneur Joseph Rodenstock. In 1877 he had already set up a workshop in Würzburg, where he made barometers, precision

inventa un procédé pour fabriquer de l'air liquide, en 1902 de l'oxygène liquide et, un an plus tard, il construisit le premier appareil servant à fabriquer de l'azote pur. Non seulement ses découvertes furent révolutionnaires mais en plus elles eurent des conséquences dans d'autres domaines. L'industrialisation de la fabrication de la bière et ainsi une restructuration du secteur des brasseries se mirent en route, les grandes brasseries d'aujourd'hui virent le jour. La nouvelle technique de refroidissement liée à une amélioration des possibilités de transport ouvrit d'autres débouchés même en outre-mer. Georg Pschorr fut le premier propriétaire de brasserie à faire installer en 1893 des chambres froides sur les bateaux à vapeur allant en Amérique du Nord ce qui permit d'exporter de la bière même en été.

Au début du 20ème siècle, le progrès technique croissant conduisit à la naissance de nouveaux domaines principaux dans l'industrie électrotechnique et de la mécanique de précision, dans la construction automobile et aéronautique.

Dans l'industrie optique et de mécanique de précision, plusieurs entreprises virent le jour qui purent se monter grâce aux connaissances acquises par les célèbres instituts von Fraunhofer et Reichenbach. Pour cette industrie basée sur la relation entre la recherche scientifique et l'habilité manuelle, Munich s'avérait un site extrêmement bien équipé. Déjà en 1900, la ville arrivait en tête pour la fabrication d'instruments astronomiques et géodésiques, les objectifs photographiques et les téléobjectifs. L'entrepreneur engagé, Joseph Rodenstock, fut vivement attiré par Munich. Il avait ouvert à Wurzbourg en 1877 un atelier de mécanique de précision pour les baromètres, balances de précision, verres et montures de lunettes et, deux ans plus tard, il put déjà faire inscrire son premier brevet. En 1891, il transféra son entreprise à Munich, le centre de l'optique

installare delle celle frigorifere su navi a vapore destinate alla navigazione verso l'America del Nord per consentire il commercio della birra anche durante i mesi estivi.

Il costante progresso tecnologico portò, agli inizi del XX secolo, alla nascita di nuovi «baricentri» dell'industria ottica, elettrotecnica, della meccanica di precisione e delle costruzioni automobilistiche ed aeronautiche.

Per quanto riguarda il settore ottico e della meccanica di precisione, nacquero diverse imprese che trassero profitto dai metodi sviluppati negli istituti Fraunhofer e Reichenbach. Monaco era la sede ideale per ospitare quest'industria basata sul connubio tra ricerca scientifica ed abilità artigiana. Infatti, già nel 1900 la città era leader nel settore della produzione di strumenti astronomici e geodetici, di obiettivi fotografici e cannocchiali. Per questo motivo Monaco esercitò una forte attrattiva su un imprenditore appassionato di nome Joseph Rodenstock. Questi aveva aperto nel 1877, a Würzburg, un'officina per la fabbricazione di barometri, bilance di precisione, lenti e montature per occhiali da vista, riuscendo a depositare il suo primo brevetto dopo soli due anni. Nel 1891 trasferì la sua azienda in quello che era considerato il centro per eccellenza delle ricerche scientifiche e della produzione in campo ottico – a Monaco. Oggi, Rodenstock produce un'ampia gamma di prodotti ottici di altissima qualità ed è presente sul mercato mondiale con 22 società affiliate.

La fabbrica di macchine e carri F. X. Meiller raggiunse fama mondiale con la costruzione dell'autocarro Meiller con cassone ribaltabile, il noto «Meiller-Kipper». Il dispositivo di ribaltamento idraulico fu la prima invenzione rivoluzionaria dell'azienda; a questa seguì il rimorchio Meiller con asse oscillante ed autotelaio tubolare. E pensare che gli inizi erano stati tutt'altro che facili: nel 1850, quando era ancora un fabbro, Lorenz Meiller rilevò una fucina sul Tegernsee. Ma l'ambizioso imprenditore aspirava a trasferirsi

Letzte Weltneuheit von Beissbarth: ein optoelektronisches System, das unsichtbare Reifenschäden sichtbar macht.

The most recent Beissbarth innovation: an optoelectronic system making visible invisible tire defects.

Dernière nouveauté mondiale de Beissbarth: un système optoélectronique permettant de voir les dégâts invisibles d'un pneu.

Ultima novità mondiale firmata Beissbarth: un sistema optoelettronico che rende visibili i danni invisibili sul battistrada delle ruote.

Die Beissbarth-Fabrik an der Tegernseer Landstraße in München um 1914

The Beissbarth Factory at Tegernseer Landstraße in Munich, in about 1914

L'usine de Beissbarth dans la Tegernseer Landstraße à Munich vers 1914

Lo stabilimento della Beissbarth sulla Tegernseer Landstraße a Monaco di Baviera intorno al 1914

Beissbarth – seit 100 Jahren erfolgreich in der Autobranche

Am 14. April 1899 haben die Kaufleute Daniel und Hermann Beissbarth von der Königlich Bayerischen Polizeidirektion in München den ersten amtlichen Fahrschein und das wohl erste registrierte Autonummernschild der Welt für ihren Wartburg-Motorwagen erhalten: ein handtellergroßes gelbes Schild mit einer schwarzen Nr.1. Noch im gleichen Jahr wurde die erste Autofabrik Bayerns ins Leben gerufen: die Motorfahrzeug- und Karosseriebaufirma „Gebrüder Beissbarth".

Heute kann die Beissbarth GmbH in München mit ihren 360 Mitarbeitern, die 1998 rund 160 Millionen DM erwirtschaftet hat, auf ein bewegtes Unternehmensleben zurückblicken: 100 Jahre Tätigkeit im automobilen Wirtschaftssektor.

In den 100 Jahren ihres Bestehens hat die Beissbarth GmbH immer wieder neue Maßstäbe in der Servicegerätetechnik gesetzt: Bereits in den 50er Jahren wurden erste Radwuchtmaschinen, Stoßdämpferprüfstände und Achsmessgeräte entwickelt. 1990 gelang dem Unternehmen als weltweit erstem Hersteller die Entwicklung eines elektronischen Fahrwerksvermessungssystems mit PC-Technik, CCC-Messsensorik und Infrarotdatenübertragung, das den automobilen Servicebereich revolutionierte. Es wird heute von allen namhaften Automobilherstellern weltweit empfohlen. Den letzten Innovationspreis des deutschen Wirtschaftsministeriums erhielt Beissbarth 1998 für die Entwicklung eines optoelektronischen Servicegerätes, das unsichtbare Reifenschäden über einen PC-Monitor sichtbar macht.

Der Vertrieb der Beissbarth Automobilservicegeräte erfolgt über eigene Niederlassungen in Australien, Belgien, Bulgarien, China, Frankreich, Großbritannien, Italien, Österreich, USA und über 50 weitere Vertriebspartner rund um den Globus.

Beissbarth – successful in the automotive branch for 100 years

On 14 April 1899 Daniel and Hermann Beissbarth, two businessmen from Munich, received their first driving licence and probably the world's first registered licence plate for their Wartburg motor coach from the Royal Bavarian Police Headquarters: a palm-sized yellow sign with a black 1 on it. In the same year Bavaria's first car factory was founded: the car and bodywork manufacturer "Gebrüder Beissbarth".

Today the Beissbarth GmbH in Munich, which employs 360 persons and achieved a turnover of DM 160 million in 1998, looks back on an eventful career: 100 years of operating in the automotive sector.

In the 100 years of its existence the Beissbarth GmbH has repeatedly set new standards in servo technology: as early as the 1950s the firm developed the first implements for balancing wheels, test stands for shock absorbers, and wheel alignment indicators. In 1990 the enterprise was the first producer – worldwide – of an electronic system for measuring moving gears; it comprised PC technology, CCC measuring sensors and infrared data transfer which revolutionized automotive services. Today this system is recommended worldwide by all renowned car manufacturers. In 1998 Beissbarth was awarded the most recent innovation prize of the German Ministry of Economics for developing an optoelectric service appliance which by means of a PC monitor makes visible invisible tire defects.

Beissbarth service implements are sold through the enterprise's own agencies in Australia, Belgium, Bulgaria, China, France, Great Britain, Italy, Austria, and the United States, as well as by 50 additional sales partners around the globe.

Beissbarth enregistre depuis 100 ans un grand succès dans le secteur automobile

Le 14 avril 1899, les commerciaux Daniel et Hermann Beissbarth reçoivent de la Königlich Bayerische Polizeidirektion (bureau de police bavarois) à Munich le premier permis de conduire officiel et la première plaque d'immatriculation enregistrée du monde pour leur voiture à moteur

Wartburg. Il s'agissait d'une plaque de la taille d'une sous-tasse sur laquelle était inscrit en noir n°1. La même année, la première usine de voitures de Bavière fut créée. C'était la société de construction de voitures et de carrosserie «Gebrüder Beissbarth».

Aujourd'hui la société Beissbarth GmbH à Munich comptant 360 employés et ayant réalisé en 1998 un chiffre d'affaires de 160 millions de DM environ peut jeter un regard en arrière sur une vie d'entreprise fort agitée. En effet, 100 ans d'activité dans le secteur de l'automobile.

Au cours de ses 100 ans d'existence, la Beissbarth GmbH a toujours posé de nouveaux jalons dans la technique des appareils de service. Déjà au cours des années 50, les premières machines servant à vérifier l'équilibrage des roues, les bancs d'essai à amortisseurs et les appareils de mesure d'alignement des roues ont été mis au point. En 1990, la société fut le premier fabricant mondial à développer un système de mesure de châssis avec une technique de PC, une sensorique CCC et une transmission des données par infrarouge ce qui révolutionna le secteur du service automobile. Il est aujourd'hui recommandé par tous les grands constructeurs automobiles du monde. Beissbarth reçut en 1998 le prix de l'innovation du ministère allemand de l'économie pour le développement d'un appareil de service optoélectronique qui permet de voir, via un écran d'ordinateur, les dégâts invisibles d'un pneu.

La distribution des appareils de service automobile de Beissbarth s'effectue par ses propres filiales implantées en Australie, Autriche, Belgique, Bulgarie, Chine, France, Grande-Bretagne, Italie, et aux USA ainsi que par plus de 50 autres partenaires de distribution à travers le monde.

Beissbarth – 100 anni di successi nel settore automobilistico

Il 14 aprile 1899 i commercianti Daniel e Hermann Beissbarth ricevevano dal Comando di Polizia Reale della Baviera in Monaco la prima patente ufficiale e la prima targa automobilistica registrata del mondo per la loro autovettura Wartburg: una targhetta gialla delle dimensioni del palmo di una mano con la cifra 1 stampata in nero. Sempre nello stesso anno fu creata la prima fabbrica automobilistica della Baviera: la «Gebrüder Beissbarth», costruttori di autovetture e carrozzerie.

Oggi la Beissbarth GmbH di Monaco di Baviera, con i suoi 360 dipendenti ed un fatturato che ha raggiunto circa 160 milioni di marchi nel 1998, ha alle spalle un percorso imprenditoriale movimentato: 100 anni di attività nel settore automobilistico.

Nei suoi 100 anni di attività la Beissbarth GmbH ha imposto sempre nuovi standard tecnici per quanto riguarda le attrezzature di controllo: già negli anni 50 vennero sviluppate le prime equilibratrici per ruote, i primi banchi di prova per gli ammortizzatori ed i primi apparecchi per controllare l'avantreno. Nel 1990 la Beissbarth è stata la prima azienda al mondo a sviluppare un sistema di misurazione dell'autotelaio che facesse uso della tecnologia computerizzata, del sistema di rilevazione mediante sensori CCC e della trasmissione dei dati a raggi infrarossi, un sistema che ha rivoluzionato il settore dei dispositivi di controllo per l'industria automobilistica. Questo sistema viene raccomandato ancora oggi, in tutto il mondo, dalle case automobilistiche più rinomate. L'ultimo premio per «importanti innovazioni tecniche» la Beissbarth l'ha ricevuto dal Ministero tedesco per il Commercio nel 1998 per lo sviluppo di un dispositivo optoelettronico grazie al quale i danni al battistrada delle ruote, fino ad allora invisibili all'occhio umano, possono essere resi percepibili attraverso il monitor di un computer.

La vendita delle apparecchiature e dei dispositivi di controllo della Beissbarth per il settore automobilistico avviene attraverso le filiali operanti in Australia, Belgio, Bulgaria, Cina, Francia, Gran Bretagna, Italia, Austria, USA e attraverso una fitta rete di 50 venditori associati sparsi in tutto il mondo.

Das Produktionsprogramm von Beissbarth umfasst ausschließlich computerunterstützte Geräte für den Automobilservice.

The product range of Beissbarth comprises computer aided compliances for the automotive service.

La gamme de production de Beissbarth englobe essentiellement des appareils assistés par ordinateurs et servant au service automobile.

Il programma di produzione della Beissbarth comprende esclusivamente apparecchiature e dispositivi di controllo computerizzati per l'industria automobilistica.

---

eine große Anziehungskraft aus. Er hatte 1877 in Würzburg eine feinmechanische Werkstatt für Barometer, Präzisionswaagen, Brillengläser und -fassungen eröffnet und konnte bereits zwei Jahre später sein erstes Patent anmelden. 1891 verlegte er sein Unternehmen in das Zentrum der wissenschaftlichen Optik – nach München. Heute produziert Rodenstock eine breite Palette optischer Erzeugnisse mit höchstem Qualitätsanspruch und ist mit 22 Tochtergesellschaften weltweit präsent.

Die F. X. Meiller Maschinenfabrik und Wagenbauanstalt wurde 1925 durch den „Meiller-Kipper" weltbekannt. Die hydraulische Kippeinrichtung war die erste revolutionäre Erfindung des Unternehmens; ihr folgte der Meiller-Anhänger mit Schwingachse und Rohrfahrgestell. Dabei war der Anfang gar nicht so leicht gewesen: Am Tegernsee hatte der Schmied Lorenz Meiller 1850 scales, spectacle lenses and frames, and where he applied for his first patent two years later. In 1891 he moved his enterprise to the centre of optical science, to Munich. Today Rodenstock produces a wide range of optical articles catering to the most exacting demands. The firm is represented throughout the world by 22 subsidiaries.

The F. X. Meiller Maschinenfabrik und Wagenbauanstalt in 1925 became famous thanks to the "Meiller-Kipper". This hydraulic tilling or tipping device was the first revolutionary invention of this enterprise. It was followed by the Meiller-Trailer boasting a floating axle and a tubular chassis. But the enterprise's early years had been rather difficult: Smith Lorenz Meiller had taken over a hammer mill at Lake Tegernsee in 1850. The ambitious entrepreneur wanted, however, to move his mill to the Bavarian capital. It took him more than ten years to ac-

scientifique. Aujourd'hui, Rodenstock produit une vaste gamme de produits optiques de la plus haute qualité. A l'échelle mondiale, la société est représentée par 22 filiales.

La société F. X. Meiller Maschinenfabrik und Wagenbauanstalt devint célèbre en 1925 par la «benne basculante Meiller». L'unité à bascule hydraulique fut la première invention révolutionnaire de l'entreprise, puis suivit la remorque Meiller avec un essieu flottant et un châssis en tube. Pourtant les débuts furent difficiles: Le forgeron Lorenz Meiller avait repris en 1850 au lac de Tegernsee une forge à marteaux. L'entrepreneur ambitieux voulait cependant s'installer dans la capitale bavaroise. Ce n'est que dix ans plus tard qu'il put acheter une licence professionnelle et transférer son entreprise à Munich. D'abord forge à marteaux et à armes, puis en plus forge pour les réparations de voitures,

nella capitale bavarese. Dovettero trascorrere, tuttavia, oltre 10 anni prima che egli potesse ottenere la licenza professionale e trasferire la sua azienda a Monaco. Quella che all'inizio era una fucina ed una fabbrica d'armi divenne, in seguito, anche un'officina di riparazione per carri e poté infine fregiarsi del titolo di «Fabbrica di Utensili della Corte Reale di Baviera».

Nel settore della fisica, i due ricercatori e colleghi di studi Lothar Rohde e Hermann Schwarz riuscirono a sviluppare, all'inizio degli anni '30, uno strumento rivoluzionario. Costruirono un frequenzimetro di precisione per la banda di 100 kHz. Ciò consentì di effettuare, per la prima volta, misurazioni esatte su materiali ceramici all'epoca di nuova concezione; si delineava già un collegamento con il settore industriale. Nel 1933 i due amici fondarono il laboratorio di sviluppo fisico-tecnico Dr. Rohde & Dr.

eine Hammerschmiede übernommen. Der ehrgeizige Unternehmer wollte aber in die bayerische Hauptstadt. Erst nach über zehn Jahren gelang es ihm, die Berufslizenz zu erwerben und seine Firma nach München zu verlegen. Zunächst Hammer- und Waffenschmiede, später zusätzlich Schmiede für Wagenreparaturen, durfte sich das Unternehmen nun „Königlich Bayerische Hof-Werkzeugfabrik" nennen.

Auf dem Gebiet der physikalischen Technik gelang den zwei Physikern und Studienfreunden Lothar Rohde und Hermann Schwarz Anfang der dreißiger Jahre eine bahnbrechende Entwicklung. Sie konstruierten einen Präzisionsfrequenzmesser für den Bereich von 100 kHz. Damit waren zum ersten Mal exakte Messungen an damals neuartigen keramischen Materialien möglich; die Verbindung zur Industrie war geschaffen. 1933 gründeten die Freunde das Physikalisch-Technische Entwicklungslabor Dr. Rohde & Dr. Schwarz (PTE). Die anfänglich bescheidene technische Einrichtung bestand aus selbst gebauten Geräten und Messinstrumenten von Altwarenlagern. Im Laufe der Zeit entstand daraus ein gefragter Spezialbetrieb für elektronische Messtechnik, aus dem einstigen PTE wurde das heutige Unternehmen Rohde & Schwarz. Einer der ersten Auftraggeber nach dem Zweiten Weltkrieg war der Bayerische Rundfunk, für den der europaweit erste frequenzmodulierte UKW-Hörfunksender seiner Art entwickelt wurde. Rohde & Schwarz – der Name des ältesten Münchner Elektronikunternehmens – steht mittlerweile weltweit für Spitzenleistungen in der Mess-, Nachrichten- und Funktechnik mit einem Exportanteil von über 50 %.

In der Luftfahrt machte sich Willy Messerschmitt einen Namen. Anfang des 20. Jahrhunderts begann der Flugzeugkonstrukteur zunächst mit der Entwicklung von Segelflugzeugen, wobei er die Testflüge meist selbst unternahm. 1925 konstruierte er – 27 Jahre alt – sein erstes Motorflugzeug.

quire the necessary license and to finally transfer his shop to Munich. Starting out as a hammer and weapon mill, operating later as a smithy for waggons and carts, it now bore the title of "Königlich Bayerische Hof-Werkzeugfabrik" – Royal Bavarian Court Tool Factory.

In the early 1930s, two physicists and fellow students – Lothar Rohde and Hermann Schwarz – succeeded in starting a pioneering development in the field of physical technology. They constructed a precision frequency meter for the 100 kHz range. Their invention allowed the taking of exact measurements of the ceramic material developed at that time. Thus a link with industry was established. In 1933 the two friends founded the "Physikalisch-Technische Entwicklungslabor Dr. Rohde und Dr. Schwarz (PTE)". The initially very modest equipment consisted of home-made apparatuses and of measuring devices picked up at a dumpyard. In the course of time a renowned special enterprise for electronic mensuration techniques developed, and the former PTE became the present-day Rohde & Schwarz enterprise. One of its first customers after the Second World War was the Bavarian Broadcasting Station for which the firm developed the first frequency modulated USW stations in Europe. Today this oldest electronic enterprise based in Munich is well-known globally for its top achievements in measuring, communication and radio technology. It boasts an export share of more than 50 %.

Willy Messerschmitt made a name for himself in aviation. In the early 20th century this airplane constructor started developing gliders which he normally tested himself. In 1925 he designed – only 27 years old – his first mechanical plane. In 1943 a brand-new jet-propelled type of plane was tested, the world's first rocket fighter plane constructed by Messerschmitt. Travelling at a speed of 800 km/h, it was 200 kilometres faster than the fastest

l'entreprise put se doter du titre de «fabrique d'outillage de la cour royale de Bavière».

Dans le secteur de la technique physique, deux physiciens et amis d'études Lothar Rohde et Hermann Schwarz connurent au début des années trente une réussite extraordinaire. Ils construisirent un fréquencemètre de précision pour le domaine des 100 kHz. C'était la première fois que des mesures exactes étaient possibles à l'époque sur des matières céramiques tout nouvelles; la liaison avec l'industrie était réussie. En 1933, ces amis créèrent le Physikalisch-Technische Entwicklungslabor Dr. Rohde & Dr. Schwarz (PTE) (laboratoire de recherches physiques et techniques). L'installation, assez sobre à ses débuts, se composait d'appareils fabriqués par leurs soins et d'instruments de mesure provenant de dépôts de vieux matériaux. Au cours du temps, elle se transforma en une usine spécialisée très demandée pour la technique de mesure électronique et l'ancien PTE devint l'entreprise Rohde & Schwarz d'aujourd'hui. Un des premiers mandataires après la Seconde Guerre mondiale fut la Bayerische Rundfunk (radio bavaroise) pour lequel le premier émetteur à l'échelle européenne de grandes ondes fut mis au point. Rohde & Schwarz – le nom de la plus ancienne société munichoise d'électronique – est maintenant au niveau international synonyme de prestations d'excellente qualité dans la technique des mesures, d'information et de la radio. Son taux à l'exportation dépasse 50 %.

C'est dans l'aéronautique que Willy Messerschmitt se fit un nom. Au début du 20ème siècle, le constructeur d'avions commença d'abord par le développement de planeurs et il effectuait généralement lui-même les vols d'essai. A l'âge de 27 ans, il construisit en 1925 son premier avion à moteur. En 1943, il put tester un tout nouveau type d'avion avec une propulsion par réaction, le premier chasseur à réaction du monde créé par Messerschmitt.

Schwarz (PTE). La modesta attrezzatura di cui disponevano all'inizio consisteva in apparecchi da essi stessi costruiti e in strumenti di misura recuperati da depositi di oggetti usati. Con il passare del tempo, il laboratorio divenne un'azienda specialistica molto richiesta per le misurazioni elettroniche, e il PTE si trasformò nell'odierna Rohde & Schwarz. Uno dei suoi primi committenti dopo la Seconda Guerra Mondiale fu la Radiotelevisione Bavarese (Bayerischer Rundfunk), per la quale fu costruita la prima emittente radiofonica ad onde ultracorte in Europa. Rohde & Schwarz – il nome della più antica azienda di elettronica di Monaco – è oggi conosciuta in tutto il mondo per le sue prestazioni di altissima qualità nel settore della tecnica di misura, delle telecomunicazioni e della radiotecnica. L'azienda vanta una quota export superiore al 50 %.

Willy Messerschmitt, un progettista di aerei, fu un personaggio di grande rilievo nel settore dell'aeronautica. All'inizio del XX secolo egli si dedicò alla progettazione di alianti eseguendo egli stesso gran parte dei voli di prova. Nel 1925, all'età di 27 anni, costruì il suo prima aeroplano a motore. Nel 1943 inventò un aereo di concezione completamente nuova con propulsione a reazione. Si trattava del primo caccia a reazione del mondo. Con una velocità di 800 km/h esso superava di 200 km/h il caccia più veloce degli USA. Anche il primo aeroplano a razzo costruito in serie fu progettato da Messerschmitt.

Le personalità qui elencate rappresentano solo esempi simbolici di tutti quegli imprenditori che, con il loro impegno, il loro coraggio, la loro disponibilità a percorrere strade innovative e la loro creatività, hanno dato un'impronta fondamentale alla storia economica della città. Grazie a loro, Monaco è diventata un sito industriale di grande rilievo. Ciò è documentato dal fatto che «global player» come la Siemens e la BMW hanno continuato a man-

1943 konnte ein ganz neuer Flugzeugtyp mit Strahlantrieb erprobt werden – der von Messerschmitt entworfene erste Düsenjäger der Welt. Mit 800 km/h Geschwindigkeit war er 200 km/h schneller als das schnellste Jagdflugzeug der USA. Auch das erste in Serie hergestellte Raketenflugzeug geht auf ihn zurück.

Die hier genannten Persönlichkeiten stehen exemplarisch für all diejenigen, die die Wirtschaftshistorie der Stadt durch Engagement, Wagemut, Innovationsbereitschaft und Kreativität geprägt haben. Sie begründeten den heutigen Stellenwert Münchens als Unternehmensstandort. Dieser wird auch dadurch dokumentiert, dass „global player" wie Siemens und BMW hier nach wie vor ihr Stammhaus haben. Während BMW als Münchner Traditionsunternehmen seit seiner Gründung im Jahre 1916 am Oberwiesenfeld ansässig ist, verlagerte Siemens nach dem Zweiten Weltkrieg seinen Hauptsitz von Berlin nach München und legte damit den Grundstein für die Entwicklung der Hochtechnologie und Elektronik in der Region.

München hat sich den ständig wechselnden Anforderungen des internationalen Wirtschaftsgeschehens stets durch schnellen Strukturwandel angepasst und sich so seine Attraktivität als Unternehmensstandort bewahrt. Heute ist die Stadt ein bedeutendes internationales Zentrum für innovative Technologien, für Forschung und Entwicklung sowie für hochqualifizierte Dienstleister wie die Unternehmensberatung Roland Berger & Partner. Als Sitz aller führenden deutschen Venture-Capital-Fonds bietet es ausgezeichnete Startbedingungen für Unternehmer. Allein 1998 wurden mehr als eine Milliarde DM an Risikokapital zur Verfügung gestellt. Mit jährlich rund 15 000 Unternehmensneugründungen gilt München heute als wichtiges Gründerzentrum.

Roland Berger

American fighter planes. Messerschmitt also invented the first rocket-assist airplane.

The famous men described above are only a few of the many entrepreneurs who have influenced the city's economic history with their dedication, daring, joy of innovation, and creativity. They set the standards for Munich's present-day status as an industrial centre, which is best proved by the fact that global players such as Siemens and BMW still have their parent companies in the Bavarian capital. BMW as a traditional Munich enterprise has been based at the "Oberwiesenfeld" since its founding in 1916; Siemens moved its main office from Berlin to Munich after the Second World War and thus laid the foundation for the development of high technology and electronics in this region.

Munich has always adapted very quickly to the constantly changing demands of international economy by introducing structural changes and has thus retained its attraction as an industrial centre. Today the city is an important international location for innovative technologies, for research and development, and for highly qualified service enterprises such as the Roland Berger & Partner consulting firm. As a seat of all the leading German Venture-Capital-Funds, Munich offers excellent starting conditions to new enterprises. In 1998 alone more than DM 1 billion venture capital was provided. With approximately 15,000 new enterprises per year, Munich is today regarded as one of the most significant industrial founding centres.

Roland Berger

Doté d'une vitesse de 800 km/h, sa vitesse dépassait de 200 km/h l'avion le plus rapide des USA. C'est encore lui qui produisit le premier les avions-fusées en série.

Les personnalités mentionnées ici ne sont que quelques exemples de toutes celles qui ont marqué l'histoire de l'économie de la ville par leur engagement, leur courage, leur sens de l'innovation et leur créativité. Elles jetèrent la base à la position actuelle de Munich comme site industriel. Celui-ci est aussi étayé par le fait que des «global players» comme Siemens et BMW gardèrent leur siège social à Munich. Alors que BMW, une entreprise traditionnellement munichoise, est implantée depuis sa création en 1916 à Oberwiesenfeld, Siemens transféra après la Seconde Guerre mondiale son siège principal de Berlin à Munich et posa ainsi les jalons au développement de la technologie de pointe et de l'électronique dans la région.

Munich sut toujours s'adapter aux exigences changeantes de la situation économique internationale par une mutation structurelle rapide et sut garder une grande attractivité comme site industriel. Aujourd'hui, la ville est un centre international important pour les technologies novatrices, la recherche et le développement ainsi que pour les prestataires de service d'excellente qualité comme la société conseil Roland Berger & Partner. Comme siège de tous les fonds venture-capital allemands majeurs, elle offre des conditions de départ idéales pour les entrepreneurs. Rien qu'en 1998, plus d'un milliard de DM de capital de risque fut mis à disposition. Avec environ 15 000 créations d'entreprises chaque année, Munich est aujourd'hui un centre important pour les nouvelles entreprises.

Roland Berger

tenere qui la loro sede centrale. Mentre la BMW, un'azienda che è diventata parte integrante della tradizione monacense, risiede presso l'Oberwiesenfeld fin dal 1916, anno della sua fondazione, la Siemens ha trasferito la sua sede da Berlino a Monaco dopo la Seconda Guerra Mondiale ponendo, in tal modo, la prima pietra del futuro sviluppo dell'alta tecnologia e dell'elettronica della regione.

Monaco è sempre riuscita ad adattarsi ai cambiamenti continui delle esigenze del mercato internazionale adeguando rapidamente le proprie strutture e riuscendo a conservare, in tal modo, la sua particolare attrattiva come sito industriale. Oggi, la città è un importante punto di riferimento, su scala mondiale, per le tecnologie innovative, la ricerca e la progettazione, nonché per aziende di servizi altamente qualificate quali, ad esempio, l'impresa di consulenza aziendale Roland Berger & Partner. Trovandosi qui la sede di tutti i maggiori fondi di investimento di venture capital della Germania, Monaco offre agli imprenditori eccellenti condizioni di partenza per le loro attività. Ad esempio, nel solo 1998 è stato messo a disposizione capitale di rischio per oltre un miliardo di marchi. Con circa 15 000 nuove aziende all'anno Monaco può venir considerata indubbiamente un importante centro di sviluppo imprenditoriale.

Roland Berger

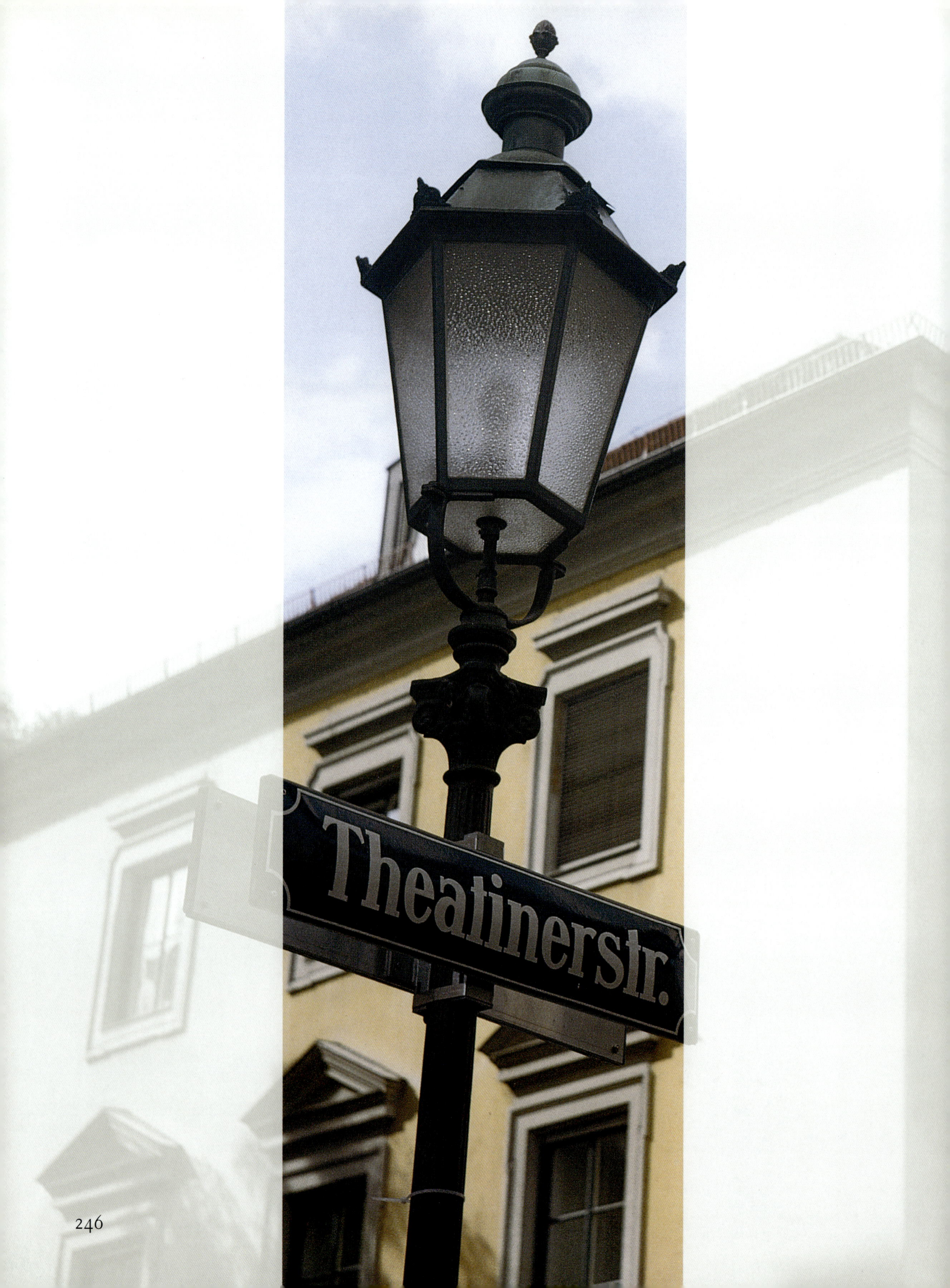
Theatinerstr.

Einkaufen in München

Shopping in Munich

Le shopping à Munich

Fare shopping a Monaco

Ist vom Einkaufen in München die Rede, denkt man an die Innenstadt – an die Fußgängerzone, den Stachus, den Marienplatz oder an die Theatiner- und Maximilianstraße; vielleicht auch an eine der vielen Nebenstraßen, wo man ein Geschäft kennt, in dem man Besonderes sucht und findet. Diese Innenstadt innerhalb des Altstadtringes ist 1,4 Quadratkilometer groß. Ja, Sie haben richtig gelesen, sie ist nur 1,4 Quadratkilometer groß, und trotzdem spielt sich hier so viel des Münchner Alltags ab. Hier befinden sich die Hauptgeschäftslagen des Einzelhandels. Hier gibt es Wirtschafts- und Dienstleistungsunternehmen, Kunst und Kultur ebenso wie eine vielfältige Gastronomie und natürlich auch die Behörden. Das Straßenbild prägen die Menschen, die hier einkaufen oder hier arbeiten und nicht zuletzt die Besucher aus aller Welt.

Wie eine das Publikum faszinierende Bühne lebt auch solch eine Stadt von einer überzeugenden, perfekten Inszenierung. Voraussetzung dafür war, dass München gut und problemlos zu erreichen ist und dass sich die Menschen in den großen Fußgängerbereichen der Innenstadt wohlfühlen können. Dafür haben Stadtplaner und Kommunalpolitiker vorbildlich gesorgt. Das Nahverkehrsnetz verläuft sternförmig zum Mittelpunkt der Stadt. Wer z. B. am Starnberger See in die S-Bahn einsteigt, ist in 30 Minuten am Marienplatz, der von einem Münchner Stadtteil aus mit der U-Bahn in 15 Minuten zu erreichen ist.

Um München zu erleben, um hier zu arbeiten, einzukaufen oder die Freizeit zu genießen, benutzen 75 % der Bürger den öffentlichen Personennahverkehr. Wer will, kann auch per Auto in die Innenstadt kommen: Eine Stunde Kurzparken an den Straßen kostet so viel wie eine Tasse Kaffee; für Langzeitparker gibt es Parkhäuser.

München ist eine pulsierende, internationale Stadt mit einer

When talking of shopping in Munich, we automatically think of the city centre – the pedestrian zone, the Stachus, Marienplatz, Theatinerstraße or Maximilianstraße; we might include in our shopping area one of the numerous side streets where we have found a store offering some special or unusual articles. The centre of Munich – surrounded by the "Altstadtring", a ring road encircling this oldest part of Munich – covers only 1.4 square kilometres. Yes, it is true, only 1.4 square kilometres; but a considerable part of Munich's everyday life takes place in this area. Here you find the most important retail stores; commercial and service enterprises; art and culture; a wealth of restaurants, cafés and pubs; and, naturally, many of the municipal authorities and public offices. The cityscape is formed by the people shopping and working here, and by the visitors from all parts of the world.

Like a fascinating theatre stage a city also lives off and through a convincing and perfect setting; in the case of Munich, this setting required easy access and large pedestrian zones in the centre which "natives" and guests could enjoy. City planners and the local politicians have provided the necessary advantages in an exemplary way. The short-distance transport network leads radially to the suburbs with Marienplatz as the hub. If you board a suburban train at Lake Starnberg you reach Munich in 30 minutes; it takes only 15 minutes to get from one of the city districts to the town centre by subway.

75 % of the local people use the public transport system to get to their working places, to shop, go sightseeing or enjoy their leisure-time in Munich. You can certainly go by car as well: to park for an hour along one of the streets costs as much (or as little) as a cup of coffee. And if you intend to remain longer, you can leave your vehicle in one of the multi-storey car parks.

Dès qu'il s'agit de shopping à Munich, on pense tout de suite au centre ville, à la zone piétonne, le Stachus, la Marienplatz ou aux rues Theatiner et Maximilian, éventuellement aussi à une des nombreuses rues adjacentes où l'on connaît une boutique dans laquelle on peut chercher et trouver quelque chose de spécial. Ce centre ville situé au sein de l'ancien boulevard de ceinture s'étend sur 1,4 kilomètre carré. Oui, vous avez bien lu, il s'étend seulement sur 1,4 kilomètre carré

Quando si parla di shopping a Monaco si pensa subito al centro città – alla zona pedonale, a Stachus, a Marienplatz o alla Theatinerstraße e alla Maximilianstraße; forse anche ad una delle tante stradine secondarie dove si trova il tal negozio in cui vendono qualcosa di particolare. Il centro di Monaco, che è compreso all'interno dell'anello del centro storico, ha un'ampiezza di 1,4 chilometri quadrati. Sì, avete letto bene, solo di 1,4 chilometri quadrati, e ciononostante buona par-

modernen und zukunftsorientierten Konzeption, wobei die Stadtplaner darauf bedacht waren und sind, die architektonische Optik Münchens als Residenzstadt, als Kunst- und Kulturstadt zu bewahren.

Was aber macht den unverwechselbaren Charakter dieser Stadt aus? Im Gehbereich der City stehen der Alte Peter, Münchens älteste Kirche, und der Liebfrauendom; unweit davon das Alte und Neue Rathaus mit dem Glockenspiel, die Asam- und die

Munich is a pulsating international city with a modern and future-oriented atmosphere; nevertheless the city planners have always tried carefully to preserve Munich's architectural flair as a former royal residence and as a centre of art and culture.

What makes Munich so unique and unmistakable in character? Attractions like the "Alte Peter" (Munich's oldest church) and the "Liebfrauendom" (the cathedral); the Old Town Hall and the New Town Hall with its carillon; Asam-

et, malgré tout, la plus grande partie du quotidien de Munich s'y joue. C'est là que se trouvent les principaux magasins du commerce de détail. Sans oublier les sociétés de l'économie et du secteur tertiaire, l'art et la culture mais aussi une gastronomie très variée et bien entendu les administrations. La présentation des rues marque les personnes venant y faire leur shopping ou y travailler, il en va de même pour les visiteurs du monde entier.

te della vita quotidiana di Monaco si svolge proprio qui, dove si trovano i migliori indirizzi del commercio al minuto. Hanno sede qui imprese commerciali e di servizi, qui si svolge la vita artistica e culturale della città, ma si trovano anche una ricca scelta di negozi di specialità gastronomiche e, naturalmente, gli uffici amministrativi della città. Il quadro delle vie di Monaco è infine caratterizzato dalle persone che vengono qui ad effettuare i propri acquisti, a lavorare e, non da ultimo, dai

Einkaufen in München – Angebot und Umgebung machen es zum Vergnügen.

Shopping in Munich - pleasurable offer and surroundings

Le shopping à Munich – L'offre et l'ambiance en font un vrai régal.

Fare shopping a Monaco – l'assortimento proposto e l'ambiente lo trasformano in un vero divertimento.

Patrona Bavariae und Frauentürme grüßen uns.

Greetings from the Patrona Bavariae, patron saint of the Land, and the towers of the cathedrale

Patrona Bavariae et les tours de la cathédrale nous saluent.

Il benvenuto di Patrona Bavariae e dei campanili del Duomo

Theatinerkirche, die Oper, die Staatstheater und die Residenz, das Stadtmuseum und der Wittelsbacher Brunnen und noch sehr viel mehr. Und hier befinden sich auch die Hauptgeschäftslagen: eine Atmosphäre, die man selbstverständlich in keinem Shoppingcenter auf der grünen Wiese erleben kann.

Kommen wir auf die Inszenierung zurück: Die Bühne der Einkaufsstadt München ist perfekt. Was machen die vielen Einzelhändler als Regisseure mit ihren Ensembles? Was erlebt das sogenannte Publikum? Gehen wir auf den Viktualienmarkt. Sein Lokalkolorit ist ein Glanzstück in der Darstellung Münchens und nur wenige Schritte vom Rathaus entfernt. Welch andere Stadt hat in ihrem Herzen einen so großen täglichen Markt für Lebensmittel zu bieten? Zauberhaft gestaltet, präsentiert er sich mit einer Angebotsfülle in höchster Qualität. Damit der Besucher diese Atmo-

kirche and Theatinerkirche (two outstanding churches); the opera house, the state theatres and the "Residenz" (the former royal palace); the municipal museum; Wittelsbach Fountain, and many other spectacular sights, which can all be reached on foot. And between them you find the best shopping areas, permeated with an atmosphere you will certainly not find in a shopping centre in a green field location.

But let us get back to our scenery; the stage of the shopping centre of Munich is perfect. How do the local retailers (in their function as stage directors) handle their actors? How do the spectators (the public) react to the "play"? Let us take a look at "Viktualienmarkt", a market only a few steps from the Town Hall, whose local colour is one of the highlights in the presentation of Munich. Is there any other city which boasts such a large daily food market right in its centre? Beautifully arranged, the wealth of high-quality merchandise catches every eye. To allow visitors to enjoy this atmosphere to the fullest, a beer garden has been established where guests can have a snack in the shade of large chestnut trees; all around them they can admire poultry straight from the farm; delicious herbs and spices from every part of the world; crayfish from Lower

Comme une scène fascinant son public, une telle ville vit également d'une mise en scène parfaite et convaincante. Pour cela, il fallait que Munich soit facilement accessible et que les personnes se sentent à l'aise dans les vastes zones piétonnes du centre ville. Les urbanistes et les politiciens communaux y ont veillé tout particulièrement. Le réseau de transport interurbain part en étoile autour de la ville. Celui qui, par exemple, monte dans la S-Bahn (RER) au lac de Starnberg met 30 minutes pour arriver à la Marienplatz et rejoint de là en un quart d'heure de métro d'autres quartiers de Munich.

Pour connaître Munich, aller au travail, faire du shopping ou pour profiter de leurs loisirs, 75 % des citoyens utilisent les moyens de transport collectif. Il est également possible d'accéder au centre ville en voiture: une heure de parking à courte durée dans les rues coûte autant qu'une tasse de café, pour des durées plus longues, des parkings sont à disposition.

Munich est une ville animée et internationale, de conception moderne et futuriste bien que les urbanistes aient tout fait pour garder l'optique architectonique de Munich comme ancienne ville de résidence de la cour de Bavière, comme ville artistique et culturelle.

Mais d'où vient le caractère unique de cette ville? A quelques pas du centre, se trouvent l'Alter Peter (l'église St. Pierre), la plus vieille église de Munich, et la cathédrale Notre-Dame; à côté le nouveau et l'ancien hôtel de ville avec le jacquemart, l'église Asam et l'église des Théatins, l'opéra, les théâtres nationaux et la Residenz, le musée municipal et la fontaine des Wittelsbach et bien d'autres encore. Et c'est également là que se trouvent les principaux magasins: une atmosphère que l'on ne retrouve certainement pas dans un centre commercial implanté aux abords de la ville.

visitatori che provengono da tutto il mondo.

Come un palcoscenico che affascina il proprio pubblico, così Monaco vive e gode di un perfetto e convincente allestimento. Ciò è consentito dal fatto che la città è facilmente raggiungibile da ogni direzione e che le persone possono sentirsi a proprio agio nelle grandi zone pedonali del centro. A ciò hanno provveduto in modo esemplare gli ingegneri urbanistici e i politici comunali. La rete del traffico locale si snoda a stella fino a raggiungere il centro della città. Chi sale, ad esempio, sulla ferrovia urbana (S-Bahn) alla fermata del Lago di Starnberg può essere a Marienplatz in 30 minuti, una destinazione raggiungibile comunque in 15 minuti da qualsiasi quartiere di Monaco con la metropolitana.

Il 75% degli abitanti di Monaco utilizza i servizi di trasporto pubblico per vivere, lavorare, fare compere o per godere del proprio tempo libero. Chi lo preferisce, può raggiungere il centro città

Mais revenons à la mise en scène: la scène Munich, ville de shopping par excellence, est parfaite. Que font les détaillants comme metteurs en scène avec leurs ensembles? Que vit le public? Allons faire un tour sur le Viktualienmarkt (marché aux victuailles). Son coloris local est une merveille dans la présentation de Munich et est seulement à quelques pas de l'hôtel de ville. Quelle autre ville peut se targuer d'un aussi grand marché quotidien d'alimentation en son centre? Magnifiquement conçu, il présente une offre incroyable de produits de la plus haute qualité. Afin que le visiteur puisse également jouir de cette atmosphère, un jardin de la bière invite à prendre une collation à l'ombre de ses châtaigniers. Et cela entre les volailles de la ferme, les herbes et les épices odorantes venant des quatre coins du monde, entre les crabes de Basse-Bavière et une offre de fromages à la parisienne. Ce marché aux victuailles est une fête des sens où les grands chefs cuisiniers de Munich croisent les Munichois et de nombreux touristes.

Les grandes zones piétonnes offrent une fête des sens d'un tout autre genre. Les économistes prétendent que l'espace piétonnier s'étendant entre la Marienplatz et le Karlstor est une des rues commerçantes les plus anche con l'auto: un'ora di sosta nei parcheggi lungo le strade costa quanto una tazzina di caffè; per soste più lunghe si può lasciare la propria macchina negli autosilo.

Monaco è una città pulsante ed internazionale, di concezione moderna ed orientata al futuro, progettata tuttavia con l'obiettivo di mantenere l'ottica architettonica di Monaco quale Residenzstadt (città sede della Residenza dei duchi di Baviera) e di città delle arti e della cultura.

Ma cosa rende così inconfondibile il carattere di questa città? Nell'ampia zona pedonale si trovano l'Alter Peter, la chiesa più antica di Monaco, e la Cattedrale della Nostra Signora; non lontano da qui vi sono il Vecchio Municipio e il Nuovo Municipio con il famoso orologio-carillon, la Chiesa di Asam e la Chiesa dei Teatini, l'Opera di Stato bavarese, il Teatro di Stato bavarese e la Residenza, il Museo Comunale, la Fontana dei Wittelsbach e molto ancora. E qui si trovano anche i negozi più «in»: un'atmosfera che non si può ritrovare, ovviamente, in nessun centro commerciale sulla «grüne Wiese».

Ma ritorniamo alla messa in scena: il palcoscenico di questa città è perfetto per lo shopping. Come orchestrano i loro «ensembles» i tanti commercianti al dettaglio – registi della città? A cosa

Der Viktualienmarkt, berühmte Lebensmittel-Oase Münchens und zugleich lebendigstes und originellstes Viertel der Stadt

The Viktualienmarkt, Munich's famous food oasis and also most vivid and original district of the town

Le Viktualienmarkt, une oasis célèbre et en même temps le quartier le plus animé et le plus original de la ville

Il Mercato delle Vettovaglie, l'oasi di generi alimentari monacense famosa e, contemporaneamente, il quartiere più vivace ed originale della città

sphäre auch genießen kann, lädt ein Biergarten unter schattigen Kastanien zur Brotzeit ein. Und dies zwischen Geflügel vom Bauernhof, köstlichen Kräutern und Gewürzen aus aller Herren Länder, zwischen niederbayerischen Krebsen und einem Käseangebot à la parisienne. Dieser Viktualienmarkt ist ein Fest für die Sinne, wo Münchner Meisterköche mit den Münchnern und den vielen Touristen aufeinandertreffen.

Ein Fest für die Sinne ganz anderer Art sind die Fußgängerbereiche. Von der Fußgängerzone zwischen Marienplatz und dem Karlstor sagen die Wirtschaftsforscher, dass es die am meisten besuchte Einkaufsstraße Deutschlands sei. Wie auch immer, an manchen Tagen kann man – oder muss man – in diesem Fußgängerbereich ein Bad in der Menge nehmen. Weniger eng ist es in der eleganten Theatiner- und Maximilianstraße. Hier flaniert man weltstädtisch.

Der Einzelhandel präsentiert seinem Publikum sozusagen eine internationale Bühne: von der weltweiten Vielfalt der qualitativ hochwertigen Mode bis zum professionellen In-Artikel des Sports, von den Düften der Parfümerien bis zu den Kostbarkeiten des Bavaria; and a cheese assortment à la parisienne. At Munich's Viktualienmarkt where the city's chief cooks and the local people and visitors meet, you cannot only feast your eyes but also your other senses.

Entirely different sensual experiences can be gained in the city's pedestrian zones. Economic experts tell us that the area between Marienplatz and the "Karlstor" gate is Germany's most popular shopping mile. You will in any case be caught in the throng of shoppers on certain days, whether you want to or not. In elegant Theatinerstraße and Maximilianstraße the squeeze is less pronounced; here you can stroll at greater leisure in a cosmopolitan atmosphere.

The retail trade presents to the public something like an international stage: here you find everything – from the creations of high visitées d'Allemagne. Quoi qu'il en soit, emprunter cette rue revient certains jours à prendre un bain de marée humaine. Dans les élégantes rues Theatiner ou Maximilian, la foule y est moins dense. Ici on flâne dans une métropole.

Le commerce de détail présente à son public une scène internationale qu'il s'agisse de la variété mondiale de la mode de grande qualité ou des dernières nouveautés professionnelles du sport, des senteurs des parfumeries ou des merveilles des bijoutiers, de la tradition bavaroise ou de l'art moderne dans 50 galeries, de la technologie électronique ou des vins d'Afrique du Sud.

Et comme toute scène a ses acteurs, il en va de même sur la scène du commerce de détail à Munich: des magasins de réputation ultrarégionale qui sont devenus de véritables institutions assiste il cosiddetto pubblico? Andiamo al Viktualienmarkt (mercato dei generi alimentari freschi). Il suo colorito locale è un cavallo di battaglia nella rappresentazione di Monaco e dista solo pochi passi dal municipio. Quale altra città può offrire nel proprio cuore un mercato quotidiano così grande di generi alimentari? Strutturato in modo incantevole, si presenta con una vasta gamma di offerte di alta qualità. Affinché il visitatore possa anche godere di questa atmosfera, può rinfrescarsi all'ombra dei castani di una birreria all'aperto e fare uno spuntino. E tutto questo in mezzo a pollame di fattoria, erbe deliziose e spezie provenienti da tutti i paesi, gamberi della Bassa Baviera e una scelta di formaggi «à la parisienne». Questo Viktualienmarkt è una festa per i sensi, dove i chef di Monaco si ritrovano insieme ai monachesi e a molti turisti.

Theatinerstraße – elegante Geschäfte und gemütliche Lokale laden zu einem Bummel ein.

Theatinerstraße – elegant shops and cozy restaurants invite to a stroll.

La rue Theatinerstraße – des boutiques élégantes et des restaurants conviviaux vous invitent à la promenade.

La Theatinerstraße – eleganti negozi e confortevoli locali invitano a farvi un giro

*Seit über 400 Jahren findet man den Namen **Oberpollinger** in den Statuten der Stadt verzeichnet. Aus einer Bräustätte wurde später eine Gaststätte und ein Hotel. 1905 eröffnete das Kaufhaus Oberpollinger, erbaut von Prof. Littmann. 1927 übernahm Karstadt den „Oberpollinger". Heute ist das Haus Oberpollinger mit ca. 40 000 m² das größte Warenhaus Bayerns und zählt zu den Flaggschiffen des Karstadt-Konzerns.*

*For more than 400 years the name of **Oberpollinger** has figured in the city statutes. A brewery was first turned into a restaurant and hotel. In 1905 the Oberpollinger Department Store – built by Prof. Littmann – opened its doors to the public. In 1927 Karstadt took over the Oberpollinger Store. Having a floor space of approximately 40,000 square metres, this building is today Bavaria's largest department store and one of the Karstadt Concern's major showpieces.*

*Le nom **Oberpollinger** est mentionné depuis plus de 400 ans dans les statuts de la ville. L'ancienne brasserie fut transformée en restaurant et hôtel. Le grand magasin Oberpollinger construit par le Prof. Littmann fut inauguré en 1905. Il fut repris en 1927 par Karstadt. La maison Oberpollinger est le plus grand magasin de grand détail de Bavière avec une superficie de 40 000 m² environ et compte parmi les plus beaux fleurons du groupe d'entreprises Karstadt.*

*Il nome **Oberpollinger** si trova registrato negli statuti della città da oltre 400 anni. L'originaria fabbrica di birra diventò, più tardi, ristorante ed albergo. Nel 1905 aprì i battenti il grande magazzino Oberpollinger, costruito dal Prof. Littmann. Nel 1927, l'«Oberpollinger» venne rilevato dalla Karstadt. Oggi l'«Haus Oberpollinger», con i suoi 40 000 mq, è il grande magazzino più esteso della Baviera e viene annoverato tra le «ammiraglie» del Gruppo Karstadt.*

Juweliers, vom bayrisch Traditionellen bis zu moderner Kunst in 50 Galerien, von der E-Technologie bis zum südafrikanischen Wein.

Und wie jede Bühne ihre Hauptdarsteller hat, gibt es solche auch auf der Einzelhandelsbühne in München: überregional bekannte Geschäfte, die zur Münchner Institution geworden sind, wie Hugendubel als größter Buchhändler Deutschlands, Loden-Frey für traditionelle und moderne Bekleidung, Dallmayr, das Feinkosthaus für höchste Ansprüche, Ludwig Beck am Rathauseck als „Kaufhaus der Sinne" oder Hirmer, das anerkannt größte Geschäft für Herrenmode. Auch die Warenhäuser in München sind anders, weil sie alle als „Nr.1-Häuser" der Konzerne geführt werden. Zu den Anziehungspunkten der Innenstadt zählen aber auch die vielen kleinen Geschäfte. Man entdeckt sie zum Teil in Nebenstraßen, nur einen Sprung vom Fußgängerstrom entfernt.

Dies also ist die unverwechselbare Einzelhandelsbühne Münchens. Insgesamt eine Bühne, die das Publikum anregt, selbst fashion to trend articles of professional sports; from the exquisite scents in drugstores to the treasures in jewellery stores; from traditional to modern works of art in 50 local galleries; and from E-technology to South-African wine.

And just as every stage has its famous actors, the retail "stage" boasts its own stars as well: stores renowned far beyond the regional limits which have become standard fixtures of Munich: Hugendubel, for instance, Germany's biggest book dealer; Loden-Frey, famous for traditional and modern clothing; Dallmayr, a delicatessen catering to the most exacting palates; Ludwig Beck am Rathauseck which is called the "Kaufhaus der Sinne"; and Hirmer, the admittedly biggest men's outfitter. Even Munich's department stores are different from those in other cities, for all of them enjoy the status of "Nr.1 stores" of their respective groups. But also the numerous small shops attract many customers; they can be discovered in side streets only a few steps from the large crowds in the main shopping malls.

munichoises comme Hugendubel, la plus grande librairie d'Allemagne, Loden-Frey pour la confection traditionnelle et moderne, Dallmayr, l'épicerie fine satisfaisant les exigences les plus élevées, Ludwig Beck am Rathauseck, au coin de l'hôtel de ville et surnommé le «grand magasin des sens» ou Hirmer, jouissant d'un grand renom pour la confection masculine. Et les grands magasins sont également différents à Munich car tous les grands groupes les dirigent comme les «numéros un» de leur établissement. Mais les nombreuses petites boutiques sont des points d'attraction non négligeables du centre ville. On les découvre parfois dans les rues adjacentes, à quelques pas des grandes artères piétonnes.

Voilà donc la scène unique du commerce de détail de Munich. En fait une scène motivant le public à devenir lui-même acteur et qui donne – du moins espérons le – l'impression aux visiteurs de se dire «cela a encore valu la peine d'être là».

Les journalistes ont toujours affublé Munich de surnoms satiri-

Una festa per i sensi, ma di tutt'altro tipo sono le zone pedonali. La zona pedonale tra Marienplatz e Karlstor è definita dagli economi come la via per lo shopping in assoluto più visitata di tutta la Germania. Sia come sia, in alcuni giorni in questa via è possibile – o si deve – fare un bagno di folla. Si sta un po' meno stretti nella Theatinerstraße o nella Maximilianstraße, dove si passeggia in un'atmosfera più metropolitana.

Il commerciante al dettaglio presenta, per così dire al suo pubblico, un palcoscenico internazionale: dalla varietà di scelta della moda di alta qualità agli articoli «in» e professionali per lo sport, dai profumi ai gioielli, dagli articoli tradizionali bavaresi all'arte moderna (vi sono ben 50 gallerie), dalla tecnologia elettronica ai vini sudafricani.

E così come ogni palcoscenico ha il suo attore principale, ci sono attori principali anche sul palcoscenico del commercio al dettaglio di Monaco: negozi conosciuti oltre i confini regionali, diventati ormai un'istituzione, come Hugendubel, la più grande libreria della Germania, Loden-Frey per vestiti tradizionali e moderni, Dallmayr, il negozio di specialità gastronomiche per i clienti più esigenti, Ludwig Beck, all'angolo del municipio, conosciuto come «il grande magazzino dei sensi», o ancora Hirmer, conosciuto come il più grande negozio per la moda maschile. Anche i grandi magazzini sono diversi a Monaco, in quanto sono ciascuno il «N° 1» del rispettivo gruppo. Ma tra i punti di maggiore attrazione del centro devono essere ricordati anche i tanti piccoli negozi che rimangono quasi nascosti nelle vie secondarie, ad un tiro di schioppo dalla via principale.

Questo è dunque l'inconfondibile palcoscenico del commercio al dettaglio di Monaco. Riassumendo, un palcoscenico che stimola il pubblico a diventare esso stesso attore e che spera di dare ai visitatori quella sensazione che «anche questa volta è valsa la pena di essere stati qui».

Alles unter einem Dach: links im „pep" Einkaufs-Center Neuperlach, rechts im Flughafen München

Everything under one roof: on the left in the "pep" shopping mall in Neuperlach, on the right in Munich's airport

Tout sous un toit : à gauche au «pep» au centre commercial de Neuperlach, à droite a l' aéroport de Munich

Tutto sotto lo stesso tetto: a sinistra lo shopping center «pep» di Neuperlach, a destra all'aeroporto di Monaco

zum Akteur zu werden und den Besuchern hoffentlich das Gefühl gibt, „es hat sich wieder einmal gelohnt, dagewesen zu sein".

Von Journalisten hat München immer wieder satirische oder anerkennende Beinamen erhalten: Isar-Athen, Millionendorf, Bierstadt, Weltstadt mit Herz, heimliche Hauptstadt, Residenzstadt usw. Zuletzt konnte man auch „Hauptstadt des Konsums" lesen. Je nach Standpunkt oder Situation kann man solche Bonmots mögen oder vergessen. Aber dass Konsum, dass Einkaufen in der überzeugend inszenierten Stadt München schön, interessant und günstig ist und außerdem Spaß macht, das wissen Münchner, das weiß das Umland der Stadt und das wissen Münchens Besucher aus aller Welt. Deshalb: „Grüß Gott, Hallo, Ciao, Servus und Tschüss in München!"

Hermann Rückl

This is Munich's unmistakable "retail stage" – a stage which induces spectators to turn into actors themselves and to say, well-satisfied: "It was worth to have come to Munich."

Journalists have bestowed many satirical or appreciatory epithets on Munich over and over again: they have called it the "Isar Athens", "Village with One Million Inhabitants", "Beer City", "Metropolis with a Heart", "Secret Capital", "Residence" etc. Lately it was even named "Capital of Consumption". You may like or dislike such appellations according to your views or situation. But the inhabitants of the city and its environs, as well as the visitors from all parts of the world know that shopping in the convincingly staged city of Munich is pleasant, interesting and advantageous and, additionally, a lot of fun. We therefore greet you in Munich only with a hearty "Grüß Gott, Hello, Ciao, Servus and Tschüss".

Hermann Rückl

ques ou élogieux: l'Athènes de l'Isar, le village de plus d'un million d'habitants, la ville de la bière, la métropole au grand cœur, la capitale secrète, la ville de Residenz etc. Dernièrement, on pouvait également lire «la capitale de la consommation». En fonction de son opinion ou de la situation, on peut apprécier ou oublier ces bons mots. Mais que la consommation, que le shopping dans Munich, ville mise en scène de manière convaincante, soient agréables, intéressants, abordables et un véritable plaisir, les Munichois le savent, les environs de Munich le savent et les visiteurs venant des quatre coins du monde le savent aussi. C'est pourquoi, nous saluons la ville: «Grüß Gott, Hallo, Ciao, Servus et Tschüss à Munich.»

Hermann Rückl

I giornalisti hanno da sempre affibbiato a Monaco appellativi lusinghieri e non: Atene sull'Isar, il paese di un milione di abitanti, la città della birra, la metropoli con sentimento, la capitale segreta, la città della Residenza, ecc. Da ultimo, la si può chiamare anche «capitale del consumo». A seconda del punto di vista o della situazione, questi soprannomi possono piacere o essere dimenticati. Ma che i negozi e lo shopping in questa città, allestita in modo così convincente, siano belli, interessanti, convenienti e divertenti lo sanno gli abitanti stessi, lo sanno quelli dei paesi circostanti e i visitatori provenienti da tutto il mondo. Quindi: «Grüß Gott, Hallo, Ciao, Servus e Tschüss a Monaco!»

Hermann Rückl

Istanbul
Lissabon
Rom
Berlin/Tegel
Budapest
Florenz
Frankfurt/Main
Köln/Bonn
Nizza
RTM-Antwerpen
Mailand/Linate
Triest
Verona
Bologna
Lufthansa

Weltstadt mit „Hub"

Metropolis with Hub

La ville mondiale et sa «plaque-tournante»

Una metropoli e il suo scalo

Millionen Geschäftsreisende und Touristen aus allen Teilen der Erde strömen Jahr für Jahr nach München, und ihre Zahl wächst kontinuierlich. Betrachtet man die Besucherfrequenz in Relation zur Einwohnerzahl, so liegt die Stadt unangefochten an der Spitze der deutschen Metropolen.

Münchens grenzüberschreitende Anziehungskraft ist auch daran zu erkennen, dass der Anteil ausländischer Besucher stabil über 40 % liegt. Unter den internationalen Gästen der Landeshauptstadt stellen die Amerikaner nach wie vor die größte Gruppe. Für sie - wie für zahlreiche andere Besucher aus dem In- und Ausland - beginnt der Aufenthalt an der Isar mit der Landung auf dem Münchner Flughafen. Als moderne Infrastruktureinrichtung, aber auch als repräsentative „Empfangshalle" der Landeshauptstadt, gehört der Flughafen damit buchstäblich zu den ersten Adressen Münchens.

Der am 17. Mai 1992 in Betrieb genommene Airport hat sich binnen weniger Jahre zu einer der zehn größten europäischen Verkehrsdrehscheiben entwickelt. Rund 80 Fluggesellschaften, die den Flughafen München regelmäßig ansteuern, sorgen für eine optimale Anbindung der bayerischen Landeshauptstadt an das weltumspannende Luftverkehrsnetz. In alphabetischer Folge vereint der Flugplan des Münchner Airports von Abu Dhabi bis Zürich ein breites Spektrum von attraktiven Destinationen, die von München aus schnell und bequem zu erreichen sind. Neben innerdeutschen und europäischen Reisezielen bietet das dicht geknüpfte Streckennetz auch zahlreiche Non-Stop-Verbindungen im Interkontinentalverkehr.

Seit 1995 baut die Deutsche Lufthansa den Münchner Flughafen schrittweise zu ihrem zweiten Knotenpunkt aus. Als ein sogenanntes „Hub" des internationalen Luftverkehrs zieht München Verkehrsströme an, die über das originäre Einzugsgebiet des Flughafens hinausgehen. Der Umsteiger, früher ein gern aber selten gesehener Gast auf dem Münch-

Millions of businessmen and tourists from all parts of the globe flock to Munich every year, and their number is increasing steadily. If we consider these figures in relation to the number of inhabitants we find that Munich is the undisputed leader of all German metropolises as far as visitors are concerned.

Munich's cross-border attraction is also evidenced by the fact that the share of foreigners coming to the city has remained stable at more than 40 % for quite some time, Americans constituting the largest group. For them and for numerous visitors from Germany and abroad their stay starts with their arrival at Munich Airport. In its function as a modern element of the local infrastructure and as the very impressive "reception hall" of the Bavarian capital, the airport is one of Munich's best addresses.

Opened on 17 May 1992, Munich Airport has become one of Europe's ten most important traffic turnstiles within a few years. Approximately 80 airlines, which serve Munich Airport regularly, provide optimum integration into the worldwide network of air routes. The flight schedule comprises - in alphabetical order from Abu Dhabi to Zurich - a wide range of attractive destinations, all of which can be reached quickly and comfortably from Munich. In addition to domestic and European destinations the dense flight network also offers numerous non-stop connecting flights within the intercontinental traffic network.

Since 1995 the German Lufthansa has developed - step by step - Munich Airport to turn it into its second main flight centre. As a so-called "hub" of international air traffic, Munich attracts masses of passengers who no longer come from the airport's original "catchment" area. People changing their plane in Munich, who were welcome but rare in former days, have by now become a significant factor for traffic planners. Today their share of the entire passenger incidence

Des millions d'hommes d'affaires et de touristes des quatre coins du monde viennent chaque année à Munich et leur nombre n'arrête pas d'augmenter. Si l'on considère la fréquence des visiteurs par rapport au nombre d'habitants, la ville arrive largement en tête de toutes les métropoles allemandes.

Le pouvoir d'attraction transfrontalier de Munich se manifeste aussi dans le fait que le pourcentage des visiteurs étrangers dépasse constamment les 40 %. Parmi les visiteurs internationaux séjournant dans la capitale de la Bavière, les Américains forment encore le groupe le plus représenté. Pour eux, ainsi que pour de nombreux autres visiteurs allemands et étrangers, le séjour aux bords de l'Isar commence par un atterrissage à l'aéroport de Munich. Comme installation d'infrastructure moderne mais aussi comme «salle d'accueil» représentante de la capitale du land, l'aéroport compte vraiment parmi les premières adresses de Munich.

L'aéroport, qui entra en fonction le 17 mai 1992, est devenu en quelques années une des dix plus importantes plates-formes européennes. Environ 80 compagnies aériennes, desservant régulièrement l'aéroport de Munich, assurent la liaison optimale de la capitale bavaroise avec le vaste réseau aérien international. Par ordre alphabétique, l'aéroport de Munich propose une vaste offre de destinations attrayantes allant d'Abu Dhabi à Zurich qui sont facilement et rapidement joignables de Munich. Outre les destinations en Allemagne et en Europe, le réseau dense propose également de nombreuses liaisons intercontinentales directes.

Depuis 1995, la compagnie aérienne Deutsche Lufthansa fait peu à peu de l'aéroport munichois son deuxième centre stratégique. Tout comme un «plaque-tournante» de la navigation aérienne internationale, Munich attire des courants de circulation dépassant le rayon d'action habituel de l'aéroport. Les passagers

Milioni di persone in viaggio d'affari e di turisti da tutte le parti del mondo affluiscono anno dopo anno a Monaco, e il loro numero cresce in continuazione. Se si considera la frequenza di visitatori rapportata al numero degli abitanti, la città si trova incontestabilmente al primo posto della classifica tra le metropoli tedesche.

L'attrattiva internazionale esercitata da Monaco di Baviera può venir individuata anche nella percentuale di visitatori stranieri che supera costantemente il 40 %. Il gruppo più consistente tra gli ospiti internazionali del capoluogo del Land è rappresentato, come di consueto, dagli americani. Per loro - così come per numerosi altri visitatori provenienti dall'estero ma anche dalla Germania - il soggiorno sull'Isar inizia con l'atterraggio all'aeroporto di Monaco. Sia come infrastruttura moderna che come «sala d'accoglienza» di rappresentanza del capoluogo del Land l'aeroporto fa parte di uno dei primi punti di riferimento della città.

Inaugurato il 17 maggio 1992 l'aeroporto si è sviluppato, in pochi anni, fino a diventare uno dei dieci maggiori snodi europei per il traffico aereo. Circa 80 compagnie aeree, che fanno rotta regolarmente sull'aeroporto di Monaco, provvedono a collegare il capoluogo bavarese, in modo ottimale, alla rete di trasporto aereo mondiale. L'orario dei voli dell'aeroporto di Monaco parte, in ordine alfabetico, da Abu Dhabi ed arriva fino a Zurigo raggruppando un ampio spettro di destinazioni estremamente attraenti che possono venir raggiunte facilmente e comodamente da Monaco stessa. Oltre a destinazioni in Germania ed Europa la fitte rete di voli offre numerosi voli non-stop intercontinentali.

Dal 1995 la Lufthansa è impegnata a trasformare gradualmente l'aeroporto di Monaco nel suo secondo nodo aeroportuale. Considerato come uno dei «perni» del traffico aereo internazionale, Monaco attira flussi di traffico che hanno ormai superato la

ner Flughafen, ist längst zu einer wichtigen Größe für die Verkehrsplaner geworden. Inzwischen liegt sein Anteil am gesamten Fluggastaufkommen in München bereits bei mehr als 25 %, Tendenz weiter steigend.

Der Flughafen München wächst mit seinen Aufgaben. Durch den bedarfsgerechten Ausbau des Airports werden die Voraussetzungen dafür geschaffen, dass sich

München Airport Center (MAC), zukunftweisende Architektur des berühmten Architekten Helmut Jahn

Munich Airport Center (MAC), trendsetting architecture by the famous architect Helmut Jahn

München Airport Center (MAC), une architecture futuriste signée par le célèbre architecte Helmut Jahn

Il München Airport Center (MAC), architettura futuristica realizzata dal famoso architetto Helmut Jahn

en transit, bien vus mais autrefois rares à l'aéroport de Munich, sont devenus depuis longtemps une grandeur non négligeable pour les planificateurs. Leur pourcentage sur l'ensemble des passagers aériens à Munich dépasse maintenant les 25 % et la tendance est à la hausse.

L'aéroport de Munich grandit en même temps que ses fonctions. Grâce à l'agrandissement

copertura operativa iniziale: Il passeggero in transito, un tempo ospite gradito ma raro dell'aeroporto di Monaco, è diventato ormai, da molto tempo, un'entità importante per i gestori del traffico aereo. Nel frattempo la sua percentuale, rapportata al numero complessivo di viaggiatori che transitano per Monaco, supera già oggi il 25 % ed è destinata a salire ancora.

die rasante Entwicklung fortsetzen kann und die Hubfunktion des Luftverkehrsstandortes München weiter gestärkt wird. Im Juni 1999 wurde das München Airport Center (MAC) in Betrieb genommen. Als ebenso attraktiver wie facettenreicher „Marktplatz" des Flughafens verbindet das MAC vom Einzelhandel über die Gastronomie bis hin zu hochwertigen Büroflächen und modern gestalteten Konferenz- und Tagungsstätten eine Vielzahl unterschiedlicher kommerzieller Angebote, die man in dieser Dichte sonst nur in der Innenstadt antrifft. Wenn im Jahr 2003 das zweite Terminal seinen Betrieb aufnimmt, wird diese „Airport-City" zugleich den unmittelbaren Übergangsbereich zwischen den beiden Terminals bilden.

Das zweite Terminal – auf eine Anfangskapazität von 15 Millionen Fluggästen pro Jahr ausgelegt – soll exklusiv von der Lufthansa und ihren Partnern genutzt werden. Die Flughafen München GmbH (FMG) und die Lufthansa haben zum Bau und Betrieb dieses Abfertigungsgebäudes Tochterunternehmen gegründet, an denen die FMG jeweils mit 60 und die Lufthansa mit 40 % beteiligt sind. In gemeinsamer unternehmerischer Verantwortung verwirklichen FMG und Lufthansa hier ein leistungsfähiges Abfertigungssystem mit kurzen Wegen, hohem Service-Standard und einer optimalen Infrastruktur für den Umsteigerverkehr.

Der bedarfsgerechte Ausbau des Münchner Flughafens erschöpft sich nicht in einer bloßen Aufstockung von Kapazitäten. Es handelt sich vielmehr um die konsequente Weiterentwicklung einer Verkehrsanlage zu einem multifunktionalen Dienstleistungszentrum von internationalem Rang. Diese Weiterentwicklung ist die Voraussetzung dafür, dass sich der Flughafen München im schärfer werdenden Wettbewerb der großen europäischen Verkehrsdrehscheiben auch behaupten kann. Als permanent wirksamer Standortfaktor liefert der Münchner Flughafen seit seinem Be-

already amounts to 25 % in Munich and tends to increase even more.

Munich Airport grows along with its duties. By enlarging and improving it to meet increasing demands, one provides the means for further rapid development and for further strenghtening Munich's hub function in air traffic. In June 1999 the Munich Airport Centre (MAC) was put in operation. As the airport's attractive and equally valuable "market place", the MAC has available a great number of commercial offers – from retail stores and gastronomic facilities, to high-class office space and modern conference and meeting places – which can only be found in similar numbers in the city centre. When the second terminal will start operating in 2003, this "Airport City" will at the same time serve as a direct passage between the two terminals.

The second terminal, initially planned to cope with approximately 15 million passengers per year, is to be used by the Lufthansa and its partners exclusively. Flughafen München GmbH (FMG) and Lufthansa have founded a subsidiary for the construction and operation of this clearance building in which FMG participated with 60 % and Lufthansa with 40 %. Together FMG and Lufthansa are putting into practice an efficient dispatch and clearing system of short distances, a high service standard, and a perfect infrastructure for change-over passengers.

The passenger-friendly development of Munich's airport is not restricted to increasing capacities. It rather means turning a traffic facility into a multifunctional service centre of international rank. This further development is to provide Munich Airport with the preconditions for retaining its position in the increasingly keener competition among Europe's major flight turnstiles. As a permanently effective locational factor Munich Airport has since its founding supplied important stimuli for the economy, the labour

nécessaire de l'aéroport, les jalons sont posés pour que le développement extrêmement rapide puisse se poursuivre et que la fonction de plaque-tournante de Munich en tant que site de la navigation aérienne soit encore renforcée. En juin 1999, le München Airport Center (MAC) entra en fonction. Tout aussi attrayant que varié, le MAC, la «place du marché» de l'aéroport, s'étend du commerce de détail à la gastronomie en passant par les bureaux de grand standing et des salles de conférences et de réunion de conception moderne, il réunit ainsi une multitude d'offres commerciales différentes que l'on ne trouve autrement dans cette densité qu'en centre ville. Lorsqu'en 2003 le deuxième terminal fonctionnera, cette «airport-city» formera en même temps l'espace transitoire direct entre les deux terminaux.

Le deuxième terminal, prévu pour pouvoir recevoir jusqu'à 15 millions de passagers par an, sera exclusivement réservé à la Lufthansa et à ses partenaires. La société Flughafen München GmbH (FMG) et la Lufthansa ont créé pour la construction et le fonctionnement de ce bâtiment d'embarquement une filiale dont la FMG détient 60 % et la Lufthansa 40 %. Dans une responsabilité commune, la FMG et la Lufthansa réalisent un système d'embarquement avec de courts déplacements, un service standard de qualité élevée et une infrastructure optimale pour le transit.

Répondant à une nécessité, l'agrandissement de l'aéroport munichois ne se limite pas à une simple augmentation des capacités. Il s'agit bien plus de la métamorphose conséquente d'une installation de communication en un centre multifonctionnel de prestations de service de rang international. Ce développement est la condition sine qua non pour que l'aéroport de Munich puisse s'affirmer face à la concurrence accrue des grandes plates-formes aériennes européennes. En tant que facteur permanent efficace du site de

L'aeroporto di Monaco cresce proporzionalmente all'aumentare dei suoi compiti. Attraverso il suo ampliamento funzionale vengono creati i presupposti per la continuazione dello sviluppo dinamico e per il consolidamento della funzione centrale dello scalo monacense. Nel giugno 1999 è stato inaugurato il München Airport Center (MAC). Questa «piazza del mercato» in aeroporto, ricca di attrattive e dalle numerose sfaccettature, concentra una tale varietà di offerte commerciali, dalla vendita al dettaglio di prodotti gastronomici ad uffici prestigiosi e a spazi moderni per conferenze e convegni, quali si potrebbero trovare solo al centro di Monaco. Nel 2003, quando entrerà in servizio il secondo terminale, questa «Airport-City» funzionerà anche da collegamento diretto tra i due terminali.

Il secondo terminale – concepito per una ricettività iniziale di 15 milioni di passeggeri all'anno – sarà destinato ad uso esclusivo della Lufthansa e dei suoi partner. Per la costruzione e la gestione di questo terminale, la Flughafen München GmbH (FMG) e la Lufthansa hanno costituito delle società affiliate alle quali la FMG partecipa sempre con il 60 % e la Lufthansa con il 40 %. Attraverso questa iniziativa imprenditoriale congiunta, la FMG e la Lufthansa hanno intenzione di realizzare un terminale passeggeri efficiente con percorsi brevi, alti standard dei servizi ed un'infrastruttura ottimale per il traffico dei passeggeri in transito.

L'ampliamento funzionale dell'aeroporto di Monaco di Baviera non si esaurisce in un semplice rafforzamento delle sue capacità. Si tratta, piuttosto, dell'evoluzione coerente di un'infrastruttura adibita prevalentemente al traffico di passeggeri in un centro multifunzionale di servizi di importanza internazionale. Questa evoluzione rappresenta il presupposto affinché l'aeroporto di Monaco si possa affermare anche misurandosi con la concorrenza sempre più accesa tra i grandi snodi europei per il traffico

Münchens „erste Adresse" für Millionen von Gästen aus aller Welt ist der im Mai 1992 eröffnete Flughafen. Als bedeutende europäische Luftverkehrsdrehscheibe mit hohem Servicestandard und einer faszinierenden Architektur ist der **Flughafen München** *eine ebenso freundliche wie repräsentative „Empfangshalle" für die bayerische Landeshauptstadt.*

Munich's "first address" for millions of visitors from all parts of the world is the airport opened to traffic in May 1992. As an important European aviation turnstile boasting a very high standard of services and a fascinating architecture, the **Munich Airport** *serves as a friendly and at the same time impressive reception hall for the Bavarian capital.*

Pour des millions de personnes venant des quatre coins du monde, la «première adresse» de Munich est l'aéroport inauguré en mai 1992. En tant que plate-forme aéronautique importante de l'Europe, **l'aéroport de Munich** *offre un standard de services élevé et une architecture fascinante. Il symbolise un premier contact tout aussi sympathique que représentatif avec la capitale bavaroise.*

Il primo punto di riferimento a Monaco di Baviera è rappresentato, per milioni di visitatori provenienti da tutto il mondo, dall'aeroporto inaugurato nel maggio 1992. **L'aeroporto di Monaco** *non è solo un importante snodo europeo per il traffico aereo internazionale, dotato di alti standard di servizi e con un'architettura affascinante, ma rappresenta anche una piacevole sala d'accoglienza e di rappresentanza del capoluogo bavarese.*

---

stehen wichtige Impulse für die Wirtschaft, den Arbeitsmarkt und die Landesentwicklung im Großraum München. Der wegen seiner zukunftweisenden Architektur mehrfach preisgekrönte, moderne Airport zählt darüber hinaus zu den populärsten Sehenswürdigkeiten in Oberbayern und zieht pro Jahr mehr als eine halbe Million Besucher an. Die prognostizierte Fortsetzung der Wachstumserfolge des Münchner Flughafens bietet die beste Gewähr dafür, dass der Airport seine Rolle als „Aktivposten" der bayerischen Landeshauptstadt auch weiterhin erfüllen wird.

Willi Hermsen

market and the overall development of Greater Munich. This modern airport, repeatedly awarded prizes for its futuristic architecture, is also one of Upper Bavaria's most popular landmarks, which attracts more than half a million sightseers every year. The fact that forecasts predict further success and growth for Munich's airport guarantees that it will keep on playing its role as one of Munich's biggest assets in future too.

Willi Hermsen

Munich, l'aéroport fournit depuis sa création des impulsions importantes à l'économie, au marché du travail et au développement du land dans la grande agglomération de Munich. Par ailleurs, l'aéroport moderne et primé plusieurs fois pour son architecture futuriste compte parmi les curiosités les plus populaires de Haute-Bavière et attire chaque année plus d'un demi million de visiteurs. La poursuite prévue de la courbe de réussite de l'aéroport de Munich offre la meilleure garantie pour que l'aéroport continue également à jouer son rôle de «poste actif» de la capitale du land de Bavière.

Willi Hermsen

aereo. Fin da quando è stato costruito, l'aeroporto di Monaco rappresenta un elemento di primaria importanza in grado di fornire impulsi significativi all'economia, al mercato del lavoro e allo sviluppo generale dell'area di Monaco. Premiato più volte per la sua architettura d'avanguardia, esso è inoltre una delle mete turistiche più importanti dell'Alta Baviera ed attira ogni anno più di mezzo milione di visitatori. Le previsioni di crescita dell'aeroporto di Monaco rappresentano la migliore garanzia affinché esso continui a svolgere, anche in futuro, il suo ruolo di «voce attiva» nel bilancio del capoluogo bavarese.

Willi Hermsen

MESSE MÜNCHEN INTERNATIONAL

Eingang West
Entrance West

Messeplatz München
Die Zukunft im Visier

Munich – Fair and Exhibition Centre
Planning for the Future

Munich – Centre de foires et d'expositions
Vue sur l'avenir

Monaco – Centro fieristico internazionale
Il futuro nel mirino

In der langen Geschichte des Messeplatzes München ist das Jahr 1998 von besonderer Bedeutung: Am 12. Februar 1998 wurde die Neue Messe München, eines der modernsten Messegelände der Welt, eröffnet. Im gleichen Jahr, am 9. Oktober, konnte im Rahmen der Neuen Messe München auch das Internationale Congress Center München – ICM in Betrieb genommen werden. Damit hat die Messe München die Weichen gestellt, um auch über das Jahr 2000 hinaus einen guten Platz unter den sechs führenden Messegesellschaften in Deutschland und den zehn wichtigsten weltweit einzunehmen.

Bereits im Jahr der Inbetriebnahme wurden mehr als 30 000 Aussteller und ca. 2,7 Millionen Besucher bei über 30 Messen und Ausstellungen der Unternehmensgruppe Messe München International sowie einer Reihe von großen und kleineren Gastveranstaltungen registriert. Alles spricht dafür, dass die internationale Nachfrage am Messeplatz München noch zunehmen wird, nicht zuletzt auch deshalb, weil neben der modernen Infrastruktur ein attraktives Veranstaltungsprogramm geboten wird. Dabei handelt es sich vor allem um Fachmessen für Investitionsgüter des Bauwesens und der

IFAT 99 - Messe im Zeichen des Umweltschutzes

IFAT 99 - the fair for environmental protection

IFAT 99 - la foire pour la protection de l'environnement

IFAT 99 - una fiera all'insegna della tutela dell'ambiente

In the long history of the fair and exhibition centre of Munich the year 1998 was of special importance: on 12 February 1998 the "Neue Messe München" was inaugurated, one of the world's most modern fair sites. On 9 October of the same year the "Internationale Congress Center München" (ICM) was opened within the scope of the Neue Messe München. Thus Messe München has paved the way for maintaining – even after the turn of the millennium – its position as one of Germany's six leading fair companies and as one of the ten most important of the world.

In the opening year more than 30,000 exhibitors and approximately 2.7 million visitors were already registered at more than 30 fairs organized by the Messe München International Group and at a series of large-scale and smaller guest events. There is every indication that international demand will continue to increase, last but not least because Munich

Au cours de la longue histoire de la ville de foires de Munich, l'année 1998 s'avère particulièrement importante. Le 12 février 1998 marqua l'ouverture de la Neue Messe München, un des parcs d'expositions les plus modernes du monde. Le 9 octobre de la même année, le centre international des congrès, Internationales Congress Center München – ICM, entra également en fonction dans le cadre de la Neue Messe München. La Foire de Munich a ainsi posé les jalons pour occuper également après l'an 2000 une bonne place parmi les six plus grands organismes de foires d'Allemagne et parmi les 10 plus grands du monde.

Au cours de l'année de mise en fonction, plus de 30 000 exposants et environ 2,7 millions de visiteurs ont déjà été enregistrés lors de plus de 30 foires et expositions du groupe d'entreprises Messe München International ainsi qu'une série de manifestations privées de taille plus ou moins importante. Tout indique que la demande internationale pour la ville de foires de Munich augmentera encore d'autant plus que l'infrastructure moderne est accompagnée d'un attrayant programme de manifestations. Il s'agit ici avant tout de salons spécialisés dans les biens d'investissement du bâtiment et de la technique de l'environnement, de la technique des boissons, de la logistique et des transports, de la sylviculture et de l'artisanat ainsi que de salons spécialisés pour l'électronique, l'informatique et les nouvelles technologies ou des manifestations pour des biens de consommation de luxe comme les articles de sport et la mode sportive, les bijoux et les montres.

Nella lunga storia di Monaco come centro fieristico, l'anno 1998 è stato particolarmente importante: il 12 Febbraio 1998 è stato inaugurato il Nuovo Centro Fiere di Monaco, uno dei più moderni del mondo. Nello stesso anno, il 9 Ottobre, nell'ambito del Nuovo Centro Fiere di Monaco è stato avviato anche il Centro Congressi Internazionale di Monaco (ICM). In questo modo, la fiera di Monaco ha posto i presupposti per occupare anche nel 2000 una buona posizione tra le sei principali società fieristiche tedesche e le dieci maggiori organizzazioni fieristiche del mondo.

Già nell'anno dell'inaugurazione, sono stati registrati più di 30 000 espositori e ca. 2,7 milioni di visitatori delle oltre 30 fiere ed esposizioni del gruppo imprenditoriale Messe München International (Fiera Internazionale di Monaco), oltre ad una serie di eventi straordinari di grandi e piccole dimensioni. Tutto lascia prevedere che la richiesta internazionale di essere presenti a Monaco crescerà ancora, non da ultimo in quanto, oltre ad infrastrutture moderne, la città è in grado di offrire un programma di manifestazioni di grande attrattiva. Si tratta soprattutto di fiere specializzate per quanto riguarda l'edilizia e le tecniche ambientali, bevande, logistica e trasporti, l'industria forestale e l'artigianato, infine l'elettronica, l'informatica e le nuove tecnologie o manifestazioni per beni di consumo di alto livello quali gli articoli sportivi e la moda sportiva, o ancora gioielli ed orologi.

Il Nuovo Centro Fiere di Monaco è stato accolto con un giudizio estremamente positivo dall'economia internazionale. I sondaggi condotti sulla funzionalità e sull'ambiente l'hanno premiato con i voti migliori. A causa della forte richiesta, è stato necessario iniziare già nel 1998 la costruzione di due ulteriori padiglioni per una superficie complessiva di circa 20 000 mq. A partire dall'autunno del 2000, la Fiera di Monaco potrà mettere a dispo-

Umwelttechnik, der Getränketechnik, der Logistik und des Transportwesens, der Forstwirtschaft und des Handwerks sowie um Fachmessen für Elektronik, Informatik und Neue Technologien oder Veranstaltungen für gehobene Konsumgüter wie Sportartikel und Sportmode, Schmuck und Uhren.

Die Neue Messe München wurde von der internationalen Wirtschaft sehr gut angenommen. Funktionalität und Ambiente wurden in den Umfrageergebnissen jeweils mit Bestnoten beurteilt. Aufgrund der starken Nachfrage musste bereits 1998 mit dem Bau von zwei weiteren Hallen mit einer Fläche von insgesamt 20 000 m^2 begonnen werden. Ab Herbst 2000 wird die Messe München eine Hallenkapazität von 160 000 m^2 zur Verfügung stellen können.

Mit dem Internationalen Congress Center München – ICM gehört die Stadt zu den fünf größten Kongresszentren Deutschlands und steht mit einer Kapazität von insgesamt 7 000 Sitzplätzen an zweiter Stelle. Die rege Nachfrage schon vor der Eröffnung und die langfristigen Buchungen zeigen deutlich, dass mit dem ICM eine Marktlücke für große internationale Kongressveranstaltungen am Standort München geschlossen wurde.

Im Rahmen der systematischen und kontinuierlichen Branchenbetreuung ergänzt das „M,O,C, – Münchener Order-und Veranstaltungs-Center" die Branchenereignisse am Messeplatz München. Seit 1993 bietet es Herstellern und Handelsvertretern von Sportartikeln, Sportmode und Schuhen Gelegenheit, über die Weltmesse der Sportartikelindustrie ISPO hinaus ihren Kunden ganzjährig in eigenen Räumen aktuelle Ware zu präsentieren. Gleichzeitig hat das M,O,C, auch die Aufgabe eines Entwicklungszentrums für neue Veranstaltungen der Messe München, z. B. für die Bereiche Museums- und Ausstellungstechnik, Film- und Postproduktion, Golf oder Immobilien.

offers – in addition to an ultramodern infrastructure – an attractive events programme. It comprises largely trade fairs for the capital goods and building sectors; for environmental technology; beverage technology; logistics and the transport sector; forestry and the crafts; electronics; informatics and new technologies. But also exhibitions of luxury consumer goods such as sports equipment, fashion, jewellery and watches.

Neue Messe München was very well accepted by the international economy. Its functionality and pleasant ambiente were awarded top grades at opinion polls. Because of brisk demand, the construction of two additional halls covering altogether 20,000 square metres was already started in 1998. From autumn 2000 on Messe München will be able to offer 160,000 square metres of hall space.

With the ICM (International Congress Center München) the city has become one of Germany's largest congress centres, holding second place thanks to the ICM's capacity of 7,000 seats. The interest shown even before the centre's inauguration and the long-term bookings since then prove clearly that the ICM has closed a gap in Munich's congress scene by providing a highly attractive venue for international meetings.

The M,O,C, – Münchener Order- und Veranstaltungs-Center – complements with systematic and continuous services the branch events at the Munich fair centre. Since 1993 it has offered producers and representatives of sports equipment, sports fashions and shoes the opportunity to present to their customers (in addition to the ISPO = International Sports Fair) new merchandise in special facilities and throughout the year. At the same time the M,O,C, also serves as a development centre for new events of Messe München, for instance for the sectors of museum and exhibition technology; film and

La Neue Messe München fut chaleureusement accueillie par l'économie internationale. Le côté fonctionnel et l'ambiance remportèrent dans les sondages les meilleures notes. En raison de la forte demande, il a fallu commencer dès 1998 la construction de deux autres halls affichant une superficie totale de 20 000 m^2. A partir de l'automne 2000, la Messe München offrira une capacité de halls de 160 000 m^2.

Avec l'Internationales Congress Center München – ICM, la ville figure parmi les cinq plus grands centres de congrès d'Allemagne et, avec une capacité de 7 000 places assises, elle se range à la deuxième place. La forte demande qui s'est manifestée déjà avant l'ouverture et les réservations faites longtemps à l'avance montrent clairement que l'ICM occupe une place de choix pour les grands congrès internationaux sur le site de Munich.

Dans le cadre d'un suivi systématique et continuel des secteurs, le «M,O,C, – Münchener Order- und Veranstaltungs-Center» vient compléter les manifestations qui se tiennent dans les divers secteurs à Munich, centre de foires et d'expositions. Depuis 1993, il permet tout au long de l'année aux fabricants et aux représentants commerciaux d'articles de sport, de mode sportive et de chaussures de présenter à leur clientèle dans leurs propres espaces les derniers modèles et ce, en dehors de la foire mondiale de l'industrie des articles de sport ISPO. Parallèlement, le M,O,C, sert aussi de centre de développement pour les nouvelles manifestations de la Messe München, p.ex. pour les secteurs de la technique des musées et des expositions, la production de films et la postproduction, le golf ou l'immobilier.

Un objectif essentiel des foires de Munich est également le suivi systématique des différents secteurs dans les marchés éloignés. La Messe München veut avant tout aider les petites et moyen-

Messeturm, weithin sichtbares Symbol der Neuen Messe München

The tower at the exhibition sites, impossible-to-miss landmark of Munich's new exhibition centre

La tour de la foire, un symbole se voyant de loin du nouveau du centre de foires.

La Torre della Fiera, un simbolo riconoscibile da lontano della Nuova Fiera di Monaco

sizione ben 160 000 mq di superficie espositiva.

Con il Centro Congressi Internazionale di Monaco (ICM), la città può essere annoverata tra i cinque maggiori centri congressuali della Germania ed è al secondo posto per quanto riguarda il numero complessivo di posti a sedere (7 000). Le richieste, arrivate in misura massiccia già prima dell'apertura, e le prenotazioni a lungo termine mostrano chiaramente che con il centro ICM è stato riempito un vuoto, quello che aveva riguardato le manifestazioni congressuali internazionali fino a quel momento.

Nell'ambito dell'assistenza sistematica e continuativa, il «M,O,C, – Centro Operativo Fieristico di Monaco» integra gli eventi di settore che hanno luogo al Centro Fiere di Monaco. Dal 1993, il M,O,C, offre a produttori e rappresentanti di commercio di articoli sportivi, moda sportiva e scarpe la possibilità di presentare la nuova merce ai propri clienti nell'ambito dell'ISPO, la Fiera Mondiale dell'Industria degli Articoli Sportivi. Contemporaneamente, svolge anche le funzioni di centro di sviluppo per nuove manifestazioni della Fiera di Monaco, ad esempio per i settori delle tecniche per l'allestimento

*Die **Neue Messe München** wurde am 12. Februar 1998 in Betrieb genommen. Ihre filigrane Architektur sowie die ästhetische Kombination aus Stahl, Glas und Holz sorgen für eine lichte, warme und sympathische Atmosphäre in den Hallen und Gebäuden. Dies schätzen auch die mehr als 30 000 Aussteller und ca. 2,5 Millionen Besucher, die jährlich am Messeplatz München registriert werden.*

***Neue Messe München** was put into operation on 12 February 1998. The complex' filigree architecture and aesthetic combination of steel, glass and wood provide a light, warm, and attractive atmosphere in halls and buildings which is greatly appreciated by the more than 30,000 exhibitors and approximately 2.5 million visitors who are registered at Munich's fair grounds every year.*

*Le nouveau parc d'exposition **Neue Messe München** est entré en service le 12 février 1998. Son architecture filigrane ainsi que la combinaison esthétique d'acier, de verre et de bois créent une atmosphère lumineuse, chaude et sympathique dans les halls et les bâtiments. C'est aussi ce qu'apprécient les quelque 30 000 exposants et 2,5 millions de visiteurs qui sont enregistrés chaque année au parc d'exposition de Munich.*

*La **Neue Messe München** è entrata in funzione il 12 febbraio 1998. La sua architettura così leggera ed essenziale nonché la combinazione di alto valore estetico di acciaio, vetro e legno contribuiscono a creare, nei padiglioni e negli edifici annessi, un'atmosfera luminosa, calda e simpatica. Ciò viene apprezzato anche dagli oltre 30 000 espositori e dai 2,5 milioni di visitatori circa che ogni anno vengono registrati sulla piazza fieristica di Monaco di Baviera.*

*Die größte Fachmesse der Welt, die **bauma**, zeigt alle drei Jahre auf über 400 000 m² Fläche die modernsten Maschinen und Ausrüstungen für die Bauwirtschaft.*

*Every three years the **bauma**, the world's largest trade fair, shows the latest machines and equipment for the building sector on an area covering 400,000 square metres.*

*Le plus grand salon spécialisé du monde, la **bauma**, présente tous les trois ans sur plus de 400 000 m² de surfaces exposées les toutes dernières machines et les plus récents équipements du bâtiment.*

*Il più grande Salone del mondo, il **bauma**, presenta ogni tre anni, su oltre 400 000 mq di superficie espositiva, i più moderni macchinari ed allestimenti del settore edile.*

Foto: Max Prugger, München, Nr. 200,81

Im Rahmen des Gesamtprojektes Neue Messe München wurde auch ein hochmodernes, multifunktionales Kongresszentrum errichtet, das **Internationale Congress Center München – ICM**. Damit gehört München zu den fünf größten Kongresszentren Deutschlands und steht mit einer Kapazität von insgesamt 7 000 Sitzplätzen an zweiter Stelle.

Within the overall project Neue Messe München an ultra-modern, multi-functional congress centre was also constructed – **the Internationale Congress Center München – ICM**. As a result, Munich has become one of Germany's largest congress centres – ranking second, at present, with a capacity of 7,000 seats.

Dans le cadre du projet global Neue Messe München, un centre de congrès ultramoderne et multifonctionnel a également été construit, l'**Internationale Congress Centrer München – ICM**. Ainsi, Munich fait partie des cinq plus grands centres de congrès d'Allemagne et, avec une capacité de 7 000 places assises, elle se range à la deuxième place.

Nel quadro del progetto globale della Neue Messe München è stato realizzato anche un modernissimo centro congressi multifunzionale, l'**Internationale Congress Center München – ICM**. Quest'opera ha catapultato Monaco di Baviera tra i cinque maggiori centri congressi della Germania, il secondo a livello nazionale per numero di posti a sedere (7 000 unità).

Ruhe- und Erholungszonen zum Entspannen tragen zum persönlichen Wohlbefinden der Messeteilnehmer bei: Das Atrium bildet den grünen Mittelpunkt des Messegeländes und ist von allen Hallen aus direkt zugänglich.

Recreation zones for resting and relaxing contribute to the well-being of fair visitors; the Atrium is the green nucleus of the fair site, directly accessible from all the exhibition halls.

Des aires de repos et de détente contribuent à ce que les participants se sentent bien: l'atrium forme l'espace vert du parc d'exposition et est accessible de tous les halls.

Per assicurare il benessere fisico dei frequentatori delle manifestazioni fieristiche sono state realizzate apposite aree relax e ricreative: il cuore verde del quartiere fieristico è rappresentato dall'atrio, accessibile direttamente da tutti i padiglioni.

Ein wesentliches Ziel des Münchner Messewesens ist es, Branchen auch in entfernteren Märkten systematisch zu betreuen. Die Messe München will vor allem mittelständische und kleinere Unternehmen dabei unterstützen, sich dem Globalisierungsprozess zu stellen. Um die weitere Internationalisierung ihrer Aktivitäten zu erreichen, hat die Messe München zwei strategische Richtungen festgelegt: verstärkte Zusammenführung der internationalen Angebots- und Nachfragepotentiale im Rahmen der Globalmessen am Standort München und bedarfsorientierte Aktivitäten in aufstrebenden Marktregionen anderer Staaten und Kontinente. So werden z. B. spezielle Messeveranstaltungen in zukunftsorientierten Marktregionen wie Ost- und Südostasien, Sibirien oder Mexiko durchgeführt.

Um das vorhandene Know-how sowie die Personal- und Finanzpotentiale zu bündeln und die Risiken der Auslandsaktivitäten zu teilen, wurden darüber hinaus mit deutschen, europäischen und außereuropäischen Partnern kooperative Projekte zum Vorteil der internationalen Wirtschaft entwickelt. Dazu gehören beispielsweise der Bau und Betrieb eines Messegeländes in Shanghai gemeinsam mit den Messegesellschaften von Hannover und Düsseldorf sowie anderen Partnern in Europa und China. Zielsetzung ist es, effektive Kommunikations- und Informationsplattformen auch für mittelständische und kleinere Unternehmen aufzubauen, die ihre Absatzchancen auf den ostasiatischen Märkten wahrnehmen wollen.

Auch die seit 1995 bestehende und von der Messe München initiierte Kooperation der zehn Messegesellschaften Mittel- und Südosteuropas hat das Ziel, der beteiligten Wirtschaft einen besseren Service zu bieten. Auch bei dieser Kooperation geht es der Messe München und ihren Partnern vor allem um die Vorteile ihrer Kunden bei der Wahrneh-

post- production; as well as golf and real estate.

The Munich fair sector also concentrates on systematically assisting industrial branches in more remote markets. Messe München tries to help primarily medium-sized and small enterprises to come to terms with globalization. To help them internationalize their activities more effectively, Messe München has worked out two strategies: 1st to combine the individual demand and supply potentials better during global fairs in Munich; and 2nd to start demand-oriented activities in the up-and-coming market regions of other countries and continents. It organizes, for example, special fairs in future-oriented market regions such as eastern and southeastern Asia, Sibiria, and Mexico.

To concentrate the available know-how of personnel and finance potentials and to split up the risks of foreign activities, M,O,C, has developed cooperative projects with German, European and non-European partners which are to benefit the international economy. They include, for instance, constructing and operating a fair site in Shanghai together with the Hanover and Düsseldorf fair companies, and with other partners in Europe and China. They are also to provide efficient communication and information platforms for medium-sized and small enterprises that wish to profit from the opportunities offered by east-Asian markets.

The cooperation initiated by Messe München between the ten fair companies of central and southeastern Europe (which has existed since 1995) also aims at offering the participating enterprises better services. In this cooperation Messe München and its partners concentrate primarily on their customers' taking advantage of their market opportunities in the respective economic areas.

The IMAG subsidiary also operates in accordance with the global services offered at and by the fair centre of Munich. IMAG organizes yearly - partly in co-

nes entreprises à se positionner par rapport au processus de mondialisation. Afin d'obtenir une internationalisation supplémentaire de leurs activités, la Messe München se fixa deux orientations stratégiques: le regroupement intensif des potentiels internationaux de l'offre et de la demande dans le cadre des foires globales se tenant sur le site de Munich et des activités orientées sur les besoins dans des régions présentant un marché en plein essor et situées dans d'autres pays et continents. Ainsi, des foires spéciales se tiendront par exemple dans des régions de marché à l'avenir prometteur comme l'Asie de l'est et du sud-est, la Sibérie ou le Mexique.

Afin de réunir le know-how existant avec les potentiels en personnel et en moyens financiers et afin de partager les risques des activités internationales, des projets de coopération en faveur de l'économie internationale furent, en outre, élaborés avec des partenaires allemands, européens et autres. Cela englobe par exemple la construction et le fonctionnement d'un parc d'expositions à Shanghai en commun avec les organismes de foires de Hanovre et Düsseldorf ainsi que d'autres partenaires européens et chinois. Le but est également de mettre au point des plates-formes de communication et d'information efficaces pour les petites et moyennes entreprises voulant saisir leurs chances de débouchés sur les marchés de l'Asie de l'est.

Existant depuis 1995 et née de l'initiative de la Messe München, la coopération des dix organismes de foire d'Europe Centrale et du sud-est veut proposer un meilleur service à l'économie concernée. Au sein de cette coopération, la Messe München et ses partenaires se concentrent avant tout sur les avantages de leurs clients lorsqu'ils tentent leurs chances sur les marché des différents espaces économiques.

C'est dans le sens d'une prestation de service globale, qui est proposée au centre de foires et

di musei e di mostre, dell'industria cinematografica o della postproduzione, e infine del golf e degli immobili.

Uno degli scopi primari dell'organizzazione fieristica di Monaco è di fornire un servizio sistematico anche ai settori di marcati più lontani. La Fiera di Monaco intende aiutare soprattutto le piccole e medie imprese ad inserirsi nel processo di globalizzazione. Per conseguire un'ulteriore internazionalizzazione delle proprie attività, la Fiera di Monaco ha stabilito due indirizzi strategici: l'intensificazione dell'incontro tra i potenziali internazionali di domanda e offerta nell'ambito delle fiere globali di Monaco, e attività mirate nelle regioni economiche emergenti di altri stati e continenti. È così che vengono, ad esempio, organizzate fiere speciali in nuove piazze economiche quali l'Asia orientale e meridionale, la Siberia o il Messico.

Per raggruppare il know-how presente e i potenziali di forza lavoro e finanziari, e per dividere i rischi rappresentati dall'esportazione delle attività all'estero, sono stati inoltre sviluppati dei progetti comuni con partner tedeschi, europei ed extra-europei a vantaggio dell'economia internazionale. A questi appartengono, ad esempio, la costruzione di un Centro Fiere a Shanghai in cooperazione con le società fieristiche di Hannover e di Düsseldorf e di altri partner in Europa e in Cina. L'obiettivo è di costruire piattaforme di comunicazione e di informazione per piccole e medie imprese che intendono approfittare delle possibilità di esportazione dei propri prodotti sui mercati dell'Asia orientale.

Anche la cooperazione tra le 10 società fieristiche dell'Europa centrale e sud-orientale, iniziata dalla Fiera di Monaco nel 1995, ha l'obiettivo di offrire un servizio migliore ai settori economici interessati. Il fine di questa cooperazione tra la Fiera di Monaco e i suoi partner rimane sempre quello di offrire una valida assistenza ai loro clienti nell'individuazione delle potenzialità d'es-

Küche muss gute Laune machen!

Nach dieser Devise praktiziert Mario Gamba in seinem **Acquarello**-Restaurant in München-Bogenhausen italienische Kochkunst auf höchstem Niveau. Sowohl bodenständige als auch von der Zeit beeinflusste Gerichte begeistern das internationale Publikum, zu dem Berühmtheiten wie Céline Dion, Elton John und Til Schweiger gehören. Gambas Klassiker Vitello Tonnato, Ravioli mit Walnuss- Ricotta-Füllung oder Rinderschmorbraten werden auch nach 5 Jahren von seinen Stammgästen geliebt.

Food must make happy!

This motto inspires Mario Gamba to offer in his Bogenhausen Restaurant **Acquarello** Italian cuisine of superior quality. Native as well as modern dishes thrill his international clientele, comprising such renowned stars as Céline Dion, Elton John, and Til Schweiger . His "regulars" are still enthusiastic about Gamba's classic specials like Vitello Tonnato, Ravioli filled with walnut-Ricotta, and braised beef – even after five years.

La cuisine doit mettre de bonne humeur!

C'est d'après cette devise que Mario Gamba pratique, dans son Restaurant **Acquarello** dans le quartier de Bogenhausen à Munich, l'art de la cuisine italienne au plus haut niveau. Des plats aussi bien du terroir que répondant à la tendance du moment sont proposés au plus grand plaisir du public international qui compte des célébrités comme Céline Dion, Elton John et Til Schweiger. Les grands classiques de Gamba comme le vitello tonnato, les ravioli fourrés à la noix et à la ricotta ou le bœuf braisé reçoivent toujours, même après cinq ans encore, les faveurs des habitués.

La cucina deve mettere il buonumore addosso!

È questo il motto che ispira Mario Gamba nel suo Ristorante **Acquarello** di Monaco di Baviera-Bogenhausen, dove egli pratica l'arte culinaria italiana ai massimi livelli. Il pubblico internazionale che lo frequenta e di cui fanno parte celebrità come Céline Dion, Elton John e Til Schweiger si entusiasma sia per i piatti tradizionali che per quelli che si ispirano alle tendenze del momento. I classici di Mario Gamba, vitello tonnato, ravioli con ripieno di noci e ricotta o lo stufato di manzo vengono amati dai clienti fissi del ristorante anche dopo 5 anni di attività.

---

mung ihrer Marktchancen in den jeweiligen Wirtschaftsräumen.

Im Sinne der globalen Dienstleistung, die am Messeplatz München wie auch vom Messeplatz München ausgehend angeboten wird, agiert auch die Tochtergesellschaft IMAG. Sie führt – teilweise in Zusammenarbeit mit der Messe München – jährlich rund 100 Fachmessen, Messebeteiligungen und Branchentermine auf allen Kontinenten durch.

Mit diesen alten Aktivitäten am Standort München und weltweit, selbstständig oder in Kooperation mit anderen Partnern, will die Messe München vor allem für kleinere und mittelständische Unternehmen globale Dienstleistungen erbringen, die es ihnen ermöglichen, im Rahmen globaler Marktabläufe Absatzchancen leichter zu finden und wahrzunehmen.

Manfred Wutzlhofer

operation with Messe München – roughly 100 trade fairs, fair participations and branch meetings in all continents.

With these activities, carried out independently or in cooperation with partners in Munich and worldwide, Messe München wishes to provide global services mainly for small and medium-sized enterprises which help them to find – and make use of – sales opportunities in worldwide marketing.

Manfred Wutzlhofer

expositions de Munich et également offertes par celui-ci, que la filiale IMAG opère également. Elle gère, quelquefois en coopération avec la Messe München, chaque année environ 100 salons spécialisés, participations à des foires et calendriers des secteurs sur tous les continents.

Avec toutes ces activités sur le site de Munich et à l'échelon mondial, qui se font de manière autonome ou en coopération avec d'autres partenaires, la Messe München apporte surtout des prestations globales de services aux petites et moyennes entreprises ce qui leur permet de trouver et de saisir plus facilement des débouchés dans le cadre des procédés globaux de marchés.

Manfred Wutzlhofer

portazione dei loro prodotti nei diversi spazi economici.

Sempre nell'ambito di un'offerta di servizi globali opera anche la IMAG, una società affiliata del Centro Fiere di Monaco. Questa organizza ogni anno circa 100 fiere specialistiche, partecipazioni a fiere ed appuntamenti di settore su tutti i continenti – in parte in collaborazione con la Fiera di Monaco.

Attraverso queste attività, condotte ormai da molto tempo sia a Monaco che nel mondo e gestite in modo indipendente o congiuntamente con altri soci, la Fiera di Monaco intende soprattutto offrire alle piccole e grandi imprese dei servizi globali che consentano loro di individuare più facilmente e di approfittare delle possibilità di sbocco nell'ambito di un mercato sempre più globale.

Manfred Wutzlhofer

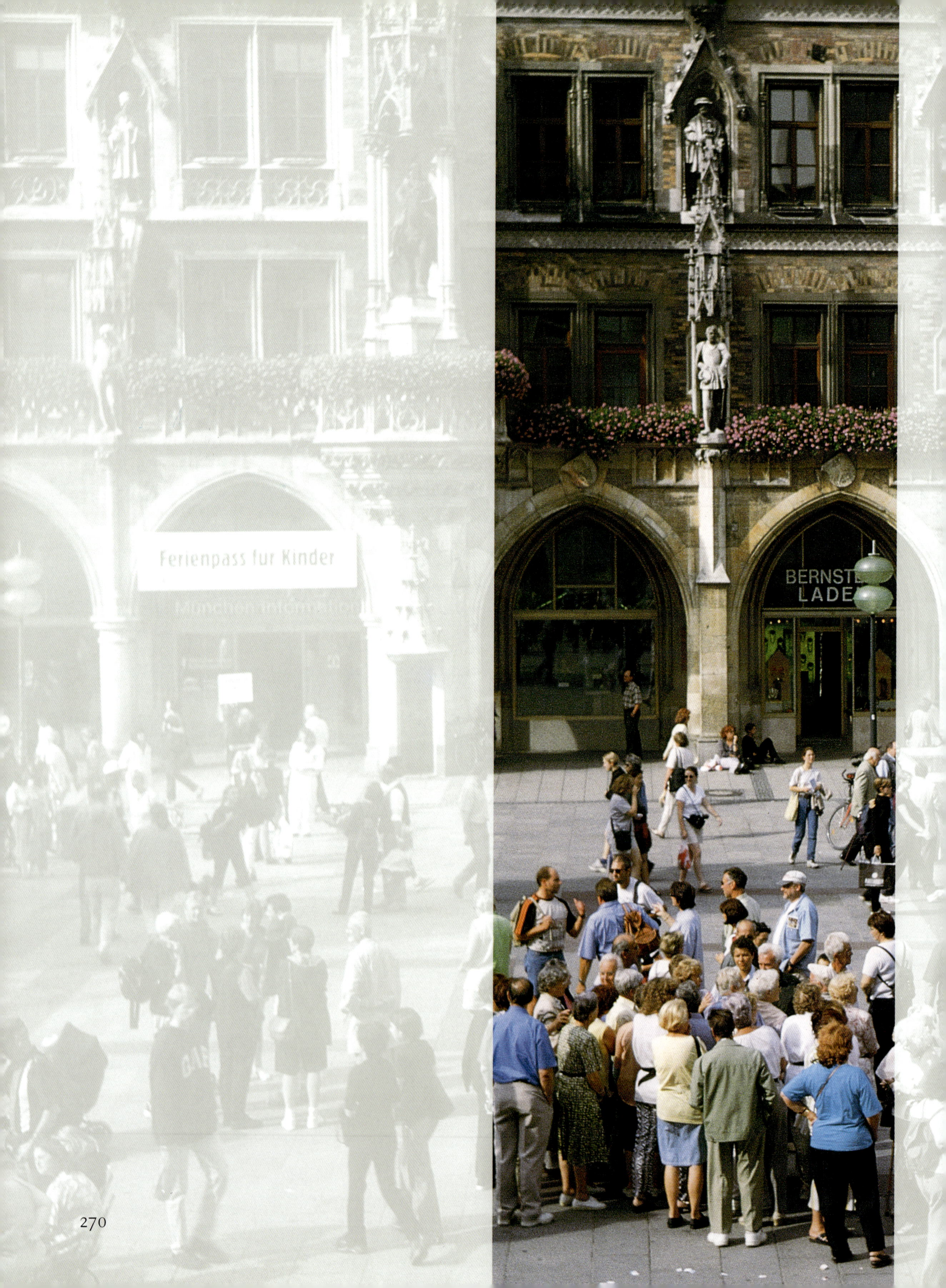
Ferienpass fur Kinder

*München –
Ziel für die Welt*

*Munich –
International Destination*

*Munich –
une destination pour le monde*

*Monaco di Baviera –
una meta da tutto il mondo*

„Ab nach München!" Dieser ekstatische Ausruf der Malerin Gabriele Münter gilt für fast 60 Millionen Gäste aus aller Welt, die das Jahr über die Stadt an der Isar aufsuchen – als Tagesausflügler oder als übernachtende Besucher.

Mit diesem Potential liegt München an der Spitze der europäischen und internationalen Reiseziele. Unangefochten und relativ krisensicher mit seiner heterogenen Struktur im Tourismus spielt die Isarmetropole seit Jahren in der Spitzenliga der gastgebenden Städte mit.

"Let's be off to Munich!" Echoing this ecstatic appeal of paintress Gabriele Münter, nearly 60 million tourists from all parts of the world flock to the city on the Isar River every year, either for a day or for a longer period of time.

Thanks to these impressive figures Munich heads the list of European and international tourist destinations. Its heterogeneous structure enables the Bavarian metropolis to play an undisputed and relatively crisis-proof role in tourism, so that it has been able to hold a dominant position in the top league of "host towns" for many years.

«En route pour Munich!» Ce cri extasié de la peintre Gabriele Münter prévaut pour les 60 millions de visiteurs des quatre coins de la planète qui viennent passer dans l'année un ou plusieurs jours dans la ville aux bords de l'Isar.

Avec ce potentiel, Munich arrive en tête des destinations de voyage en Europe et dans le monde. Incontestée et relativement à l'abri des crises grâce à sa structure hétérogène dans le tourisme, la métropole fait partie depuis des années des villes les plus visitées.

«Andiamo a Monaco!» Questo grido estatico della pittrice Gabriele Münter vale per quasi 60 milioni di ospiti provenienti da tutto il mondo che visitano la città sull'Isar lungo tutto l'arco dell'anno – chi rimanendo solo per la giornata, chi scegliendo di fermarsi anche per la notte.

Con questo potenziale, Monaco è in cima alla lista delle mete turistiche europee ed internazionali. Da anni la metropoli sull'Isar gioca nella serie A delle città ospitanti, una posizione incontestata e relativamente sicura da crisi grazie alla sua struttura turistica eterogenea.

Und was macht München so anziehend? 70 % der gewerblichen Übernachtungen sind geschäftlich motiviert (27 % Geschäftsreisende allgemein, 25 % Kongress- und 18 % Messebesucher), bei den restlichen 30 % handelt es sich um Gäste, deren Interesse der Kunst, Kultur oder diversen Veranstaltungen gilt. Im Vergleich zu anderen deutschen Großstädten hat München damit den größten rein touristischen Anteil an Übernachtungen.

Hoch dekoriert in der Tourismusbranche, wurde München 1999 wieder als „Lieblingsstadt der Deutschen" mit dem Goldenen Globo ausgezeichnet, auf den

What is it that makes Munich so attractive? Well, on the one hand business is responsible for 70 % commercial overnight stays (27 % of them concerned with general business, 25 % with congresses and 18 % with fairs and exhibitions). On the other hand, tourists interested in art, culture and sundry events constitute 30 %. Compared with other big German cities, Munich thus boasts the largest share of strictly "touristic" overnight stays.

Having received numerous touristic prizes in the past years, Munich in 1999 was once more awarded the "Golden Globe" on

Qu'est-ce qui rend Munich si attirant? 70 % des nuitées en hôtel ont des motifs de travail (27 % voyagent pour leur travail, 25 % assistent à des congrès et 18 % visitent des foires), les 30 % restants sont des touristes s'intéressant à l'art, la culture et à diverses manifestations. Comparée à d'autres villes allemandes, Munich compte le plus fort pourcentage de nuitées purement touristiques.

Hautement récompensée dans le secteur touristique, Munich se vit à nouveau décerner le Globo d'or comme la «ville préférée des allemands», ce qui devient d'ailleurs presque une tradition. Pour attribuer ce prix, des lecteurs

Ma cosa rende Monaco così attraente? Il 70 % dei pernottamenti sono per viaggi d'affari (27 % di commessi viaggiatori in generale, 25 % di congressisti e 18 % di visitatori di fiere); per il restante 30 % si tratta di ospiti interessati prevalentemente all'arte, alla cultura o a diverse manifestazioni. In confronto ad altre grandi città tedesche, Monaco vanta la quota maggiore di pernottamenti per scopi puramente turistici.

Altamente decorata nel ramo turistico, Monaco è stata insignita del Globo d'Oro quale «città più amata dai tedeschi», un premio al quale sembra essersi quasi abbonata e che viene conferito dai lettori di una rivista di viaggi.

Ein reicher Bürger namens Rosipal stiftete für das Neue Rathaus, erbaut in mehreren Etappen von 1867 bis 1905, ein Glockenspiel mit Turnier und Schäfflertanz, heute eine der größten Touristenattraktionen Münchens.

A rich citizen named Rosipal donated for the New City Hall which was erected in several stages from 1867 to 1905 a carillon depicting a tournament and the local coopers' dance, today one of Munich's most popular tourist attractions.

Un riche citoyen, portant le nom de Rosipal, dota le nouvel hôtel de ville, édifié en plusieurs étapes entre 1867 et 1905, d'un carillon représentant un tournoi et la danse des tonneliers, aujourd'hui l'une des plus grandes attractions touristiques de Munich.

Un ricco cittadino di nome Rosipal donò per il Nuovo Municipio, costruito a più riprese tra il 1867 ed il 1905, un carillon che riproduceva un torneo cavalleresco e la danza dei bottai e che oggi rappresenta una delle maggiori attrazioni turistiche monacensi.

die Stadt schon beinahe ein Abonnement hat. Bei diesem Publikumspreis wählen die Leser einer Reisezeitschrift stets ihre Lieblingsstadt. Immerhin – fast 55 % der Gäste kommen aus dem Inland.

which the city seems to have a monopoly; this public award is bestowed on the "favourite German city" selected by the readers of a large travel magazine. The surprising fact is that nearly 55 % of the visitors are Germans.

d'une revue touristique élisent leur ville préférée. Il faut noter que presque 55 % des visiteurs sont allemands.

Parmi les visiteurs étrangers, qui représentent environ 45 % de l'ensemble des visiteurs, Munich

che scelgono ogni anno la loro città preferita. Comunque, quasi il 55% degli ospiti proviene dalla Germania.

Ma anche per i visitatori provenienti dall'estero (presenti con una percentuale del 45 % sul to-

*Vor mehr als 25 Jahren hatte Viktor Hepting die Idee – seiner Liebhaberei entsprechend – den Münchnern Austern aufzutischen. Er wurde bald zum Pionier und Vorreiter in der deutschen Gastronomieszene. Gemeinsam mit seinen Partnern, Alexander Knobl und Chef Martin Klieber, verwöhnt er inzwischen seine Gäste mit kulinarischen Genüssen wie frischen Stonecrabs, Riesengarnelen oder Mahimahi, internationale Spezialitäten, die fangfrisch eingeflogen werden. Lange schon gehört der **Austernkeller** in der Stollbergstraße zu den Topadressen für Meeresspezialitäten aus der ganzen Welt.*

Serviert werden die feinen Gaumenfreuden in maritimer Atmosphäre: Von Anbeginn an befindet sich das Seafoodrestaurant in einem stilvollen Kellergewölbe aus der Jahrhundertwende, in dem im Laufe der Zeit eine prachtvolle Dekoration aus Muscheln, Austern und Krebstieren sowie Geschirr und Tafelgeräten rund ums Meer entstanden ist.
Von links/left to right: Viktor Hepting, Küchenchef Martin Klieber, Alexander Knobl

*More than 25 years ago Viktor Hepting had the idea of turning a private hobby into a business by serving oysters to the local people. He soon became a pioneer in Germany's gastronomic scene. Together with his partners Alexander Knobl and Chef Martin Klieber he has been catering to his guests with such culinary treats as fresh stone crabs, giant prawns, and mahimahi – all international specialties which are flown straight from the coast to Munich. For quite some time the **Austernkeller** at Stollbergstraße has been one of the top addresses for special seafood from all parts of the world.*

The exquisite delicacies are served in a maritime atmosphere: the restaurant has always been located in a stylish vault dating from the turn of the century, which has gradually been decorated very ingeniously with seashells, oysters and crabs; even the china and tableware commemorate the sea.

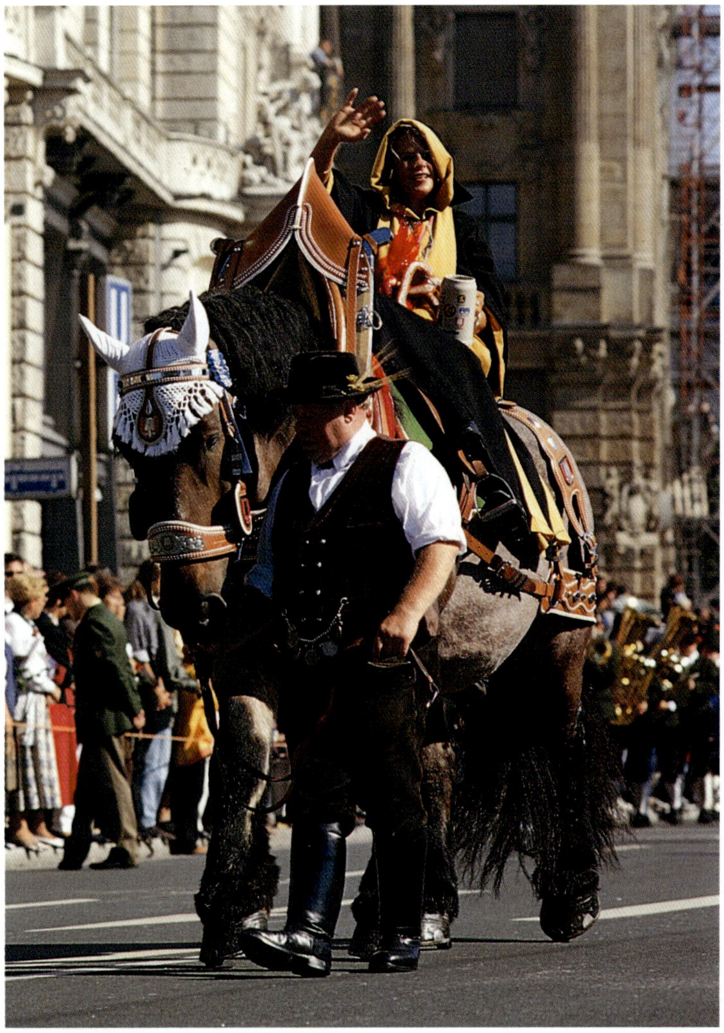

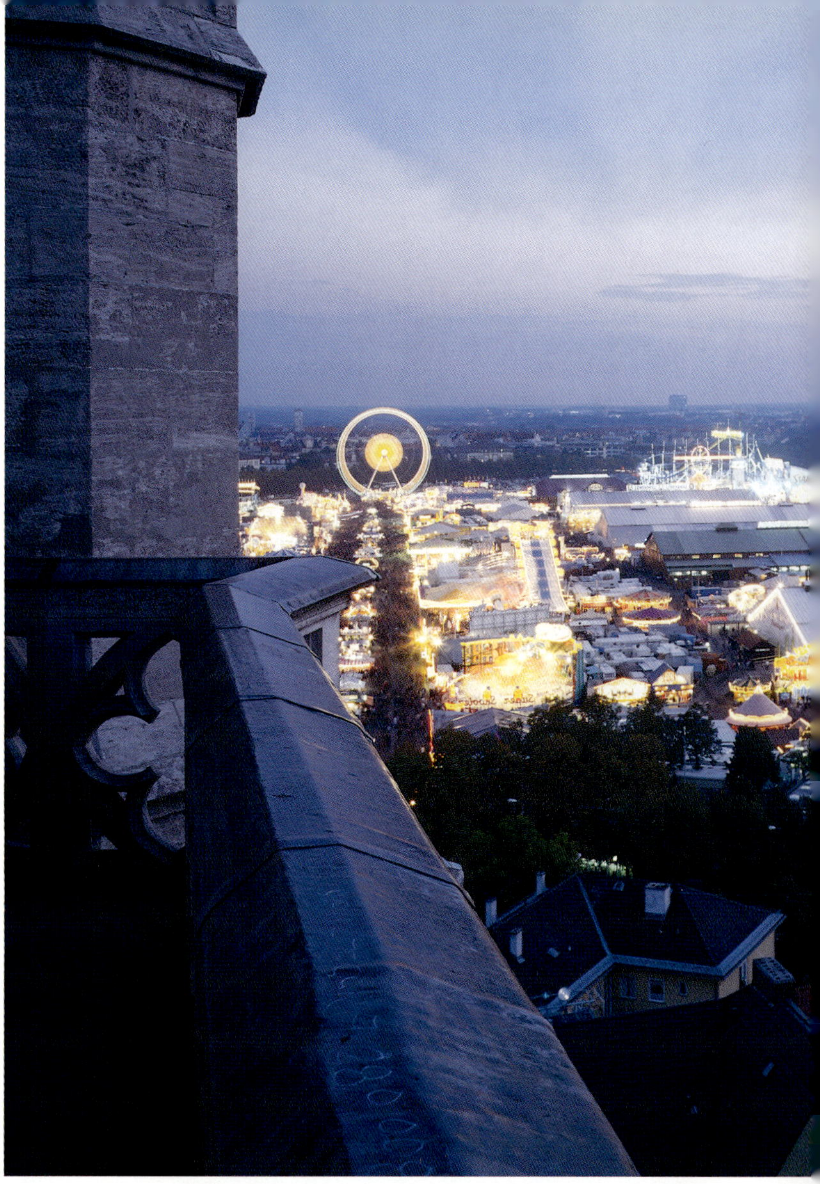

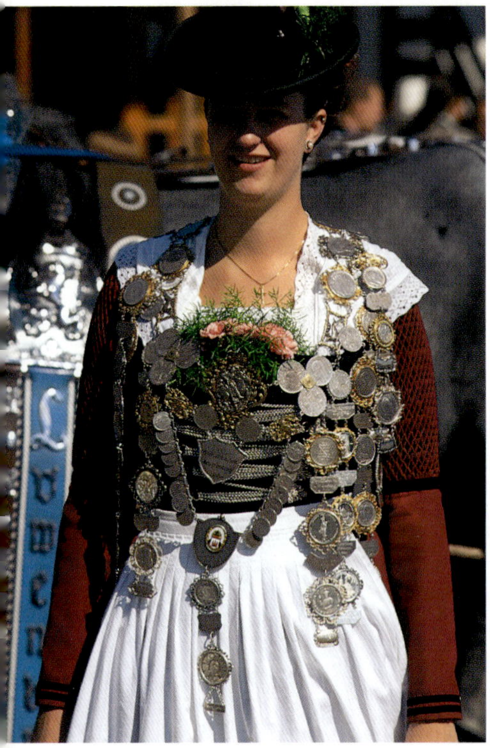

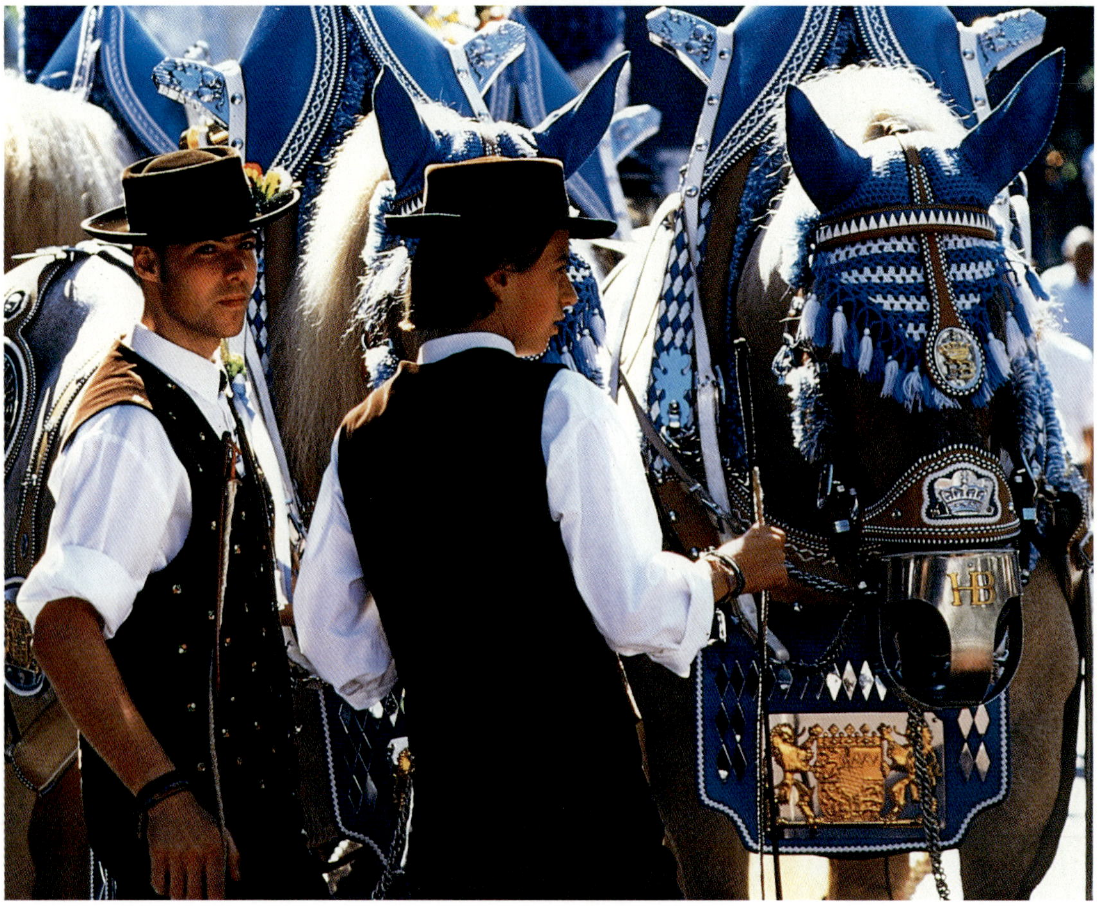

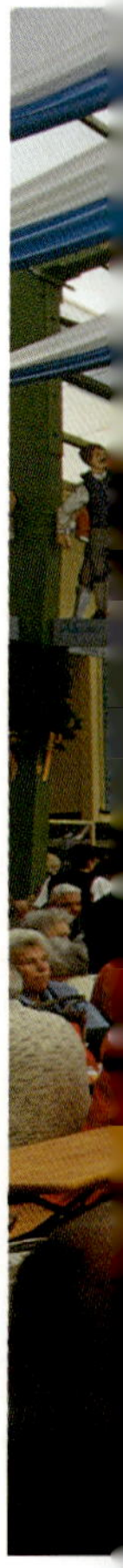

*Oktoberfest –
Ausdruck der Lebensfreude
von Jung und Alt*

*The Oktoberfest –
a symbol of joie-de-vivre
of young and old alike*

*La fête de la Bière –
manifestation de la joie de vivre
des jeunes et des moins jeunes*

*La Festa della Birra –
espressione di gioia di vivere
per ogni fascia di età*

Aber auch bei den ausländischen Besuchern, die nahezu 45 % der Gäste ausmachen, steht München unter den deutschen Städten an der Spitze. Da kann die Konkurrenz nicht mithalten.

Traditionell stark vertreten sind in München die Amerikaner, es folgen unsere südlichen Nachbarn, die Italiener, dann die Japaner und Gäste aus Großbritannien. Überhaupt ist die Landeshauptstadt das Lieblingsziel der Besucher aus Asien: Japan führt mit fast 174 000 Übernachtungen, China mit Hongkong folgten mit mehr als 38 000 und Taiwan mit fast 13 000 Übernachtungen. Die Gäste aus den Arabischen Golfstaaten sind mit über 75 000 Übernachtungen vertreten, „Down under"-Gäste aus Australien, Neuseeland und Ozeanien mit über 66 000 Übernachtungen.

Der Tourismus bringt München Milliarden ein. Eine Untersuchung des Deutschen Wirtschaftswissenschaftlichen Institutes für Fremdenverkehr an der Universität München (DWIF) kommt für 1998 zu einem fremdenverkehrsbedingten Umsatz von über sechs Milliarden Mark. Der Tourismus stellt also einen beträchtlichen Wirtschaftsfaktor dar. Hier entstehen Umsätze, die sich direkt auf das Gewerbe auswirken und damit auch auf die Einkommen der hier Beschäftigten. Über die Hälfte des von den Besuchern ausgegebenen Geldes entfällt auf das Gastgewerbe, ein Drittel fließt in den Einzelhandel. Den Rest teilen sich der Veranstaltungs- und Ausstellungssektor, touristisch relevante Dienstleistungsanbieter, öffentliche und private Verkehrsbetriebe. – Der Fremdenverkehr sichert rund 68 000 Arbeitsplätze.

1998 fanden in München rund 14 000 Kongresse, Tagungen und Seminare mit 860 000 Besuchern statt. Seinen Höhepunkt erreichte das Kongressjahr im Oktober mit der Eröffnung des Internationalen Kongress Centers München „ICM" München wird seinen Platz unter den ersten Adressen der Kongressstädte auch künftig behaupten und ausbauen können, nicht zuletzt dank der optimalen

But also foreign visitors (who represent nearly 45 %) prefer Munich to the other German cities, in fact none of them can compete with the Bavarian capital. American tourists are, traditionally, the largest group of foreign tourists; they are followed by the Italians, our southern neighbours; Japanese and British visitors take third place. Munich is, in fact, a very popular destination with most Asian tourists: Japan takes the lead, with nearly 174,000 overnight stays, followed by China with 38,000, and Taiwan with 13,000. Visitors from the Arabian Golf states account for more than 75,000 overnight stays; and "down-under" guests from Australia, New Zealand, and Oceania (the Pacific area) for more than 66,000.

Tourism is one of Munich's major sources of income and an important economic factor: a study by the German Scientific Institute for Tourism at Munich University (DWIF) computed a tourist-based turnover of more than DM six billion for 1998 – an amount which has a direct effect on trade and, consequently, on the incomes of the people working in this sector. Gastronomy accounts for more than half of the money spent by tourists, retail for one third of it. The rest is divided up among the exhibition and events sector, service enterprises connected with tourism, and public and private transport services. Thus tourism provides approximately 68,000 jobs.

In 1998 about 14,000 congresses, meetings and seminars attracting 860,000 visitors took place in Munich. The climax of the congress year was the opening of the International Congress Center Munich (ICM) in October 1998. Thanks to the ICM's excellent infrastructure Munich will be able to retain and even improve its leading position among the major congress centres in future too. Science and research, economic organizations and large-scale enterprises, as well as Munich's status as a media

arrive en tête des villes allemandes. La concurrence n'arrive pas à faire aussi bien. Traditionnellement, les Américains sont présents en grand nombre, arrivent ensuite les voisins méditerranéens, les Italiens, puis les Japonais et les visiteurs de Grande Bretagne. De plus, la capitale du land est la destination préférée des Asiatiques. Le Japon culmine avec près de 174 000 nuitées, la Chine et Hong Kong suivent avec plus de 38 000 nuitées et Taiwan affiche près de 13 000 nuitées. Les visiteurs des Etats du Golfe arabique représentent plus de 75 000 nuitées, viennent ensuite les visiteurs d'Australie, de Nouvelle-Zélande et d'Océanie avec plus de 66 000 nuitées.

Le tourisme rapporte des milliards à Munich. Une étude faite à l'université de Munich du Deutsches Wirtschaftswissenschaftliches Institut für Fremdenverkehr (Institut économique et scientifique du tourisme) avance pour 1998 un chiffre d'affaires inhérent au tourisme de l'ordre de six milliards de DM. Le tourisme représente donc un facteur économique considérable. Les chiffres d'affaires ont une influence directe sur les professions touristiques et par conséquent aussi sur les revenus des personnes actives dans ce secteur. Plus de la moitié des dépenses faites par les touristes arrivent dans les caisses de la gastronomie et de l'hôtellerie, un tiers va au commerce du détail. Le reste revient au secteur des manifestations et des expositions, aux prestataires de service inhérents au tourisme, aux moyens de transports publics et privés. Le tourisme assure environ 68 000 emplois.

En 1998, 14 000 congrès, conférences et séminaires se sont tenus à Munich et ont enregistré 860 000 visiteurs. L'apogée a été atteint en octobre avec l'ouverture de l'Internationales Kongress Center München (ICM), le centre international des congrès de Munich. A l'avenir encore, Munich pourra confirmer et conforter sa place parmi les meil-

tale dei visitatori), Monaco rappresenta la meta preferita tra le città tedesche, di cui non teme la concorrenza.

Gli stranieri più numerosi sono tradizionalmente gli americani: seguono i nostri vicini del sud, gli italiani, quindi i giapponesi e gli inglesi. Ma la capitale bavarese è soprattutto la meta preferita dagli asiatici: la classifica è guidata dal Giappone, con quasi 174 000 pernottamenti, seguita da Cina e Hongkong con più di 38 000 pernottamenti e da Taiwan con quasi 13 000 pernottamenti. Gli stati arabi del Golfo sono presenti con oltre 75 000 pernottamenti, mentre gli ospiti «down under» provenienti da Australia, Nuova Zelanda e Oceania raggiungono un totale di 66 000 pernottamenti.

Il turismo frutta miliardi a Monaco. Una ricerca condotta dall'Istituto tedesco delle Scienze Economiche per il Turismo dell'Università di Monaco (DWIF) ha accertato che il fatturato derivante dai proventi dell'industria turistica ha superato nel 1998 i sei miliardi di marchi. Il turismo rappresenta dunque un rilevante fattore economico, dato che si tratta di un giro d'affari che influisce direttamente sul commercio della città e sul reddito delle persone occupate nel settore. Più della metà dei proventi deriva dall'industria alberghiera, un terzo va al commercio al dettaglio. La parte rimanente viene suddivisa tra i settori delle manifestazioni e delle fiere, i servizi turistici e i servizi di trasporto pubblici e privati. – Nel complesso, il turismo garantisce circa 68 000 posti di lavoro.

Nel 1998 si sono svolti a Monaco circa 14 000 congressi, convegni e seminari con 860 000 visitatori. Il culmine è stato raggiunto in ottobre con l'inaugurazione del Centro Congressi Internazionale di Monaco («ICM»). Anche in futuro Monaco potrà mantenere e potenziare la propria posizione ai vertici delle città congressuali, non da ultimo grazie all'infrastruttura ottimale dell'ICM. Scienza e ricerca, associazioni industriali e grandi aziende, così

Ob auf dem Oktoberfest, im sonnigen Biergarten oder in einer traditionsreichen Gaststätte – die Münchner Brauereien Paulaner und Hacker-Pschorr der **Schörghuber Unternehmensgruppe** *bieten für heimische und internationale Gäste Münchner Gastlichkeit und bayerische Lebensart in bester Form.*

No matter whether they cater to people at the Oktoberfest, in a sunny beer garden, or in a restaurant looking back on a long tradition – the Paulaner and Hacker-Pschorr breweries of the **Schörghuber Corporate Group** *always offer local and foreign guests the outstanding hospitality and life style typical of Bavaria.*

Das Seehaus im Englischen Garten

The Seehaus in the English Garden

Le restaurant Seehaus dans le Jardin anglais

Il locale Seehaus nel Giardino Inglese

Das Paulaner im Tal

The Paulaner im Tal

Le restaurant Paulaner im Tal

Il locale Paulaner im Tal

Que ce soit à la fête de la bière, dans un jardin de la bière ou dans une brasserie riche en traditions, les brasseries munichoises Paulaner et Hacker-Pschorr appartenant au **Groupe d'entreprises Schörghuber** *offrent aux clients munichois et internationaux un bel exemple de la convivialité munichoise et de l'art de vivre bavarois.*

Che si tratti della Festa della Birra, di un' assolata birreria all'aperto o di un ristorante ricco di tradizione, le fabbriche di birra monacensi Paulaner e Hacker-Pschorr del **Gruppo Schörghuber** *offrono ai frequentatori sia del posto che di tutto il mondo la tipica ospitalità che contraddistingue Monaco ed il «savoir vivre» bavarese nella sua forma migliore.*

Das Hacker-Pschorr Oktoberfest-Zelt

The Hacker-Pschorr tent at the Oktoberfest

Le chapiteau de Hacker-Pschorr à la fête de la bière

Il tendone della Hacker-Pschorr alla Festa della Birra

*München
im Dezember:
„Man" trifft sich
auf dem stim-
mungsvollen
Christkindlmarkt
und erfüllt sich
hier so manchen
Wunsch.*

*Munich
in December:
Nobody wants to
miss the wonderful
atmosphere of the
Christmas market
where many a wish
can get fulfilled.*

*Munich
en décembre :
«on» se rencontre
sur le marché
de Noël plein de
charme et on
s'achète un petit
cadeau.*

*Monaco
in dicembre:
ci si incontra al
suggestivo Merca-
tino di Natale dove
e possibile soddis-
fare l'uno o l'altro
desiderio.*

Das **Asam-Schlössl** im Münchener Stadtteil Thalkirchen – 1724-1739 Landsitz des Hofmalers Cosmas Damian Asam – wurde 1993 nach liebevoller Renovierung durch die Augustiner Brauerei von der Münchener Wirtin Birgit Netzle übernommen. Gehobene Gastronomie und Tradition vereinen sich hier auf perfekte Art. Neben der gemütlichen Tiroler Stube bietet das Schlössl stilvolle Nebenräume für Festlichkeiten sowie einen idyllischen Wirtsgarten.

The **Asam-Schlössl** located in the part of Munich called Thalkirchen used to be the country seat of court painter Cosmas Damian Asam; it was lovingly restored in 1993 by the Augustiner brewery and is run today by landlady Birgit Netzle from Munich. Here, excellent cuisine and tradition go together perfectly. In addition to the cosy Tyrolean room the Schlössl offers stylish side rooms for festivities as well as an idyllic beer garden.

Die genuesische Fassade der historischen Gastwirtschaft **Bamberger Haus** im Schwabinger Luitpoldpark stammt ebenfalls aus dem 18. Jahrhundert. 1995 wurde es von der Augustiner Brauerei übernommen und umgebaut. Schlössl-Wirtin Birgit Netzle serviert seit 1997 in den gepflegten Räumen kulinarische Köstlichkeiten. Von bayerisch bis barock und elegant bietet das Haus auf drei Etagen Räumlichkeiten für jeden erdenklichen Anlass.

The Genoese façade of the historic restaurant **Bamberger Haus** in the Luitpold Park in Schwabing (part of central Munich) dates back to the 18th century as well. It was taken over and restructured by the Augustiner brewery in 1995. Since 1997 the landlady of the Schlössl, Birgit Netzle, has served culinary delicacies in an unpretentious atmosphere. The house has three stories and offers rooms, decorated in Bavarian to baroque to elegant style, for every occasion.

Alljährlich im Juni wird die Gründung der Stadt München (14.6.1158) mit einem Fest gefeiert.

Every year Munich celebrates a festival in honour of its foundation on June 14th, 1158.

Chaque année, la date de création de la ville (14 juin 1158) est célébrée par une fête.

Ogni anno, in giugno, viene celebrata con una festa in ricordo della fondazione della città di Monaco avvenuta il 14 giugno 1158

Das Grillstüberl des **Bratwurstherzl** *mit seinem 350 Jahre alten Gewölbe. Hier werden auf dem offenen Buchenholzgrill die im Hause hergestellten Rostbratwürstchen gebraten.*

120 Plätze bietet der Biergarten des Bratwurstherzl am Viktualienmarkt, wo man im Sommer das Edelhell vom Holzfass im Freien genießen kann.

The "Grillstüberl" room of the **Bratwurstherzl** *with its 350-year-old vault. Here the sausages are grilled on an open beechwood flame.*

The beer garden of the Bratwurstherzl on Viktualienmarkt offers room for 120 guests; in summer you can enjoy – outdoors – the "Edelhell" beer fresh from the wooden barrel.

Le «Grillstüberl» du **Bratwurstherzl** *avec ses voûtes vieilles de 350 ans. C'est sur le grill fonctionnant au bois de hêtre que les saucisses faites maison seront cuites.*

Sur le Viktualienmarkt, le jardin de la bière du Bratwurstherzl offre 120 places permettant, en été, de déguster en plein air la bière blonde tirée d'un tonneau en bois.

La «Grillstüberl» del **Bratwurstherzl**, *con la sua volta del 1650. Qui, su una griglia in legno di faggio, vengono arrostiti i würstel di produzione propria.*

Nel giardino della birra del Bratwurstherzl, che dà sul Viktualienmarkt e ha una capienza di 120 posti, è possibile gustare all'aria aperta, in estate, la nobile birra chiara spillata direttamente dalla botte di legno.

Infrastruktur des ICM. Wissenschaft und Forschung, Wirtschaftsverbände und Großfirmen sowie der Rang Münchens als Medienzentrum werden das Ihre dazu beitragen.

Stadt der Lebensfreude und der Feste

Neben Wissenschaft, Forschung, Technologie und Industrie kommt in der Isarmetropole auch die Lebensfreude nicht zu kurz. So wurde München im Spannungsfeld zwischen Tradition und Moderne, zwischen Bodenständigem und Hightech zu einem Traumziel für eine weltweite Gästeschar. Berge, Seen und Schlösser bilden dabei die Traumkulisse. Mit seinem hohen Freizeitwert zieht die Stadt gleichermaßen Kulturinteressierte wie Sportbegeisterte an.

Vermarktet wird die Tourismusdestination München durch das Fremdenverkehrsamt der Landeshauptstadt. Das im vierten Jahrzehnt bestehende, mittlerweile traditionsreiche Amt hat ein weltcentre will certainly contribute their share to reaching this goal.

A City of Joie de Vivre and Festivals

In addition to science, research, technology and industry the wholehearted enjoyment of life also plays an important part in Munich. With its contradicting forces of tradition and modern life, of indigenous structures and high-tech, the metropolis on the Isar has become a mecca for guests from all parts of the world. Mountains, lakes, castles and palaces provide a spectacular background for this field of tension. Because of its high recreational value, Munich attracts culture lovers and sports fans alike.

The local tourist office is responsible for "marketing" the city successfully. Set up more than 30 years ago, this by now traditional office has established a worldwide network of contacts. Additionally, it organizes popular festileures adresses des villes de congrès, en particulier grâce à l'excellente infrastructure du ICM. La science et la recherche, les associations économiques et les grandes entreprises ainsi que la place de Munich comme centre médiatique y apporteront une contribution non négligeable.

Ville de la joie de vivre et des fêtes

Outre la science, la recherche, la technologie et l'industrie, la métropole aux bords de l'Isar est connue pour sa joie de vivre. Munich, tanguant entre tradition et modernité, entre son côté rustique et sa haute technologie, est devenue la destination de rêve d'une foule de touristes. Les montagnes, les lacs et les châteaux forment ici une coulisse féerique. En misant sur les loisirs, la ville attire aussi bien les passionnés de culture que de sports.

Munich, comme destination touristique, est commercialisée par l'office de tourisme de la come l'importanza di Monaco come centro dei media, daranno inoltre il loro contributo.

Città della gioia e di festa

Accanto a scienza, ricerca, tecnologia ed industria non manca certo la gioia di vivere nella metropoli sull'Isar. E' così che Monaco, divisa tra tradizione e modernità, valori locali e alta tecnologia è diventata una meta da sogno per migliaia di turisti provenienti da tutto il mondo. Lo scenario è costituito da un paesaggio meraviglioso di montagne, laghi e castelli. Per l'alto valore attribuito al tempo libero, la città attira in egual misura le persone interessate alla cultura e gli appassionati di sport.

La commercializzazione di Monaco come meta turistica avviene attraverso l'Ente per il Turismo della città. Costituito negli anni quaranta, pur mantenendo le proprie caratteristiche tradizionali l'ente ha allacciato una rete di contatti a livello mondiale. E' inoltre preposto all'organizzazione

Der Christopher-Street-Day 1999 in München

Christopher-Street-Day 1999 in Munich

Défilé du Christopher-Street-Day en 1999 à Munich

Il Christopher-Street-Day 1999 a Monaco

*Direkt am idyllischen Isar-Hochufer zwischen München-Harlaching und Grünwald präsentiert sich der denkmalgeschützte, traditionsreiche **Gutshof Menterschwaige**. Das ehemals königliche Gut mit dem Lola-Montez-Haus, in dem König Ludwig I. seine Geliebte Lola Montez versteckte, wird heute von den Wirten Christian Schottenhamel und Michael Schamberger betrieben. Zusammen mit der Löwenbräu-Brauerei haben sie dem Gutshof zu neuem Glanz verholfen.*

Für Anlässe jeder Art bietet die Menterschwaige stilvolle Räumlichkeiten: im alten Gewölbe mit Nischen, Ecken und offenem Kamin für 120 Gäste, in der Jagdstube und in der Lola-Montez-Stube für je 45 und im König-Ludwig-Saal für 160 Personen. Regionale sowie internationale Spezialitäten verheißen Gaumenfreuden.

*Directly at the idyllic steep banks of the Isar between München-Harlaching and Grünwald lies the **Gutshof Menterschwaige**, a protected building with a long tradition. The formerly royal residence with the Lola Montez House, where king Louis I of Bavaria hid his mistress Lola Montez, is jointly run today by the two innkeepers Christian Schottenhamel and Michael Schamberger. Together with the Löwenbräu brewery they have given the place new glory.*

The Menterschwaige offers stylish function rooms for all occasions: the old vaults with nooks and crannies and an open hearth for up to 120 guests, the Jagdstube (hunters' den) and the Lola-Montez-Stube for up to 45 and the König-Ludwig-Saal for up to 160 persons. Regional and international specialities are certain to tickle your palate.

*Für positive Schlagzeilen am laufenden Band sorgt das **Park Café** am Alten Botanischen Garten, seitdem Thomas Jadrnicek, Michael Schamberger und Christian Schottenhamel den Club, das Park-Café Kitchen und den Biergarten übernommen haben. Rauschende Feste werden hier im Münchner Szene-Nachtclub gefeiert. Im Park-Café Club, der sich mit der einstigen New Yorker Edel-Diskothek Studio 54 durchaus messen kann, verkehrt Prominenz aus dem In- und Ausland. Das Park-Café Kitchen wurde mit dem Star-Designer Jacobo Foggini umgebaut. Alles was in und trendy ist, trifft sich hier zum Frühstück, Lunch, zur Happy Hour oder zum Dinner mit mediterraner Küche.*

Der Biergarten mit über 2 500 Plätzen unter Kastanienbäumen bietet bayerische Schmankerl. Also ... nichts wie hin!

*The **Park Café** at the Alte Botanische Garten has received constant positive press coverage since Thomas Jadrnicek, Michael Schamberger and Christian Schottenhamel took over the Club, the Park-Café Kitchen and the beergarden. Dazzling fetes are celebrated at Munich's scene nightclub. The Park-Café Club which can certainly be compared to New York's former in-discotheque Studio 54 is frequented by celebrities from Germany and abroad. The Park-Café Kitchen was remodelled by the star designer Jacobo Foggini. Everyone who is hip and trendy comes here to enjoy Mediterranean cuisine for brunch, lunch or dinner.*

At the beergarden which seats more than 2,500 guests Bavarian delicacies are offered under chestnut trees. Let's go ... what are you waiting for!

Die Auer Dult, der traditionelle Jahrmarkt auf dem Auer Kirchplatz, beliebt wegen seiner Atmosphäre und seinem vielfältigen Angebot

The Auer Dult, the traditional Bavarian fair on the churchyard in the Au district, is popular because of its atmosphere and wide variety of merchandise on offer.

L'Auer Dult, la kermesse traditionnelle sur la place de l'église dans le district de l'Au. On apprécie son atmosphère et la variété de son offre.

L'Auer Dult, la tradizionale fiera annuale sulla piazza della chiesa del quartiere di Au molto amata per la sua atmosfera e per la sua variegata offerta

*Alfred Hugo Boettner meldete anno 1901 im Tal Nr. 5 einen Austern- und Teehandel an. Bereits 1905 wurde das florierende Geschäft in die Theatinerstraße verlegt, wo es seither als eine der feinsten Adressen Münchens galt. So ist das **Restaurant Boettner's** einzigartig, hat es doch beinahe ein ganzes Jahrhundert überlebt, ohne seinen unnachahmlichen Stil zu verlieren. Auch in der vierten Generation ist es noch im Besitz der Gründerfamilie, wobei seine Leitung in der Hand von Frank Hartung liegt.*

1998 musste das renommierte Restaurant den Umbauplänen in der Theatinerstraße weichen und zog mit dem gesamten Interieur in das wenige Minuten entfernte, soeben sanierte Orlandohaus in der Pfisterstraße 9 um, wo die lange Tradition hervorragender Gastronomie fortgeführt wird.

*Alfred Hugo Boettner had his oyster and tea shop at Tal Nr. 5 registered in 1901. He did a brisk business and moved his shop to Theatinerstraße as early as 1905 where it has since been one of Munich's choicest addresses. Thus the **Restaurant Boettner's** is unique because it has survived almost a century without losing its incomparable style. The business is family-run now by the fourth generation with Frank Hartung in charge of the management.*

In 1998 the famous restaurant had to clear its premises due to extensive reconstruction work on Theatinerstraße and moved with its complete interior decoration to the Orlandohaus on Pfisterstraße 9 which is only a few minutes away and has been refurbished recently. There it will continue its long tradition of haute cuisine.

---

weites Netz von Kontakten geknüpft. Es ist zudem Veranstalter der Volksfeste, auch des berühmten Oktoberfestes.

Das Bild, das sich die Menschen von unserer Stadt machen, ist eng verknüpft mit dem Oktoberfest, dem Fest der Feste. Die Wiesn, das größte Volksfest der Welt, prägt das Image Münchens und trägt auch zum wirtschaftlichen Erfolg der Stadt bei. Viele Jahre war es als Inbegriff von Gemütlichkeit und Lebensfreude Aushängeschild der Fremdenverkehrswerbung. Mittlerweile ist das Oktoberfest ein Selbstläufer geworden, es steht nicht mehr im Zentrum der aktiven Stadtwerbung.

Auch Dulten, Stadtgründungsfest, Christkindlmarkt und viele liebenswerte Stadtteilfeste sowie das unverwechselbare Flair, die nostalgischen Attraktionen und die sprühende Lebensfreude, die sich Gästen wie Bewohnern in dieser Festkultur mitteilen, tragen dazu bei, dass die Bayernmetropole

vals, among them the famous "Oktoberfest".

The impression most people gain of Munich is, of course, strongly influenced by the Oktoberfest, the top event of all the local festivities. "Die Wies'n" (as this biggest festival in the world is called in the vernacular) has shaped Munich's image and contributed greatly to the city's economic success. For many years it was used as a kind of figurehead in touristic advertising, being considered the embodiment of joie de vivre and of "Gemütlichkeit". Today the Oktoberfest is managed independently and no longer plays a major part in the general city advertising.

But also "Dulten" (local kirmesses), the anniversary of the city's founding, the "Christkindlmarkt" (Christmas Market) and numerous attractive district festivals help Munich to preserve its lead in the tourist sector; this status is also supported by Munich's special flair, nostalgic attractions and exuberant zest for life which

capitale du land. Existant depuis quatre décennies, cet office, maintenant riche en traditions, a noué un réseau de contacts à travers le monde. De plus, il s'occupe de l'organisation des fêtes populaires, y compris de la célèbre fête de la Bière.

L'image que se font les gens de notre ville est étroitement liée à la fête de la Bière, la fête des fêtes. La «Wiesn», la plus grande fête populaire du monde, marque l'image de Munich et contribue au succès économique de la ville. Pendant de nombreuses années, elle a été le symbole de la convivialité et de la joie de vivre, et a servi de support à la publicité touristique. Entre-temps, elle est devenue une entité en soi et n'est plus le centre des activités publicitaires municipales.

Les kermesses, les fêtes annuelles de fondation de la ville, les marchés de Noël et de nombreuses petites fêtes de quartiers sans oublier le charme inégalable, les attractions nostalgiques et une pétillante joie de vivre que se

delle feste popolari, tra le quali anche la famosa Oktoberfest.

Il quadro che molte persone si fanno della nostra città è strettamente collegato all'Oktoberfest, la festa delle feste. Definita, in gergo popolare, anche «Wiesn», la più grande festa popolare del mondo, dà un'impronta inconfon-

Die weltberühmten Münchner Philharmoniker in der Philharmonie im Gasteig

The world famous Munich philharmonic orchestra in the concert hall at Gasteig

De réputation internationale, l'orchestre philharmonique de Munich à la philharmonie du Gasteig

L'Orchestra Filarmonica di Monaco, famosa in tutto il mondo, nella sala della Philharmonie del Gasteig

AUGUSTINER GROSSGASTSTÄTTEN
Eine ausgezeichnete regionale Küche, ein gepflegtes Augustiner Bier und die herzliche Atmosphäre machen die AUGUSTINER GROSSGASTSTÄTTEN zu einem Ort traditioneller Gastlichkeit.

AUGUSTINER GROSSGASTSTÄTTEN
The restaurant's excellent cuisine, tasty Augustiner beer, and a hearty atmosphere make the AUGUSTINER GROSSGAST-STÄTTEN a centre of traditional hospitality.

AUGUSTINER GROSSGASTSTÄTTEN
Proposant une excellente cuisine régionale, une bière Augustiner soignée et une agréable atmosphère, les grandes brasseries AUGUSTINER GROSSGASTSTÄTTEN offrent un endroit de restauration traditionnel.

AUGUSTINER GROSSGASTSTÄTTEN
Un'eccellente cucina regionale, una birra Augustiner di prima qualità ed un'atmosfera di grande cordialità rendono le AUGUSTINER GROSSGASTSTÄTTEN un luogo dalla tradizionale ospitalità.

pole ihren Standortvorteil im Tourismus behauptet.

Werbung und Public Relations des Fremdenverkehrsamtes konzentrieren sich selbstverständlich auch auf Kunst und Kultur, die dem Besucher hier auf Schritt und Tritt begegnen. Zwei Werbethemen – „München, Stadt der Musik" und „München, Stadt des Sports" – sollen dem Fremdenverkehr an der Schwelle ins 21. Jahrhundert neue Impulse geben. Thema Nummer eins wird durch drei internationale Stardirigenten – James Levine, Zubin Metha und Lorin Maazel – eindrucksvoll präsentiert. Für Thema Nummer 2 eröffnet sich mit dem Interaktiven Erlebniszentrum Olympic Spirit – einer Weltneuheit – eine neue Dimension.

Ein weiterer Schwerpunkt in der Werbung ist München als Stadt der Museen. Mit der Pinakothek der Moderne, der alten und der neuen Pinakothek, der benachbarten Glyptothek und der Antikensammlung entsteht hier

entices visitors and natives during these festivities.

The local tourist office's efforts in the fields of advertising and public relations also concentrate – of course – on the city's wealth of art and culture which abound wherever visitors go in Munich. Two new slogans – "Munich, City of Music", and "Munich, City of Sports" are to provide new touristic stimuli at the threshold of the 21st century. The first title, "Munich, City of Music", is convincingly supported by three international star conductors, i. e. James Levine, Zubin Metha, and Lorin Maazel. The second one, "Munich, City of Sports", is effectively given a new dimension with the "Interaktive Erlebniszentrum Olympic Spirit", an innovative institution which is unique throughout the world.

A further central topic of advertising is Munich's wealth of museums. One of the globe's largest museumscapes – comprising the Pinakothek der Moder-

communiquent les touristes tout comme les habitants lors de cette culture des fêtes contribuent à ce que la métropole bavaroise confirme son avantage comme site touristique.

La publicité et les relations publiques de l'office de tourisme se concentrent bien évidemment sur l'art et la culture que le visiteur rencontre partout. Deux thèmes publicitaires «Munich, ville de la musique» et «Munich, ville du sport» doivent donner de nouvelles impulsions au tourisme au seuil du 21ème siècle. Le premier thème est présenté de manière éblouissante par trois chefs d'orchestre internationaux James Levine, Zubin Metha et Lorin Maazel. Le deuxième thème ouvre avec la nouveauté mondiale, le centre d'attractions interactif Olympic Spirit, une nouvelle dimension.

La publicité se concentre également sur Munich en tant que ville des musées. Avec la Pinakothek der Moderne, l'an-

dibile all'immagine di Monaco e contribuisce anche al successo economico della città. Per molti anni è stata sinonimo di giovialità e di gioia di vivere ed è servita da richiamo per i turisti sulle pubblicità della città. Nel frattempo, l'Oktoberfest è diventata una manifestazione a sé stante e non è più al centro delle campagne pubblicitarie per la città.

Anche le sagre, la festa per l'anniversario della fondazione della città, il «Christkindlmarkt» (mercatino di Natale) e le tante piacevoli feste popolari nei vari quartieri della città, così come il suo inconfondibile «flair», le attrazioni nostalgiche e l'esuberante gioia di vivere che si impadronisce dei visitatori e degli abitanti, fanno sì che la metropoli bavarese mantenga la sua posizione di centro turistico di primaria importanza.

L'attività promozionale e di pubbliche relazioni dell'Ente per il Turismo si concentrano ovviamente anche sull'arte e sulla

MÜNCHENS HARMONISCHE KÜCHE

Das Wildrestaurant **Halali** *in der Schönfeldstraße gleich neben der Staatsbibliothek war schon vor der Jahrhundertwende bei den Münchnern beliebt. Seit der Renovierung 1982 bildet das Traditionslokal mit seiner dunklen Holztäfelung, säulengestützten Rundbögen und einer exklusiven Tisch- und Tafelkultur den Rahmen für die von Inhaber Hans Mair präsentierten Gaumenfreuden. Der Keller - eine Liebhaberei des Hausherrn - besticht mit einer Auswahl österreichischer Edeltropfen.*

The game and venison restaurant **Halali** *on Schönfeldstraße directly next to the national library was highly popular with the people in Munich even before the turn of the century. Since its renovation in 1982 the traditional restaurant with dark wooden panelling and a vaulted ceiling supported by columns has been a place of unpretentious elegance to delight in the culinary joys presented by the owner Mr Hans Mair. The cellar - the owner's passion - impresses with an excellent range of best Austrian wines.*

eine der größten Museumslandschaften der Welt.

Die Zeichen im München-Tourismus stehen auf Zuwachs. Rund 340 Hotels mit 37 000 Betten, mehr als 110 Tagungsstätten mit rund 100 000 Sitzplätzen, 50 Museen und Sammlungen, darunter das größte technische Museum der Welt, 160 Galerien und 56 Theater, zum Beispiel die weltweit renommierte Bayerische Staatsoper, über 5 000 Restaurants, ein Flughafen als internationales Drehkreuz von hohem Rang, das modernste Messegelände Europas – all das bildet das Fundament für den touristischen Mythos München, die „Weltstadt mit Herz".

Doch auch hier sind Impulse für den Weg in das nächste Jahrtausend gefragt, denn gerade im Tourismus muss den neuen ne, the Old and New Pinakothek, the adjoining Glyptothek and the Antique Collection – is at present developing in the Bavarian capital.

Munich's tourist sector augurs further growth. About 340 hotels offering 37,000 beds; more than 110 conference centres boasting 100,000 seats; 50 museums and collections (among them the world's largest technological museum); 160 art galleries and 56 theatres (including the internationally acclaimed Bavarian State Opera); more than 5,000 restaurants; an airport and international aviation turnstile of major importance; and Europe's most modern fair site – all that provides the foundation for the touristic myth of Munich, the "Weltstadt mit Herz" (Metropolis with a Heart).

But here, as well, new stimuli are required to lead Munich into the new millennium. For particularly in tourism one has to pay attention to cienne et la nouvelle Pinakothek, la Glyptothek voisine et la Antikensammlung (collection d'antiquités), Munich propose un des plus grand choix de musées du monde.

Dans le secteur touristique de Munich, les signes sont à la hausse. Environ 340 hôtels avec 37 000 lits, plus de 110 centres de conférences avec environ 100 000 places assises, 50 musées et collections, dont le plus grand musée de la technique du monde, 160 galeries et 56 théâtres, par exemple l'opéra national à la réputation mondiale, plus de 5 000 restaurants, un aéroport servant de plate-forme internationale de haut rang, le centre de foires le plus moderne d'Europe, tout cela sert de base à la création du mythe touristique de Munich, la «ville mondiale au grand cœur».

Mais là aussi, des impulsions pour le passage au prochain millénaire sont demandées, car justement le tourisme

cultura di cui la città è pervasa. Sono due i temi principali di promozione della città – «Monaco, città della musica» e «Monaco, città dello sport» – temi che daranno nuovi impulsi all'Ente per il Turismo alla soglia del XXI secolo. Il primo tema viene presentato con grande effetto da tre direttori d'orchestra di fama internazionale – James Levine, Zubin Metha e Lorin Maazel. Per quanto riguarda il secondo tema, con il Centro Sportivo Interattivo Olympic Spirit, una novità mondiale, si apre tutta una nuova dimensione.

Un altro tema pubblicitario fondamentale è «Monaco, città dei musei». Grazie alla Galleria Nazionale di Arte Moderna, alla Vecchia e alla Nuova Pinacoteca, alla vicina Gliptoteca e alla Collezione Nazionale di Antichità, Monaco può essere considerata come uno dei maggiori panorami culturali del mondo.

Il turismo a Monaco è in crescita. Circa 340 alberghi con 37 000 posti letto, più di 110 sale convegni per un totale di circa 100 000 posti a sedere, 50 musei e collezioni, tra i quali il maggiore museo per la tecnica del mondo, 160 gallerie e 56 teatri, ad esempio l'Opera di Stato bavarese, oltre 5 000 ristoranti, un aeroporto che rende la città un cro-

Oper in München: nicht nur während der Festspiele ein Kunstgenuss

The opera in Munich: an artistic treat not only during the Festivals

L'opéra à Munich: un plaisir également en dehors des festivals

L'opera lirica a Monaco: un piacere artistico non solo durante il Festival

Standards Rechnung getragen werden. Durch eine noch engere Verbindung des touristischen Marketings mit Kulturaktivitäten, Partnerschaften und Events wird München, die alte Residenz- und moderne Hightech-Stadt, auch im neuen Jahrtausend seine führende Rolle behaupten. Internationale Großveranstaltungen wie die Leichtathletik-Weltmeisterschaften 2002 und die Bundesgartenschau 2005 werden das Ihre dazu beitragen.

Den gestiegenen Ansprüchen an Service und Betreuung wird durch zielgruppenspezifische Angebote wie „Hits für Kids" oder die Einführung der „München Welcome Card" Rechnung getragen. Komplettangebote, zusammengefasst im „Münchner Schlüssel", erlauben ein bequemes Kennenlernen der Stadt. Schon aus ökologischen Gründen ist eine intensive Zusammenarbeit zwischen dem öffentlichen Personennahverkehr und Anbietern von umweltschonenden

new standards. By linking even more closely touristic marketing with cultural activities, partnerships, and attractive events, the former court city and present-day high-tech centre of Munich will maintain its leading role in the new millennium as well. International large-scale events such as the World Athletics Competition in 2002, and the Federal Garden Show in 2005 will contribute their share to realizing this aim.

More exacting demands made on service and care are already being met with target-group-specific offers like "Hits for Kids", or by introducing the "Munich Welcome Card". Package offers, combined in the so-called "Münchner Schlüssel" (Key to Munich), make it possible to get to know Munich in a comfortable and convenient way.

Intensive cooperation between public short-distance transport and the organizers of environment-friendly city tours will become even more significant in

doit s'adapter aux nouveaux standards. Par une relation encore plus étroite du marketing touristique avec les activités culturelles, les partenariats et les événements, Munich, l'ancienne ville de la Résidence et la ville moderne de la haute technologie, doit confirmer son rôle de leader dans le nouveau millénaire. De grandes manifestations internationales comme les championnats du monde d'athlétisme en 2002 et l'exposition d'horticulture en 2005 y contribueront.

Les exigences accrues de service et de suivi trouvent leurs réponses dans des offres orientées sur des groupes cibles comme «Hits für Kids» ou l'introduction de la «München Welcome Card». Des offres complètes, réunies dans «Münchner Schlüssel» (la clé de Munich) permettent de faire connaissance de manière agréable avec la ville.

Déjà pour des raisons écologiques, une collaboration intense entre les transports interurbains

cevia internazionale di primaria importanza, il centro fieristico più moderno di tutta l'Europa – tutto ciò costituisce la base per il mito di Monaco, la «metropoli con sentimento».

Ma anche qui si richiedono nuovi impulsi per l'entrata nel nuovo millennio, perché proprio il settore turistico deve adeguarsi ai nuovi standard. Grazie ad un rapporto ancora più stretto del marketing turistico con attività culturali, compartecipazioni ed eventi, Monaco, l'antica città della Residenza e moderna città high-tech, riuscirà a mantenere il suo ruolo di leader anche nel prossimo millennio. Grandi eventi internazionali come i Mondiali di Atletica Leggera nel 2002 e l'Esposizione Nazionale di Giardinaggio nel 2005 daranno il loro contributo.

Alle richieste sempre più esigenti di servizi e di assistenza si cerca di far fronte con offerte mirate, quali ad esempio «Hits für Kids» o mediante l'introduzione della «Welcome Card di Monaco».

*Das kleine, familiär geführte Restaurant **Buon Gusto** in der Münchener Altstadt hält, was sein Name verspricht: feine italienische Küche, gekocht vor den Augen der Gäste, um die sich Wirt Rinaldo Talamonti liebevoll kümmert und die er mit ausgefallenen Gerichten aufs Angenehmste überrascht.*

*The small restaurant **Buon Gusto** in Munichs old town is run like a family business and does its name justice: excellent Italian cuisine cooked directly in front of the guests by Rinaldo Talamonti who looks after his customers with great care and surprises them with unusual and delicious meals.*

*Situé dans la vieille ville de Munich, le petit restaurant familial **Buon Gusto** fait honneur à son nom. Une délicate cuisine italienne, préparée sous les yeux des clients. Le restaurateur Rinaldo Talamonti est aux petits soins pour sa clientèle et la surprend agréablement avec des mets extraordinaires.*

*Il piccolo ristorante a conduzione familiare **Buon Gusto**, nel centro storico di Monaco, mantiene la promessa evocata dal suo nome, proponendo una cucina italiana le cui prelibatezze vengono preparate davanti agli occhi degli ospiti. Di questi ultimi si prende cura amorevolmente il titolare Rinaldo Talamonti, sorprendendoli continuamente con pietanze decisamente ricercate.*

Das Gasthaus *„Zum Brunnwart"* in der Biedersteinerstraße am Rande des Englischen Gartens in München gelegen, nur ein paar Gehminuten entfernt von Schwabings berühmter Leopoldstraße, blickt zurück auf über 130 Jahre Wirtsbetrieb. Die dezent renovierte Innenausstattung hat nichts von ihrem ursprünglichen Charme verloren. Die betont unaufdringliche, bayerisch-anheimelnde Atmosphäre trägt die Handschrift der Wirte Karin Goll und Alfons Harlander. Sie beide beherrschen perfekt die Rolle der Gastgeber.
Das Gasthaus zum Brunnwart bietet vorwiegend traditionelle Gerichte zu moderaten Preisen. Besonders hervorzuheben ist der aufmerksame, stets liebenswürdige Service.
All das wissen die vielen Stammgäste und die einheimische Prominenz zu schätzen, die auch zahlreich zu den hauseigenen Veranstaltungen erscheinen.
Schon lange ist der Biergarten ein Geheimtip. Vom ersten Sonnenstrahl bis spät in den Herbst hinein genießt man hier das unverwechselbare Ambiente, das nur in Bayern zufinden ist.

Stadttouren für den Tourismus zukunftweisend. Für einen schnellen Informationsfluss sorgt zusätzlich the future, mainly for ecological reasons. Additionally, the internet provides a rapid flow of informa- de personnes et les agences proposant des visites de la ville respectant l'environnement mon- Pacchetti di offerta completi, raccolti nella brochure «Chiave di Monaco», consentono di avere a disposizione uno strumento comodo per conoscere la città. Sia, soprattutto, per motivi ecologici, ma anche per il prosperare del turismo, è auspicabile che ci sia in futuro una collaborazione intensiva tra i servizi di trasporto pubblici e le organizzazioni dei tour ambientalistici della città. Infine, Internet fornisce un flusso

Straßenmusikanten gehören zum Stadtbild.

Street musicians are a common part of the town.

Les musiciens ambulants font partie du paysage urbain.

I musicisti per le strade fanno parte della fisionomia cittadina.

Resümee

Auch im 21. Jahrhundert wird München seine lange Tradition als Fremdenverkehrsmetropole fortsetzen. Dank seiner Lage im Herzen Europas, im Ansichtskartenland Oberbayern, mit seiner hochkarätigen Wirtschafts- und Wissenschaftsstruktur, einer lebendigen Kultur gepaart mit altbayerischer Tradition und weißblauem Charme, wird die Isarmetropole weiterhin Traumziel für Menschen aus aller Welt sein.

Dr. Gabriele Weishäupl

Summing up

Munich will continue its long tradition as a tourist centre in the 21st century as well. Thanks to its location in the heart of Europe and in the picture-book country of Upper Bavaria, to its top-grade economic and scientific structure, to a lively contemporary cultural scene coupled with old-Bavarian traditions, and to its "white-and-blue charm", the metropolis on the Isar will continue to be a magic destination for people from all parts of the world.

Dr. Gabriele Weishäupl

Résumé

Au 21ème siècle, Munich poursuivra encore sa longue tradition de métropole du tourisme. Grâce à sa position au cœur de l'Europe, dans cette magnifique région de Haute-Bavière, avec son excellente structure économique et scientifique, sa culture vivante liée aux anciennes traditions bavaroises et au charme des couleurs bavaroises bleu-blanc, la métropole aux bords de l'Isar continuera d'être la destination de rêve des gens de toute la planète.

Dr. Gabriele Weishäupl

Sintesi

Anche nel XXI secolo Monaco continuerà la sua lunga tradizione di metropoli turistica. Grazie alla sua posizione al centro dell'Europa, nell'incantevole Alta Baviera, con la sua struttura economica e scientifica di prim'ordine ed una cultura vivace abbinata alle antiche tradizioni bavaresi e al suo innato charme bianco-blu, la metropoli sull'Isar continuerà ad essere la meta turistica sognata in tutto il mondo.

Dr. Gabriele Weishäupl

*Die von Staatsschauspieler Peter Fricke zum Leben gebrachte **Brasserie buñuel** in **München-Grünwald** liegt im Bannkreis der Bavaria-Filmstudios und ist mit ihrem Pariser Flair und ihrer exzellenten französischen Küche von Andrée Marmion und seiner Tochter Madeleine Puzenat ein beliebter Künstlertreff.*

Regelmäßige Showauftritte, Lesungen sowie Live-Musik montags ab 21 Uhr!

*The **Brasserie buñuel** in **München-Grünwald** which lies in the sphere of influence of the Bavaria-Filmstudios, is run and filled with life by the famous German actor Peter Fricke. With its Parisian flair and excellent French cuisine of Andrée Marmion and its daughter Madeleine Puzenat it has become a popular meeting place for artists.*

Performances and readings in regular intervals as well as live music on Mondays from 9pm!

*Mise en route par le comédien Peter Fricke, la **Brasserie buñuel** à **München-Grünwald**, se trouve à proximité des studios de cinéma Bavaria-Filmstudios et s'avère, grâce à son flair parisien et son excellente cuisine française proposée par Andrée Marmion et sa fille Madeleine Puzenat, un lieu de rencontre apprécié des artistes.*

Spectacles réguliers, lectures et musique en direct, tous les lundis à partir de 21 heures !

294

Die Münchner
Brauereien

Munich's
Breweries

Les brasseries
munichoises

Le fabbriche di birra
di Monaco

Augustiner-Bräu Wagner KG, Hacker-Pschorr-Bräu GmbH, Löwenbräu AG, Paulaner Brauerei GmbH & Co KG, Spaten-Franziskaner-Bräu KgaA und Staatliches Hofbräuhaus in München heißen die sechs Münchner Großbrauereien offiziell, die heute noch den Ruf der Stadt München als der heimlichen Hauptstadt des Bieres dokumentieren.

Spätestens seit dem Sankt-Andreas-Tag im Jahr 1487 sind diese Brauereien die Garanten für reines Bier. Damals verlangte Herzog Albrecht der Weise von den Brauherren seiner Residenzstadt einen „Aid" darauf, dass sie „zu jedem pier allain gersten, hopfen und wasser nehmen… und nicht andern darein tun". 30 Jahre später, 1516, erweiterte sein Sohn Wilhelm das Reinheitsgebot auf ganz Bayern, das seit Anfang dieses Jahrhunderts bis heute in ganz Deutschland gilt.

In der Tradition von 1487 erneuern die Münchner Brauer alle zwei Jahre am Münchner Brauertag den „Preu-Aid" vor den Bürgern auf dem Viktualienmarkt.

Munich's six largest breweries are officially called Augustiner-Bräu Wagner KG, Hacker-Pschorr-Bräu GmbH, Löwenbräu AG, Paulaner Brauerei GmbH & Co KG, Spaten-Franziskaner-Bräu KgaA, and Staatliches Hofbräuhaus; they still uphold Munich's reputation as the "Secret Capital of Beer".

Since Sankt-Andreas Day in 1487 at the latest these breweries have been warrantors of pure beer. At that time Duke Albrecht the Wise had the brewers of his residential city swear that they "would only put barley, hop and water into their beer and nothing else". 30 years later, in 1516, his son Wilhelm extended this law to all of Bavaria. And since the beginning of our century it has been valid throughout Germany.

In commemoration of the oath of 1487, Munich's brewers on the so-called "Brewers' Day" renew the "brewing oath" to the citizens on Viktualienmarkt, an event that takes place every two years. During this ceremony the

Augustiner-Bräu Wagner KG, Hacker-Pschorr-Bräu GmbH, Löwenbräu AG, Paulaner Brauerei GmbH & Co KG, Spaten-Franziskaner-Bräu KgaA et la Staaliches Hofbräuhaus sont à Munich les six grandes brasseries officielles qui prouvent aujourd'hui encore la réputation de la ville de Munich comme capitale régionale de la bière.

Depuis au plus tard le jour de la Saint André en 1487, les brasseries se portent garant d'une bière pure. A l'époque, le duc Albrecht le Sage exigea des brasseurs de sa ville résidentielle de porter serment affirmant qu'ils «n'utiliseront pour toute bière que de l'orge, du houblon et de l'eau … et rien d'autre». 30 ans plus tard en 1516, son fils Guillaume étendit le commandement sur la pureté de la bière à l'ensemble de la Bavière. Au début de ce siècle, il fut étendu à toute l'Allemagne et prévaut jusqu'à aujourd'hui.

Dans la tradition de 1487, les brasseurs munichois renouvellent tous les deux ans leur serment, à savoir devant les citoyens le jour

Augustiner-Bräu Wagner KG, Hacker-Pschorr-Bräu GmbH, Löwenbräu AG, Paulaner Brauerei GmbH & Co KG, Spaten-Franziskaner-Bräu KgaA e Staatliches Hofbräuhaus in München, queste le denominazioni sociali ufficiali delle sei grandi fabbriche di birra di Monaco di Baviera che documentano, ancora oggi, la fama della città come capitale segreta della birra.

Al più tardi a partire dal giorno di Sant'Andrea dell'anno 1478 queste fabbriche di birra sono le grandi garanti della birra pura. All'epoca, il duca Alberto il Saggio pretese dai titolari delle manufatture birraie della sua città-residenza che essi prestassero un giuramento di «prendere per ciascuna birra solo orzo, luppolo e acqua … e non aggiungervi nient'altro». 30 anni dopo, nel 1516, suo figlio Guglielmo estese la Legge sulla purezza della birra all'intera Baviera, che dall'inizio del XX secolo fino ad oggi vale nell'intera Germania.

Fedeli alla tradizione del 1487, i fabbricanti di birra monacensi

Der von den Münchner Brauereien gestiftete Maibaum auf dem Viktualienmarkt: Durchmesser 0,8 Meter, Länge 34 Meter. Auf den bunten Tafeln finden sich neben Standl-Frau, Schäfflern und Biergartenszenen die Logos der sechs Münchner Brauereien auf einem klassischen Bierfuhrwerk.

The may pole on the victuals market which was donated by Munich's breweries has a diameter of 0.8 metres and a height of 34 metres. On the colourful plaques there are the market women, coopers and scenes from a beergarden and also the trademarks of the six Munich's breweries on a classic horse-drawn cart.

Sur le Viktualienmarkt, le mat de cocagne offert par les brasseries munichoises affiche un diamètre de 0,8 mètre et une longueur de 34 mètres. Ses tableaux décoratifs représentent la marchande les tonneliers et les scènes de jardins de la bière tout comme les logos des six brasseries munichoises sur un attelage classique de transport de la bière.

L'Albero di Maggio sul Viktualienmarkt donato dalle fabbriche di birra monacensi: diametro 0,8 metri, lunghezza 34 metri. Sulle variopinte insegne sono riportati, oltre alle donne del mercato, ai bottai e alle scene da birreria all'aperto, anche i logotipi delle sei fabbriche di birra monacensi su un classico carro che trasporta i fusti di birra.

*Blick vom Stiglmeierplatz auf das Bräustüberl von **Löwenbräu**, München, den Löwenbräukeller und seinen gemütlichen Biergarten*

*View from Stiglmeierplatz to the "Bräustüberl" of **Löwenbräu**, Munich, the Löwenbräukeller and its cosy beer garden*

*Vue de la place Stiglmeier sur la brasserie **Löwenbräu** de Munich et son agréable jardin de la bière*

*Vista, dalla Stiglmeier-platz, sulla Bräustüberl della **Löwenbräu** di Monaco, sulla Löwenbräukeller e sulla sua frequentatissima birreria all'aperto*

Blick von der Marsstraße auf Münchens älteste bürgerliche Brauerei, **Spaten-Franziskaner-Bräu**. *Sie steht für München und seine Brautradition seit 1397*

Looking from Marstraße to Munich's oldest civilian brewery – the **Spaten-Franziskaner-Bräu**. *It has represented Munich and the city's brewing tradition since 1397.*

Vue de la rue Marsstraße sur la plus vieille brasserie munichoise, la **Spaten-Franziskaner-Bräu**. *Elle représente Munich et sa tradition de brassage depuis 1397.*

Vista, dalla Marsstraße, sulla più antica fabbrica di birra privata di Monaco di Baviera, la **Spaten-Franziskaner-Bräu**. *Essa è sinonimo della tradizione birraia monacense fin dal 1397.*

Dabei werden die kostbaren Brauerinsignien gezeigt, und nach einem Festgottesdienst in der ältesten Stadtpfarrkirche St. Peter zieht ein Festzug, der von Brauereigespannen, Trachtengruppen, Musikkapellen sowie den Honoratioren der Stadt begleitet wird, durch Münchens Straßen. An diesem Tag werden auch die Auszubildenden von den Brauherren und dem Oberbürgermeister feierlich in den Gesellenstand verabschiedet. Unter dem von den Münchner Brauern gestifteten Maibaum wird bei Freibier getanzt und gelacht.

Der Qualitätsbegriff „Münchner Bier", den es nur einmal gibt, wird von den örtlichen Brauern hart verteidigt. Daran kann auch der Spruch des Europäischen Gerichtshofes von 1987 nichts ändern, der die gesetzliche Verankerung des Reinheitsgebotes zum Teil außer Kraft gesetzt hat. Selbst wenn nunmehr Zusatzstoffe erlaubt sind, verzichten die Münchner Brauereien weiterhin auf solche Stoffe und werden ihr Bier auch künftig nur aus Wasser, Malz und Hopfen – und aus nichts anderem – herstellen.

Und was wäre das Oktoberfest, die Wies'n, ohne das „Münchner Bier"? Erst das spezielle, von den Münchner Brauereien eingesottene Oktoberfestbier mit mindestens 13,5 % Stammwürze macht das Fest zum Oktoberfest, zum „Fest des Münchner Bieres".

Über ein Fünftel des bayerischen Bieres wird in München gebraut, was auch den wirtschaftlichen Aspekt für die Landeshauptstadt unterstreicht. Wirtschaftlich wie kulturell sind die Münchner Brauer mit der Stadt verbunden. Seit jeher fördern sie Wissenschaft, Kunst und Kultur, engagieren sich in städtischen Gremien und öffentlichen Institutionen, waren und sind Wegbereiter von Technik und Sicherheit. Ihre Familien stellten Komponisten wie Richard Strauss oder Gründer des heutigen TÜV wie Gabriel Sedlmayr.

Ein guter Teil des Münchner Bieres wird in den für München einzigartigen Biergärten konsu-

precious brewers' insignias are exhibited and after a special service in Munich's "Peterskirche", the city's oldest parish church, a festive procession displaying colourful teams of horses and brewery waggons, folklore groups and brass bands accompanied by the city's notabilities, moves through Munich's streets. On this day the local apprentices are pronounced journeymen by the brewers and the First Mayor. Afterwards the "natives" enjoy the free beer, dancing and making merry under the maypole donated by the brewers.

The unique quality badge "Münchner Bier" has always been defended persistently by the local brewers. It will certainly not be affected by a decision made by the European Court of Justice in 1987, which partly repealed the legal foundation of the purity law. Even though additions are permitted now, Munich's breweries will in future, too, do without such additives and continue brewing their beer only with water, malt and hop, and nothing else.

What would the "Oktoberfest" – in Bavaria called "Wies'n" – be without "Münchner Bier"? It is the special October Festival beer – containing at least 13.5 % of the "Stammwürze" – which turns this event into a genuine Beer Festival.

More than a fifth of all the Bavarian beer is brewed in Munich, a fact that underlines its economic significance for the state capital. Munich's brewers are closely linked with the city economically as well as culturally. They have always promoted the sciences, art and culture, are represented in municipal bodies and public institutions, and have always been pioneers of technology and safety. Their families produced such outstanding citizens as composer Richard Strauss or the founder of the present-day car-inspection service "TÜV" – Gabriel Sedlmayr.

des brasseurs munichois sur le Viktualienmarkt. Les précieux insignes des brasseurs sont exhibés à cette occasion et, après une messe célébrée dans l'ancienne église paroissiale St Pierre, un défilé parcoure les rues de la ville et est composé des attelages des brasseurs, de groupes folkloriques, d'orchestres ainsi que des personnalités de la ville. Ce jour là, les apprentis sont officiellement élevés par les brasseurs et le maire au rang de compagnons. Sous l'arbre de mai (mât de cocagne) offert par les brasseurs munichois, place est faite à la danse et aux rires et la bière coule à profusion.

Le terme de qualité «Münchner Bier» (bière munichoise) qui est unique est ardemment défendu par les brasseurs locaux. Et la sentence de la cour européenne de justice prononcée en 1987, qui a partiellement levé la tradition légale du commandement sur la pureté de la bière, ne peut rien y changer. Même si maintenant des substances supplémentaires sont autorisées, les brasseurs munichois les refusent toujours et continueront à l'avenir encore de fabriquer leur bière avec de l'eau, du malt et du houblon, et rien d'autre.

Et que serait la fête de la Bière, la Wies'n sans la «bière munichoise»? Les brasseurs

rinnovano ogni due anni, nella «Giornata del birraio monacense» il «Giuramento della birra» davanti ai cittadini al «Mercato delle Vettovaglie». In tale occasione vengono esibite le preziose insegne dei birrai, e dopo una messa solenne nella chiesa di San Pietro, la più antica chiesa parrocchiale della città, un corteo accompagnato da carri delle fabbriche di birre addobbati a festa, da gruppi in costume folkloristico nonché dai notabili della città sfila per le vie della città. In questa giornata avviene anche l'elevazione solenne degli apprendisti birrai al rango di artigiani ad opera dei titolari delle fabbriche di birra e del borgomastro della città. E sotto l'«Albero di Maggio» donato dalle fabbriche di birra della città viene offerta birra gratuitamente, si balla e ci si diverte.

La denominazione di qualità «Münchner Bier» (Birra di Monaco), di cui ne esiste solo una nel mondo, viene difesa a spada tratta dai birrai locali. Questa situazione non è stata minimamente intaccata neanche dalla sentenza della Corte di Giustizia Europea del 1987 che ha parzialmente revocato il carattere normativo della Legge sulla purezza della birra. Anche se ora è ammesso l'impiego di additivi, le

Bereits seit dem Jahre 1950 ist der Name der Familie Kreitmair eng verbunden mit dem großen **Paulaner Festzelt „Winzerer Fähndl"** auf dem Münchner Oktoberfest. Seit 1965 trägt es die Handschrift von Willi Kreitmair. Der Wiesnwirt und seine Ehefrau Helga kümmern sich ganz persönlich um das Wohl ihrer Gäste, indem sie zum Beispiel jedes Detail selbst aussuchen. Das gilt ebenso für den traditionsreichen Gasthof Kreitmair mit seinem schattigen Biergarten in Keferloh bei München.

Schon von weitem für jeden Oktoberfestbesucher sichtbar ist die Attraktion des Winzerer Fähndls: der 25 Meter hohe Turm am Haupteingang, auf dessen Dach sich ein riesiger Paulaner Maßkrug dreht. Festzelt und Gasthof sind Stammplatz vieler Prominenter aus Politik, Wirtschaft, Kultur und Sport. Ihnen bieten die engagierten Wirtsleute neben dem berühmten Paulaner Bier bayerische Köstlichkeiten wie Kalbs- und Schweinshaxe vom Grill, knusprige Brathendl und Enten oder Junghirschbraten an.

Der von Willi Kreitmair jeden Abend persönlich angeführte traditionelle Spanferkel-Zug gegen 19.30 Uhr macht darüber hinaus den Besuch im Winzerer Fähndl zu einem unvergesslichen Erlebnis.

Already since 1950 the name of the Kreitmair family has been closely connected with the great **Paulaner beer hall "Winzerer Fähndl"** on Munich's Oktoberfest. Since 1965 it has been primarily influenced by landlord Willi Kreitmair. He and his wife Helga take good care of their guests personally by individually selecting every detail. The same can be said of the traditional restaurant Kreitmair with its shady beergarden in Keferloh on the outskirts of Munich.

Visitors coming to the Oktoberfest can see the landmark of the Winzerer Fähndl on first sight: a 25 metre high tower in front of the beer hall with a gigantic Paulaner mug revolving on top. The beer hall as well as the restaurant are frequented by many celebrities from politics, culture, sports and the economy. In addition to the famous Paulaner beer the dedicated landlord and landlady offer them Bavarian delicacies such as barbecued knuckles of veal and pork, crisp roasted chicken, ducks or venison.

In addition the traditional piglet parade, personally led by Willi Kreitmair around 7.30 pm every day makes a visit of the Winzerer Fähndl an unforgettable event.

Depuis déjà 1950, le nom de la famille Kreitmair est étroitement lié au grand **chapiteau Paulaner «Winzerer Fähndl»** trônant à la fête de la Bière. Depuis 1965, il porte la signature de Willi Kreitmair. Celui-ci et sa femme Helga s'occupent personnellement de leur clientèle et veillent par exemple eux-mêmes aux moindres détails. Cela prévaut également pour le restaurant Kreitmair riche en traditions, doté d'un jardin de la bière ombragé et situé à Keferloh près de Munich.

A la fête de la Bière, l'attraction du Winzerer Fähndl se voit de loin, à savoir une tour de 25 mètres de haut située à l'entrée principale et faisant tourner sur son faîte une immense chope à bière Paulaner. Le chapiteau et le restaurant sont le lieu privilégié de nombreuses personnalités du monde politique, économique, culturel et sportif. Les restaurateurs engagés leur proposent, outre la célèbre bière Paulaner, des spécialités bavaroises comme le jarret grillé de veau ou de porc, le poulet ou le canard grillés et croustillants ou le rôti de jeune cerf.

Par ailleurs, le défilé traditionnel du cochon de lait mené personnellement par Willi Kraitmair à 19h30 chaque soir fait de la visite de la fête de la Bière un souvenir inoubliable.

È già dal 1950 che il nome della famiglia Kreitmair è strettamente legato al grande **tendone «Winzerer Fähndl» della birra Paulaner** all'«Oktoberfest». Dal 1965, la gestione del tendone è stata assunta da Willi Kreitmair. Egli e sua moglie Helga si prendono cura in prima persona dei propri ospiti, ad esempio scegliendo ogni dettaglio dell'allestimento del locale. Ciò vale, in egual misura, per il ristorante Kreitmair di Keferloh presso Monaco, un locale ricco di tradizione che dispone anche di un'ombrosa birreria all'aperto.

Chi si reca alla Festa della Birra può ammirare l'attrazione del Winzerer Fähndl già da lontano: si tratta di una torre di 25 metri, presso l'entrata principale del tendone, sulla cui sommità gira un gigantesco boccale di birra Paulaner. Sia il tendone dell'Oktoberfest che il ristorante sono i ritrovi abituali di numerose personalità del mondo della politica, dell'economia, della cultura e dello sport. Ad essi i due titolari propongono, oltre alla famosa birra Paulaner, anche manicaretti della cucina bavarese come lo stinco di vitello e di maiale alla griglia, fragranti polli ed anatre arrosto o l'arrosto di cerbiatto.

Inoltre, la tradizionale «sfilata delle porchette» delle ore 19.30 ogni sera, con in testa Willi Kreitmair in persona, fa della visita al Winzerer Fähndl un evento indimenticabile.

miert. In dieser seit ca. 1725 für alle Gesellschaftsschichten existierenden Einrichtung zelebrieren die Menschen ihr individuelles Biergartenzeremoniell, denn die Brotzeit darf mitgebracht werden. Hier lebt man, denn wo kann man noch sagen: „Hier bin ich Mensch, hier darf ich's sein", wenn nicht in einem Münchner Biergarten.

Dr.-Ing. Peter Kreuzpaintner

A large portion of the beer brewed in Munich is consumed in the city's unique "beer gardens". In these institutions, which have existed since roughly 1725 and cater to all social classes, the local people celebrate an individual beer garden ceremony, for they are allowed to bring along their own snacks. Here one is able to really live, for where can one say with Goethe "hier bin ich Mensch, hier darf ich's sein", (here I can really be a human being) if not in a Munich beer garden.

Dr.-Ing. Peter Kreuzpaintner

munichois brassent pour la fête d'octobre une cuvée spéciale, la bière contient en effet au moins 13,5 % de moût et fait de la fête d'octobre la «fête de la Bière munichoise».

Plus d'un cinquième de la bière bavaroise est brassé à Munich ce qui souligne l'aspect économique de ce secteur pour la capitale du land. Au niveau économique et culturel, les brasseurs munichois sont étroitement liés à la ville. Depuis la nuit des temps, ils assurent la promotion de la science, de l'art et de la culture, s'engagent dans les réunions municipales et les institutions publiques. Ils ont montré et montrent encore les voies de la technique et de la sécurité. Leurs familles déclinent des noms de compositeurs comme Richard Strauss ou le fondateur de l'actuel TÜV comme Gabriel Sedlmayr.

Une bonne partie de la bière munichoise est consommée dans les jardins de la bière absolument typiques de Munich. Dans ces jardins existant depuis 1725 environ et destinés à toutes les classes sociales, les habitants célèbrent leur cérémonie individuelle du jardin de la bière car il est permis d'amener son «casse-croûte». Ici on vit car où peut-on encore dire: «ici je suis un homme, ici je peux l'être», si ce n'est dans un jardin de la bière munichois.

Dr.-Ing. Peter Kreuzpaintner

fabbriche di birra monacensi continuano a rifiutare tali sostanze e produrranno la loro birra, anche il futuro, solo con acqua, malto, e luppolo ... e nient'altro.

E cosa ne sarebbe della Festa della Birra, dell'Oktoberfest, senza la «Münchner Bier»? Infatti, è proprio la birra dell'Oktoberfest, concepita volutamente dalle fabbriche locali con un tenore alcoolico del mosto originario del 13,5 %, a fare dell'Oktoberfest la «Festa della Birra Monacense».

Oltre un quinto della birra bavarese viene fabbricata a Monaco, e questo sottolinea l'importanza che questo aspetto riveste per l'economia della città. Le fabbriche di birra sono legate alla città sia da un punto di vista economico che culturale. Esse, infatti, promuovono da sempre la scienza, l'arte e la cultura, i suoi esponenti sono impegnati in diversi organismi comunali ed istituzioni pubbliche, sono stati e continuano ad essere pionieri nel campo della tecnica e della sicurezza. Dalle famiglie dei birrai sono scaturiti compositori come Richard Strauss o anche Gabriel Sedlmayr, uno dei fondatori dell'odierno Istituto di Controlli Tecnici «TÜV».

Una buona parte della birra di Monaco viene consumata nelle birrerie all'aperto così uniche e tipiche di Monaco. In questa vera e propria istituzione, esistente dal 1725 circa ed aperta a tutti i ceti della popolazione, la gente celebra il suo rituale enogastronomico personalizzato, anche perché la merenda può venir portata da casa. Qui si vive, nel vero senso della parola. In quale altro posto se non in una birreria all'aperto, infatti, si può ancora affermare: «Qui sono uomo, qui posso esserlo.»

Dr.-Ing. Peter Kreuzpaintner

„Wenn es in München keinen Biergarten gäbe, dann müsste man ihn sofort erfinden..." So beginnt 1996 ein Bericht über die Entstehung einer der beliebtesten Münchner „Institutionen".

Heide Volm in Planegg ist eine dieser Institutionen. Der Traditionsbiergarten wurde 1994 von der Wirtsfamilie Heide umgebaut und bietet seither 1 500 Plätze – davon 300 mit Bedienung –, eine Pilsbar, eine Steckerlfischbude, einen Kiosk mit Salatbar sowie einen großzügigen Spielplatz. Die Bewirtung beginnt am späten Vormittag, um 16 Uhr wird der Fischgrill angeheizt und die Pilsbar eröffnet.

Bei gutem Wetter spielt bei Heides in Planegg natürlich auch die Musik: an Feiertagen und in regelmäßigen Abständen donnerstags.

Heide Volm liegt jenseits der Stadtgrenze. Die hohe Qualität der Speisen und Getränke und der ausgezeichnete Service bieten jedoch einen besonderen Anreiz, wodurch für unzählige Besucher der Aufenthalt unter den riesigen, Schatten spendenden Kastanien zum unvergesslichen Erlebnis wird.

"If Munich didn't have its beergardens they would have to be invented instantly..." This is the beginning of a report written in 1996 about the emergence of Munich's most popular "institutions".

Heide Volm in Planegg is one of these institutions. The traditional beergarden was remodelled by the innkeepers, the Heide family, in 1994, and since then has offered 1,500 seats - of which 300 are attended to by waiters -, a Lager bar, a stand for barbecued fish, a kiosk with a salad buffet as well as a spacious playground. Food service begins late in the morning, at 4pm the barbecue for the fish is lit and the Lager bar opens.

Weather permitting of course there is also live music at Heide's in Planegg: on holidays and in regular intervals on Thursdays.

Heide Volm is situated beyond the city boundaries. The excellent quality of the foods and beverages as well as an impeccable service are a special treat which makes the stay of the countless visitors who come to sit in the shade of the enormous chestnut trees an unforgettable one.

«Si le jardin de la bière n'existait pas à Munich, il faudrait l'inventer immédiatement...» C'est ainsi que commence en 1996 un rapport sur l'histoire d'une des «institutions» munichoises les plus appréciées.

A Planegg, Heide Volm est une des ces institutions. Le jardin de la bière traditionnel a été réaménagé en 1994 par la famille de restaurateurs Heide et offre depuis 1 500 places, dont 300 avec service, un bar à Pils, un stand de poissons cuits au bois, un kiosque avec buffet de salades ainsi qu'une grande aire de jeux. Le service commence en fin de matinée, vers 16 heures le grill à poissons est mis en route et le bar à Pils ouvert.

Par beau temps, la musique est également au rendez-vous chez Heide, il en va de même les jours fériés et à intervalles réguliers les jeudis.

Heide Volm est situé en dehors des limites de la ville. Ses plats et boissons de grande qualité, son excellent service offrent cependant un charme particulier qui fait que de nombreux visiteurs viennent passer un moment inoubliable à l'ombre des immenses châtaigniers.

«Se a Monaco non esistessero le birrerie all'aperto, bisognerebbe reinventarle quanto prima...» Così inizia un articolo del 1996 sulla nascita di una delle «istituzioni» monacensi più amate.

Una di queste istituzioni è la **Heide Volm di Planegg**. La birreria all'aperto, ricca di tradizione, è stata ristrutturata nel 1994 dalla famiglia di gestori Heide ed offre, da allora, 1 500 posti a sedere – 300 dei quali con servizio al tavolo –, un «pils bar», una bancarella che vende pesce allo spiedo, un bancone delle insalate nonché un grande campo giochi. La ristorazione inizia nella tarda mattinata; e alle ore 16 viene riscaldata la griglia per il pesce ed aperto il pils bar.

Tempo permettendo, la Heide Volm propone anche musica dal vivo: ad esempio, nei giorni di festa nonché, a intervalli di tempo regolari, anche di giovedì.

La Heide Volm si trova fuori dal territorio comunale di Monaco. L'ottima qualità delle sue proposte enogastronomiche e l'eccellente servizio rappresentano, però, uno stimolo particolare che induce innumerevoli visitatori a soggiornare sotto i giganteschi, ombrosi ippocastani e fare della permanenza un'esperienza indimenticabile.

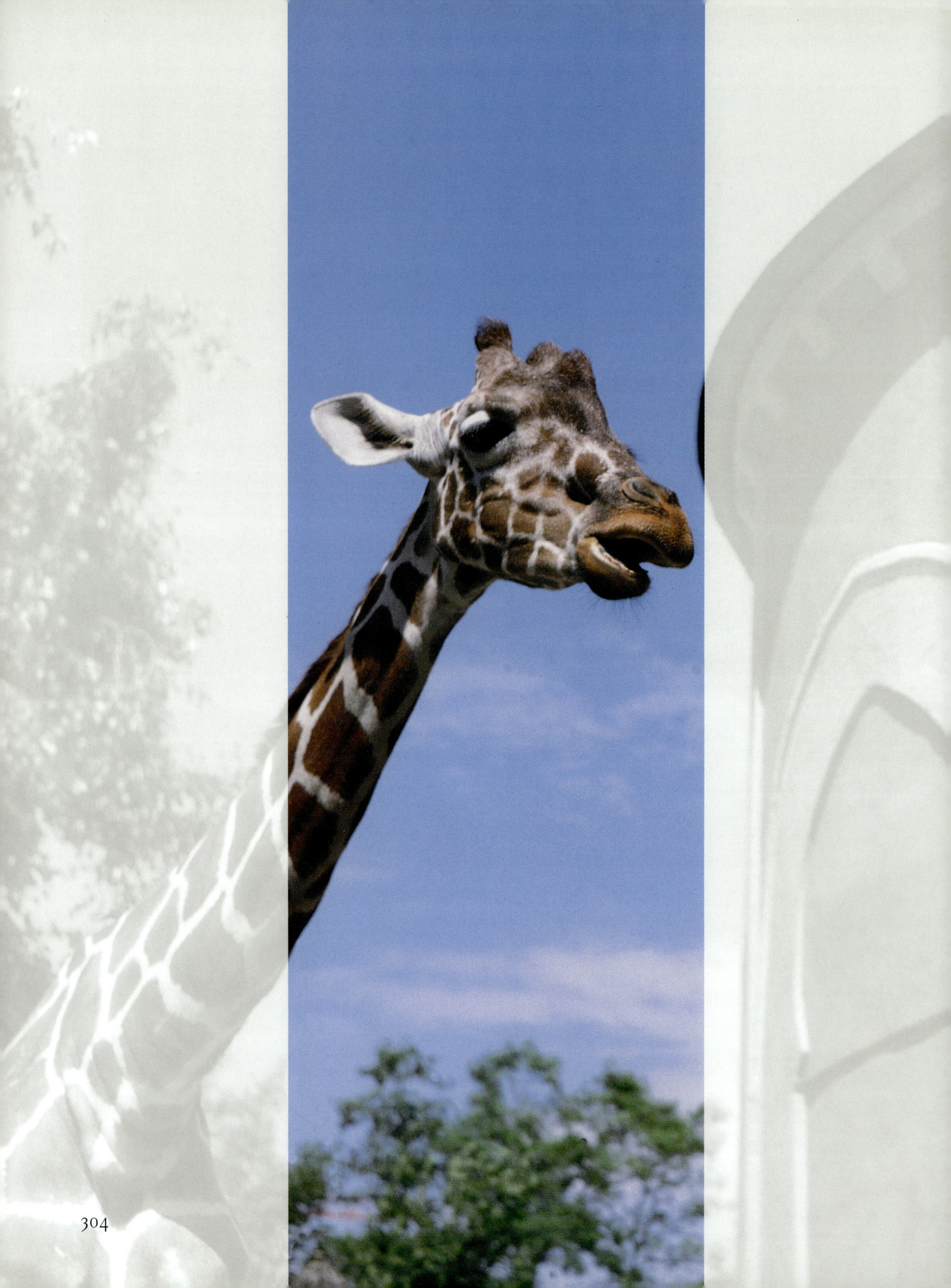

*Zoo der Zukunft:
der Münchner Tierpark Hellabrunn*

*Zoo of the Future:
Munich's Tierpark Hellabrunn*

*Le zoo de l'avenir:
le Tierpark Hellabrunn à Munich*

*Lo zoo del futuro:
il Tierpark Hellabrunn di Monaco*

Im Landschaftsschutzgebiet der Isarauen liegt der Tierpark Hellabrunn, der 1911 als erster Geo-Zoo der Welt gegründet wurde. Zahlreiche Quellen, ein lebhafter Mühlbach und stille Altwasserarme lassen den Park in der Tat zu einem „hellen Brunnen" werden. Der lichtdurchflutete Auwald mit seinem alten Baumbestand bietet einen idealen Lebensraum für viele geschützte Tierarten.

In the landscape preserve of the Isar's water meadows lies the "Hellabrunn Tierpark", founded in 1911 as the first geo-zoo worldwide. Numerous springs, a rapidly flowing brook and quiet sidearms of stagnant water turn the park into a veritable "heller Brunnen", i. e. a bright fountain. The river forests suffused with light and full of old trees offer an ideal habitat for many protected species.

C'est dans la zone protégée des paysages, au bord de l'Isar, qu'est situé le zoo Hellabrunn qui fut fondé en 1911 comme le premier géo-zoo du monde. De nombreuses sources, le ruisseau très vif de Mühlbach et de tranquilles bras morts transforment le parc en une véritable «fontaine claire» (heller Brunnen). Avec son vieux peuplement forestier, la forêt inondée de lumière offre un cadre

Nell'area a tutela paesaggistica lungo il corso del fiume Isar si trova lo zoo di Hellabrunn, il primo «Geo-Zoo» del mondo realizzato nel 1911. Numerose sorgenti, una gora vivace e tranquilli bracci di fiume trasformano il parco in una vera e propria «fontana di vita». Il bosco rivierasco inondato di luce offre, con il suo antico patrimonio arboreo, uno spazio

Robbenbecken im Polarium

Pool for the seals in the Polarium

Le bassin des phoques au polarium

La vasca delle foche nel Polarium

Eisbäranlage im Polarium

Polar bear panorama in the Polarium

Les installations pour les ours polaires au polarium

L'area degli orsi polari nel Polarium

Indische Elefanten vor dem Großen Warmhaus

Indian elephants in front of their extensive quarters

Eléphants indiens devant la grande maison chaude

Elefanti indiani davanti al Grande «Warmhaus»

Durch die harmonisch in die Landschaft eingebundenen Freigehege entstand hier, unmittelbar vor den Toren Münchens, ein Natur- und Tierparkparadies, in dem jährlich ca. 1,4 Millionen Besucher Entspannung, Muße und Erholung finden.

Das Wohlergehen der Zootiere in Menschenhand ist die wichtigste Voraussetzung einer guten Zootierhaltung. Der Besucher von

By integrating open-air preserves into the landscape one has created, right in front of Munich's gates, a nature and zoo paradise in which annually approximately 1.4 million visitors find recreation, leisure and relaxation.

The welfare of the animals held captive by man is the most important precondition for proper zoo keeping. Today's visitors, longing for unspoiled and unmarred

de vie idéal à de nombreuses espèces animales protégées.

Grâce aux installations à ciel ouvert harmonieusement intégrées dans le paysage, il a été possible de créer directement aux portes de la ville de Munich un paradis naturel et un jardin zoologique qui reçoit chaque année 1,4 million de visiteurs venant y chercher détente, loisirs et repos.

vitale ideale per molte specie animali protette.

Grazie all'impiego di recinti inseriti armoniosamente nel paesaggio è stato creato qui, direttamente alle porte di Monaco, un paradiso naturale e zoologico nel quale ogni anno trovano distensione, quiete e riposo circa 1,4 milioni di visitatori.

Il benessere degli animali affidati alle cure dell'uomo costitui-

Das Niederaffenhaus mit Außenanlage

Facility for the lower apes with outdoor enclosure

La maison des singes avec les installations extérieures

La casa delle scimmie con area all'aperto

307

heute mit seiner Sehnsucht nach unverfälschter, intakter Natur kommt zudem mit sehr hohen Erwartungen in den Tierpark. Dies mag auch damit zusammenhängen, dass unser Einfühlungs- und Vorstellungsvermögen gegenüber dem faszinierenden Phänomen Leben in dem Maße eingeschränkt wird, wie wir uns von der Natur entfernen. Vor allem für die Kinder bleibt dabei der hautnahe Kontakt zum Mitgeschöpf Tier auf der Strecke.

Die moderne Zoostrategie möchte dem Besucher die Artenvielfalt der Tiere und deren Verhaltensweise in naturnahen Landschaften näherbringen. Im Zoo erschließt sich damit eine neue, einmalige Welt, die entdeckt und mit allen Sinnen erobert werden will. Sei es in der großen Freiflugvoliere, im tropischen Dschungelzelt, die 23 Meter lange Ameisenrallye im Reptilienhaus, die „Villa Dracula" mit freifliegenden, tropischen Fledermäusen oder die vielen anderen Attraktionen, die große und kleine Besucher immer aufs Neue begeistern. Welches Kinderherz würde nicht schneller schlagen beim Reiten auf dem Kamel oder gar auf dem Elefanten? Interaktive Tierprogramme mit freifliegenden Adlern und Falken sowie eine spezielle Seelöwendarbietung runden einen Besuch in dem beliebten Zoo ab. Das Aquarium mit seinen traumhaften Unterwassergärten, ein Juwel modernster Aquaristik,

nature, enter a zoo full of high expectations. This may also be connected with the fact that faced with the fascinating phenomenon of life our sensibility and imagination is restricted to the same extent as we get farther and farther away from nature. Particularly our children lose the ability to keep close contact with animals, our fellow creatures.

Modern zoo strategy tries to make visitors familiar with the rich variety of species and their behaviour by presenting the animals in natural surroundings. Thus, in a modern zoo, one meets a new and unique world which must be discovered and taken in with all one's senses. Young and old people are equally thrilled by Munich's large free-flight volary in the tropical jungle tent; by the 23-metre-long ant rallye in the reptile house; by the "Villa Dracula" with free-flying tropical bats; and by the numerous other attractions. Every child's heart beats faster when it is offered a ride on a camel or even on an elephant. Interactive animal programmes starring free-flying eagles and falcons or performing seals round off a visit to this much-beloved zoo. The aquarium with its marvellous underwater gardens – a jewel of ultramodern aquaristics –

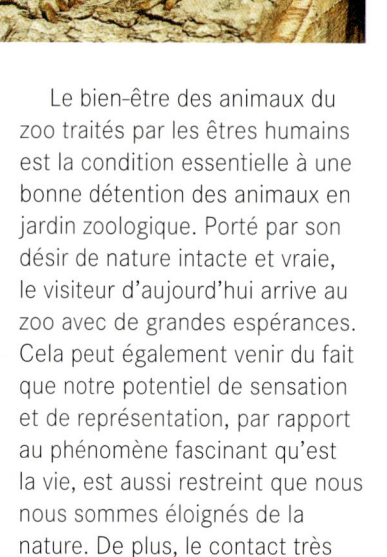

Le bien-être des animaux du zoo traités par les êtres humains est la condition essentielle à une bonne détention des animaux en jardin zoologique. Porté par son désir de nature intacte et vraie, le visiteur d'aujourd'hui arrive au zoo avec de grandes espérances. Cela peut également venir du fait que notre potentiel de sensation et de représentation, par rapport au phénomène fascinant qu'est la vie, est aussi restreint que nous nous sommes éloignés de la nature. De plus, le contact très proche avec les animaux est impossible pour les enfants.

La stratégie zoologique moderne tente de sensibiliser le visiteur à la variété des animaux et à leur comportement dans des paysages proches de la nature. Au zoo, un nouveau monde extraordinaire est créé qui veut être découvert et conquis par tous les sens.

Qu'il s'agisse de l'immense volière en plein air, de la tente renfermant une jungle tropicale, des 23 mètres de tube servant de rallye aux fourmis dans la maison aux reptiles, la «Villa Dracula» avec des chauves-souris tropicales volant en

sce la premessa più importante per il buon funzionamento di uno zoo. Inoltre, il visitatore di oggi, con la sua nostalgia per una natura autentica ed intatta, arriva qui con grandi aspettative. Ciò può essere dovuto al fatto che la nostra capacità di immedesimazione e di immaginazione nei confronti dell'affascinante fenomeno della vita viene tanto più limitata quanto più ci allontaniamo dalla natura. Soprattutto i bambini hanno perso l'abitudine al contatto vivo ed immediato con gli animali.

La strategia di uno zoo moderno è volta ad avvicinare il visitatore ad una varietà di specie e di comportamenti animali che si manifestano in un ambiente quanto più naturale possibile. In tal modo lo zoo apre le porte ad un mondo nuovo, unico, che vuole essere scoperto e conquistato da tutti i nostri sensi: la grande voliera, la tenda della giungla tropicale, il rally delle formiche lungo 23 metri, la casa dei rettili, la «Villa Dracula» con pipistrelli tropicali che volano in assoluta libertà e le numerose altre attrazioni che entusiasmano sempre i visitatori di ogni età. Quale bambino non si emozionerebbe per una cavalcata su un cammello o addirittura su un elefante? Programmi interattivi sugli animali, con aquile e falconi che volano liberamente, ed uno speciale spettacolo con leoni marini completano la visita allo zoo. L'acquario, con i suoi fantastici giardini sommersi, un gioiello della più moderna acquariologia, impressiona tanto l'esperto quanto il profano.

Dschungelzelt mit Raubtieraußenanlage

Tent-like jungle habitat with outdoor enclosure for the wild animals

La tente de la jungle avec les installations extérieures des fauves

Il tendone della giungla con area all'aperto per animali da preda

Großvoliere mit gärtnerischer Innenanlage

Spacious landscaped aviary

Immense volière avec jardin intérieur

La grande voliera con area coperta adibita a giardino

Pinguinschwimmbecken im Polarium

Pool for the penguins in the Polarium

Bassin des pingouins au polarium

La vasca natatoria dei pinguini nel Polarium

besticht den Fachmann ebenso wie den Laien.

Darüber hinaus ist Hellabrunn als wissenschaftlich geleiteter Zoo eine wichtige Stätte der Bildung und der praxisbezogenen Forschung. Eigens entwickelte interaktive Computerprogramme sowie große Bildtafeln vermitteln auf anschauliche Weise überraschende Kenntnisse vom Leben der Tiere. Ein spezielles Narkosemittel, die „Hellabrunner Mischung", wurde hier entwickelt und zugleich das Blasrohrsystem zur Praxisreife perfektioniert. Diese tierschonende, schmerzlose Methode wird weltweit in Zoos und in der Wildtierforschung angewandt.

Und nicht zuletzt erfüllt Hellabrunn als Zuchtstätte bedrohter Tierarten eine wichtige „Arche Noah"-Funktion. Dank der erfolgreichen Wiedereinbürgerungsaktionen des Zoos leben heute in München geborene Przewalski-Urwildpferde wieder in chinesischen Schutzgebieten, durchstreifen Mhorr-Gazellen wieder die Nationalparks von Tunesien und Marokko – beides Arten, die durch Menschenhand in freier Wildbahn ausgerottet waren und nur in den Zoos überleben konnten.

Prof. Dr. Henning Wiesner

fascinates experts as well as laymen.

Furthermore, Hellabrunn as a scientifically-run zoo is an important educational and practice-oriented research centre. Specially-developed computer programmes and large illustration boards explain in a descriptive way surprising facts about animal life. A special anaestethic – the so-called "Hellabrunn Blend" – was developed in the Munich zoo, and the blowpipe system was perfected for practical use. This painless and gentle method is at present used in zoos and in the research of wild animals throughout the world.

Last but not least Hellabrunn is an important breeding centre for threatened species and thus has the function of a modern "Noah's Ark". Thanks to the Munich zoo's successful resettlement programme, primeval wild horses born in Hellabrunn are once more living in Chinese preserves today, and Mhorr gazelles again roam the national parks in Tunesia and Marocco; both species had been extirpated in their wild, original habitat and have survived only in zoos.

Prof. Dr. Henning Wiesner

Schauaquarium mit lebenden Korallen

Aquarium with live corals on display

Aquarium de spectacle avec des coraux vivants

L'acquario-esposizione con i coralli viventi

*Am Bronzeelefanten
im Kinderzoo*

*Bronze elephant statue
of the children's zoo*

*Près de l'éléphant de bronze
au zoo des enfants*

*Presso l'elefante bronzeo
nello zoo dei bambini*

toute liberté et de nombreuses autres attractions qui ravissent toujours les petits comme les grands. Quel cœur d'enfant ne battrait pas la chamade en étant juché sur un chameau ou même un éléphant? Des programmes d'animaux interactifs avec des aigles et des faucons volant en toute liberté ainsi qu'une représentation spéciale de phoques viennent compléter la visite de ce zoo très apprécié. Avec sa magnifique flore sous-marine, l'aquarium, un bijou de tout ce qui se fait actuellement de mieux en matière d'aquarium, séduit l'expert tout comme le novice.

Par ailleurs, Hellabrunn, en tant que zoo dirigé de manière scientifique, est un centre important de sciences et de recherches proches de la pratique. Des programmes informatiques interactifs mis au point ici ainsi que de grands tableaux illustrés permettent de transmettre de manière claire d'étonnantes connaissances sur la vie des animaux. Un narcotique spécial, le «mélange Hellabrunn», fut élaboré ici, de même, le système de tuyau à vent fut perfectionné ici pour sa mise en pratique. Cette méthode, protégeant l'animal et sans douleur est utilisée à l'échelle mondiale dans les zoos et dans la recherche sur les animaux sauvages.

Il ne faut pas oublier non plus qu'Hellabrunn occupe une importante fonction d'Arche de Noé en tant que centre d'élevage d'espèces animales menacées. Grâce au succès des actions de réintroduction, des chevaux sauvages de Przewalksi, nés au zoo de Munich, vivent maintenant à nouveau dans les sites protégés chinois, des gazelles Mhorr d'Hellabrunn parcourent à nouveau les parcs nationaux de Tunisie et du Maroc, deux espèces qui à l'état sauvage avaient été exterminées par l'homme et qui ne purent survivre que dans les jardins zoologiques.

Prof. Dr. Henning Wiesner

Oltre a ciò lo zoo di Hellabrunn, che viene gestito con criteri scientifici, rappresenta un importante punto di riferimento per la formazione e la ricerca pratica. Appositi programmi interattivi sviluppati in proprio nonché grandi tavole illustrative hanno il compito di trasmettere visivamente, in modo estremamente chiaro, informazioni sorprendenti sulla vita degli animali. Qui è stato, inoltre, sviluppato uno speciale narcotico, la «mistura di Hellabrunn», ed è stato messo a punto il sistema di iniezione dei narcotici mediante cerbottana, entrambi strumenti utili per la pratica della ricerca scientifica. Questo sistema delicato ed indolore viene impiegato negli zoo di tutto il mondo e per gli studi sugli animali selvatici.

Infine, Hellabrunn svolge un'altra funzione importante, quella di essere una specie di «Arca di Noè», ovvero un luogo di riproduzione di tutte le specie animali in estinzione. Grazie alle operazioni di reintegrazione condotte con successo dallo zoo, oggi nei parchi protetti della Cina vivono nuovamente esemplari della razza antica di cavalli Przewalski nati nel parco di Monaco, mentre le gazzelle Mhorr di Hellabrunn corrono agili nei parchi nazionali della Tunisia e del Marocco. Entrambe queste specie animali erano state sterminate dalla mano dell'uomo nel loro habitat naturale e hanno potuto sopravvivere solo grazie agli zoo.

Prof. Dr. Henning Wiesner

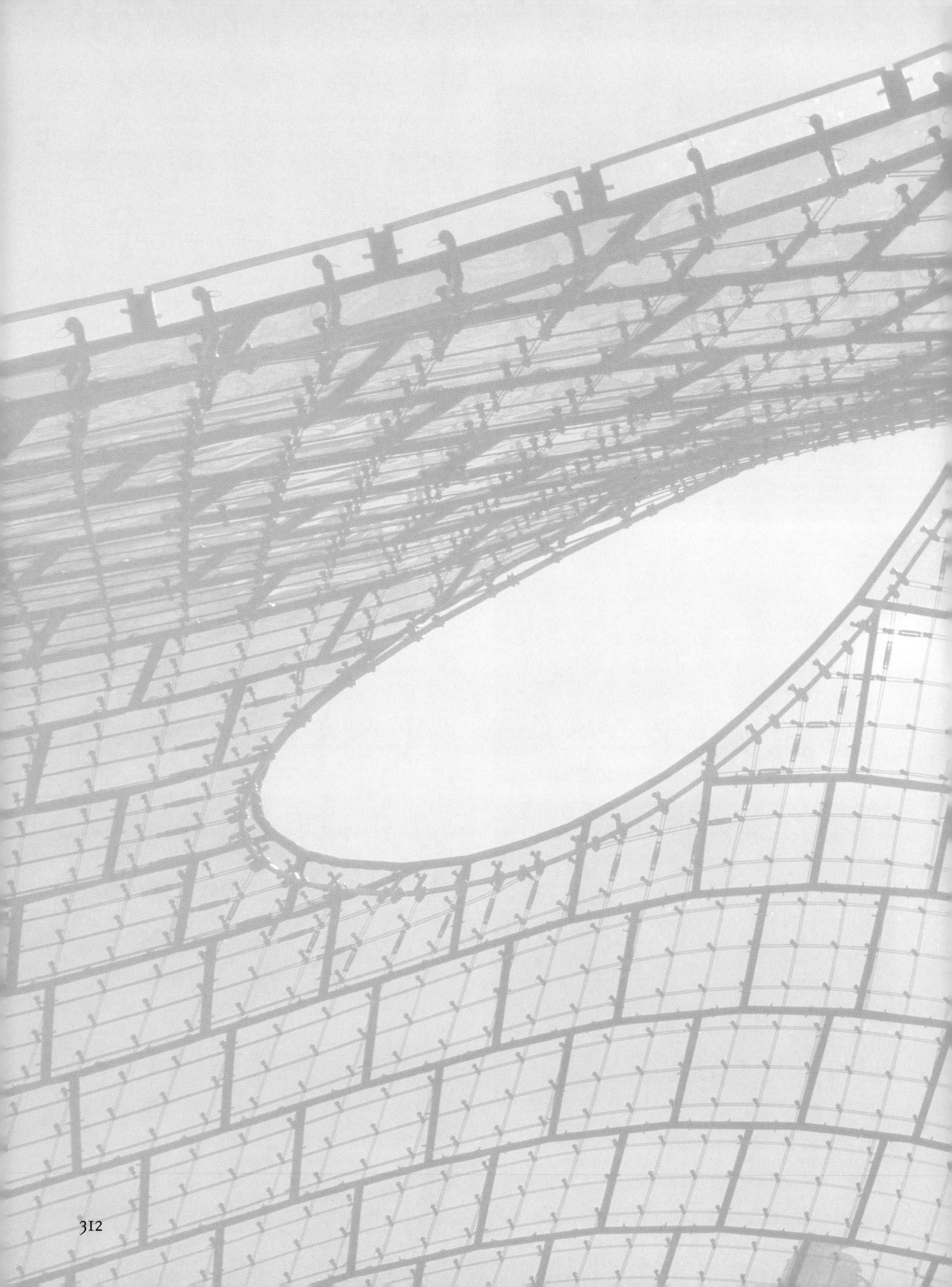

*München –
Stadt des Sports*

*Munich –
City of Sports*

*Munich –
ville du sport*

*Monaco –
città dello sport*

Ein „bedeutendes Münchner Wahrzeichen griechischer Herkunft", zu bewundern nicht etwa in der Glyptothek, sondern auf dem Oberwiesenfeld? Keine Frage: der Olympiapark! Mittendrin das imposante Stadion mit seinem von Architekt Günter Behnisch konzipierten schwingenden Dach aus Acrylglas. Unter ihm sei „das Feuer der Begeisterung niemals erloschen", heißt es in der Werbebroschüre. In der 69 250 Besucher fassenden Arena wurden 1972 die Olympischen Spiele als heiter-beschwingtes Fest des Sports gefeiert. Hier flog die 16-jährige Hochspringerin Ulrike Meyfarth zum Olympiasieg, ehe der blutige Anschlag palästinensischer Terroristen auf die israelische Mannschaft die Freude auf den Gesichtern erstarren ließ.

Zwei Jahre nach Olympia erzielte Gerd Müller vom FC Bayern im Finale der Fußballweltmeisterschaft auf dem beheizbaren Rasen das entscheidende Tor zum 2:1-Sieg der deutschen Nationalmannschaft über die Niederlande. Mit dabei weitere fünf Münchner: Franz Beckenbauer, Sepp Maier, Uli Hoeneß, Paul Breitner und Hans-Georg Schwarzenbeck. Seitdem stürmt das Team des FC Bayern erfolgreich auf fußballhistorischem Grund, gewann 14 deutsche Meistertitel, dreimal den Europacup der Landesmeister sowie Uefa-Cup, Europacup der Pokalsieger und Weltcup: Die mit Edelsteinen verzierten Trophäen funkeln auf blauem Samt im Klubzentrum an der Säbener Straße.

Aber macht eine Metropole zur Sportstadt, wenn sie Olympische Spiele und Fußball-WM veranstaltet hat und einen weltberühmten Fußballklub beherbergt? Keineswegs! Eher die Tatsache, dass Stadion, Schwimmhalle, Eissportzentrum, das zum Erlebnis-Center Olympic Spirit umgebaute Radstadion, die Regattastrecke in Schleißheim und die Schießanlage beispielhafte nacholympische Nutzung durch Hochleistungsathleten und Freizeitsportler gefunden haben. Zur Belebung und

Do you know a Munich landmark of Greek descent which can be admired not in the Glyptothek Museum but on the Oberwiesenfeld? Of course, the Olympiapark! Right in its centre of this park you find the imposing stadium with its famous tent-like roof of acrylic glass designed by architect Günther Behnisch. The advertising folder assures us that "under this roof the fire of enthusiasm has never died out". In 1972 the Olympic Games took place in this arena holding 69,250 visitors – a sports event celebrated under the motto "cheerful and lively". Here 16-year-old Ulrike Meyfarth won the gold medal in high-jumping just before the attack on the Israeli team by Palestine terrorists shocked the spectators.

Two years after the Games, in the finals of the World Football Championship, Gerd Müller from the FC Bayern shot the decisive goal for the German national team's 2:1 victory over the Netherlands. Five more players from Munich were among the winners: Franz Beckenbauer, Sepp Maier, Uli Hoeneß, Paul Breitner, and Hans-Georg Schwarzenbeck. Since then the FC Bayern team has successfully continued the tradition of this historical sports field by winning the German Championship 14 times, the European Cup of National Champions three times, and additionally the UEFA Cup, the European Cup of the Cup Winners, and the World Cup. The club's sparkling, gem-studded trophies are exhibited on blue velvet in the FC Bayern's club centre at Säbener Straße.

But does a town deserve to be called a "sport city" just because it has been the scene of Olympic games and world football championships, and because it shelters a football club of global renown? Of course not. It is far more likely that this title was bestowed on Munich because the stadium, swimming hall, skating rink, the cycling stadium which was turned into the "Olympic Spirit" adventure centre, the regatta course in Schleißheim, and the shooting

Admirer un «symbole important de Munich d'origine grecque», non pas à la Glypothek mais sur le terrain de l'Oberwiesenfeld? Pas de doute: le Parc olympique! Au centre, le stade imposant avec sa toiture suspendue en plexiglas conçue par l'architecte Günter Behnisch. Sous elle «le feu de l'enthousiasme ne s'est jamais éteint», voilà ce qui est écrit dans la brochure publicitaire. C'est dans l'arène pouvant accueillir 69 250 visiteurs que les Jeux olympiques de 1972 ont été célébrés comme une fête du sport gaie et enthousiaste. C'est ici qu'Ulrike Meyfarth, championne de saut en hauteur, remporta à 16 ans son titre olympique avant que l'attentat sanglant des terroristes palestiniens sur l'équipe israélienne ne vienne ternir la joie sur les visages.

Deux ans après les Olympiades, lors de la finale de la coupe du monde de football, Gerd Müller du FC Bayern marqua le but signant la victoire de 2 à 1 de l'équipe d'Allemagne contre les Pays-Bas. Cinq autres Munichois étaient de la partie: Franz Beckenbauer, Sepp Maier, Uli Hoeneß, Paul Breitner et Hans-Georg Schwarzenbeck. Depuis, l'équipe du FC Bayern n'en finit pas d'écrire les pages de son succès: elle remporta 14 fois le titre national, trois fois la coupe d'Europe des clubs champions ainsi que la coupe UEFA, la coupe d'Europe des vainqueurs de coupe et le championnat du monde. Les trophées sertis de pierres précieuses brillent sur le velours bleu dans le club-house de la rue Säbener.

Mais est-ce qu'organiser les Jeux olympiques et la coupe du monde de football, posséder un club de foot de renommée internationale suffisent à une métropole pour devenir une ville du sport? En aucun cas! Disons plutôt le fait que le stade, la piscine olympique, la patinoire, le vélodrome transformé en centre d'aventures Olympic Spirit, le parcours de régate de Schleißheim et le stand de tir furent utilisés après les Jeux par des athlètes

È mai possibile ammirare un «significativo emblema monacense di origine greca» non nella Gliptoteca ma all'Oberwiesenfeld? Ma certo: si tratta del Parco Olimpico! Al centro c'è l'imponente stadio con il suo tetto oscillante in vetro acrilico concepito dall'architetto Günter Behnisch. Sotto tale tetto «il fuoco dell'entusiasmo non si è mai spento», si legge in un opuscolo pubblicitario. Nel 1972, in questa arena sportiva in grado di ospitare fino a 69 250 spettatori vennero celebrati, come festa sportiva all'insegna della serenità e dell'allegria, i Giochi Olimpici estivi. Fu qui che la 16enne saltatrice in alto Ulrike Meyfarth volò a conquistare l'alloro olimpico, prima che il cruento attentato perpetrato da un gruppo di terroristi palestinesi contro la squadra israeliana facesse raggelare il sangue nelle vene dei partecipanti e di quanti seguivano l'evento.

Due anni dopo l'Olimpiade, sul terreno riscaldabile dello stadio Gerd Müller del FC Bayern di Monaco mise a segno, nella finale dei Mondiali di calcio qui disputati, il gol decisivo del 2 a 1 della Nazionale tedesca contro l'Olanda. Tra i protagonisti dell'evento figuravano altri cinque monacensi: Franz Beckenbauer, Sepp Maier, Uli Hoeneß, Paul Breitner e Hans-Georg Schwarzenbeck. Da allora, la squadra dell'FC Bayern ha compiuto con successo le sue gesta su questo terreno così denso di storia calcistica, aggiudicandosi 14 titoli tedeschi, tre Coppe dei Campioni nonché Coppa UEFA, Coppa delle Coppe e Coppa Intercontinentale. I trofei, ornati di pietre preziose, brillano su velluto blu nella sede del sodalizio situata nella Säbener Straße.

Ma affinché una metropoli possa acquisire il titolo di «città dello sport» è sufficiente che essa organizzi Giochi Olimpici e Mondiali di calcio e vanti una società calcistica di fama mondiale? Niente affatto! Questa denominazione deriva piuttosto dal fatto che lo stadio, la piscina, gli stadi del ghiaccio, il velodromo riadat-

Finanzierung tragen nicht allein FC Bayern und TSV 1860 mit jährlich über 1,5 Millionen Besuchern bei, sondern neben anderen sportlichen Großereignissen auch Open-Air-Konzerte, Kirchentage, Papst-Messe, Parteitage, Oper und Zirkus. Bis Ende 1998 lockten 1159 Veranstaltungen 32,9 Millionen Zuschauer ins Olympiastadion, das seit dem 12. September 1972 187-mal ausverkauft war. 11,2 Millionen Besucher des Olympiaparks besichtigten die Betonschüssel unter dem Zeltdach. In die große Halle strömten 17,4 Millionen zu 1 444 Veranstaltungen und in die Schwimmhalle, Europas größtes Gartenhallenbad, 11,9 Millionen.

Den Sport haben die Münchner aber nicht erst Anfang der Siebziger Jahre entdeckt, sondern bereits 1827. Damals berief König Ludwig I., ein Förderer nicht nur der schönen Künste, Hans Ferdinand Maßmann, einen Freund und Schüler des „Turnvaters" Friedrich Ludwig Jahn, in seine Residenz und erteilte ihm den Auftrag, auf dem „Oberen Wiesenfeld" einen Turnplatz zu errichten. Dort, am „Maßmannsbergl", wurde später eine Turnhalle gebaut, die erste öffentliche Turnstätte Deutschlands.

In den Jahren nach dem Zweiten Weltkrieg entstanden in München 26 Bezirkssportanlagen, auf denen sich nicht nur die 453 000 Mitglieder der 656 Münchner Sportvereine betätigen können; die Sportstätten stehen jedem Bürger offen. Neben der Trabrennbahn in Daglfing und der Galopprennbahn in Riem hat die Stadt das Dantestadion nebst Freibad und den früher auch sportlich genutzten Rundbau des Circus Krone aufzuweisen.

Im Schatten von König Fußball fristet der Leistungssport trotz städtischer Förderung in fast allen anderen Sportarten ein kümmerliches Dasein. Münchner Olympiasieger wie der Turner Inno Stangl, der Eiskunstläufer Manfred Schnelldorfer oder die Leichtathletin Gisela Mauermayer haben keine Nachfolger gefunden. Die Handballer des ehe-

range have subsequently been used in an exemplary manner by top athletes and amateur sportsmen. Not only the FC Bayern and the TSV 1860 contribute to the maintenance and financing of these facilities with more than 1.5 million visitors, but also other large-scale sports events as well as open-air concerts, Church meetings, the mass held by the Pope, party conventions, and opera and circus performances. Up to late 1998, 1,159 events drew 32.9 million spectators to the Olympic Stadium, which was sold out 187 times after 12 September 1972. 11.2 million Olympiapark visitors came to see the concrete bowl under the tent roof. 17.4 million saw 1,444 performances in the large hall, and 11.9 million people visited the swimming hall – Europe's largest inside garden pool.

It was, however, not in 1972 but as early as 1827 that Munich discovered the attraction of sports. At that time King Ludwig I, who was not only a friend of the fine arts, called Hans Ferdinand Maßmann, a friend and "disciple" of "Turnvater" Friedrich Ludwig Jahn, to his residence and entrusted him with the setting up of a gymnastics centre at the Obere Wiesenfeld. On this "Maßmann hill" a gymnasium was later erected, which was Germany's first public sports facility.

In the years following the Second World War 26 district sports facilities were established in Munich which were not only used by the 453,000 members of 656 Munich sports clubs, but were open to every citizen. In addition to the trotting course in Daglfing and the galloping race course in Riem the city also boasts the Dante Stadium complete with outdoor pool, and the circular building of the Krone Circus, which was formerly also used for sports events.

Overshadowed by "King Football", nearly all sectors of competitive sports struggle for existence in spite of generous municipal support. Olympic gold medal winners like gymnast Inno Stangl,

de haut niveau et des sportifs amateurs. Le FC Bayern et le TSV 1860 ne sont pas les seuls à contribuer à l'animation et au financement en attirant chaque année plus de 1,5 million de visiteurs. Il faut également mentionner les grands événements sportifs, mais aussi les concerts en plein air, les journées religieuses, la messe pontificale, les journées des partis, l'opéra et le cirque. Jusqu'à la fin de l'année 1998, 1 159 manifestations ont attiré 32,9 millions de visiteurs dans le stade olympique qui, depuis le 12 septembre 1972, a joué 187 fois à guichets fermés. 11,2 millions de visiteurs du Parc olympique ont admiré la cuve en béton sous le toit en forme de tente. Dans la grande salle, 17,4 millions de visiteurs ont assisté à 1 444 spectacles et 11,9 millions sont allés à la piscine, le plus grand complexe européen de piscine couverte avec jardin.

Mais les Munichois n'ont pas découvert le sport qu'au début des années soixante-dix, mais déjà en 1827. A l'époque, le roi Louis 1er, un promoteur non seulement des beaux-arts, fit venir Hans Ferdinand Maßmann, un ami et élève de «l'inventeur de la gymnastique» Friedrich Ludwig Jahn, dans sa résidence et lui demanda de construire sur la «oberes Wiesenfeld» un terrain de gymnastique. Plus tard, sur le «Maßmannsbergl», une salle de sports a été érigée, le premier centre sportif public d'Allemagne.

Dans les années suivant la Seconde Guerre mondiale, 26 complexes sportifs ont vu le jour à Munich qui accueillaient les 453 000 membres des 656 associations sportives de Munich. Les centres sportifs étaient ouverts à tout le monde. Outre la piste de course de trot de Daglfing et la piste de course de galop de Riem, la ville peut se targuer du stade Dante doté d'une piscine en plein air et de la construction ronde du cirque Krone qui servait avant également au sport.

A l'ombre du roi foot, les sports de compétition présentent, malgré les subventions munici-

tato ad event center per l'iniziativa «Olympic Spirit», il centro di canottaggio di Schleißheim ed il poligono di tiro hanno conosciuto un esemplare sfruttamento postolimpico da parte di atleti sia agonistici e dopolavoristici. Ad animare e finanziare le attività del Parco Olimpico contribuiscono non solo le partite dei due sodalizi calcistici FC Bayern e TSV Monaco 1860 con oltre 1,5 milioni di spettatori all'anno ma, oltre ad altri grandi eventi sportivi, anche concerti open air, convegni ecclesiastici, messe celebrate dal Papa, congressi di partiti, rappresentazioni operistiche e circensi. Fino alla fine del 1998, 1 159 manifestazioni hanno attirato nello Stadio Olimpico 32,9 milioni di spettatori; dal settembre 1972, lo stadio ha registrato il «tutto esaurito» 187 volte. 11,2 milioni di persone hanno preso posto sotto il tetto a tendone. Nel grande palazzetto dello sport sono affluiti 17,4 milioni di persone per assistere a 1 444 manifestazioni, mentre la piscina, che è la più grande struttura coperta con annesso giardino in Europa, ha registrato 11,9 milioni di presenze.

La scoperta dello sport da parte dei monacensi, però, non risale all'inizio degli anni Settanta ma al 1827. All'epoca, re Ludovico I, che si dintinse come promotore anche di attività che esulavano dall'ambito delle belle arti, convocò nella sua residenza Hans Ferdinand Maßmann, un amico ed allievo del «padre della ginnastica» Friedrich Ludwig Jahn, e gli conferì l'incarico di costruire un centro per la ginnastica sull'«Oberes Wiesenfeld». Lì, su quella che poi venne definita la «Collina Maßmann» venne edificata una palestra per la ginnastica, la prima struttura pubblica per la ginnastica in Germania.

Negli anni che seguirono alla Seconda Guerra Mondiale nacquero, a Monaco, 26 impianti sportivi di quartiere che da allora possono venir sfruttati non solo dai 453 000 iscritti alle 656 società sportive monacensi, ma

Olympiapark München

Magnet für Münchner und Touristen

Der Olympiapark München pulsiert. Rund 5,8 Millionen zahlende Besucher aus aller Welt finden in jedem Jahr den Weg in das Gelände um Olympiaturm und Coubertinplatz. Allein 4 Millionen Menschen kommen durchschnittlich zu den mehreren Hundert Großveranstaltungen in Olympiahalle, Olympiastadion und den weiteren Anlagen des Olympiaparks.

Damit setzen wir Maßstäbe – allen Besuchern an dieser Stelle ein herzliches Dankeschön. Doch der Erfolg verpflichtet: Der Olympiapark muss auch künftig ein attraktives Ziel bleiben.

Das jüngste Kind des Olympiaparks heißt Olympic Spirit München, eine groß angelegte Erlebniswelt, modern und jugendlich gestaltet. Sämtliche olympischen Sportarten präsentieren sich hier mit ausgereiften Computersimulationen und Multimediadarstellungen, die den Besuchern ein täuschend echtes Gefühl vermitteln – ein olympisches Museum des Sports, analog zum Deutschen Museum der Technik.

Neben dem Olympiaturm stehen den Münchnern und ihren Gästen die drei Eishallen des Olympia-Eissportzentrums, die Olympia-Schwimmhalle sowie diverse Trainingsplätze und eine ausgedehnte Tennisanlage zur Verfügung.

Besondere Erwähnung verdient eine nicht enden wollende Reihe hochkarätiger Veranstaltungen, die Olympiahalle und Olympiastadion zu einem der wichtigsten Veranstaltungszentren der Welt werden lassen. Konzerte – von den Rolling Stones bis zu den drei Tenören –, Shows wie Holiday on Ice und natürlich sportliche Leckerbissen wie die Spiele der Fußball-Bundesliga und der Champions League oder die Leichtathletik-Europameisterschaften 2002 sorgen für einen gut ausgelasteten und immer lebendigen Olympiapark.

Wilfrid Spronk

The Olympic Park in Munich

A Magnet Attracting Natives and Tourists

The Olympic Park Munich is booming. Roughly 5.8 million paying visitors from all parts of the world pour into the area around the Olympic Tower and Coubertin Square every year. Four million people attend the hundreds of large-scale events taking place in the Olympic Hall, the Olympic Stadium and the numerous other facilities of the Olympic Park.

With these figures we certainly set standards – and would therefore like to thank all the visitors who have come to see Munich's Olympic Site. But success is also an obligation: the Olympic Park must remain an attractive destination in future as well.

The youngest "offspring" of the Olympic Park is called Olympic Spirit München – a large-scale adventure world in modern and youthful make-up. All the Olympic disciplines are shown here by means of expert computer simulations and multimedia presentations, which communicate to visitors the feeling of taking part in these events themselves. One could call it an "Olympic Museum of Sports", analogous to the German Museum of Technology.

In addition to the Olympic Tower, local people and their guests find at their disposal the three skating rinks of the Olympic Ice Sports Centre, the Olympic swimming pool, several training facilities and numerous tennis courts.

An everlasting succession of top events, which turn the Olympic Hall and the Olympic Stadium into one of the world's most important entertainment centres, deserves special mention here. Concerts featuring everything from the Rolling Stones to the Three Tenors, shows like Holiday on Ice, and, of course, sport treats such as the football games of the German Bundesliga and the Champions League, or the European Championships in Athletics which will take place in 2002, guarantee that the Olympic Park will remain busy and full of life.

Wilfrid Spronk

Le Parc Olympique de Munich

Un pôle d'attraction pour les Munichois et les touristes

Le Parc Olympique de Munich connaît une vive animation. Environ 5,8 millions de visiteurs payants venant du monde entier prennent chaque année le chemin des installations autour de la tour olympique et la place Coubertin. En moyenne 4 millions de personnes assistent à plusieurs centaines de grandes manifestations qui se jouent dans la Salle Olympique, le Stade Olympique et dans d'autres centres du Parc Olympique.

Nous posons ainsi des jalons et remercions ici vivement tous les visiteurs. Mais succès oblige : le Parc Olympique doit à l'avenir encore rester un but attrayant.

Le petit dernier du Parc Olympique s'appelle Olympic Spirit München, un monde d'aventures de grande ampleur, à la conception moderne et jeune. Toutes les disciplines sportives olympiques se présentent ici avec d'excellentes simulations par ordinateur et des présentations multimédiales transmettant aux visiteurs un sentiment trompeur de réalité – un musée olympique du sport, analogue au musée allemand de la technique.

A côté de la Tour Olympique, les Munichois et leurs invités ont le choix entre trois patinoires du Centre Olympique des sports de glace, la Piscine Olympique ainsi que divers centres d'entraînement tout comme un vaste complexe de terrains de tennis.

Il ne faut pas oublier ici de citer une liste sans fin de manifestations de renom qui font de la Salle Olympique et du Stade Olympique un des centres les plus importants de manifestations du monde. Les concerts, qu'il s'agisse des Rolling Stones ou des trois ténors, des spectacles comme Holiday on Ice et bien entendu des grands moments sportifs comme les matchs de première division allemande, la coupe des clubs champions ou les championnats d'Europe d'athlétisme en 2002 permettent au Parc Olympique d'être bien rempli et lui assurent une vive animation.

Wilfrid Spronk

Il Parco Olimpico di Monaco

Un «catalizzatore» di monacensi e turisti

Il Parco Olimpico di Monaco pulsa di vita. Circa 5,8 milioni di visitatori paganti provenienti da tutto il mondo si riversano, ogni anno, sull'area che circonda la Torre Olimpica e la Coubertinplatz. Solo le diverse centinaia di grandi manifestazioni nella Olympiahalle, nello Stadio Olimpico e negli altri impianti del Parco Olimpico vengono frequentate, ogni anno, da 4 milioni di persone.

In questo modo noi definiamo nuovi standard – e a tutti i visitatori vorrei esprimere il mio ringraziamento. Ma il successo genera un nuovo impegno: il Parco Olimpico deve rimanere una meta attraente anche in futuro.

L'ultima «creatura» del Parco Olimpico si chiama Olympic Spirit München, un mondo di eventi da vivere concepito con criteri moderni e rivolto ai giovani. Qui, le discipline sportive olimpiche si presentano con simulazioni computerizzate e rappresentazioni multimediali molto avanzate che trasmettono al visitatore una sensazione quasi autentica – una sorta di museo olimpico dello sport sulla falsariga del «Deutsches Museum».

Oltre alla Torre Olimpica, i monacensi ed i loro ospiti hanno a disposizione tre stadi del ghiaccio del Centro Olimpico dello sport sughiaccio, la Piscina Olimpica nonché diversi campi di allenamento ed una vasta area dedicata al tennis.

Merita di essere menzionata la serie interminabile di manifestazioni di alto livello che fanno dell'Olympiahalle e dello Stadio Olimpico due dei principali teatri di manifestazioni a livello mondiale. Concerti – dai Rolling Stones ai Tre Tenori –, show come Holiday on Ice e, naturalmente, gli «appetitosi» appuntamenti sportivi come le partite della Serie A di calcio tedesca e della Champions League o i Campionati Europei di Atletica Leggera del 2002 fanno del Parco Olimpico un'area con un buon grado di sfruttamento degli impianti e sempre viva.

Wilfrid Spronk

1972 galt das weltberühmte Zeltdach des Architekten Behnisch als gewagt und architektonisch mutig. Heute ist es zum Wahrzeichen des Olympiaparks und zu einem der weltweit meistfotografierten Bauwerke geworden.

In 1972 the world-famous tent roof designed by architect Behnisch was regarded as a daring feat of architecture. Today it has become the landmark of the Olympic Park and one of the most frequently photographed buildings worldwide.

En 1972, le toit en forme de toiles de tente et mondialement célèbre de l'architecte Behnisch paraissait osé et d'une certaine audace architecturale. Aujourd'hui, il est devenu l'image de marque du Parc Olympique et un des édifices les plus photographiés au monde.

Nel 1972, il famoso «tetto a tendone» dell'architetto Behnisch era considerato una realizzazione azzardata e decisamente coraggiosa sotto il profilo architettonico. Oggi è diventato l'emblema del Parco Olimpico ed una delle opere edili più fotografate del mondo.

Nicht nur Münchens Traditionsclubs feiern in einem der schönsten Stadien der Welt ihre Erfolge, auch internationale Top-Spiele wie das Finale der Champions League 1997 finden im Olympiapark statt.

Not only Munich's traditional football clubs celebrate their victories in this stadium – one of the most beautiful in the world; international top events like the finals of the Champions League in 1997 also take place in the Olympic Park.

Ce ne sont pas uniquement les clubs munichois traditionnels qui célèbrent leur succès dans un des plus beaux stades du monde, de grandes rencontres internationales se tiennent également dans le parc olympique comme la finale de la coupe des clubs champions en 1997.

Non sono solo i sodalizi monacensi dalla lunga tradizione a celebrare i loro successi in uno degli stadi più belli del mondo. Nel Parco Olimpico hanno luogo anche partite di richiamo internazionale, come la finale della Champions League nel 1997.

Die Golf-Legende Severiano Ballesteros bei den BMW International Open in München Nord-Eichenried, 1999

The legendary golf player Severiano Ballesteros during the BMW International Open in the north of Munich-Eichenried, 1999

La légende du golf, Severiano Ballesteros, lors de l'Open International BMW à Munich Nord-Eichenried, 1999

La leggenda golfistica Severiano Ballesteros ai BMW International Open del 1999 svoltisi ad Eichenried, a nord di Monaco

maligen Europacupsiegers TSV München-Milbertshofen spielen viertklassig in der Oberliga, die deutschen Meistermannschaften der Milbertshofener im Volleyball und der Maddoggs im Eishockey wurden aufgelöst, die einst ruhmreichen Leichtathleten der Sechziger retteten sich in eine Fusion mit Nürnberg/Fürth.

Das Olympiastadion – vor einem Vierteljahrhundert eine architektonische Sensation – scheint inzwischen den gehobenen Ansprüchen der Fußballklientel nicht mehr zu genügen. 1999 drohte der FC Bayern München, nahe der Neuen Messe

skater Manfred Schnelldorfer, or light athletic champion Gisela Mauermayer have not found successors. The hand ball team of the former European Cup winner TSV München-Milbertshofen now plays in the fourth-class Upper League; the volley ball team of Milbertshofen – formerly German masters, and the "Maddoggs" ice hockey team were dissolved; and the once renowned light athletic sector of the 1860 club survived only by fusing with Nuremberg/Fürth.

By now the Olympic stadium, which was considered an architectural sensation 25 years ago,

pales dans presque toutes les autres disciplines sportives, un triste bilan. Les champions olympiques munichois comme le gymnaste Inno Stangl, le patineur artistique Manfred Schnelldorfer ou l'athlète Gisela Mauermayer n'ont pas trouvé de successeurs. Les joueurs de handball de l'ancien vainqueur de coupe d'Europe TSV München-Milbertshofen offrent un jeu de quatrième ordre dans la Oberliga, les équipes championnes d'Allemagne comme Milbertshofen en volley-ball et les Maddoggs en hockey sur glace ont été supprimées, les athlètes autrefois célèbres des Sechziger

anche da ogni singolo cittadino. Oltre alla pista di trotto di Daglfing e a quella di galoppo di Riem il Comune vanta anche il «Dantestadion», con annessa piscina all'aperto, e l'edificio circolare del Circus Krone, che anni addietro veniva utilizzato anche come impianto sportivo.

All'ombra di «re Calcio», però, lo sport agonistico conduce in quasi tutte le altre discipline sportive una magra esistenza, nonostante l'opera di promozione effettuata dal Comune. I vincitori olimpici originari di Monaco come il ginnasta Inno Stangl, il pattinatore artistico Manfred Schnelldorfer o l'atleta Gisela Mauermayer non hanno trovato adeguati seguaci. La compagine di pallamano del TSV Monaco-Milbertshofen, a suo tempo vincitrice della Coppa Europa, disputa ora nella quarta serie tedesca; le squadre già campioni di Germania del Milbertshofen (pallavolo) e dei Maddoggs (hockey su ghiaccio) sono state sciolte, e gli atleti un tempo famosi del Monaco 1860 si sono salvati fondendosi con il sodalizio di Norimberga/Fürth.

Lo Stadio Olimpico – che un quarto di secolo fa aveva destato sensazione per la sua architettura – sembra non soddisfare più, nel frattempo, le accresciute esigenze della clintela calcistica. Nel 1999 il FC Bayern di Monaco ha minacciato di costruire, di propria iniziativa, un'arena multifunzionale nelle vicinanze della Nuova Fiera di Monaco, nel caso in cui il suo desiderio di realizzazione

Riem in eigener Regie eine multifunktionelle Arena zu errichten, sollte sein Wunsch nach einem Umbau mit Lounges und VIP-Räumen und der Entfernung der Rundbahn nicht erfüllt werden. Einschneidende bauliche Maßnahmen würden jedoch zu einer Zerstörung des Ensembles führen. Das Eröffnungsspiel der Fußball-WM 2006 soll voraussichtlich in München stattfinden. Ob im Olympiastadion oder in der geplanten Bayern-Arena oder überhaupt, ist ungewiss, denn der Deutsche Fußballbund war 1999 nur Bewerber.

Hans Eiberle

seems to no longer satisfy the more exclusive demands of Munich's football fans. In 1999 the FC Bayern München threatened to build a multi-functional arena of its own near the new Munich Fair site if one refused to meet its demand for a reconstruction including lounges and VIP facilities and for removing the circular cycle track. But any radical architectural changes would destroy the overall concept. The opening game of the World Football Championships 2006 is expected to take place in Munich. It is, however, still uncertain whether it will grace the Olympic Stadium or the planned Bavarian arena, or whether it will take place at all – for the German Football Association was only one of the candidates in 1999.

Hans Eiberle

n'ont pu perdurer qu'en fusionnant avec Nuremberg/Fürth.

Le stade olympique, une sensation architecturale il y a un quart de siècle, ne semble plus satisfaire les exigences élevées des amateurs de football. En 1999, le FC Bayern a menacé de construire lui-même une arène multifonctionnelle près du centre de foire Neue Messe à Riem si son désir de transformation avec salles privées et espaces VIP n'était pas satisfait et si le problème de l'éloignement du public par rapport au terrain n'était pas résolu. Des mesures de transformation radicale détruiraient cependant l'ensemble. Le match d'ouverture de la coupe du monde de football en 2006 devrait se jouer à Munich. Que ce soit dans le stade olympique ou dans l'arène bavaroise en projet est encore incertain vu que la fédération allemande de football a juste présenté sa candidature en 1999.

Hans Eiberle

di lounge ed aree riservate ai VIP e di ristrutturazioni per eliminare la distanza degli spalti dal terreno di gioco dovuta alla presenza della pista di atletica non fosse stato esaudito. Interventi edili radicali, però, comporterebbero la distruzione dell'intero complesso. La partita inaugurale dei Mondiali di calcio del 2006 dovrebbe venir disputata, con ogni probabilità, a Monaco. Ferma restando che la Federcalcio tedesca diventi l'ente organizzatore (nel 1999 era ancora solo nella rosa dei candidati); e che si decida se il terreno di gioco sarà quello dello Stadio Olimpico o della prevista «Arena del Bayern».

Hans Eiberle

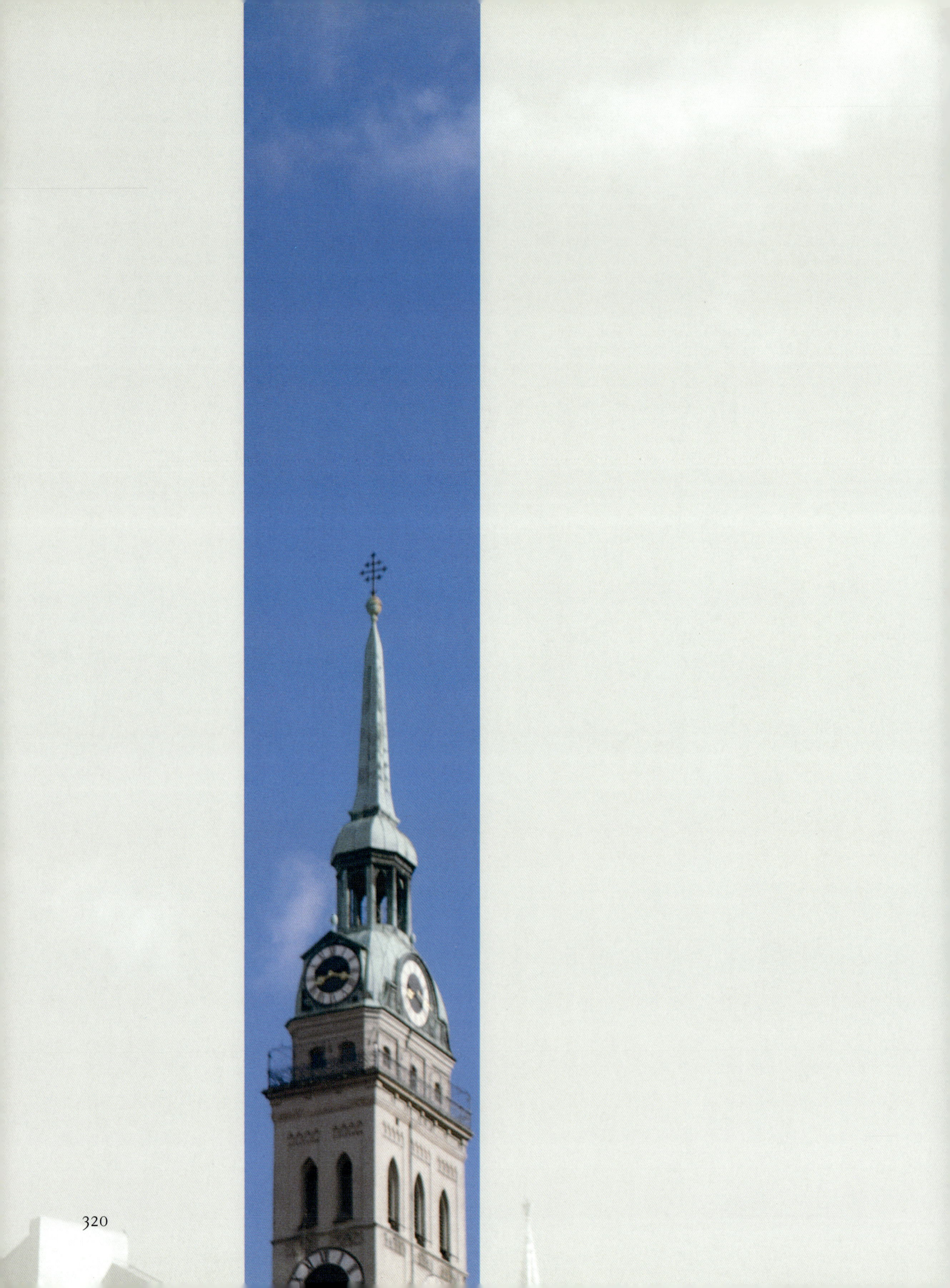

München ist nicht nur München
Die Vielfalt der Volkskultur in der bayerischen Landeshauptstadt

Munich is not only Munich
The great variety of popular culture in the Bavarian capital

Munich n'est pas seulement Munich
La variété de la culture populaire dans la capitale bavaroise

Monaco non è solo Monaco
La varietà della cultura popolare nella capitale della Baviera

Wenn von der Geschichte München gesprochen wird, gerät meist in Vergessenheit, dass die zwischen 1854 und 1942 einverleibten 29 Städte und Gemeinden ihre eigene Entwicklung durchgemacht haben. Die vom Hof, dem Adel und den Bürgern geprägte Residenzstadt hatte dabei auf die Dörfer im Umland keinen Einfluss. Der Anteil des alten München am heutigen Stadtgebiet beträgt schlichte 5,2%.

Die Dörfer um München entwickelten sich ihrerseits recht unterschiedlich. Bis in das 19. Jahrhundert hinein war nämlich die gesamte Volkskultur mit der Tracht, dem Brauchtum, der Volksmusik, dem Volkstanz, der Mundart und der Hausform nach den umliegenden Landgerichten orientiert.

Aus diesem Grund gibt es im heutigen München vier verschiedene Trachtenbereiche: die Münchner Bürgertracht, die Ampertaler bzw. Dachauer Tracht im Münchner Norden und Westen, die Tracht im Münchner Osten und die Tracht im Münchner Süden. Dazu kommen noch seit 1884 die „Gebirgs-Trachten-Erhaltungs-Vereine" und zahlreiche andere Gruppen mit unterschiedlichen Trachten.

Von den über 1200 Volkskulturgruppen und -vereinen in der bayerischen Landeshauptstadt gehören allein zwei Drittel zur Musikalischen Volkskultur. München war und ist das Zentrum der bairischen Volksmusik schlechthin. Da waren z.B. die seit dem 14. Jahrhundert bestehenden Stadtmusikanten, die „Musikbanden" in den Wirtschaften und vor allem die beliebten Redouten mit ihren fast jährlich wechselnden Modetänzen.

Aus biedermeierlichen „Gesellschaften" gingen in München die ersten privaten Orchester und Chöre hervor, so 1840 die heute noch bestehende Bürgersängerzunft, u.a. mit Konrad Max Kunz (1812-75), dem Komponisten der Bayern-Hymne (1862), als musikalischem Leiter. Bei dem 1864 gegründeten Laienorchester „Wilde Gungl" brachte deren erster

Talking of Munich's history, we tend to forget that the 29 towns and communities incorporated into the city between 1854 and 1942 all developed independently. This residential city of the kings and electors, shaped by the court, the aristocracy and the citizens, had practically no influence on the surrounding villages, for the city of old covered only 5.2% of the present-day city area.

The villages in Munich's vicinity developed, however, in very different ways. Up to the 19th century the entire popular culture – including costumes and customs, folk music and dancing, idioms and the building style of homes – was influenced by the respective "Landgerichte" (regional courts) to which they belonged.

In present-day Munich we therefore find four different areas of "Trachten" or costumes: the Tracht of the Munich citizens; the Amper Valley or Dachauer Tracht in the northern and western parts; the Tracht of the eastern part of Munich and that typical of the southern part. Since 1884 there have additionally been "Gebirgstrachten-Erhaltungs-Vereine" (societies dedicated to preserving the Alpine costumes), and other groups sporting different Trachten.

Two-thirds of the more than 1,200 popular culture groups and societies within the Bavarian capital concentrate on folk music. Munich has always been the undisputed centre of Bavarian folk music. The so-called "Stadtmusikanten", for instance, a band of town musicians, date back to the 14th century; there were music bands playing in pubs and inns, and the greatly cherished "Redouten", masked balls introducing fashionable dances which were replaced by more recent ones nearly every year.

The first private orchestras and choirs developed out of the social gatherings so popular in the Regency Period; in 1840, for example, the "Bürgersängerzunft" (Citizens' Choral Society) was founded, which has survived until

Quand il est question de l'histoire de Munich, on oublie généralement que les 29 villes et communes intégrées entre 1854 et 1942 connurent elles-mêmes leur propre développement. La ville résidentielle marquée par la cour, la noblesse et la bourgeoisie n'avait aucune influence sur les villages des alentours. Le pourcentage du Munich d'autrefois par rapport à la ville actuelle s'élève seulement à 5,2 %.

Les villages autour de Munich se développèrent de manière fort différente. Jusqu'au 19ème siècle, l'ensemble de la culture populaire avec ses costumes, ses traditions, sa musique folklorique et ses danses populaires, son langage et la forme de ses maisons s'orientait en fonction des circonscriptions des tribunaux voisins.

Pour cette raison, il existe dans le Munich d'aujourd'hui quatre groupe de costumes traditionnels: le costume bourgeois de Munich, le costume de la vallée de l'Amper ou de Dachau au nord et à l'ouest de Munich, le costume de l'est de Munich et le costume du sud de Munich. Il faut y ajouter les associations pour le maintien des costumes de montagne et de nombreux autres groupes avec des costumes différents.

Parmi les quelques 1 200 groupes et associations de culture populaire présents dans la capitale du land de Bavière, près de deux tiers se consacrent à la culture de la musique folklorique. Munich a été et est le centre incontesté de la musique folklorique bavaroise. Citons par exemple les musiciens de ville existant depuis le 14ème siècle, les «Musikbanden» dans les restaurants et en particulier les bals masqués avec leurs danses modernes changeant presque toutes les années.

Les premiers orchestres et chorales privés viennent de «sociétés» de l'époque des Biedermeier, comme en 1840 la corporation des chanteurs existant encore aujourd'hui avec entre autres Konrad Max Kunz (1812-75) et le compositeur de l'hymne

Quando si parla della storia di Monaco si dimentica spesso che i 29 comuni e città incorporati tra il 1854 ed il 1942 si erano sviluppati, fino all'epoca, in maniera autonoma. La città, residenza eletta dei duchi Wittelsbach ed in seguito capitale del regno di Baviera, fu improntata sui fasti della vita di corte, della nobiltà e dei suoi cittadini, ma non ebbe nessuna influenza sulla vita dei paesini confinanti. La Monaco originaria contribuisce, oggi, solo al 5,2 % del territorio della città.

I paesi intorno a Monaco ebbero, a loro volta, uno sviluppo alquanto differenziato. Fino al XIX secolo, infatti, l'intera cultura popolare, con i suoi costumi tradizionali, gli usi, la musica e la danza folcloristica, il dialetto e l'architettura, era orientata agli usi e costumi dei distretti circostanti.

E' per questo motivo che nella Monaco odierna si incontrano quattro differenti costumi tradizionali appartenenti a quattro zone specifiche della città: il costume borghese di Monaco, il costume della valle dell'Amper e di Dachau, caratteristico delle zone rispettivamente settentrionale ed occidentale della città, il costume della zona est e quello della zona sud di Monaco. A questi si sono aggiunti, a partire dal 1884, i costumi delle varie «Associazioni per la salvaguardia dei costumi montani» e di numerosi altri gruppi.

Degli oltre 1 200 gruppi ed associazioni di cultura popolare della capitale bavarese solo i due terzi coltivano e si dedicano alla musica folcloristica. Monaco è stata ed è il centro per antonomasia della musica popolare bavarese. Già nel XIV secolo esistevano, ad esempio, i musicanti di città e le «bande di musica» che suonavano nelle osterie; da non dimenticare, poi, i popolari balli in maschera in occasione dei quali veniva lanciata, quasi ogni anno, una nuova danza alla moda.

Dalle associazioni monacensi ispirate al «Biedermeier» scaturirono le prime orchestre ed i primi cori privati, come la «Corporazio-

musikalischer Leiter Franz Strauss die Jugendwerke seines Sohnes Richard Strauss (1864-1949) zur Uraufführung.

Nachdem die Künstler die Alpen und ihre Bewohner „entdeckt" hatten, wurden Gebirgslieder gesammelt und gesungen. In München wirkte besonders der Kreis um Maximilian Herzog in Bayern (1808-88) als Vorreiter einer „Alpenhaftigkeit", die bis heute nachwirkt. Durch ihn, den populären „Zithermaxl", fand die technisch verbesserte Zither in weiten Kreisen Verbreitung.

Die Redouten erreichten in den neuen riesigen Sälen der Bierkeller um 1900 ihre zweite Blütezeit. Und zwischen 1870 und 1930 hatten die beliebten Münchner Volkssänger regen Zulauf. Ihre satirischen, witzigen oder kritischen Couplets wurden zu Tausenden gedruckt und bald nachgesungen.

Mit August Hartmann (1846-1917) und Hyacinth Abele (1823-1916) setzte 1876 von München aus die wissenschaftliche Volksliedforschung in Bayern ein. Nach dem Ersten Weltkrieg führten ausgedehnte Sammelunternehmen zur Veröffentlichung des überlieferten Liedguts, vor allem durch den Kiem Pauli (1882-1960) und Prof. Kurt Huber (1893-1943). Gleichzeitig betrieb der Münchner Georg von Kaufmann (1907-72) in ganz Oberbayern eine Volkstanzpflege mit großer Breitenwirkung.

Dem ungezwungenen Singen und Musizieren (ohne Bühne, ohne Programm, ohne Ansager, ohne Eintritt, ohne Honorar!) dient seit 1981 mit anhaltendem Erfolg der von dem Münchner Volkskulturpfleger Volker D. Laturell eingeführten „Boarische Hoagart'n", ein monatliches offenes Sänger- und Musikantentreffen in Münchner Wirtshäusern.

Ende November werden alljährlich im Rahmen des traditionellen „Cäcilienfests der Münchner Musikanten" im Alten Rathaussaal Personen, die sich besondere Verdienste um die Volks-

today. One of its leaders was Konrad Max Kunz (1812-1875) who composed the Bavarian anthem in 1862. The conductor of the amateur orchestra "Wilde Gungl" (established in 1864), Franz Strauss, first presented the early works of his son Richard Strauss (1864-1949) to the Munich public.

After the local artists had "discovered" the Alps and their inhabitants, one started to collect and sing mountain songs with great enthusiasm. In Munich the group around Maximilian Duke of Bavaria (1808-1888) paved the way for an "Alpine Awakening" which still has its impact today. Thanks to the Duke - lovingly called "Zithermaxl" - this instrument was improved technically and thus became widely popular.

In about 1900 the masquerades were revived in the new halls of the beer cellars. And between 1870 and 1930 the popular "Volkssänger" attracted masses of people. Their satirical, funny, or critical songs were printed by the thousands and shortly afterwards sung by the local people.

bavarois (1862) comme chef d'orchestre. Le premier chef d'orchestre de l'orchestre d'amateurs «Wilde Gungl» fondé en 1864, Franz Strauss, fit, lors de la première, jouer les premières œuvres musicales de son fils Richard Strauss (1864-1949).

Après que les artistes ont «découvert» les Alpes et leurs habitants, les chansons montagnardes furent rassemblées et chantées. A Munich, le cercle du duc bavarois Maximilian (1808-1888) démontra en premier un vif «engouement pour les Alpes» qui perdure jusqu'à aujourd'hui. Grâce à lui, le populaire «Zithermaxl», une cithare améliorée techniquement se trouva acceptée dans tous les milieux.

Vers 1900, les bals masqués connurent dans les nouvelles salles immenses des brasseries leur deuxième période de gloire. Et entre 1870 et 1930, les chanteurs populaires munichois appréciés étaient très courus. Leurs couplets satiriques, amusants ou critiques étaient publiés par milliers et rechantés peu après.

ne dei cantori civici» (Bürgersängerzunft) del 1840, che esiste ancora oggi e di cui fu direttore artistico, tra gli altri, Max Kunz (1812-75), il musicista che compose l'inno bavarese nel 1862. L'orchestra amatoriale «Wilde Gungl», fondata nel 1864 e diretta inizialmente da Franz Strauss, presentò per la prima volta le opere giovanili del figlio di questi, Richard Strauss (1864-1949).

Quando gli artisti «scoprirono» le Alpi e gli abitanti delle montagne, si iniziò a collezionare e a cantare canti montanari. La cerchia monacense che faceva capo a Maximilian Herzog (1808-88) fu precursore in Baviera della «cultura alpina», che ha lasciato la sua impronta fino ai nostri giorni. Grazie a Maximilian Herzog, conosciuto dal popolo come «Max, il suonatore di cetra», questo strumento, tecnicamente migliorato, ebbe un'ampia diffusione.

I balli in maschera ebbero un secondo periodo di grande popolarità nel 1900, quando furono aperte le nuove ed enormi sale delle birrerie. E tra il 1870 ed 1930 riscossero grande successo anche i tanto amati Cantori Popolari di Monaco. I loro couplet satirici e divertenti vennero pubblicati con tirature di diverse migliaia di copie e canticchiati ovunque.

Nel 1876, a Monaco ebbe inizio, per opera di August Hartmann (1846-1917) e Hyazinth Abele (1823-1916), la ricerca scientifica sui canti popolari in Baviera. Nel periodo che seguì alla Prima Guerra Mondiale vennero pubblicate numerose raccolte voluminose di canti tradizionali, grazie soprattutto a Kiem Pauli (1882-1960) e al Prof. Kurt Huber (1893-1943). Contemporaneamente, il monacense Georg von Kaufmann (1907-72) si dedicò alla divulgazione su vasta scala delle danze folcloristiche in tutta l'Alta Baviera.

musik in München erworben haben, vom Oberbürgermeister mit Ehrenmedaillen und Urkunden ausgezeichnet.

Anlässlich des Jubiläums „200 Jahre Englischer Garten" 1989 fand nach 85jähriger Pause auf Initiative von Volker D. Laturell wieder der im vorigen Jahrhundert beliebte „Kocherlball" am Sonntagmorgen am Chinesischen Turm statt. Inzwischen kommen hier um 6 Uhr in der Früh' am 3. Sonntag im Juli wieder bis zu 20000 volkstanzbegeisterte Frühaufsteher zusammen.

Das echte Volks-Theater hatte in München schon große Bedeutung, ehe sich im 16./17. Jahrhundert ein Berufsschauspielertum entwickelte. Die Tradition des Volksschauspiels reicht von der mittelalterlichen Poetenschule über das barock-pompöse Jesuitentheater, das Kindertheater und die Passionsspiele im 18. Jahrhundert sowie die Liebhaberbühnen im 19. Jahrhundert bis heute. Die derzeit rund 150 Münchner Volkstheater, Amateurbühnen, Laienspielgruppen usw. haben sich nahezu aller Sparten der darstellenden Kunst angenommen: Theater mit und/oder für Kinder, Figuren- und Puppentheater, religiöse Stücke, klassische Stücke und Dramen, Musiktheater, Krimis, fremdsprachige Stücke und Ausländer-Theater, gesellschaftskritische Stücke, Komödien und Lustspiele, bayerisches Bauerntheater, Tanz und Pantomime, Kabarett und Kleinkunst und natürlich die traditionsreiche Münchner Volkssängerbühne.

Die Bindung der Dörfer an die alten Landgerichte endete 1803, als rund um die Haupt- und Residenzstadt das neue Landgericht München entstand. Nach Eingemeindung von Teilflächen schluckte München 1854 mit Au, Giesing und Haidhausen erstmals ganze Gemeinden. Bis zum Ersten Weltkrieg folgten dann elf weitere Gemeinden und die Städte Schwabing und Milbertshofen. Die nächste Eingemeindungswelle zwischen 1930 und 1942 brachte München einen Zuwachs von

The scientific research of folksongs started in Munich in 1876 under August Hartmann (1846-1917) and Hyazinth Abele (1823-1916). After the First World War these traditional songs were intensively collected and printed, particularly by Kiem Pauli (1882-1960) and Prof. Kurt Huber (1893-1943). At the same time Georg von Kaufmann (1907-1972) from Munich promoted folk-dancing throughout Upper Bavaria.

In 1981 Volker D. Laturell, a protector and fosterer of popular culture, introduced with great success the so-called "Boarische Hoagart'n", an open meeting of singers and musicians taking place once a month in Munich's pubs. It offers completely informal musical performances without stage, programme, annoucers, entrance fees and pay.

Every year in late November persons who have earned special merit in the field of folk music in Munich are awarded medals and certificates by the mayor on the occasion of the "Cäcilienfest der Münchner Musikanten" in the Old Town Hall.

During the celebration of the 200th anniversary of the English Garden in 1989 Volker D. Laturell - after 85 years - revived the "Kocherlball" at the Chinese Tower which had been very popular in the 18th century. Up to 20,000 folk dance enthusiasts and early risers meet at 6 a.m. on the 3rd Sunday in July.

The original folk drama already played an important part in Munich before the professional theatre developed in the 16th and 17th centuries. The folk drama tradition started with the medieval school of poets, and continued with the ostentatious Baroque theatre of the Jesuits, the children's theatre, the passion plays of the 18th century, the amateur groups of the 19th century until today. Munich's roughly 150 popular theatres, amateur groups and companies cover nearly all the different types of drama: plays with and for children, puppet shows, religious

Avec August Hartmann (1846-1917) et Hyazinth Abele (1823-1916), la recherche scientifique sur la chanson populaire en Bavière commença à Munich en 1876. Après la Première Guerre mondiale, de grandes actions de recherche conduirent à la publication des chansons récoltées, en particulier par Kiem Pauli (1882-1960) et le prof. Kurt Huber (1893-1943). A la même époque, le Munichois Georg von Kaufmann (1907-1972) s'engagea dans la préservation dans toute la Haute-Bavière des danses populaires.

Chanter et faire de la musique «sans façons» (sans scène, sans programme, sans annonce, sans entrée, sans cachet!) continuent avec succès depuis 1981 à soutenir l'action «Boarische Hoagart'n» engagée par Volker D. Laturell, spécialiste munichois du maintien de la culture populaire, et qui consiste en une rencontre mensuelle ouverte aux chanteurs et musiciens dans les cafés de Munich.

A la fin novembre, dans le cadre de la traditionnelle «Cäcilienfest der Münchner Musikanten» (Fête de la Ste Cécile des musiciens munichois), des personnes ayant connu des mérites particuliers au niveau de la musique folklorique à Munich, recevront du maire des médailles d'honneur et des certificats.

Depuis 1989, à l'occasion des «200 ans du Jardin Anglais», le «Kocherlball» très apprécié au siècle dernier a, après une pause de 85 ans, été réintroduit sur l'initiative de Volker D. Laturell, et se tient à nouveau le dimanche matin à la Tour Chinoise. Depuis, le 3ème dimanche du mois de juillet à 6 heures du matin plus de 20 000 lève-tôt et amateurs de danses folkloriques se retrouvent.

Le vrai théâtre populaire était déjà très important à Munich avant que ne se forme au 16ème/17ème siècle une troupe de comédiens professionnels. La tradition du théâtre populaire englobe l'école des poètes du Moyen Age, le théâtre des Jésuites baroque et pompeux, le théâtre pour enfants,

L'attività canora e concertistica spontanea ed informale (senza palcoscenico, senza programma, senza presentatore, senza biglietto d'ingresso ... e senza compenso per chi si esibiva!) fu introdotta nel 1981 da un cultore appassionato della cultura popolare, Volker D. Laturell, con manifestazioni canore e musicali pubbliche, chiamate «Boarische Hoagart'n», che si svolgono ogni mese nelle osterie di Monaco riscuotendo un immutato successo.

Nell'ambito della cosiddetta «Festa di Santa Cecilia dei musicisti monacensi», che si tiene ogni anno a fine novembre nella sala del vecchio municipio, coloro che si sono distinti per meriti nel campo della musica popolare vengono premiati dal sindaco della città con medaglie onorifiche e certificati di riconoscimento.

Nel 1989, dopo una pausa di ben 85 anni, in occasione dei «200 anni del Giardino Inglese» Volker D. Laturell ripristinò il cosiddetto «Kocherlball», molto popolare nel secolo scorso. Il ballo si svolse una domenica mattina presso la Torre Cinese; da allora, nella terza domenica di luglio si riuniscono qui ogni anno, alle 600 del mattino, fino a 20 000 persone (decisamente mattiniere) appassionate di danze folcloristiche.

A Monaco, il teatro popolare autentico rivestiva una grande importanza già prima che, nel XVI/XVII secolo si sviluppasse una vera e propria scuola di attori professionisti. La tradizione del teatro popolare risale ancora alla scuola dei poeti medievali ed è continuata, poi, con il teatro barocco e pomposo dei gesuiti, il teatro dei bambini, i misteri della passione del XVIII secolo e le compagnie filodrammatiche del

Der traditionelle „Kocherlball" am Chinesischen Turm

The traditional "Kocherlball" at the Chinese Tower

Le traditionnel «Kocherlball» à la Tour Chinoise

Il tradizionale «Kocherlball» presso la Torre Cinese

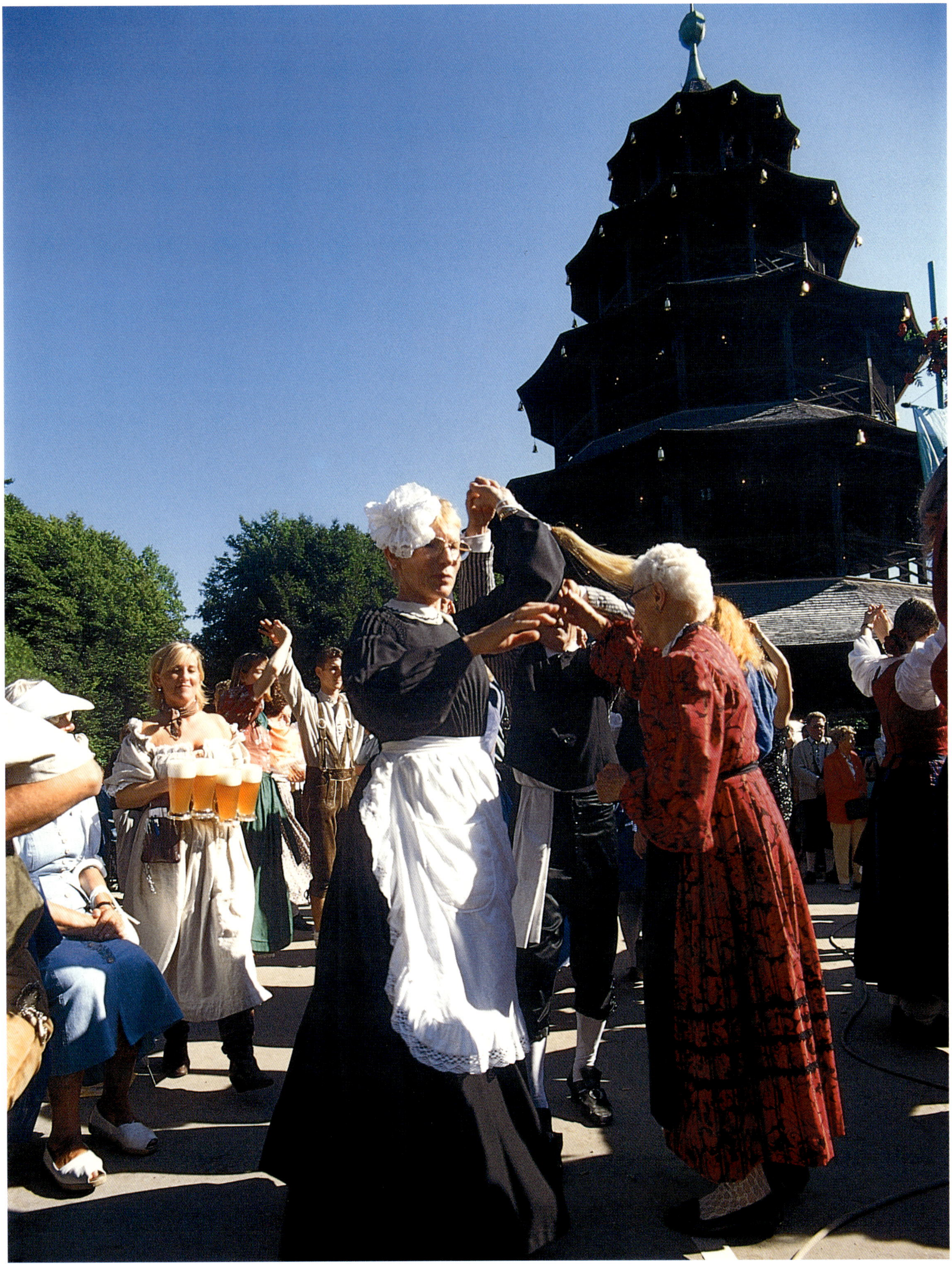

noch einmal zwölf Gemeinden und der Stadt Pasing. Gerade diese zuletzt einverleibten Gemeinden haben ihr ländliches Aussehen und ihr bäuerliches Brauchtum teilweise bis heute erhalten, allen voran Feldmoching, das „einzige Bauerndorf der Welt mit U-Bahn-Anschluss".

So erweist sich das Brauchtum in der Stadt nach seiner Herkunft immer noch als städtisch-bürgerlich, während es draußen in den Stadtvierteln unverändert ländlich-bäuerlich geprägt ist. Obwohl es in der Stadt die Zünfte längst nicht mehr gibt, stehen beispiels-

plays, classical plays and tragedies, musical theatre, mysteries, foreign plays, socio-critical plays, comedies and farces, Bavarian country-style theatre, dancing and pantomime, varieté and cabaret, and – of course – the "Volkssängerbühne" so extremely rich in tradition.

The villages' affiliation with the regional courts of old ended in 1803, when the new Landgericht München was established. After incorporating several small individual parts, the city in 1854 for the first time swallowed up entire communities – i. e. Au, Giesing

les jeux de la passion au 18ème siècle ainsi que les scènes d'amateurs du 19ème siècle jusqu'à aujourd'hui. Les quelques 150 théâtres populaires, théâtres amateurs, groupes amateurs de Munich s'adressent à toutes les formes de cet art, qu'il s'agisse de théâtre pour enfants ou avec des enfants, de théâtre de marionnettes, de pièces religieuses, de pièces et de drames classiques, de théâtre musical, policier, de pièces en langue étrangère et de théâtre jouant des pièces étrangères, de pièces sur la société, de comédies et de théâtre

XIX secolo fino a giungere ai giorni nostri. Oggi esistono circa 150 teatri popolari, amatoriali, compagnie filodrammatiche ecc. che si dedicano a pressoché tutti gli indirizzi dell'arte figurativa: il teatro con i bambini e/o per i bambini, il teatro delle marionette, le opere religiose, classiche e i drammi, il teatro musicale, i gialli, le opere in lingua straniera o per stranieri, le opere con contenuti di critica sociale, le commedie, le opere rustiche bavaresi, le danze e le pantomime, il cabaret e la rivista di avanspettacolo, e, naturalmente, il teatro dei cantori

„Die Schäffler", Szene aus dem Wies'n-Festzug, der alljährlich zu Beginn des Oktoberfestes stattfindet

"Die Schäffler", scene from the festive parade which opens the Oktoberfest every year

«Die Schäffler», scène du défilé précédant l'ouverture annuelle de la Fête de la bière

«Die Schäffler», scena tratta dalla sfilata annuale in occasione dell'inizio della Festa della Birra

weise der Brauertag und der Gärtnertag ebenso im jährlichen Münchner Brauchtumskalender wie der alle sieben Jahre stattfindende Schäfflertanz. Vor allem auch die Maidult (um den 1. Mai), die Jakobidult (letzte Juliwoche) und die Kirchweihdult (3. Oktoberwoche) auf dem Auer Mariahilfplatz und schließlich der Christkindlmarkt auf dem Marienplatz (im Advent) können auf eine jahrhundertelange Geschichte zurückblicken. Das inzwischen weltberühmte Oktoberfest, hervorgegangen aus einem Pferderennen zur Huldigung der Wittelsbacher,

and Haidhausen. Up to the First World War eleven additional communities and the towns of Schwabing and Milbertshofen followed. During the next wave of incorporations between 1930 and 1942, twelve further communities and the city of Pasing became parts of Munich. Particularly this last group of communities has preserved its rural appearance and peasant customs until today – most of all Feldmoching which is called the "world's only farming village with a subway connection".

According to their origin, the city's customs still bear urban features, while those of the city districts still indicate rural and peasant influence. Although the guilds have long ceased to exist, celebrations like the "Brewers' Day" and the "Gardeners' Day" are still as much integral parts of Munich's calendar of events as the "Schäfflertanz", which takes place every seven years. But also the "Maidult" (about 1 May), the "Jakobidult" (last week in July), the "Kirchweihdult" (third week in October), and the "Christkindlmarkt on Marienplatz" (during the Advent season) look back on century-old traditions. The internationally famous "Oktoberfest", which actually dates back to a horse race honouring the Wittelsbach Dynasty, was first held in 1810.

de boulevard, de théâtre paysan bavarois, de danse et de pantomime, de cabaret et de café-théâtre et bien entendu de théâtre des chanteurs populaires connaissent une grande tradition à Munich.

La liaison des villages avec les anciennes circonscriptions des tribunaux s'acheva en 1803 lorsque tout autour de la capitale et de la ville résidentielle, la nouvelle circonscription du tribunal d'instance fut créée. Après l'incorporation d'une partie des terrains, Munich incorpora pour la première fois en 1854 des communes entières avec Au, Giesing et Haidhausen. Jusqu'à la Première Guerre mondiale, onze autres communes suivirent ainsi que les villes de Schwabing et Milbertshofen. La prochaine vague d'incorporation qui eut lieu entre 1930 et 1942 permit à Munich de grandir encore de 12 communes et de la ville de Pasing. Les communes incorporées en dernier ont quelquefois gardé leur apparence rurale et leur tradition paysanne jusqu'à aujourd'hui et ici, Feldmoching arrive en tête et est surnommé «le seul village rural du monde doté d'une ligne de métro».

Ainsi la tradition en ville reste, en fonction de son origine, toujours bourgeoise alors que dans les quartiers de la ville elle garde toujours un caractère rural et paysan. Bien que les corporations n'existent plus depuis longtemps en ville, le Brauertag et le Gärtnertag (jour des brasseurs respectivement des jardiniers) sont par exemple toujours dans le calendrier des traditions munichoises comme la «Schäfflertanz» qui n'a lieu que tous les sept ans. Les kermesses Maidult (vers le 1er mai), Jakobidult (dernière semaine de juillet) et la Kirchweihdult (3ème semaine d'octobre) sur la place Mariahilfplatz dans l'Au et enfin le marché de Noël sur la Marienplatz (pendant l'avent) reposent sur une tradition séculaire. La fête de la Bière, mondialement célèbre, qui débuta par une course de chevaux lors du serment de fidélité

popolari monacensi che vanta una ricca e lunga tradizione.

I vincoli dei paesini con le antiche giurisdizioni cessarono nel 1803 con l'istituzione di un nuovo tribunale di Monaco con giurisdizione sull'intera area intorno alla capitale del regno di Baviera. Dopo l'incorporamento di aree parziali, nel 1854 Monaco iniziò ad inglobare interi comuni come Au, Giesing e Haidhausen, cui seguirono, prima della Prima Guerra Mondiale, altri 11 comuni e le città di Schwabing e di Milbertshofen. L'ondata successiva, tra il 1930 e il 1942, arricchì Monaco di altri 12 comuni e della città di Pasing. E sono proprio questi ultimi comuni che hanno mantenuto, in parte fino ad oggi, il loro aspetto rurale ed i loro usi contadini, in modo particolare Feldmoching, «l'unico paese di contadini del mondo servito da una metropolitana».

Sotto questo aspetto, gli usi e costumi della città rivelano l'impronta della loro provenienza civico-urbana, mentre la periferia conserva tuttora un immutato carattere rurale e campagnolo. Sebbene le corporazioni artigiane non esistano più in città da molto tempo, la Festa dei Birrai e la Festa dei Giardinieri, ad esempio, fanno parte tuttora del calendario delle usanze di Monaco, come anche il Ballo dei Bottai che si tiene ogni sette anni. Soprattutto la Fiera di Maggio (intorno al 1º maggio), la Fiera di San Giacomo (ultima settimana di luglio), la Fiera della Consacrazione della Chiesa (terza settimana di ottobre) che si svolge sulla «Mariahilfplatz» nel quartiere di Au, ed infine il Mercatino di Natale sulla «Marienplatz» (nel periodo dell'Avvento) vantano una tradizione centenaria. La Festa della Birra, famosa ormai in tutto il mondo e le cui origini vanno ricercate in una corsa di cavalli in onore dei Wittelsbach, esiste fin dal 1810.

Quasi sconosciuto, invece, è il fatto che a Monaco ebbero inizio anche le funzioni mariane in Germania: la prima di esse in terra tedesca fu celebrata nel 1841 in

ist immerhin bereits 1810 entstanden.

Kaum bekannt ist, dass die Tradition der Maiandachten in Deutschland ihren Anfang in München nahm: 1841 wurde die erste Maiandacht auf deutschem Boden in einem Kloster in dem Münchner Vorort Haidhausen und am Vorabend zum 1. Mai 1843 in der Herzogspitalkirche die erste Maiandacht innerhalb der Stadt gefeiert. Noch heute hat die hauptsächlich auf den größten Marienverehrer unter den Wittelsbachern, Kurfürst Maximilian I. (reg. 1597–1651), zurückgehende Marienverehrung im katholischen München ihre Bedeutung. Die Aufstellung der großartigen, von Hans Krumper entworfenen Figur der zur „Patrona Bavariae" erhobenen Muttergottes 1616 an der Residenzfassade war Vorbild für die Bürger und Bauern im ganzen Land, an ihrem Haus ebenfalls eine Marienfigur anzubringen. Mit der Mariensäule auf dem Schrannenplatz (seit 1854 „Marienplatz") übergab der Kurfürst 1638 den Münchnern ein zweites Standbild der Landespatronin. Übrigens gehen alle Kilometerangaben nach München bis zur Mariensäule.

Auch viele andere Kirchenfeste werden noch (oder wieder!) mit Bräuchen begangen, denken wir nur an das „Einascheln" am Aschermittwoch, die „Palmweihe" am Palmsonntag, die Prozession an Fronleichnam, die „Kräuterweihe" an Mariä Himmelfahrt und die Martinsumzüge am 11. November. Gerade die Feste der populären Heiligen werden gefeiert, vor allem wenn sie Patron einer Kirche oder gar der ganzen Stadt sind, wie Mitte Juni am Dom mit dem Fest des Stadtpatrons St. Benno.

Diesen vielen pfarreilichen Kirchweihfesten steht am 3. Sonntag im Oktober die „Allerwelts"-Kirchweih gegenüber. Als nämlich den Aufklärern Anfang des 19. Jahrhunderts die vielen Kirchweihfeste im Land zu viel wurden, führten sie 1806 diesen Einheitstermin ein, mit der Folge, dass es seither zwei Kirchweih-

Few people know that the German tradition of "Maiandachten" (a service held in honour of the Holy Virgin) first started in Munich: the first one to take place on German soil was held in 1841 in a monastery in the suburb of Haidhausen; the first one taking place within the city limits was held on the eve of May first 1843 in the Herzogspitalkirche. The veneration of the Virgin Mary, which dates back primarily to Elector Maximilian I (1597-1651), the most devoted Virgin worshipper of all the Wittelsbachers, is still widespread in the Catholic city of Munich. When in 1616 the magnificent statue of the Holy Virgin (designed by Hans Krumper and given the name and rank of a "Patrona Bavariae") was set up in front of the façade of the residential palace, it induced numerous Bavarian citizens and peasants to follow this example. In 1638 the Elector presented the "Mariensäule" (a column bearing the figure of the Virgin Mary) to his subjects; it was originally placed on "Schrannenplatz", but was moved to Marienplatz in 1854. By the way, all road distances to Munich are given in relation to the Mariensäule as Munich's central point.

Numerous other church events are still (or again) connected with old customs: the "Einascheln" ceremony (having a black (ash) cross put on the forehead on Ash Wednesday); the consecration of willow (palm) branches on Palm Sunday; the Corpus Christi Procession; the consecration of herbs on Assumption Day; and the St. Martin Procession on 11 November. The birthdays of popular saints are also celebrated with enthusiasm – particularly if they are patron saints of local churches or of the city itself, like St. Benno; his festival takes place in mid-June in Munich's cathedral.

The numerous parish fairs and kirmesses are complemented by a universal fair taking place on the third Sunday in October. When in the early 18th century the enlightened authorities found that there were too many indivi-

aux Wittelsbach, remonte tout de même à l'an 1810.

Il est peu connu que l'origine de la tradition des nuits de mai en Allemagne se trouve à Munich. En 1841, la première nuit de mai eut lieu sur sol allemand dans un couvent situé à Haidhausen dans la banlieue munichoise et, la veille du 1er mai 1843 dans l'église Herzogspital, la première nuit de mai fut fêtée dans la ville. Aujourd'hui encore, la vénération de la vierge Marie, qui revient en force dans la ville catholique de Munich, est principalement à mettre au compte du plus grand vénérateur de Marie, le prince électeur Maximilian 1er (reg. 1597–1651). L'installation de l'extraordinaire statue créée par Hans Krumper de la Mère de Dieu élevée au rang de «Patrona Bavariae» en 1616 sur la façade de la Résidence montrait l'exemple aux bourgeois et aux paysans de tout le land et les invitait eux aussi à installer une statue de Marie sur leur façade. Avec la Mariensäule (colonne à Marie) sur la place Schrannen (appelée depuis 1854 Marienplatz), le prince électeur donna aux Munichois en 1638 une deuxième image de la sainte de leur land. De plus, toutes les indications kilométriques de Munich vont jusqu'à la Mariensäule.

De nombreuses autres fêtes religieuses sont accompagnées encore (ou à nouveau!) de traditions. Pensons par exemple à «l'Einascheln» le mercredi des cendres; le «baptême des rameaux» le dimanche des Rameaux, la procession de la Fête-Dieu, la «Kräuterweihe» à l'Ascencion et les défilés de la St. Martin le 11 novembre. Les fêtes des saints populaires sont justement bien célébrées, encore plus s'il est le patron d'une église ou même de la ville entière, comme à la mi-juin à la cathédrale avec la fête du patron de la ville, St. Benno.

Se tenant le 3ème dimanche d'octobre, la Kirchweih générale fait face à toutes les autres fêtes de Kirchweih religieuses. Lorsqu'au début du 19ème siècle, les

un convento del sobborgo monacense di Haidhausen, e la vigilia del 1 maggio 1843 si tenne, per la prima volta, una funzione mariana all'interno della città nella «Herzogspitalkirche». Il culto mariano, risalente principalmente a colui che fu il cultore più fervente di Maria nel casato dei Wittelsbach, il principe elettore Massimiliano I (regnò dal 1597 al 1651), riveste ancora oggi grande importanza nella Monaco cattolica. La grandiosa rappresentazione della Madonna, eseguita nel 1616 da Hans Krumper sulla facciata della Residenza ed elevata a «Patrona Bavariae», fu il modello per i cittadini ed i contadini di tutto il paese che seguirono l'esempio adornando le loro case con un'effige di Maria. Con la Colonna di Maria, fatta erigere dal principe elettore nel 1638 sulla Schrannenplatz (dal 1854 «Marienplatz» – Piazza di Santa Maria), gli abitanti di Monaco ebbero una seconda statua della patrona del paese. A proposito, tutte le indicazioni chilometriche per Monaco arrivano fino alla Colonna di Maria.

Anche molte altre feste religiose vengono ancora (o nuovamente) accompagnate da usanze antiche: basti pensare all'imposizione delle ceneri il mercoledì omonimo, alla «benedizione delle palme» nella domenica che precede la Pasqua, alla processione del Corpus Domini, alla «Benedizione delle Erbe» in occasione della festa dell'Assunzione della Vergine e alle processioni di San Martino l'11 novembre. I santi popolari vengono festeggiati nel giorno della loro ricorrenza, soprattutto se sono santi protettori di una chiesa o addirittura della città, così come avviene a metà giugno nel Duomo per la festa di San Benno, il patrono della città.

Alle tante feste parrocchiali si contrappone, nella terza domenica di ottobre, la benedizione della chiesa «universale». All'inizio del XIX secolo gli illuministi ritennero, infatti, che esistessero troppe sagre ed istituirono pertanto, nel 1806, questa ricorrenza unitaria. La conseguenza fu che, da

feste im Jahr gibt, wobei das Brauchtum am „Kirta" im Oktober weitgehend weltlich geprägt ist. Dazu gehört vor allem der „Kirchweihtanz".

Und dieser ist wiederum Bestandteil der gerade in München sorgsam gepflegten großen brauchtümlichen Tanztermine. Das beginnt schon in dem seinerseits recht traditionellen Fasching mit den „Redouten" im Alten Rathaus, das ja eigentlich nie Rathaus war, vielmehr 1470-80 als städtisches Tanzhaus errichtet wurde und jahrhundertelang als solches diente. Denn genau dort fanden 1717 die ersten Münchner Faschingsredouten statt, die auch von Kurfürst Max II. Emanuel (reg. 1679-1726) und seiner Gemahlin Therese Kunigunde besucht wurden. Hier finden jeweils auch am 30. April der „Maitanz" und am Kirta-Samstag der erwähnte „Kirchweihtanz" statt.

Da sind aber noch viele andere wichtige Termine für den Münchner im Kalender: Die Starkbierzeit im Frühjahr, das Aufstellen der Maibäume am 1. Mai, der Stadtgeburtstag Mitte Juni - irgendwas wird immer gefeiert in München.

Volker D. Laturell

dual fairs, they introduced this collective kirmess date in 1806 to do away with all the rest. As a result, there are now two fairs per year, the October "Kirta" (Bavarian for Church Fair) having a more mundane flair, as it offers the popular "Kirmes Dance".

And this event is, in turn, one of the important dates in Munich's carefully cultivated dance calendar, whose festivities start in the traditional "Fasching" (carnival) with the masquerades in the Old Town Hall; this picturesque building actually never served as an administrative centre but was built as a dance hall from 1470 to 1480 and was used for this purpose for centuries. Here Munich's first masquerades took place in 1717, balls that were attended even by Elector Max II Emanuel (1679-1726) and his wife Therese Kunigunde. Here the "May Dance" takes place on 30 April, and the earlier mentioned "Kirchweihtanz" (Kirmess Dance) on "Kirta Saturday".

But Munich's festivity calendar has much more to offer: the strong beer time in the spring; setting up the maypoles on first May; the city anniversary in mid-June - there is always a reason for celebrating in Munich.

Volker D. Laturell

rationalistes en eurent assez de toutes ces fêtes de Kirchweih (consécration de l'église) dans le land, ils décidèrent de cette date unique en 1806. Le résultat est qu'il existe depuis deux fêtes de la consécration par an et le «Kirta» (tradition du jour de Kirchweih) en octobre est nettement plus répandue. La danse «Kirchweichtanz» en est un des moments forts.

Et elle fait à son tour partie des dates de danses traditionnelles très bien respectées à Munich. Cela commence déjà durant le carnaval traditionnel avec les «bals masqués» dans l'ancien Hôtel de Ville, qui ne fut en fait jamais un hôtel de ville, et qui fut érigé en 1470-1480 comme maison de danse municipale et fonctionna pendant des siècles. C'est justement là qu'eurent lieu les premiers bals masqués du carnaval de Munich en 1717 auxquels assistèrent également le prince électeur Max II Emanuel (reg. 1679-1726) et son épouse Therese Kunigunde. C'est là que se tiennent chaque fois le 30 avril la «Maitanz» et, le samedi de Kirta, la «Kirchweihtanz» déjà mentionnée.

Mais il existe encore bien d'autres rendez-vous dans le calendrier des Munichois: la période de la bière de mars au printemps, la mise en place des mâts de cocagne de mai (Maibaum) le 1er mai, l'anniversaire de la ville à la mi-juin. Il y a toujours quelque chose à fêter à Munich.

Volker D. Laturell

allora, esistono due feste di benedizione della chiesa all'anno, delle quali il cosiddetto «Kirta» ha un'impronta piuttosto secolare. Ad esso si rifà soprattutto il «Ballo della Sagra».

E questo, a sua volta, fa parte della serie di grandi balli tradizionali molto sentiti a Monaco. Si inizia nel periodo di carnevale, già di per sé ricco di tradizione, con i suoi balli in maschera (Redouten) nel Vecchio Municipio (Altes Rathaus) che, a dire il vero, non svolse mai la funzione di municipio, bensì fu costruito come casa da ballo e servì a questo scopo per secoli. Infatti, fu proprio in questo luogo che si tennero, nel 1717, i primi balli in maschera di carnevale di Monaco, ai quali presero parte anche il principe elettore Massimiliano II Emanuele (regnò dal 1679 al 1726) e sua moglie Teresa Kunigunde. E, sempre qui, si svolge anche il «Ballo di Maggio» ed il già citato «Ballo della Sagra» in ottobre nel sabato del «Kirta».

Ma ci sono ancora tanti altri importanti appuntamenti nel calendario di Monaco: il «periodo della birra forte» in primavera, ad esempio, la festa dei ciliegi il 1º maggio e la festa di compleanno della città a metà giugno. Insomma, a Monaco c'è sempre un'occasione per festeggiare.

Volker D. Laturell

„Blasius der Spaziergänger", alias Sigi Sommer, Journalist und Schriftsteller, Chronist des Münchner Lebens

"Blasius der Spaziergänger", alias Sigi Sommer, journalist and writer, chronicler of the life in Munich

«Blasius der Spaziergänger», alias Sigi Sommer, journaliste et écrivain, chroniqueur de la vie munichoise

«Blasius der Spaziergänger», al secolo Sigi Sommer, giornalista e scrittore, attento cronista della vita cittadina

330

*Eine Stadt
im Aufbruch*

*A City on the
Way to New Horizons*

*Une ville
en plein essor*

*Una città
in atmosfera
neopionieristica*

Als ich 1994 etwas verwegen „eine neue Münchner Gründerzeit" ankündigte, ist dieser große Anspruch noch auf heftige Skepsis gestoßen. Ist München nicht ganz im Gegenteil dabei, so fragten viele, wesentliche Entwicklungen zu verschlafen? Wird nicht in der Planungsbehörde eine Bauverhinderungspolitik betrieben? Ist nicht der rot-grünen Stadtratsmehrheit die Verbesserung von Luft und Wasser und die Durchsetzung von mehr Grün in der Stadt viel wichtiger als die wirtschaftliche Prosperität? Solche Fragen stellt heute niemand mehr. Selbst der konservative „Münchner Merkur" bringt seine Reportagenserie über die Neubauten und Projekte der Landeshauptstadt unter dem Motto: „Die neue Gründerzeit". Beinahe allwöchentlich beweisen Grundsteinlegungen, Richtfeste und Eröffnungsfeiern, dass die weißblaue Metropole tatsächlich gegenwärtig einen Bauboom erlebt wie schon lange nicht mehr.

Der München-Besucher kann sich schon bei einem Altstadtbummel von der Aufbruchstimmung auf dem Bausektor überzeugen. Am Altstadtring, neben der Staatskanzlei, hat die Max-Planck-Gesellschaft, die gemäß ihrer Satzung den Sitz eigentlich im wieder vereinigten Berlin haben müsste, ihre Hauptverwaltung errichtet: ein auffälliges Symbol an prominenter Stelle für die Bedeutung der Wissenschaften in dieser Stadt. München beherbergt nicht nur drei Universitäten (die Ludwig-Maximilians-Universität, die Technische Universität und die Universität der Bundeswehr vor den Toren der Stadt), sondern auch viele Fachhochschulen, Forschungsinstitute der Max-Planck-Gesellschaft und auch die Hauptverwaltung der Fraunhofer Gesellschaft sowie bedeutsame private Forschungs- und Entwicklungsabteilungen, beispielsweise bei Siemens und BMW.

Apropos Siemens: Dieser Weltkonzern müsste aus historischen Gründen seinen Sitz ebenfalls im wieder vereinigten Berlin haben,

When in 1994 I announced somewhat rashly that Munich was about to enjoy a new "Gründerzeit", this ambitious forecast met with widespread scepticism. Many people asked whether sleepy Munich was not rather missing essential developments? Or whether the city planners were not pursuing a policy of preventing construction? Or whether the Red-Green majority in the city council did not find it more important to improve Munich's air and water quality and to enlarge the green zones than to better economic prosperity? Nobody asks these questions today. Even the conservative "Münchner Merkur" newspaper heads its series of reports on the city's new buildings and projects "The New Gründerzeit". Nearly every week cornerstone and topping-out ceremonies as well as inaugurations of finished buildings go to prove that the "white-blue" metropolis of Munich is enjoying the most impressive building boom in many decades.

A stroll through the old city centre will convince visitors that Munich is really setting out for new horizons in the building sector. At the "Altstadtring", next to the "Staatskanzlei", the Max-Planck-Gesellschaft has erected its new headquarters, although (according to its charter) it should have its main office in reunited Berlin: a striking symbol of the important status which the sciences enjoy in Munich. For Munich not only boasts three universities (Ludwig-Maximilians-Universität, the Polytechnic and the University of the Bundeswehr outside the city gates), but also numerous Fachhochschulen (institutes of higher learning), research institutes of the Max-Planck-Gesellschaft, the main office of the Frauenhofer Gesellschaft, and very important private research facilities, for instance those of Siemens and BMW.

As far as Siemens is concerned, this global concern also ought to have its headquarters in reunited Berlin, but it is at present also building its central office –

Lorsqu'en 1994 j'annonçais avec audace «une nouvelle ère de construction pour Munich», cette immense prétention se heurta à un lourd scepticisme. Beaucoup se demandaient si Munich, au contraire, n'était pas en train de rater des développements essentiels? L'office de la planification ne pratiquait-il pas une politique visant à empêcher la construction? La majorité socialiste et écologique du conseil municipal n'attachait-elle pas plus d'importance à l'amélioration de la qualité de l'air et de l'eau et à une augmentation des espaces verts dans la ville qu'à la prospérité économique? Aujourd'hui, personne ne pose plus ces questions. Même le quotidien conservateur «Münchner Merkur» présente une série de reportages sur les nouveaux bâtiments et les projets de la capitale du land en l'intitulant «la nouvelle ère de construction». Presque toutes les semaines, les fêtes marquant la pose de la première pierre, la fin de la construction de la charpente et l'inauguration prouvent que la métropole bleu-blanc connaît actuellement un véritable boom de la construction comme elle n'en a pas vécu depuis longtemps.

A Munich, le visiteur peut se rendre compte en se promenant dans la vieille ville de tout ce qui passe au niveau de la construction. La société Max-Planck, qui d'après ses statuts devrait en fait siéger dans la ville de Berlin réunifiée, a établi son siège administratif sur l'ancien périphérique, à côté de la chancellerie. Il s'agit d'un symbole voyant, installé à une place de choix et soulignant l'importance des sciences dans cette ville. Munich abrite non seulement trois universités (l'université Ludwig-Maximilian, l'université technique et l'université de l'armée située aux portes de la ville), mais encore de nombreuses écoles supérieures, instituts de recherche de la société Max-Planck ainsi que le siège administratif de la Fraunhofer Gesellschaft sans oublier d'importants départements privés de recher-

Quando, nel 1994, annunciai con un pizzico di audacia l'inizio di una «nuova era di sviluppo industriale a Monaco» raccolsi commenti improntati ad un forte scetticismo per questa grande aspirazione. Molti si chiesero se la città, in piena contraddizione con l'annuncio fatto, non stesse già ignorando completamente alcuni sviluppi essenziali. Nell'ente comunale di pianificazione non veniva, forse, attuata una politica di ostruzionismo verso i progetti edili? La maggioranza rosso-verde che costituiva la giunta non anteponeva, forse, il miglioramento delle condizioni ambientali e la creazione di più spazi verdi alla prosperità economica? Queste domande, oggi, non le pone più nessuno. Anche il quotidiano conservatore «Münchner Merkur» ha divulgato recentemente una serie di reportage sulle nuove opere edili e sui progetti futuri che interessano il capoluogo bavarese al motto di «La nuova era di sviluppo industriale». Quasi settimanalmente, cerimonie di posa della prima pietra, feste di ultimazione delle strutture portanti di edifici e nuove inaugurazioni testimoniano come, attualmente, la metropoli bianco-azzurra stia effettivamente vivendo un boom edilizio che non conosceva più da tempo.

Il visitatore di Monaco può convincersi dell'atmosfera neopionieristica che regna nel settore edile facendo una semplice passeggiata lungo l'anello di circonvallazione del centro storico («Altstadtring»). Qui, vicino alla Cancelleria di Stato bavarese ha istituito la propria sede centrale la Società Max Planck, sebbene essa, per statuto, dovrebbe trovarsi nella Berlino riunificata: un indizio evidente, peraltro in un'ubicazione di prim'ordine, dell'importanza che le scienze rivestono in questa città. Monaco non solo ospita tre atenei (l'Università Ludwig-Maximilian, il Politecnico e l'Università dell'Esercito alle porte della città), ma anche numerosi istituti superiori parauniversitari, istituti di ricerca della Società Max Planck e la sede centrale della Società Fraunhofer

baut jedoch seine Zentrale, das „Siemens-Forum" nach den Plänen des New Yorker Architekten Richard Meier auch am Münchner Altstadtring. Der kühl-elegante Bau in gleißendem Weiß soll noch 1999 in Betrieb genommen werden.

An der Kreuzung des Altstadtrings mit dem Altmünchner Prachtboulevard Maximilianstraße errichtete ein Immobilienfonds ein Verwaltungsgebäude, das einerseits das historische und durch die Verkehrsschneise zeitweise beschädigte Maximiliansforum wieder vollendete und andererseits den Altstadtring mit einem Aluminium-Glas-Gebäude bestückte. In unmittelbarer Nachbarschaft wird Münchens größte Bauunternehmung, die Bayerische Hausbau, auf immer noch brachliegenden Flächen weitere Bauten errichten.

Die fusionierte HypoVereinsbank gestaltet gleich mehrere Blöcke der Altstadt (zwischen Theatinerkirche und Dom) grundlegend um, und hierbei wird erfreulicherweise nicht altstädtische kleinteilige Struktur durch langweilige, aber zweckmäßige Monostruktur verdrängt (was in so vielen Innenstädten zur Verödung beigetragen hat), sondern im Gegenteil eine abweisende Konglomeration von Bürogebäuden abgelöst durch eine auf Durchlässigkeit und Vielfalt angelegte Baustruktur mit vielen Höfen und Passagen, Restaurants, Cafés und verschiedenen Geschäften.

Die Kultur kommt beim Bauboom im Herzen der Stadt keineswegs zu kurz: Die größte kommunale Investition von fast 150 Millionen Mark gilt dem Probengebäude der Kammerspiele (nach den Plänen des Wiener Architekten Gustav Peichl) und der Sanierung des Schauspielhauses. Am Salvatorplatz, vis-à-vis des Kultusministeriums, entstand in historischem Gemäuer das Literaturhaus, das der Münchner Architekt Uwe Kiessler um eine moderne Etage ergänzte.

Zu den ärgerlichsten Baulücken der Altstadt zählt der Ja-

the "Siemens Forum" – at the Altstadtring, according to plans made by architect Richard Meier from New York. This cool, elegant and stark-white building is to be ready for operation in 1999.

At the crossing of the Altstadtring and the magnificent Boulevard of Maximilianstraße a major property company has constructed an administration building which has not only completed the historic "Maximiliansforum" that had been temporarily been damaged by the traffic route leading through it, but has also provided the Altstadtring with an impressive building of glass and aluminium. In its vicinity Munich's largest construction firm, the "Bayerische Hausbau" enterprise, is going to set up additional buildings on a still vacant lot.

The recently fused HypoVereinsbank is just reconstructing several blocks in the old city centre between Theatinerkirche and the cathedral; but, fortunately, here one is not replacing the historic small-scale structures with monotonous but functional, uniform buildings (a habit which has contributed greatly to making city centres desolate) but is trying, on the contrary, to turn an uninspiring conglomeration of office buildings into a transparent and variable building structure comprising numerous courtyards, passages, restaurants, cafés and shops.

Culture also profits from this building boom in the heart of the city: the most generous communal investment amounting to nearly DM 150 million is being spent on the rehearsal building of the "Kammerspiele" theatre (planned by the Viennese architect Gustav Peichl) and on the redevelopment of the Schauspielhaus. On Salvatorplatz, opposite the Ministry of Culture, the "House of Literature" has been established within historic walls; this building has been topped with an additional modern storey by architect Uwe Kiesler from Munich.

One of the building gaps in the city centre most offending to

che et de développement comme par exemple chez Siemens et BMW.

A propos de Siemens: Pour des raisons historiques, ce groupe mondial devrait en fait avoir également son siège dans le Berlin réunifié. Cependant, il construit sa centrale, le «Siemens-Forum», d'après les plans de l'architecte new-yorkais Richard Meier également sur l'ancien périphérique de Munich. D'un blanc brillant, l'édifice dégageant une impression froide et élégante, doit entrer en service en 1999.

Au carrefour de l'ancien périphérique avec le splendide boulevard de la Maximilianstraße, un fonds immobilier a édifié un bâtiment administratif qui, d'une part, termine à nouveau le Maximiliansforum endommagé au cours de l'histoire et parfois aussi par les voies de communication et, d'autre part, décore l'ancien périphérique avec un bâtiment alliant aluminium et verre. A proximité immédiate, la plus grande entreprise munichoise du bâtiment, la Bayerische Hausbau, va construire d'autres bâtiments sur des terrains encore en friche.

La HypoVereinsbank, qui vient de fusionner, reconçoit parallèlement et de fond en comble plusieurs blocs de la vieille ville (entre l'église des Théatins et la cathédrale) et, il est agréable de constater que les petites structures si typiques aux vieilles villes ne laissent pas leur place à une monostructure fonctionnelle mais ennuyeuse (ce qui a souvent entraîné la désertion de nombreux centres villes). Au contraire, une conglomération repoussante de bâtiments administratifs est remplacée par une structure de construction aérée et variée dotée de nombreux passages et cours, restaurants, cafés et autres magasins.

Au sein de ce boom de construction au cœur de la ville, la culture n'est de reste non plus: l'investissement communal majeur frôlant les 150 millions de DM concerne le bâtiment de répétition des Kammerspiele d'après les plans de l'architecte

nonché importanti enti privati di ricerca e sviluppo, ad esempio presso la Siemens e la BMW.

A proposito di Siemens, anche questo gruppo internazionale dovrebbe avere la sua sede, per ragioni storiche, nella Berlino riunificata; anch'esso, però, attualmente sta costruendo il suo punto di riferimento centrale, il «Siemens-Forum», sull'Altstadtring secondo il progetto dell'architetto newyorchese Richard Meier. L'inaugurazione dell'edificio sobrio ed elegante in bianco luccicante è prevista entro la fine del 1999.

All'incrocio tra l'Altstadtring e la «Maximilianstraße», una sostuosa strada di antica tradizione, un fondo immobiliare ha istituito un edificio uso uffici che, da un lato, ha nuovamente completato lo storico «Maximiliansforum» temporaneamente danneggiato dalla direttrice del traffico, e dall'altro ha dotato l'Altstadtring di un edificio in alluminio e vetro. Nelle immediate vicinanze, la più grande impresa edile monacense, la Bayerische Hausbau, costruirà ulteriori edifici su superfici ancora inutilizzate.

La HypoVereinsbank, l'istituto bancario nato da una recente fusione, sta attualmente sottoponendo ad un ampio riadattamento architettonico diversi isolati del centro storico tra la Chiesa dei Teatini ed il Duomo, senza però, fortunatamente, limitarsi alla semplice sostituzione delle piccole strutture edili, tipiche del centro storico, con monostrutture monotone anche se rispondenti alle necessità d'uso (cosa che ha contribuito a rendere squallide le zone centrali di numerose città) ma, al contrario, rimpiazzando un agglomerato di edifici uso uffici tutt'altro che invitanti con una struttura edile «permeabile» e molto variegata con numerosi cortili interni e gallerie, ristoranti, caffè e diversi negozi.

Ma anche nella situazione di boom edilizio che interessa il cuore della città, la cultura non viene trascurata. Il più grande investimento comunale, con un ordine di grandezza di circa

333

kobsplatz vor dem Stadtmuseum im historischen Zeughaus. Hier sind nach schmerzvoller Planungsgeschichte und vergeblichen städtebaulichen Wettbewerben jetzt endlich die Weichen gestellt worden für die künftige Nutzung und Gestaltung des Platzes: Die erfreulicherweise durch Zustrom aus dem Osten wieder wachsende jüdische Gemeinde soll hier ein im Stadtbild deutlich hervorragendes Zentrum erhalten mit Synagoge, Gemeinderäumen, koscherem Restaurant und möglicherweise auch Kindergarten und Schule. Die Stadt wird mit einem Jüdischen Museum unter anderem an die bedeutende Geschichte des Judentums an der Isar erinnern, aber auch aktuelles Leben dokumentieren und Perspektiven aufzeigen.

In der Nachbarschaft des Jakobsplatzes stand einmal eines der bedeutendsten Denkmäler der Industriekultur, die gusseiserne Schrannenhalle. Dieses noch im Original vorhandene Zeugnis der Baukultur des 19. Jahrhunderts soll an seinen Originalstandort zurückkehren, wenn auch nicht in voller Länge. Die Investoren wollen Gastronomie, Kultur und Markt bieten und mit einem attraktiven Treffpunkt zur weiteren Belebung der Altstadt beitragen.

Genug der Beispiele! Der Bauboom wird von den einst über angebliche „Bauverhinderung" oder „Schlafmützigkeit" grantelnden Münchnern ja gar nicht mehr in Frage gestellt, sondern wegen Baulärm, Baustellenverkehr und Umleitungen fast schon wieder beklagt.

Zum Glück beschränkt sich aber die Aufbruchstimmung keineswegs auf die Altstadt. München war zwar gegen Ende der 80er Jahre fast schon an das Ende der Fahnenstange seiner baulichen Entfaltungsmöglichkeiten gestoßen, hat dann aber durch verschiedene glückliche Umstände plötzlich gigantische neue Chancen erhalten, die man allesamt unter dem sehr nüchternen Schlagwort „Umnutzung" zu-

the eye is the Jakobsplatz in front of the Municipal Museum in the historic arsenal. After painful planning failures and futile competitions one has finally decided how this square is to be used in the future: here the Jewish community, which has fortunately increased again through immigration from the eastern part of Europe, is to receive a centre complete with a synagogue, community facilities, a kosher restaurant and, possibly, a Kindergarten and school of its own. The city plans to commemorate the significant history of the Jewish race with a Jewish Museum at the Isar, but will also document the present-day life and future perspectives of its Jewish citizens.

In the neighbourhood of Jakobsplatz you once found one of the most important monuments of industrial culture – the cast-iron Schrannenhalle. This still existing example of 19th century architecture will be returned to its former location, but not in full length. The investors intend to offer gastronomy, culture and a market in these premises and hope that with another attractive meeting place they can further revitalize the old city centre.

These examples should suffice to convince even the last sceptic. Most of the natives who formerly nagged about Munich's sluggishness and attempts to prevent construction have certainly become aware of the building boom; in fact they have already started to complain about it because of the unpleasant noise, traffic and detours connected with it.

Fortunately, the spirit of awakening is not restricted to the city centre. Although Munich in the late 80s reached more or less the end of its possibilities for further architectural development, it discovered gigantic new chances which can best be expressed by the slogan "redeployment". Below a few of the most significant examples:

In 1992 Munich's airport moved from the eastern part of the city to the district of Freising in the north. The former airport

viennois Gustav Peichl et l'assainissement du théâtre. Sur la place Salvatorplatz, en face du ministère de la culture, la Literaturhaus a vu le jour dans des murs historiques et a été complétée d'un étage moderne par l'architecte munichois Uwe Kiessler.

Parmi les vides les plus déprimants de la vieille ville citons la place Jakobsplatz devant le Stadtmuseum (musée municipal) dans la Zeughaus historique. Après de nombreux déboires de planification et des appels d'offres, les

150 milioni di marchi, è riservato all'edificio delle prove dei «Kammerspiele» (realizzato secondo il progetto dell'architetto viennese Gustav Peichl) ed al risanamento dello «Schauspielhaus». Sulla Salvatorplatz, di fronte al Ministero Bavarese della Pubblica Istruzione, è stato realizzato, in un ambiente di significato storico, il «Literaturhaus», che l'architetto monacense Uwe Kiessler ha arricchito di un piano moderno.

Uno dei punti non edificati del centro storico che crea da tempo grandi irritazioni è la Jakobsplatz

sammenfassen kann. Ich nenne nur die wichtigsten Beispiele:

1992 ist der Münchner Flughafen vom Osten der Stadt umgezogen in den nördlich gelegenen Landkreis Freising. Dadurch stand das Flughafengelände plötzlich für neue Nutzungen zur Verfügung. Stadt und Staat haben gemeinsam mit einer finanziellen Kraftanstrengung von 2 Milliarden Mark (zuzüglich 700 Millionen für den optimalen U-Bahnanschluss) die Neue Messe München geschaffen, südlich davon kann auf über 500 Hektar die große Mes-area was, consequently, available for other uses. Pooling their funds, the city authorities and the State of Bavaria raised DM two billion (plus DM 700 million for an optimum subway connection) which were invested in the "Neue Messe München". South of this fair and exhibition site a large "Fair City" will be established on an area of 500 hectares, which will eventually offer room for 16,000 inhabitants and 13,000 jobs. South of this "Messestadt", which is being realized step by step but will take at least 15 years jalons sont enfin posés pour l'utilisation future et la conception de la place. La communauté juive, connaissant un agrandissement bienvenu depuis l'ouverture vers l'est, doit recevoir ici un centre nettement plus important avec synagogue, maison des œuvres, restaurant kascher et possibilités également de jardin d'enfants et d'école. La ville veut rappeler entre autres avec un musée juif l'importante histoire du judaïsme aux bords de l'Isar, documenter la vie actuelle et présenter des perspectives.

dirimpetto allo «Stadtmuseum» nello storico arsenale militare («Zeughaus»). Qui ora, dopo una «dolorosa» fase di progettazione e gare comunali di appalto senza esito, sono state poste le basi per la realizzazione urbanistica ed il futuro utilizzo della piazza. Per la comunità ebraica, che grazie all'afflusso dai paesi dell'Est sta nuovamente crescendo, verrà allestito qui un centro con una sua fisionomia ben precisa nel quadro urbanistico monacense e dotato di sinagoga, locali di riunione, ristorante cascer e, probabilmente, anche di un asilo e di una scuola. Con l'istituzione di un Museo Ebraico («Jüdisches Museum») il comune intende, tra l'altro, ricordare la significativa storia dell'ebraismo sulle rive dell'Isar, ma anche documentare la vita attuale ed indicare prospettive per il futuro.

Nelle vicinanze della Jakobsplatz si trovava, un tempo, uno dei più significativi monumenti della cultura dell'industrializzazione: il vecchio mercato coperto («Schrannenhalle»). Questa testimonianza della cultura edile del XIX secolo, realizzata in ghisa e, peraltro, ancora disponibile in originale, dovrà tornare alla sua

170 Müllfahrzeuge finden hier Platz. Es handelt sich um den zweigeschossigen Carport des im September 1999 eingeweihten neuen Domizils des Amtes für Abfallwirtschaft in unmittelbarer Nachbarschaft des Olympiastadions.

There is room for 170 waste disposal trucks. This is the double-story carport of the new domicile of the office of waste management inaugurated in September 1999 neighbouring the Olympic stadium.

170 camions d'enlèvement des ordures ménagères trouvent leur place ici. Il s'agit du parking à deux étages du nouveau domicile, inauguré en septembre 1999, de l'office de la gestion des déchets à proximité immédiate du stade olympique.

Qui trovano posto 170 veicoli della nettezza urbana. Si tratta del deposito automezzi a due piani presso la nuova sede dell'Ufficio della Nettezza Urbana inaugurata nel settembre 1999 nelle immediate vicinanze dello Stadio Olimpico.

sestadt errichtet werden, die einmal Raum bieten soll für 16 000 Bewohner und 13 000 Arbeitsplätze. Südlich von dieser Messestadt, die derzeit schrittweise realisiert wird, aber noch mindestens 15 Jahre bis zu ihrer Vollendung benötigt, schließt sich ein beispielloser 220 Hektar großer Landschaftspark an, der den Blick auf das Alpenpanorama freihält und im Jahr 2005 Schauplatz der Bundesgartenschau sein wird.

Weil die Messe umgezogen ist, können an ihrem alten Platz hinter der zumindest Ende September/Anfang Oktober weltberühmten Theresienwiese auf der Theresienhöhe 1 600 Wohnungen gebaut und viele vor allem mittelständische Unternehmen angesiedelt werden. In den denkmalgeschützten Gabriel-von-Seidl-Hallen des alten Messegeländes wird das Deutsche Museum seine Verkehrsschau unterbringen; damit ist sichergestellt, dass München die Heimat des Deutschen Museums bleibt und dass auf dem alten Messegelände auch künftig ein Publikumsmagnet wirken wird.

to be finished, a unique nature park covering 220 hectares adjoins, which will offer an unrestricted and stunning view of the Alps and will be the scene of the Federal Garden Show in 2005.

As the Munich Fair has moved to a new site, its former location "Theresienhöhe" (which is internationally famous in late September and early October when the October Festival takes place on "Theresienwiese") is available for

Dans le voisinage de la Jakobsplatz se dressait autrefois un des monuments majeurs de la culture industrielle, la Schrannenhalle en fonte. Ce témoignage originel de la culture de construction du 19ème siècle doit revenir à son site originel même si ce n'est pas dans toute sa longueur. Les investisseurs veulent réunir gastronomie, culture et marché et contribuer, avec un point de rencontre attractif, à donner encore plus d'animation à la ville.

sistemazione originaria, anche se non nella sua lunghezza complessiva. Gli investitori vogliono offrire gastronomia, cultura e mercato e contribuire, con un accattivante punto d'incontro, all'ulteriore rilancio del centro storico.

Ma ora, basta con gli esempi! Oggi, il boom edilizio non viene più messo in discussione dai monacensi, che un tempo brontolavano dell'«ostruzionismo» o delle lentezze burocratiche e che oggi, invece, quasi lamentato

Modell der noch im Bau befindlichen Pinakothek der Moderne (Planung: Stephan Braunfels Achitekten, München)

Model of the Pinakothek of modernity currently under construction (planning by Stehpan Braunfels Architekten, München)

Modèle de la Pinakothèque des Modernes encore en cours de construction (planification de Stephan Braunfels Architekten, München)

Modellino della Pinacoteca di Arte Moderna attualmente in costruzione (progetto: Stephan Braunfels Architekten, München)

Das allergrößte Entwicklungsgebiet der Stadt ist aber dem Rückzug der Bahn zu verdanken – zwischen dem Hauptbahnhof und dem westlich gelegenen Stadtteil Pasing. Auf einer Gesamtfläche von 173 Hektar mit einer Gesamtlänge von 8 Kilometern sind Bauflächen von 80 Hektar und fast genauso viele Grün- und Erholungsflächen vorgesehen. In der Summe sollen 8 500 Wohnungen und knapp 12 000 Arbeitsplätze entstehen. Dass die Stadt in

new projects: eventually 1,600 flats will be erected here and, additionally, numerous mainly medium-sized enterprises are to settle in this area. In the Gabriel von Seidl Halls on the old fair site, which are protected as monuments, the German Museum is going to establish its Traffic Exhibition, a fact which guarantees that the German Museum will remain in Munich and that the old fair site will boast an attractive tourist sight in future too.

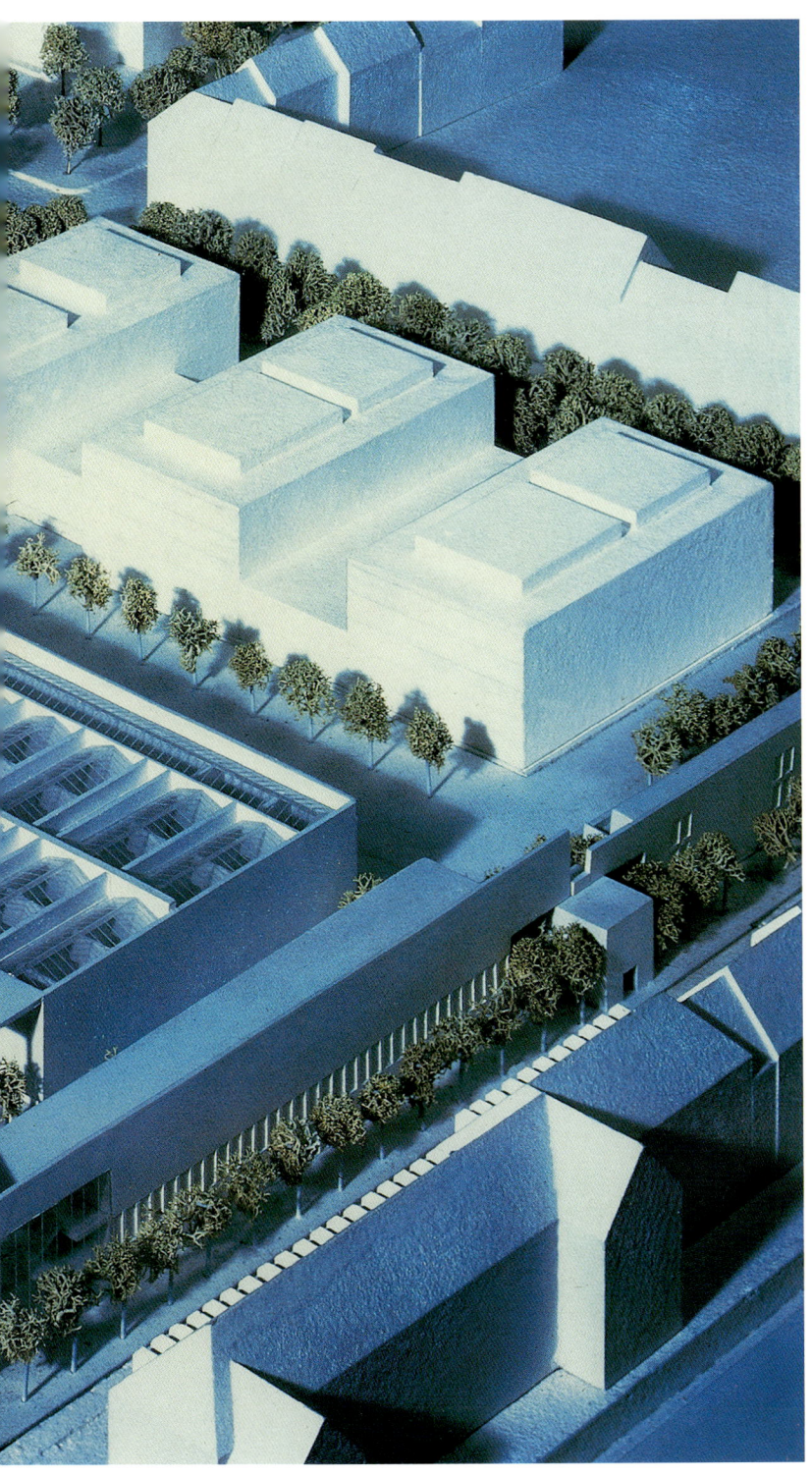

Mais laissons les exemples de côté! Le boom de construction que connaît Munich n'est même plus mis en doute par les Munichois qui se plaignaient autrefois de «l'empêchement à construire» ou de «la torpeur» de la ville mais qui se plaindraient presque maintenant du bruit, de la gêne pour la circulation et des déviations causés par les chantiers.

Mais il est heureux que cet essor ne se limite pas à la vieille ville. Certes, Munich, à la fin des années quatre-vingt, arrivait presque au maximum de ses possibilités de développement en matière de construction mais a reçu, grâce à différentes circonstances heureuses, des possibilités gigantesques que l'on peut toutes résumer avec le terme sobre d'«utilisation différente». Je ne cite que les exemples majeurs:

En 1992, l'aéroport de Munich a déménagé de l'est de la ville pour s'implanter dans l'arrondissement de Freising situé au nord. Le terrain de l'ancien aéroport était alors libre pour de nouvelles utilisations. La ville et l'Etat ont fourni en commun un effort financier de 2 milliards de DM (plus 700 millions pour les accès par le métro) et ont créé le nouveau centre des congrès, la Neue Messe München. Au sud de cet emplacement, sur plus de 500 hectares, la Messestadt, la «ville de foire», voit le jour qui offrira bientôt un cadre à 16 000 habitants et 13 000 emplois. Au sud de la Messestadt, qui est actuellement réalisée au pas à pas, et qui mettra au moins 15 ans pour prendre sa forme définitive, il y a un parc paysager unique de 220 hectares laissant ouvert la vue sur les Alpes et qui accueillera en 2005 le salon national de l'horticulture.

Comme le palais des congrès a déménagé, 1 600 appartements ont pu être construits sur son ancien emplacement à la Theresienhöhe, derrière la célèbre Theresienwiese connue mondialement à la fin septembre/début octobre avec la fête de la Bière, et de nombreuses entreprises en

nuovamente il rumore, il traffico degli automezzi da cantiere e le deviazioni per gli utenti della strada.

Fortunatamente, però, l'atmosfera neopionieristica non si limita affatto al centro storico. Verso la fine degli anni Ottanta, Monaco aveva quasi raggiunto il punto terminale delle sue possibilità di sviluppo edilizio; poi, però, per tutta una serie di circostanze propizie la città ha potuto sfruttare improvvisamente nuove opportunità di grandi dimensioni, la cui essenza può venir sintetizzata, a livello generale, con il concetto di «modifiche di sfruttamento». Vorrei citare solo gli esempi principali.

Nel 1992, l'aeroporto di Monaco si è trasferito dalla sua ubicazione originaria, ad est della città, nel circondario di Freising a nord. Ciò ha reso improvvisamente disponibile la vecchia area aeroportuale per un nuovo utilizzo. Qui, con uno sforzo finanziario di 2 miliardi di marchi (cui ne vanno aggiunti 700 milioni per l'allacciamento ottimale alla linea della metropolitana) il Comune e lo Stato bavarese hanno creato la Nuova Fiera di Monaco, a sud della quale verrà costruita, su oltre 500 ettari di terreno, la grande Città Fieristica, che nei progetti dovrà ospitare 16 000 abitanti ed offrire lavoro a 13 000 persone. A sud di questa Città Fieristica, che attualmente è in fase di graduale realizzazione ma che verrà completata non prima di 15 anni a partire da oggi, sorgerà, a sua volta, un parco all'inglese senza precedenti dell'estensione di 220 ettari con veduta del panorama alpino e con i migliori presupposti per ospitare, nel 2005, la Mostra Federale di Giardinaggio.

Il trasferimento della Fiera dalla sua ubicazione sulla Theresienhöhe, situata dietro la «Theresienwiese» che almeno tra fine settembre ed inizio ottobre assurge a fama mondiale a causa dell'Oktoberfest, rende possibile la costruzione sul posto di 1 600 abitazioni e l'insediamento di numerose imprese, soprattutto di medie dimensioni. Nei capannoni

Zeiten kommunaler Finanznot überhaupt ein derart großes städtebauliches Projekt in Angriff nehmen kann, ist den Grundsätzen der „Sozialgerechten Bodennutzung" zu verdanken: Die Grundstückseigentümer haben sich nach einem komplizierten Regelwerk an den Kosten der Infrastruktur zu beteiligen, die durch die Ausweisung des neuen Baurechts notwendig wird. Da der Wertzuwachs durch neues Baurecht immer noch erheblich höher ist als der Beitrag zu den Folgekosten, haben die großen Grundstückseigentümer (wie im vorliegenden Fall die Bahn), aber auch Investoren und Bauträger, Banken und Versicherungen dieses Regelwerk akzeptiert, mit dem es der Stadt gelungen ist, einen aus Gründen der Finanznot drohenden Baustopp abzuwenden und wirtschaftlich mit großen Projekten Gas zu geben.

But Munich owes its largest development area to the German railways, which have ceded a huge piece of land between the main railway station and the western part of Pasing to the city. Of a total area of 173 hectares with a total length of 8 kilometres, 80 hectares are to be used for housing construction and the same amount for parks and recreational facilities. Al-

majorité de taille moyenne ont pu s'implanter. Dans les halls Gabriel von Seidl de l'ancien palais des congrès, classés monuments historiques, le Deutsches Museum va y installer son exposition sur la circulation. Cela permet d'assurer que le Deutsches Museum restera à Munich et que le public sera attiré comme un aimant par l'ancien site du palais des congrès.

del vecchio Centro Fieristico «Gabriel von Seidl» e posti sotto la tutela delle Belle Arti, il Museo Tedesco della Scienza e della Tecnica («Deutsches Museum») allestirà la sua «Mostra sul Traffico»; ciò assicura la «paternità» di Monaco sul Deutsches Museum e la peculiarità di «catalizzatore di pubblico», seppure in un'altra veste, al vecchio Centro Fieristico.

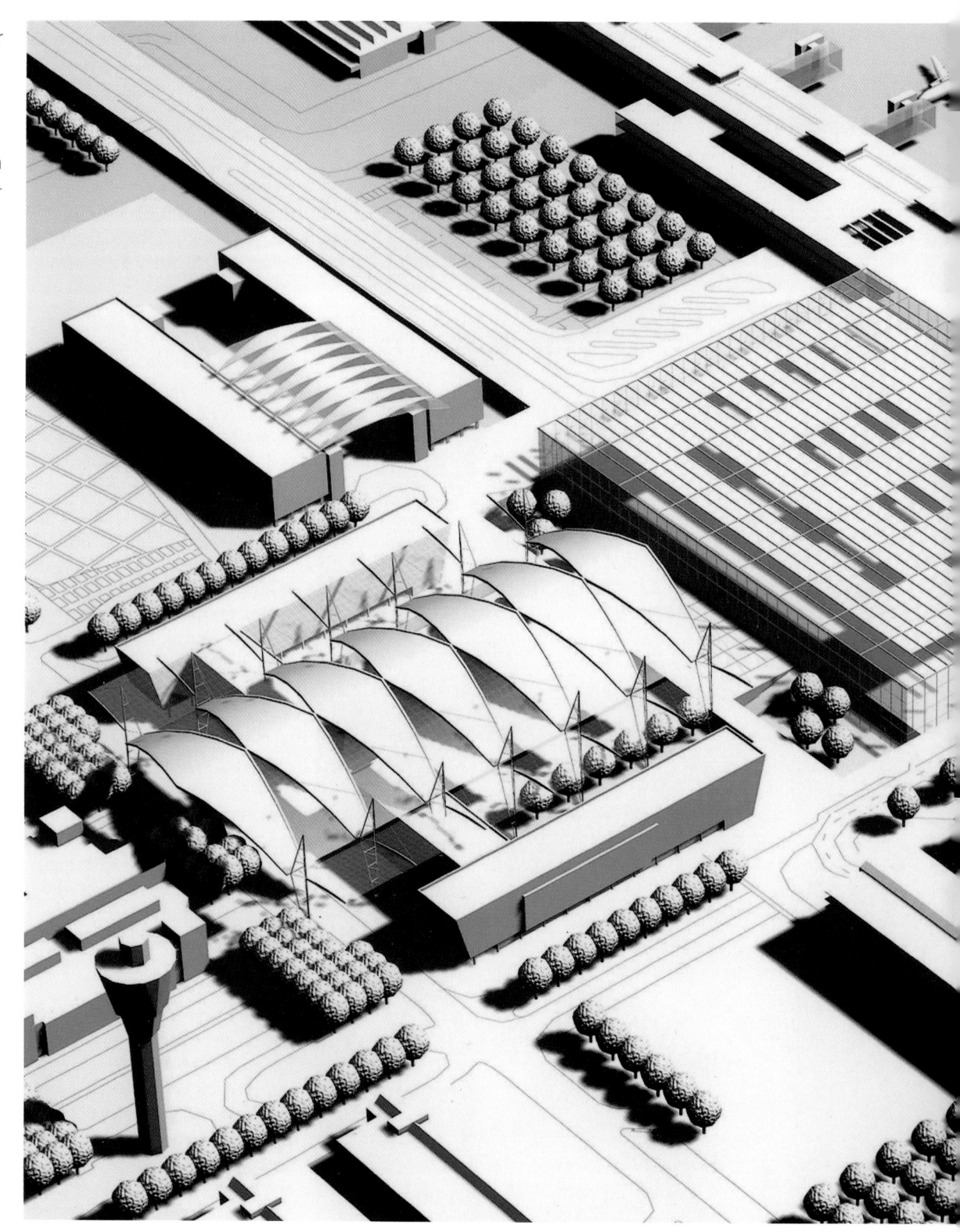

Flughafen München – Terminal 2:
Planung Architekturbüro Koch und Partner, München; voraussichtliche Fertigstellung im Jahre 2003

Munich airport – Terminal 2:
Planning: Architekturbüro Koch und Partner, München; anticipated completion in 2003

L'aéroport de Munich – le terminal 2 : planification du bureau d'architectes Koch et Partner, Munich ; mise en service prévue pour 2003

Aeroporto di Monaco – terminale 2: progetto dello studio di architetti Koch und Partner, Monaco; ultimazione prevista per il 2003

Den Grundsätzen der „Sozialgerechten Bodennutzung" wird auch das neue Medienzentrum im Norden der Stadt zu verdanken sein, das mit einem Hochhaus des Langenscheidt-Verlags Münchens Bedeutung als Verlagsstadt unterstreichen und für alle aus dem Norden kommenden Autofahrer die Stadteinfahrt markieren wird. Über 10 000 Arbeitsplätze, vor allem der Medienbranche, together 8,500 flats and roughly 12,000 new jobs are to be provided. It is the principle of "socially fair land utilization" which enables the city to start such a huge project in spite if its present financial problems: the property owners must – in accordance with a complicated system – take over a share of the infrastructural costs which are imposed as soon as the new building permit is

Mais le plus grand espace de développement, nous le devons au repli de la société des chemins de fer, entre la gare principale et la ville de Pasing située à l'ouest. Sur une surface de 173 hectares et une longueur de 8 kilomètres, des constructions de 80 hectares et presque autant d'espaces verts et de détente sont prévus. Environ 8 500 logements et 12 000 emplois doivent être créés. Le fait que la ville en cette période de restriction financière puisse entreprendre un projet d'urbanisme d'une telle ampleur est à mettre au compte des principes «de l'utilisation sociale et équitable des sols». Les propriétaires des terrains doivent participer, en respectant une série de directives, aux coûts de l'infrastructure qui s'avère nécessaire en raison de la définition de la nouvelle législation en matière de construction. Comme, avec cette nouvelle législation, la plus-value reste toujours nettement supérieure à la contribution des frais subséquents, les grands propriétaires fonciers (comme dans le cas présent la société des chemins de fer) mais aussi les investisseurs, promoteurs, banques et assurances ont accepté ces directives qui permirent à la ville d'éviter un stop de la construction menacée par les finances et de donner le feu à de grands projets économiques.

Les principes de «l'utilisation sociale et équitable des sols» donneront également le jour au nouveau centre médiatique au nord de la ville qui souligne, par un gratte-ciel de la maison d'édition Langenscheidt, l'importance de Munich comme ville de l'édition et qui marquera pour tous les visiteurs arrivant par le nord l'entrée de la ville. Plus de 10 000 emplois, en particulier dans le secteur médiatique, verront le jour sur cette aire qui jusqu'à présent était réservée aux marchands de matériaux de récupération et de charbon, ateliers et marchés aux puces. Derrière les bureaux, il sera possible de créer un habitat à l'abri du bruit.

Ma la nascita della più grande area di sviluppo della città è da ricondurre al «ritiro» delle Ferrovie Federali dalla zona compresa tra la Stazione Centrale ed il quartiere di Pasing ad ovest della città. Su una superficie complessiva di 173 ettari e per una lunghezza totale di 8 chilometri sono previste superfici edificabili di 80 ettari ed un'area verde e ricreativa di dimensioni analoghe. Complessivamente è prevista la realizzazione di 8 500 abitazioni e la creazione di 12 000 posti di lavoro. Il fatto che il Comune, in un periodo di difficoltà finanziarie per gli enti locali, sia in grado di affrontare un progetto urbanistico di tali dimensioni si deve ai principi dello «Sfruttamento sociale del terreno». I proprietari dei terreni interessati sono tenuti, sulla base di un complicato regolamento, a partecipare ai costi dell'infrastruttura necessaria perché venga applicato il nuovo diritto edilizio. Visto che il plusvalore generato dal nuovo diritto edilizio è, pur sempre, di gran lunga superiore del contributo ai costi indotti, i grandi proprietari dei terreni (nella fattispecie, le Ferrovie Federali), ma anche investitori e costruttori, banche ed assicurazioni hanno accettato questo regolamento con il quale il Comune è riuscito a scongiurare l'incombente blocco del progetto per mancanza di finanziamenti e a premere sull'acceleratore dei grandi progetti cautelandosi, contemporaneamente, sotto il profilo economico.

Ai principi dello «Sfruttamento sociale del terreno» si rifà anche il nuovo «Centro mass media» a nord della città, che con il grattacielo della casa editrice Langenscheidt sottolineerà il significato di Monaco come città editoriale e contrassegnerà l'entrata della città per tutti gli automobilisti provenienti da nord. Sull'area prevista per la realizzazione del progetto, che attualmente ospita rigattieri e commercianti di carbone, officine e mercatini dell'usato, è prevista la creazione di oltre 10 000 posti di lavoro, soprattutto del settore mass media. Dietro

sollen auf diesem bislang von Altwaren- und Kohlenhändlern, Werkstätten und Flohmärkten genutzten Areal entstehen. Hinter den Bürogebäuden wird lärmgeschütztes Wohnen möglich sein.

Nicht zuletzt dem Bauboom und den Auswirkungen der Neuen Messe, die für Münchens innovative Unternehmen einen gigantischen Standortvorteil darstellt, ist es zu verdanken, dass München unter den deutschen Großstädten eine einsame Spitzenstellung einnimmt. Andere Ursachen kommen freilich noch hinzu, so beispielsweise
- der hohe Anteil von Hightech-Betrieben, um deren Ansiedlung sich zweifellos auch der Freistaat Bayern verdient gemacht hat,
- das rasante Wachstum der Medienbranche, bei der sich in zwölf Jahren die Zahl der Betriebe, der Umsätze und der Beschäftigten mehr als verdoppelt hat,
- der hohe Anteil des Handwerks, das einen ausgesprochenen Stabilitätsfaktor auf dem Arbeitsmarkt darstellt, jeden siebten Arbeitsplatz und sogar jeden fünften Ausbildungsplatz der bayerischen Landeshauptstadt beisteuert,
- sowie die Attraktivität des Fremdenverkehrs, der selbst 1997 und 1998 Zuwächse verzeichnen konnte, als die Tourismuszahlen bundes- und landesweit stagnierten oder gar rückläufig waren.

Hier einige Zahlen und Beispiele, die den hohen Anspruch einer „einsamen Spitzenstellung" tatsächlich belegen können:
- Die Arbeitslosigkeit lag in München Ende 1998 bei 5,7 %, schon in der Franken-Metropole Nürnberg 3 Prozentpunkte höher, in Berlin sogar dreimal so hoch!
- Die Zahl der Gewerbebetriebe stieg in den letzten Jahren von 79 000 auf über 100 000! München gilt als „Mekka der Existenzgründer", was maßgeblich den Hochschulabsolventen zu verdanken ist.

granted. Since the added value of new building rights is considerably higher than the contribution to the later costs, big property owners (as the railways in our case) as well as investors, builders, banks and insurance companies have accepted this system, which enables the city to prevent a threatening building stop and to go ahead with large-scale projects.

The new Media Centre in the northern part of the city will also owe its existence to this system of "Sozialgerechte Bodennutzung". Comprising the high-rise building of the Langenscheidt publishing firm, it will underline Munich's significance as a publishers' city and mark the entrance to the city for all motorists coming from the north. More than 10,000 working places – primarily in the media sector – are to be provided in this area, which was formerly dominated by second-hand dealers, coal merchants, work-shops and flea markets. Behind the office buildings people will be able to live in flats shielded from city noises.

It is mainly the building boom and the benefits of the Neue Messe Munich – both of which constitute gigantic advantages for Munich's innovative enterprises – to which the city owes its unique position in Germany. But there are several other reasons, a few of which I would like to mention here:
- the large percentage of high-tech firms, for which the Free State of Bavaria earns the credit,
- the rapid growth of the media sector where the number of firms and of employees, as well as turnovers have more than doubled in only twelve years,
- the considerable number of craftsman's enterprises which not only provide stability in the labour market, but also every seventh job, and every fifth training position in the Bavarian capital,
- the attractive tourist sector which registered an increase

Le boom de la construction et les répercussions de la Neue Messe, qui présente un atout gigantesque pour les entreprises novatrices de Munich, font entre autres en sorte que Munich continue d'occuper une place de choix parmi les grandes villes allemandes. Les autres raisons sont par exemple:
- Le fort pourcentage des entreprises actives dans la haute technologique. L'Etat libre de Bavière n'ayant pas ménagé ses efforts pour leurs implantations.
- La croissance extrêmement rapide du secteur médiatique dont le nombre de sociétés, le chiffres d'affaires et le nombre des employés ont plus que doublé en douze ans.
- Le fort pourcentage de l'artisanat qui s'avère un véritable facteur de stabilité sur le marché du travail et fournit un emploi sur sept et même une place d'apprentissage sur cinq dans la capitale de Bavière.
- Ainsi que l'attractivité du secteur touristique qui a même pu enregistrer des croissances en 1997 et 1998 alors que les chiffres du tourisme étaient stagnants ou en recul dans le land et le pays.

Citons ici quelques chiffres et exemples prouvant les exigences élevées posées par une «chevauchée en tête»:
- Le taux de chômage se chiffrait à Munich à la fin de l'année 1998 à 5,7 %. Il était de 3 % supérieur dans la métropole de la Franconie, à Nuremberg et même trois fois plus élevé à Berlin!
- Le nombre des entreprises artisanales, commerciales et industrielles est passé, au cours des dernières années, de 79 000 à 100 000. Munich est connue comme la Mècque des créateurs d'entreprises ce qui est en grande partie dû au nombre des étudiants sortant des universités.
- La capitale du land investit par habitant plus du double que la moyenne des grandes villes allemandes. C'est ainsi que la

gli edifici uso uffici verranno realizzate abitazioni con protezioni fonoassorbenti.

Si deve, non da ultimo, al boom edilizio e alle positive ripercussioni della Nuova Fiera, che per le aziende innovative monacensi rappresenta un enorme vantaggio geografico, se nella graduatoria delle grandi città tedesche Monaco occupi uno dei primissimi posti. Ciò, naturalmente, ha anche altre cause come, ad esempio,
- l'elevata quota di aziende high tech, il cui insediamento è stato promosso indubbiamente anche dal Libero Stato di Baviera;
- la rapida crescita del settore dei media, in cui nel giro di dodici anni il numero delle aziende, i fatturati e gli organici sono più che raddoppiati;
- l'elevata quota di aziende artigianali, che rappresentano decisamente un fattore di stabilità per il mercato occupazionale vantando un posto di lavoro su sette e, addirittura, un posto di apprendistato su cinque di quelli disponibili nel capoluogo bavarese;
- nonché l'attrattiva del turismo, che ha conosciuto uno sviluppo in crescita anche negli anni 1997 e 1998 in cui il turismo, invece, ha accusato un ristagno o, addirittura, un andamento recessivo sia a livello nazionale che regionale.

Ecco qualche cifra ed esempio che dimostrano la fondatezza dell'aspirazione di «primato indiscusso» tra le città tedesche:
- la disoccupazione ha registrato a Monaco, a fine 1998, una quota del 5,7 %; a Norimberga, metropoli della Franconia, essa segnava il 3 per cento in più, e a Berlino era il triplo più alta;
- il numero delle aziende commerciali è salito, negli ultimi anni, da 79 000 ad oltre 100 000 unità! Grazie alla preparazione dei neolaureati degli atenei della città, Monaco viene considerata una vera e propria «mecca della neoimprenditoria»;
- il Comune di Monaco attua investimenti pro capite della

- Die Landeshauptstadt investiert pro Kopf der Bevölkerung mehr als doppelt so viel als der Durchschnitt der deutschen Großstädte. Damit wurde beispielsweise der kommunale Beitrag zum neuen Flughafen, zur Neuen Messe, zum U-Bahn- und Wohnungsbau ermöglicht.
- Trotz dieser außerordentlichen Investitionstätigkeit konnte die Stadt dank neuerdings wieder sprudelnder Gewerbesteuern 1998 und 1999 auf jede Neuverschuldung verzichten, ja sogar Schuldenlasten real zurückführen.

Trotz alledem ist München natürlich keine „Insel der Glückseligen", sondern eine Stadt im zunehmend härter werdenden Standortwettbewerb. Auch in München haben in den neunziger Jahren Zehntausende Beschäftigte ihren Arbeitsplatz in der Produktion verloren, und es wird immer schwieriger, dies mit einem Wachstum im Dienstleistungsbereich zu kompensieren. Schlimmer noch: Bedingt durch Fusionen und Rationalisierungen droht Personalabbau jetzt auch im Dienstleistungssektor, und dies trifft die Bankenstadt und das Versicherungszentrum München ganz besonders hart. Deshalb gibt es nicht den geringsten Grund, sich entspannt zurückzulehnen und auf den Lorbeeren der Nummer Eins unter den deutschen Städten auszuruhen, sondern allen Anlass, Wachstumsbranchen wie den Mediensektor oder Genforschung und Biotechnik und neueste Entwicklungen bei den Informations- und Kommunikationstechnologien zu fördern. München ist dafür gut gerüstet.

Christian Ude

even in 1997 and 1998, when tourist figures stagnated or even receded throughout Bavaria and Germany.

Below a few figures and examples emphasizing Munich's top position:
- in late 1998 Munich's unemployment rate was at 5.7%; in the Frankonian metropolis of Nuremberg it was 3 points higher, and in Berlin three times as high!
- The number of industrial enterprises has increased in the past few years from 79,000 to more than 100,000! Munich is regarded as the mecca of company-founders, to a large extent thanks to university graduates.
- Munich's per capita investment rate is twice as high as that of the average German city.
- Despite these extraordinary investments the city has lately been able – thanks to more substantial trade tax proceeds – to do without new credits in 1998 an 1999, in fact it has even reduced its debts.

Nevertheless Munich is not an oasis of bliss, but rather a city involved in a steadily more intensive locational competition. In Munich, too, ten thousands of employees have lost their job in the 90s, and it becomes more and more difficult to compensate this deficit by the noticeable growth in the service sector. But there is worse to come: due to fusions and rationalization measures in the service sector as well, personnel cuts are now imminent in the tertiary sector too, and this will hit the banking and insurance centre of Munich particularly hard. We must therefore not relax and rest on past laurels, but have to promote growth branches such as the media sector, gene research, biotechnology, and the newest developments in information and communication engineering. And for these tasks Munich is well prepared.

Christian Ude

contribution communale permit la naissance du nouvel aéroport, de la Neue Messe, de l'agrandissement du réseau métropolitain et la construction de logements.
- Malgré son extraordinaire activité d'investissement, la ville peut renoncer, grâce aux nouveaux impôts sur les bénéfices des professions industrielles, commerciales et artisanales collectés en 1998 et 1999, à un nouvel endettement, et même réduire la charge de l'impôt.

Malgré tout, Munich n'est pas une «île de la félicité», mais une ville où la concurrence avec les autres sites devient de plus en plus aiguë. A Munich aussi, au cours des années quatre-vingt-dix, dix mille employés ont perdu leur emploi dans le secteur de la production et une compensation avec une croissance dans le secteur tertiaire s'avérera de plus en plus difficile. Bien pire encore: étant donné les fusions et les rationalisations, une réduction du personnel se fait sentir également dans le secteur tertiaire et cela touche tout particulièrement la ville bancaire et le centre des assurances qu'est Munich. C'est pourquoi, il n'existe pas la moindre raison pour se renverser confortablement dans son fauteuil et pour se reposer sur ses lauriers de numéro un parmi les villes allemandes. Il s'agit de promouvoir absolument tous les secteurs comme le secteur médiatique ou la recherche génétique, la biotechnique et les derniers développements dans les technologies de l'information et de la communication. Pour tout cela, Munich est bien équipée.

Christian Ude

popolazione di oltre il doppio rispetto alla media delle grandi città tedesche. Ciò, ad esempio, ha reso possibile il contributo dell'amministrazione locale alla realizzazione del nuovo aeroporto, della Nuova Fiera, della metropolitana e delle opere di edilizia residenziale;
- Nonostante questi investimenti straordinari, nel 1998 e 1999 il Comune è riuscito, grazie al nuovo gettito provocato recentemente dalle imposte sulle attività industriali, a rinunciare ad ogni forma di nuovo indebitamento e, addirittura, a ridurre l'onere debitorio in termini reali.

Nonostante tutto ciò, Monaco naturalmente non è un'«isola felice» ma una città impegnata in una concorrenza sempre più dura con le altre città industriali. Negli anni Novanta, anche a Monaco decine di migliaia di dipendenti hanno perso il posto di lavoro; e col tempo diventerà sempre più difficile compensare questo andamento con una crescita delle attività del terziario. Anzi, a causa delle fusioni e delle razionalizzazioni in corso l'abbattimento di personale rischia di coinvolgere anche l'area dei servizi, e questo colpisce duramente Monaco come città delle banche e delle assicurazioni. Per questo non c'è il benché minimo motivo di rilassarsi e cullarsi sugli allori del primato tra le città tedesche, ma diventa giocoforza sfruttare l'occasione di promuovere i settori in crescita come quello dei media o della ricerca genetica e le biotecnologie nonché gli sviluppi più recenti nelle tecnologie informatiche e della comunicazione. Monaco è attrezzata per farlo.

Christian Ude

Autoren und Fotografen

Authors and photographers

Auteurs et photographes

Autori ed fotografi

Dr. Reinhard Bauer
Roland Berger
Hans Eiberle
Dr. Sabine Glaser
Willi Hermsen
Dr.-Ing. Peter Kreuzpaintner
Jürgen Kuhr
Volker D. Laturell
Dr. Hans F. Nöhbauer
Hermann Rückl
Heinrich Traublinger
Christian Ude
Dr. Gabriele Weishäupl
Prof. Dr. Henning Wiesner
Hermann Wilhelm
Prof. Ernst-Ludwig Winnacker
Manfred Wutzlhofer

Peter Ackermann, München
Seite 334/335

Toni Angermayer, Holzkirchen
Seite 306, 307 oben, 308 oben, 309, 310, 311

Bayerische Staatsgemälde-sammlung, München
Seite 12/13, 54, 58

Stephan Braunfels Architekten, München
Seite 336/337

Flughafen München GmbH,
Seite 256/257, 259, 338/339

Moni Gaul, München
Seite 302 unten, 308 links

Heinz Gebhardt, München
Umschlag Bildleiste 1. und 2. Motiv von rechts, Seite 28/29, 34/35, 40/41 42/43, 44/45, 59, 65, 66 oben, 74, 75, 76/77, 86, 97, 104/105, 216, 248/249, 250, 254, 255, 272/273, 274, 276 unten rechts, 276/277 oben Mitte, 277 unten rechts, 284, 286, 288, 297, 302 oben, 325, 326/327, 329

Norbert Höchtlen, München
Seite 114/115

Wilfried Hösl, München
Seite 64

IABG AG, Ottobrunn,
Seite 120/121

Laboratorium für Molekulare Biologie, Genzentrum, München, Seite 220, 221

Landeshauptstadt München, Stadtarchiv,
Seite 23

Volker D. Laturell, München
Umschlag Bildleiste 4. Motiv von rechts, Seite 201, 323

Leonhard Lenz, München
Seite 318

Messe München/LOSKE,
Seite 264

Münchner Stadtmuseum,
München, Seite 11, 16, 17

Oda Sternberg, München
Seite 66 unten

Martha Schlüter, München
Seite 46/47

Klaus Wagenhäuser, München
Umschlag Bildleiste 3. Motiv von rechts, Seite 19, 50, 52, 53, 56, 60/61, 67, 70, 83, 84/85, 88/89, 91, 96, 97, 101 unten links, 102/103, 106/107, 108, 110/111, 207, 212/213, 236/237, 250/251, 252, 276 oben links und unten links, 277 oben rechts und unten links, 280, 282, 287, 290, 292, 296, 300

Wilhelm Zeitlmeir, München,
Umschlag Hauptmotiv, Seite 8/9, 24/25, 26/27, 30/31, 32/33, 36/37, 38/39, 48/49, 71, 79, 80/81, 94/95, 99, 100, 101 oben und rechts, 109, 112, 113, 114 links, 118/119, 204/205, 208, 214, 223, 230/231, 246/247, 262/263, 265, 270/271, 294/295, 304/305, 307 unten rechts, 308 unten und rechts, 312/313, 320/321, 330/331

Verzeichnis der PR-Bildbeiträge

Index of PR Photographs

Index des photographies destinées aux relations publiques

Indice delle fotografie PR

Nachstehende Unternehmen haben mit ihren PR-Bildbeiträgen das Zustandekommen dieses Buches in dankenswerter Weise gefördert.

The contribution of PR photographs from the following companies has been a form of support for the realization of this book which is much appreciated.

Nous remercions les entreprises ci-après d'avoir contribué avec leurs photographies à la réalisation de cet ouvrage.

Ringraziamo le aziende indicate qui a fianco per aver contribuito, con le loro fotografie PR, alla realizzazione del presente libro.

Aquarello GmbH
München
Seite/page/page/pagina 269

Asam-Schlössl
München
Seite/page/page/pagina 281

Augustiner Großgaststätten GmbH
München
Seite/page/page/pagina 288

Austernkeller „Die Auster" Gaststättenbetriebs-GmbH
München
Seite/page/page/pagina 275

Bamberger Haus
München
Seite/page/page/pagina 281

Magnus Bauch Metzgerei, Groß- und Einzelhandel
München
Seite/page/page/pagina 238/239

Bayerische Beamten Versicherung
München
Seite/page/page/pagina 164/165

Bayerische Landesbank
München
Seite/page/page/pagina 167

Bayerische Motoren Werke Aktiengesellschaft
München
Seite/page/page/pagina 234/235

Bayerischer Rundfunk
München
Seite/page/page/pagina 152/153

Beissbarth GmbH
München
Seite/page/page/pagina 242/243

Bertelsmann Buch AG
München
Seite/page/page/pagina 174

Böhmler im Tal Einrichtungshaus GmbH
München
Seite/page/page/pagina 233

Boettner's Restaurant
München
Seite/page/page/pagina 287

Bratwurstherzl am Viktualienmarkt
München
Seite/page/page/pagina 283

Brasserie Bunuel
München
Seite/page/page/pagina 293

BSH Bosch und Siemens Hausgeräte GmbH
München
Seite/page/page/pagina 140/141

Buon Gusto Talamonti
München
Seite/page/page/pagina 291

Hubert Burda Media
München
Seite/page/page/pagina 149

cine motion Film- und Fernsehproduktion GmbH
Haar b. München
Seite/page/page/pagina 130

Circus Krone
München
Seite/page/page/pagina 69

Compaq Computer
Dornach
Seite/page/page/pagina 134/135

DaimlerChrysler Aerospace AG
Ottobrunn
Seite/page/page/pagina 224 bis 227

DEMOS Wohnbau GmbH & Co. KG
München
Seite/page/page/pagina 168/169

Deutsches Museum
München
Seite/page/page/pagina 218/219

Dresdner Bank AG
München
Seite/page/page/pagina 57, 161

DSF Deutsches Sportfernsehen GmbH
Ismaning
Seite/page/page/pagina 158

Emprise Consulting München GmbH
Seite/page/page/pagina 143

Europäisches Patentamt
München
Seite/page/page/pagina 210/211

Flughafen München GmbH
Seite/page/page/pagina 261

Fraunhofer Management GmbH
München
Seite/page/page/pagina 209

Gutshof Menterschwaige
München
Seite/page/page/pagina 285

Hacker-Pschorr-Bräu GmbH
München
Seite/page/page/pagina 303

Halali Restaurant
München
Seite/page/page/pagina 289

Handwerkskammer für München und Oberbayern
München
Seite/page/page/pagina 202/203

IABG Industrieanlagen-Betriebsgesellschaft mbH
Ottobrunn
Seite/page/page/pagina 147

Investa Projektentwicklungs- und Verwaltungs GmbH
München
Seite/page/page/pagina 171

Karstadt AG Haus Oberpollinger
München
Seite/page/page/pagina 253

Kirby Direktion GmbH & Co. KG, Wolfgang Mahling
Oberhaching
Seite/page/page/pagina 173

KirchMedia GmbH & Co. KGaA
Ismaning
Seite/page/page/pagina 156/157

Knorr-Bremse AG
München
Seite/page/page/pagina 176

Kufner KG – Holding
München
Seite/page/page/pagina 123

LfA Förderbank Bayern Landesanstalt für Aufbaufinanzierung
München
Seite/page/page/pagina 163

MAN Aktiengesellschaft
München
Seite/page/page/pagina 144/145

Messe München GmbH
München-Riem
Seite/page/page/pagina 266/267

Motorola GmbH
München
Seite/page/page/pagina 126/127

MTU Motoren- und Turbinen- Union München GmbH
Seite/page/page/pagina 228/229

Andreas Mühlbauer Bau GmbH
München
Seite/page/page/pagina 189

Münchner Symphoniker
München
Seite/page/page/pagina 63

NAIS Euro Matsushita Electric Works AG
Holzkirchen
Seite/page/page/pagina 125

Neles Automation Group, Valmet Automation GmbH
Oberhaching
Seite/page/page/pagina 129

Nourypharma GmbH
Oberschleißheim
Seite/page/page/pagina 217

Olympiapark München GmbH
München
Seite/page/page/pagina 316/317

Omega See Software Vertriebs Gmb
Oberschleißheim
Seite/page/page/pagina 139

Optimol Ölwerke Industrie GmbH
München
Seite/page/page/pagina 181

Osram GmbH
München
Seite/page/page/pagina 183

Park Cafe
München
Seite/page/page/pagina 285

Paulaner Brauerei GmbH & Co. KG
München
Seite/page/page/pagina 301

Plaza Media GmbH
Ismaning
Seite/page/page/pagina 159

ProSieben Media AG
Unterföhring
Seite/page/page/pagina 154

Johann Rettinger GmbH Präzisions-Anlagenbau- München
Seite/page/page/pagina 137

Sanofi-Synthelabo
München
Seite/page/page/pagina 215

Sankyo Pharma GmbH
München
Seite/page/page/pagina 192/193

Schoeller Packaging Systems GmbH
Pullach b. München
Seite/page/page/pagina 186

Schörghuber Unternehmensgruppe
München
Seite/page/page/pagina 179, 279

Siemens AG
München
Seite/page/page/pagina 133

Spaten-Franziskaner-Bräu KGaA, Gabriel Sedlmeyr
München
Seite/page/page/pagina 298/299

Spinner GmbH Elektrotechnische Fabrik
München
Seite/page/page/pagina 185

Süddeutscher Verlag
München
Seite/page/page/pagina 150

Münchener Tierpark Hellabrunn AG
München
Seite/page/page/pagina 304-311

Tollwood
München
Seite/page/page/pagina 73

Zum Brunnwart
München
Seite/page/page/pagina 292